from The Dovekeepere —
"I now understood it was our duty
as human beings to see behind the veil
to the inside of the world, to the heart
of things."

DATE			
6-3			
8/06 27x			

EXISTENTIALISTS
AND
MYSTICS

EXISTENTIALISTS

AND

MYSTICS

WRITINGS ON
PHILOSOPHY AND
LITERATURE

IRIS MURDOCH

ALLEN LANE
THE PENGUIN PRESS

ALLEN LANE
THE PENGUIN PRESS
Published by the Penguin Group
Penguin Putnam Inc., 375 Hudson Street,
New York, New York 10014, U.S.A.
Penguin Books Ltd, 27 Wrights Lane,
London W8 5TZ, England
Penguin Books Australia Ltd, Ringwood,
Victoria, Australia
Penguin Books Canada Ltd, 10 Alcorn Avenue,
Toronto, Ontario, Canada M4V 3B2
Penguin Books (N.Z.) Ltd, 182–190 Wairau Road,
Auckland 10, New Zealand

Penguin Books Ltd, Registered Offices:
Harmondsworth, Middlesex, England

First American edition
Published in 1998 by Allen Lane The Penguin Press,
a member of Penguin Putnam Inc.

1   3   5   7   9   10   8   6   4   2

LIBRARY OF CONGRESS CATALOGING-IN-PUBLICATION DATA
Murdoch, Iris.
Existentialists and mystics : writings on philosophy and literature / Iris Murdoch ;
edited and with a preface by Peter Conradi ; foreword by George Steiner.
p.   cm.
Includes bibliographical references and index.
ISBN 0-7139-9225-5   (alk paper)
1. Philosophy.   2. Criticism.   I. Conradi, Peter J., 1945–
II. Title.
PR6063.U7A6   1998
824'.914—dc21   97-39579

This book is printed on acid-free paper.

Printed in the United States of America
Set in Sabon

*'Man is a creature who makes pictures of himself,
and then comes to resemble the picture.'*
Iris Murdoch, 'Metaphysics and Ethics'

Contents

Foreword
by George Steiner

With the exception of formal and symbolic logic or analytic studies of the foundations of mathematics, all philosophy is part of natural language. However abstruse, whatever its resort to technical terms or neologism, a philosophic argument belongs to verbal and written discourse. This entails questions of 'style'. Different philosophies, different philosophers have their differing styles. A metaphysics, an epistemology will have its voice, often immediately recognisable. In turn, there have been among philosophers literary masters. At the outset, ancient Greek thought did not separate the poetic from the philosophical. The poem, as in the case of Parmenides or Empedocles, was a legitimate means of philosophic argument, even of a technical nature. Lucretius and Dante inherited this unison. Prose came to prevail in philosophy, but often of an inspired and highly personal order. There is scarcely a greater dramatist of reason or, perhaps, dramatist *tout court*, than Plato. The most characteristic of French prose remains Cartesian to this day. Nietzsche compelled German to clarities, to a lyric terseness which few other writers have matched. There is something eerie in the aphorismic inventiveness, in the almost surrealist wit of Wittgenstein's 'pictures' and thought-experiments (cf. Paul Klee).

Concomitantly, poetry, drama, fiction have had their philosophic passions. I have already cited Dante, where any 'partition' would be absurd. On which side of the divide, if any, do we situate Rousseau or the poems and parables of Valéry? The dynamics of reciprocity between Bergson and Proust, between Thomas Mann and Schopenhauer, are organic. The fiction is informed by abstractions of a philosophic-systematic kind given executive forms by the actions, by the speech of the characters. Today, even philosophers of science recognise in Musil's *Man Without Qualities* a text immediate to

[ix]

their own concerns. In the history of English-language literature, and notably in that of the novel, such symbiosis is rarer. English-American literary sensibility is wary of abstraction and of doctrine. It flinches from intellectual technicality or that which 'has a palpable design upon us' (where Keats's warning can serve as a natural definition of moral philosophy). There have been exceptions. George Eliot was steeped not only in theology, but in the philosophies of history and of the applied sciences. Her ability to articulate, not only in her novels, the philosophic-epistemological debates of the day was of the first strength. Iris Murdoch often refers to her great predecessor. She does not, unless I am mistaken, cite a spirit in fact much closer to her own: that of Santayana, the melancholy Platonist, whose *The Last Puritan* is, in many formal and conceptual regards, a Murdoch fable *avant la lettre*.

In the professional life, in the compendious *oeuvre* of Iris Murdoch, philosophy and literature have been strictly inseparable. She taught philosophy at Oxford with distinction during some fifteen years. She published papers and essays and reviews in moral philosophy, in aesthetics and the history of thought. A number of these appeared in the senior journals 'in the trade'. Her Gifford Lectures remain a memorable occasion. In at least three fields, the study of Platonic and Kantian ethics, the introduction to British students and readers of French existentialism and its Kierkegaardian roots, and in the inquiry into the nature of art and of beauty, Iris Murdoch has made contributions which, alone, would ensure something of her international stature. It is, therefore, of signal importance and fascination to have this ample collection in hand.

But nearly at every point, the essays and lectures here harvested, point not only to a prodigal philosophic content, but to Murdoch the novelist. This bearing is manifold. 'Thinkers' – the designation is significantly askew in common English – figure largely and dramatically throughout her fiction, from the time of *Under the Net*, *The Sandcastle* and *The Flight from the Enchanter* to that of *The Green Knight* and *Jackson's Dilemma*. The game of recognitions is tempting. A Sartre, a Canetti (himself a novelist-philosopher), a Donald MacKinnon, that most searching of modern British moral philosophers, declare themselves in the *personae* of the novels as, one ventures to suppose, they did in the author's own biography. Central to Iris Murdoch's imaginings are the strangeness, the solitude, the psychological and social risks inherent in the 'examined life'. She possesses, in the rarest measure, a gift of which Valéry's *Monsieur Teste* and Musil's epic are the supreme instances: that of dramatising, of making figurative, the act of thought. This act, its damaging human context, its inward eroticism irradiate such books as *The Bell*, *The Black Prince*, that unnerving and too often overlooked 'colossus' *The Sea, The Sea* and *The Philosopher's Pupil* (a title which is of itself a *summa*). A Platonist through and through – Plato 'is our best philosopher' – Murdoch has long been fascinated by the phenomenon of the 'coven', of the cult, of the mimetic apprenticeship which has surrounded certain masters of thought (*maîtres à penser*) from Pythagoras and Plato's academy to the time of Wittgenstein. Hence her penetrating, both poignant and ironic, evocations of discipleship, of the ambiguities of *charisma* in *The Bell*, and throughout the later fictions. Where Hegel sets Master and Servant at the core of phenomenology, Iris Murdoch places the teacher and the taught, the *guru* and the adept. Here the 'don' and the artist are fused.

The range of reference and of occasion in this gathering is extensive. The expanded Romanes Lecture of 1976, 'The Fire and the Sun' is a monograph *per se*. Nevertheless, the philosophic writings of Iris Murdoch pivot on what is close to being a single theme (thus we find in these pages a persistent, moving repetitiveness).

What is at stake throughout is the definition of the Good with a view to conducting our lives in its light. The two philosophers who have posed this question in abiding depth are Plato and Kant. It is to them, to Plato first and foremost, that Murdoch turns with untiring attention and wonder, where 'attention' and 'wonder' are themselves, and very precisely, instruments of moral perception. But to inquire of the Good, to proclaim axiomatically that 'the Good, not will, is transcendent', in manifest opposition to Schopenhauer, to Nietzsche, is to solicit a galaxy of ancillary problems. What relations has the Good to religion, to faith in God, whatever mode such faith may adopt? Is the determination of the Good contingent, this is to say dependent on a particular cultural-historical-social context, or is it in Plato's sense a 'universal' or, as Kant would put it, 'a categorical imperative' independent of altering circumstance? Is the Good a legitimate object of intellectual-epistemological dialectic, or the yield of intuition, of immediacies of inward disclosure grounded in the largely inaccessible impulses of the unconscious (this will be where Freud enters the scene)? To examine, to pursue the definition of the Good in the legacy of Plato, of Neo-Platonism, of the Enlightenment and of modern logic, is, inevitably, to engage in political choices, in discriminations of ideology. Crucially so in what Dame Iris qualifies as our 'untheological time'. It is to take into account, albeit obliquely and with a somewhat troubling decorum, the barbarism of this twentieth century and the collapse of liberal, humanistic comforts under the impact of the inhuman (the world of the death-camps, the resurgence of torture and enslavement in myriad and technological forms). At their best, Murdoch's papers, lectures, reviews are like a light-house: the beam circles around and around the central axis of the Good taking in, at each successive sweep, a vast and diverse horizon.

But the light itself is unwavering. Language itself 'is a moral medium'; metaphor is a prime instrument of ethical illumination. Only 'clearness of experience' and 'exactness of concept' will help us in our quest. The voice in this book, the patience are those of a renowned teacher. And of a teacher who takes generous pleasure in citing her masters.

The partners in discourse are four-fold. First, the classics, among whom Plato towers, as I have indicated, together with Kant. An argument on ethics and its rational foundations must also engage Aristotle. There are significant references to Hume, whose robust clarity and unworried good sense clearly appeal to Dame Iris. The second cluster is that of 'Oxbridge', of the moralists, logicians and language-analysts among her predecessors and contemporaries. G. E. Moore matters because of his particular aura of 'transcendent empiricism', of ethical idealism underwritten by a recurrent appeal to the everyday facts of bodily experience. The names of Ryle, of Hare, of Hampshire, of Ayer, of Charles Stevenson figure frequently. A good number of the lectures, review-articles and essays contributed to collective volumes, form a distinguished part of the philosophic climate, notably at Oxford, in the post-war decades.

Moore, whom Murdoch entitles somewhat surprisingly the 'father of modern philosophy', and Wittgenstein look in, as it were from Cambridge. The matters at issue are characteristic of their moment and academic milieu. What light does linguistic analysis throw on the legitimacy and verifiability of ethical propositions? How do such propositions translate into the practice of personal and social conduct? Are there ways in which we may bring into fruitful interplay the absolutism of Platonic 'Forms' or Kantian imperatives with the findings of modern psychology and scientific rationalism? What has logical positivism in the Oxbridge vein to contribute to the major currents of metaphysical and ethical debate? This latter question sees Iris Murdoch concurring with, dissenting from and, in part, reverting to her British peers.

A third 'cast' is that of continental existentialism, of Sartre in particular whom Murdoch was among the very first to introduce to British philosophers and readers. His literary genius, the force of his political engagements, clearly fascinated Iris Murdoch. It is poignant to know that Dame Iris's most recent and incomplete work was to bear on Heidegger. Sartre's strictly philosophic tomes are an extended footnote to Heidegger's *Sein und Zeit*, and it is just this key dimension which is absent from the presentations of existentialism included in this collection.

Fourth are the 'Mystics'. The seminal impulse is utterly paradoxical. After intense study, and despite Sartre's *La Nausée* which she ardently prizes, Murdoch came to feel that the existentialist commitment to the actual world was, in some deep sense, spurious. Existentialist ontology and models of consciousness were abstractions, dogmatic mythologies of closure (*No Exit*). Equally to be rejected was Bertrand Russell's celebrated opposition between 'Mysticism' and 'Logic'. Properly grasped, the 'mystical' pursuit of the Good, of perfect unison with moral truths, arises out of a rootedness in common humanity, in 'ordinary' being, far more concrete than either the 'language-games' of analytic-academic philosophers or the ideologies of the existentialist. For Iris Murdoch, there is in 'mysticism', when it is attached to life, a deep-lying utilitarianism. In all this, the absolutely key *persona* is that of Simone Weil. It is Weil's concept of *enracinement*, it is her invocation of solid weight (*pesanteur*) when applied to grace, it is the sacrificial tenor of her wretched existence which, for Iris Murdoch exemplify and re-insure the otherwise contradictory ideal of immanent transcendence, of down-to-earth 'rapture' or illumination. This, of course, is the *Leitmotif* throughout Iris Murdoch's principal novels. In turn, Weil leads back to the distant font of Pascal and, contiguously, to Kierkegaard. Dame Iris's relations to Kierkegaard constitute, of themselves, an intriguing 'mini-drama'. His paramount rôle in the development of modern religious psychology and phenomenology, his anticipation of European existentialism, his stature as a witness, are obvious to Murdoch. Yet she cannot but think him 'tiresome' and 'queer'; the strictures of the Oxford tutor come through. It is Simone Weil who prevails: 'To read her is to be reminded of a standard' (alas, it is to be reminded also of one of the ugliest cases of blindness and intolerance in the vexed history of Jewish self-hatred).

Two other tutelary presences inspire these pages. Whatever the catastrophe of its distorted, exploitative applications, the genius of Marx, the cognitive pertinence of Marxism are obvious to Murdoch. There, she is at one with Sartre and 'continental' in a forceful sense. It is precisely against the high temptations of Marxism that a liberal-pluralist hope must articulate its legitimacy and *praxis*. The subtle modes of instrumentality of psychoanalysis in Murdoch's philosophy and novels remains to be defined. One intuits their problematic ubiquity. What references at many points in these essays make plain is Iris Murdoch's awareness of Freud's status as a philosopher of culture as well as a writer. More especially, it is Freud's modulation of the myth of the 'Fall of Man' into secular terms, his stoicism, never untinged by hope, in the face of the desolation of our private and social circumstance, which Murdoch finds concordant with her own persuasions.

*

Against this manifold background, Iris Murdoch spells out her *credo*.

> Art and morals are ... one. Their essence is the same. The essence of both of them is love. Love is the perception of individuals. Love is the extremely difficult realisation that something other than oneself is real. Love, and so art and morals,

is the discovery of reality. What stuns us into a realisation of our supersensible destiny is not, as Kant imagined, the formlessness of nature, but rather its unutterable particularity; and most particular and individual of all natural things is the mind of man.

Luminous shades of Blake's 'holiness of the minute particular'. Then again:

We need a moral philosophy which can speak significantly of Freud and Marx, and out of which aesthetic and political views can be generated. We need a moral philosophy in which the concept of love, so rarely mentioned now by philosophers, can once again be made central.

And most incisively:

But because of the muddle of human life and the ambiguity and playfulness of aesthetic form, art can at best explain only partly, only reveal almost: and of course any complex work contains impurities and accidents which we choose to ignore. Even the Demiurge will never entirely understand. Although art can be so good for us, it does contain some of those elements of illusion out of which its detractors make so much of their case. The pierced structure of the art object whereby its senses flow into life is an essential part of its mortal nature. Even at its most exquisite art is incomplete ... Art, like (in Plato's view) philosophy, hovers about in the very fine air which we breathe just beyond what has been expressed.

Note the exact felicity of 'pierced object' (would that Dame Iris had alluded to its source, which is the famous kabbalistic trope of the 'pierced vessels' of divine creation).

These three quotations come from texts composed across many years. It is their essential concordance which is telling. A fundamental act of moral-aesthetic vision is circumscribed and re-stated. Art is our supreme 'clue to morals' (an arresting phrase). Both direct the spirit towards the *mysterium* of love. The programme is precisely that mapped in Neo-Platonism, in Augustine and in Dante's *Paradiso*. But with a formidable difference. It does not postulate 'God'. There is no need for any formal creed, let alone any generalised diffuse deism. Murdoch has a deeply courteous respect for those who believe 'supersensibly' – a precisian's term, very much in the register of Oxford linguistic philosophy, a donnish term charged with scrupulous monition. But Dame Iris argues for a morality of love, of individualised reciprocity whose foundations can, ought to be those of rational humanism. Or indeed, as a number of her most intricate fictions suggest, of a remembered paganism, of myth and of allegory as metaphors of ethical possibility.

I happen to wonder whether this 'eros of soul' is adequate in the face of Dostoevski's challenge that 'if there is no God all is allowed'; or to sense an unsettling proximity to the aestheticism of Pater and the domestic comforts of E.M. Forster's 'only connect'. 'Sweetness' is an epithet which Murdoch assigns in what seems to me to be excessive praise. None the less, there can be no doubt as to the urgent seriousness, as to the compassionate clear-sightedness in her position.

Throughout the broad currents of these texts, we come on remarks *en passant* of the most stimulating and provoking kind (the senior common room at its rare best). 'It takes a foreigner like Nabokov or an Irishman like Beckett to animate prose language into an imaginative stuff in its own right.' Or: 'even *Hamlet* looks second-rate compared with *Lear*' (is it the deliberate acrobatics with theological evil in Hamlet's decision not to dispatch Claudius when at prayer which unnerves Iris Murdoch?). Or: 'Plato's work is in fact full of pleasing jokes and is pervaded by a light of humour and sweet-tempered amusement' (yet Murdoch has, we know, pondered Book X of *The Laws*). A judgement introduced by the observation that 'Christ makes witty remarks but not jokes'. Surely, some of these *apodicta* will turn up on future Schools or Tripos examination-papers, followed by the ominous injunction: 'discuss'.

But it is not the academic note which prevails; it is that of the major novelist.

Like D. H. Lawrence and F. R. Leavis, Iris Murdoch is certain that, in the final analysis, it is the novelist who is 'the greatest truth-teller'. That most elusive and vital of goals, 'to find a satisfactory method for the explanation of our own morality and that of others', is in reach, if at all, not so much of systematic or generalised investigation, as it is of the novel. Or of great literature in general. The dynamics of consciousness in regard to the self and the world have been explored and made cogently figurative by Tolstoy before Ryle or Sartre argued their epistemologies. Indeed it is Shakespeare and Tolstoy who are Dame Iris's touchstones (an ironic conjunction in view of Tolstoy's animadversions on Shakespeare). It is in their fictions, it is in eminent poetry, that the human condition, with its conflictual ethical matrix, is rendered with both 'freedom' and 'tolerance'. The two nouns are cardinal. It is the unfettered play of imagination in great artists which is free to create freedom, this is to say which empowers the men and women in drama, in narratives, autonomous stature and spontaneous action. It is the tolerance of a Shakespeare towards his *dramatis personae* and the prodigal variousness of mortal circumstance which constitutes both an inexhaustible reality and wisdom. When she assigns to literature this final excellence, Murdoch echoes the turn to Wordsworth, to the poetic, of John Stuart Mill, a systematic thinker she often cites.

Is this to take sides in the archetypal quarrel between philosopher and poet, between 'truth' and 'fiction', as it is, seminally, hammered out in Plato? Is it to rescind Plato's banishment of the 'non-truth tellers' and mimes lest they corrupt the moral and political authority of the Good in the city of man? Plato's ostracism and its full epistemological implications have been at the centre of Iris Murdoch's works and, one suspects, of her personal being. They quicken her novels and her philosophy. They are debated explicitly throughout this book, most notably in 'The Fire and the Sun' and in the Platonic dialogues of 1986. Murdoch's considerations are subtle and equitable. She never sells short the force, the high gravity of Plato's indictment (to which the late Tolstoy converted, albeit in a fundamentalist Christian vein). On the other hand, she presses home her faith in the transcendant truth-saying of the arts and of the masters of literary imagining. Plato has thought to efface – perhaps in some self-ironising critique of his own poetic-dramatic genius – the ways in which Homer and the Greek tragedians enact, 'body forth', as Shakespeare would have it, the moral-metaphysical questioning and exemplification made abstractly propositional by philosophy. Freud is mistaken in urging human consciousness to 'outgrow' the basically infantile day-dreams of the poet.

[xvii]

But this is not, in any urbane or didactic sense, to settle the issue, to resolve the non-linear equation. Only a very impatient young romantic could proclaim that 'beauty is truth, truth beauty' and that we need know no more. The Platonic challenge will justly confront the creative imagination so long as philosophy and literature co-exist. That co-existence remains charged with the informing tension of the unfinished. Nowhere more so than in the achievement of Iris Murdoch.

George Steiner, March 1997.

Editor's Preface

Dame Iris Murdoch is both a very distinguished novelist and also a notably influential moral philosopher. Before describing how this collection of essays has been organised to illustrate her particular philosophical journey, it is worth remarking on how she came to think of herself as a philosopher, and how large a role a wider sense of Europe may have played in this. Between 1938 and 1942 Iris Murdoch read 'Greats' (ancient history, Greek, Latin, and philosophy) at Somerville College, Oxford. Had the war not supervened, she recounts that she might have continued her studies as a Renaissance art historian. Instead, in 1947, she opted to continue her study of philosophy with a Sarah Smithson studentship at Newnham College, Cambridge, and published her first book, on Sartre, in 1953. She had briefly met Sartre in Brussels in 1945, and recalls that he drew larger audiences than Chico Marx.*

Why the change of plan? Auden wrote of Yeats that mad Ireland 'hurt' him into poetry. It might be surmised that the madnesses of Europe hurt Iris Murdoch into moral philosophy. She spent the period 1944–6 as an Administrative Officer with the United Nations Rehabilitation and Relief Association (UNRRA), in Belgium and in Austria. There she witnessed a 'total breakdown of human society', that she was later to term 'instructive', while helping refugees and camp-survivors find food and blankets, among other matters.†

In addition to her experience at UNRRA, she was successively

---

* Iris Murdoch, *Sartre: Romantic Rationalist*, new introduction to 2nd ed. (London, 1987).
† J. Haffenden, *Interviews with Novelists* (London and New York, 1985) pp. 191–209.

close to two victims of Hitler, both of whom died young and tragically. The first was Frank Thompson, a contemporary at Oxford and incidentally E. P. Thompson's older brother, whom it was assumed she would marry. He was parachuted into Macedonia during the war, and marched with the Partisans towards Sofia, Bulgaria. He was captured, regularly beaten and finally executed by the Nazis. A volume of poems by Catullus, and a Byzantine coin found in his pocket when arrested were later presented to Dame Iris by the Bulgarians. The second, the poet and anthropologist Franz Bauermann Steiner, a gentle, scholarly Czech-Jewish refugee from Prague, a poet and anthropologist, never recovered from the deaths in a concentration camp of the parents he had left behind. The suitcase containing his doctorate on the sociology of slavery was stolen from the luggage van on the London to Oxford train, in 1942. He had kept no notes and had to do all the work again. The year that he re-submitted, in 1949, he had a coronary from which he never fully recovered. He died in November 1952. Recalling their love many years later, Murdoch recounted that she was with him the evening before his death. 'In spite of his melancholy, he was always a cheerful, happy person, very tender, very full of feeling. He was a good man, a religious man in a deep sense. I still miss him.'*

Murdoch has always insisted adamantly that she draws no characters 'from life', but equally that life, in some generalised sense, nonetheless inspires her art. Is it an impertinent speculation to find something owed to Franz Steiner in the gentle, scholarly and dying Peter Saward, a character in Murdoch's second published novel *The Flight from the Enchanter* (1956) whose work, in an early draft of the novel at Iowa University, is on the history of the Jews rather than the decoding of an ancient script? Or in Mischa Fox, the enchanter himself, something owed to the book's dedicatee, Elias Canetti? *The Flight from the Enchanter* was in fact completed before the publication of *Under the Net* (1954) and has as much claim to be her *Ur*-novel. It is full of refugees, and meditates on displacement and uprooting.

In the 1969 essay entitled 'On "God" and "Good" ' (Part Seven

* See Jeremy Adler's 'An Oriental in the West: The originality of Franz Steiner as poet and anthropologist', *TLS*, 7 Oct. 1994, pp. 16–17; and 'The Lost Loves of Iris Murdoch', *Mail on Sunday*, 5 June 1988, pp. 17–20.

of this book) Iris Murdoch twice asks what it might be that could make a man behave unselfishly in a concentration camp. What, in a post-Christian world, are good and evil? What is courage? (What mysterious force, one might interpolate, specifically motivated such as the Polish-Jewish children's writer Janusz Korczak in Treblinka, or the Catholic Pole Maximilian Kolbe in Auschwitz, to give their lives for others?) How is it that a few fanatics – Nazis in Weimar Germany, Communists in post-war Europe, the IRA – can drive their cultures mad? Such preoccupations connect the first of her light comic novels of the early fifties with those darkly comic novels written decades later, for example *The Good Apprentice* (1985) and *The Message to the Planet* (1989), which have their own Holocaust meditations. The enchanters and maguses of her fiction belong on an international stage, and have always a political dimension, from the Central European Hugo Belfounder in *Under the Net*, who is half-Wittgenstein, half-Prince Myshkin out of Dostoevsky's *The Idiot,** onwards.

Iris Murdoch is a European and indeed an international, not a narrowly 'English' thinker, with a substantial following in, for example, France, Russia and Japan. Her literary models are as much Russian as English. Tolstoy and Dostoevsky, as well as Shakespeare, Henry James and Proust, matter fundamentally to her.† The two essays in Part Six of this book – 'The Sublime and the Beautiful Revisited' and 'Against Dryness' – have a boldness of conception, a polymath fluency, and a confident, ambitious breadth of reference that are distinctly un-English. Dame Iris began her philosophical career with the first book in any language on Sartre – *Sartre: Romantic Rationalist*, published in 1953 – and was almost certainly the first English philosopher to take him seriously. Her most recent work-in-progress, as yet unfinished, is a weighty study of Heidegger.

---

* For evidence of Dostoevsky as a model throughout, see P. Conradi: 'Iris Murdoch and Dostoevskii' in *Dostoevskii and Britain*, ed. W. Leatherbarrow (Oxford, 1995), pp. 277–93.
† See John Fletcher, 'Iris Murdoch: The Foreign Translations' in *Encounters with Iris Murdoch*, ed. R. Todd (Amsterdam, 1988), pp. 21–36. And see R. Todd, *Iris Murdoch: The Shakespearian Interest* (New York and London, 1979).

Before discussing the organisation of this collection, a word about the title, which is also the title of a key essay in Part Five. Iris Murdoch's taking Sartre seriously came out of her deep dissatisfaction with Anglo-Saxon philosophy, which had in her view largely abandoned fruitful discussion of either 'consciousness' or 'moral value'. Existentialism promised to find room for both. And yet, as this collection shows, the promise proved a dubious one. Despite some admiration for Sartre, Murdoch was critical of existentialism from her first encounter with it. As early as 1950 she wrote of existentialist novels, 'This fact alone, that there is no sense of mystery, would falsify their claim to be true pictures of the situation of man' ('The Existentialist Hero'), and in another early essay she wrote that existentialism enshrines '. . . a dramatic, solipsistic, romantic and anti-social exaltation of the individual' ('Existentialist Bite'). Indeed, both words of the sub-title of her study of Sartre – *Romantic Rationalist* – carried at least a sceptical if not a pejorative charge, and might have suggested the diagnosis of a double pathology, as much as a neutral description.

Mary Warnock nonetheless recently characterised Iris Murdoch as 'roughly' an 'existentialist' philosopher.[*] Despite acknowledging Murdoch's being 'highly critical' of existentialism, Warnock argues that Murdoch shares with existentialists 'an immersion in the real world'. This claim, though prefigured by certain critics,[†] now looks doubtful and inattentive. Iris Murdoch's scepticism about existentialism is not an incidental matter. Her urge to find an alternative and more accurate description of our condition than it can provide, has long driven both her fiction and her philosophy.[‡]

[*] *Women Philosophers*, ed. M. Warnock (London, 1996), p xliii.

[†] See A. S. Byatt in *Degrees of Freedom* (2nd ed. London, 1994), pp. 308–9, who argues interestingly that Murdoch's early novels, if they 'ask Sartrean questions . . . do not offer Sartrean answers' but 'are engaged in a meaningful game with the Sartrean universe'. The 1986 postscript to Byatt's excellent *Writers and their Work* pamphlet, included in the same edition, argues that Murdoch's late interests shift towards religion.

[‡] For one account of this, see Diogenes Allen's fine 'Two Experiences of Existence: Jean-Paul Sartre and Iris Murdoch', *International Philosophical Quarterly*, June 1974, pp. 181–7. Allen contrasts the way that 'contingency' affronts and provokes in Sartre the egotistical response of 'nausea' with the

The title essay of this collection suggests that this more accurate description might be found in Plato, and might broadly be termed 'mystical'. It is true that both existentialism and mysticism *appear* to emphasise a full inhabiting of the present moment. Yet existentialism, as the present collection of essays shows, comes more and more to play the role of principal ideological opponent, and precisely because the existentialist is not immersed in the real world at all. It is the mystic who is so immersed, while the existentialist moment of choice is described in terms of the *discontinuity* between the moral agent and his/her world. The succession of essays in this volume clarifies this vital opposition, with consequences for her thinking about both philosophy and fiction.

For philosophy and fiction, even if they should not be related reductively, are related nonetheless. From the very first philosophical essays collected here, Murdoch uses *exempla* from literature – Stendhal, Dostoevsky, Rilke, Flaubert, George Eliot – as if they were as valid as *exempla* from life. The two essays in Part Six suggest how a recovery of 'character' in literature could help philosophy in its attempt to recuperate 'introspectabilia'. And Iris Murdoch gave, for example, her own early essay, 'Nostalgia for the Particular', to Rozanov, the eponymous philosopher in *The Philosopher's Pupil* (1983), as the title of a major book.

Indeed, the Platonist Max Lejour in chapter twelve of Iris Murdoch's novel *The Unicorn*, published in 1963, says that 'Good ... is the unimaginable object of our desire ... That is the idea which is vulgarized by existentialists and linguistic philosophers when they make good into a mere matter of personal choice'. The passage makes clear to what, or to whom, her Plato is opposed, conflating existentialist and linguistic philosophies together as a common foe. That novel itself also shows unequivocally that she is

awe and reverence ('the Sublime') that what is 'other' provokes in Murdoch. See also *Metaphysics as a Guide to Morals* (London, 1992), p. 377, where 'Sartre's "*nausée*" expresses the horror of those who can no longer love or attend to or even really *see* the contingent, and fear it as a threat to their imaginary freedom and self-regarding "authenticity" '; and p. 463, where the other person is 'envisaged by Sartre as the enemy'. See also 'The Critique of Freedom', Chapter One of David Gordon's *Iris Murdoch's Fables of Unselfing* (London and Columbia, 1995).

a Platonist by the early 1960s.* Both the central image of incarceration, and then the whole weirdly beautiful Gothic atmosphere and plot machinery alike, are all designed to subvert and educate a facile view of freedom. *The Unicorn*'s 'existentialist' fool Effingham Cooper, in one of the key passages in Murdoch's oeuvre, learns for a short moment while nearly drowning in a bog to *look* rather than to *leap* – indeed, 'to look and look until one exists no more'; and that 'with the death of the self the world becomes quite automatically the object of a perfect love' (p. 198). A crude and simplified account of her thinking might identify existentialism with the self-centred picture of moral choice as a 'leap of the will', mysticism with the other-centred picture of moral choice as dependent on the agent's ability to look.

As for the 'mystical' alternative, Bertrand Russell, in a famous essay, opposed 'Mysticism' to 'Logic'. This is an opposition that Murdoch would surely reject. The mystic is neither irrationalist nor dreamer. The mystic may well reject God yet seek to keep religion, possessing 'the certitude and power which are the gifts of faith'.† S/he helps the world in practical ways. Hence the title of Part Five – Towards a Practical Mysticism. The mystic, so far from inhabiting an alternative reality, is the person most attuned to the here-and-now. In the title essay the mystic is indeed close to utilitarianism. '[T]he mystical is an ever-present moral idea, that of extending ordinary decent morals indefinitely in the direction of perfect

---

* Murdoch declared in interview with W. K. Rose, *Shenandoah* 19.2 (1968), pp. 59–63, 'I once was a kind of existentialist and now I am a kind of platonist [sic]. What I am concerned about really is love . . .'. Peter Conradi, *Iris Murdoch: The Saint and the Artist* (2nd ed., London, 1989) suggests that she is a Platonist when she writes *The Bell* in 1957. Her novel *The Black Prince* (1973) is in part a Neoplatonic manifesto. 'I was never an existentialist,' Murdoch said later to William Slaymaker, 'Interview with Iris Murdoch', Papers in *Language and Literature* 21 (Fall 1985), pp. 425–32.

† See R. Heyd, 'An Interview with Iris Murdoch', *University of Windsor Review*, xxx (1963), pp. 61–82. Compare also Hans-Georg Gadamer in *Dialogue and Dialectic*, tr. P. C. Smith (New Haven & London, 1980) a thinker who also finds in the Platonic myths not an ecstasy that transports us to another world, but an ironic counter-image of the process by which we attain a more accurate perception of this one.

[xxiv]

goodness. The "ordinary" good man, aware of the magnetism of good as well as the role of duty, is thus connected to a mystical ideal whether or not he is, in the traditional sense, religious . . ." 'That's what we want to know, how conduct can be changed and how consciousness can be changed', Murdoch once remarked.[†] The interested reader can find here a concern with ordinary moral issues and decisions that everyone faces. How, for example, might you deal with the dislike of a close relative based on jealousy ('The Idea of Perfection')? How do you recover from a slight to your vanity?; and how do you fall out of love ('On "God" and "Good" ')? How can you deal with the itch to be better ('The Sovereignty of Good Over Other Concepts')?

As to exactly how Murdoch herself is a mystical/Platonic rather than an existentialist novelist: this is a question for literary criticism.[‡] The problem of organising these essays to tell a sequential story is vexed by the fact that the phases of a philosopher's thinking do not, of course, neatly follow one another like one reign following another, with one sovereign idea passing away, before the next can be enthroned. Murdoch does not, for example, wait for the demise of existentialism before searching for an alternative. The careful dating of each part clearly displays such overlapping, and certain themes recur in each decade.

The question as to how moral philosophy can discuss and reclaim 'consciousness', 'experience' or 'introspectabilia'; the question as to

---

[*] Iris Murdoch, *Metaphysics as a Guide to Morals*, p. 355.

[†] M. Bellamy, 'An Interview with Iris Murdoch', *Contemporary Literature*, xviii (Spring 1977), pp. 129–40.

[‡] For varying accounts of Murdoch's Platonism, see F. Baldanza, *Iris Murdoch* (New York, 1974); Lorna Sage. 'The Pursuit of Imperfection' in *Critical Quarterly*, xix, no. 2 (Summer 1977), pp. 67–87; E. Dipple, *Iris Murdoch: Work for the Spirit* (Chicago, 1982); W. Bronzwaer, 'Images of Plato' in *Encounters with Iris Murdoch*, ed. R. Todd (Amsterdam, 1988), pp. 55–67; P. Conradi, *Iris Murdoch: The Saint and the Artist*, op.cit.; also 'Iris Murdoch and Plato' in A. Baldwin & S. Hutton, eds. *Plato and the English Imagination* (Cambridge, 1994), pp. 330–42; C. Bove, *Understanding Iris Murdoch* (Columbia, 1993); D. Gordon (as above); and M. Antonaccio and W. Schweiker (eds), *Iris Murdoch and the Search for Human Goodness* (Chicago and London, 1969).

who exactly deserves to be the model of the good man in our age – these run throughout. The opposition between those ('existentialist') descriptions of the moment of moral choice which, on the one hand, emphasise 'will' or 'movement', and those ('mystical') descriptions which, on the other hand, emphasise vision, gazing, and attention; the Kantian sublime; the significance of G. E. Moore – these also recur. Then there is the question of free will. We know free will to be circumscribed – consider Freud and Marx – so what is the exact extent and real nature of the free will remaining to us? Must we be condemned always to oscillate between the illusion of complete determinism and the equal, opposed illusion of total free will, like so many twentieth-century thinkers and, indeed, fictional heroes? 'An unexamined sense of the strength of the machine is combined with an illusion of jumping out of it' ('On "God" and "Good" ').

À propos such recurring preoccupations, Iris Murdoch herself says in the Prologue below, 'Philosophy is a matter of getting hold of a problem and holding on to it and being prepared to go on repeating oneself as one tries different formulations and solutions. This patient relentless ability to stay with a problem is a mark of the philosopher; whereas a certain desire for novelty usually marks the artist.' No editing of such small overlaps has therefore been attempted. There is a difference between arranging the essays so that they 'tell a story', and bullying them into doing so. It should be possible to read these essays independently, as well as sequentially, so that the essays also remain self-contained and self-explanatory.

The organisation of this book tells the story of a philosopher trained at Oxford and at Cambridge, who admires the lucidity of analytic philosophy, and masters this clarity early. Part Two, Nostalgia for the Particular, documents her simultaneous unease with Anglo-American philosophy, which had abandoned the study of consciousness, and outlawed certain kinds of discussion of moral value. Part Three, Encountering Existentialism, chronicles her growing certainty that French existentialism offers an unreal alternative. From the time that she wrote 'The Idea of Perfection' (Part Seven), the word 'existentialism' has come indeed to stand for the inadequacies *both* of Anglo-Saxon *and* Continental European philosophies – solipsism, moral relativism, and the unreal and romantic oscillation between behaviourism and free will. Existentialism 'makes your responsibility absolute, or it abolishes it'. Part Four, The Need for Theory, records how her dissatisfaction with existing moral philosophy drew her towards Simone Weil, whose importance for Murdoch is much larger than this single essay would suggest. Weil probably introduced her to the Christian mystics and to Buddhism and Hinduism.

Reading Simone Weil certainly led Murdoch to a new view of Plato. As a student herself at Oxford, Iris Murdoch recounts that, 'there was no wide consideration of [Plato], he was simply misunderstood. I learnt nothing of value about him as an undergraduate (he was regarded as "literature"!). Yes, reading SW helped me very much.'[*] After encountering Weil, she was increasingly to come to see Plato as our contemporary, speaking directly to our condition; and the culmination of this collection concerns her re-readings of Plato.

While Iris Murdoch writes with exemplary lucidity throughout, various means have been used to make this collection more accessible to the lay reader who may lack formal philosophical training. The use of parts accompanied by appropriate dates and epigraphs is one. Within each part the order generally follows dates of original publication; but in Part Seven, Rereading Plato, 'On "God" and "Good" ', first published in 1969, is placed before 'The Sovereignty of Good Over Other Concepts', which was first published in 1967. This follows Dame Iris's own practice in the collection she made of these essays when they were published together as The Sovereignty of Good.[†] A similar minor change is made within the ordering of Part Two. Footnoting policy has been to add brief explanatory comments for philosophical figures whose names might not be familiar to all readers. Nietzsche, Kierkegaard, Kant and Hegel do not get footnotes. Oakeshott and McTaggart

---

[*] Correspondence with the editor, 13 January 1992.
[†] This book was incidentally dedicated with typical generosity to Stuart Hampshire, whose thinking it contested. The Fire and the Sun (Oxford, 1976) was dedicated to Murdoch's husband, John Bayley; Acastos: Two Platonic Dialogues (London, 1986), which comprised the two plays which appear in this collection under their individual titles (see Part Seven) was dedicated to Michael Kustow.

do. For more detailed information on the philosophical scene Iris Murdoch entered around 1950, see John Passmore's helpful *One Hundred Years of Philosophy* (London, 1957).

'Thinking and Language' in Part Two came from a symposium of that title with A. C. Lloyd and Gilbert Ryle, but stands on its own; 'Vision and Choice in Morality' formed part of a discussion with a Mr Hepburn, and has been cut to be free-standing. At the same time two long symposia in which Dame Iris's contribution, though potent in significance, was relatively small in length, have regrettably had to be left out: 'Freedom and Knowledge', a discussion between Iris Murdoch, D. F. Pears, P. K. Gardiner and Stuart Hampshire (*Proceedings of the Aristotelian Society*, 25, 1951, 130–5),* and 'Philosophy and Beliefs', a discussion between Anthony Quinton, Stuart Hampshire, Iris Murdoch and Isaiah Berlin (*Twentieth Century*, June 1955, 495–521).† Reviews – generally considered ephemeral in comparison with longer article-reviews – have also been omitted, with the single exception of Part Three where, for reasons already touched upon, it was felt necessary fully to document Murdoch's growing scepticism and hostility towards existentialism.

In the Prologue below, Iris Murdoch remarks that the number of influential philosophers is small. Hence, perhaps, 'conversation' between them is possible. From the etiquette of some of the Aristotelian Society symposia held at 21 Bedford Square around 1950, it is hard to escape the conclusion that this was a conversation among gentlemen, who observe the convention that a bare surname is an adequate form of address, a habit on occasion vexing to bibliographical enquiry. Into this enclave at about the same time came a generation of five extraordinary women philosophers: Elizabeth Anscombe, Phillipa Foot, Mary Midgley, Iris Murdoch and Mary Warnock. Iris Murdoch retains the short form of address decades later, and it caused this editor headaches. For

* Iris Murdoch argues here that reason and feeling are not separate, pointing out that feelings can pressure reason and the will may be impotent; human beings can accordingly drift into decisions. She expresses reasoned doubts both about the value of self-awareness, and the possibility of self-knowledge.
† In this symposium Iris Murdoch questions linguistic philosophy for offering a commonplace, 'watered-down' morality, and for dividing fact from value.

example, in *The Fire and the Sun*, does she refer to D.M. or to John McDowell? I have tried to identify the correct figures and to add their initials throughout.

It was decided to start the volume with Iris Murdoch's conversation with the philosopher and broadcaster Bryan Magee, originally shown on BBC television in 1978, but substantially reworked by Iris Murdoch before publication. Interesting in itself, the interview provides a good road-map to some of the issues that follow. Some, but not all. The Magee interview makes no mention of existentialism. It is hard to escape the conclusion that by the late 1970s Iris Murdoch had helped to render existentialism out of date. Not merely was it, as she suggests in Part Five below 'the natural mode of being of the capitalist epoch', so that its political credentials as a critique of capitalism look unconvincing; but also, as her husband Professor John Bayley, whose influence on her thinking especially in the Part Six essays is palpable, put the matter, 'The tenets of existentialism, apparently so pitiless and so searching, have become the opiate of the sub-intelligentsia, the props on which the common reader interested in ideas can cheerfully recline.'* Much of its apparent rebelliousness now also seemed imitative and self-regarding.

By 1978 and her interview with Magee, structuralism (and post-structuralism) had started to emerge as her chief philosophical adversary, an opposition she elaborates on in her book *Metaphysics as a Guide to Morals* (London, 1992). It might be, however, that existentialism and structuralism are distantly related. Both tend towards and encourage moral relativism and solipsism. Both arrogantly divide the world between determinism and free will: between a mass too stupid to understand that they are 'spoken by' the conventions (existentialism) or alternatively are 'spoken by' language (structuralism); and an élite who, naturally, 'escape ... from the fate of the codified'.†

The sub-title of this book – 'Writings on Philosophy and Literature' – is an approximation. It does not convey the true

---

* John Bayley, *Tolstoi and the Novel* (London, 1966), p. 184.
† Iris Murdoch's introduction to the second (1987) edition of her *Sartre*, p. 37.

diversity of sources gathered here. The wide variety of original modes of dissemination includes two radio broadcasts from 1950 (four years before Iris Murdoch published her first novel *Under the Net*), one television broadcast, one play performed at the National Theatre and one unperformed play, a symposium, both Leslie Stephens and Romanes Lectures, reviews and article-reviews, an address to the Aristotelian Society at 21 Bedford Square in 1951, and addresses to universities. Moreover, not all deal exclusively with 'Philosophy and Literature'. Two also concern politics: 'The Existentialist Political Myth' and 'A House of Theory'. To term oneself a mystic does not have to mean being a-political – consider the examples of Walter Benjamin and, indeed, Simone Weil herself. Murdoch often in this collection expresses doubts about a *direct* role for politics in art, yet might be said in some very general sense to have brought mysticism and politics together in her superb (unpublished) short radio opera, *The One Alone* (BBC Radio 3, 13 February 1987), which concerned the spiritual struggles of a brave opponent of political tyranny, subject to solitary confinement.

I should like to acknowledge the help of my kind colleagues at Kingston University, John Clarke, and Anne Rowe, and of Alison Samuel at Chatto & Windus. For all full details of original publication, see Acknowledgements & Sources on p. 532. John Fletcher and Cheryl Bové's massive *Iris Murdoch: A Descriptive Primary and Annotated Secondary Bibliography* (New York and London, 1994) has been of great help and is recommended to the serious student, who may also be interested in the Iris Murdoch Society, which publishes an annual Newsletter. North American readers should contact Tony Bové, 1716 Timberview Drive, Marion, Indiana 46952, USA; readers in Europe should write to Dr Anne Rowe, 21 Upper Park Road, Kingston-upon-Thames, Surrey, KT2 5LB, UK.

Peter Conradi, January 1997

PART ONE

Prologue

'Literature entertains, it does many things, and philosophy does one thing.'

Men of Ideas, Some Creators of Contemporary Philosophy,
1978

Literature and Philosophy: A Conversation with Bryan Magee

MAGEE: Some great philosophers have been also great writers in the sense of great literary artists – I suppose the outstanding examples are Plato, St Augustine, Schopenhauer and Nietzsche. Others, if not in quite their class, were certainly very good writers: Descartes, Pascal, Berkeley, Hume and Rousseau spring to mind. In our own time Bertrand Russell and Jean-Paul Sartre have both been awarded the Nobel Prize for Literature. Yet there have been great philosophers who were bad writers, two of the very greatest – Kant and Aristotle – being two of the worst. Others were just pedestrian – one thinks of Aquinas and Locke, for example. As for Hegel, his work has become a byword for obscurity, almost a joke in that regard. I think he must be the most difficult to read of all world-famous writers.

What these examples show is that philosophy is not, as such, a branch of literature: its quality and importance rest on quite other considerations than literary and aesthetic values. If a philosopher writes well, that's a bonus – it makes him more enticing to study, obviously, but it does nothing to make him a better philosopher. I state this firmly at the outset because in this discussion I am going to consider some of the respects in which philosophy and literature do overlap, together with someone whose experience spans both worlds. Iris Murdoch is now a novelist of international reputation, but for many years before she became a successful novelist – and indeed for some years after, making a total of fifteen altogether – she was a tutor in philosophy at Oxford University.

MAGEE: When you are writing a novel on the one hand and philosophy on the other, are you conscious that these are two radically different kinds of writing?

MURDOCH: Yes, I am. Philosophy aims to clarify and to explain, it states and attempts to solve very difficult highly technical problems and the writing must be subservient to this aim. One might say that bad philosophy is not philosophy, whereas bad art is still art. There are all sorts of ways in which we tend to forgive literature, but we do not forgive philosophy. Literature is read by many and various people, philosophy by very few. Serious artists are their own critics and do not usually work for an audience of 'experts'. Besides, art is fun and for fun, it has innumerable intentions and charms. Literature interests us on different levels in different fashions. It is full of tricks and magic and deliberate mystification. Literature entertains, it does many things, and philosophy does one thing.

MAGEE: Having read several of your books, including your philosophical books, it strikes me that the sentences themselves are different. In your novels the sentences are opaque, in the sense that they are rich in connotation, allusion, ambiguity; whereas in your philosophical writing the sentences are transparent, because they are saying only one thing at a time.

MURDOCH: Yes. Literary writing is an art, an aspect of an art form. It may be self-effacing or it may be grand, but if it is literature it has an artful intention, the language is being used in a characteristically elaborate manner in relation to the 'work', long or short, of which it forms a part. So there is not one literary style or ideal literary style, though of course there is good and bad writing; and there are great individual thinkers who are great writers, whom I would not call philosophers, such as Kierkegaard and Nietzsche. Of course philosophers vary and some are more 'literary' than others, but I am tempted to say that there is an ideal philosophical style which has a special unambiguous plainness and hardness about it, an austere unselfish candid style. A philosopher must try to explain exactly what he means and avoid rhetoric and idle decoration. Of course this need not

[4]

exclude wit and occasional interludes; but when the philosopher is as it were in the front line in relation to his problem I think he speaks with a certain cold clear recognisable voice.

MAGEE: The number of people who have engaged in both activities at a professional level must be tiny. You are among the very few who can characterise from personal experience what the difference is. Can you say more about it?

MURDOCH: Philosophical writing is not self-expression, it involves a disciplined removal of the personal voice. Some philosophers maintain a sort of personal presence in their work, Hume and Wittgenstein for instance do this in different ways. But the philosophy has a plain impersonal hardness none the less. Of course literature too involves a control of the personal voice and its transformation. One might even set up an analogy between philosophy and poetry, which is the hardest kind of literature. Both involve a special and difficult purification of one's statements, of thought emerging in language. But there is a kind of self-expression which remains in literature, together with all the playfulness and mystification of art. The literary writer deliberately leaves a space for his reader to play in. The philosopher must not leave any space.

MAGEE: You said a moment ago that the aim of philosophy is to clarify whereas the aim of literature, very often, is to mystify: I suppose it is central to what the novelist or playwright is doing that he is trying to create an illusion, whereas it is central to what the philosopher is doing that he is trying to dispel illusion.

MURDOCH: Philosophy is not aiming at any sort of formal perfection for its own sake. Literature struggles with complex problems of aesthetic form, it tries to produce a kind of completeness. There is a sensuous thingy element in every art form. Even fragmentary literary writing shows some sense of a complete whole. Literature is (mostly) 'works of art'. Works of philosophy are quite different things. Very occasionally a work of philosophy may also be a work of art, such as the *Symposium*, but these are exceptional cases; and it is in the light of other parts of Plato's philosophy that we read the *Symposium* as a philosophical statement. Most philosophy, as compared with literature, seems rambling and formless, even when the philosopher is explaining something of great formal complexity. Philosophy is a matter of getting hold of a problem and holding on to it and being prepared to go on repeating oneself as one tries different formulations and solutions. This patient relentless ability to stay with a problem is a mark of the philosopher; whereas a certain desire for novelty usually marks the artist.

MAGEE: With the making of the contrast in mind, how would you characterise literature as distinct from philosophy?

MURDOCH: It might take a long time to 'define' literature, though we all know roughly what it is. It is the art form which uses words. Journalism can be literature if it is also art, scholarly writing can be literature. Literature is various and very large, whereas philosophy is very small. The problems stated at the beginning are mostly the same problems which occupy us today, and although the problems are vast, there are in a sense not all that many of them. Philosophy has had a tremendous influence, but the number of philosophers exerting the influence has been comparatively small. This is because philosophy is so difficult.

MAGEE: Your point about the continuity of philosophical problems since the beginning was hit off strikingly by [A.N.] Whitehead when he said that all Western philosophy is merely footnotes to Plato.

MURDOCH: Yes indeed. Plato is not only the father of our philosophy, he is our best philosopher. Of course the methods of philosophy change, but we have not left Plato behind, which is also to say that philosophy does not make progress in the way that science does. Of course literature does not make progress either. Nobody is better than Homer. But literature has no continuous task, it is not in that sense a kind of 'work'. It is indeed something in which we all indulge spontaneously, and so might seem to be nearer to play, and to the vast irresponsible variety of play. Literary modes are very natural to us, very close to ordinary life and to the way we live as reflective beings. Not all literature is fiction, but the greater part of it is or involves fiction, invention, masks, playing roles, pretending, imagining, story-telling. When we return home and 'tell our day', we are artfully shaping material into story form. (These stories are very often funny, incidentally.) So in a way as word-users we all exist in a

[6]

literary atmosphere, we live and breathe literature, we are all literary artists, we are constantly employing language to make interesting forms out of experience which perhaps originally seemed dull or incoherent. How far reshaping involves offences against truth is a problem any artist must face. A deep motive for making literature or art of any sort is the desire to defeat the formlessness of the world and cheer oneself up by constructing forms out of what might otherwise seem a mass of senseless rubble.

MAGEE: Your remark about cheering oneself up brings to the fore the fact that one of the chief aims of literature has always been to entertain; and I don't think that is an aim which has anything to do with philosophy.

MURDOCH: Philosophy is not exactly entertaining but it can be comforting, since it too is an eliciting of form from muddle. Philosophers often construct huge schemes involving a lot of complicated imagery. Many kinds of philosophical argument depend more or less explicitly upon imagery. A philosopher is likely to be suspicious of aesthetic motives in himself and critical of the instinctive side of his imagination. Whereas any artist must be at least half in love with his unconscious mind, which after all provides his motive force and does a great deal of his work. Of course philosophers have unconscious minds too, and philosophy can relieve our fears; it is often revealing to ask of a philosopher, 'What is he afraid of?' The philosopher must resist the comfort-seeking artist in himself. He must always be undoing his own work in the interests of truth so as to go on gripping his problem. This tends to be incompatible with literary art. Philosophy is repetitive, it comes back over the same ground and is continually breaking the forms which it has made.

MAGEE: You've now said a number of things about literature which, by implication, contrast it with philosophy, but I'd like to draw out the contrasts more explicitly. For instance, you said story-telling is natural – we all do it in everyday life, and we all like to be told stories. I suppose, by contrast, philosophy is counter-natural. Philosophy involves us in the critical analysis of our beliefs, and of the presuppositions of our beliefs, and it's a very striking fact that most people neither like doing this nor like having it done to them. If the assumptions on which their beliefs rest are questioned it makes them feel insecure, and they put up a strong resistance to it.

MURDOCH: Yes. I think philosophy is very counter-natural, it is a very odd unnatural activity. Any teacher of philosophy must feel this. Philosophy disturbs the mass of semi-aesthetic conceptual habits on which we normally rely. Hume said that even the philosopher, when he leaves his study, falls back upon these habitual assumptions. And philosophy is not a kind of scientific pursuit, and anyone who resorts to science is falling straight out of philosophy. It is an attempt to perceive and to tease out in thought our deepest and most general concepts. It is not easy to persuade people to *look* at the level where philosophy operates.

MAGEE: Bertrand Russell once said that philosophy consists of the questions we don't know how to answer. Isaiah Berlin also takes this view.

MURDOCH: Yes, that we do not know *how* to answer, or perhaps even quite how to ask. There are plenty of questions we cannot answer, but we know how they might be answered. Philosophy involves seeing the absolute oddity of what is familiar and trying to formulate really probing questions about it.

MAGEE: You said just now that philosophy is not science, and I agree. But it has certain very basic things in common with science. One of these is that both are attempts to understand the world, and to do so in a way that does not consist of expressing personal attitudes. In other words, in both activities one submits oneself to criteria outside oneself; one tries to say something that is *impersonally* true. This relates to another important difference between philosophy and literature. Just now you said something that seemed to imply that whereas your novel writing reveals a distinctive literary personality you wouldn't mind if your philosophical writing did not. It strikes me that almost the most important thing about an imaginative or creative writer is the possession of a personality in that sense. If he hasn't got one we're not interested in reading him. Whereas with philosophers that is simply not the case. You could read all the works of Kant with impassioned interest, and at the end of it have very little idea what Kant was like internally, as a human being.

MURDOCH: You mean what interests us is the personality expressed in the work? The writer himself is something else again; he might be dull though his work was not, or vice versa. I am not sure about 'literary personality'. We want a writer to write well and to have something interesting to say. Perhaps we should distinguish a recognisable style from a personal presence. Shakespeare has a recognisable style but no presence, whereas a writer like D. H. Lawrence has a less evident style but a strong presence. Though many poets and some novelists speak to us in a highly personal manner, much of the best literature has no strongly felt presence of the author in the work. A literary presence if it is too bossy, like Lawrence's, may be damaging; when for instance one favoured character is the author's spokesman. Bad writing is almost always full of the fumes of personality. It is difficult to make rules here. The desire to express oneself, to explain and establish oneself, is a strong motive to art, but one which must be treated critically. I do not mind owning a personal style, but I do not want to be obviously present in my work. Of course a writer has to reveal his morality and his talents. This sort of self-revelation happens in philosophy too, but there we ask, is the conclusion true, is the argument valid?

MAGEE: When talking to friends who may be very intelligent and well educated without knowing much about philosophy, I find that they often betray the assumption that philosophy is a branch of literature – that a philosopher is somehow expressing a personal view of the world in the same sort of way as an essayist might, or a novelist; and it's not always easy to explain why this is not so. I suppose the reason is partly that philosophical problems have histories, and each philosopher comes to the scene at a certain stage in that developing history; and if he is to make a contribution at all he has to make it at that point, otherwise there simply isn't a contribution to be made. In that respect, again, he is like a scientist.

MURDOCH: Yes, that is true. And perhaps that is something which distinguishes the 'true philosopher' from other reflective thinkers and moralists. The philosopher engages with the philosophical field in the form which it has when he appears on the scene. There is a definite body of doctrine to which he must react, and he enters into what is in some ways a rather narrow dialogue with the past. The artist by contrast seems an irresponsible individual. He may be deeply related to his time and to the history of his art, but he has no given problems to solve. He has to invent his own problems.

MAGEE: Perhaps partly for that reason the writing of art – the writing of plays, novels and poems – engages far more of the personality, both of the writer and of the reader, than philosophy does. Philosophy is a more narrowly intellectual activity. Literature, to be literature at all, must move one emotionally, whereas the philosopher – like the scientist – is positively trying to eliminate emotional appeal from his work.

MURDOCH: Yes. I think it is more fun to be an artist than to be a philosopher. Literature could be called a disciplined technique for arousing certain emotions. (Of course there are other such techniques.) I would include the arousing of emotion in the definition of art, although not every occasion of experiencing art is an emotional occasion. The sensuous nature of art is involved here, the fact that it is concerned with visual and auditory sensations and bodily sensations. If nothing sensuous is present no art is present. This fact alone makes it quite different from 'theoretical' activities. Moreover much art, perhaps most art, perhaps all art is connected with sex, in some extremely general sense. (This may be a metaphysical statement.) Art is close dangerous play with unconscious forces. We enjoy art, even simple art, because it disturbs us in deep often incomprehensible ways; and this is one reason why it is good for us when it is good and bad for us when it is bad.

MAGEE: So far we've been talking about the differences between philosophy and literature, and I think it's important that we should stress them: but there are also some significant things in common, aren't there? I know from previous conversations with you, for example, that you think notions of truth are near the centre of both.

MURDOCH: Yes, indeed, I think that though they are so different,

philosophy and literature are both truth-seeking and truth-reveal-
ing activities. They are cognitive activities, explanations. Literature, like other arts, involves exploration, classification, discrimination, organised vision. Of course good literature does not look
like 'analysis' because what the imagination produces is sensuous,
fused, reified, mysterious, ambiguous, particular. Art is cognition
in another mode. Think how much thought, how much truth, a
Shakespeare play contains, or a great novel. It is illuminating in
the case of any reflective discipline to see what kind of critical
vocabulary is directed against it. Literature may be criticised in a
purely formal way. But more often it is criticised for being in
some sense untruthful. Words such as 'sentimental', 'pretentious',
'self-indulgent', 'trivial' and so on, impute some kind of falsehood, some failure of justice, some distortion or inadequacy of
understanding or expression. The word 'fantasy' in a bad sense
covers many of these typical literary faults. It may be useful to
contrast 'fantasy' as bad with 'imagination' as good. Of course
philosophy too is an imaginative activity, but the statements at
which it aims are totally unlike the 'concrete statements' of art,
and its methods and atmosphere, as those of science, inhibit the
temptations of personal fantasy. Whereas creative imagination
and obsessive fantasy may be very close almost indistinguishable
forces in the mind of the writer. The serious writer must 'play
with fire'. In bad art fantasy simply takes charge, as in the
familiar case of the romance or thriller where the hero (alias the
author) is brave, generous, indomitable, lovable (he has his faults
of course) and ends the story loaded with the gifts of fortune.
Fantasy is the strong cunning enemy of the discerning intelligent
more truly inventive power of the imagination, and in condemning art for being 'fantastic' one is condemning it for being untrue.

MAGEE: But that conception of truth is very different, is it not, from
what the philosopher is trying to get at?

MURDOCH: I want to say that literature is like philosophy in this
respect because I want to emphasise that literature too is a truth-
seeking activity. But of course philosophy is abstract and
discursive and direct. Literary language can be deliberately
obscure, and even what sounds like plain speaking is part of some
ulterior formal imaginative structure. In fiction even the simplest

[11]

story is artful and indirect, though we may not notice this because we are so used to the conventions involved, and we are all to some extent literary artists in our daily life. Here one might say that it is the directness of philosophy which strikes us as unnatural, the indirectness of the story as natural. It is not easy to describe what philosophical mistakes are like. Sometimes there is a logical or quasi-logical fault in a chain of argument, but more often philosophy fails because of what might be called imaginative or obsessive conceptual errors, false assumptions or starting points which send the whole investigation wrong. The notion of the 'sense datum', or the distinction between evaluative and descriptive language, are arguably examples of such errors. The test of truth in philosophy is difficult because the whole subject is so difficult and so abstract. It may not be clear what is supposed to verify what, since the phenomena which justify the theory have also to be described by the theory. The philosopher must fear tautology and constantly look back at the less strictly conceptualised 'ordinary world'. There is an analogous problem in art, but it is different and often invisible because of the natural closeness of art to the world. The test of truth in philosophy is difficult because the subject is difficult, the test of truth in literature may be difficult because in a way the subject is easy. We all feel we understand art, or a lot of it anyway. And if it is very obscure it can numb the critical faculties; we are prepared to be enchanted. As I said, philosophy does one thing, literature does many things and involves many different motives in the creator and the client. It makes us happy, for instance. It shows us the world, and much pleasure in art is a pleasure of recognition of what we vaguely knew was there but never saw before. Art is mimesis and good art is, to use another Platonic term, anamnesis, 'memory' of what we did not know we knew. Art 'holds the mirror up to nature'. Of course this reflection or 'imitation' does not mean slavish or photographic copying. But it is important to hold on to the idea that art is about the world, it exists for us standing out against a background of our ordinary knowledge. Art may extend this knowledge but is also tested by it. We apply such tests instinctively, and sometimes of course wrongly, as when we dismiss a story as implausible when we have not really understood what sort of story it is.

MAGEE: Let us move on now to consider philosophical ideas about literature. You have just been talking about fantasy in the bad sense – which I take to be a form of self-indulgence, usually incorporating false values such as the worship of power, status or wealth, and hence being closely involved with vulgarity in art. This is intimately linked with the reason why some philosophers have actually been hostile to art, isn't it? And indeed your last book, *The Fire and the Sun*, was about Plato's hostility to art. It would be interesting to hear you say something about why such a great philosopher as Plato – who himself used artistic forms, such as the dialogue: there's obviously a lot of fiction in Plato – should have been antagonistic to art.

MURDOCH: Plato was notoriously hostile to art. As a political theorist he was afraid of the irrational emotional power of the arts, their power to tell attractive lies or subversive truths. He favoured strict censorship and wanted to banish the dramatists from the ideal state. Also he was afraid of the artist in himself. He was a very religious man and he felt that art was hostile to religion as well as to philosophy: art was a sort of egoistic substitute for the discipline of religion. The paradox is that Plato's work is great art in a sense which he does not theoretically recognise. He says that there is an old quarrel between philosophy and poetry; and we must remember that in Plato's time philosophy as we know it was just emerging out of all sorts of poetic and theological speculation. Philosophy does make progress by defining itself as not being something else. In Plato's time it separated itself from literature, in the seventeenth and eighteenth centuries from natural science, in the twentieth century from psychology. Plato thought art was mimesis, but he thought it was bad mimesis. And it is true that there is always more bad art around than good art, and more people like bad art than like good art. Plato believed that art was essentially personal fantasy, celebrations of unworthy things or distortions of good things. He saw it as trivial copying of particular objects with no general significance, and of course this is what a great deal of art is. Imagine what Plato would have thought of television. One ought to look at the real world and think about it and not be content with trivial images and unsavoury dreams. This is not totally unlike Freud's view of art as a substitute for power and 'real life' satisfactions. Freud sometimes suggests that art is the fantasy mind of the artist speaking directly to the fantasy mind of the client. Art is private consolation. I think this is a profound idea and a serious charge. One can see how the thriller or the sentimental picture may be simply a stimulus to the private fantasies of the reader or viewer. Pornography is the extreme instance of this private use of 'art'.

MAGEE: But surely these criticisms apply only to bad art. Admittedly most art, as you say, is bad art. But good art – which is really the art that endures, one hopes – isn't subject to them.

MURDOCH: I suppose a client can always try to use art for his own purposes, only good art may resist bad purposes more successfully. I mean, someone might go to the National Gallery just looking for pornographic images. What we call bad art is asking to be used badly and cannot be understood any other way. A general practice of art which produces the good will necessarily produce the bad too, and it need not be all that bad. Critics can be too austere and puritanical. I am very hostile to pornography, I think it is really damaging and degrading. But people are fairly harmlessly employed enjoying ordinary mediocre art. A sentimental novel can be a decent rest from one's troubles, though one might be even better off reading *War and Peace*.

MAGEE: There's a widespread view today, isn't there, that good art is good for one in another sense: that it sharpens one's sensibilities, that it increases one's powers of understanding and therefore one's capacity for empathy with other people.

MURDOCH: I think good art is good for people precisely because it is not fantasy but imagination. It breaks the grip of our own dull fantasy life and stirs us to the effort of true vision. Most of the time we fail to see the big wide real world at all because we are blinded by obsession, anxiety, envy, resentment, fear. We make a small personal world in which we remain enclosed. Great art is liberating, it enables us to see and take pleasure in what is not ourselves. Literature stirs and satisfies our curiosity, it interests us in other people and other scenes, and helps us to be tolerant and generous. Art is informative. And even mediocre art can tell us something, for instance about how other people live. But to say this is not to hold a utilitarian or didactic view of art. Art is larger than such narrow ideas. Plato at least saw how tremendously important art is and he raised interesting questions about it. Philosophers on the whole have not written very well about art, partly because they have regarded it as a minor matter which must be fitted in with their general theory of metaphysics or morals.

MAGEE: That is generally true, but there is one philosopher I would exempt from the charge: Schopenhauer. Unlike nearly all other philosophers he did regard art as being central to human life and had some genuinely profound things to say about it.

MURDOCH: Yes, certainly. Schopenhauer disagreed with Plato, in fact he turned Plato's view upside down. Plato saw art as giving intellectual pleasure to the selfish stupid part of the soul. Whereas the nobler part of the soul sought for knowledge of reality through what Plato called Ideas, which were universal rational conceptions or sources of enlightenment, and to be contrasted with unintelligible particular things. So according to Plato art was meanly particular and knowledge was rationally general. Schopenhauer on the other hand says that art actually seeks and can convey the Ideas, which he pictures as intelligible forms which are partly realised in nature, and which the imagination of the artist tries to elicit. Schopenhauer says that art removes the veil or mist of subjectivity and arrests the flux of life and makes us see the real world and this shock is the experience of beauty. This is an attractive and lofty view of art since it pictures it as moral and intellectual striving, and as being like philosophy in that it attempts to explain the world. It also suggests the way in which good art is both very general and very particular. Eastern religions present views which are in some ways similar. However I cannot accept these 'Ideas', even as offering a metaphor of how the artist works. Of course our minds may be said to 'impose form' on the world, and philosophers have always been looking for built-in affinities between us and nature. I do not hold any general philosophical view on this matter, and I think that here an analogy between philosophy and art could go too far. The working artist confronts, and may glory in, a lot of unintelligible random stuff; and perhaps great artists only seem to 'explain the world', though they do explain parts of it. Kant's more muddled, less lofty, picture of art which Schopenhauer 'corrects' is in some ways more realistic. Art is not all that 'intelligible'. But I do find Schopenhauer's view sympathetic in that it portrays art as a high use of the intellectual and moral faculties, and as an attempt to overcome the self and see the world.

Schopenhauer is something of an exception among philosophers in that he clearly loves and values art. A lot of philosophical theorising on the subject is less imaginative, concerned with opposing one rather limited view to another one, as in: is art for art's sake or for society's sake?

MAGEE: One of the troubles with almost any philosophy of art is that it is exclusive. Once you think that all art has got to be of a certain kind to fit your particular theory, then it follows that everything that does not fit in with your theory is not art.

MURDOCH: Fortunately artists do not pay too much attention to philosophers. But sometimes philosophy can damage art, it can make people blind to some kinds of art, or only able to produce some kinds.

MAGEE: One outstanding example, in the modern world, of a philosophy which has been damaging to art is Marxism. According to Marxist theory art has a specific role, which is to be an instrument of social revolution. There is a very great deal of Marxist art of all kinds – novels, plays, paintings, sculpture and so on – I have to say I regard most of it as rubbish. It is rubbish because the impulse that created it has not been a genuinely artistic impulse at all. It is a branch of propaganda.

MURDOCH: I certainly do not believe that it is the artist's task to serve society. Marxists, I suppose, do believe this, though there have been famous controversies about how it is to be done. Some Marxists would hold that art should be virtually pamphlets or posters for the present state of the revolution, that novelists and painters should attack 'social enemies' and glorify the kind of people society needs now. Modern Soviet pictures of noble farm workers or girl scientists are cases of this thoroughly sentimental form of art. There is a more intelligent and liberal Marxist view of literature as deep analysis of society. George Lukács took that sort of view before he was forced to admit he was 'mistaken'. He made a distinction between 'realism', which was an imaginative exploration of social structure, and 'naturalism' which was trivial or sensationalist copying; and he described the great nineteenth-century novelists as realists, in that they told us deep important truths about society. I think he is right to praise these novelists in this way. But analysis of society in a way interesting to a Marxist was not the main aim of these writers nor the only thing they were doing. As soon as a writer says to himself, 'I must try to change society in such and such ways by my writing,' he is likely to damage his work.

MAGEE: But how can we fit Dickens in here? He seems to have had genuinely social aims – among other aims, no doubt – and he does appear to have had quite a considerable social influence.

MURDOCH: Yes, Dickens manages to do everything, to be a great imaginative writer and a persistent and explicit social critic. I think the scandals of his society were closely connected with the kind of ferment and social change which engaged his imagination most deeply. He is able to swallow all these things into his genius, and you rarely feel he is 'getting at you' with some alien social point. But one might note all the same that his most 'abstract' novel *Hard Times* is one of his less successful, and that his most effective criticisms of society are made through live and touching characters such as the sweeper boy Joe in *Bleak House*. Dickens is a great writer because of his ability to create character, and also because of deep frightful imaginative visions which have little to do with social reform. *Edwin Drood* is a better novel than *Hard Times*. A deliberate or anxiously surreptitious attempt to persuade usually removes a work to a more superficial level. One feels this sometimes in George Eliot who does not 'get away with it' as well as Dickens does.

MAGEE: In such cases the work of art is not only ceasing to be an end in itself, it is being made a means for a lesser end than itself.

MURDOCH: Yes. As I said, I do not think that the artist, *qua* artist, has a duty to society. A citizen has a duty to society, and a writer might sometimes feel he ought to write persuasive newspaper articles or pamphlets, but this would be a different activity. The artist's duty is to art, to truth-telling in his own medium, the writer's duty is to produce the best literary work of which he is capable, and he must find out how this can be done. This may seem a rather artificial distinction between artist and citizen, but I think it is worth reflecting in this way. A propaganda play which is indifferent to art is likely to be a misleading statement even if it is inspired by good principles. If serious art is a primary aim then some sort of justice is a primary aim. A social theme presented as art is likely to be more clarified even if it is less immediately persuasive. And any artist may serve his society incidentally by revealing things which people have not noticed or understood. Imagination reveals, it explains. This is part of what is meant by saying that art is mimesis. Any society contains propaganda, but it is important to distinguish this from art and to preserve the purity and independence of the practice of art. A good society contains many different artists doing many different things. A bad society coerces artists because it knows that they can reveal all kinds of truths.

MAGEE: We've discussed, first, the distinction between philosophy and literature; then philosophical ideas about literature; let us now move on to philosophy in literature. I mean several things by that. Let us take novels as our example. First, there have been some famous philosophers – or thinkers very like philosophers, such as Voltaire – who have been themselves novelists: Rousseau, for instance, or in our own time Jean-Paul Sartre. Then, among other novelists, there are some who have been influenced by philosophical ideas. Tolstoy appends an epilogue to *War and Peace* in which he explains that he's been trying in this novel to express a certain philosophy of history. Dostoevsky is quite often described by existentialists as the greatest of all existentialist writers. Proust, in *A la recherche du temps perdu*, is deeply concerned with problems about the nature of time, which is also one of the classic concerns of philosophers. Can you make any observations on the sort of role philosophy can play in novels?

MURDOCH: I see no 'general role' of philosophy in literature. People talk about Tolstoy's 'philosophy' but that is really a *façon de parler*. And Bernard Shaw is a terrible instance of a writer quite mistakenly imagining that he has 'a philosophy'. Fortunately his 'ideas' do not harm his plays too much. When T. S. Eliot says that it is not the poet's task to think and that neither Dante nor Shakespeare could do so, I understand him although I would not put it that way. Of course writers are influenced by the ideas of their time and may be interested in philosophical change, but the amount of philosophy they succeed in expressing is likely to be small. I think as soon as philosophy gets into a work of literature it becomes a plaything of the writer, and rightly so. There is no strictness about ideas and argument, the rules are different and truth is differently conveyed. If a so-called 'novel of ideas' is bad art its ideas if any would have been better expressed elsewhere. If it is good art the ideas are either transformed or else appear as little chunks of reflection (as in Tolstoy) which are put up with cheerfully for the sake of the rest of the work. Great nineteenth-century novelists get away with a lot of 'idea play' in their work, but one could not regard it as philosophy. Of course artists writing as critics and theorising about their own art may not be very 'philosophical' but they can be more interesting than the philosophers! Tolstoy's book *What Is Art?* is full of oddities, but it expresses one profound central idea, that good art is religious, that it embodies the highest religious perceptions of the age. One might say that the best art can somehow *explain* the concept of religion to each generation. I feel great sympathy with this idea though it is not philosophically presented.

MAGEE: I'm not sure I go along with you entirely. In *War and Peace* Tolstoy tells us that the articulation of a particular philosophy of history is one of the things his novel came into existence to do. Or take a major English novel like Laurence Sterne's *Tristram Shandy*. Not only was that directly influenced by Locke's theories about the association of ideas: this is actually mentioned in the novel, and in terms which clearly refer to the novel itself. In other words Sterne was consciously doing something which he *himself* related to Locke's theory of the association of ideas. So there really are great novels in which the use of philosophical ideas is part of the structure.

MURDOCH: Perhaps it is partly that I feel in myself such an absolute horror of putting theories or 'philosophical ideas' as such into my novels. I might put in things about philosophy because I happen

[19]

to know about philosophy. If I knew about sailing ships I would put in sailing ships; and in a way, as a novelist, I would rather know about sailing ships than about philosophy. Of course novelists and poets *think*, and great ones think supremely well (and T. S. Eliot is not literally right) but that is another matter. Tolstoy or someone may say that he is writing to 'express a philosophy' but why should we think he has succeeded? The novels by Rousseau and Voltaire are certainly robust cases of 'novels of ideas' and have been very influential books in their time. Now they seem dated and rather dead, and that is the penalty of the form. I can think of one good philosophical novel which I admire very much, Sartre's *La Nausée*. That does manage to express some interesting ideas about contingency and consciousness, and to remain a work of art which does not have to be read in the light of theories which the author has expressed elsewhere. It is a rare object. Of course it is still philosophically 'fresh'.

MAGEE: All right, let's take Jean-Paul Sartre's *La Nausée*. I agree with you, I think it's a magnificent novel. Surely it also articulates a philosophical theory? To articulate a philosophical theory so successfully in the form of a work of fiction may be a unique achievement, but the fact that it has been done shows that it can be done. I think there is an important difference of opinion between you and me which we may simply not be able to resolve in this discussion. You, it seems to me, are trying to say that philosophy as such has no place in imaginative writing, except in so far as it can be material as anything else can be material. Whereas I want to say that some major novels make use of philosophical ideas not just as material in that sense, but in ways which are structural to the whole undertaking.

MURDOCH: The case of Sartre may be a special one. There is a literary 'feel' about his earlier philosophy, *L'Etre et le néant* is full of 'pictures and conversations'. Sartre emphasises the more dramatic aspects of the philosophy of Hegel, which is full of historical instances and in which the movement of thought itself is seen in terms of formal oppositions and conflicts. 'Ideas' often seem more at home in the theatre, though (as in the case of Shaw) there may be an illusion involved here. I am not sure how far

Sartre's plays are, or are not, damaged by having strong theoretical motives. Certainly one sees from Sartre's other novels, and the novels of Simone de Beauvoir, and I admire all these, how, as soon as the 'existentialist voice' is switched on, the work of art rigidifies. In general I am reluctant to say that the deep structure of any good literary work could be a philosophical one. I think this is not just a verbal point. The unconscious mind is not a philosopher. For better and worse art goes deeper than philosophy. Ideas in art must suffer a sea change. Think how much original thought there is in Shakespeare and how divinely inconspicuous it is. Of course some writers reflect much more overtly but as in the case of Dickens their reflections are *aesthetically* valuable in so far as they are connected, through character for instance, with substructures which are not abstract. When we ask what a novel is *about* we are asking for something deep. What is Proust about, and why not just read Bergson? There is always something moral which goes down further than the ideas, the structures of good literary works are to do with erotic mysteries and deep dark struggles between good and evil.

MAGEE: If the fiction writer is dealing with 'something moral which goes down further than the ideas' this must mean that fiction unavoidably involves the writer in presuppositions of not only a moral–philosophical but even a moral–metaphysical sort. One of the things I have in mind is this. Any kind of story at all, and any kind of description at all, are bound to incorporate value judgements, not just in the words you use but in what you choose to narrate, or describe, at all. So there simply is no way in which value judgements can *not* be structural to the writing. Any investigation of what these value judgements are is a philosophical activity, at least in part, as is even merely any seriously critical discussion of them. If your story is a serious one about people and the relations between people there will be no way in which you can avoid revealing moral presuppositions of many, complex and deep kinds.

MURDOCH: I agree, one cannot avoid value judgements. Values show, and show clearly, in literature. There are important moral presuppositions, for instance about religion and society, which belong to changing 'climates of ideas'. The disappearance of a general faith in religion and social hierarchy has affected literature profoundly. Our consciousness changes, and the change may appear in art before it receives its commentary in a theory, though the theory may also subsequently affect the art. We might mention here a contemporary school of critics who are especially interested in recent changes of consciousness. I mean the literary formalists who have tried to develop a literary criticism out of structuralist philosophy. 'Structuralism' is the name of a very general philosophical attitude which originated in linguistics and anthropology with thinkers such as Saussure and Lévi-Strauss.*

MAGEE: As you say, it originated in linguistics. We could illustrate it this way. You and I are communicating by uttering sentences each of which contains comparatively few words. But for somebody to understand us it isn't enough for him to know just the words we are using: he's got to be acquainted with a whole language system, in this case the English language. The point being made is a reaction against an idea that arose in the nineteenth century as a result of the development of science, the idea that to understand something you should isolate the phenomenon and, so to speak, look at it through a microscope. The basic thought of structuralism is a reaction against that, which says: 'No, the only way you can *really* understand phenomena is by relating them to larger structures. In fact the very notion of intelligibility itself involves relating things to structures.' The application of this view to literature has resulted in each piece of writing being viewed primarily as a word-structure.

MURDOCH: Yes. This view expresses a sort of anxious self-consciousness about language which has been evident in literature at least since Mallarmé. It has also found expression in linguistic philosophy. One could say that Wittgenstein was a 'structuralist'. 'What signs fail to express, their application shows.'† Many aspects of the theory are not new; it has heterogeneous literary

---

* [Saussure, Ferdinand de (1857–1913), Swiss linguist, father of modern linguistics, who argued that language is a closed system of signs within which exist 'only differences'. The French anthropologist Claude Lévi-Strauss (b. 1908), took Saussurian principles and applied them to the comparative study of societies and cultures.]

† *Tractatus*, 3.262

and philosophical ancestors such as the phenomenologists, the surrealists, and Sartre. It is not a closely unified doctrine. The 'change of consciousness' which interests the formalists is consequent upon our becoming aware of ourselves as sign-using animals who 'constitute' the world and ourselves, by our significance-bestowing activity. This is a case of a philosophical, or quasi-philosophical, assumption which can affect literature, just as Marxist assumptions can affect literature. It is a kind of literary idealism or literary monism. The formalists want to cure us of what might be called 'the realistic fallacy' whereby we imagine we can look through language into a separate world beyond. If language makes the world it cannot refer to the world. The writer must realise that he lives and moves within a 'significance-world', and not think that he can pass through it or crawl under the net of signs. This theory involves many formalists in an attack on the realistic novel, and on the familiar conventions of 'easy' literature which affects to use language as a simple transparent medium. The classical story, the classical object, the classical self with its mass of solid motives, are all 'pseudo-wholes' constituted by a misunderstanding of language. The idea that the self is not a unity goes back to Hume, and the suspicion that language itself is a sort of primal fault goes back to Plato. A number of literary writers since the Romantic Movement have gradually interested themselves in these ideas and played with them. Formalism is the latest systematic attempt to describe and explain what is by now quite a long and heterogeneous process. Such an attempt is bound to be valuable and interesting, but I myself find its atmosphere and its terminology too constricting. I think literary change is more mysterious and less unitary, and literary forms more profoundly versatile than such critics seem to suggest. In its more extreme manifestations formalism can become a metaphysical theory which denies, as such theories often do, a useful and necessary distinction, in this case the distinction between self and world and between more and less referential (or 'transparent') uses of language. Any artist knows what it is to look at the world, and the distance and otherness thereof is his primary problem. When Dr Johnson 'refuted' Berkeley by kicking a stone he was rightly protesting against a metaphysical attempt to remove a necessary distinction. The writer will make his own choice, and use language as he pleases and as he can, and must not be bullied by a theory into imagining that he cannot now tell a plain tale, but must produce self-consciously verbal texts which fight against ordinary modes of intelligibility. As part of their prescriptive doctrine some formalists have tried to develop a 'poetics', a neutral quasi-scientific theory related to literature as linguistics is related to a natural language. But such a 'meta-language' would depend upon some neutral method of identifying fundamental elements in the material to be analysed, and it is not clear what the 'elements' in literature could be agreed to be. It seems to me that all the interesting and important differences of opinion would be likely to break out at the earliest stage and thus 'infect' the meta-language with value judgements; so that unless such a theory was extremely abstract and simple (and thus inadequate) it would prove to be merely literary criticism by other means. We have so many *kinds* of relation to a work of art. A literary work is an extremely heterogeneous object which demands an open-minded heterogeneous response. Moreover aesthetic criticism combines a certain generality with an 'ostensive' relation to a particular object at which the hearer looks while the critic talks. Of course students often want to be reassured by a 'theory of criticism', and simplifications ease the hard work of original thought. But critics are better off without any close-knit systematic background theory, scientific or philosophical. A good critic is a relaxed polymath. Nor would I accept the dangerous argument that having no particular theory means having a 'bourgeois' theory. Of course we live as we must within historical limitations. But as critics and thinkers and moral agents we can attempt to understand our instincts and our attitudes and to distinguish true values from local prejudices and blinkered conventions. The 'bourgeois era' has brought us certain moral conceptions, such as the idea of rights and the freedom of the individual, which we are able to judge as permanently valuable. It is also produced a great literature which displays dated assumptions but also celebrates values which are still our own. We may appeal here to a conception of human nature which goes back to the Greeks. It is an important fact that we can understand Homer and Aeschylus. Literature is indeed the main carrier and creator of this wide-ranging understanding. Any theory which cuts people off from the great literature of the past deprives them of a historical and moral education and also of a great deal of pleasure.

MAGEE: In practice, literature written under the influence of formalist theories tends to be literature for a circle of cognoscenti, not literature which can appeal very widely. The common-sense assumption that language relates to a world of things and of people seems to me a necessary basis for any literature that is going to have a wide readership – and it is certainly a fact that most of the very greatest writers, from Shakespeare downwards, have been widely understood and appreciated. I have to confess that I am very much on one side of this controversy. Neither in literature nor in philosophy do I greatly care to see words made themselves the object of interest. I think they should be seen, in both activities, as a medium through which one relates to the world, whether it be a world of people, or of things, or of nature, or of problems, or of ideas, or of works of art.

MURDOCH: Yes, but I think it is up to the artist to decide how he is to use words. Writers who have never heard of formalism may write in ways which attract formalists. *Tristram Shandy* and *Finnegans Wake* are justified as art without any theory. We rightly judge theories by their ability to explain states of affairs with which we are already familiar, and if the theory attacks our phenomena we must take sides. I know who are great writers in the past and I will not surrender them to a theory but rather consider the theory in their light. Of course, if one may pick up the word 'form' here, literature is art and is thus the creation of formal and in a sense self-contained objects. A poem, play or novel usually appears as a closed pattern. But it is also open in so far as it refers to a reality beyond itself, and such a reference raises the questions about truth which I have already mentioned. Art is truth as well as form, it is representational as well as autonomous. Of course the communication may be indirect, but the ambiguity of the great writer creates spaces which we can explore and enjoy because they are openings on to the real world and not formal language games or narrow crevices of personal fantasy;

and we do not get tired of great writers, because what is true is interesting. Tolstoy's idea that art is religious is at home somewhere here. As I said, any serious artist has a sense of distance between himself and something quite other in relation to which he feels humility since he knows that it is far more detailed and wonderful and awful and amazing than anything which he can ever express. This 'other' is most readily called 'reality' or 'nature' or 'the world' and this is a way of talking that one must not give up. Beauty in art is the formal imaginative exhibition of something true, and criticism must remain free to work at a level where it can judge truth in art. Both artist and critic look at two things: representation and 'other'. This looking is of course not simple. Training in an art is largely training in how to discover a touchstone of truth; and there is an analogous training in criticism.

MAGEE: My last point was about certain kinds of self-consciousness in the use of language: I'd like now to raise a question about another one. An outstanding feature of philosophy in the twentieth century, especially in the Anglo-Saxon world, has been a completely new kind of concern with language, and in consequence a new self-consciousness about the use of language which can result in the most refined and scrupulous use of words. Has this in any way infected the novel? You personally, as someone who trained first of all as a philosopher and only then became a novelist – has it influenced the way you write your novels?

MURDOCH: It is true that there has been a kind of crisis in our relation to language, we are much more self-conscious about it, and that does affect writers.

MAGEE: One inevitable consequence of this is that you can no longer write like the novelists of the nineteenth century.

MURDOCH: Of course we are not anything like as good as the nineteenth-century novelists, but also we write differently.

MAGEE: This is an exceedingly interesting question. Can you say more about *why* you can't write like them?

MURDOCH: It is very difficult to answer that question. There are obvious differences to do with the standpoint of the author and his relationship to his characters. An author's relation to his characters reveals a great deal about his moral attitude, and this technical difference between us and the nineteenth-century writers is a moral change but one which it is hard to analyse. In general, our writing is more ironical and less confident. We are more timid, afraid of seeming unsophisticated or naïve. The story is more narrowly connected with the consciousness of the author who narrates through the consciousness of a character or characters. There is usually no direct judging or description by the author speaking as an external authoritative intelligence. To write like a nineteenth-century novelist in this respect now seems like a literary device and is sometimes used as one. As I said earlier, I think literature is about the struggle between good and evil, but this does not appear clearly in modern writing, where there is an atmosphere of moral diffidence and where the characters presented are usually mediocre. Many things cause literary change, and self-consciousness about language may be more of a symptom than a cause. The disappearance or weakening of organised religion is perhaps the most important thing that has happened to us in the last hundred years. The great nineteenth-century novelists took religion for granted. Loss of social hierarchy and religious belief makes judgement more tentative, interest in psychoanalysis makes it in some ways more complex. All these changes are so remarkable and so challenging that it sounds as if we ought to be better than our predecessors, but we are not!

MAGEE: [. . .] I'd like to go a little more fully [. . .] into the question of what an author's relation to his characters reveals about his moral standpoint.

MURDOCH: It is important to remember that language itself is a moral medium, almost all uses of language convey value. This is one reason why we are almost always morally active. Life is soaked in the moral, literature is soaked in the moral. If we attempted to describe this room our descriptions would naturally carry all sorts of values. Value is only artificially and with difficulty expelled from language for scientific purposes. So the novelist is revealing his values by any sort of writing which he may do. He is particularly bound to make moral judgements in so far as his subject matter is the behaviour of human beings. I suggested earlier that a work of art is both mimetic and formal, and of course these two requirements sometimes conflict. In the novel this conflict may appear as a struggle between characters and plot. Does a writer limit and constrain his characters to suit the plot or to suit his own judgements and his theme? Or does he stand back and let the characters develop independently of him and of each other without regard to plot or any general overriding 'tone'? In particular, how does the writer indicate moral approval or disapproval of his characters? He has to do this, consciously or unconsciously. How does he justify the good man, how does he present him or even hint at his existence? The author's moral judgement is the air which the reader breathes. One can see here very clearly the contrast between blind fantasy and visionary imagination. The bad writer gives way to personal obsession and exalts some characters and demeans others without any concern for truth or justice, that is without any suitable aesthetic 'explanation'. It is clear here how the idea of reality enters into literary judgement. The good writer is the just, intelligent judge. He justifies his placing of his characters by some sort of *work* which he does in the book. A literary fault such as sentimentality results from idealisation without work. This work of course may be of different kinds, and all sorts of methods of placing characters, or relation of characters to plot or theme, may produce good art. Criticism is much concerned with the techniques by which this is done. A great writer can combine form and character in a felicitous way (think how Shakespeare does it) so as to produce a large space in which the characters can exist freely and yet at the same time serve the purposes of the tale. A great work of art gives one a sense of space, as if one had been invited into some large hall of reflection.

MAGEE: Does what you are saying mean, in the last analysis, that imaginative writing must, although it is imaginative, be rooted in some kind of acceptance of things as they are, and even respect for things as they are?

MURDOCH: Well, artists are often revolutionary in some sense or other. But the good artist has, I think, a sense of reality and might be said to understand 'how things are' and why they are. Of course the term 'reality' is notoriously ambiguous in philosophy and I have used it to suggest both that the serious artist looks at the world and that he sees more of the world. The great artist sees the marvels which selfish anxiety conceals from the rest of us. But what the artist sees is not something separate and special, some metaphysically cut-off never-never land. The artist engages a very large area of his personality in his work, and he works in and normally accepts the world of common sense. Art is naturally communication (only a perverse ingenuity can attempt to deny this obvious truth) and this involves the joining of the farthest-out reality to what is nearer, as must be done by any truthful explorer. This is something which the critic must be watching too. When is abstract painting bad art, when is it not art at all? Abstract painting is not just wilful fantasy or provocation, it is connected with the nature of space and colour. The abstract painter lives, and his pictures are seen, in a world where colours are taken to be surfaces of objects, and his consciousness of this is a part of his problem. Such tensions between aesthetic vision and 'ordinary' reality may give rise to very refined and difficult judgements. Literature is connected with the way we live. Some philosophers tell us that the self is discontinuous and some writers explore this idea, but the writing (and the philosophy) takes place in a world where we have good reasons for assuming the self to be continuous. Of course this is not a plea for 'realistic' writing. It is to say that the artist cannot avoid the demands of truth, and that his decision about how to tell truth in his art is his most important decision.

MAGEE: Do you think this acceptance of reality implies anything conservative with a small 'c'? What I have in mind is the sort of acceptance of things and people as they are which can arise out of intense interest and is also related to love. As regards people, at least, perhaps a better word than 'conservative' would be 'tolerant'.

MURDOCH: I would like to say that all great artists are tolerant in their art, but perhaps this cannot be argued. Was Dante tolerant? I think most great writers have a sort of calm merciful vision because they can see how different people are and why they are different. Tolerance is connected with being able to imagine centres of reality which are remote from oneself. There is a breath of tolerance and generosity and intelligent kindness which blows out of Homer and Shakespeare and the great novelists. The great artist sees the vast interesting collection of what is other than himself and does not picture the world in his own image. I think this particular kind of merciful objectivity is virtue, and it is this which the totalitarian state is trying to destroy when it persecutes art.

This conversation with Bryan Magee, philosopher and broadcaster, was originally shown on British television, 28 October 1977. Substantially reworked, as above, it was published in Magee's *Men of Ideas*, 1978.

PART TWO

Nostalgia for the Particular, 1951–57

'In fact, any experience is infinitely rich and deep. We feel it to be intrinsically significant because we can brood upon it; but the same brooding shows it to be endlessly various in meaning.'

'Nostalgia for the Particular', 1952

Thinking and Language

I want to consider language as a kind of thinking, and to do this I shall first attempt a description of thinking. I set aside all philosophical theories, old and new, about the nature of thinking: theories such as that it is having representations, or cognising propositions, or manipulating symbols or behaving in certain ways. I shall assume, as we all do when we are not philosophising, that thinking is a private activity which goes on in our heads, that it is a 'content of consciousness'. Even those philosophers who are most opposed to the 'inner life' view of thinking allow such 'contents' to exist, though with an extremely curtailed role, under the title of imagined monologues, images, or sentences uttered to oneself. I shall take activities of this sort to be what is meant by thinking and shall attempt first of all to describe them, and to consider their relation to 'language'. (By language I shall mean verbal language throughout.) Such a description will clearly not cover all that we mean by 'mental concepts'. It will not be intended to cover habitual and unreflective modes of activity which may nevertheless be called intelligent. My concern is with those kinds of mental activity (and which exactly they are will be evident) which in ordinary English are called 'thinking'.

I shall be assuming (as, again, we all do) for purposes of this description that within limits we all have similar 'mental' experiences. After offering the description I shall consider its logical status, its purpose, and what light it may throw upon the nature of language.

We might at first be tempted to say that thought is the uttering of mental words. We could then divide the mental region between obscure drifting images and clear verbal thought whose meaning is determined in accordance with simple overt criteria. But this will not do. Words do not occur as the content of thought as if they were cast upon a screen and there read off by the thinker. If we explicitly imagine the uttering of a verbal message to ourselves this contrasts with the more confused way in which words do occur 'in our minds'. Also, if we were to hear and see words uttered inwardly we might wonder what they meant; this sort of wondering is an experience which does occur sometimes, as when Bunyan ponders the sense of a text which he suddenly hears ringing in his ears, but this is unlike what we usually call thought. A machine which gave us a verbal version of another person's thought might tell us very little; and even if we remember in our own case what we 'said to ourselves' on a certain occasion, we should be ill-informed unless we could remember too in what frame of mind, with what intention, we had said it. The meaning-character of uttered speech often demands an awareness of gesture, tone, and so on, as well as of context, for its full understanding. This is clearly so too, *mutatis mutandis*, for inward 'speech'. The thought is not the words (if any) but the words occurring in a certain way with, as it were, a certain force and colour.

Reflection on this may lead us toward two provisional conclusions, both of which I shall pick up again later. The first is that if we want to stick naïvely to a description of 'what occurs' we shall be unwise to divide words and other imagery sharply from each other at the outset. Word experience in thinking may have various kinds of image-like character. (What kinds, whether visual or dynamic, may depend on personal peculiarities and is not here important.) We may indeed distinguish at two extremes the vague floating images which are pliant and indescribable, which as it were tell us nothing new, and the fully verbalised thought, ready for exposure to someone else, the formulation of which was perhaps a development of some vaguer reflection. The former are the most private, the latter the most public, i.e., readily exposable, parts of any inner monologue. This indicates, incidentally, the crystallising role which the occurrence of words, and the determining role which the availability of names, may play in thought. In between the two however there is the region where words occur but in a more indeterminate imaging manner (indeterminacy is a main characteristic of the mental image) and not at all like a rehearsed inner speech.

The second point to be noticed is the serious empirical unsuitability of anything like a mathematical model for language. Mathematical symbols are correctly considered as not occurring as contents of consciousness. The symbols which constitute our ordinary language may, and I shall argue should, be considered. This is not to deny that for some purposes we may adequately think of language as an internally self-determining set of public symbols or (the *Tractatus* picture) as a determinate mirror of the structure of the world. In the context however of a description of thinking we cannot consider language as a set of grooves into which we slip. Here language cannot be considered as saying itself; it is not 'p' that says p, but I who say 'p' meaning p. Language is a set of occurrences.

We might imagine a tribe whose private thoughts consisted entirely of mathematical calculations, simple observation and induction verbally conducted, and exclamations. For such a people thinking would indeed be the private manipulation of exposable symbols; and for them a simple division of language into descriptive and emotive uses would be appropriate. Here too it would be easier to make sense of the idea that it was a matter of accident into which series of mental events a particular symbolic configuration had got itself. ('If it's a calculation anyone could do it, if not you might as well spin a coin.') It is an important fact about us that we are not like these people.

Let us now continue the description. Considered as a content of thought, language may have a revelatory role (as when in *La Chartreuse de Parme* Mosca fears the *mention* of the word 'love' between Fabrice and the duchess) or it may have the opposite role. We have already had reason to think that a thought cannot necessarily be characterised by its verbal content. Language and thought are not co-extensive. That this is so is obvious if we consider the experience of attempting to break through a linguistic formulation grasped as inadequate in relation to an obscurely apprehended content. We know too what it is like for thought to be stifled by a conventional description, or for a verbal summary to replace a memory image. Experience of this kind may lead to neurotic or metaphysical views about language ('consciousness is the gaps in language') where it is thought of as a coarse net through which experiences slip. ('Thought seeks the unique, language gets in the way.') This experience may be connected with the nostalgia for the particular* and the search for the concrete universal. Not all our new concepts come to us in the context of language; but the attempt to verbalise them may result not in frustration but in a renewal of language. This is *par excellence* the task of poetry. So there is give and take; words may determine a sense, or a fresh experience may renew words. (I am not distinguishing here between words which I originate, and the words of another which I think through and make my own.)

Finally let me turn to another aspect of the problem and then be done with this question-begging description. It seems that a thought may be described as an experience into which words enter variously or not at all. Now it may be said, why should we want to characterise an individual thought? Why should we regard it as a mental datum? What we look at when using mental words is context and conduct, not inner events. This is true up to a point (and I shall discuss its relevance further below). But in fact, to us (as opposed to the external observer naming our goings on), our imagined monologues are not always unimportant, and we *do* attempt to characterise particular events which occur in them. In *Daniel Deronda* when Gwendolen hesitates to throw the lifebelt to her detested husband, who subsequently drowns, it matters very much to her to know whether or not at that moment she intended his death. It is also remarkable that another person, Deronda, thinks that he too is able to come to a true conclusion about Gwendolen's intention. Such a conclusion obviously depends upon a wide consideration of context, but what it appears to be *about* is a particular mental event. I shall examine this notion further in what follows; at present I only point out that this is how we behave.

When it is of interest to us to characterise a past thought, how do we do it? I may answer the question: what were you thinking then? by a sentence which purports to offer the content of the thought. This may or may not imply that I was using verbal images 'at the time'. Or else I may reply by some statement about my intention or state of mind, which I may characterise in metaphorical terms. Analogies and metaphors readily spring up in such a context (the

* [See next essay, 'Nostalgia for the Particular'.]

pages of psychological novels and of books of art criticism are covered with them) and they are usually accepted or even developed by the interlocutor. We are not at a loss here – nor do we (unless there are special reasons) question the accuracy of the description offered. We can easily give ourselves an example both of the way in which a thought experience overflows its verbal content and of the naturalness of a metaphorical description of the experience by attempting to characterise the experience of reading certain lines of poetry. To take an instance at random, Clare's lines about the snail:

> Frail brother of the morn,
> That from the tiny bents and misted leaves
> Withdraws his timid horn
> And fearful vision weaves.

To take such an example is convenient because it constitutes a sort of public object which we can all handle, whereas communication of certain other types of mental experience is often only possible in limited societies, sometimes only in societies of two. Here we may attempt to describe our experience on reading these lines in terms say of a smooth delicate suspense followed by an enormous sense of chaotic expansion at the last line. What is important is not that we necessarily offer each other the same descriptions, but that we naturally use a metaphorical mode of speech, and that yet we can understand each other and even come to influence what the other experiences.

I shall now discuss the status and purpose of the descriptions which I have been offering. I have used the word 'experience' throughout – which we have been advised against doing. We are so advised, I think, for several reasons. It is held, on the one hand, that accidental introspective contents are of no interest in connection with determining the meaning of mental terminology, since we cannot detect or identify any stable kind of datum of which these terms are the name. On the other hand, mental terms do have clear and determinate conventions of use in connection with modes of overt behaviour. If it cannot be shown that something *must* have occurred in order for a certain use of a mental term to be an accurate use then that something is not regarded as part of the meaning of the term; and the things which 'must occur' are then demonstrated to be observable conduct and not unobservable inner experience.

I think one may challenge both the criterion of meaning used here and certainly the 'ontological' conclusions which appear to be drawn from it. It may be true both that we do not learn mental words in connection with inner experiences, and also that we verify, or justify, propositions which contain these words (when they refer to other people) by reference to conduct. It does not follow from this that there is 'no such thing' as the inner experience or that it is not (in some cases at any rate) what is meant by the mental words, in a perfectly familiar sense, of 'meant'. The notion of meaning which goes with strict justification (or verification) demands an observable or identifiable something which shall by a universal convention be that which justifies the use, and this is to be detected from an objective impersonal standpoint. From such a standpoint 'the mind' is inevitably seen as divided between obscure private communings about which nothing can be said, and overt cases of intelligent, etc., conduct; and the language which this investigation illuminates is a public symbolism taking its sense from an open network of social conventions. But it is surely important that the users of mental words would often indignantly deny that 'what they meant' was the overt and not the inner. Such an 'idea of meaning' proves, moreover, a perfectly acceptable basis for communication, and one without which the use would sensibly alter. (Imagine a people who *really* held that what happened 'in their heads' was irrelevant to the use of words such as 'decide'.) The reaction to this should not be to denounce an illusion and suggest that the inner *is nothing*, or is at best shadowy and nameless. One should attempt a new description.

In doing so the choice must be rejected between logical behaviourism and the private theatre. An ontological approach, which seeks for an identifiable inner stuff and either asserts or denies its existence, must be avoided. An account of meaning which rests on a search for hard verificatory data (the *Tractatus* approach) breaks down in certain regions, and there seems no good reason to maintain it *à tout prix*. What is observable is that we need and use the idea that thoughts are particular inner experiences. This is an idea which connects up with our notion of the privacy and unity of our 'selves' or 'personalities'. There is here, if I may borrow a psychological term, an important and necessary 'illusion of immanence'; only to call it an 'illusion' risks giving the description an ontological flavour. It is rather a necessary regulative idea, about which it makes no sense to ask, is it true or false that it is *so*? It is for us *as if* our thoughts were inner events, and it is *as if* these events were describable either as verbal units or in metaphorical, analogical terms. We constantly recover and fix our mental past by means of a descriptive technique, a sort of story-telling, whose justification is its success. We know too of ways in which to adjust and check, in ourselves and others, the accuracy of this technique. And if a philosophical precedent be needed for this important *as if*, we have only to look to Kant's use of the regulative idea of freedom, which seems to me essentially similar and equally empirical.

What I have just been talking about is how we can characterise or describe the activity of private thought. For if one is tempted to look at language as a part of the content of such thought, one must first consider the technique of description which is available for such a study. I have suggested that we have a technique which we use naturally, as a part of our ordinary living, and that there seems to be no good philosophical reason for abandoning it. One should rather attempt to investigate it and make it if possible more accurate. Language is used to recover and 'fix' our inner mental life in such a way that we both 'have the idea' that there was a datum, while being unable to make sense of ontological questions about the datum.

An important point to notice about our experience as displayed in such a description is that it is, somehow, riddled with the sensible. Language itself, if we think of it as it occurs 'in' our thoughts, is hardly to be distinguished from imagery of a variety of kinds – hardly to be distinguished at times, one might add, from sensations, in the sense of obscure bodily feelings. Again, there seems no sense here in asking for a clear ontological classification. This is what thinking is like. This is to be connected with the fact that we naturally use metaphors to describe states of mind, or to describe 'thought processes', in those cases where a sentence giving the verbal content of the thought is felt to be inadequate. In such a context metaphor is not an inexact *faute de mieux* mode of expression, it is the best possible. Here metaphor is not a peripheral excrescence upon the linguistic structure, it is its living centre. And the metaphors which we encounter, and which illuminate us, in conversation and in poetry, are offered and are found illuminating because language also occurs in thinking in the way that it does. We do not 'suddenly' have to adopt the figurative mode; we are using it all the time. That is, both the actual occurrence of words in thought and our private conceptual fixing of our states of mind, is experienced in an imaging, semi-sensible mode, particular examples of which we are not unable to discuss successfully with other people. The core of 'experience' upon which the conceptualising *as if* is at work to produce a version more precise than anything which strict memory can detect is itself sensible in character – and the language which does the 'fixing' is already soaked in the sensible, from its occurrence in the strugglings of private thought. I am not sure if this description is a good one; what is philosophically important here is that it may be accepted (by some people at least) as a plausible account of what is the case, and one which can be improved upon by mutual agreement.

This may suggest a new view of concepts – or rather the renovation of an old view. We naturally create metaphors in the context of certain kinds of attempt to describe. As when, for instance, we speak of having a bond with somebody which remains unbroken through times of emptiness or even of hostility. Such a mode of speech is so natural to us that we might be surprised when its metaphorical character is pointed out. This is typical of our use of language to fix in a semi-sensible picture some aspect of our activities – and such fixing is using, or creating, concepts. This is not to say, again, that the notion of a concept as 'how a word is used' is not a useful, even essential, one. It is to say it is perhaps not the only one of philosophical interest. If we think of conceptualising rather as the activity of grasping, or reducing to order, our situations with the help of a language which is fundamentally metaphorical, this will operate against the world-language dualism which haunts us because we are afraid of the idealists. Seen from this point of view, thinking is not the using of *symbols* which designate absent *objects*, symbolising and sensing being strictly divided from each other.

Thinking is not designating at all, but rather understanding, grasping, 'possessing'.

I said earlier that it made no sense, when retrospectively characterising such a content of thought, to ask whether what was asserted was 'really so' or not. It makes no sense, that is, in the context of a scientifically minded verificatory enquiry. It does make sense however in the context of the individual's self-examination, and in certain cases (e.g., the *Deronda* case) other people may significantly ask and answer the question too. I spoke above of an 'experience', sensible in character, upon which the conceptualising thought is at work – and such a core may often be detected. We know what it is like to try to recall a state of mind – it is *as if* there is something there the exact character of which we cannot yet quite descry. What, it may be asked, are the criteria here of a true description? That is, what are the criteria for me (or, rarely, for you) – what will satisfy me that I have hit the mark? I am not sure how much use it is to ask this question. What, after all, satisfies me, objective corroboration apart, that I have remembered anything correctly? One might speak here (particularly in such a case as the *Deronda* example) of adequacy, richness, flexibility, which will depend upon the subject's inducing a truthful and imaginative state of mind in the present. We know what it is to attempt to do this. If the 'truth' involved here cannot be even pictured in terms of correspondence, this is but another case of the breaking down of the dualism. And if it looks as if one approaches a sort of idealism here, it seems to me that that cannot be avoided. The idealists after all did attempt (with metaphysical implications of which one may well disapprove) to characterise concepts in a way which a purely empirical consideration of what thinking is like should suggest, even now, to the unprejudiced. There seems no reason why one should not model a description of experience upon its fullest moments, just as much as on its emptiest moments, if one can show such a description to be of philosophical interest.

I have attempted such a description here, and tried to draw from it one or two ideas which I fear I have not been able to develop very far. How far they can be developed, and what is the best way to do it, is still unclear to me. What is important I think, to sum up, is the following. It need not be assumed that a certain kind of logical technique offers the only method of dealing with 'mental phenomena'. This technique moreover goes with a verificationist attitude and a dualistic view of language and the world which may be challenged. A more naïvely empirical approach may reveal to us problems, about the characterisation of thought, the nature of concepts, the role of metaphor, which are still worth investigation. It will also suggest to us the method of investigation, which will involve a study, a developing and vindicating of our ordinary and familiar linguistic habits.

This paper came from a symposium entitled 'Thinking and Language', between Iris Murdoch, Gilbert Ryle and A. C. Lloyd, 1951.

Nostalgia for the Particular

We have got used to the idea that the region of personal 'experience' or 'consciousness' resembles the silence of the law in the *Leviathan*. Here, *anything* may go on, it doesn't matter what, so long as the public rules are not broken; and what goes on is of no interest except to the individual. Hume and Locke thought that there must be some constant and rigid connection between language and experience. In ceasing to believe this we have, perhaps too readily, let the notion of 'experience' drop out of sight altogether. The 'mental event' has been abandoned for two reasons which it is worthwhile to distinguish; partly because we do not need it and partly because we cannot find it. Only the revelation about not needing it has taken the interest out of the attempt to find it. Since we do not require the mental event either to make language significant or to provide a referent for remarks about the mind, we have not examined further what precisely it is that is wrong with the idea of the mental event. The arguments in *The Concept of Mind* [Gilbert Ryle] are largely demonstrations that we are not really referring to inner mental happenings when we speak of intelligent activity; it is assumed almost by the way that there are no such happenings. This movement occasions a certain haunting sense of loss which might be investigated further; a sense too of an unbridgeable gulf between the 'meaning' which is investigated by linguistic analysis, and the 'meaning' involved in poetry, or investigated by psychoanalysis, which seems inextricably linked with experience. Here a number of problems lie closely side by side and we must recover what has been jettisoned in order to separate them.

The mental event was needed partly to constitute the stuff and contents of the mind and be the guarantee of the intelligent character of action, and partly to provide a world composed of recurrent and intrinsically meaningful entities which should also be the basis of language. We cease to want it to play the first role when we see that what determines the use of words about the mind are features of the overt context; the rigidity that creates meaning lies in the social framework and not in the relation to an inward utterance. We lose interest in the second role when we see that acts of meaning (for instance in the form of images) do not necessarily accompany intelligent uses of words and that even if they did they would only be rendered unambiguous by the use which we made of them. And we no longer want to solve the problem of universals by thinking of experience as providing units of meaning which we can pack up and take away.

We can speak of facts without speaking of experiences. But, the objector may argue, can we really? We may surrender the idea of 'the particular experience', understood in the senses mentioned, but have we not merely shifted its position? It must now appear as that which ultimately *justifies* rules for the use of words. And is this not obviously true? In a way it is; and yet this notion dissolves in our hands in a manner similar to the manner in which the problem about the content (as opposed to the form) of other people's experience dissolves. What does a man *lack* who, without understanding the word 'red', always manages (for some reason or other, say because he has been hypnotised) to use it correctly? Well, he lacks the real justification, the experience. *What* experience? Here the problem falls away in either of two directions. Either the experience eludes identification except via the convention which it was intended to illuminate, or else, if we really examine a case of 'the experience which justifies' we find, not that there is too little to say about it, but that there is too much. If we consider what justifies in its full-blooded reality and not simply in its justifying role, it becomes indefinitely rich. The sensation is an experience, yes – but as such it can be described, characterised, in an indefinite number of ways and it seems fruitless to insist that it compactly *holds* at a given moment all that could truly be said of it. The ideas of 'knowing' and 'observing' which go with the idea of 'the specific' depend upon an ability to describe which may be exercised thus or thus upon any given experience. These arguments are familiar.

But, the objector will continue, does this mean more than that there are certain problems you need not raise about experiences, and problems which you cannot solve by reference to them. The experiences remain, palpable and inward, and surely there is more than this which needs to be said about them. Here it is necessary to distinguish two problems which may be in the mind of someone who feels that there is more to be said about experience. The first is: do we have 'mental' experiences which are perfectly specific and able to be described unambiguously in the way in which 'physical' experiences can be described? The second is: are there mental experiences which are somehow self-describing, which have intrinsic sense, which are sources of, or experiences of, sense? One result of our having 'dropped' the mental event so abruptly is that these two problems tend to become confused with each other. I shall now look at the first one, before going on to see if any precise meaning can be given to the second one.

Much of the distress and opposition occasioned by *The Concept of Mind* arises from a desire to retain the identifiable mental event; though much of the confusion in the criticism of this book comes from a failure to distinguish this item from the act of meaning. Surely, it is felt, when I am jealous or angry something quite particular happens within me, and it is this that *makes* an angry or jealous condition. Something happens, yes. But it is still the outward context and not the precise nature of the inner feeling, however intense this may be, which determines the name which we give to the condition as a whole. Could we imagine a machine which induced 'jealous feelings' in the absence of any jealousy context? It is in a particular *situation* that we call a thought jealously toned. And if we look closely at 'feelings' here, what are they? It is the physical concomitants which provide the core of the notion of an event. These physical phenomena may be taken as a test of the genuineness of the feeling, and may give a date to the feeling, but they do not determine the meaning of the feeling. The thing inside the box gives weight to the box, but it does not give shape to the box, and in a way it does not matter what is inside. There is an impact, and there is a convention, and it is to the latter we look for meaning.

But, it may still be objected, there *are* mental events which have a perfectly definite character and one which is not to be either scattered into the context or identified with a physical concomitant. I may agree that no such event necessarily occurs when I recognise a red thing, nor even when I feel jealous; but when, for instance, I feel that I am morally responsible for having had a particular thought, what I am concerned with here is one such self-contained event. Or if I suddenly make a decision, or solve a problem, though I were to die the next moment it would still be true that a particular mental movement had been made. Such mental events are *there*, God sees them, and they are just as compact and determinate as physical events, though possibly harder to describe. If I shoot my landlord the event itself does not depend on the context for its existence, though it may in a sense depend on the context for its meaning (e.g., was it blameworthy?). Similarly if I suddenly conceive the idea of shooting my landlord this event does not depend on the context for its existence though it may (in exactly the same sense as in the other case) for its meaning. When we introspect we look at contexts but this is not because there are no events. What exactly is the trouble here?

Now it is true that what is called 'having an idea' or 'solving a problem' or 'making a decision' often does not even appear to be a particular event. But all that the defender of the inner life is now maintaining is that it sometimes does. Moreover, certain remarks about the mind do seem to refer to particular mental events, and to suggest that such remarks are really about behaviour is to suggest a radical alteration of their sense. Yet, on the other hand, there does seem to be a difficulty involved in describing or identifying the inner events. What sort of difficulty is this? After all, *any* experience, the experience of a physical event just as much as the experience of a mental event, may be hard to describe. It is difficult to describe the smell of the Paris metro or what it is *like* to hold a mouse in one's hand – except by using the words already used. Is it the same in the case of the experience of the decision to shoot the landlord, or is there some other difficulty? 'But we don't experience decisions, we make decisions.' Yet if you want to characterise the thing as an event, it's an experience like another, you can describe it thus or thus; and why is describing it so hard?

Professor Ayer (in *Thinking and Meaning*) divides the mental region between overt public conventions (which govern that inward utterance of words which is all that 'thinking' can properly consist in) and obscure private phenomena, devoid of 'meaning', except possibly as material for psychological study. Professor Ryle (in *The Concept of Mind*) makes in effect the same division; the 'conventions' now cover a greater variety of patterns of behaviour, and though the phenomena get an occasional mention, Ryle never troubles to define his attitude towards them since he regards them as not required in connection with determining the sense of descriptions of the mind. In his paper in the recent symposium on *Thinking and Language,*[*] however, Ryle attends to this region of phenomena, and sub-divides it again. He distinguishes here between two modes in which the description of a 'mental process' may be offered. One mode (which he calls a chronicle) is the itemising of 'brute' psychological happenings (mental pictures, verbal imagery); the other mode (which he calls a history) consists in graphic description ('I was in a fog', 'I saw it in a flash'), such as one might spontaneously offer to describe a period of cognition.

The defender of the inner life will not be really satisfied. He will feel that the second sub-division is on the same pattern as the first and that once more the item which he wishes to preserve is lost between the two halves. The activity of the mind (considered now as a phenomenon among others) is not so easily disposed of. There are identifiable mental events the proper characterisation of which does not consist either in the listing of odd items of consciousness or in the offering of loose metaphorical descriptions which seem to have no real core which they are the descriptions of. On the one hand, metaphors are (*prima facie* at any rate) neither here nor there. We often spontaneously give metaphorical descriptions of situations (such as being lost on Hampstead Heath) of which we could, for other purposes, give more exact non-metaphorical descriptions. No one disputes the fact that, for everyday purposes, we are satisfied with the characterisation of our thoughts by unreflective metaphors or verbalised end-products. The question here is, can we not give a more exact description of the actual occurrences involved in thinking, whose existence has been denied or neglected? If we

[*] [See previous essay 'Thinking and Language'.]

examine the 'chronicle' we find that too little is offered. Or rather, if we really try to compile the list of merely 'psychological' items, we find that (unless the description is to be intolerably abstract and inexact) we have to put in a number of features which Professor Ryle seems not to have reckoned with. We cannot mention, say, an image as a psychological happening without saying, for instance, what it is an image of. (Something which might be by no means evident from an exact pictorial representation of the image.) There is also, perhaps, the way in which it emerges (suddenly, cloudily) and its relation to the thought process of which it is a part. Then there are more subtle aspects of the matter, such as the emotional 'tone' or 'colour', if any, of the image, or perhaps a sense of direction or urgency of which it is the bearer. It is here perhaps that we shall find ourselves compelled to use irreducible metaphors, which may or may not be the same as ones which might be offered in the 'history'.

Let this be admitted, as I think it must be, that we can sometimes detect mental happenings for which the more elaborate type of description which I have suggested is the appropriate (or at any rate a possible) one. Does anything special follow from this? Let us examine the situation more closely. The shyness and elusiveness of the mental event is real but not insuperable, either logically or in fact. 'Thoughts' are peculiar phenomena in a way in which ordinary sensations, however hard the latter may be to describe, are not. (Sensations, considered as experiences, may of course approximate toward being 'thoughts'.) To begin with, thoughts have, as it were, a life and dynamic of their own. They are not always, or not altogether, under our conscious control. They emerge unexpectedly, they become hazy or clear for no apparent reason. They display a sense of direction which may go beyond what the conscious mind can account for. All this will sound familiar to anyone who has reflected at all upon the matter. It follows that they are hard to 'pin down' or to describe precisely. They elude close observation (though so do many physical sensations), they are difficult to sum up (so is the smile of the Mona Lisa), their movement is hard to characterise (so is that of the waves), they have to be defined in terms of their intention (so would a sketchy drawing) and described as part of a total process (so would a movement made as part of a game).

Is there anything which, granted all this, still puts 'thoughts' into a special category? All experiences are 'private' and may be hard to describe. The further we move away from the situation where the *descripta* are 'ordinary' experiences, the harder it may be to find suitable descriptive terms in the public language. And this will be the case whether the experiences concerned are 'thoughts' or inward bodily sensations or sensations of the 'external world'. In the case of the latter (when what is required is an objective description and not one with a personal reflective colour) there is of course the 'outer correlate': there is the fact that others 'see the same', there is the possibility of pointing, the resort to the objective check, and so on; and it is in this situation that terms in the public language are able to apply unambiguously and constitute an adequate and full description. In the case of experiences of the inner (sensation or thought) this is not so, and this is part of what it means for something to be inner. Yet this does not mean that we shall *necessarily* feel that our verbal descriptions are less good; it might well be harder to describe the experience of a texture or a movement than to describe the experience of a pain or the solving of a problem. Although in the latter case (apart from e.g. the possibility of defining inner sensations 'ostensively' by inducing them) we shall lack certain modes of representation and explanation (pointing or the use of the camera).

'But won't the description of the inner have to be indirect and metaphorical in a way in which the other descriptions needn't be?' Part of our feeling that the inner is 'peculiar' resides here. The metaphorical (and hence indirect) nature of our descriptions of thought is not however something which strikes us forcibly except in a reflective context. When Burke says* that the fact that we all use similar metaphors to characterise mental states is 'evidence' for the states concerned being *really* similar, this sounds slightly odd: partly because we do not (for reasons referred to above) necessarily feel that all mental states are determinate conditions, and partly because, when we feel that they are (the case under discussion), our

* *Essay on the Sublime and the Beautiful.*

[49]

ordinary metaphors are so deadened by use that we find it hard to conjure up the idea of an event of which we are giving but a picturesque representation. What Burke has in mind, of course, are graphic descriptions of the 'historical' kind such as would be offered in ordinary conversation. If we raise the problems which ordinary language conceals of the 'real' character of the mental event, and consider the more exact style of description which is now in question, we may still be struck by the natural and spontaneous way in which certain metaphors impose themselves. (Various modern theorists will tell us reasons, philological or psychoanalytical, for not being surprised at this.) We often do not feel that the description is indirect ('I leapt from there to the conclusion', 'The two ideas slowly came apart') – and to say that it is metaphorical is simply to say that there is no outer correlate.*

When I say of a pain that it is 'piercing' or of a decision that it is 'firmly fixed' or of a thought that it is 'cloudy' there is no peculiar kind of gap here between the subject and the words; the object is not 'something quite else' of which the words only indirectly tell us, speaking in riddles like the Delphic sibyl. The idea that this is so arises partly from an expectation (connected with notions I shall discuss later) that the mental event will be odd, and partly from a mistaken conception of metaphor as being necessarily the comparison of one 'given' structure with another. Our language is littered with expressions of the mental in terms of the physical which (whether or not we regard them as 'original' meanings belonging to some pre-logical stage of language) should enable us to give adequate descriptions of mental processes. The movement of thought *is* a sort of leap, its obscurity *is* a sort of cloud. If we can accept 'movement' and 'obscurity' here, we should be able to take 'leap' and 'cloud' also, without beginning to feel that language has become, in some special way, parted from its object. Such then are the difficulties attaching to the description of mental events. Particular cases of description may raise particular problems. Sometimes, since thoughts are queer phenomena, we may find it

---

* At this point I should like to acknowledge a debt to the remarks made by Professor Price at the Aristotelian Society Symposium on *Thinking and Language*. [See previous essay.]

hard to offer a clear and unambiguous description – but this will be true in the same way of other kinds of queer phenomena with which we have to deal. Sometimes too we may be puzzled about how exactly to relate the event-character of a thought to its meaning-character in the description. But there is nothing here which points to the presence of a special sort of item which is sharply separate from other items of experience. The mental event, as an experience, is not connected with 'meaning' in a way which is different from that in which any other experience may be connected with meaning. It may be a struggle toward a sense obscurely grasped – but so may be the experience of looking hard at something to decide what it is, and the description of both events could follow the same pattern. If a thought is ever an experience, the experience may be (as others are) more or less sharp and clear, and may be (as others are) described thus or thus according to our interests and purposes.

The objector may feel at this point that he has been put off with a valueless concession, and that the matter has been closed without his difficulty having been properly met. What is conceded is that there are mental events which have the quasi-physical character which prompts us to use certain metaphorical descriptions when we are pressed to say what they are like. This is to say that all that differentiates the 'thought' is something to do with its phenomenal character as an experience. A thought may be a describable 'impact', in the same way as a sensation. This is true enough, the objector will say; but what you have been discussing is the difference between experience of the outer and experience of the inner. What I want to hear discussed (and what is covered up here by the word 'experience') is the way in which (sometimes if not always) I may be said to discover, or create, within a sensation or a thought, a specific significance which is immediately presented.

To say this is to raise the second of the two questions which I distinguished earlier, namely, the question: are there not mental events which are self-describing, which are experiences of meaning? This question becomes confused with the question which I have hitherto been discussing in this way. We are tempted to want a series of intrinsically self-describing experiences as a basis for language and as a filling for the mind. Those who point out that these items are not required neglect, or by implication deny, the existence of mental events in any sense. The lost object then becomes the container of both problems. I shall now turn to the second of these and attempt to give it a more exact sense.

Surely, it will be said, I have absolutely specific experiences (at any rate sometimes) in both sensation and thought. There is something definite which recurs. I can give myself examples of this at any time. Experiences announce themselves, determinacy isn't just a matter of words. Someone who speaks in this way may be quite prepared to admit two things. Firstly he may admit that we do *not* need the idea of constant acts of recognition as a basis for language. It is not the case that unless experience has immediate sense language is done for. Language can operate independently. Recognising something moreover need not mean going deeply into its intrinsic character, or noting a real recurrence; what happens here may be 'thin' and not 'deep', the touching of a spring, a mere reflex. Secondly, it may be admitted that in order to describe an experience I shall have to use the language which I have learnt in public contexts, and that my description will be one of various possible ones. But, it will be added, although language may sometimes react upon experience in that it may help us to make it precise, to observe more, and so on, the definiteness of experience does not depend on language. What concerns us here is our power to communicate, not with others, but with ourselves. After all, there are experiences with private faces and no public names; and even readily nameable experiences need not be just a matter of touching off the spring of a public convention, a reflex that jerks one into a groove of language. They may be, not impacts which a convention defines, but determinate entities of which if I say 'it's the same again' I am either right or wrong.

There seems to be something true here, but what is it? If we frankly cut experience loose from language our temptation to say that experiences recur exactly diminishes, and what constitutes an experience seems in doubt. An important feature of experiences is that they occur one at a time, and that we cannot get at past ones to compare them with present ones. Photographs, diaries, gramophone records may build up an impression; but these things have to be interpreted. On the other hand we hate to think that there is no cast-iron guarantee in the matter. If we think that a certain experience is the same as a past one we *must* be right or wrong: God can see the similarity even if we can't. Can we not be sure of ourselves when we pick out some broad similarity of structure between two experiences? We may feel sure, yes; but the 'structure' will consist of a number of 'simple' judgements of sameness which we can analyse no further, and then there is the whole living tone and quality of the experience about which we shall have to make an even more precarious judgement of sameness. Nothing can reproduce an experience (even a very good photo is only a reminder) and nothing can be really like an experience except another experience; and here what we want is an infallible criterion of sameness and this is just what we cannot find. (The problem of universals: there is nothing that we can take away from one occasion to make us quite certain on the next occasion.) Here we are tempted to draw in to help us the notion of 'an intrinsic sense'. We hate to think that it is all a matter of what we feel inclined to say; and of course in a way it isn't.

Yet the way in which it isn't is unsatisfying too. Of course there is 'definiteness', but it is not an immediate and self-describing definiteness. Experience does verify and falsify, but it does this without displaying an explicit and unambiguous sense within itself. One reason why we feel that it does display such a sense is because there are conclusive verifications. But we forget that verification takes place within a context, and that it is in particular situations that certain events are taken as showing that certain propositions are true. It is the context which decides what is the specific utterance of an experience. Another reason for our feeling, and this perhaps is a more compelling one, is that we seem able to brood upon experiences (as we constantly do when doing philosophy), giving ourselves examples of this and that particular one, and pointing out the examples to ourselves. 'It is like *this*'; what could be more definite?

We must distinguish the clearness of experiences from the exactness of concepts. Experiences can be as specific as you please, in the sense of clear (not cloudy), vivid, impressive – but they can still be described in this way or in that. 'Brown' is less exact than 'burnt sienna', and less exact in what seems another way than 'circular'. We want to feel that the burnt sienna exactness is not

conventional in the way in which, strictly, the circular exactness is –
i.e., that it rests directly on experience. (We are not yet inclined to
accept a definition of burnt sienna in light wave terms.) But
however specific the experience I may take it won't help. (From here
too can be seen what is wrong with the case of the missing shade of
blue.) The concept is clear – but the experience? Well, look and see.
There are situations where one verifies, and situations where one
broods, or where the 'sensum' has an emotional or reflective
content. All these can be described thus or thus. The definiteness of
concepts depends on the *possibility* of certain ideally defined (e.g.,
experimental) experiences being definite (i.e., such that we accept
them as a verification or a justification). But this still does not give
us an experience with immediately self-contained unambiguous
sense. In fact any experience is infinitely rich and deep. We feel it to
be intrinsically significant because we can brood upon it; but the
same brooding shows it to be endlessly various in meaning. The
combination of the feeling that meaning must in the end be
something that we can corner and survey with a realisation that
such meaning is not to be found in sense experience is a motive of
idealism.

Here there is the cue for a renewed attempt. If the notion of the
self-describing particular cannot be defended in length, then
perhaps it can be defended in depth. Why should there not be
moments of significance, determinate though not necessarily
recurrent? Surely, when we set aside the problems which arise from
the attempt to bind language and experience rigidly together, we see
that there *are* such? Consider our enjoyment of the 'language' of a
Persian rug. Here there is not the thin light touch of recognition but
a deep gazing. (Gazing is here the master image.) Here too we can
refine our experience, making it more and more specific, seeing
more and more deeply into the sense which is before us. What is
required here is that an immediate experience should have an inner
complexity and rigidity sufficient to enable it to withstand the flux
of attention. The definiteness which we would find here is then not
the definiteness which goes with verification (which we may admit
to be a construct) but an intrinsic and experienced definiteness.
'Ordinary' experiences may not have been 'determinate at the time',
or it may seem pointless to argue about whether they were. These

are crustaceans who keep their distinguishing shell upon the outside. But the experiences now in question, rigid objects of contemplation, are vertebrates, their structure is inside them. If indeed we consider how contemplation may discover (or create) an immediate form within its object we may even feel it possible to re-establish the significance of the world by turning all experience into contemplation. (Husserl said that by a 'change in the shading' we could transform 'a pure psychology of the inner life into a self-styled transcendental phenomenology'.)

Now even those who feel doubtful whether all experience could be seen to have immediate structure if looked at with the right kind of introspective penetration may well feel that *some* experience does have such a structure. The aesthetic experience is surely something radically different in kind and will provide for those who still feel the nostalgia for the particular both an explanation of and a justification for their continued dissatisfaction. The phrase 'signifi-cant form' comes very naturally to mind here. An explanation, yes – but a justification? A work of art does not simply 'hit' us, or if it does *that* is not an aesthetic experience. Even a significant form has to be traced. The notion of the aesthetic experience is a compound one, which flourishes most in connection with small-scale visual art, and its main components are these.

A work of art is a self-contained structure which we set ourselves, in a certain mood of detachment and with a previous knowledge and acceptance of certain conventions, to consider as a whole. This consideration will often be (depending on the complexity of the work of art) a sustained exercise of the discursive intelligence, and subject to all the accidents which may attend upon any period of cogitation. This exercise of the intelligence may be pleasurable on the whole (though not necessarily in a sense different from that in which any exercise of intelligence might be pleasurable) – and in the course of it there *may* be moments of excitement and emotion. These moments however depend upon their context for the kind of thrill which they give us, in so far as this is grasped as significant. (When in *The Brothers Karamazov* we read the words, 'Gentlemen, I have had a good dream', we are moved – but the significance of what moves us depends on the whole work.) It is only where a very simple work is concerned – a line of poetry or a small visual object –

that we can feel that we have before us anything like an immediate or self-contained bearer of meaning; and even that is an illusion. The impact is momentary; but the impact is still an experience like another, which we can describe thus or thus, and its connection with meaning is not different in kind from that of any other experience. In any case, as soon as we find ourselves compelled to look for aesthetic experiences in the simplest aesthetic units and to raise questions about how long a single act of attention may be sustained, we must realise that we are on the wrong track. What is special about art is not to be found by examining the quality of the moment to moment experiences which we have when attending to it.

The objector may now say: all right, let us drop the notion of aesthetic experience in general, and concentrate upon these moments of impact, which have been much too casually put aside. Is there not here perhaps that which we are seeking: a momentary experience with an inner structure? It may be agreed that such moments are not essential concomitants of aesthetic attention, and that on the other hand they may occur in non-aesthetic contexts – when, for instance, I am struck or impressed by something immediate. Such an experience is described by Rilke in one of his letters where he writes:

Looking is such a marvellous thing, of which we know but little; through it we are turned absolutely toward the outside, but when we are most of all so, things happen in us that have waited longingly to be observed, and while they reach completion in us, intact and curiously anonymous, *without our aid* – their significance grows up in the object outside: a powerful, persuasive name, the only name these inner events could possibly have . . . Suddenly, in the shadow of a street, a face is held out to you, and you see, under the influence of the contrast, its essence with such clarity . . . that the momentary impression involuntarily assumes the proportions of a symbol.

Here we may pick up the word 'symbol'. Rilke's words describe something which we can recognise. Much of our experience is poor and thin, but some of it is rich and pregnant in the way described;

and there is a use of the word 'symbolic' which covers just this sense of structure and extended meaning being given in immediate experience. This is to be distinguished from the automatic employment of conventional 'symbolisms' on the one hand, and from the reading of natural signs on the other. For here there does appear to be an *experience* of *significance*. Such experience may be conveyed to us either by natural objects or by forms of art. Its characteristic is the depth and resonance of the impression. We are moved in a manner which (initially at least) we are at a loss to explain; and the impression often proves inexhaustibly fertile for subsequent comment. Within this region fall the symbols of symbolist poetry and psychoanalysis.

But in what sense does the significance *lie in* the impression? It is retrospectively that we give the thing a structure. It is just a fact that we have found out (and indeed lately) that a further account can be given of certain impacts. If no account can be given, no reasons found for an impression, we do not call it 'significant'. Or if we are determined to say that nevertheless it *is* significant and there must be reasons, this will be because we are being influenced by a theory. ('Nothing in the psyche is accidental'.) In any case, the account which we choose to give when 'unpacking' an impression will be one among other possible ones. I may decide to agree with William Empson that the *frisson* which I receive from a particular poem arises from the presence of the ambiguities he detects in it. But if I tried I could doubtless think of other plausible 'reasons' for my experience. It will be a matter for my *decision* what kind of exploration of my experience I choose to attend to; and on this will depend too the structure of the object experienced. (This is connected with the nature of all 'appreciation' of the arts.)

The objector, still unsatisfied, will say: why tie 'meaning' up with verbal explanation in this way? The experience (as you have admitted) is more than the explanation can cover. And the experience is what it is, it speaks itself. (When I listen to music I hear its meaning.) It was never denied that experiences are what they are. All that is contended is that we should not think of them as possessing intrinsically the kind of definiteness which belongs with verbal explanation. An aesthetic impression may be definite and vivid and clearly structured, but so may a non-aesthetic impression.

Modern analytic techniques appear to lift the sense out of immediate experience in order to scatter it over the conventional context of that experience. We may be tempted to try to reinstate this sense by seeking for a particular and immediate kind of significance which should be independent of our ordinary modes of understanding. We fail to discover this; but what we do discover are those features of experience which inspire the quest – features which analysis has neglected or denied. If all experience were thin and unfocused we would be that much less tempted to insist that it 'says itself'. If there were no inward mental happenings we should not be led to imagine that all significant awareness consisted of such events. Phenomena such as 'thoughts' and 'symbolic experiences' must find their place too in any philosophical description of the mind. It is such happenings, heavily weighted as they so often are with a content which seems to go beyond consciousness, that give to the idea of 'immediate experience' that inexhaustible richness the neglect of which prompts both resentment and vain investigation.

This paper was read at a Meeting of the Aristotelian Society at 21 Bedford Square, London, 9 June 1952.

Metaphysics and Ethics

What should a philosophical study of morals be like? This is a question concerning which there is a certain amount of doubt among modern philosophers. When I speak about modern philosophers and modern philosophy I shall be meaning that present-day version of our traditional empiricism which is known as linguistic analysis – and although a lot of what I have to say will be critical of recent developments in that tradition, the criticisms which I make will also come, I believe, out of the tradition. To understand current moral philosophy it is necessary to understand its history. And here it is convenient to begin from the moment when G. E. Moore made a certain distinction. Moore said we should distinguish between the question, what things are good? and the question, what does the word 'good' mean? On this second question Moore had important things to say. He claimed that 'good' was indefinable, and that previous moral philosophers, because they had failed to distinguish those two questions from each other, had fallen into the error of defining 'good', or 'valuable', in terms of some other non-valuable entity, whether a natural entity, such as pleasure, or a metaphysical entity, such as rationality. If asked, what *things* are good, one might indeed answer this question by pointing to pleasure or to rationality – but one could not answer the question what is *good itself* in this way. Moore convinced his readers of this very simply by pointing out that it made *sense* always, given any proposition of the form 'X is good', to withdraw thoughtfully and ask – 'But is X really good?' That is, the notion of 'good' could significantly be attached to or withdrawn from anything whatever, and the things to which it happened to be attached did not form part of its meaning.

This simple argument of Moore's produced a complete change of perspective in moral philosophy. It transformed the central question of ethics from the question, 'What is goodness?' – where an answer was expected in terms of the revelation of some real and eternally present structure of the universe – into the question – 'What is the activity of "valuing" (or "commending")?', where what is required is to see what is in common to people of all ages and societies when they attach value to something. This phrase 'attach value' is itself significant of the change of attitude. The philosopher is now to speak no longer of the Good, as something real or transcendent, but to analyse the familiar human activity of endowing things with value. If we want to place the definitive breach with metaphysical ethics at any point, we can place it here.

Moore himself, however, was not wholly of the modern time in that although he pointed out that 'good' was not the second name of any other natural or metaphysical property, he could not rid himself of the conviction that it was nevertheless the name of *a* property, the unanalysable non-natural property of goodness, which inhered in certain actual states of affairs – so that although any proposition of the form 'X is good' could *make sense*, such a proposition would only be *true* if X really possessed the property of goodness.

Philosophers after Moore retained Moore's distinction of the two questions, and Moore's linguistic approach. They took it that the central question of ethics was the question 'What does "good" *mean*?' – but they refrained from answering the question 'What things are good?' and made it clear that this was a matter for the moralist, and not for the philosopher. Concerning the meaning of 'good', things then moved fast. What is known as the verificationist view of meaning, entering philosophy from the side of natural science, made a violent impact upon ethics. If the meaning of a proposition is the method of its verification, and if verification has to be in terms of observation of sensible events, then clearly ethical propositions could not have meaning in this way – and it was no use appealing to a mysterious property, not open to ordinary observation, to give them significance. Moore's non-natural property disappeared, in this more sceptical atmosphere, together with many other would-be metaphysical entities. Ethical propositions were clearly and firmly separated from other types of propositions and have remained so ever since. They were not, it was claimed, true or false, they did not state facts: they did not state *natural* facts, for the reason that Moore had given, and they did not state *metaphysical* facts, for the same reason, and also because there were none to state. It was then said that the ethical propositions expressed emotions. They did not have *descriptive*, or factual, meaning, they had *emotive* meaning.

The emotive theory of ethics was not created as the result of a patient scrutiny of ethical propositions. It arose largely as the by-product of a theory of meaning whose most proper application was in other fields. The emotive theory was overthrown partly by a return to common sense; it was felt that, surely, ethical statements must somehow be regarded as rational, defensible by argument and by reference to fact. Partly, the theory disappeared as a result of two other philosophical developments: first, the notion that meaning should be analysed not in terms of method of verification, but in terms of *use*, and second, what might roughly be summed up as 'the disappearance of the mind'.

The notion that the meaning of a word is its use – a notion which in other fields we may associate with the name of Wittgenstein – did, I think, arise independently in the field of ethics, as a development and refinement of the emotive theory. Ethical statements were now said, not to express emotion, but to evoke emotion and more generally to persuade.

This is the view which we find most fully explained by Stevenson in his book *Ethics and Language.** Hard upon this development, however, and associated with the same change in our conception of meaning, there followed the revolution in our attitude to psychological concepts. When we speak of 'the mind', it was now maintained, we are not speaking of a set of inner entities such as faculties and feelings, which are open to introspection, we are speaking of observable actions and patterns of behaviour. We learn and we apply mental concept words on the basis of what we can openly observe. This new view, which was made widely known by Professor [Gilbert] Ryle's book *The Concept of Mind*, had consequences for moral philosophy. Previously a moral statement

---

* [Charles L. Stevenson (b. 1908), Professor of Philosophy at the University of Michigan, and author of *Facts and Values*.]

had been said to express an *attitude*, where this was conceived of in terms of the speaker's feelings, and, possibly his wish to influence the hearer's feelings. Now, if a moral statement was said to express an attitude, this was to be analysed rather in terms of the speaker's conduct, and his intent to influence the hearer's conduct. Moral statements had been treated first as exclamations and then as persuasions – now they were called imperatives or prescriptions or rules.

To adopt this analysis had the technical advantage of allowing the philosopher to express the essence of morality in a purely logical manner, without reference to either metaphysical or psychological entities, and in such a way that the old dilemma about whether moral remarks were subjective or objective was completely resolved. If a moral remark is not really a statement but a rule, then it cannot be subjective or objective, or true or false either. In this way two objections were met which had been made to Moore's ethics: it was now shown in the analysis that moral judgements were essentially practical (answers to the question 'What shall I do?') and not in any way factual. Whereas Moore had treated moral remarks as expressions of moral insight, not as instances of moral advice, and he had clung to the idea that they were still in some sense factual. The new analysis corrected both these points. There remained the question, concerning which Moore's view had also been far from satisfactory, of the *rationality* of ethical judgements. This was met by a further refinement of technique. The distinction between 'descriptive' meaning (meaning *via* reference to fact) and 'evaluative' meaning, as it was now called, which had previously been only a distinction made between types of proposition, was now pressed into the structure of individual moral words. The meaning of the word 'good', for instance, was to be divided into an evaluative and a descriptive part. The descriptive part would consist of reference to the facts in virtue of which the speaker called something valuable – and the evaluative part would consist of the prescription – 'choose this one'. In this way the analysis could allow that a moral judgement might be discussed and defended by stating of facts – without itself becoming a factual statement.

Thus in a complex way, and by the successive correction of a series of theories, we have reached our present position – and the discussion goes on. This present position has, I think, been most clearly expounded in Mr R. M. Hare's book *The Language of Morals*, and may be summed up as follows. A man's morality is seen in his conduct and a moral statement is a prescription or rule uttered to guide a choice, and the descriptive meaning of the moral word which it contains is made specific by reference to factual criteria of application. That is, in a moral statement we quasi-command that a particular thing be done, and are ready to say in virtue of what facts it ought to be done. We are also ready, if our moral statement is sincere, to do it ourselves in the appropriate circumstances. I think it is fair to take Mr Hare's book as expressing the current position, although his book is under attack in many quarters. Most of these attacks, in my view, are upon the details of Mr Hare's analysis and not upon its deep assumptions. What these assumptions are I shall discuss shortly.

Now this piece of our philosophical history might be described as the elimination of metaphysics from ethics. We are certainly now presented with a stripped and empty scene. Morality is not explained in terms of metaphysical concepts such as the rational will, nor in terms of psychological concepts such as moral feelings. It is not pictured by the philosopher, nor defended by philosophical arguments, as being attached to any real natural or metaphysical structure. It is pictured without any transcendent background. It is presented simply in terms of exhortations and choices defended by reference to facts. Now what has happened here exactly, and what have we been let in for? Let us look more closely.

The present view emerges from a very finely knit complex of mutual supporting arguments. To unravel this complex a bit, I suggest that we distinguish three types of argument on which this view may be said to rest. These are: *first*, a general critical argument to the effect that there are no metaphysical entities, *second*, a special critical argument, to the effect that even if there were, we could not base an analysis of morality upon them since it is impossible to argue from *is* to *ought*, from facts to values. *Third*, there are arguments, involving an appeal to our experience of morality, which support the various details of the analysis – the notion of guiding a choice, arguing, referring to facts, judging a man by his conduct, and so on.

About the first argument, which I shall call 'the anti-metaphysical argument', I shall be very brief. The criticism of metaphysics, which was always a part of our own tradition, and which was made systematic by Kant, is an established aspect of modern philosophy and has unavoidable implications for ethics. This is not to say, of course, that great moral conceptions such as 'the rational will' are senseless or useless, but simply that they cannot be established by certain familiar types of philosophical argument. This is a point I shall return to later. I go on now to argument number two.

This argument, which I shall call 'the anti-naturalistic argument', to the effect that we cannot derive values from facts is the most important argument in modern moral philosophy – indeed it is almost the whole of modern moral philosophy. Now this argument, as it has appeared in recent years, has a certain complexity about it. It is sometimes presented as if it were the exposure of a logical fallacy. When Moore called argument from 'is' to 'ought' 'the Naturalistic Fallacy' he implied just this – and in Mr Hare's book the central argument, which is this same argument, is expressed in logical terms. To reach an imperative conclusion we need at least one imperative premiss. We may also be encouraged to think of the argument in this way because of its original very striking formulation by Hume – and because Moore's formulation of it, which has so much caught our imagination, was made *à propos* of an obviously fallacious argument by John Stuart Mill: that is, Mill's argument that what in fact is desired is *ipso facto* what ought to be desired.

Now if the anti-naturalistic argument is designed merely to point out that a statement of value cannot be derived directly, and with no further help, from an ordinary statement of fact, then perhaps it may be called the exposure of a logical fallacy. But the trouble is that arguments of the crudity of Mill's argument are fairly rare in moral philosophy. If we want *pure* examples of this type of argument we are more likely to find them in the work of psychologists and sociologists than in the work of moral philosophers. What the great moral philosophers, in the past, have usually been doing is something much more complicated. They present a total metaphysical picture of which ethics forms a part. The universe, including our own nature, is like *this*, they say. Now this picture may be attacked by argument number one – that is straight philosophical criticism designed to show that the philosopher in question is not able to establish, by the argument he uses, the structure that he describes. But it is not so clear (although Moore, for instance, seems to have thought that it was) that such a picture of the place of morality can always be attacked by the second argument, the anti-naturalistic argument. Now it may be said – but surely the anti-metaphysical argument settles the matter. If we cannot establish transcendent metaphysical structures by philosophical argument then such structures cannot be the basis of ethics. But this is not so clear. What the moral philosopher professes to do nowadays is to analyse the essence of *any* morality, to display the logic of *any* moral language. But what place the concept of the transcendent may have in the structure of a morality is something which is *not* entirely settled by either the anti-metaphysical argument, or by the anti-naturalistic argument in its purely logical form. This narrow form of the anti-naturalistic argument I shall call 'the logical argument'. These arguments only prove that we cannot picture morality as issuing directly from a *philosophically established* transcendent background, or from a factual background. But this is not yet to say that the notion of *belief* in the transcendent can have no place in a philosophical account of morality.

Why has it been so readily assumed that the stripped and behaviouristic account of morality which the modern philosopher gives is imposed on us by philosophical considerations? I think this is because the anti-metaphysical argument and the logical argument have been very closely connected in the minds of those who used them with a much more general and ambiguous dictum to this effect: you cannot attach morality to the substance of the world. And this dictum, which expresses the whole spirit of modern ethics, has been accorded a sort of logical dignity. But, why can morality not be thought of as attached to the substance of the world? Surely many people who are not philosophers, and who cannot be accused of using faulty arguments since they use no arguments, do think of their morality in just this way? They think of it as continuous with some sort of larger structure of reality, whether this be a religious structure, or a social or historical one.

Now I suggest there is another type of answer to the question, why not attach morality to the substance of the world? – and that is a moral answer. If you do this you are in danger of making your morality into a dogma, you are in danger of becoming intolerant of the values of others, and of ceasing to reflect on your own values through taking them too much for granted. In short, if you start to think of morality as part of a general way of conceiving the universe, as part of a larger conceptual framework, you may cease to be reflective and responsible about it, you may begin to regard it as a sort of fact. And as soon as you regard your moral system as a sort of fact, and not as a set of values which only exist through your own choices, your moral conduct will degenerate. This fear of moral degeneration through lack of reflexion is to be found in many modern writers on ethics, notably in the work of Mr Hare, whose book I have already mentioned. It is also to be found, more positively asserted, in many existentialist writers – and it may be found, at what I take to be one of its sources, in that great pamphlet of Liberalism, Mill's *Essay on Liberty*.

Now *this* sort of objection to picturing morality as part of a systematic understanding of the world is of a quite different type from the other objections. This is not a logical or philosophical objection, it is a straight moral objection to the effect that certain bad results follow in practice from thinking about morality in a certain way. We may agree with this. But to say it is of course *not* to say that morality cannot under any circumstances be part of a general system of belief about how the world is, or about transcendent entities. It is *not* to say that anything which involves such beliefs is not a morality – it is merely to maintain that the holding of such beliefs is morally and socially dangerous.

I am suggesting that modern philosophers have tended to take their stripped, behaviouristic and non-conceptual picture of morality as the only possible picture because they have joined the anti-metaphysical argument and the logical argument to a *moral* argument of a different type – a moral argument which properly belongs in the propaganda of Liberalism. Why has this happened? I think it is not difficult to see if we consider the amount of support which what I have briefly called the behaviouristic view of morals can gain from a study of the actual morality of our own society. Of the three arguments which support the current view of morals, I have so far discussed the anti-metaphysical argument – and the anti-naturalistic argument, which I suggested should be divided into (*a*) a rather narrow logical argument, and (*b*) a much more general moral argument. I come now to the third argument, or group of arguments, the appeal to our general conception of what morality is like.

Now clearly, if this appeal is made with the morals of our own liberal society in mind, there is a great deal in the behaviouristic picture of morals which receives immediate confirmation. We, in our society, believe in judging a man's principles by his conduct, in reflecting upon our own values and respecting the values of others, in backing up our recommendations by reference to facts, in breaking down intuitive conclusions by argument, and so on. Our morality is, on the whole, conceptually simple. We approach the world armed with certain general values which we hold *simpliciter* and without the assistance of metaphysics or dogmatic theology – respect for freedom, for truth, and so on. We study the facts, and we make our choices in the light of the facts and our values. Our disagreements among ourselves concern the application of principles – our disagreements with other societies concern what principles to hold. There are, of course, persons and groups among us whose morality is *not* conceptually simple, but metaphysical and dogmatic (for instance, some Christians and all Communists) – but these people are in the minority. It is therefore the case that the logical formula presented by the modern moral philosopher is on the whole a satisfactory representation of the morality most commonly held in England. The simplest moral words ('good' and 'right') are selected for analysis, their meaning is divided into a descriptive and an evaluative part, the descriptive part representing the factual criteria, the evaluative part representing a recommendation. And once the largely empirical disagreements about application of principles and classification of cases have been cleared up, ultimate moral differences will show as differences of choice and recommendation in a common world of facts. What the modern moral philosopher has done is what metaphysicians in the past have always done. He has produced a model. Only it is not a model of any morality whatsoever. It is a model of his own morality.

I want now to proceed with my discussion and to attempt to say more exactly what I think the philosopher's attitude ought to be towards what I have rather vaguely called conceptual or metaphysical frameworks within which morality may be placed. In order to do this I want to distinguish three different questions. These three questions are: *One*, Is morality to be seen as essentially and by its nature centred on the individual, or as part of a general framework of reality which includes the individual? *Two*, What kinds of arguments could establish the existence of such a general framework? and *Three*, What should the method of the moral philosopher now be like? I shall consider them in order.

First – Is morality to be seen as essentially centred on the individual? Now our tradition of thought tends to take it for granted that morality must be self-contained; and we can also invoke here the patronage of Kant, who says that the moral will is autonomous, and that morality cannot be founded on anything but itself. But equally, if we can come out of the trees and see the wood for a moment, it is clear that this is only one type of view of morality – roughly a Protestant; and less roughly a Liberal, type of view. Kant himself is the source not only of this Liberal morality, but also of a modern version of its opposite, which I shall call, with an old name, Natural Law morality, and about which I shall have more to say in a moment.

If we consider our own assumptions here we may discover many ways in which our empiricist tradition goes with the view of the moral will as something essentially separate and autonomous. None of our philosophers, apart from the idealists, has presented any elaborately metaphysical view of ethics. This is not surprising. Ethics and epistemology are always very closely related, and if we want to understand our ethics we must look at our epistemology. I think the most important person here is Hume. It is from him more than anyone else that we have derived a philosophical tendency, which is still with us, to see the world in terms of contingently conjoined simples, to see it as a totality of ultimate simple facts which have no necessary connection with each other. In so far as we imagine that the world does contain necessities, and that real connections exist between these simple elements, this is merely the result of habit and custom, which are themselves the work of Nature. It is only in reflective moments that we can see the ultimately disjoined character of the world. It is habit which gives to us, according to Hume, both our objective material world, and our moral world. Moral attitudes are habits of sentiment built up in society, and they do not need, and cannot have, any greater sanction. Since Hume was conservative in morals and politics he had no objection to morality continuing to be a matter of habit. But since he was also the empiricist that he was, he presents this habit as covering up the world of disconnected facts that lies behind it. *This* is what reflection would discover, to the moral consciousness as to the scientific consciousness.

With this the stage is set for the history of ethics in this country. We oscillate between habit and reflection – the conservative side stressing habit, the progressive side stressing reflection. But notice still how much there is in common. Reflection is not metaphysical speculation, it is return to the facts. Burke, who was a great defender of tradition as a basis of morals, did not argue from a systematic or metaphysical background; indeed a rejection of system was a part of his outlook. Tradition and custom were to be taken as facts, as present realities, which were to be respected as such. Our traditionalists have not been metaphysicians, and neither have our progressives. The ideals which have inspired our society have been utilitarian ideals. And the utilitarians, when they wished to break down habit and custom by reflection, did not refer us to any metaphysical structure, but referred us to certain simple values and, above all, back again to the facts. The oscillation between habit and reflection may be seen today in moral philosophy itself in the contrast between, for instance, Professor Ryle and Professor Oakeshott* on the one hand, both of whom hold that morality is and ought only to be a matter of habit, and Mr [T.D.] Weldon and Mr [R.M.] Hare on the other, who hold that morality is a matter of studying the facts and then making a reflective choice.

So, I suggest that in answering the question concerning whether morality is to be centred on the individual, we have been influenced partly by our own moral outlook and partly by our philosophical

---

* [Michael Joseph Oakeshott (1901–90), British philosopher, political sceptic, author of *Experience and its Modes*, *Rationalism in Politics* and *On Human Conduct*.]

empiricism into assuming that it is of the *essence* of morality to be centred in this way. Nothing, we tend to assume, can *contain* the individual, except possibly his habits and his tradition, and these are merely facts like other ones, and capable of being reflectively examined. But this is only one way, roughly a Protestant, liberal, empiricist, way, of conceiving morality. What I have called Natural Law moralists – Thomists, Hegelians, Marxists, and less reflective persons who are camp followers of these doctrines – see the matter in a quite different perspective. The individual is seen as held in a framework which transcends him, where what is important and valuable is the framework, and the individual only has importance, or even reality, in so far as he belongs to the framework.

We may notice here some points of contrast between the Natural Law view and the Liberal view. On the Liberal view we picture the individual as able to attain by reflection to complete consciousness of his situation. He is entirely free to choose and responsible for his choice. His morality is exhibited in his choice, whereby he shows which things he regards as valuable. The most systematic exposition of modern Liberal morality is existentialism. Contrast the Natural Law picture. Here the individual is seen as moving tentatively *vis-à-vis* a reality which transcends him. To discover what is morally good is to discover that reality, and to become good is to integrate himself with it. He is ruled by laws which he can only partly understand. He is not fully conscious of what he is. His freedom is not an open freedom of choice in a clear situation; it lies rather in an increasing knowledge of his own real being, and in the conduct which naturally springs from such knowledge.

I would emphasise here that the contrast which I am remarking is not just a contrast between two philosophies; it is a contrast between two types of moral outlook. And here it should be added that of course not everyone in our society holds the liberal view in a pure form. Indeed the man in the street, and this goes for most ordinary non-philosophical Christians, is often a sort of non-metaphysical objectivist. That is, he believes that moral values are real and fixed – that is why he is so scandalised by the emotivists and the existentialists – but he has no clear view of nature or of history which is to explain the fixing of the values – and in this respect of course he differs, for instance, from the Marxist.

The logical picture of morality, which our modern philosophy has presented us with, shows no awareness of the importance of the contrast of which I have been speaking. We have been led to adopt a method of describing morality in terms of which all moral agents are seen as inhabiting the same world of facts, and where we are unable to discriminate between different types of morality, except in terms of differences of act and choice. Whereas, I am arguing, it is possible for differences to exist also as total differences of moral vision and perspective. From the Liberal point of view it seems axiomatic that however grandiose the structure may be in terms of which a morality extends itself, the moral agent is responsible for endowing this totality with value. The Liberal concentrates his attention on the *point of discontinuity* between the chosen framework and the choosing agent – and it is this moment of discontinuity which the modern philosopher has tried to catch in a formula. But for the individual, whether he be a Marxist or a Christian, who takes up a Natural Law point of view the scene looks completely different. Here there is no axiom of discontinuity. The individual's choice is less important, and the interest may lie in adoration of the framework rather than in the details of conduct. And here if the Liberal philosopher just goes on insisting that the moral agent is totally free by definition and is responsible for endowing the framework with value, and that 'ought' cannot be derived from 'is', this merely results in a colossally important difference of outlook being left unanalysed.

I now pass on to the second question, what kind of argument can establish whether or not there exists a transcendent non-empirical framework within which morality is to find its place? Here I shall be brief. It seems fairly clear that much of the criticism of traditional metaphysics, which modern philosophy has made its task, must stand. In addition there is the task of criticising types of modern quasi-philosophy or semi-scientific metaphysics which seek to present the human mind as enclosed within social, historical, or psychological frames. I have in mind a great variety of views deriving from a study of Marx, Freud, the behaviour of calculating machines, and so on. It is in the criticism of such views that the logical argument (you can't derive 'ought' from 'is') is most often properly in place. The task of philosophy here may be said to be the definition and re-definition of human freedom *vis-à-vis* the various forces which, it is argued by arguments which are often more philosophical than empirical, may be said to threaten it. A recent example in this kind of defensive negative criticism is Mr Isaiah Berlin's lecture *Historical Inevitability*, in which, in accents which remind us of Kierkegaard's attacks on Hegel, he argues that the individual cannot be shown to be enclosed by any framework of inevitable laws. This definition of freedom, which it is so important for philosophy to concern itself with, is achieved partly by such negative criticism. Is it also to be achieved by more positive means? This leads me to the last and most difficult question.

It is not at all clear, to me at any rate, what sort of philosophical method should now be used in the study of morals and politics. It has been assumed by moral philosophers that they have to be descriptive analysts as well as critics, that is, that they are to produce some sort of positive philosophical characterisation of morality; and it seems that this is a reasonable requirement. But how is it to be done? I think that the implications for ethics of doing philosophy by the linguistic method have not yet become entirely clear. Words are tricky things and must be handled with care. We must not be too impressed by them – on the other hand, we must take them seriously enough. I think philosophers were too impressed by words when they assumed that all that was needed to effect the change-over in ethics from the old to the new régime was to put the word 'good' in inverted commas. The analysis of this concept has been made the centre of modern ethics. This has been done partly under the influence of former metaphysical theories of ethics, and partly as a result of the concentration on act and choice, rather than descriptive or speculative discussion, as being the essence of morality. It has been assumed tht moral argument always takes the form of pointing to facts, rather than the form of analysing or explaining concepts. On the current view, freedom is conceived as freedom of overt choice, and there is a corresponding lack of interest in differences of belief. Moral language is taken as closely related to choice – that it recommends to action is its defining characteristic – and all this can then be offered as an analysis of the meaning of the word 'good'. 'This is good' equals 'choose this'. But our freedom is not just a freedom to choose and act differently, it is also a freedom to think and believe differently, to see the world differently, to see different configurations and describe them in different words. Moral differences can be differences of concept as well as differences of choice. A moral change shows in our vocabulary. How we see and describe the world is morals too – and the relation of this to our conduct may be complicated.

We were too impressed by words when we assumed that the word 'good' covered a single concept which was the centre of morality. We were not impressed enough when we neglected less general moral words such as 'true', 'brave', 'free', 'sincere', which are the bearers of very important ideas. The concept of 'goodness', for reasons which it would be interesting to investigate, is no longer a rich and problematic concept. Whereas the concept of 'truth', for instance, contains tangles and paradoxes the unravelling of which would show us really interesting features of the modern world. It is in terms of the inner complexity of such concepts that we may display really deep differences of moral vision.

It is, of course, always the philosopher's task to study the writings of philosophers of the past impartially, and compare and contrast them with ourselves. There has been of late something of a tendency to read back into the great metaphysicians our own logical formulae, and to treat them as if they were trying ineptly to do what we have done successfully. But the main task is the task on which moral philosophy is in fact engaged – the analysis of contemporary moral concepts, through moral language. I have suggested that this task has been too narrowly conceived. We have not considered the great *variety* of the concepts that make up a morality. Nor have moral philosophers made any satisfactory frontal attack on the question of how belief in the transcendent may modify the meaning of ethical statements. This question, so far as it has come up, has mainly risen as a by-product of criticism of theological statements.

Would this sort of analysis, in its more extended form, be itself a kind of metaphysics? In a way obviously not. It does not involve the postulation of transcendent entities established by philosophical arguments; on the contrary, it is critical of all such arguments, and if it speaks of such entities they are considered as objects of faith or belief. Modern philosophy is profoundly anti-metaphysical in spirit.

Its anti-metaphysical character may be summed up in the *caveat*: There may be no deep structure. This is the lesson of Wittgenstein – and one which, incidentally, has not yet been taken enough to heart by those who want to reduce morality to a single formula.

On the other hand, to analyse and describe our own morality and that of others may involve the making of models and pictures of what different kinds of men are like. Moral philosophers in the past differed concerning what they supposed themselves to be doing. Some (e.g. Plato) attempted to reveal a truth which was not accessible to all men. Others (e.g. Kant), tried to analyse the morality of any ordinary conscientious person. Philosophers who attempted the latter have usually found themselves bound to coin new concepts in making the attempt, and have not in the past been shy of doing so. And it is here that description moves imperceptibly into moralising. An instance of a modern moral philosopher, not in our tradition, who coins new and persuasive concepts in the course of offering a description is Gabriel Marcel.* Indeed all the existentialists do this. So, in a more sober way, did some of our own fairly recent philosophical ancestors – A. E. Taylor and Joseph,† for instance. Even, in a way, Moore. But we have been shy of such extensive description and shy of coining concepts because we are anxious not to moralise, and because we think that ethics should study the logical structure of moral language and have the neutrality of logic. If I am right, this has merely had the result that philosophers have done their moralising unconsciously instead of consciously.

Philosophers have usually tended to seek for universal formulae. But the linguistic method, if we take it seriously, is by its nature opposed to this search. Logic, whatever that may be determined to be, has its own universality; but when we leave the domain of the purely logical we come into the cloudy and shifting domain of the

---

* [Gabriel H. Marcel (1889–1973), French Christian philosopher who reluctantly accepted the title 'Christian existentialist'. See Part Three, 'The Image of Mind', below.]

† [A. E. Taylor (1869–1945), English philosopher and authority on Plato, whose *Laws* he translated. H. W. B. Joseph (1867–1943), best known for *An Introduction to Logic*. He followed Prichard (see p. 76 below) in attacking empirical psychology.]

concepts which men live by – and these are subject to historical change. This is especially true of moral concepts. Here we shall have done something if we can establish with tolerable clarity what these concepts *are*. We should, I think, resist the temptation to unify the picture by trying to establish, guided by our own conception of the ethical in general, what these concepts *must be*. All that is made clear by this method is: our own conception of the ethical in general – and in the process important differences of moral concept may be blurred or neglected. Can the moral philosopher, once he stops being critical and begins to be positive, establish anything at all in the nature of a universal truth? If by universal truth is meant something which has a sort of logical universality, then I think the answer is no. The current would-be logical analysis of moral judgements is certainly not such a truth. The difficulty is, and here we are after all not so very far from the philosophers of the past, that the subject of investigation is the nature of man – and we are studying this nature at a point of great conceptual sensibility. Man is a creature who makes pictures of himself and then comes to resemble the picture. This is the process which moral philosophy must attempt to describe and analyse.

I think it still remains for us to find a satisfactory method for the explanation of our own morality and that of others – but I think it would be a pity if, just because we realise that any picture is likely to be half a description and half a persuasion, we were to deny ourselves the freedom in the making of pictures and the coining of explanatory ideas which our predecessors have used in the past. After all, both as philosophers and as moral beings we are concerned with the same problems with which they were concerned: What is freedom? Can it be shown that men are free? What is the relation of morality to social realities? What is the relation of morality to what we believe concerning God and the hereafter? It is a merit of modern philosophers to be more conscious than their predecessors of what the philosopher's activity is. We can become more patient and historical in analysing other moralities and more daring and imaginative in exploring our own without losing the benefit of that greater consciousness.

First published in *The Nature of Metaphysics*, ed. D. F. Pears, 1957.

[75]

Vision and Choice in Morality

[. . .] It is a peculiarity of ethics that the initial segregation of the items to be studied is less easy than in other branches of philosophy [. . .] Now it has been assumed, roughly since Moore, that we can distinguish two questions: 'What is my morality?' and 'What is morality as such?' After an initial period of excitement over this distinction, ethics is moving in the direction of finding it less simple. When we survey the feuds of our recent ancestors who are not in the linguistic tradition, for instance, the differences of opinion of Joseph, Taylor, Ross, Prichard,* it is easy to see that these philosophers had very different interests and attitudes to the world, and were concerned accordingly to display different aspects of the moral life. Can it be safely assumed that linguistic philosophers are immune from such partiality, being able to derive from the study of language some sort of initial definition and subsequent analysis of morality which shall have the prestige and neutrality of logic? Here it is especially important to attend to the initial delineation of the field of study, observing where and in what way moral judgements may be involved, and then to consider the relations between the selected phenomena and the philosophical technique used to describe them. A narrow or partial selection of phenomena may suggest certain particular techniques which will in turn seem to lend support to that particular selection; and then a circle is formed out of which it may be hard to break. It is therefore advisable to return frequently to an initial survey of 'the moral' so as to reconsider, in the light of a primary apprehension of what morality is, what our

* [Sir W. D. Ross (1877–1971), with H. A. Prichard (1871–1947) and H. W. B. Joseph (see p. 74 above) are accounted the major figures in Oxford moral theory in the first half of the twentieth century.]

technical devices actually *do* for us. Why do we do moral philosophy anyway? For the sake of 'completeness'? [. . .]

I shall begin by outlining the view with which I want to bring our fresh evidence into relation, and perhaps into conflict, emphasising its main points of interest and attraction. It may be that no one individual completely adheres to this position, but I think that it will sound familiar and may pass as a summary of what has quite lately been maintained and not authoritatively or as a whole displaced. I shall call it, with apologies to those who do not hold it, the 'current view'. The remote ancestors of this view are Hume, Kant, and Mill; its more immediate determinants are Rylean behaviourism and the view of meaning, together with its anti-metaphysical corollaries, which we connect with the 'verification principle', but which also has its background in the works of Russell and the British empiricists. On this view, the moral life of the individual is a series of overt choices which take place in a series of specifiable situations. The individual's 'stream of consciousness' is of comparatively little importance, partly because it is often not there at all (having been thought to be continuous for wrong reasons), and more pertinently because it is and can only be through overt acts that we can characterise another person, or ourselves, mentally or morally. Further, a moral judgement, as opposed to a whim or taste preference, is one which is supported by reasons held by the agent to be valid for all others placed as he [is], and which would involve the objective specification of the situation in terms of facts available to disinterested scrutiny. Moral *words* come into the picture because we not only make choices, but also guide choices by verbal recommendations. This group of words have their meaning, in accordance with the situation outlined above, through the two elements of recommendation and specification (evaluative and descriptive meaning). The specification (of good-making criteria) will differ according to the moral code of the agent, while the element of recommendation will remain constant. A moral concept then will be roughly an objective definition of a certain area of activity plus a recommendation or prohibition.

The charms of this view are obvious. It displays the moral agent as rational and responsible and also as free; he moves unhindered against a background of facts and can alter the descriptive meaning of his moral words at will. The view thus combines the philosophical insight of Hume (we live in a world of disconnected facts) with that of Kant (morality is rational and seeks universally valid reasons), while more surreptitiously it embodies the morality of Mill ('a creed learnt by heart is paganism'). All this is achieved, moreover, by a 'linguistic' method which provides a meaning for moral words which eschews earlier errors and construes these words as nearly as possible on the model of empirical terms, giving them definite factual criteria of application, and without reference to transcendent entities or states of consciousness. Morality can then be shown to be rational after its own fashion,* while at the same time a method is provided whereby we can analyse any morality, reflective or unreflective, our own or someone else's. This neatly reconciles the opposite ways in which Hume and Kant reached the same conclusion about heteronomy of the will. The points in this, I am afraid very condensed, account which I should like to emphasise for future reference are these: the behaviouristic treatment of the 'inner life', the view of moral concepts as factual specifications plus recommendations, the universalisability of the moral judgement, and the accompanying picture of moral freedom [. . .]

In a philosophical analysis of morality what place should be given to the 'inner life'? [. . .] What must here be clearly separated is the notion of inner or private psychological phenomena, open to introspection, and the notion of private or personal vision which may find expression overtly or inwardly. There has, I think, been some tendency for the discrediting of the 'inner' in the former sense to involve the neglect of the 'inner' in the latter sense. Recent philosophy has concentrated upon the task of resolving 'the mind' into sets of identifiable activities, where the problem is first, how to isolate and identify such of these activities as are purely introspectible ones, and second, how to assess the importance of these inner proceedings as criteria for the application of words descriptive of the mind. The arguments on both these points are familiar.

---

* Those who prefer Burke to Mill may find the 'unconscious' version of the model more attractive, wherein morality appears as habit, and moral remarks are rules for beginners.

Introspectible entities present difficulties of identification; however, it may be conceded that 'mental events' exist, in the sense that there are mental images, speeches uttered to oneself, and perhaps more obscure occurrences which ask for metaphorical descriptions.* These events, however, are in no way privileged, either as being causes of more outward activity or as being the hidden core or essence of individual minds. The concepts which we use to comprehend and describe the mind depend almost entirely on overt criteria.

How does this affect ethics? On the one hand, in a legitimate way through the elimination of hypostatised and non-observable 'qualities', 'sentiments' or 'acts of will' which might have been thought to be bearers of moral value. On the other hand, our by now fairly modified mental behaviourism has tended, in the field of ethics, to lend support to a more rigid moral behaviourism, which has much more extensive implications; this is partly because, as we have constantly seen, modern ethics lags behind other branches of philosophy and assimilates their findings at first in a crude form, and partly because of more or less conscious *moral* attitudes which favour a behaviouristic picture. That is, it has been readily assumed that in assembling the data (initial definition) for the moral philosopher to work on, we can safely leave aside not only the inner monologue and its like, but also overt manifestations of personal attitudes, speculations, or visions of life such as might find expression in talk not immediately directed to the solution of specific moral problems. In short, the material which the philosopher is to work on is simply (under the heading of behaviour) acts and choices, and (under the heading of language) choice-guiding words together with the arguments which display the descriptive meaning of these words. Here two philosophical conceptions reach out towards each other and, in a hazy region, seem to meet. On the one hand, there is no inner life, and moral concepts too must have meaning through definite external criteria. On the other hand, morality is choice, and moral language guides choice through factual specification. The result is a picture, which seems to have the authority of the modern view of the mind, of the essence of the

---

* See Professor Ryle in *Aristotelian Society*, supplementary volume (1951).

moral life as sets of external choices backed up by arguments which appeal to facts. The picture is simple, behaviouristic, anti-metaphysical, and leaves no place for commerce with 'the transcendent'. It gathers force too from the evaluation which it implicitly contains and which may be put in the form of an appeal to 'the moral life as we know it': surely we see that morality is essentially behaviour. 'If we were to ask of a person "what are his moral principles?" the way in which we could be most sure of a true answer would be by studying what he *did*."

Now clearly, as a piece of moral advice it might be wise to tell somebody: don't speculate, just concentrate on *this* state of affairs and see what is to be done. It is an important fact that our lives occur temporally in the way that they do, and that we tend, for purposes of getting on to the next thing, to construct them into a series of situations. However, if one is, as a moral philosopher, exclusively interested in this fact one will miss certain important aspects of morals. I suggested earlier that care must be taken in the initial assembly of data, as this may affect the subsequent techniques which will in turn seem to endorse the data. I shall now briefly discuss the area in question (the 'inner life' in the sense of personal attitudes and visions which do not obviously take the form of choice-guiding arguments) from the point of view of its claim to form part of the data of ethics; and I shall then go on to discuss the compatibility of these data with current techniques.

Ethics need not have any quarrel with the argument against the inner in its most modified form. At any rate, I do not at this point wish to propose any quarrel. The data in question are all 'events' and 'activities' which are either overt (conversation, story-telling) or if introspectible are identifiable and in principle exposable (private stories, images, inner monologue). Now activities of this kind certainly constitute an important part of what, in the ordinary sense, a person 'is like'. When we apprehend and assess other people we do not consider only their solutions to specifiable practical problems, we consider something more elusive which may be called their total vision of life, as shown in their mode of speech or silence, their choice of words, their assessments of others, their

* R. M. Hare, *The Language of Morals*, p. 1.

conception of their own lives, what they think attractive or praiseworthy, what they think funny: in short the configurations of their thought which show continually in their reactions and conversation. These things, which may be overtly and comprehensibly displayed or inwardly elaborated and guessed at, constitute what, making different points in the two metaphors, one may call the texture of a man's being or the nature of his personal vision. Now with regard to this area various attitudes may be adopted by the moral philosopher. It may be held that these elusive activities are irrelevant to morality which concerns definite moral choices and the reasons therefor. It may be held that these activities are of interest in so far as they make choices and their reasons more comprehensible. It may be held that these activities can be regarded as being themselves moral acts resulting from responsible choices and requiring reasons. All these three positions would be in different ways compatible with the current view. Or finally, it may be held that these activities are themselves direct expressions of a person's 'moral nature' or 'moral being' and demand a type of description which is not limited to the choice and argument model.

It may be said at once (in answer to the first of the four views mentioned above) that we do to a considerable extent include the area in question in our moral assessments of others and indeed of ourselves, and we usually know very well in practice how to balance definite performance against apprehended 'being' in our judgements. The question is, what technique is suitable to the analysis of such material. It is proposed on the current view that we regard moral differences as differences of choice, given a discussable background of facts. Moral arguments will be possible where people have similar criteria of application (share descriptive meanings of moral terms) and differ about what exactly the facts are. Moral arguments will be difficult or impossible where the differences are differences of criteria. This picture seems plausible if we take as the centre of 'the moral' the situation of a man making a definite choice (such as whether to join a political party) and defending it by reasons containing reference to facts. It seems less plausible when we attend to the notion of 'moral being' as self-reflection or complex attitudes to life which are continuously displayed and elaborated in overt and inward speech but are not separable temporarily into situations.

Here moral differences look less like differences of choice, given the same facts, and more like differences of vision. In other words, a moral concept seems less like a movable and extensible ring laid down to cover a certain area of fact, and more like a total difference of *Gestalt*. We differ not only because we select different objects out of the same world but because we see different worlds [. . .] [There are those who would] suggest that morality is understanding, interpretation and reflection as well as 'choice'. [. . .] Whereas I would argue that we cannot accommodate this aspect of morals without modifying our view of 'concepts' and 'meaning'; and when we do this the idea of choice becomes more problematic. In construing meaning for purposes of ethics, philosophers have been anxious to keep as near as possible to a model suitable for simple empirical terms. 'Good' is to have meaning in the same way as 'red', except that the factual criteria may vary and a recommendation is added. This is one result of assuming that moral philosophy can be made linguistic simply by putting 'good' into inverted commas. That this is insufficient may be overlooked so long as we construe the moral life behaviouristically as strings of choices and recommendations backed up by reference to facts. In such a world 'good' and 'right' *could* be the only 'moral words'. But if we attend to the more complex regions which lie outside 'actions' and 'choices' we see moral differences as differences of understanding (and after all, to view them so is as old as moral philosophy itself), more or less extensive and important, which may show openly or privately as differences of story or metaphor or as differences of moral vocabulary betokening different ranges and ramifications of moral concept. Here communication of a new moral concept cannot necessarily be achieved by specification of factual criteria open to any observer ('Approve of *this* area!') but may involve the communicaton of a completely new, possibly far-reaching and coherent, vision; and it is surely true that we cannot always *understand* other people's moral concepts.* If we take the view that moral differences are in this sense 'conceptual' and not exclusively behaviouristic we shall also be able to see moral philosophy itself as

---

* On this and related topics see Mrs [Philippa] Foot's excellent paper in *Aristotelian Society*, Supplementary Volume, 1954.

a more systematic and reflective extension of what ordinary moral agents are continually doing, and as able in its turn to influence morality. Great philosophers coin new moral concepts and communicate new moral visions and modes of understanding.*

It is not difficult to see why such a view of morals and of moral philosophy is regarded in some quarters with suspicion. Briefly, there are at least three reasons, two of them predominantly moral, and one more philosophical. First, it is felt to be dangerous to regard morality as insight (or understanding or sensibility) rather than as action plus argument closely related to action. This view is partly perhaps a reaction against emotivism, which tended to confuse insight with emotion; mainly, however, it represents a determination to value action as against understanding or meditation. Notice with what passion philosophers hastened to correct the error of Moore, who separated insight from action. Here, all I can say is that in this complicated matter most moral agents know how to proceed. Moral insight, as communicable vision or as quality of being, *is* something separable from definitive performance, and we do not always, though doubtless we do usually, require performance as, or allow performance to be, the test of the vision or of the person who holds it. The second point concerns freedom. On the current view the moral agent is free to withdraw, survey the facts, and choose again. There is, moreover, an open field for argument of an empirical fact-investigating kind among those who have similar principles. This view is Kantian in atmosphere: moral beings, or those of them who can communicate, live in the same world. It is also Humian: only carelessness and inattention, that is habitual and

---

* We may reflect here upon the attitude which certain modern philosophers take up toward their predecessors. Mr [T.D.] Weldon (*Vocabulary of Politics*) argues that most political philosophies are tautologous conceptual structures surrounding empirical recommendations. Mr [R.M.] Hare (*Proceedings of the Aristotelian Society*, 1954–5) speaks of 'the oldest and most ineradicable vice of moralists – the unwillingness to make moral decisions'. (Hence the search for Golden Rules and other such simplifications.) It is easy to see how both these attitudes arise from the current view of morality as surveying the facts and making a choice. But great moral and political philosophers offer us new concepts with which to interpret the world, and they simplify because they are philosophers. What these linguistic analysts mistrust is precisely langauge.

traditional attitudes, separate us from 'the facts'. Argument or tradition may then be stressed, according to taste. If, however, we hold that a man's morality is not only his choices but his vision, then this may be deep, ramified, hard to change and not easily open to argument. It is also less realistic to say that it is itself something which we choose; and then it may seem that our conception of moral freedom is in danger. Here it may be said that those who think that freedom is absolute in the 'withdraw and reflect' sense confuse the wish with the fact – and that in any case there is no need to equate the freedom needed to ensure morality with a complete independence of deep conceptual attitudes. It may be argued that we *ought* always to assume that perfect communication and *disinterested* reflection about facts can precede moral judgement, and it is true that such an attitude may often be desirable. But this is itself a Liberal ideal. Finally, the notion that moral differences are conceptual (in the sense of being differences of vision) and must be studied as such is unpopular in so far as it makes impossible the reduction of ethics to logic, since it suggests that morality must, to some extent at any rate, be studied historically. This does not of course imply abandoning the linguistic method, it rather implies taking it seriously.

So far I have been attempting to bring certain moral data [. . .] into conflict with two related dogmas: moral behaviourism and the descriptive-evaluative view of moral concepts. I shall now go on to the cases [. . .] of more coherent personal fables, and attempt to bring these data into conflict with certain current views about universal rules. I shall want here to distinguish the personal fable as such from 'personal vision' or 'moral being', on the one hand, which I have just been discussing, where differences may be conceptual without being uniquely personal or pictorial, and from theological structures on the other hand, which may be thought of as 'transcendent realities', and which I shall be discussing later. Here my first argument will be brief and negative: why insist on forcing moral attitudes into the 'universality' model when this is contrary to appearances? My second argument will be to the effect that certain moralities make use, positively, of a quite different model [. . .]

Now clearly any fable, if it is connected with practice, and is not merely a private film show *à la* Walter Mitty, will imply rules since a discipline is required to put any plan into action. The question which we need to answer in order to relate this phenomenon to the current view is whether a morally important fable will always imply universal rules. It has been powerfully argued, especially by Mr Hare* that a *moral* decision is one which is supportable by reasons which are universalisable. Here we may get the full force of what is meant by a philosophical model. We are being asked to conceive of a structure of would-be universal reasoning as lying at the core of any activity which could properly be called moral.

How do we decide whether a fable is morally important? If my argument (which forms an internally connected edifice, just as the current view does) is accepted so far, then it will be conceded that a considerable area of personal reflection is morally important in the sense of constituting a person's general conceptual attitude and day-to-day 'being', which will in turn connect in complex ways with his more obviously moral 'acts'. And here must be included a man's meditation upon the conception of his own life, with its selective and dramatic emphases and implications of direction. Again, we have in practice ways of distinguishing fables which are morally relevant from those which are more purely decorative,† and it suffices for the argument if fables are sometimes of the former kind. Such fables may be more or less closely and more or less obviously connected with 'action' and 'choice'.

For purposes of the present question let us consider the cases where fables are fairly closely related to action. Now clearly a fable may very well have practical implications which *can* be regarded as universal rules. This will be so especially when the fable expresses some sort of generally accepted and comprehensible social pattern. Parables of widely held religions, which have the concreteness of

* *Proceedings of the Aristotelian Society* (1954–5).
† There are forms of unity in life stories which can safely be said to be purely of aesthetic interest. Vladimir Nabokov, for instance, in his autobiography, *Speak, Memory*, tells how General Kuropatkin, who once played with matches with him as a child, was recognised by his father years later, when disguised and fleeing from the Bolsheviks, by a flaring match light. Nabokov adds, 'The following of such thematic designs through one's life should be, I think, the true purpose of autobiography.' The king of this region is Proust.

personal fables, may have universalisable implications for similar reasons. Such will, however, not so obviously be the case, either where the fable is elaborately personal, or where the fable includes the conception that the individual is unique. If one is Napoleon one does not think that everyone should do as one does oneself. Let us consider these cases.

A man may penetrate his life with reflection, seeing it as having a certain meaning and a certain kind of movement. Alternatively, and in fact the alternatives can shade into each other, a man may regard himself as set apart from others, by a superiority which brings special responsibilities, or by a curse, or some other unique destiny. Both these fables may issue in practical judgements, possibly of great importance. Now, does the question whether these are moral decisions really depend on the answer to the question: would you wish anyone else so placed to act similarly? If faced with this somewhat surprising query the fable-makers might reply, 'Yes, I suppose so'; or possibly they might reply (in the first case), 'But nobody could be in *this* position without being *me*', or (in the second case), 'No, for nobody else has *my* destiny'. It will then also be so that, when asked for reasons for their actions, the first man will answer, 'You wouldn't understand', and the second man will give reasons which will only be cogent if one agrees that he is unique. My point is that here the 'universal rules' model simply no longer describes the situation. One can force the situation into the model if one pleases, but whatever is the point of doing so? To do so is to blur a real difference, the difference between moral attitudes which have this sort of personal background and those which do not. Whether such attitudes seem to us desirable or praiseworthy is quite another question.

I leave my negative argument here and go on to the second argument. It is at this point that one may raise the question [. . .] of the contrast between art and morals [. . .]. Some people stress the dissimilarity between art and morals because they want to insist that morality is rational, in the sense of legislating for repeatable situations by specification of morally relevant facts. Other people stress the similarity between art and morals because they want to insist that morality is imaginative and creative and not limited to duties of special obligation. Is there a conflict here? Let us consider the latter case. In the paper already mentioned* Mr Hare excellently emphasises the importance of distinguishing the pair general and specific from the pair universal and particular. Accepting this distinction, one may say that a moral agent may explore a situation imaginatively and in detail and frame a highly specific maxim to cover it, which may nevertheless be offered as a universal rule. This would seem to reconcile the two parties mentioned above [. . .]

I have already argued that there are kinds of moral outlook which it seems pointless to crush at all costs into the universal rules formula. I want now to consider whether there are not positive and radical moral conceptions which are unconnected with the view that morality is essentially universal rules. I have in mind moral attitudes which emphasise the inexhaustible detail of the world, the endlessness of the task of understanding, the importance of not assuming that one has got individuals and situations 'taped', the connection of knowledge with love and of spiritual insight with apprehension of the unique. Such a description would in fact roughly fit types of moral attitude in other ways very dissimilar; certain idealist views, certain existentialist views, certain Catholic views.[†]

Now it may be argued that one may well meditate upon the mysteriousness and inexhaustibility of the world, but meanwhile one has continually to make judgements on the basis of what one thinks one knows, and these, if moral, will claim to be universal. Here again, let us pause and consider what after all a philosophical model is for. If we give in here and agree that somebody whose

---

* *Proceedings of the Aristotelian Society* (1954–5).
† I regret mentioning without expounding, but to elaborate these themes here would take too long. Miscellaneous examples of the kind of view I have in mind, may be found in [M.] Nedoncelle, *Vers une philosophie de l'amour*; [G.] Marcel, *Etre et avoir*, [J.] Rousselot, 'Synthèse aperceptive et philosophie de l'amour', *Revue de Philosophie* (1910). Behind the current views lies British empiricism. Behind these views lie idealism and perhaps certain aspects of Thomism. See Marcel on his debt to [F.H.] Bradley in the *Journal Méta-physique*. It is Kierkegaard who most specifically, though in some ways tiresomely, displays the transformation of an idealist philosophy into a phenomenology of individual moral struggle.

belief and moral inspiration was of the kind mentioned above would of course, when he acts, wish others so placed to act as he does, what does it profit us? We have won a similarity, but we have lost a much more important and interesting difference. There are people whose fundamental moral belief is that we all live in the same empirical and rationally comprehensible world and that morality is the adoption of universal and openly defensible rules of conduct. There are other people whose fundamental belief is that we live in a world whose mystery transcends us and that morality is the exploration of that mystery in so far as it concerns each individual. It is only by sharpening the universality model to a point of extreme abstraction that it can be made to cover both views.

One may suspect, in fact, that much of the charm of 'universality' is borrowed surreptitiously from 'generality'. Mr Hampshire,* for instance, who does not explicitly make Mr Hare's distinction, emphasises the repeatability of moral situations; and Mr Hare himself says 'we steer a middle course' between the 'hidebound inflexibility' of the man who never adjusts rules to situations, and the 'neurotic indetermination' of the man who always hesitates because he fears he has not understood.† But who steers this middle course? To select the middle course is itself a moral choice: the choice which, transformed into a description of morality, Mr Hare wishes us to make true by definition. We do continually have to make choices – but why should we blot out as irrelevant the different background of these choices, whether they are made confidently on the basis of a clear specification of the situation, or tentatively, with no confidence of having sufficiently explored the details? Why should attention to detail, or belief in its inexhaustibility, necessarily bring paralysis, rather than, say, inducing humility and being an expression of love?

Mr Hare and Mr Gellner‡ caricature a person whom they call

* [Stuart Hampshire,] 'Logic and Appreciation' in *Aesthetics and Language*, ed. William Elton.
† *Proceedings of the Aristotelian Society* (1954–5), p. 310.
‡ Also in *Proceedings of the Aristotelian Society* (1954–5) [Ernest Gellner (1925–95), author of *Words and Things*, reviewed by Iris Murdoch, *Observer*, 29 November 1959. Originally a philosopher who 'moved' to anthropology, he attacked analytical philosophy.]

an 'existentialist' who seems to have nothing to say for himself except that he thinks he has a duty to do a certain action, but has no views on whether anyone else so placed should act similarly. With no further explanation this view seems absurd, especially when we contrast it with everyday ideas of morality as rules which are not only universal but also general. However, no real existentialist is so tongue-tied. Any attitude may be made to look absurd if its conceptual background is removed. A morality, if I am right, is a ramification of concepts, and this only appears, in current writings, not to be so because on the one hand the key concepts of our general social morality (freedom, tolerance, factual arguments, etc.) have become practically unconscious and are taken for granted, and on the other hand because the concepts are what they are (insistence on specification of generally observable facts, etc.) whereas, a man who hesitated, always acted with an air of doubt, thought it meaningless to legislate for others, and so on, might well be able to explain his conduct rationally in terms of different concepts.

Here again, it is not difficult to see why such views are met with hostility and why the current model is defended with passion. Doubtless 'everyday morality', in our society at any rate, is of the kind currently described, where rules are universal, fairly general without being too general, and where clear and above-board factual reasoning is required to justify choices. It is felt (Mr Gellner obviously feels)* that other attitudes will tend to be non-rational and possibly non-democratic; whereas Hare would perhaps suspect that a refusal to accept his picture constituted a sort of moral evasion, an attempt to avoid responsibility by pretending that everything is too difficult: and clearly there are views and attitudes which would justify both fears. However, on the one hand, even a disreputable view may still be a moral view,† and on the other hand, if we look with understanding, these alternative views are not

---

* Mr Gellner contrasts U-type evaluations (which claim universality) with E-type ones (which do not), and connects the former with rational argument, and the latter with disreputable things such as the *Führerprinzip*, *credo quia absurdum*, and romantic love.

† It may be noted that Mr Gellner regards both the systems which he describes as 'moralities', and admits that he does not see 'by what standard external to both one could choose between them'.

by any means so sinister or so unusual. Let us consider in more detail some of the reasons for mistrust.

It may be held that views which emphasise 'particularity' and 'inexhaustibility' will involve inability to describe and specify and hence breakdown of communication, and it may be felt that this will at best condone slackness and at worst encourage violence. Mr Hare says briskly that individuals (and doubtless situations) 'can be described as fully and precisely as we wish'. Now, with the best will in the world, this is not always so. There are situations which are obscure and people who are incomprehensible, and the moral agent, as well as the artist, may find himself unable to describe something which in some sense he apprehends. Language has limitations and there are moments when, if it is to serve us, it has to be used creatively, and the effort may fail. When we consider here the role of language in illuminating situations, how insufficient seems the notion of linguistic moral philosophy as the elaboration of the evaluative-descriptive formula. From here we may see that the task of moral philosophers has been to extend, as poets may extend, the limits of the language, and enable it to illuminate regions of reality which were formerly dark. Where the attempt fails, and one has to choose without having understood, the virtues of faith and hope have their place. It is very well to say that one should always attempt a full understanding and a precise description, but to say that one can always be confident that one has understood seems plainly unrealistic. There are even moments when understanding *ought* to be withheld.

The insistence that morality is essentially rules may be seen as an attempt to secure us against the ambiguity of the world. Rules may be ambiguous in that we have to decide how to apply them, but at least in attempting an ever more detailed specification one is moving in the direction of complete clarity. If I am right, however, this cannot properly be taken as the only structural model of morality. There are times when it is proper to stress, not the comprehensibility of the world, but its incomprehensibility, and there are types of morality which emphasise this more than is customary in utilitarian Liberal moralities. We may consider here the importance of parables and stories as moral guides [. . .]. How ambiguous a parable appears to be will depend on the coherence of the moral world in which it is being used. Certain parables or stories undoubtedly owe their power to the fact that they incarnate a moral truth which is paradoxical, infinitely suggestive and open to continual reinterpretation. (For instance, the story in the New Testament about the woman who broke the alabaster box of very precious ointment, or the parable of the prodigal son.) Such stories provide, precisely through their concreteness and consequent ambiguity, sources of moral inspiration which highly specific rules could not give.* Consider too the adaptability which a religion may gain from having as its centre a person and not a set of rules. (For a determined rejection of such 'concrete' guidance, see Kant's remarks about Christ in the *Grundlegung*.) It may be said, that a moral attitude which lays emphasis on ambiguity and paradox is not for everyday consumption. There are, however, moments when situations are unclear and what is needed is not a renewed attempt to specify the facts, but a fresh vision which may be derived from a 'story' or from some sustaining concept which is able to deal with what is obstinately obscure, and represents a 'mode of understanding' of an alternative type. Such concepts are, of course, not necessarily recondite or sophisticated; 'hope' and 'love' are the names of two of them. And there are doubtless some people who direct their whole lives in the latter way. The 'moral' dangers of such attitudes are plain. All that can be said is that we know

---

* Mr Hare says that it is odd that existentialists like to discuss moral questions by writing novels since 'no work of fiction can be about a concrete individual' (*Proceedings of the Aristotelian Society* [1954–5], p. 310). This seems a strange view. We *imagine* fictitious characters as concrete individuals and although it is true that the information which we have about them is limited, this may be so also in the case of real people, and anyway the information is endlessly open to reinterpretation. In fact, we may, in the course of time, alter our assessment of a fictitious character. We do not see the same Stavrogin or the same Charlus at forty that we saw at twenty. Why existentialists like writing novels is plain. A novelist can readily *represent* a situation in which the agent is immersed, which he only partly understands, and whose solution may involve a clash of irreconcilable moral viewpoints. Whether and in what circumstances such a 'representation' constitutes an 'explanation' is, of course, another question.

roughly how to deal with these dangers and part of the moral life is dealing with them.*

I come now at the end of my paper to a matter of great importance which must, however, be dealt with briefly. What I have attempted to do so far is, by appeal to a certain range of 'moral data', to suggest that the current model illuminates and describes only a certain type or area of moral life, and that if we attempt to construe all moral activities in terms of it we are led to ignore important differences. In order properly to analyse these differences, I argued, it was necessary to think of morality not solely as choice and fact-specifying argument, but as differences between sets of concepts – where an exclusive emphasis on choice and argument would be itself one conceptual attitude among others. What I have said so far has been said without raising the question of naturalism.

I think that a good deal of the power of the current view derives from a feeling that it constitutes a defence against the fallacy of naturalism; and it does appear to do this, since patently no argument can proceed directly from fact to value if it has to go *via* the agent's choice of good-making criteria. Let us, however, see how the position is affected by the alternative view I have outlined above. Is there in fact a knockdown argument against naturalism? The argument against it may be divided, I suggest, into the following components. (1) An argument against metaphysical entities. This may come in a strong form which claims that all concepts of metaphysical entities are empty, or in a weak form which merely holds that the existence of such entities cannot be

---

* If time and space permitted it would be tempting to digress here on the subject of 'symbols'. Symbols ('the language of the unconscious') may play, in ways which are still largely obscure, a spiritually liberating role. Jung (*Answer to Job*, p. 172) contrasts the maternal attitude of the Catholic church, which 'gives the archetypal symbolisms the necessary freedom and space in which to develop' with the paternal attitude of Protestantism with its more rationalistic rule-conscious viewpoint. Whether or not one cares for Jung's general attitude (which seems to make absolute some rather dubious concept of 'psychic vitality') there is a contrast here and an interesting one. A deeper realisation of the role of symbols in morality need not involve (as certain critics seem to fear) any overthrow of reason. Reason must, however, especially in this region, appear in her other *persona* as imagination.

philosophically established. (2) A closely related dogma concerning meaning, which I have discussed above, to the effect that empirical terms have meaning *via* fixed specification of empirical criteria, and moral terms have meaning *via* movable specification of empirical criteria, plus recommendation. This will imply that a moral term cannot be defined by a non-moral term. (3) The use of these insights to point out that any argument which professes to move directly from fact to value contains a concealed evaluative major premiss. (4) A *moral* argument or recommendation of a Liberal type: don't be dogmatic, always reflect and argue, respect the attitudes of others. Behind the first two points lie the assumptions of British empiricism, and behind the fourth lie the moral attitudes of Protestantism and Liberalism.

The total argument has sometimes been presented as if it were the exposure of a quasi-logical mistake: if we dismember it, however, we can see that only (3) has a strictly logical air. We can also more coolly decide which parts are acceptable and what it is able to prove. For myself, I accept the weak form of (1). (For instance: there are no philosophical proofs of the existence of God, but it is not senseless to believe in God.) Where (2) is concerned I have attempted to offer an alternative view of moral concepts which shows moral differences as differences of vision not of choice. What effect does a modified acceptance of (1) and a rejection of (2) have upon one's view of alleged arguments from fact to value? Such arguments, it would be currently held, can be faulty either because they involve a definition of moral terms in non-moral terms (the case dealt with by (2)) or because they are elliptical (the case dealt with by (3)). These alleged mistakes are closely related but not identical. Someone who says 'Statistics show that people constantly do this, so it must be all right' (pattern of certain familiar arguments) should have it pointed out that he is concealing the premiss 'What is customary is right.' He must also realise (it would be argued) that 'What is customary is right' is a moral judgement freely endorsed by himself and not a definition of 'right'. The notion that 'customary' defines 'right' may be the psychological cause of, or the would-be reason for, the curtailing of the argument, but it is not the same thing as the curtailing of the argument. The man may publicise his premiss, still insisting on the definition. In many cases, of course, the exposure of the premiss destroys the appeal of the argument, which may depend (as in the example above) upon the hearer's imagining that he has got to accept the conclusion or deny the plain facts; and I would certainly want to endorse many arguments of type (3) whose purpose is solely to achieve such an exposure. I turn now to the other contention, which is the more interesting one.

Why can moral terms not be defined in non-moral terms? The answer to this question is given by the world picture which goes with the current view, and whose purpose at this point is to safeguard a certain conception of freedom. The descriptive-evaluative distinction is simply another way of saying that moral terms cannot be *defined* in non-moral terms because the agent *freely* selects the criteria. The moral word cannot *mean* the empirical state of affairs it commends since it can be used to commend others without change of essential meaning. This can be plausibly illustrated in the case of 'good'. If, however, we do not accept the current view of moral concepts as commendations of neutral areas, and consider rather the way in which a moral outlook is shown in ramifications of more specialised concepts which themselves determine a vision of the world, then the prohibition on defining value in terms of fact loses much of its point. It is, of course, the case that moral arguments may proceed by appeal to facts; but what may be lost to view, especially if we consider only simple utilitarian arguments, is that such arguments take place within a moral attitude where some sovereign concept decides the relevance of the facts and may, indeed, render them observable. The too rigid affirmation of a link between certain facts and an evaluation could appear here either as a *moral* error or as a *linguistic* error. The moral error could be, for instance, 'lack of realism' (lack of a suitably wide and reflective attitude to facts) and would be judged as such in the light of a rival moral attitude concerning what was morally relevant. The linguistic error could be, for instance, a failure to understand the customary degree of generality of a moral word; although here one might need further information before deciding whether an unusual use of a word represented a linguistic misunderstanding rather than a moral difference. My point is that if we regard the current view, not as a final truth about the separability of fact and value, but as itself representing a type of moral attitude, then we shall not think that there is a *philosophical* error which consists in merging fact and value. On the alternative view which I have suggested fact and value merge in a quite innocuous way. There would, indeed, scarcely be an objection to saying that there were 'moral facts' in the sense of moral interpretations of situations where the moral concept in question determines what the situation is, and if the concept is withdrawn we are not left with the same situation or the same facts. In short, if moral concepts are regarded as deep moral configurations of the world, rather than as lines drawn round separable factual areas, then there will be no facts 'behind them' for them to be erroneously defined in terms of. There is nothing sinister about this view; freedom here will consist, not in being able to lift the concept off the otherwise unaltered facts and lay it down elsewhere, but in being able to 'deepen' or 'reorganise' the concept or change it for another one.* On such a view, it may be noted, moral freedom looks more like a mode of reflection which we may have to achieve, and less like a capacity to vary our choices which we have by definition. I hardly think this a disadvantage.

It is from here that we can see what the problem of naturalism really is. We have noted the anti-metaphysical argument (1), the argument against concealment of premisses (3), and the dogma about the essential separability of fact and value (2). There remains a question which is fundamentally an evaluative one concerning how we picture morality and its source. I think that much of the impetus of the argument against naturalism comes from its connection with, and its tendency to safeguard, a Liberal evaluation (4). It is felt to be important that morality should be flexible and argumentative, centred upon the individual, and that no alleged transcendent metaphysical realities, such as God, or History, or the Church, should be allowed to overshadow the moral life. But, and this is the point to which I have been wanting to get, if I am right in

---

* In certain cases, whether we speak of deepening or of changing a concept will be a, not necessarily unimportant, question of words. When we deepen our concept of 'love' or 'courage' we may or may not want to retain the same word.

accepting the weaker version of (1) and in rejecting (2), then there is nothing in the so-called argument against naturalism to prove that *belief* in the transcendent can form no point of a system of morality.

We may now turn back to the real world and consider with an open mind what part such belief does play in morals. There is surely an important and philosophically interesting difference between the man who believes that moral values are modes of empirically describable activity which he endorses and commends and the man who believes that moral values are visions, inspirations or powers which emanate from a transcendent source concerning which he is called on to make discoveries and may at present know little. Whether such deep differences of outlook correlate with obvious differences of moral procedure will depend on further details of the beliefs and society in question. It has been possible to ignore such differences in England partly because the Protestant Christian and the Liberal atheist have, for historical reasons, so much in common. If, however, we interest ourselves in the conceptual background of choice, and the 'vision' and 'moral being' of the chooser, we shall see naturalism not as a fallacy but as a different system of concepts. The current model, so far from refuting naturalism, merely summarises a non-naturalistic moral attitude. The true naturalist (the Marxist, for instance, or certain kinds of Christian) is one who *believes* that as moral beings we are immersed in a reality which transcends us and that moral progress consists in awareness of this reality and submission to its purposes.

The defender of the current view may maintain that in so far as the naturalist's arguments are not erroneous philosophical ones (which we have already excluded) they are mere blind appeals to non-rational conceptions and cannot be called proper moral reasons. Here I can only reply that I do not accept the implied definition of 'rational' and 'moral' and have already argued this at length. Whether a particular argument is rational or (in some sense of 'seriously offered') moral is something which we decide, in ways which are hard to summarise, by considering the weight and coherence of the total attitude – and we may assess in this way arguments which conform to the current pattern just as much as those which do not.

The final argument of the defender of the current view will be the deep one that whatever set of concepts incarnate a man's morality, that man has *chosen* those concepts, and so at one remove the familiar pattern can re-emerge. It may be felt that this argument at least is inescapable [. . .]. Here one can only come back again to the question: what is a philosophical model for? The Liberal wants all the time to draw attention to the *point of discontinuity* between the choosing agent and the world. He sees the agent as central, solitary, responsible, displaying his values in his selection of acts and attitudes. The naturalist on the other hand, differs from the Liberal precisely in *not* seeing the moral agent in this way; and whereas the Liberal thinks that the naturalist has certain erroneous beliefs and fails to realise the responsibility which he nevertheless has, the naturalist thinks that the Liberal fails to understand the truth about the universe and wrongly imagines himself to be the source of all value. (Remember Belloc's remark about the lady who decided to give the universe a piece of her mind.) Different conceptions of moral freedom, which would need to be explained at length, go with these two views. Why should they be planed down and assimilated to each other?

[. . .] Philosophers have been misled, not only by a rationalistic desire for unity, but also by certain simplified and generalised moral attitudes current in our society, into seeking a single philosophical definition of morality. If, however, we go back again to the data we see that there are fundamentally different moral pictures which different individuals use or which the same individual may use at different times. Why should philosophy be less various, where the differences in what it attempts to analyse are so important? Wittgenstein says that 'What has to be accepted, the given, is – so one could say – *forms of life.*'* For purposes of analysis moral philosophy should remain at the level of the differences, taking the moral forms of life as given, and not try to *get behind them* to a single form.

I suggested above that ethics had in the past, in one of its aspects, been continuous with the efforts of ordinary moral agents to conceptualise their situations. This kind of imaginative exploration of the moral life is being practised by contemporary continental

* *Untersuchungen* [*Philosophical Investigations*], 226e.

philosophers, often without special metaphysical pretensions; and there is no reason why such exploration should be combined with erroneous philosophical arguments. It has been largely abandoned in this country since philosophers have been under the impression that ethics must be neutral analysis or nothing. I have argued that in so far as ethics sets out to be analysis rather than exploration it can attain only a precarious neutrality, like that of history, and not the pure neutrality of logic. This will also imply that ethics is in certain important respects discontinuous with the rest of philosophy, as political philosophy, with its more detailed historical implications, is usually conceded to be. Ethics surely is in fact, as it has always *mutatis mutandis* been, both exploration and analysis; nor can we assume that even if we try explicitly to separate these two activities we shall necessarily be successful.

Here, if we abandon the notion of a pure formula, we shall be able once again to see how deeply moral attitudes influence philosophical pictures of morality. (This present writing is doubtless no exception.) There is perhaps in the end no peace between those who think that morality is complex and various, and those who think it is simple and unitary, or between those who think that other people are usually hard to understand and those who think they are usually easy to understand. All one can do is try to lay one's cards on the table.

Proceedings of the Aristotelian Society: Dreams and Self-Knowledge,
30, 1956.

PART THREE

Encountering Existentialism, 1950–59

'This fact alone, that there is no mystery, would falsify their claim to be true pictures of the situation of man.'

'The Existentialist Hero', 1950

'A dramatic, solipsistic, romantic and anti-social exaltation of the individual.'

'Existentialist Bite', 1957

The Novelist as Metaphysician

I am going to talk about what some French critics have called 'the phenomenological novel'. We may well ask, is this really a new kind of novel? Surely it does most of the things that other novels do. Yet there is to it a very special flavour which is due to a definite theory held by the novelist. It is this theory which I want to discuss; and the novelists I have especially in mind are Jean-Paul Sartre, Simone de Beauvoir, and Albert Camus. These writers have also produced books on philosophy which they regard as related to their work in literature; and their literary critic in chief is the philosopher Maurice Merleau-Ponty.

What lies behind this *rapprochement* of literature and philosophy? It is not the first time that there has been such a *rapprochement*. And I do not just mean that 'every novelist has his philosophy', in some vague sense of the word 'philosophy'. The Romantic movement in literature obviously has a connection with the philosophical thought of the nineteenth century. Kierkegaard might be called a great romantic, though a queer one. And the writers I am going to discuss owe a debt to the romantic tradition too, though they also have highly unromantic characteristics, which I shall mention later. Yet the relation of Sartre and company to philosophy is clearly different from that of their literary predecessors; and this is not simply because they are in fact doing philosophy as well as writing novels. These writers would claim that they are philosophers in the main tradition of European philosophy – and that their use of literary means is symptomatic of the turn that philosophy as a whole is now taking.

The word 'phenomenology' is still a stranger over here. It gives the title to a major work of Hegel: *The Phenomenology of Mind*. I suppose Hegel is the founder of phenomenology as a self-conscious philosophical discipline; though some phenomenologists like to claim earlier philosophers, such as David Hume, as their forerunners. And Hume has, I should think, as good a claim to be the ancestor of phenomenology as of British empiricism. Since Hegel, phenomenology has been the main stream of philosophical thought on the Continent. But though it is strictly Hegel's child, it received an injection in extreme infancy from Hegel's enemy, Kierkegaard; it never recovered from this, and it developed in consequence what its parent would probably regard as curious deformities. The great names in phenomenology after Hegel are Husserl, Jaspers, Heidegger and Sartre. There is another line of descent from the *Phenomenology of Mind* via Marx's *Capital*, the work which stood Hegel's book on its head. So that the existentialists and the Marxists are really philosophical cousins.

What is phenomenology? If one wanted a bold formula one might say that it was an *a priori* theory of meaning with a psychological flavour and a highly developed descriptive technique. I am not going now to criticise phenomenology as a philosophical method; I want only to describe it as a key to the thought of Sartre and the others considered as novelists. In England the study of meaning has become the province chiefly of linguistic philosophers or of semantics merchants. Meaning is explained in terms of the position of words in the language and their relation to that more or less conventional framework of behaviour which ekes out the language. A recent example of this kind of analysis is Professor [Gilbert] Ryle's book, *The Concept of Mind*. The phenomenologist does not regard meaning only as a function of our language; nor does he, on the other hand, take it, with the Aristotelians, to be somehow inherent in things themselves, nor with the Platonists, as residing in a transcendent intelligible world. He regards it as dependent upon the activity of the subject.

'Meaning is conferred by the subject'. This is said. But who is the subject? Is this a sort of metaphysical subject which is identical in all of us? A frame which imposes *a priori* conditions of objectivity? Or is the subject which confers meaning the empirical psychological subject, you and me in short? Or is it something between the two? The crucial step towards the phenomenological viewpoint is made when we leave Kant and turn to Hegel. Kantian subjects are beings each endowed with the same faculty of reason, and whose rational wills are thought of as harmonising in a Kingdom of Ends. But in the Hegelian world reason has a history, that is the subject has a history, and is in a state of war with his environment and with other subjects. With Hegel the real subject enters philosophy. It is true that Hegel holds that 'all is ultimately reconciled in the Absolute'. But what interests Hegel, at any rate in the *Phenomenology*, is not the goal but the way – and on the way, at any time before the end of history, there are contradictions that remain unresolved.

In this perilous Hegelian universe, full of substance and colour and dialectical change, the modern phenomenologist first begins to feel at home. Hegel's *Phenomenology* is a remarkable book. It can be taken as a world history of ideas, as a world history of societies, as a possible history of an individual consciousness, or as a metaphysic. How exactly one is to understand this work does not now concern me, fortunately. The aspect of it which is relevant here is this: it describes various general modes in which the subject grasps, sees or understands his world. Hegel presents us with a series of portraits of a self which is at various stages of self-alienation and self-knowledge. At first it is pictured as merely divided against itself, then it is seen at war with other selves, mastering them or being mastered; later on it advances to realise an ethical and then a religious meaning in the world about it. Now this is in many ways the same self whose adventures we meet with again in Sartre's book *L'Etre et le néant* – but with important differences.

Behind the story of the Hegelian self lies the dialectic, the self-development of reason, or, if not that, then the intelligible onward march of history, as the Marxists would say. The Hegelian self, for all its historical and psychological colour, has no fundamental structure, and no fundamental predicament, for it is not ultimately an independent irreducible entity at all. In the end there will have been nothing but the different phases of the Absolute – and these phases are not phases of anything independent of the phase. The self whose structure Sartre describes in *L'Etre et le néant*, and whose adventures he relates in that book and in his novels, is however an independent entity, and it has, like the self of Kierkegaard, one fundamental predicament. Sartre's novels and plays have a strictly didactic purpose. They are intended to make us conscious of this predicament, so that we may pursue sincerely and with open eyes our human *métier* of understanding our world and conferring meaning upon it.

What is this predicament? The outlines of it, as pictured by Sartre, are perhaps by now familiar. We all readily seek out pictures whereby to understand ourselves. This can be a dangerous game, but it is certainly a natural one, and the picture offered by Sartre does have an immediate appeal to many people. The nature of consciousness, he says, must be understood by contrast with the nature of things. The thing is in-itself, *en-soi*; the consciousness is for-itself, *pour-soi*. That is, it *is* nothing; it is not a substance and it has no meaning, although it is the source of all meaning. Its fundamental character is its nothingness, that is, its freedom; its fundamental predicament is the realisation of its freedom: *Angst, angoisse*, dread. It is, however, also conscious that it has to contend, not only with the world of things, but with other selves who are only too ready to make it an object in their universe and to give it their alien significance.

To get the full flavour of this drama I think that the keyword is 'ambiguity', a word which one associates particularly with Kierkegaard. The free and lonely self, whose situation Sartre pictures in these somewhat Kierkegaardian terms, discovers the world to be full of ambiguities. These have to be, and are resolved by action, or by that species of action which we call inaction. That is, we are condemned to choose; we choose our religion or lack of it, our politics or lack of it, our friends or lack of them. Within the wide limits of our historical situation we choose one world or another one.

The existentialists have generalised and given a philosophical form to something which, piecemeal, most of us can recognise in the crises of our own lives, and which some novelists have already been at pains to display. If we want more scientific material to study we may turn to the case histories of the psychoanalyst. What is the analyst doing? Is he laying bare a pre-existing structure, or is he persuading the patient to give a fresh meaning to his past experience? The liberating and therapeutic character of analysis would seem to arise not simply from revelation and instruction on the part of the analyst, but from the creation by the patient of a new view of his personality and his own free assent to this view.

In *L'Etre et le néant* we find a chapter called 'existentialist psychoanalysis'. This is a procedure we all indulge in when we question ourselves – as we perhaps rarely do – concerning our *projets fondamentals*. Are we accepting too readily the standards of our society or of our church? Is our picture of the world distorted by an unwillingness to face unpleasant facts about ourselves? These questions are asked in the context of a fundamental loneliness of the individual, where there is no answer to the questioning except a decision, an affirmation of meaning the objectivity of which nothing certifies. We ask: Is what we value really valuable? We must answer – and yet this cannot be in terms of objective values, for there are none.

This begins to sound oddly familiar. It is interesting that by dissimilar paths the existentialists and the logical positivists have reached positions which are in some ways strikingly alike. Consider this:

> There is nothing to be done about it, except look at the facts, look at them harder, look at more of them, and then come to a moral decision. Then asking whether the attitude that one has adopted is the right attitude comes down to asking whether one is prepared to stand by it. There can be no guarantee of its correctness, because nothing counts as a guarantee. Or rather, something may count for someone as a guarantee, but counting something as a guarantee is itself taking up a moral standpoint.

This is not Sartre but Professor A. J. Ayer writing in a recent number of *Horizon*. The fundamental moral predicament is the same for both of them. This viewpoint was strikingly expressed long ago in Wittgenstein's *Tractatus*:

> The sense of the world must lie outside the world. In the world everything is as it is and happens as it does happen. In it there is no value – and if there were it would be of no value. If there is a value which is of value, it must lie outside all happening and being-so. For all happening and being-so is accidental.

It was the negative aspect of this text that the linguistic philosophers first emphasised. Ethical propositions are not really propositions, so they must be a kind of exclamations, and so on. Later they cottoned on to its positive aspect, and changed over from being enlightened materialists who said that value was a fiction to being the defenders of the true concept of value. It is in emphasising that real value is a function of a free act of valuing, not an objective quality of the world, that the existentialists come closest to this line of thought. Both sides have been charged with corrupting the youth. It is easy to see why.

The next moves, though, are different. The linguistic moral philosopher (the positivist) is concerned only with analysing propositions about moral concepts and with showing, for instance, that such propositions are ultimately connected with our attitudes to life, and are not ordinary statements of fact. Sartre, who is a phenomenologist rather than a logician, and a moralist as well as a moral philosopher, wishes to go on and to display in detail the adventures of the beings who are in this situation of having no guarantee. Sartre is profoundly serious about ethics, and his works have a piercing and illuminating character which, to my mind, contrasts favourably with the abstract nature of a careful book such as Charles Stevenson's *Ethics and Language*. Stevenson sets about describing attitudes at the level of conventional morality and without an adequate terminology. The conflicts which Sartre describes are the ones which go to the root. His terminology may offend because of its metaphysical implications. But even where it is unacceptable it is illuminating. And can we really describe (I would emphasise *describe*) what moral disagreements are like without on the one hand making some concessions to the notion of a substantial self, and on the other using the real concepts which are causing the real trouble? Political concepts, for instance. We may or may not decide that it is the moral philosopher's task to conduct such a description. But rather than do it in Stevenson's terms I would prefer that we should assume that the matter ends with Professor Ayer's article in *Horizon*.

Sartre's novels, then, describe the drama of people who are reacting more or less consciously and in various modes to the predicament of their ethical loneliness and their state of war with other selves. And it is not only ethical loneliness that is described. *La Nausée*, which is certainly one of Sartre's most remarkable books, describes what one might call a sort of logical loneliness. Meaning is suddenly seen as withdrawn not from a world of objective values, but from physical objects themselves. This is a plunge into the absurd. If indeed we confer meaning, not only upon ethical and religious systems, but upon the physical world too, in that we see it as the correlative of our needs and intentions, then this meaning could in principle vanish, leaving us face to face with a brute and nameless nature. This is the predicament of Antoine Roquentin, the hero of *La Nausée*. And one might say, the purpose of the book is to reveal to us our real situation by contrast with one from which a familiar element has been removed. A similar device is used in the play *Huis-clos*. We might compare Kant's use of the notion of intellectual intuition, or the contemporary philosopher's games with the queer logics of imagined languages. The same vanishing of meaning, only applied this time to social convention, is described in *L'Etranger* of Albert Camus. In Simone de Beauvoir's book *L'Invitée*, the drama concerns the meaning of action: what is the real meaning of my act, that which I see or that which others see? In Sartre's novel sequence, *Les Chemins de la liberté*, there are many themes, but the chief one is political: is there a meaning in history, and what is the individual who cannot answer this question to do about it?

One may ask, *en fin de compte*, why all this fuss, all this talk about 'meaning'? Is not this the sort of thing that novelists have always been doing, is this really a candidate for being a new kind of novel? I think it is, in the sense that the writer's attention is focused on this unusual point, this point at which our beliefs, our world pictures, our politics, religions, loves and hates are seen to be discontinuous with the selves that may or may not go on affirming them. It is this focusing of the attention, the bringing to light of this aspect of our experience, that gives to the writings of Simone de Beauvoir, Camus and Sartre, their disquieting character. It is for this that they are attacked as immoral. It is this that Maurice Merleau-Ponty celebrates when he says that with Miss de Beauvoir there ends the era of *la littérature morale*, and there begins the era of *la littérature métaphysique*.

Broadcast on the BBC Third Programme, March 1950, the first of two radio talks on existentialism.

The Existentialist Hero

Maurice Merleau-Ponty said that with Simone de Beauvoir the era of moral literature ended and the era of metaphysical literature began. He was referring, I think, to the fact that in an existentialist novel the interest is focused upon the ambiguity of the characters' situation, and upon how the characters choose to resolve this.

Let us look at an example: Simone de Beauvoir's novel *L'Invitée* for instance (translated into English under the title *She Came to Stay*). The theme of *L'Invitée* is this. Pierre and Françoise, both mature people of the theatre world, aged about thirty, are *des amoureux fort rationels** used to sharing all secrets and discussing frankly their relations with other people. This rational couple befriend a far from rational young woman called Xavière, aged twenty, for whom Pierre develops a serious attachment. For the first time Françoise finds that there is something in Pierre's life which she cannot share. Attempts to find a solution *à trois* break down – and later on Françoise has a love affair with a young man called Gerbert in whom Xavière also has an interest. Xavière has throughout regarded Françoise as an older woman, eaten up with bitterness and envy – and she sees this move purely as an act of revenge. At the end of the book, in a rather surprising climax, the highly rational Françoise kills Xavière. Why? Because she could not endure the fact that Xavière's conception of her (Françoise) was both completely unjust and completely inaccessible.

Françoise discovers that rationality is not enough. The world of perfect communication which she had established with Pierre is destroyed. Though Pierre does not wish it, inevitably he and Xavière form *un couple* over against Françoise. She has fallen back

---

* [Thoroughly rational lovers.]

into the normal human condition where each one is lonely and every other one is a menace – the Hegelian battlefield, where one denies one's being-for-others at one's peril. There is no safety in rationality and frankness. Sooner or later there come the experiences which cannot be communicated. Perfect love and understanding cannot be maintained. Ultimately one is alone. Françoise may never again imagine that any act of hers is perfectly understood by another, but she may well feel, too, the need to make for herself another world of her own. There follows the affair with Gerbert – which is seen by Françoise as something simple and sincere, but of course is regarded by Xavière as revenge. What is the meaning of an action? What we see or what others see? It is part of our predicament that we feel responsible for what other people think we are, – even if we feel that they are wrong. The final act of violence, which I find sadly out of character, does not solve Françoise's problem. Xavière herself may cease, but nothing can now blot out her judgement of Françoise. Only Xavière herself could have done that. Was Françoise's conduct guided throughout simply by unacknowledged jealousy? Miss de Beauvoir makes Françoise a sympathetic character; but she leaves nevertheless a certain ambiguity in the matter.

It is not surprising that this book has been regarded, in certain quarters, as shocking and immoral. Yet the very qualities which make it shocking to some endear it to others; endear it, for instance, to M. Merleau-Ponty. What is so shocking and so endearing is that the characters act and talk with a simple directness and an absence of concern for or remarks about traditional morality.

These are people from after the deluge. The values of the nineteenth century are gone. The destruction for which Nietzsche called has taken place. And, on the other hand, there is none of either the satanism or the cynicism which marked the novels of the 1920s – Evelyn Waugh's early works, for instance. Cynical frivolity is the reaction of those who are still under the sway of the morality which they deny. But Pierre and Françoise are something new in the immoralist line. They are not uneasy rebels against the social code, nor are they exactly oblivious of it. They are detached from it, and they make their own morality as they go along.

What is the moral light that guides Françoise throughout this would-be edifying story? This is not moral literature, that is a literature with an ordinary accepted moral code – it is metaphysical literature. We are being taken one step further back, as it were, to be shown the universal human predicament; and it is also indicated how we are to conduct ourselves therein. Well, how? The answer would seem to be, with complete sincerity and simplicity, and remembering that we are surrounded by other free beings. This message seems at first glance to be tediously simple; but at second glance it is problematic. We are told that we are lonely individuals in a valueless and meaningless world. Yet it is also hinted that, when placing our own values and meanings, certain moves are preferable to certain others. The Sartrian existentialist is particularly hard to assess as a thinker because of just this mixture of philosophy and preaching in his thought. He is doing two things, *describing* what he takes to be the character of man's relations with the world, and *recommending* certain lines of conduct.

Miss de Beauvoir's Françoise is interesting because she illustrates the ethic at its purest, or one might say at its emptiest, where it is concerned only with personal relations, and where the dogmatic and didactic element is least imposing. There is in the situation of Françoise that element of real ambiguity which one would expect *a priori* to find in existentialist novels, and which in fact one does not find, for reasons which I shall suggest in a minute.

When we come to the analysis of political action, here we find the writings of Miss de Beauvoir particularly becoming much more specific and more persuasive. There is also at last a distinctly hopeful note. This may be in part a function of Miss de Beauvoir's wartime experience. A resistance movement can show one an unselfish purity in human action which is memorable. I think that there is a broader explanation, though, for the emphasis on politics as being the most important kind of ethics – and that is that the Sartrian existentialist has acquired a profoundly Marxist outlook. He is not only Hegelian in his philosophical technique, he is Marxist in his immediate reactions to the world. The existentialist shares with the Marxist a feeling of responsibility for the condition of men, a conception of life as perpetual warfare, and a willingness to engage his weapons as a thinker in the battle. Literature too, must be in the fight, it must be *engagée*. The most urgent battles are those which are to be fought out on the political field. Personal questions can wait. Such questions may be modified by the solution of our political difficulties – though I doubt if Sartre and de Beauvoir think that the warfare of personalities will be much ameliorated by the coming of socialism.

The average Marxist must, nevertheless, present to the existentialist eye a spectacle of complete *mauvaise foi* [bad faith] – that is, the Marxist regards his analysis, with its key concepts such as the dialectic, the role of the proletariat, and so on, as recording objective facts about the nature of the universe. The Marxist, the average Marxist that is, is doing metaphysics in the old pre-Kantian sense. The existentialist, on the other hand, sees the meaning of the world as a function of the consciousness of mankind. The Marxist might well object that the existentialist neglects the historical character of that consciousness, and makes its present form into an absolute. The Marxist is more struck, however, by the idealist appearance of the existentialist analysis – and also by the sinister nature of its influence.

At the end of that otherwise rather bad little book, *L'Existentialisme est un humanisme*, which Sartre brought out some years ago, there is an interesting discussion between Sartre and a Marxist. In the course of the argument the Marxist says, first, that existentialism denies causality, and that this divides it radically from Marxism; and, secondly, that existentialism is in effect a resurrection of liberalism, only it is not an optimistic nineteenth-century liberalism, but a tortured liberalism, more suited to the present age. These two remarks between them sum up the Marxist objections to existentialism. There are philosophical objections and political objections. Existentialism is philosophically wrong because it denies the picture of the sure development of history with which the Marxist works. Its talk of freedom as the fundamental human characteristic seems to make the meaning of history both arbitrary and precarious. The existentialist has, moreover, as the speaker in this reported argument shrewdly remarked, *un mépris des choses*. Contempt for things. The Marxist is *chez soi* in the universe. In his universe nothing is absurd. There is an intelligible unity of man and nature. Nature has its own dialectical history, and its own rationally explicable and developing interactions with the activities of man. The existentialist, however, is both unMarxist and unromantic; he regards nature as the brute and meaningless scene into the midst of which man is inexplicably cast. The existentialist tends to find nature absurd.

The existentialist is philosophically wrong, thinks the Marxist, and so he is politically dangerous. As a political factor he is inevitably a liberal. In fact, Sartre's own politics have always been left-wing, and at one time even *communisant* [fellow traveller]. The existentialist tells us that we are free, and that the meaning of the universe depends on us – but he also admits tht we enter into a situation which is already partly formed. We must both engage in some consistent course of action, and keep on remembering that nothing guarantees that we are right. The temper required here is heroic. Such a man as T. E. Lawrence, for instance, is an existentialist model because he was a world-changer who never lost his capacity to doubt.

It is now easy to see why the Marxists regard such thoughts as dangerous. Men are not all of this heroic temper – and if everyone is encouraged to doubt then some may be paralysed into inactivity and others may come to any old conclusion. And then the truth may not prevail. The Marxist regards the existentialist as tainted by a Christian morality, in that he is fundamentally concerned about the individual's sincerity, and so one might say the saving of his soul – and is less concerned with the salvation of society by mass action. The Christians on the other hand regard the existentialists as materialists and class them with the Marxists.

The existentialist, however, can reply that the Marxist may pay too high a price for putting doubt to sleep. Men who have lost their capacity to have doubts themselves or to understand doubts in others may lose both the freshness of their intellect and the purity of their idealism.

> Too long a sacrifice
> Can make a stone of the heart.[*]

Not only may they lose their qualities of humane generosity and sympathy. This in itself might well be a sacrifice required from one

[*] [W. B. Yeats, 'Easter, 1916'.]

generation for the sake of the next. But there is also the danger that such men may lose their sense of direction. Love and brotherhood may initially have pointed out the goal. But if the way is hatred and oppression, it may be that the goal will be altered or lost sight of. The mechanism of means and ends is not as simple as the Marxist imagines. Nor is it, for instance, with the inevitability of a law of nature that the proletariat will assume its historic role. It might well assume not the Marxist role but some quite other one. If it is to be indeed the vanguard of world socialism it must be led to take up this burden freely and consciously. So the existentialist will argue, and with some justice. Yet there is justice too in the Marxist view that doubt paralyses action, and that the risks of dogmatism are risks that must be run.

I think that Sartre is quite keenly aware of this dilemma and that it forms in fact the central theme of *Les Chemins de la liberté*. There are plenty of other problems which are dealt with in *Les Chemins*, but the political theme is the unifying one – and will, I expect, receive an even clearer development in the last of the four volumes – the one called *La Dernière Chance*, which is yet to appear. Since volume one (*L'Age de raison*) we have been acquainted with Brunet, the Communist; a sympathetic character. We have also witnessed Mathieu's vague and inconclusive thoughts about joining the Communist Party. Mathieu is no doubt what the Marxist feels everyone would tend to become under existentialist influence: a drifting intellectual, full of doubts and scruples; politically useless, and, because he is both over-sensitive and inconsistent, a menace even to his friends. But Sartre is as well aware of Mathieu's faults as he is of Brunet's.

What can become of such a person? In the third volume, *La Mort dans l'ame*, we see Mathieu at the time of the fall of France. After months of inactivity behind the line he suddenly joins a small suicide squad who decide to resist the German advance. The situation is known to be hopeless. Why does he do it? He is not moved by any notions about glory or patriotism. He does it – for nothing. He might well have done the opposite. Or perhaps there is in his mind, if anything is, some vague notion of human dignity. His death is not actually related in *La Mort dans l'ame* but we last see him facing the German light artillery and making an extremely existentialist farewell speech. So I doubt if we shall encounter Mathieu again. At last he has made his dent upon the face of the universe.

I think that Sartre certainly attaches a value to Mathieu's final move – however vague its motives may be. But Sartre is not a champion of *actes gratuits*. He does not approve of caprice any more than he approves of dogmatism. Neither Mathieu nor Brunet is what he would wish a human being to be. I suspect that the interest is now to shift to a mysterious character called Schneider, who appears in the last part of *La Mort dans l'ame*. Schneider is someone whom Brunet meets in a German prison camp. Brunet is, of course, busy contacting other party members in the camp, and trying to keep alive some spark of anger in the defeated army. Schneider is not a party man. He is prepared to join forces with Brunet – but he does not share Brunet's belief that the working class will necessarily triumph over fascism and bring in a socialist way of life. Nor does he share Brunet's contempt for the weak and confused 'human material' which surrounds them. Schneider then, who respects his fellows, who is uncertain about the shape of the future and the meaning of the present, and who nevertheless prepares himself for action, has more of the makings of the existentialist hero than anyone else Sartre has drawn in the novels.

There is, however, another character who has, full scale, all the qualities which are shown in this sketch of Schneider – I mean Bernard Rieux in Albert Camus's novel, *La Peste*. Rieux is perhaps the perfect instance of the existentialist hero. He is a person with no illusions and no certainties. He does his job and he loves his fellows and serves them as far as he can. One might say that Schneider is a Marxist *manqué*, and that Rieux is a Christian *manqué*. In Camus's first novel, *L'Etranger*, we saw the world of human relations reduced to its absurd condition, with its meaning removed. Rieux, we feel, is one who is forever conscious of the possibility of the absurd, but who does not relax his grip nevertheless.

For myself, I find these people extremely appealing: Françoise, Mathieu, Schneider, Rieux. The only thing one might say is that these characters and the universes which they inhabit are made excessively transparent. We can see a little too precisely what is being done. These people are appealing, but they are never enchanting – and the worlds in which they live are without magic and without terror. There is here none of the enticing mystery of the unknown, as we find it in a writer like Alain-Fournier, and none of the demonic powers we feel in Dostoevsky. There is not even the nightmarishness of the absurd which Kafka expresses. Sartre's nightmares are thoroughly intelligible. This is, after all, an unpoetical and unromantic literary tradition. The works which it produces lack the concreteness and the opaque character of poetry. They are designed to show and to persuade. They are not ends in themselves. They are like thoughts and not like objects. In these worlds there is ambiguity but there is no mystery. And this alone would condemn them in the eyes, for instance, of a rival existentialist, Gabriel Marcel. This fact alone, that there is no mystery, would falsify their claim to be true pictures of the situation of man.

However that may be, the existentialist hero does present an interesting and touching symbol of the plight of modern man. And to this in part he owes his popularity. As a recent writer in *Horizon* put it, we are in a world which is becoming as absurd as Kafka's world. Only our relation to it is not the same as that of Kafka's heroes. We are not yet resigned to absurdity – and our only salvation lies in not becoming resigned.

Broadcast on the BBC Third Programme, March 1950, the second of two radio talks on existentialism.

Sartre's The Emotions: Outline of a Theory

Sartre describes this essay[*] as an exercise in phenomenological psychology. It is one of his early works, first published in 1939, and markedly under the influence of Husserl. The task which Sartre sets himself is to define the essence of emotion. Psychologists, he says, have made implicit use of this concept in their descriptions of mental phenomena; he proposes to examine it explicitly. He uses the Husserlian terminology, but an acquaintance with Husserl is not necessary for an understanding of what he is up to. We can put it this way: we use the word 'emotion' and we give names to particular emotions and do something which we might call identifying or recognising these within ourselves. What is the essential character of that which we so identify?

Sartre begins by rejecting the more or less behaviouristic theories of James and Janet.[†] He then examines what he calls the psychoanalytic view of emotion. He agrees with the analysts, as against the behaviourists, in regarding emotion as a significant and purposive response to a situation, but he objects to their mode of explanation in that it allows a fact of consciousness to have a meaning of which we are unconscious. What the consciousness 'sees' is, for example, the symbolic realisation of a repressed desire. The emotional phenomenon is not a meaningless piece of behaviour; but on the other hand its meaning is not necessarily open to the consciousness at the time that it occurs. 'It is the profound contradiction of all psychoanalysis to introduce a bond of causality

[*] [Jean-Paul Sartre, *The Emotions: Outline of a Theory* (New York, 1948).]
[†] [William James (1842–1910), American philosopher and psychologist, who played a significant role in establishing experimental psychology. Pierre Janet (1859–1947), French psychologist and neurologist who influenced Freud.]

and a bond of comprehension between the phenomena which it studies.' Sartre then offers his own phenomenological theory which, he claims, retains the view of emotion as significant and purposive, while solving the problem of how it is that we do not seem to be conscious of it as such.

He opens his exposition by discussing the notion of reflective activity. Action does not necessarily involve transition from unreflective consciousness of the world to reflective consciousness of our minds and then back again to the world. Our action may be an unreflective grasping of one or other of two 'shapes' of the world which offer themselves 'out there', and we need not return into ourselves to make the choice. Similarly, Sartre says, emotional consciousness is not normally reflective. Psychologists err who regard emotion as reflective consciousness of ourselves as moved. Emotion is primarily consciousness of the world as qualified in a certain way. The change to the emotional consciousness is to be seen as an instance of a familiar type of unreflective change, where we grasp a given reality in a new manner. (Sartre uses the example of the puzzle picture wherein we search for and suddenly see the hidden form.) Only here there is a special purposiveness in our creation of the new *gestalt*; emotion is a believed-in magical transformation of the world to confer upon it tension-relieving properties. (Sartre uses the word 'magical' to mark the contrast with 'deterministic' or 'natural'.) Thus his answer to the question: If emotion is purposive why are we not aware of this? is that we are aware of it in that we are conscious of the configuration we have framed to achieve the purpose, but we are not reflectively aware of it, any more than we are reflectively aware of our intentions when we perform some simple action. 'This finality is not unconscious; it exhausts itself in the constitution of the object.'

This theory has at first glance a certain daring and illuminating attractiveness; but at a second look it is seen to be full of difficulties.* Sartre has two theories: that emotion is purposive and

---

* One might say this of most of Sartre's philosophical writings. The present text is enriched by many more interesting examples and suggestions than I have had space to comment on. It is a pity that the translation is often graceless, and here and there seriously inaccurate.

that we are conscious of this. These are independent of each other in the sense that the former could be held as a psychological working hypothesis even if the latter could not be made philosophically respectable. Let us look first at the former. Sartre assumes much too readily that we know what is meant by an emotional state, or a world 'coloured by emotion'; but this is just what has to be made clear. The concept of emotion is immensely broader in its limits and more subtle in its special cases than Sartre allows. He concentrates, and this is what enables him to make his view plausible, on certain typical instances of clearcut emotional states, particularly those where a 'defence mechanism' pattern is to be detected, i.e., where a definite purpose suggests itself. (She sobs so as not to tell.) This purpose is then achieved by a conferring of qualities or predicates upon the world. But not all emotional states are as 'pure' as the examples he has chosen; there are emotional moods of an indeterminate kind where we are unable even to name the emotion and certainly not able to make precise either the change which the world has undergone or the purpose for which this could have been brought about. The theory seems equally inapplicable to aesthetic or religious emotions where the emotional colour appears as one aspect of a complex situation which cannot be simplified in terms of purpose. Emotional moods may indeed issue in judgements where we do definitely predicate something of the world. Yet here there is another difficulty; there are many instances of judgements (of which ethical judgements are the most interesting) which have emotional colour, where we would reject the notion of purpose, not because it cannot be made precise, but because these judgements have a claim to objectivity which is incompatible with their being covertly purposive.

This brings us to the question of our consciousness of emotion. Here there are two problems, one concerned with the transparency of emotion, and the other with the objectivity of emotional predicates. First, what does Sartre mean by saying, in his attack on the analysts, that the 'meaning' of a state of consciousness must be a constitutive part of that consciousness? We may agree, that there is a distinction between the 'meaning', in conventional or 'regularity' terms, of a natural object, and the meaning of a conscious condition. (The meaning relation in the first case is external to the object and exists *for* an onlooker, while in the second case this is not so.) We may agree, too, that where a patient never accepts the offered diagnosis, the analyst can only continue to maintain its correctness at the price of mistaking a peculiar kind of working hypothesis for a piece of established scientific fact. But even when the patient accepts the diagnosis, is it clear what has occurred? Very rarely will this appear as the revelation of something which was there all along. The acceptance of the diagnosis will often involve considerable imaginative effort on the patient's part. (Consider, for instance, the cure reported in Layard's 'The Lady of the Hare'.) Only the simplest and most formalistic interpretation of 'the cogito', that which says that my consciousness at a given moment consists simply of that which I 'see' to be there, would enable one to condemn the analysts out of hand. Sartre concludes that an outsider cannot know better than I the meaning of my state of mind; but he does not consider what is, for me, the meaning of my state of mind. He seems to treat meaning as a given constituent of the transparent cogitatio. But 'meaning' here can have at least two senses, and it is a bad Cartesian tendency to consider states of consciousness as a series of separate windows through which we look at red patches and the like that makes Sartre miss this. Such formalistic reflections on the cogito have made Descartes in effect the father of phenomenalism. The meanings with which the analyst is concerned are not perceptual meanings enclosed within an instantaneous cogitatio. If we insist here that a fact of consciousness must take its explanation only from consciousness, we must understand 'explanation', not as something immediate and self-evident, but as a complicated history of shifting conceptualisations. (Sartre seems more alive to this in *L'Etre et le néant*, where he discusses the historical character of the *pour-soi*.) We need not instance abnormal states of mind to see that we do not in fact regard consciousness as a transparent medium whose 'meaning', including our subsequent conceptualising in terms of attitudes, values, real intentions, etc., must at each moment be contained implicitly 'within' it.

It is within this Cartesian context that Sartre places the question of our awareness of emotion, and offers his ingenious explanation in terms of unreflective consciousness of a 'purposive object'. But even if his purposive theory were psychologically plausible (and I have suggested that it is not), his analysis of consciousness could not be made to carry it. This analysis rests upon the distinction between conscious and reflective activity. Sartre says that emotion is unreflective consciousness of the world as qualified in a purpose-serving manner (e.g., I see it as insurmountably difficult in order to justify myself in doing nothing). 'This finality is not unconscious; it exhausts itself in the constitution of the object.' But it is only the subjective idealism of Sartre's whole terminology that gives this the air of being an explanation. There are no such pure emotional subjects which have to do only with pure emotional objects, and emotion is only one aspect of a situation where the question of truth is still to be raised in one form or another.* Hence, as we would expect, emotional conditions respond to reflection in very various ways. Even in the 'purest' type of case, that which most closely follows the pattern which makes Sartre's view plausible, our consciousness of the emotional purpose could not be shown to be of the same type as our ordinary unreflective consciousness of purpose in everyday activity. If on reflection we reverse our judgement this implies that the emotional object is 'unreal' in a sense in which the ordinary purposive object is not. The notion of the 'emotional purpose' remains a fruitful psychological type of explanation which we may use in certain cases when we wish to explain to ourselves, with or without the help of an analyst, the meaning of our own emotional reactions.

Sartre's errors here (and they are also those of Husserl), are of three kinds: Platonic, Berkeleyan, and Cartesian; and they are worth reflecting on since they illustrate the dangers of giving to a philosophical 'theory of consciousness' the close-knit character of a psychological picture. It becomes clear that it is a mistake to demand a single clear essence for a vague concept, that the question of objectivity or truth cannot be excluded at any point from an analysis of our consciousness of the world, and that the notion that

* I think Sartre later did justice to this point if I rightly understand him at *L'Etre et le néant*, p. 28, where he accuses Husserl of a similar error: 'Dès le moment qu'il fait du noème un irréel, corrélatif de la noèse, et dont l'esse est un peroipi, il est totalement infidèle à son principe.' ['From the moment when he turns the noema into an unreality, a correlative of the noesis, and whose being is to be perceived, he is totally unfaithful to his principle.']

on the whole we know what we are up to must be interpreted widely enough to meet the empirical facts of normal consciousness and need not involve an atomistic view where each state of mind holds its total significance, including our subsequent explanations, implicitly within itself.

Review in *Mind*, 59, April 1950.

De Beauvoir's The Ethics of Ambiguity

The difficulty for the existentialist moral philosopher, among whose mutually incompatible ancestors are Kant, Hegel, Kierkegaard, and Husserl, is the derivation of the 'ought' which he presses upon us from the 'is' of his phenomenological description of the self, without the intermediary of a dogmatic metaphysic. (Such as Kant's ultimately *was*, the existentialist would say.) Simone de Beauvoir's little book*, which might be described as a treatise on ethics, an exercise in phenomenology, or a political pamphlet, does not confront this problem. She presupposes, rather than argues, Sartre's view of the self, and produces her imperatives therefrom without discussion. Freedom is the foundation of all value, man founds and maintains all the values he recognises. The existentialist lesson is that, since he is the sort of being that he is, he ought to do this in 'anguish', with lucid consciousness of his responsibility, reaffirming his values, while knowing that they depend only on him. This position, as held by Miss de Beauvoir and other popular existentialist writers such as Camus, defines itself more as a polemical attack on the *esprit de sérieux* (the viewpoint of those who unquestioningly take their values as 'given', e.g. the bourgeois, the dogmatic party member), than as an attempt to work out a philosophical view of moral action. It is at this point that one most feels the slightness of Miss de Beauvoir's book. If freedom founds all values why *ought* I to will my own freedom and also (for this too is an imperative, in fact the fundamental one) the freedom of others? Is 'freedom' to be defined in terms of my attitude (anguish), or in terms of what I choose – and if the latter does this not involve a

* [Simone de Beauvoir, *The Ethics of Ambiguity*, trans. Bernard Frechtman (New York, 1948).]

distinction between true and false values which cannot in turn be derived from the concept of free choice? The existentialists may reply that they, like other moral philosophers, base their 'how man should live' on their 'what man is like'. (He is 'naturally' an other-regarding being.) But some fuller account of moral reflection and decision is needed to link these two, as well as a franker discussion of the 'dogmatic' character of the Sartrian picture of the self. As it is we have Hegelian and Husserlian phenomenology on one hand and Kierkegaardian preaching on the other.

Miss de Beauvoir does not linger over these questions, but goes on to a diagnosis of political attitudes. (One sometimes has the feeling that she regards politics as the only kind of practical ethics.) She 'psychoanalyses' various types of attitude to social relations (the sub-man, the nihilist, the adventurer, etc.) and offers diagnoses of types of *mauvaise foi* (the Communist who oscillates in argument between a dialectical and a deterministic view of necessity). These sketches are crude but it is worth reflecting on what they attempt to do. In a way they are 'aids to moral reflection', in a way they are quasi-proofs of the metaphysical position adopted. Is it a task of the moral philosopher to diagnose and describe the attitudes and concepts in terms of which the moral conflicts of his age are fought out? (Ethical concepts are *not* timeless.) I would wish to say yes. But in what sort of language is this to be done, can it be done 'neutrally'? (Are Stevenson's descriptions of attitudes neutral?) Miss de Beauvoir's descriptions are certainly not neutral, but are coloured both by her metaphysical presuppositions and by certain passionate beliefs.

Perhaps the experience which has most coloured the author's approach to ethics is that of the Resistance and of the post-war disillusionment; the 'purity' of the moment of action followed by the hardening of a living faith into 'earnestness'. The problems which seem to her most important are those of mass political action, the relation of a man to his party, and of the party to the people it serves; the problem of how to win freedom by violent means that temporarily deny it. How is the Liberal (or Christian) spirit of individualism to survive a long era of ideological warfare? Miss de Beauvoir puts the problem with an admirable fierceness, though her discussion of it is not prolonged or deep enough. It is worth noting that almost the only contemporary individual mentioned with approval in her book is T. E. Lawrence. Lawrence is an existentialist hero because he was a man of action who kept his doubts alive. (Compare Rieux in Camus's *La Peste*.) Should he be taken as the model of the 'good man' for this age? This question too is worth reflecting on. The Marxists are probably right in regarding the existentialists as the latest theorists of liberalism. Lawrence was able to act in spite of his doubts; but most men are not Lawrences, and if they are to act they must put doubt to sleep. (Dialectical materialism, as much as 'bourgeois complacency', excludes anguish.) The Marxist will argue that in fact the existentialist plays into the hands of the reactionary; for the average man constant reflection hinders action. The existentialist will reply that the Marxist buys action at the cost of killing the power to reflect and losing sight of the end.

The Marxist–Liberal debate, which is surely of immense importance for any student of ethics or political theory, is sketched but not satisfactorily discussed by Miss de Beauvoir. She is inclined to take the notion of 'freedom' as not in itself problematic; but can we really deduce our political duties *now* from the command 'set men free', however much in the 1930s we may have thought we could? The Marxist and the Liberal views of the 'free man' are not alike, and with this goes a difference of value judgements into which Miss de Beauvoir does not enter. She seems to assume (and is this so far from Kant's Kingdom of Ends?) that 'ultimately' we shall all, if we act freely, be choosing compatible things.

Review in *Mind*, 59, April 1950.

The Image of Mind

What does M. Marcel* think that philosophy is? He uses various phrases to describe it in his first volume of Gifford lectures. It is a reflective quest inspired by a metaphysical uneasiness. It is the reinstating of a proper description of experience. It examines that in the life of the individual which claims an absolute worth and which seems to resist other kinds of classification. It is concerned with the relation of living to truth.

It is not easy to state the central idea of the descriptive analysis which Marcel offers in fulfilment of this programme. The effect is rather that of floating with a current (an image he uses at one point). One might say that the description aims at two things, one negative and one positive: to dissuade us from conceiving human experience in terms of certain crude dualisms (necessary or contingent, empirical or noumenal, subjective or generalised, abstract or successive, inner or outer, immanent or transcendent) and to reveal to us (conceptualise for us) how what we value most is felt as a mysterious bond which links what we are with something which belongs to us and yet lies beyond us. Personal relations, particularly family relations, provide the key idea of Marcel's philosophy. Kantian or Humian pictures of the mind will not serve our attempt to describe these full and complex aspects of our experience. The mind is not a series of impressions, nor is it the abstract kernel of an empirical shell. Mental activity, experience, is a constantly renewed reflection, in the course of which the facts and circumstances of my life become the facts and circumstances of *my*

* Gabriel Marcel, *The Mystery of Being*, vol. 1, *Reflection and Mystery* ([London], 1951).

life by being appropriated or interiorised by me. (Marcel acknowledges his debt to Bradley.* He takes over much of the Bradleian phenomenology without the Bradleian metaphysic.) In the course of this reflection there is demanded of me a certain sensibility or respect for an *otherness* to which I find myself related, the varying nature of which Marcel attempts to conjure up for us by such terms as 'mystery', 'presence', 'essence'. This otherness is felt, in the last analysis, as being connected with a 'supra-empirical' source – and this, no doubt, will be further discussed by Marcel in the second volume of the Giffords, which has not yet appeared.

The kind of search for truth with which this philosophy is concerned, and of which it is itself an instance, does not produce conclusions which can be separated from the 'working' which leads up to them; the truths in which it issues are personal appropriations, not universally valid propositions. This Marcel admits, indeed points out. How are we to judge it then, and can we relate it to the Oxford and Cambridge universe of philosophical discourse? One could sketch a vague relation between Marcel's work and, say, Gilbert Ryle's *The Concept of Mind* by pointing out that in both cases what is attempted is a descriptive analysis of 'mental experience', using arguments which are persuasive rather than demonstrative, and which attempt clarification of ordinary language (familiar ideas) with the liberal use of examples. Both, moreover, are concerned to maintain the unity of experience in the face of dualistic theories. Marcel differs from Ryle however in that the 'experience' in which he is interested is more complex, his technique for describing it more elaborate, and he is interested in drawing certain metaphysical conclusions from his description.

What chiefly gives Marcel's writings their obscure metaphysical flavour is his use of special concepts such as mystery, availability, participation. These are essential to his description – and either they will help the reader to *see* something in his own experience or they will not. The revelatory power of these notions is often, I think, very considerable, nor do I see how one could achieve the same revelation without their use. How does this revelation differ from that which we gain from a writer such as Proust (whom Marcel frequently

---

* [F. H. Bradley (1846–1924), English Idealist philosopher whose ethical system has been called Hegelian.]

quotes)? It attempts to be more systematic and precise and also to lead toward certain conclusions. It would be a mistake however to imagine that because a comparison with Proust is in order, and because Marcel is a playwright, his writings can be dismissed from the field of philosophy as we understand it. There are points at which his argument bites directly onto our concerns: the matter, for instance, of what Marcel calls the 'non-contingency of the empirical'. My life is experienced by me as a narration, in the course of which I appropriate its 'accidents'; in this context, what use is the dualism, necessary or contingent? Marcel here points toward an analysis which might appeal to those who are unwilling to regard a person as a series of mental events each of which is contingent in relation to the series. Indeed the whole of his argument raises the question which our philosophising has not yet satisfactorily settled: what *is* a description of experience? It is not clear, to me at any rate, on what grounds the hygienic and dehydrated analysis of mental concepts which we use in this city [Oxford] can claim to be more *accurate* than the more lush efforts of M. Marcel.

We can however legitimately complain that Marcel is excessively obscure and imprecise. His argument rambles around in an impressionistic manner, and he tends to let one special concept lead us on into another one, without either having been sufficiently defined by the examples. Further, his use of unexamined metaphors is unnerving. He rightly says at one point:

> Our thought seems to come up against the obstacle of its own tendency to represent things to itself in physical terms, in images, metaphors, models, analogies; but we should be proving ourselves all the more certainly the slaves of material comparisons, if we supposed that all thought has to do is to blast such obstacles out of its way.

This kind of description cannot escape from metaphor; but unless the metaphors are accompanied by a close critical commentary the result is often vague and confusing. Truth is like a city, Marcel says: he starts to work out the comparison, drops it, and says truth is like a conversation, it is like climbing a mountain. At the close we have a vague impression, or at best an impulse to think the matter out for ourselves.

EXISTENTIALISTS AND MYSTICS

To one who asks 'What is a decription of experience?' an appropriate rejoinder is 'What is a description of experience for?' Marcel is 'bringing out' quite different features from those which interest philosophers such as Professor Ryle. Marcel's concerns are ethical and religious; he wants to analyse that in our experience which we feel to be important, valuable, irreducible – that which is threatened by psychoanalysts, sociologists and crude positivists. One might say that it is Marcel's desire to analyse our persistent concern about *truth* (in the non-scientific sense) which inspires him to transcend the mind–body dualism rather than to resolve it into its 'lower' half. (*The Concept of Mind* does not discuss sincerity and self-deception.) This lands him in difficulties, however. He says frequently that his discussion is at the level of phenomenology (that is, description of everyday experience) rather than of ontology (that is, explanation of that experience in terms of 'reality'). It is not very clear whether, and in what sense, he is accepting here a distinction between the apparent and the real; the tenor of his argument would seem to be that this distinction (together with that between immanent and transcendent) must be found within our experience. Yet in his discussion of sensation, for instance, he implies that there may be philosophical questions which a purely phenomenological approach ('our own more prosaic investigation') cannot answer. At this point agnosticism may be puzzling but innocuous (like that of Hume). But where it is a matter of 'truth', ethical, political, religious, then something more needs to be said about how the phenomenological method is being used and about the status of its conclusions. A purely phenomenological discussion of religion leaves the crucial question untouched. (The believer is not concerned with the forms and effects of belief in God but with whether, out there, there is God.) No doubt this matter will be discussed in the second volume. It is a pity however that Marcel does not tell us outright whether phenomenology ever *is* ontology (presumably not – so what are we to take ontology to be?) and that his analysis seems to slip between being purely descriptive and being normative or recommendatory. ('I emphasised the metaphysical value that attaches, or rather that should be attached, in the French language to the preposition *chez*.')

The political implications of Marcel's viewpoint cannot go unnoticed (nor is he concerned that they should). It is interesting to compare his key images with those of Sartre. Sartre represents, by contrast, a defiant rationalism, a spiritual *tabula rasa*. The hero of *La Nausée* abhors the gluey excess of the existent world, aspires toward the detached hygienic purity of circles and melodies. Sartre lives in a café and eschews intimate bonds. *L'Etre et le néant* is dominated by the image of consciousness as a perpetual escape from solidification. Marcel on the other hand values intimacy and family relations; his favourite images are of continuity, participation, merging. He values respect for natural bonds, for the inherited, for the mysterious and fruitful links with *being*, which our deracinate civilisation seems to threaten. ('We are all tending to become bureaucrats.') In this view and its political corollaries he may remind us a little of Burke – and, to come nearer home, of Michael Oakeshott,* who uses the word 'technique' in the same pejorative sense as Marcel. In both Marcel and Oakeshott hatred of Marxism, and even of socialism, is one with a mistrust of technical, scientific, rationalistic modes of thought. The dualism which Marcel does recognise is that between love and technique (mystery and problem). In this aspect of his thought (and it is an important one) Marcel seems to me to be guilty of that sort of insensitivity to the complex character of the situation of which he so readily (and often rightly) accuses others. To call Marxists mere technicians is both to underrate their moral power, and to misconstrue their moral worth.

Those acquainted with Marcel's earlier work will find little that is new in this book. His writing is, as it has always been (I think he would not object to the comparison), an unsystematic improvisation upon a certain number of themes. His genius lies in the revelatory power of the concepts which he coins to describe aspects of our experience which we will agree with him in finding important. If we have not finished with the question of how to describe our minds we might still learn something from Marcel (and indeed from Bradley, of whom he is perhaps the most distinguished disciple). His profound and suggestive technique is, I think, capable of a greater precision than he has yet cared to give to it.

Article-review in *University: a Journal of Enquiry*, 1951.

* [See p. 69 above.]

The Existentialist Political Myth

There are various ways in which one can think of existentialism as being important. One can think of it as a literature, as a morality, as a psychology, or as a piece of academic metaphysics which mixes Cartesian and Hegelian strains. The aspect of its importance which I want to consider now however is its importance as a political myth. That it plays this particular role among others has of course not escaped the attention of either its adherents or its opponents – and many on both sides may well regard this as being its central role. The Hungarian Marxist George Lukács says of existentialism that it is rapidly becoming the ideology of the European bourgeois intellectual; and the existentialists themselves return constantly, in an uneasy way, to attempt to situate themselves *vis-à-vis* the Marxists. This problem, the problem of what to think about Communism, *how* to think about Communism, is the most persistent thorn in their side. And they wage an inconclusive battle of persuasive definitions round about the concepts of Marxism, trying to draw them, as it were, into the existentialist camp.

Now there is a great deal which Marxism and existentialism have in common with each other – and there is even something which they both have in common with contemporary English philosophy. It is worth noticing the common character before going on to consider the conflicts. To indicate this character one might say in an inexact epigrammatic mode of speech: this is an age of anti-essentialist thinking, anti-Cartesian, anti-abstract, dialectical. It is an age when we are both reaping the fruits of Hegel and facing the problem of his break with Kant. Kant was a dialectical but a dualistic thinker: that is, he did not conceive of the mind's relation with its object as being that of static contemplation or the receiving of atomic impressions. He conceived the mind as struggling with reality, as seeking totality, rational satisfaction, within it; on the other hand, Kant distinguished between the shifting phenomenal show, and an unknown, or partially known, transcendent reality that lay beyond it. The task of philosophy was to examine the limitations of our thinking; to show how it was that one could never completely know the reality which nevertheless exercised upon us a constant magnetic attraction. Hegel was a dialectical but monistic thinker. For him there is nothing but the shifting phenomenal show, and this, conceived of as a closely knit rationally developing whole, is truth, reality. There is nothing outside it. Hegel is sometimes wrongly thought of as remote, airy, and metaphysical in the purely pejorative sense of that word. He could more justly be considered as the first great modern empiricist; a dialectical empiricist, as opposed to, say, Hume who might be called a mechanistic empiricist. What Hegel teaches us is that we should attempt to describe phenomena. That he cast the laws governing phenomena in logical terms is neither here nor there as far as the value of his method is concerned. In fact, he set about patiently *describing* a vast quantity of human experience, experience of individuals and of societies; and the Marxists had only to drop his logical rubric and turn the thing the other way up in order to have a mode of descriptive analysis which could then be labelled dialectical *materialism*. 'Hegel's Logic is the algebra of the revolution.' The Hegelian characteristic which Marxists, existentialists, and English logicians (or logical analysts) have in common is a non-dualistic patience with phenomena. What we are all working upon, it might be said, is *le monde vécu*, the lived world, what is actually experienced, thought of as itself being the real, and carrying its own truth criteria with it – and not as being the reflection or mental shadow of some other separate mode of being which lies behind it in static parallel. This is the revolution in philosophic method which is showing us its different faces at the present time. It is a move, one might notice, which brings the activity of the philosopher in some ways closer to that of the novelist. The novelist is *par excellence* the unprejudiced describer of *le monde vécu* – and it is not surprising that a great novelist, such as Tolstoy, found out long ago things which Sartre and Professor [Gilbert] Ryle are now offering to us in a philosophical form. With this concentration upon phenomena goes the overcoming of a crude opposition between idealism and materialism; with it goes a sense of the unity of theory and practice, a determination not to say more than we can see: in short an abandonment of the old speculative metaphysics of the Cartesian kind. Of course, one can overdo the attractive business of observing a unity of pattern in an apparently highly various region. If one were to say, for instance, that when Professor [A. J.] Ayer says that much of our mental life takes place in public he is making a Hegelian remark about 'objective spirit', this might sound paradoxical and excessive. Yet I think there *is* this unity of pattern, and that it is important.

It is true that the differences are more obvious than the similarities. It is one thing to decide that 'explanation' is the orderly observation of experience and not a looking behind experience, but it is another thing to know what to observe or how to describe. One might say, broadly, that the logical analysts describe ordinary language, and behaviour so far as it illuminates this, the existentialists describe a range of psychological phenomena connected with private personal experience, and the Marxists describe man's behaviour as a social being. Further, the purposes for which the descriptions are used are different. Yet the method has a common character, and even as far as conclusions are concerned, existentialism shares some things with logical analysis and others with Marxism. For instance, Ryle and Sartre both attack, and in very similar terms, the substantial intellectualist picture of the mind; and, if we look on the other side of existentialism, we find Sartre using Marxist categories as soon as he starts to describe man's social existence.

To sum things up in a rather shocking way: as far as method goes, we are all Hegelians nowadays; but the spectre which haunts us is Kant. The Cartesian dualism is dead, Hegel killed it long before *The Concept of Mind* was written. The problem of metaphysics today is the problem of the Kantian dualism.

Now it may seem odd, on the face of it, to describe the existentialists as anti-Cartesian, since they are constantly talking about 'the *cogito*' and claiming descent from Descartes. When I call them anti-Cartesian I am using this term as Professor Ryle used it, to mean that they are not mind–body dualists. What *is* Cartesian about them is their insistence upon the primacy and the authority of the personal consciousness. Sartre describes the human condition in a terminology and by a method which owes much to Hegel; but he wishes too to stress the solipsistic isolation of each human unit, and here he makes appeal to the Cartesian cogito. Yet the isolation which Sartre's man suffers from goes even beyond that of the Cartesian doubter; for it is also the incurable isolation of the man described by Kierkegaard. Sartre attempts both to display the general structure of human consciousness, and to indicate its absurd isolation. In attempting the former he is writing in the general tradition of philosophical endeavour which descends from Kant through Husserl; he is attempting a new deduction of the categories. Sartre's deduction has more pictures and conversations about it than that of Kant; it reads more like a psychological myth, and seems closer to Freud than to the *Critique of Pure Reason*. Yet it is a sort of transcendental deduction; Sartre is seeking in the consciousness for the *a priori* basis of objective reality. When he analyses the structure of our consciousness of others, or our emotional consciousness, he is exhibiting our fundamental categories. These 'forms' are regarded as held as it were in common between the objective and the subjective world – and they are laid bare by a technique of description, the phenomenological reduction, which puts the question of the objective reality of phenomena 'in parenthesis' so that the essential structure of the phenomena may be investigated. What is supposed to emerge is the nature of human consciousness, or, if you like, the human condition. It is here, in this sort of semi-psychological description and analysis, that existentialist writings are at their most brilliant and illuminating. The new concepts which they invent (such as Sartre's *être-pour-autrui*, Gabriel Marcel's *fidelité*) draw a line round important aspects of experience, naming what has not been named before. I am not concerned here however with the psychological subtlety and finesse of these descriptions, nor with any logical criticism of their more dubious philosophical corollaries. I am concerned with their character as a political myth.

We may notice to begin with how extremely recognisable Sartre's descriptions seem to a great many people – particularly perhaps on the other side of the Channel. People say: yes, this is what we are

[133]

like. And it is not far from here to: this is what man is like. Well, what is he like? We might contrast the Sartrian man with the Kantian rational being. What Kant describes is an empty consciousness, a structure of intuition, understanding, reason, which is the same in every rational creature. But Kant's man lives in a universe where there is a transcendent objective truth, although it may not be altogether knowable. Similarly the man whom Kierkegaard describes may live plunged in doubt and confusion but he lives in a universe where there is God. Sartre's man is described as an isolated non-historical consciousness, like Kant's man, and as being anguished and doubtful like Kierkegaard's man – but he is unlike both in that he inhabits a universe which contains no transcendent objective truth. Truth somehow depends on him. There is no human nature, Sartre tells us, there is only a human condition.

This condition is not described in abstract philosophical terms. Philosophical jargon sketches a framework, but the detail is filled in by concrete description, of a subtle and compelling kind, of our moment to moment awareness. The scale and method of this description are important. Sartre concentrates attention on the individual consciousness, and its immediate mental behaviour, and what emerges is a non-historical, non-social, and non-determined individual. A solipsistic picture. We might compare Sartre's method, from this point of view, with that of the logical analysts. They too look at the moment to moment character of consciousness in order to delineate the concepts used in talk about the mind. The being which they examine is a non-historical specimen. The concepts analysed are of a completely general character; one would not, for instance, expect to find here an analysis of a concept such as 'class-consciousness'. They sum up their observations in the view that knowing how has primacy over knowing that; that is, that our nature as rational creatures is best considered in terms of activities and skills rather than in terms of the contemplation of truths or the private manipulation of syllogisms. From this they profess to draw no further conclusions about man's nature; a programme which on the whole they carry out more strictly than does Sartre, who makes a similar profession. Their analyses are concerned simply to solve certain philosophical problems, and they make no metaphysical claims. Yet we may notice that in one case at least, political, if not metaphysical, conclusions are to be found connected with an analysis of this kind. I am thinking of Michael Oakeshott [who], also starting out with epistemological views exactly similar to those of Ryle, makes them lend support to a sort of traditionalistic political liberalism. The argument, crudely put, runs: if man is a knower how and not a knower that, if his rationality expresses itself in non-reflective and non-deliberate modes of activity and not in intellectual apprehension of subsistent truths – then we should not imagine that society ought to be, or can be, changed overnight with the help of a rationalistic political blueprint. Oakeshott is the opponent of everything which he calls 'rationalism in politics'; and of course the most notorious rationalists are the Marxists.

Sartre is not shy of drawing both metaphysical and political conclusions from his examination of consciousness. But his political position turns out to be very unlike that of Oakeshott. He examines the intellectualist, substantialist, picture of the self and finds it wanting; and instead of saying 'then don't let's have a picture', he invents one with the opposite characteristics. Man is not a substance, a something; so he is a *néant*, a nothing. He is a *néant* which aspires toward being, with an aspiration which is subject to no role external to itself or common to others. Sartre is not a dualist in the sense of the dualism which Ryle attacks; but he is a dualist in two other senses. There is, to use his own jargon, the dualism between the consciousness or *être-pour-soi*, and the world of things or *être-en-soi*, and there is the dualism between the consciousness and the ideal totality which the consciousness aspires to be, and which Sartre calls *être-en-soi-pour-soi*. Sartre's first novel, *La Nausée*, is a sort of metaphysical poem on the subject of the two dualisms. The hero, Roquentin, is afflicted with a dreadful sense of the contingency of the world, the brute nameless there-ness of material existence. He feels himself as an empty nothing which has been crowded out of the opaque world of objects. Compared with *them* he is *de trop pour toujours*. On the other hand, he is haunted by thoughts about melodies and circles which seem to have a perfect satisfying intelligible mode of being which lifts them out of the fallen world of existence. Toward this other world Roquentin aspires, and hopes to reach it, it appears at the end of the book, by creating a work of art. This myth, Kantian, sometimes Platonic, in its flavour, perfectly expresses Sartre's view of human life, the view to which he gave a philosophical expression in *L'Etre et le néant*. Man is an emptiness poised between two inaccessible totalities. The world of objects is impenetrable, the world of intelligible being is unattainable, even contradictory.

This rather bitter view of objective reality as 'fallen' is a persistent feature of existentialist thinking; and one which could no doubt be connected, if one cares for this sort of genealogy, with parallel or antecedent trends in Protestant and Jansenist theology. The form which this notion takes in contemporary existentialism is interesting however. Roquentin, the hero of *La Nausée*, is not only impressed by the brutish solidity of the stones on the sea shore; he feels a similar kind of horror when he contemplates the world of insincere bourgeois banality which surrounds him in the provincial town where he is living. He notices, in this world, the *mauvaise foi* [bad faith] of its inhabitants, the idolatry of state and family, the 'justification' drawn from position and wealth, in short the reification of relations and institutions. But, Roquentin thinks, the rationality and solidity of this world is a veneer, just as the rational classification and tame nameability of the world of objects is a veneer. Beneath the latter lies the brute confusion of the contingent world, and behind the former lies the non-rational, non-justifiable absurdity of the lonely consciousness. What is human and real is this lonely, empty aspiration – the bourgeois social world of technical hierarchies and rights and duties is made to conceal this unnerving solitude – and somehow it is the latter which is the true seat of value. The trend of thought is anti-rational, anti-scientific, anti-technical. The world of clear-cut rational distinctions, of techniques and positions and institutions and rights is unreal. This is the echo which we hear in the writings of thinkers as apparently far apart as Oakeshott, Camus, Marcel. It is no accident that the term 'technique' is used pejoratively by both Marcel and Oakeshott; it may be a long way from the latter's attack on rationalism to Camus' recommendation of the absurd life, but it is down the same road.

Now the comments which a Marxist would make on all this are but too clear. He would say: this is the mythology of those who reject capitalism, with its materialistic values and its deadening of human activity, and who are yet afraid to embrace socialism. They are afraid of the conclusions which a rational and scientific consideration of the scene would force upon them, and so they deny reason, and identify it with the rigid technicalities of the capitalist system. The individualistic outlook natural to capitalism can no longer ignore the rapidly changing social basis of man's life and values. A universalistic Kantian Rousseau-esque individualism is now impossible. So those who are morally sensitive and intelligent enough not to be taken in by capitalism now embrace a solipsistic and nihilistic individualism. Their own lives are absurd and pointless and their society faces annihilation; so naturally they welcome a philosophy which says that all human life is essentially senseless and that man lives *vis-à-vis du néant*. So they can feel that their miserable lot is the lot of all humanity, and not just their historical fate – and at the same time, with the help of the theological concepts furnished by their philosophy, they can maintain themselves in a state of doubt and guilt and anguish, thereby both expressing and appeasing the bad conscience which they feel at not being socialists. Such remarks are made, for instance, by the Marxist critic of existentialism, George Lukács.

Before considering the justice of these comments I want to look at the other side of the dualism. It is here that we must look to see what sort of answer Sartre himself might give to the Marxist charges. Consciousness is negation, nothingness; it makes itself by negating the given, the brute thingy world, on one side – and it makes itself also by aspiring, on the other side, toward an ideal completeness. So consciousness is both *rupture* (the break with the given) and *projet* (aspiration to totality); both these characteristics Sartre equates with freedom and the latter he connects with value. Freedom, considered as negation and project, is the main character of human consciousness. We are condemned to be free. We express this freedom by our inability to be things; however hard we may build up thingy ramparts of institutions and reified values round about us, there is an aspiration which continually breaks down these ramparts in favour of some more distant ideal, which in turn is deadened and reified when we come upon it. What we want is the impossible; that is to be a living transparent consciousness and at the same time a stable opaque being; to be both *pour-soi* and *en-soi* at the same time. This, says Sartre, is the aspiration to be God, to be *ens causa sui*, and it is innately contradictory. This, he says, is the fundamental form of all our particular projects and ambitions. Toward the end of *L'Etre et le néant* Sartre speaks in characteristically persuasive rhetorical terms about the situation of the being who aspires vainly to be God. The passion of man is the opposite of that of Christ; Christ suffered so that God should be man. Man suffers in order to be God, but since the completeness which he seeks is impossible his suffering is vain. *L'homme est un passion inutile.* Under the form of one object or another, one value or another, man seeks his own Godhead; but no project satisfies him, all tend to fall dead into the region of the reified. From the point of view of their ultimate failure to satisfy, all projects are equally vain and *ça revient au même de s'enivrer solitairement ou de conduire les peuples.*

This has an attractive ring of heroic stoicism and nihilistic despair. So we might be surprised to find Sartre, in another *persona*, preaching the ethics of social democracy and liberal individualism, and talking like any Fabian. In his pamphlet *Existentialism and Humanism* we find Sartre speaking of freedom in much more universalistic and Kantian terms. I cannot choose something as good for myself unless I choose it as good for all men. I cannot will my own freedom without willing that of all. And in *What is Literature?* he tells us that a writer, since his work is an appeal to the free assent of his audience, cannot but be an advocate of freedom. Here we see 'freedom' being used to mean not the frustrated flickerings of the isolated consciousness, but something much more like what Rousseau meant by it, more like what it means in talk about social democracy and liberalism. This contradiction, which is pointed out by Lukács, is not an unimportant slip, but represents a real dilemma.

Is it individual choice which founds freedom and value, giving to my actions a meaning which otherwise they would not have and which is *their* meaning? In this sense of freedom stone walls do not a prison make, I am free so long as I am conscious. If on the other

---

* ['It comes to the same whether you get drunk on your own, or go out and lead the peoples of the world.']

hand one thinks of freedom also in the ordinary sense of social, civil, political freedom, as a domain of personal spontaneity which might be infringed and which ought to be respected – then how is *this* to be connected with *that*? They can only be connected by assuming some sort of universal human nature, which Sartre does in *Existentialism and Humanism*, although this contradicts his earlier position. Sartre wants to have the best of both these worlds.

It may be pointed out that the first sense of liberty makes the word so general that it robs it of its meaning. A deterministic theory has the same dazing effect; if one accepts the new use of the terms one has then to think of other terms to indicate the contrast, which still seems to be there, between free and non-free. Yet this theory is not without point. It emphasises the absence of any framework which *contains* me, the individual. Neither the institutions and rights of the bourgeoisie, nor the dogma of any religion, nor any conception of historical development can confer sense from the outside upon my actions. Even the psychoanalyst can't. Meaning is egocentric. Yet, as I am infinitely free, I am also infinitely responsible. Simone de Beauvoir depicts this sense of infinite responsibility in her novel *Le Sang des autres*. The hero of this work is constantly being reminded of the crime of 'being another'. One cannot but do harm to the innocent – whether it be to the girl one fails to love, or to the hostages who are shot because one resists tyranny. The solution, the author concludes, is to struggle for a kingdom of freedom, where we shall not be forced by circumstance to do violence to each other – and where respect for one another's freedom will render innocent such inevitable conflicts as shall still remain. The novel carries as a superscription a quotation from the *Brothers Karamazov*: I am responsible for everything before everybody. Now one may feel both puzzled and uneasy at the total character of this assertion. Uttered in a religious context it may have a sense. Though one sympathises with Lukács who, looking at the works of Dostoevsky, points out how a total responsibility may take the form of a total irresponsibility. In Simone de Beauvoir's novel the sense of total responsibility does seem to lead to a certain clouding over of the notion of the ordinary virtues. The cardinal virtue for her, and for Sartre in his more Fabian *persona*, is sincerity, the exercise of one's own freedom, and a respect for and defence of that of others. This latter idea is tied on to the lonely self-justifying individual by means of an implicit notion of human nature, or else with the help of an emotionally attractive idea of responsibility. Thus Sartre is able to preach social democracy as if it were deducible from existentialism, and complain in *What is Literature?* that people are wasting their good will in personal relationships instead of setting about the task of setting humanity free, which seems to impose itself because we are what we are.

What form, one may now go on to ask, can a metaphysic of social democracy take in a world such as ours where it is increasingly impossible to think in terms of the *Contrat Social?* It has been said of existentialism that it is a myth of the Resistance. This is superficial if it means that it is a matter of a momentary fashion or slogan. But it may have a deeper sense. The picture of man which Sartre offers is of a being constantly threatened by a deadening and solidifying of his universe – a fall into the banal, the conventional, the bourgeois, the realm of *mauvaise foi* – who may rise out of this in search of a living totality but forever in vain. Such a being is at his best, his most human, when he is by an effort of sincerity breaking his bonds; yet such a moment can never be held or stabilised. What is the political cash value of such an idea? Simone de Beauvoir sums up the existentialist position when she says: *seule la revolte est pure.*[*] All achievement deadens and corrupts – living value only resides in active affirmation or the rebellious struggle. Sincerity is not a state of being. This viewpoint, plausible in a personal psychological context, has its political counterpart. It fits perfectly the ethos of a resistance movement. But once the comparative simplicity of this situation is removed, it shows itself as a fear of authority, conformity, achievement. The pure moment is something which is poised between the dead conventions of capitalist society on the one hand and the rigid dogma of the Communist Party bureaucrat on the other. There is something typically existentialist about this position. We find the same principle in Marcel and in Berdyaev.[†] The latter gave a

[*] ['Only revolt is pure.']
[†] [Nikolai Berdyaev (1874–1948), Russian Idealist philosopher sometimes identified with early existentialism, who finally rejected Marxism in favour of a Messianic spirituality.]

significant expression to it when he valued courtship above marriage and held that there should be divorce if ever the living flame should die down. In the political field this viewpoint may issue in a sort of romantic Trotskyism. It is this which George Lukács calls the politics of adolescence. It's interesting to note in passing that almost the same phrase is used by Oakeshott, for an opposite purpose, that is to describe the rationalist approach to politics. One can, I think, say what is appropriate about the label in both cases. This romantic Trotskyism, which consorts with Marxism for purposes of revolt but not for purposes of achievement, may be seen in particular in the work of Simone de Beauvoir and Maurice Merleau-Ponty, and also, though less markedly perhaps, in Sartre. Volumes III and IV of Sartre's novel *Les Chemins de la liberté* contain a curious and touching fable about this matter, where the friendship is described of the communist Bouvet with the mysterious Schneider – Schneider, who turns out to be a discredited ex-party member pointedly called 'Vicarios' and for the sake of whom Bouvet eventually breaks with the party, with whose immediate doctrines he is in conflict. The question is: should the personal and the immediate values be preferred to the long-term workings of a machine in which one can but have faith? Is the scapegoat rightly branded and excluded, and even if he is not, what is the sense in taking his part if one has nothing but an individual gesture to oppose to a planned and organised intention for good? How is one to know, after how much incursion of evil, that planned intention must be regarded as irrevocably corrupt? The (I think) deliberately Christ-like figure of Sartre's Vicarios may make one think of the great prototype of this kind of fable: the story of the Grand Inquisitor in *The Brothers Karamazov*.

I have been suggesting that existentialism can be seen as a mythological representation of our present political dilemma. I think the Marxists are right when they say that a powerful reason for the popularity of existentialism is that it makes a universal myth of the plight of those who reject capitalism but who cannot adjust themselves to the idea of socialism, and who seek a middle way. They seek it, the Marxists might add, in doubt and despair, finding no genuine political road in the centre, but only turnings away to the left and the right. To put it in Sartrian jargon, they reject the opaque brutish world of capitalist institutions and values, they are outside, or conceive themselves as outside, this *être-en-soi*; yet the ideal totality which they yearn for, the *en-soi-pour-soi* of socialism, is impossible, since all achievement corrupts and the dead hand extinguishes the pure flame. So they are left in the middle, empty and lonely and doomed to continual frustration.

Now one may ask: should we reject this myth as simply not representing how we are situated, or if we do accept it as having a political significance, is there any answer which can be made to those who are drawing extremist lessons from it? The existentialists, while possibly even accepting much of the Marxist analysis of their picture, would resist the Marxist conclusion. How is one to see this? One could think again of the Grand Inquisitor fable and put in these terms it seems clear that one must answer: I must side with Christ against the Grand Inquisitor. But what is it to side with Christ? Putting Stalin in the place of the Inquisitor and Marx or Trotsky in the place of the Messiah will not help us here.

This myth raises empirical and moral questions which, as so often in the field of politics, merge into each other. The question: are the Marxists right? can up to a point be regarded as an empirical question. We may ask: did Marx not underestimate the ideological power of the middle class? May it not be possible for the capitalist system to readjust itself and survive its internal contradictions? If the class struggle in England and America seems to be losing its sharpness, is this only a temporary phenomenon? One could attempt to answer these questions by examining facts. Yet the empirical answer does not seem to give the moral answer. Even if one were to see what history were doing one might still decide to let it get along without one. In any case, it seems clear to me that the empirical answer is clouded in such obscurity that although we must not cease to look for it, we cannot do the looking without raising the moral questions at the same time. The problem which the existentialist myth puts before us is a problem about time, about the value of the present and of the personal. If we decline to valorise the historical process, or if we cannot understand it, can we morally contract out, and what would this mean? Marxism stands for, and is, an incarnation of ideas and values. The social values of capitalism are also incarnate, but those of the Middle Way are at present not. It may be well to say: believe only in a *living* future, a future that belongs to existing human beings, and not in a rational ideal of a politically deduced future time. Do not sacrifice a human present for a problematic inhuman future. But does this leave one with only a personal morality, and with no political morality or only a negative one?

An anti-rationalist historian such as [Herbert] Butterfield reminds us too that every generation is equidistant from eternity, and adds as a final piece of advice that we should hold to Christ and let the rest take care of itself. But he does not tell us what this means or what attitude to the historical process it would involve for us at present. This was what I had in mind earlier when I spoke of the Kantian dualism. Here one's values seem not to be incarnate, either in the old or the new morality, but present themselves as transcendent. What is it to choose in this way, and may one not after all be rejecting the flesh and blood in favour of the shadow? The answer to the empirical question about history does not seem to me to be clear enough to enable one to avoid the moral, or if you like, metaphysical question. Belief in God may affect how one thinks about the matter but will, I think, not give one any easy way out of the dilemma. We seem to be faced, as Pascal was, with the necessity of betting.

This presentation may seem to an English audience utterly unreal. History condemns us to be metaphysicians or even Trotskyists? Come now! And it is true that the existentialist picture of the dilemma is one which has power on the continent but, on the whole, and for a variety of reasons, not over here. Yet I think that whether we recognise it or not, and whether or not we enjoy these romantic and dramatic pictures of it, we are in some such dilemma. The dilemma of deciding what it is the rejection of Marxism condemns us to. Here again it may be said: why put it so intensely? Let us not try to jump out of our skins. Let us go along as we have always done, making *ad hoc* moral choices and pursuing a politics of compromise. This would be all right if it were not for the fact that the present tempo of politics means more than ever that he who hesitates is lost. The only recorded remark made by the American novelist William Faulkner during his recent visit to Europe was one to the effect that: now there are no spiritual problems, there is only the problem when shall I be blown up? But indeed it is just this, the imminence of being blown up, that makes there to be spiritual problems for those who otherwise could have got along without them.

To put it at last in concrete terms: there are certain features about Marxism as it is lived in Soviet Russia which makes it morally unacceptable to many of us. There are certain *facts*: the existence of forced labour camps, the insecurity of the individual, the authoritarian direction of thought, which we find intolerable, and to which we can only say no. On the other hand, I take it for granted that any intelligent moral being will say no also to what I might call the morality of McCarthy, or the notion of a self-righteous crusade against Communism in defence of 'Western values'. What are the alternatives? One may adopt a sort of total morality of refusal, a deliberate washing of the hands, which would involve, for instance, complete pacifism. This is a perfectly intelligible position and one which must be respected. On the other hand, one may tag along, accepting the sins and the morals of one's civilisation, and waiting for the slippery side-step into war, where it will inevitably appear that the other side is the aggressor. Meanwhile, one may devote one's time to attacking such manifestations of the McCarthy morality as one encounters in public or private life. This sort of compromise is, I suppose, the one which many of us are adopting. Finally, one might make the moral effort to embrace Marxism nevertheless, accepting the forced labour camps and so on. Whether one can do this will depend partly on one's estimation of the empirical arguments, and on one's view of the capitalist alternative. The one thing we cannot with honesty say, armed with the atom bomb, is: I shall simply wait and defend England from invasion when the time comes.

If this is how we are placed, and I think it is, the existentialist mythology can be seen as, among other things, a picture of our dilemma. We want to think morally about politics but our moral categories are confused and our political categories are empty. What answer does existentialism offer? It offers no answer. Its concept of value is problematic, a question mark. But it is an expression of a passionate and sincere desire to keep to the middle way, to preserve the values of an innocent and vital individualism in a world which seems to menace them from both sides. We may well feel sympathy with this passion, and with the cry of distress which accompanies it. It is not yet clear what will show whether or not the myth represents a tragic delusion.

Essay in *Socratic Digest*, 5, 1952.

Hegel in Modern Dress

It is almost mysterious how little Hegel is esteemed in this country. This philosopher, who, while not being the greatest, contains possibly more truth than any other, is unread and unstudied here. The countrymen of David Hume have, oddly enough, a better record. But it remains the case that scarcely anything of value has been written about Hegel in England – and Oxford and Cambridge undergraduates are directed to him, if at all, as to a philosophical curiosity. It is scarcely to be expected then that Jean-Paul Sartre's remarkable book *Being and Nothingness*,* which has at last been translated, and which can profitably be regarded as a lengthy footnote to the *Phenomenology of Mind*, will make any impact.

Being and Nothingness is a very long and almost totally Hegelian work concerning the nature of human consciousness – a subject which no longer exists in British philosophy. It is impossible even to outline the argument, but something can be said about the structure of the book. Sartre begins by posing a dilemma against the background of European philosophy. How is one to characterise the relation of object and subject? Subjectivist philosophies lose the object in the subject, objectivist philosophies divide it irrevocably from the subject. The relation between the two must be seen as complex, unstable, dialectical. This unstable relation Sartre proceeds to describe in terms of what he calls being for-itself and being in-itself. Being for-itself, or consciousness, has a flickering and unsettled quality which Sartre expresses by saying that it secretes its own *néant*, or 'nothingness' as it has unhappily to be called in English. The subject does not have the mode of existence of objects. It is, however, haunted by its awareness of this other mode of

* [Jean-Paul Sartre, *Being and Nothingness*, trans. Hazel E. Barnes (London, 1957).]

existence, towards which it constantly aspires. It wishes to be in-itself. From this characteristic of consciousness there follow results, such as 'bad faith' (the consoling illusion that one can *be* something in a thinglike manner) and, in a sense, the impossibility of sincerity. In this context, too, Sartre defines 'value'. We apprehend values as a 'lack', the lack of something which would stabilise and 'thingify' our being.

Sartre has here psychologised and de-historicised Hegel's general account of 'alienation'. In what follows he performs a similar service for Hegel's famous 'Master and Slave' analysis. The relation of being for-itself to being in-itself takes on a particularly important (and in Sartre's picture distressing) form in our relations with other people: our being for-others. Other people are vital and yet unsatisfying and also dangerous to us because they hold the promise of a stabilisation of being. They are dangerous in that they may stabilise us as something which we do not wish to be (shame) – and they are unsatisfying in that even if they wish to glorify us (love), we cannot be certain of their steadfastness, and in trying to hold them to their task we objectify them and destroy the freedom which gives value to their performance.

In the later part of the book Sartre discusses freedom, and what he calls 'existential psychoanalysis'. 'The final discoveries of ontology are the first principles of psychoanalysis.' Voluntary deliberation is always faked. We have ourselves made the apparently objective considerations which we manipulate. If freedom is freedom to do otherwise – at what price? At the price of abandoning the fundamental projects which make us what we are? Our freedom lies deeper than 'will' and ordinary reflection. It *is* the fundamental nature of our *élan* toward being, and can only be uncovered by a type of analysis which avoids the reifying faculty theories and symbolisms of traditional and current psychology. (Sartre accuses Freud of treating the consciousness as a thing.) The discussion leads on to a fascinating consideration of 'quality as a revelation of being'. Why do we like filling holes? Why are we fascinated by what is slimy? Not for Freud's reasons. Sex itself mirrors something more fundamental, the fruitless desire of consciousness to be its own foundation.

The book ends with a definition of its own status. All this, Sartre tells us, has been an essay in 'phenomenological ontology'. Ontology is to metaphysics as sociology is to history. Ontology can only make models and pictures, can only say things are 'as if'. (It is as if being in-itself, in a desire to become its own foundation, gave itself the dimension of for-itself.) It is for metaphysics to say whether this is really so.

Concerning the status of this work, most English critics would be quick to say (I think rightly) that metaphysics in the sense hinted at by Sartre does not exist. All that can be done has been done. But what about the value and nature of what has been done? Is Sartre attempting the impossible: a description of 'consciousness' which reveals a universal structure, and at the same time does justice to the unstable nature of what is described? On the latter point, it is curious how far, in a superficial sense at any rate, Sartre succeeds. The flickering nature of our actual thoughts and awarenesses, the way in which we move from 'subjective' to 'objective' apprehensions, which was dramatically presented in *La Nausée*, is more systematically dealt with in *Being and Nothingness*, and we are forced to recognise ourselves in the often unnerving picture. But is any universal or fundamental structure revealed here? Has Sartre done more than produce a compelling analysis of certain moods and emotions which may or may not be common to the human race?

It is hard to judge his attempt without putting this whole type of enterprise in question. Terms such as 'being' and 'consciousness' have been dropped from Anglo-Saxon philosophy. Here the philosopher largely confines his activity to removing problems attaching to particular concepts by an examination of the functioning of language in the affected area. He eschews psychology and does not try to tell us what the whole of reality is like. Sartre attempts it in a manner which he admits to be quasi-metaphorical. What is the value of this? It seems to me that in this country our exposure of certain types of metaphysical argument has led us too readily to reject the grandiose picture-making aspects of metaphysics. Such pictures can be illuminating, in a psychological and moral sense, even if their status is dubious, and even if they are established more by a general appeal to our knowledge of human nature than by a rigorous argument.

If we look at Sartre's work in this light it is certainly edifying. It teaches us about human nature as a novel might do. It is also the case that we shall probably object, partly on empirical and partly on moral grounds, to many aspects of the analysis. The enormous metaphor certainly tells us a lot about Sartre's own obsessions and evaluations, which we may see no reason to share. The picture is exceedingly egocentric. Our existence as historical entities and as members of society is quickly shuffled aside. Our 'fundamental dilemma' is seen as that of a solitary being. Values have a solipsistic basis in the vain attempt of each consciousness to be *causa sui* – and even other individuals exist ultimately as threats or instruments. Sartre at several points makes the appeal to Kierkegaard against Hegel. The individual person demands recognition as this person, and not as part of something suprapersonal. Yet Sartre's own picture of the individual strikes one as curiously depersonalised and mechanical. It is as if the Hegelian Absolute had become a person and were striving for self-awareness in what it suspected to be a complete solitude. Other people, on Sartre's picture, appear as unassimilated parts of oneself. The death-struggle of one consciousness with another (a favourite topic of existentialist fiction) does, of course, exist. Simone de Beauvoir's *Mandarins* provides the latest variation on the theme (Paule and Henri). But if we believe that love is not necessarily fruitless, and that the apprehension of value, in personal relations, in society, and also in art, is connected with the ultimate and difficult apprehension of other persons and things as independent and *real*, then we are implicitly appealing to a conception of 'being' other than that which Sartre presents.

It is curious that although Sartre himself is a striving moralist, deeply concerned to influence his age, the most systematic version of his theory seems to make striving pointless. What appears, from *Being and Nothingness*, as being 'truly valuable'? The ordinary virtues are tainted with 'bad faith'. Possibly self-knowledge is of value, a freedom which is self-aware? There is a strong dash of stoical romanticism in Sartre's theory: we are as we are, let us at least know it. But the process of self-knowledge, as Sartre portrays it, appears negative and destructive; and his attempts elsewhere to apply 'existential psychoanalysis' to particular persons (e.g., Baudelaire) diminish the subject and do not seem to exemplify any novel mode of discovery. For polemical purposes Sartre has, in fact, had to supplement his account with, for instance, the more Kantian declarations of *Existentialism and Humanism*. The humanistic passion which he displays in his more popular writings has since led him to the brink of the Communist Party and more recently away again. He has also, since writing *Being and Nothingness*, produced his promised Ethics in the paradoxical guise of the enormous work on Genet.

Sartre's book is likely to displease philosophers by being 'metaphysical', to displease Christians by being uncompassionate, and to displease Marxists and others by being unhistorical and unsocial. But it raises many questions which are surely philosophical ones, particularly concerning the nature and function of psychology; and above all it is full of fascinating and profound analyses of human devices and desires. It is an extremely interesting book, and could prove so too for lay readers if initial horror of the Hegelian terminology can be overcome. It is certainly difficult, but it is not as impossible to understand as might appear from a casual glance. It is full of 'pictures and conversations'. It seems to me to have been very well translated by Hazel Barnes, barbaric terms like 'nihilation' being kept to a minimum. It is doubtless the case that writers of brief and meticulous articles will always look askance at writers of large, unrigorous emotional volumes; but the latter, for better or worse, have the last word.

Review in *New Statesman and Nation*, May 1957.

Existentialist Bite

Mr Everett Knight has written a polemical book* which has a touch of the true gadfly quality. He writes as a whole-hearted disciple of Sartre, and sees Sartrian existentialism as the answer to the needs of the age. Existentialism completes the work begun by the Enlightenment. Rationalism denied the older theological order, but substituted the order of science. Kant's Newtonian rules separated us from things-in-themselves. With the decay of nineteenth-century science we are left without God and without Natural Laws. True atheism is now established and its conclusions must be drawn. Mr Knight sees these conclusions in what he calls a 'return to the particular', manifested in art and philosophy alike. In visual art the 'return' may be seen in the work of Cézanne and later painters who set aside the rules (e.g., of perspective) which divided us from the thing. In philosophy the Husserlian conception of 'intentionality', which represents consciousness as exhausting itself in its object, and not as existing as a separate entity, is used by the existentialists to support a theory of 'immediacy'. Man is what he does. He exists, and has no essence.

The book begins with an account of the philosophy of Husserl, and goes on to a chapter entitled 'From Baudelaire to Sartre', which includes a discussion of Valéry. There follow three longer studies of Gide, Malraux and Saint-Exupéry, and of the philosophy of Sartre with its political and social implications.

It is difficult in a book of this sort to avoid a certain amount of generalised philosophical exposition, and Mr Knight's reader may become uneasy because a somewhat vague and rapid 'background'

* [Everett W. Knight, *Literature Considered as Philosophy: The French Example* (London, 1957).]

[151]

philosophical summary is used to support some 'foreground' generalisation which is vital to the argument. The most interesting part of the book, however, is its attempt to see in literature the emergence of a certain philosophical style and atmosphere, and here I think the author succeeds. The notion that art should concern itself with the particular is nevertheless an ambiguous one. In a sense it is the definition of any work of art, in that the artist attempts to create a self-contained union of form and content with definite limits and internal harmony. There is another sense in which art *now* seeks the particular – but even this is full of ambiguities. Mr Eliot's 'objective correlative' represents a sense of 'the particular' which is different both from Mr Knight's and from the sense in which I suggest particularity belongs to any art. Mr Knight wants to give a moral content to the (modern) artist's concern with particulars. He connects particularity with 'engagement', through intermediary notions such as immediacy and concern for the individual. There is something attractive in this rather sketchy connection, but again I suspect the situation of being far more complex. Mr Knight gives analytically, a favourable sense to 'engagement', and I cannot see that he justifies this. He regards it, too, as a modern phenomenon in virtue of its connection with particularity and return to things. But this severely limits what would seem to be the normal sense of the word. Was not Dante an 'engaged' writer?

Mr Knight dislikes laws and rules and what he calls sacrificing immediacy to concepts. We must learn to substitute the particular for the general, action for contemplation. This is why literature and art are now 'sources of truth inferior to none'. I find something emotional and inexact in these attitudes. We cannot 'do without concepts' (whatever that would mean). Existentialism is an illuminating philosophy precisely through its invention of fresh moral concepts; and we need to be told more clearly what differentiates Mr Knight's call to action from that which inspired fascism.

Mr Knight says that existentialism is 'a philosophy of action considered as a response to the immediate'. He admits that 'immediate' must be carefully interpreted. He adds, with qualifications, that 'existentialist political thought is founded upon Marxism.' He goes on to say that what we now need is a refurbished

Marxism, and that to provide this may be the great task of existentialism. I found all this very interesting. I agree that what the age requires is a refurbished Marxism. Existentialism has perhaps some contribution to make. But its *appeal* as a philosophy is at present through its most non-Marxist aspects – its dramatic, solipsistic, romantic and anti-social exaltation of the individual.

Review in *The Spectator*, July 1957.

PART FOUR

The Need for Theory, 1956–66

'The paradox of our situation is that we must have theories about human nature, no theory explains everything, yet it is just the desire to explain everything which is the spur of theory.'

'Mass, Might and Myth', 1962

Knowing the Void

There is a persistent conception of the philosopher as one who perceives the unity in different branches of knowledge and offers out of his own meditation thereon a lesson for his age. The first philosophers were of such a kind, though since their day not all have in fact conformed to this picture, and most contemporary philosophers are particularly anxious to point out that it is a false one. Simone Weil may be seen as a thinker of this type. The *Notebooks** present us with her thoughts in an unsystematic and fragmentary form which, however, makes clear the passionate way in which she strove to relate philosophy to her own personal experience. The quality of this striving, together with one at least of her doctrines, might justify the title 'existentialist' – although the sources of her thought, in ancient and oriental philosophy, are far from the customary origins of existentialism.

The complete text of the *Notebooks* is immensely more interesting than the previously published selection. Such a selection tends to read as a series of epigrams, whereas the present book, with its obsessive circling round certain ideas, shows us the fundamental directions of the author's mind. This is not something which one would be bothered to know in the case of every author, but in the case of Simone Weil it is worth knowing. She takes a vast range of European and Eastern thought as her text, yet she speaks only of what she has thoroughly understood and transformed by her own meditation. To read her is to be reminded of a standard.

There are a number of different 'tracks' leading through the *Notebooks*, some of which I know I have missed. Most obviously

* *The Notebooks of Simone Weil*, 2 vols, trans. and ed. Arthur Wills (London, 1956).

perhaps the writer can be seen as a Platonist. She believes that Good is a transcendent reality, and that Good and Evil are connected with modes of human knowledge. She is determined to regard everything as potentially related to everything else, in an intense synthesising vision which will delight some readers, and madden others: especially those who take it that the first lesson of philosophy, since Hume, is that nothing is related. 'The two essential things in Platonic dialectics: *contradiction* and *analogy*. Both are means of emerging from the *point of view*.' These are her methods, and that her goal.

We are presented with a psychology whose sources are in Plato, in Eastern philosophy, and in the disciplines of Christian mysticism, and yet which bears upon contemporary problems of faith and action. The soul is composed of parts, and justice, and also faith, consist in each part performing its own role. 'The baser parts of myself should love God, but not too much. It would not be God.' We do not know what we are – (the lesson of psychoanalysis). Until we become good we are at the mercy of mechanical forces, of which 'gravity' is the general image. If we give more than we find natural and easy we may hate the recipient. A sufferer communicates his suffering by ill-treating and distressing others. All beings tend to use all the power at their disposal. 'A virtuous action can degrade if there is no available energy at the same level.' (Need for a new concept of energy in sociology and psychology.) We make advances by resisting the mechanism: but there is no reward. Energy and imagination are on the side of the low motives. To resist gravity is to suffer the void. During our apprenticeship good appears negative and empty. We are helped by meditating on 'absurdities which project light'. When we truly realise the impossibility of good we love it, as we love the mysteries of a religion. (There is a theory of art implicit here. All art is religious.) It is upon meditation and not action that progress depends. 'Action is the pointer of the balance. One must not touch the pointer, but the weights.' 'People suppose that thinking does not pledge them, but it alone pledges us.' It is of no avail to act above one's natural level. (Lesson of the Bhagavad Gita.)

These are hard sayings and they do not compose a consoling philosophy. None knows better than Simone Weil that suffering may be pointless and is usually degrading. Her thought returns continually to the destruction of cities, the extermination of peoples, prisons and places of torture: but she observes that we can only think that suffering purifies because we see it as pure affliction, whereas the sufferer sees not the affliction but the imaginary consolation. Her concept of 'the void', which must be experienced in the achieving of detachment, differs from the *Angst* of popular existentialism, in that *Angst* is usually thought of as something which circumstances may force upon a man, whereas experience of the void is a spiritual achievement, involving the control of the imagination, that 'restorer of balances'. Spiritual progress is won through meditation: a view which is a contrast (and some may think a welcome corrective) to contemporary English ethics with its exclusive emphasis on act and choice, and its neglect of the 'inner life'. Here, oddly enough, English philosophy and popular existentialism are on the same side, with their urgent cry of 'we have to choose!' – a doctrine which is, after all, consoling for us sinners who blunder on through a life of continual mistakes. But Simone Weil emphasises 'waiting' and 'attention'. 'We should pay attention to such a point that we no longer have the choice.'

It may be felt that this is an undemocratic philosophy. Plato indeed was no democrat. His follower here is certainly non-utilitarian, and in a sense non-liberal – characteristics which will make her alien to many. She has dangerous thoughts. Why cannot science become again an image of the universe through which we can participate in reality? Astronomy and chemistry are debased forms of astrology and alchemy. In a way, the Church was right to condemn Galileo. Things have gone wrong since the Renaissance because at that time we rejected the Church in favour of a non-Christian conception of Greece. Much of this will have an unpleasant ring – especially as it is upheld by arguments in which the search for analogy seems to have carried the writer too far: for instance, in reading Christian meanings into Greek myths. On the other hand, Simone Weil is also the author of one of the very few profound and original political treatises of our time, *L'Enracinement* [*The Need for Roots*]. Considering her, our political categories break down; and this is perhaps instructive.

The personality which emerges from these writings is not always attractive, but it compels respect. She is sometimes unbalanced and scarcely accurate. She whitewashes Plato, suggesting that he really disapproved of slavery and disliked only decadent art. She refuses to say any good word for the Jews: the only city over which she does not lament is Jerusalem. 'Practically the only thing the Hebrews did was to exterminate, at any rate prior to the destruction of Jerusalem.' She seems at times almost too ready to embrace evil and to love God as its author; many readers may find a repellent and self-destructive quality in her austerity. (A figure which obsesses her is T. E. Lawrence.) She endorsed the Greek view that 'to philosophise is to learn how to die' – and it is hard not to believe that she in some way willed her own early death. Yet the other side of this is the sense of a profoundly disciplined life behind her writings: the union of a passionate search for truth with a simplicity and austerity of personal living, which gives to what she writes an authority which cannot be imitated. She is one who, like Kierkegaard's 'subjective thinker', does not simply convey information, but is most properly to be understood as an example.

She quotes with approval the remark that 'the science of religions has not yet begun'. The *Notebooks* may be recommended to those seeking hints for such a science. They show how the idea of the supernatural emerges necessarily from an intense meditation upon good and evil and death and chance. But, as Simone Weil points out, mysteries will yield truths only to a religious attention. This was her chief reason for not becoming a Christian, since other mysteries may be equally rich in truth, and indeed she found them so. Whatever one's ultimate beliefs, these 'truths' and the mode of their emergence are a reality which cannot be neglected, and of which we have yet to devise a method of study. The *Notebooks* may also be recommended to those who imagine that current philosophical techniques can readily show theological statements to be empty. 'To be able to study the supernatural, one must first be capable of discerning it.'

Article review in *The Spectator*, November 1956.

T. S. Eliot as a Moralist

A great literary critic can be a most influential moralist; and in this role Mr Eliot has been one of our more important moralists. He has influenced us most, and to an extent which is not at once apparent, so deeply have his lessons been taken to heart, in his less obviously didactic critical writings, wherein he has with some success attempted to reintroduce certain kinds of moral standards into literary criticism. He has also written a considerable number of 'pamphlets', more immediately edifying in their purpose, and as editor of the *Criterion* he constituted himself over many years a close commentator upon his times. 'In one's prose reflections one may be legitimately occupied with ideals, whereas in the writing of verse one can only deal with actuality.'* In an age when an exaggerated respect for technicians and experts has silenced many voices, Mr Eliot has been one of the few authoritative persons to continue to utter bold and simple counsels and to draw attention, in politics, to general principles. I shall in what follows be most immediately concerned with these simpler pronouncements uttered 'for edification'; but in order to understand them it will be necessary to pursue Mr Eliot's themes into his more strictly critical writings also.

How can one be a moralist in this age? What does one appeal to? To appreciate the nature of Mr Eliot's moral appeal it is necessary to see the basis of his opposition to 'liberalism'. This exercise is the more valuable since it is surely of the greatest importance for any of us in these days to examine what we take this concept to be. Mr Eliot sees liberalism as the end product of a line of thought which is to be found in Stoicism, in the Renaissance, in Puritanism, in the

* [T. S. Eliot,] *After Strange Gods* [London, 1934], p. 28.

Romantic movement and in nineteenth-century humanism. Characteristic of this line of thought is a cult of personality and a denial of authority external to the individual. In the fissure between Dante and Shakespeare lies the loss which Mr Eliot mourns; the self-dramatisation of Shakespeare's heroes foreshadows the romanticism of the modern world. The Puritans continued more insidiously to undermine tradition and authority, and with their 'thin mythology' inaugurate the age of amateur religions. Authorised by Kant,[*] inspired by Blake,[†] and more recently encouraged by Huxley, Russell, Wells and others, every man may now invent his own religion, and have the pleasures of religious emotion without the burdens of obedience or dogma. To Puritan influence, too, Mr Eliot (acknowledging a debt to Tawney) traces much of the materialism of our modern industrial society with its worship of 'success'. He himself remembers the morality in which 'it was tacitly assumed that if one was thrifty, enterprising, intelligent, practical and prudent in not violating social conventions, one ought to have a happy and "successful" life'.[‡] Romanticism, that debilitated Renaissance, with its denial of original sin and its doctrine of human perfectibility, attacking an organism weakened already by the Puritans, produces the new style of emotional individualism; and humanism, in an attempt at remedy, confounds the categories even further by offering a high-minded version of that confusion of art with religion which with the Romantics had at least remained at a more orgiastic level. So, out of Matthew Arnold, out of the 'dream world' of late romantic poetry, out of the mid-nineteenth century, that 'age of progressive degradation,'[§] issues liberalism, the imprecise philosophy of a society of materialistic and irresponsible individuals.

Mr Eliot's writings lack the note of tiresome Messianism which we find, for instance, in T. E. Hulme; but there is no doubt that he presents us with a picture of a humanity 'fallen' or 'divided' or 'alienated' (to use the Hegelian term which seems oddly apt here) in

---

[*] *The Use of Poetry and the Use of Criticism* [London, 1933], p. 135.
[†] *Selected Essays* [London, 1932], p. 321. Essay on 'William Blake'.
[‡] Preface to Djuna Barnes's *Nightwood* [New York, 1936], p. 6.
[§] *Selected Essays*, p. 427. Essay on 'Baudelaire'.

certain respects, and equally that he has his own positive conception, and one which informs his critical writings, of that unity
which has been lost and is again to be won. Art should not be 'the
expression of personality'. 'The progress of an artist is a continual
self-sacrifice, a continual extinction of personality.'* The sermons
of Andrewes are superior to those of Donne because the emotion of
Andrewes 'is not personal'. 'Donne is a "personality" in a sense in
which Andrewes is not: his sermons, one feels, are a means of "self-
expression". He is constantly finding an object which shall be
adequate to his feelings; Andrewes is wholly absorbed in the object
and therefore responds with the adequate emotion.'† Some time in
the seventeenth century poets lost the capacity for 'direct sensuous
apprehension of thought'. They no longer 'felt their thoughts as
immediately as the odour of a rose'.‡ Sensibility was dissociated,
emotion parted company with thought and broke loose on its own.
Romanticism encouraged its undisciplined expression, and as men
lost their sense of limit, poetry lost its 'hardness'. It was Baudelaire,
that true blasphemer and believer in sin, that was 'the first counter-
romantic in poetry',§ and one of the initiators of the movement,
which we connect with Imagism and notably with Mr Eliot, which
attempts to reintroduce 'precise emotion' and to draw the artist's
attention 'back to the object'. This putting of emotion in its place is
at the same time a putting of poetry in its place. Poetry cannot play
the part of religion. The more we realise what literature is, and what
it *cannot* do, the more we return soberly to a sense of our own
limitations. Baudelaire, Mr Eliot says, would surely have approved
of these words of T. E. Hulme: man

> is endowed with original sin. While he can occasionally accom-
> plish acts which partake of perfection, he can never himself *be*
> perfect. Certain secondary results in regard to ordinary human
> action in society follow from this. A[s] man is essentially bad, he
> can only accomplish anything of value by discipline – ethical and

* *Selected Essays*, p. 17. Essay on 'Tradition and the Individual Talent'.
† Ibid., p. 351. Essay on 'Launcelot Andrewes'.
‡ Ibid., p. 287. Essay on 'The Metaphysical Poets'.
§ Ibid., p. 424. Essay on 'Baudelaire'.

political. Order is thus not merely negative, but creative and liberating. Institutions are necessary.*

I give merely a sketch of what is clearly a profoundly unified attitude whose 'literary' faces have 'metaphysical' faces to correspond. (This unity of Mr Eliot's attitude is also my excuse for treating as one 'position' utterances made over a number of years.) 'Dissociation of sensibility' serves as a symbol for Mr Eliot of the loss, in some far more general sense, of a unified world: the loss of a sense of limit and of an understanding of where each thing has its place. The limiting and rendering precise of emotion is one aspect of the criticism of the messy and uninhibited 'liberal individual'. Liberalism, then, destroys tradition through challenging authority. In a society where every man's opinion is equally valuable there is no unity of outlook. This favours over-specialisation, the worship of techniques, and the division of one part of society from another. Liberalism is a creed which dissipates and relaxes; and it 'prepares the way for that which is its own negation: the artificial, mechanized or brutalized control which is a desperate remedy for its chaos'.† We have the choice of a society bound for the extremes of paganism, or a society more positively Christian than our own. Mr Eliot turns to appeal, over the head of the dominant creed of the time, to an older, purer tradition. The historical reality upon which he relies is the Anglican Church, the only instrument through which the conversion of England can be achieved; and he pictures a Christian society, inspired by a Christian élite, and reminded by the Church of standards which lie beyond the individual.

There is a revolution of our time and a 'new sensibility', in the creation of which Mr Eliot has played a major part; and before going on to consider his morals and politics more closely let us look for a moment at this scene of change. G. E. Moore, the father of modern philosophy, and incidentally a thinker hailed with approval by Hulme, placed as epigraph to his *Principia Ethica* the words of Butler: 'everything is what it is and not another thing'; and when Mr Eliot himself remarks (*à propos* of poetry and religion) that

---

* Ibid., p. 430. Essay on 'Baudelaire'.
† *The Idea of a Christian Society* [London, 1939], p. 16.

'nothing in this world or the next is a substitute for anything else'[*]
he speaks with the voice of the age. We have become increasingly,
sometimes excessively, self-conscious about our concepts and our
language, and anxious to delimit categories and prevent the spilling
over of one thing into another. Mr Eliot's is not the only eye which
looks upon the nineteenth century as an era of messy thinking, and
one can readily parallel, in other disciplines, his exasperated cry,
'Arnold does not see what poetry *is*.' Science, philosophy, history,
criticism have become more specialised, more acutely conscious of
their own limitations. Mr Eliot, too, is, in this respect, exemplary.
He has carried, one wants to say with a sort of 'heroism', his self-
awareness about language into the depths of his poetry, into 'the
intolerable wrestle with words and meanings' and the attack upon
'the general mess of imprecision of feeling'. Unlike some other poets
in the Imagist tradition, Mr Eliot has never lost his respect for
words. The desire, as Hulme put it, to 'hand over sensations
bodily'[†] has never led Mr Eliot to make war upon language after
the manner of Mallarmé or Pound. One of the deep characteristics
of his poetry is a continual concern, in the midst of difficulties, for
the referential character of words. (This one most movingly feels in
the *Four Quartets*.) As a prose writer equally Mr Eliot has shown
an exemplary sense of the limitations of his job. He does not
trespass upon the field of technical philosophy, but says what he has
to say, as critic and as moralist, precisely and appropriately. He is
aware, and shares this concern with certain contemporary moral
philosophers,[‡] that a deterioration in morals is a destruction of
concepts. If our convictions part company with our vocabulary of
justification, our controversies become empty. 'We are living at
present in a kind of doldrums between opposing winds of doctrine,
in a period in which one political philosophy has lost its cogency,
though it is still the only one in which public speech can be framed.
This is very bad for the English language . . . Good prose cannot be
written by people without convictions.'[§] In these ways, Mr Eliot is

---

[*] *The Use of Poetry and the Use of Criticism*, p. 113.
[†] *Speculations* [London, 1924], p. 134.
[‡] See, for instance, R. M. Hare's *The Language of Morals* [Oxford, 1952].
[§] *The Idea of a Christian Society*, pp. 19–20.

not alone, but belongs with other makers of his age. He is the great poet of the new sensibility, one aspect of which is categorical precision, while the other aspect is what Hulme called 'cinders' and Sartre called '*nausée*'. 'The return to the object' has its unnerving moments. 'It is essential to prove that beauty may be in small dry things,' said Hulme. 'The great aim is accurate, precise description. The first thing is to recognize how extraordinarily difficult this is.'* One is reminded of the hard, dry, piecemeal character of the philosophy of Wittgenstein. For precise description reveals to the unillusioned gaze a world reduced to pieces: 'Men and bits of paper, whirled by the cold wind.' The synthesis of the nineteenth century, that premature and shallow integration, is no longer available to us. To what can we appeal?

Mr Eliot, it seems, is very much a member of our age; but with the zeal of a 'rationalist', using that word in its popular sense, he tends to attribute his insights to the Christian tradition, narrowly considered, while he collects the contemporary vices together under the name of liberalism. In spite of his appreciation of compromise-making Anglicanism, that 'uneasy bed', Mr Eliot is more fundamentally an anti-Puritan Puritan, invoking the evil-conscious Puritanism of Hawthorne and James against the 'decayed Protestantism' of the present, in which he sees on one hand the materialism analysed by Tawney, and on the other the 'dreary hymn-singing pietism' which he attributes to D. H. Lawrence's mother. He speaks of those 'vast hosts of the dead' of whose presence James Joyce was aware; but the dead whom the political Mr Eliot venerates lie far away. Mr Eliot is notably not in the English conservative tradition. He is an eclectic moralist. One feels that the voice of Krishna, bidding us not to think of the fruit of action, rings more loudly in his ears; whereas he is less patient with that medley of voices, to which T. H. Greene, for instance, lent careful attention, which constitutes the English political creed. He praises Bradley, who is 'wise', whose philosophy (unlike that of his successors) is 'catholic, civilized and universal', and who destroyed, more surely than Arnold, the bases of contemporary Benthamism. But Mr Eliot's own political and philosophical understanding is remote from the flexible and

* *Speculations*, pp. 131–2.

concrete thinking of the Idealists. One finds in him something of that 'Jansenism of temperament' which he attributes to Pascal: Mr Eliot, with his dislike of 'untidy lives', being perhaps also one 'who cannot avoid seeing through human beings and observing the vanity of their thoughts and of their avocations, their dishonesty and self-deception, the insincerity of their emotions, their coward-ice, the pettiness of their real ambitions'.[*] One feels this disillusioned tone in Mr Eliot's political writings, especially in his attitude to 'the mob'. He declares, alarmingly, that he would prefer an illiterate audience to an audience of ill-educated or half-educated persons such as are now available.[†] And it is significant that he extends no sympathy to the English Nonconformist tradition, with its wide-reaching utilitarian and socialist connections. When Methodism receives a kind word in the book on 'Culture' it is partly because it helped to pave the way for the Oxford Movement.

With hair-raising thoroughness Mr Eliot rejects the 'stuff' of our liberal world. I find something instructive here in his attitude to certain novelists. He gives approval to Jane Austen, Dickens and Thackeray, because with them 'personality . . . was more nearly in its proper place. The standards by which they criticized their world, if not very lofty ones, were at least not of their own making.' But George Eliot unfortunately combined her profounder insights with 'the dreary rationalism of the epoch' and is 'of the same tribe as all the serious and eccentric moralists we have had since',[‡] and whom Mr Eliot deplores. But it is in D. H. Lawrence that the extremity is reached of heretical belief and unrestrained and morbid emotional-ism. Mr Eliot finds in Lawrence 'a lack not so much of information as of the critical faculties which education should give, and an incapacity for what we ordinarily call thinking'.[§] This is an astonishing judgement. Whatever *is* thinking if Lawrence couldn't think; and what is serious moral reflection if George Eliot, whatever her beliefs, does not present a most lofty instance of it? I think that this is more than a verbal question, and I would connect it, very

---

[*] *Selected Essays*, p. 414. Essay on 'The Pensées of Pascal'.
[†] *The Use of Poetry and the Use of Criticism*, p. 152.
[‡] *After Strange Gods*, pp. 53–4.
[§] Ibid., p. 58.

cautiously, with some of Mr Eliot's views on Shakespeare. Mr Eliot says that 'neither Shakespeare nor Dante did any real thinking', but 'it happened that at Dante's time thought was orderly and strong and beautiful' and so 'Dante's poetry receives a boost'.* Shakespeare is also compared unfavourably as a 'thinker' with Marlowe. I suspect that what lies behind these uses of language is a somewhat abstract and mathematical model of thinking ('orderly, strong and beautiful') which one may connect with medieval Christianity and Thomist metaphysics. And one might suggest in reply that our mixed-up modern world needs for its unravelling a type of sensitive 'concrete' understanding to which if we deny the name of thinking we are lost. But these are only hints and guesses.

Mr Eliot has rightly said that it is important in what *terms* a justification is framed. (Pagan statesmen may be 'contained' by the Christian ethos of their people: only certain justifications will serve.)† It is especially important now to keep alive such sources of moral response as remain to us. It seems to me that Mr Eliot plays dangerously when he rejects *in toto* the moral content of liberalism and appeals over its head to a conception of dogma and authority which can itself play an ambivalent role. In 1933 Mr Eliot remarked that 'it was better to worship a Golden Calf than to worship nothing'.‡ And in 1939 he said that we should object to fascism because it is pagan. Objections to oppression and cruelty are 'objections to means not to ends'. In fact, the ordinary person dislikes fascism 'because he is fearful of authority'.§ To argue in this way is to belittle that naked respect for the human person as such which one may connect with Locke and with Kant, and which one hopes has become a part of the English political tradition. Can this be set aside as a romantic over-valuation of the individual? It is at least perilous to neglect the remnants of that liberal moral absolutism which, without dogma, holds that there are certain things which cannot be done to human persons. It is to such a remnant of liberal faith that a book such as P. H. Simon's *Contre la*

---

* *Selected Essays*, p. 136. Essay on 'Shakespeare and the Stoicism of Seneca'.
† *The Idea of a Christian Society*, pp. 27–8.
‡ *Criterion* (April 1933).
§ *The Idea of a Christian Society*, pp. 20, 70.

torture is addressed, and has perhaps not altogether failed. It may be added that John Stuart Mill, that argumentative and undogmatic absolutist, was not merely 'a Romantic', but was remotely a maker, too, of that dry and critical atmosphere in which Mr Eliot among others has flourished.

Mr Eliot may reply that morality must be based on *truth*, and that he is more concerned with the promulgation of truth than with the cultivation of benevolent impulses resting on misunderstandings. It may be that the Christian tradition must be the salvation of the West; but to argue this too narrowly is to neglect aspects of liberalism which are, to put it mildly, worth preserving, and to neglect, too, the extent to which liberalism is entwined with our Christian tradition as it in reality, and as a working power, now is. We may agree profoundly with many of Mr Eliot's indictments of present-day society, and agree with him, for instance, when he says that the events of September 1938 inspired in him 'a doubt of the validity of civilization'.* And there are events since then which inspire similar doubts. But whatever our religious beliefs, we must hope that the liberal world can regenerate itself out of its own resources – and we must seek the Christian tradition, in its various forms, within that world. I would agree with F. R. Leavis who, in defending D. H. Lawrence against Mr Eliot, said, 'It is characteristic of the world as it is that health cannot anywhere be found whole'; and added that 'the sense in which Lawrence stands for health is an important one'.† We cannot now afford to squander any of our 'health', which must be sought, with discrimination, in many quarters; and to say this is, of course, to take up a liberal attitude.

At the last word, however, one must return to Mr Eliot the poet. Mr Eliot observed that 'the essential advantage for a poet is not to have a beautiful world with which to deal: it is to be able to see beneath both beauty and ugliness; to see the boredom and the horror and the glory'.‡ Mr Eliot has seen, and it is a great part of our 'health' that we have a poet who can penetrate our anxious trivial world with such a profound compassion. In his poetry Mr

* Ibid., p. 64.
† *The Common Pursuit* [London 1952], pp. 246–7.
‡ *The Use of Poetry and the Use of Criticism*, p. 106.

Eliot is no Jansenist. We need thus to be helped to 'imagine that which we know': and to say this is, of course, to take up a Romantic attitude.

Essay in *T. S. Eliot: A Symposium for his 70th Birthday*, ed. N. Braybrooke, 1958.

A House of Theory

The socialist movement in England is suffering a loss of energy: and this is a misfortune which touches the whole community. The Tories are, by their nature, not a party of ideals and moral inventions. It is rather their function, a function which liberal-minded socialists must welcome in general even if they often deplore it in particular, to check and criticise the more abstract visions of the Left. But now the salt itself seems to have lost its savour. The more progressive section of society seems able, in this time, to provide very little in the way of guidance and inspiration. There is a certain moral void in the life of the country. How has this come about?

It does not seem difficult to analyse the sources of moral energy which fed the socialist movement in the past. First and most primitive was the desire for human equality, the valuing of the poorest he with the richest he: a desire made more intense by the miseries of the Industrial Revolution. Developing later, and giving to the movement its most characteristic and probably most profound motive, was the conception of exploitation, whose technical form was the Labour Theory of Value. Joined with this was what one might call Benthamite efficiency, the desire to tidy up society, sweeping away metaphysical obscurantism and outdated tradition, and plan rationally for the happiness which was so patently lacking. To be compared and contrasted with this was Marxist efficiency, closely knit theoretical scientific socialism, offering a more complex philosophy and a more revolutionary vision. A product of this confident science was a certain determinism whose appeal was religious as well as scientific: the apocalyptic belief that capitalism was doomed, the Messianic belief in the role of the proletariat. Independent of these sources of power but mingled with all of them was a general revolt against convention, the resistance to the nineteenth-century father-figure in his many guises, the revolt against sexual taboos and restrictions, the movement for the liberation of women. With this one may connect the hatred of industrial civilisation which certainly moved many people and which sometimes led to nostalgia for the apparent simplicity of the medieval world: all that poor Morris had in mind when he cried that 'Shoddy is king!' Consolation and promise were, however, to be found in the sheer energy generated by the working men's associations themselves, the discovery of active community and common purpose, the warmth of proletarian solidarity. While common in some way to almost all, and equally Christian, Marxist and anarchist in its inspiration, was the vision of an ideal community in which work would once again be creative and meaningful, and human brotherhood would be restored; whereas now the working classes were deracinate and disinherited, human nature both in them and in their masters mutilated and divided: all that could be summed up in the Hegelian concept of 'alienation'. These – and the list could doubtless be extended and the items subdivided in different ways – were the complex and various ideals and motives of socialism.

Nearly all this great accumulation of energy has now been dissipated, by the achievement of goals which satisfied the desires in question, or by the achievement of something which made the desires less sharp. As a result largely of the working-class movement itself together with the development of new economic techniques we have the Welfare State. Many of the most obvious injustices and deprivations have been remedied. The rich are not so rich nor the poor so poor, and there has been a serious attempt to create equality of opportunity. The sense of exploitation has faded and the struggle for equality tends to take the form of the struggle for higher wages. It now seems possible that capitalism is not doomed after all, or at least not doomed in the dramatic manner once envisaged. On both the theoretical and the practical plane economists have led us to believe that capitalism can (perhaps) overcome its tendency to periodic crises, and does not inevitably (and, as was thought, increasingly) grind the faces of the poor: thus removing the sense of impending cataclysm, destroying the attraction of the Labour

Theory of Value, and blunting the socialist claim to provide the only true science of society.

The appeal of Marxism as a body of doctrine, never strong in this country, has diminished with the lengthening history of the USSR. Marx and Marxist theorising have been left to the Communists. The revolt against convention which was a sacred duty in the nineteenth century, and between the wars was at least still fun, is now, as a result of the greater flexibility of society, not obviously either. Shoddy remains king, but nobody bothers much. The vision of the ideal society, which, outside Marxism, was often associated with opposition to parliamentary methods, lingered a while in Guild Socialism, and perished with the development of the parliamentary Labour Party. The sentiments of 'proletarian solidarity' have given way to the sentiments of the trade union movement. Socialism no longer seems (as it seemed to certain favoured spirits) something essentially and profoundly Christian. The anarchists are gone. What has triumphed (with many results for which we are profoundly thankful) and what is still largely with us is Benthamite efficiency, the spirit of the Fabians. Socialism, in the course of its rapid and successful development, has lost even the oddments of theory with which it started out.

It will be argued that the absence of socialist theory is neither surprising nor deplorable. The British were never ones for theory in any case. We have always been empiricist, anti-metaphysical in philosophy, mistrustful of theoretical systems. It is true, indeed, that our political thought has been almost entirely sceptical, and could be summed up under the three heads of Tory scepticism, scientific scepticism, and liberal humanist scepticism. Hume and Burke would represent the first. (Don't theorise: let habit and tradition solve your problems.) Bentham, with some assistance from Hobbes, would represent the second. (Don't theorise: theories are troublesome metaphysical nonsense. What matters in society is the mechanics of satisfaction.) Locke and Mill, with Kant in the background, would represent the third. (Don't theorise: empirical truths are unsystematic and moral truths can't be demonstrated; so be an undogmatic but rational respecter of persons.) However, all these thinkers were themselves theorists in the minimal sense that they invented certain concepts, presented certain schemes and pictures, in terms of which we can understand their differences and conceive them as constituting a conversation. The liberals particularly set before us, unsystematically but with a power which has kept its hold upon our imagination, certain spiritual values 'fixed' in concepts such as that of Natural Rights.

Now 'socialist theory', in so far as it existed here, was not directly a product of academic thinkers. It was not in its nature to be. It consisted rather of overlapping sets of ideas argumentatively put together by bodies such as the Socialist League and the Fabian Society. We have never produced a great socialist philosopher, and we have paid very limited attention to the one whom we had in our midst. However, our socialist thinking was strongly nourished by philosophical ideas which had become to some extent common property: the ideas of Locke and the Utilitarians, as well as modified versions of Marxism and Utopian theories imported from France. A socialist philosophy does not, and should not, grow independently of the main stream of philosophical ideas. With this in mind, we turn from the 'conceptual conversation' of the past to look at the contemporary scene, where we notice, of course, a marked contrast. Developments in mathematical logic, the influence of scientific method, the techniques of linguistic analysis, have combined to produce a new philosophy even more anti-theoretical than its sceptical predecessor. The creative aspect of philosophy is reduced almost to nil, or rather tends to be limited to the invention of what one might call 'logical gadgets'. (Russell's Theory of Descriptions would be a distinguished example.) The instrument that results is for its purposes excellent, and the critical task of philosophy, of great importance in a liberal society, has never been performed with greater exactness and rigour. Many persistent philosophical problems have been solved by the new method, which represents a genuine advance and discovery. One consequence, however (and I shall argue an unnecessary one), is that a certain area of thought which was formerly influential is becoming denuded. As philosophy is steadily drawn in the direction of logic and becomes increasingly a matter for highly trained experts, it separates itself from, and discourages, the vaguer and more generally comprehensible theorising which it used to nourish and be nourished by; and the serious student who is either studying philosophy or is influenced by it (and there are many of the latter) develops an almost excessive fear of imprecision. 'Everything that can be said can be said clearly.' Outside the small area of possible clarity lies the dangerous region of 'mushy' thinking from which attention is averted. The ideal is a demonstration, however tiny, which is clean, sterile and conclusive.

In considering the way in which [. . .] modern techniques have affected moral and political theory, and through them affected a range of less specialised theorising, it is necessary to consider in more detail the 'elimination of metaphysics'. In the past philosophers had invented concepts expressive of moral belief and presented them as if they were facts concerning the nature of the mind or of the world. Philosophy since Hume has, in opposing dogmatic rationalist metaphysics in general, been critical of this tendency, but in varying ways. Briefly, criticism of metaphysics may proceed along Humian, Kantian, or Hegelian lines. Hume, who wished to maintain as rigorously as possible that we know only. what our senses tell us, denied the existence of moral 'facts' or 'realities', analysed moral concepts into non-rational feelings and imaginative habits, and was prepared to let basic empirical concepts suffer the same fate. Kant, anxious to defend both the reality of our empirical knowledge and the dignity of our moral intimations, changed Hume's habits of imagination into 'categories', or fixed formal modes of apprehension which if directed upon empirical data would yield knowledge. Other matters, such as the moral law and the destiny of the soul, could only be objects of belief, although the reality and something of the nature of the spiritual realm were suggested by the demands of conscience. Hegel altered Kant's criticism in a fundamental way when he conceived the categories as the forms not only of our knowledge of empirical objects, but also of our apprehension of social, psychological and spiritual realities, and subjected them to historical treatment, taking the pattern of their development initially from the history of the changing ideas of the human race.

These philosophers were all critical of dogmatic rationalist metaphysical arguments (such as those used by St Thomas) and so put a question mark beside moral beliefs (ethical, political, religious) which rested formerly on such arguments; but they differed significantly in the place which they assigned to beliefs of this kind under the new regime. Neither Hume nor Kant had any interest in variety of belief, nor, for these purposes, any historical sense; and they virtually removed from the scene of rational discourse all theories except those specifically accredited by their own philosophical methods. Hume, whose 'elimination' followed the simple lines of atomic empiricism, regarded all beliefs as equally irrational, but some as inevitable and convenient. Civilised life after all rested on moral instincts, and Hume described those of his own society. Kant more systematically attempted to show why our knowledge was limited to certain kinds of object, and in doing so pictured the mind as solely concerned with the objects of empirical observation and science. He allowed in addition one belief (the belief in Reason, with the related and tentative belief in God); and all other theories were classed together as superstition. Hegel differed from Hume and Kant in that he did not regard the fact that a belief or theory had rested upon a discredited type of philosophical argument as automatically denuding the theory of philosophical interest or even of truth. He did not class theories as either whole truths or total errors, but allowed to all the influential beliefs that men have held the status of interpretation and discovery of the world. All three philosophers are, of course, vulnerable themselves, though not in the essentials of what they have to say, to attacks by modern critics; all three, in different ways, can lay claim to the title of 'empiricist'.

Modern British philosophy is Humian and Kantian in inspiration. It follows Hume and Kant in regarding sense experience as the only basis for knowledge, and it follows Kant in attempting more specifically to show that concepts not so based are 'empty'. Moral and political philosophies, never the centre of modern developments, have followed in the wake. Attention was concentrated upon the error by which former philosophers imagined themselves to be making quasi-factual discoveries when really they were preaching. Since morality could not be 'proved' by philosophical argument, philosophy now aimed at studying it in a non-partisan manner, analysing the 'logic' of moral discourse in general, and leaving moral exhortation to others. Moral judgements, since they did not admit of empirical verification, were first said to be 'emotive' (a

Humian position). Later they were likened to imperatives (a Kantian position). In this second and more subtle phase Kant's single belief in Reason was refashioned into a formula which purported to give the defining characteristics of any moral judgement as such. A certain rationality, universality, consistency, was thought of (with minor variations) as defining the *form* of morality irrespective of its *content*. The variegated area of moral belief or ideology (the special religious and social concepts which guide choice, and which are in many cases a legacy from the metaphysical philosophers) was usually treated, together with the actual patterns of choice, as part of the *content*, the region of morality which is a matter of personal decision and not a proper subject for analysis. Such beliefs were not, of course, demonstrable by philosophical argument (it was the mistake of the old philosophers to think that they were) and they came to be seen as the idiosyncratic 'colour' of a moral attitude, something nebulous and hazy, which for purposes of exposition and example was best analysed away into actual choices at the empirical level. The moral agent is thus pictured, in a manner which remains essentially Kantian, as using his reason to survey the ordinary factual world, and making decisions therein which he will defend by reference to facts and to simple principles offered as patently rational. He is *not* pictured as using his reason to explore the intermediate area of concepts. Moral action, in short, is seen as the making of sensible choices and the giving of sensible and simple reasons. It is not seen as the activity of theorising, imagining, or seeking for deeper insight.[*]

Such a situation could hardly be promising for the department of ethics which deals with political concepts; and indeed whereas moral philosophy survives by the skin of its teeth, political philosophy has almost perished. Whereas some sense (misleading perhaps but just comprehensible) can be made of the idea of the 'fundamental logical form of a moral judgement', very little sense can be made of the idea of the 'fundamental logical form of a

[*] See especially R. M. Hare *The Language of Morals*, and also articles by [S.] Hampshire, [J. O.] Urmson and others. It will be noted that this position is curiously existentialist in flavour. Popular existentialism is Kantianism with Reason in the veiled role of Kierkegaard's God. All positive beliefs stand in danger of *mauvaise foi*.

political judgement'. The 'form' of political thinking cannot be thus plausibly divided from its 'content'. It is impossible not to regard political philosophy in an historical manner; and it is very difficult to extract from it the type of compact philosophical problem whose statement and attempted solution now alone count as really 'doing philosophy'. Exercises in political philosophy consist usually in carefully restricted discussion of a well-known concept (such as the General Will), attempting with brief and undetailed historical reference to illustrate the nature and 'function' of the concept. These discussions are often valuable; but they are not popular because they necessarily lack precision of a logical or near-logical variety, and their atmosphere is such as to suggest that 'political concepts' are things of the past. They are, after all, metaphysical beliefs, or, to be more exact, they are personal evaluations and social recommendations disguised as truths about the nature of man. It is the (logical and morally neutral) task of the philosopher to pierce this disguise, and to separate the solid recommendation from the conceptual mask which comes away, as it were, empty. The giving of actual political advice and the suggestion of moves in definite political dilemmas are, of course, not the business of philosophy. Here again, political activity, like moral activity, is thought of as the making of empirical choices, and not as itself an activity of theorising. The most consistent exposition of this generally favoured view is in T. D. Weldon's *The Vocabulary of Politics*. A curious result of this development is that liberal and progressive thinkers who are touched by modern philosophy come on what they take to be logical grounds to the same conclusions about political theorising to which conservative thinkers come on frankly moral grounds. Berlin and Weldon and Popper* agree with T. S. Eliot and Michael Oakeshott that systematic political theorising is a bad thing.† The former think it so because it is

* [Karl Popper (1902–1994), born in Vienna, was for a time loosely associated with the Vienna circle and with logical positivism, which he also criticised. He came to the London School of Economics in 1946. His impassioned critiques of Plato, Hegel and Marx in *The Open Society and its Enemies* caused much debate.]

† Mr Eliot forms in fact a curious counterpart in this respect to Bertrand Russell. Both share the view that *real* thinking is highly systematic (for Russell,

'metaphysical' and opinionated and obscures the scientific business of altering our society for the better. The latter think it so because it interferes with the deep operation of traditions which should not be tampered with by critical reflection. Bentham and Hume are still with us; but we are losing touch with Locke and Mill.

The discrediting of theory has, then, taken place as a result of a combination of different tendencies: Tory scepticism, Benthamite scepticism, a Kantian protestant fear of 'superstitions', and more recently a dislike of Marxism, all apparently supported by the anti-metaphysical destructive techniques of modern philosophy. It is moreover felt that theorising is anti-liberal (an idea which it is easy to extract from Kant) and that liberal-minded persons should surround their choices with a minimum of theory, relying rather on open above-board references to facts or to principles which are simple and comprehensible to all. Here it is important, in accordance indeed with the clear-headed methods of analytical philosophy, in order to see what one is doing, to separate neutral arguments from evaluations. The point, briefly made, is that the 'elimination of metaphysics', though it shows that moral beliefs were often supported by erroneous arguments, does not *ipso facto* 'discredit' the area of moral belief, properly understood as an area of conceptual moral exploration. All that the anti-metaphysical arguments make clear (and one would not wish to deny this) is that moral theorising is not the discovery of bogus 'facts', but is an

mathematics, for Eliot, Thomist theology) and accept the implication that thinking about society is another matter. Russell, when acting as a social critic, drops his rigorous philosophical *persona* and is clearly engaged in a quite different kind of activity. Mr Eliot, who reserves a unique pinnacle for Dante because (unlike Shakespeare) he combined literary ability with a background of real (i.e. systematic theological) thought denies the name of 'thinking' to social analysis such as that practised by D. H. Lawrence. Mr Eliot's theology is, however, more relevant to his social criticism than Lord Russell's mathematics is to his, and this in itself is an advantage. Right-wing thinkers may be shy of system at the political level but they are not shy of moralising. Whereas Left-wing (non-Communist) utterances must be 'scientific' or else offered as fragmentary personal notions. The greater moral solemnity of the Right (and of the extreme Left) makes them, I suspect, in certain ways profounder critics of our society at present.

activity whose purpose and justification are moral. Hegel understood and displayed this, though he also sinned by picturing moral exploration dogmatically within a rigid hierarchy of ideas. There is no philosophical (or scientific) reason why there should not be an area of theory, reflection, meditation, contemplation, *between* ourselves and the simple empirical levels of action, so long as certain arguments are eschewed, and so long as it is clearly recognised that the purpose of the theorising is moral clarification and understanding; and moral, political, and religious theories have, after all, often served this purpose in the past and have not always been 'mere superstitions'. It therefore emerges that the choice made by our intellectuals against the development of theories is a moral choice.

Is it a right choice? I think not. There is a serious and growing void in our thinking about moral and social problems. This void is uneasily felt by society at large and is the more distressing since we are now perhaps for the first time in our history feeling the loss of religion as a consolation and guide; until recently various substitutes (socialism itself, later Communism, pacifism, internationalism) were available; now there seems to be a shortage even of substitutes. The claim of socialism to be a 'science' has become, after many setbacks, a trifle less confident, and has certainly lost the spiritual appeal which it once had. Of course socialism will continue to attempt to constitute itself a science, in the sense of a highly organised investigation of the mechanics of society. But, and especially since it cannot now claim to be the scientific study of an inevitable quasi-biological development, it should, in my view, also far more frankly and more systematically declare itself a morality. Our socialist ancestors had ideals but no techniques. We are often amazed at their naïveté. We have the techniques; *these* we can explain clearly. But we can give only a rather brief and denuded explanation of our ideals. We have reached a stage where the amount of theory is decreasing while the social need for it increases. The danger represented by what is called the 'managerial society' is the danger (already diagnosed by Marx as characteristic of capitalism) of the division of the population into experts and ignorant (though perhaps contented) masses with no communication between them; and we have now the additional spectacle of the division of the experts into mutually non-comprehending groups. What is needed is an *area of translation*, an area in which specialised concepts and recommendations can be seen and understood in the light of moral and social ideas which have a certain degree of complexity and yet are not the sole property of technicians. There is a Tory contention that theorising leads to violence, and there is a liberal contention that theories are obscurantist and blinding. Now on the contrary it is the absence of theory which renders us blind and which enables bureaucracy, in all its sense, to keep us mystified; and as for violence, the absence of civilised theorising can also lead in that direction. It is dangerous to starve the moral imagination of the young. We require, in addition to our 'science', a social analysis which is both detailed and frank in its moral orientation. A more ambitious conceptual picture, thought out anew in the light of modern critical philosophy and our improved knowledge of the world, of the moral centre and moral direction of socialism would enable those of us who are not experts to pick up the facts of our situation in a reflective, organised and argumentative way: would give us what Shelley called the power to imagine what we know. Socialist thought is hampered, and the appeal of socialism is restricted, because our technical concepts are highly esoteric and our moral concepts are excessively simple and there is nothing in between. We need, and the Left should provide, some refuge from the cold open field of Benthamite empiricism, a framework, a house of theory.

In response to these ambitious desires it may be coldly argued that 'socialist theory' was a product of the working-class movement, and that the working-class movement no longer exists, whereas the trade union movement does; and that it is impossible to call up moral visions in a situation in which there is no material incentive to make people lift their eyes to the hills. Further, it will be said that a perfectly good socialist theory of a down-to-earth kind does exist and indeed fills many volumes. Those who ask for information about socialism are not left unanswered; what more is required? If it is a 'philosophy' that is wanted, that can hardly be produced on the spur of the moment and would in any case be itself something esoteric and technical.

It is doubtless true in a sense that the working-class movement as a dynamic theory-generating body with immediate objectives does not at present exist. There is less appetite for ideas. Education is no longer seen as the road to freedom; it is seen as the road to a higher salary. However, the working class exists, and with it many of the ills of capitalist society which were a scandal to our forefathers, and a large body of increasingly vague but loyal socialist opinion exists, too. The question must be continually asked: how are we to keep *thought* about socialism and *moral concern* about socialism alive in a Welfare State? Spiritual unrest and even decisive moral reactions are not lacking. 'Public opinion' is the name of a force which should control and check the development of bureaucracy; and public opinion has shown itself of late, to the dismay of certain Tories, to be still both lively and powerful. Its activity, however, has been limited to the sudden assertion of some absolute value (usually in the field of foreign affairs), obscurely grasped, without any connection of a theoretical kind being established between the occasions. A religious and moral vocabulary is the possession now of a few; and most people lack the word with which to say just [why] what is felt to be wrong is wrong.

If in the hope of finding such words we turn to the available socialist 'literature' we are likely to be disappointed. In the old days professional and amateur philosophising fed the public mind with ideas. Now, for a larger vision we have to look back to Laski or Tawney, or search for hints in eccentric and little-known works by Christians or Marxists. What we have plenty of, and what we find officially in the centre of the picture, are detailed technical books and pamphlets in which the author tells us briefly that we need public ownership in order to bring about equality, and then hurries on to the details of investment policy. The motive, the passion, in much of this literature is patently that of an expert making an efficient plan. Needless to say one is glad of such experts, and it would be an impertinence in the uninitiated to criticise what they cannot understand. But what one requires as well is a little more pausing at the first stage, a little more analysis, in terms which are not those of the economist, of an idea such as that of equality –

which is, in fact, in danger of becoming the only influential 'general idea' of contemporary socialism. More theoretical exploration of the aims of socialism, those aims to which all techniques are properly subordinate, would benefit both sides of the specialist barrier. The expert would gain that unifying vision which is needed to prompt more inspired and imaginative uses of technique. He would be less isolated, more responsible, more often compelled to explain, and having to explain, to connect, to translate, deepens understanding; while the average person would gain a more complex, and hence more influential, grasp upon what is being done on his behalf, instead of coming straightaway up against the blank wall of economics.

It is not true that 'everyone knows what is wrong with our society' and differs only over a simple choice of solutions. What we see as wrong, and our ability to express what is wrong in a profound, subtle and organised way, will influence our conception of a solution as well as providing us with the energy to seek it. We have not mended our society since its mutilation by nineteenth-century industrialism. There is less poverty but no more (in some ways less) true community life. Work has become less unpleasant without becoming more significant. The gulf remains between the skilled and creative few and the unskilled and uncreative many. What was formerly called the proletariat has lost what culture it once had, and gained no true substitute. A stream of half-baked amusements hinders thought and the enjoyment of art and even of conversation. Equality of opportunity produces, not a society of equals, but a society in which the class division is made more sinister by the removal of intelligent persons into the bureaucracy and the destruction of their roots and characteristics as members of the mass. In short, a proletariat in the fundamental sense intended by Marx still exists: a deracinate, disinherited and excluded mass of people. Only this mass is now quiescent, its manner of life largely suburban and its outlook 'petty bourgeois', and it increasingly lacks any concept of itself as deprived.

This list of grievances, whose items would be regarded as obvious in some quarters and eccentric in others, suggests to me the following, which again will seem obvious to some. The socialist movement should most explicitly bring back into the centre of its thinking its original great source of inspiration and reflection, the problem of labour: the problem, that is, of the transformation of labour from something senseless which forms no real part of the personality of the labourer into something creative and significant. To do this would involve a rethinking and regrouping on the theoretical plane of concepts such as 'exploitation' and 'alienation' which were formerly gathered about the Labour Theory of Value. The familiar ideas of 'equality', 'democracy', 'freedom' need to be understood anew in the light of the problem of labour and not treated as independent 'absolutes' whose meaning is taken for granted. To treat them so is ultimately to imperil them. Theory is needed to refresh the tired imagination of practice. Our available techniques seem uninteresting because we lack the vision to grasp their possibilities. A line of thought such as I have in mind leads very directly to problems that have been immensely discussed and considered. Can we maintain educational standards while making education more 'democratic'? Can we make technical training more universal and more humane while still meeting the demands of industry? Is the 'opposition' role of the trade unions a hindrance to 'industrial democracy'? It is not that these matters have not been studied; it is rather that they have been studied on too severely practical a level and without a sufficient consultation of our final aims. We should profit by widening the area in which they could be discussed with intelligence and interest.

A study of nationalisation, such as *Industry and Society*, for instance, representing an official attitude, combines complexity at the technical level with question-begging simplicity at the moral and theoretical level. 'Nationalisation' is spoken of in terms of redistribution of wealth, making important powers socially responsible, and enabling the State to profit from the present structure of our economy. 'Equality' is envisaged as the abolition of private shareholding and inherited position. Keynes is quoted to show that with the dissociation of ownership of industry from its control there is a 'natural line of development' in the direction of State socialism. There is a momentary reference to 'joint consultation'. Nothing whatever is said about conditions and nature of work. Whereas critics (the authors of *The Insiders*, for instance) who rightly suggest that 'public ownership must be seen in the context of the original socialist goal of industrial democracy' and who point out the extent to which *Industry and Society* takes our present economic and social structure for granted, still conceive the problem in terms of 'the democratisation of power', rather than in terms of what such a shift of power would be designed to achieve. But the fascination of the means should not obscure the end; and to *see* the end we must to some extent separate it from the often seemingly barren complexities of the means; we must to some extent lend it the remoteness and flexibility of a 'theory'. The problem of the transformation of labour is not only the original centre of socialist thought, it is the problem of the managerial society. Even to pose it with enough clarity would help to counteract the movement of talent and interest toward the levels of bureaucratic control and to send it back toward the levels of the unskilled. But for such an idea to be fruitful, a source of inspiration and controversy, it needs to be presented as an autonomous moral conception, independent of, and ultimately sovereign over, the mere notions of efficiency and rational 'tidying up' of capitalist society into which socialism is in danger of degenerating.

If we seek here for inspiration in our own tradition we have not far to look. The Guild Socialists dissented on precisely this point from their less ambitious and more purely Benthamite colleagues, in that the latter were concerned with the damage done to the consumer and the former with the damage done to the producer. The Guild Socialists were deeply concerned with the destruction of community life, the degradation of work, the division of man from man which the economic relationships of capitalism had produced; and they looked to the factories themselves, for the restoration of what was lost. Such ideas were and are easy targets for mockery, and in the old Guild Socialist form were doubtless quite impracticable; and they faded from the scene partly because they were tied to inadequate techniques, and partly because the conception of the Welfare State presented an easier and more obviously urgent and attractive target. With its achievement it is necessary to renew our study of the more difficult and fundamental problems of capitalism. We cannot live without the 'experts'. But the true 'open society' in the modern world is one in which expertise is not mysterious; and the only way to prevent it from becoming mysterious is continually to subordinate its activities to a lively and *interested* public opinion; and this in turn will languish without 'theories'. The Welfare State marks the successful end of the first road which the socialist movement in this country elected to travel. It is time now to go back and explore the other road, to go back to the point of divergence, the point not so very far back at which we retained as a living morality ideas which were common to Marx and to William Morris.

Essay in *Conviction*, ed. J. S. Mackenzie, 1958.

Mass, Might and Myth

I am not the polymath who would be the ideal reviewer of this remarkable book. To deal adequately with *Crowds and Power*[*] one would have to be, like its author, a mixture of historian, sociologist, psychologist, philosopher and poet. One is certainly confronted here with something large and important: an extremely imaginative, original and massively documented theory of the psychology of crowds.

Using heterogeneous and very numerous sources, Dr Canetti has built a structure which has the clarity, simplicity and explanatory flexibility of a metaphysical system. His view will not prove easy to 'place' in any familiar pattern or genealogy of ideas; nor has he himself given any help to would-be 'placers'. He quotes the most diverse and esoteric writers, but the names of Freud and Marx occur nowhere in his text (Freud is mentioned once in a note). This particular reticence, which reminds one of Wittgenstein, is the mark of the artist and of the confident, truly imaginative thinker; only whereas Wittgenstein had in fact not troubled to read some of his best-known predecessors, one may be pretty sure that Dr Canetti has read everything.

The book falls roughly into two halves. The first half analyses, with an amazing wealth of illustration, the dynamics of different types of crowds and of 'packs', a term used to denote a smaller, more rigidly structured and purposive crowd. The second part, which discusses how and why crowds obey rulers, deals with the psychology of the despot. The key to the crowd, and to the crowd's master, Canetti finds in his central theory of 'command' and 'survival'.

[*] Elias Canetti, *Crowds and Power*, trans. Carol Stewart (London, 1962).

A simplified account of this theory runs as follows. A fundamental human passion and a key to the nature of all power is the passion to *survive*. There is always satisfaction in the thought that it is someone else who is dead: and this satisfaction may become an addiction. This is something much more positive than a mere instinct of self-preservation. 'The lowest form of survival is killing.' In one guise or another – the meditation in the cemetery, the general 'throwing in another division' – there is deep satisfaction in the notion: 'They lie dead, I stand here alive.' This is one aspect of power.

A related aspect is 'the command'. Canetti connects command with the primitive notion of a flight from death. (The herd flees when the lion roars.) 'Beneath all command glints the harshness of the death sentence.' We are all subject to commands and each command which we obey leaves behind in us its 'sting'. This alien sting 'remains in us unchanged'. We do not forget or forgive any command. This in turn provides us with a major source of energy: the desire for a reversal, the desire to 'get rid of our stings' by making other people obey corresponding orders. This has many and varied consequences, some obvious and some not so obvious. Many promotion systems rely quite explicitly upon this primitive aspect of human nature. A man under orders will do anything because 'he does not accuse himself but the sting'. Our stings are our destiny.

In the last part of the book, Canetti introduces another concept, that of 'transformation'. This specifically human talent has many uses but is most primitively a kind of protection. It is a danger to any would-be despot, whose corresponding passion is 'to unmask'. The book ends with a discussion of the case of Schreber, a paranoiac who wrote a detailed memoir of his delusional life. In this account Canetti finds all the characteristics of power and its relation to crowds which he has been analysing. 'It is only a step from the primitive medicine man to the paranoiac and from both of them to the despot of history.'

How does one judge a large-scale theory of this sort? Clearly there is no point in just saying impatiently, well is it true or not? The question is, how much will it explain, how much light will it throw, what will it connect with what? I think Canetti's theory throws a great deal of light and precisely illuminates places which have hitherto been very dark. Marx has told us much about the dynamics of society. Freud has told us much about the human heart. But neither of them provides us with a satisfactory theoretical explanation of Hitler or an explanation, say, of the political power of a church over its adherents. Let us take two instances from Canetti. Roman Catholicism 'sees the open crowd as its enemy'. 'Communication between worshippers is hindered.' Even the communion service gives each man 'a precious treasure for himself'. 'The communion links the recipient with the vast invisible church but it detaches him from those actually present.' The only 'permitted crowd' is the crowd of the blessed, who are 'not imagined as active'.

And then (fragment of another discussion) about Germany. The German national symbol is the forest, which means also the army. The prohibition on universal military service robbed the Germans of their most essential closed crowd. This was 'the birth of National Socialism'. 'The party came to the rescue,' with its hierarchical order-uttering structure. Canetti concludes the discussion with speculations concerning the persecution of the Jews, which he connects with the German experience of inflation. The Germans felt that they had been 'depreciated', and they needed to pass this humiliation on to something else which could be, like the mark, reduced to worthlessness and thrown away by the million.

This sort of quotation and reference cannot do justice to the imaginative subtlety and variety of the analyses which Dr Canetti produces on page after page; and even if we do not always agree, we have certainly been given something to reflect *with*. One's hesitations, I think, are not at all concerned either with the importance or the scale of what is here presented, but (a characteristically philosophical question) with its relation to other types of theory. Canetti gives us no direct help with this problem, but indirectly presents us with an excellent object of study, since the case of Schreber has also been discussed by Freud. A feature of Schreber's delusion was that he imagined that he was being changed into a woman; this, which at first distressed him, he later decided was part of a plan whereby he was to redeem humanity by entering into sexual relations with God. Freud emphasises the *subsequent* nature of the religious fantasy, and finds the origin of Schreber's condition in repressed homosexuality.

Canetti disagrees: 'Processes of power always play a crucial part' in paranoia. He adds a note that 'Freud wrote in 1911, before the great wars and revolutions of our century. Had he read Schreber forty years later he would have been the first to see the limitations of his approach.' Canetti sees the case of Schreber against a background of power conceived in quasi-political terms. Schreber's sex-change is to be thought of as a device used by Schreber in a power-battle with the Almighty. Here 'religion and politics are inextricably intermingled: the Saviour of the world and the Ruler of the world are one . . . At the core of all this is the lust for power.'

One has here the profoundest hesitations. I suspect that many of us (such is the power of Freud) would tend to regard it as axiomatic that in a delusion about sex-change the purely sexual aspect must be radical. It is eminently salutary to be made to challenge such axioms. For myself, I do not want to be forced to say that Canetti's account necessarily invalidates Freud's, or vice versa. The human mind is an ambiguous thing. One hesitates here between an appeal to 'science' and an appeal to a natural metaphysic which lies at the basis of morality and which is not under orders from either science or philosophy. The paradox of our situation is that we must have theories about human nature, no theory explains everything, yet it is just the desire to explain everything which is the spur of theory. The peculiarity of contemporary philosophy is that it is so stunned by 'everything' that it has given up explaining.

Ideally a 'theory' should be both centripetal and centrifugal, and this I think Dr Canetti's theory triumphantly is. His book is full of starting points, embryo theories, sudden independent illuminations. When he says of Christianity, for instance, that it is a 'religion of lament' in which the 'hunting pack' expiates its guilt by turning into a 'lamenting pack', or when he speaks of the 'frenzy of increase' which in modern capitalism undermines the religion of lament, he is giving us new means of thinking which, as it were, contain their own ambiguities. Dr Canetti might be the first to agree that concepts as well as men should enjoy the privileges of transformation. Rich concepts have histories. And precisely because Dr

Canetti's concepts are so rich I do not think we should be in too much of a hurry to see them as rigidly systematic.

This problem of the 'necessary incompleteness' of systems occurs to one particularly in relation to the 'moral' of *Crowds and Power*. Canetti speaks of power as fundamental to human nature and he analyses power with predominantly 'political' imagery: 'Canetti's man' appears as a conscious, irritable person ruled by 'stings'. And it is incidentally a matter of 'accident' whether extreme cases turn out to be Hitlers or harmless Schrebers. Our most pressing need, as Canetti very movingly and convincingly argues at the end, is to control the 'survivor mania' of our rulers, and the key to this is 'the humanisation of command'. But how is command to be humanised? Canetti has not given us a psychology with which to picture the humanisation of command. Here rival science and indomitable morality stand ready to enter the argument. How strictly is one to understand the imagery of the 'stings'? Command has a sexual aspect which deserves analysis. (This Hegel appreciated. Dr Canetti is resolutely non-Hegelian.) Also, cannot the pain of stings be removed by love and compassion without any 'reversal'? How are we here to conceive the 'free' man? No theory of human nature can place itself beyond the attack of purely moral concepts.

Whether or not we agree, we have here that rare sense of being 'let out' into an entirely new region of thought. Canetti has done what philosophers ought to do, and what they used to do: he has provided us with new concepts. He has also shown, in ways which seem to me entirely fresh, the interaction of 'the mythical' with the ordinary stuff of human life. The mythical is not something 'extra'; we live in myth and symbol all the time.

Crowds and Power, one may add, is a marvellously rewarding book even if one were to read it without any theoretical interests at all. It is written in a simple, authoritative prose, splendidly translated by Carol Stewart, and it is radiant with imagination and humour. There are hundreds of memorable things. A matchbox derives its charm from being reminiscent of a forest: a forest fire in a matchbox. 'A menagerie of transformed clothes' is mentioned in passing. There is a beautiful discussion of the human hand, and a remarkable section on the psychology of eating. The book is full of entertainments and provocations to thought. It is also a great original work on a vitally important subject, and provides us with an eminence from which we can take a new look at Marx and Freud. A large work of scholarship which is also a completely new work of theory is rare enough: and we should remind ourselves that in the obscure and disputed field of 'the study of human nature' we cannot rely only upon the piecemeal efforts of teams of merely competent scientists. We need and we shall always need the visions of great imaginers and solitary men of genius.

Review in *The Spectator*, September 1962.

The Darkness of Practical Reason

In his book *Freedom of the Individual*[*] Stuart Hampshire argues as follows. In human beings (as opposed to things) power is a function of will and will is a function of desire. Some desires are 'thought-dependent' in that they depend on statable beliefs which, if they altered, would alter the desires, and so such desires cannot be defined by purely behavioural criteria, since the subject's conception of what he wants is constitutive of the wanting. We do not discover our thought-dependent desires inductively, by observation, we formulate them in the light of our beliefs. We have the experience of being convinced by evidence and of changing our beliefs and so willing differently, and there seems to be no set of sufficient conditions outside our thinking which could explain this situation equally well.

Here Hampshire pauses to deal with two matters which could be sources of confusion: 'the doctrine of the transcendent will' and Aristotle's problem of *Akrasia* (weakness of will, *video meliora proboque, deteriora sequor* [I see the better course and approve of it, but I follow the worse course]). The doctrine of the transcendent will (forms of which Hampshire attributes to Kant, Schopenhauer, and Wittgenstein) presents freedom as an 'ideal' movement of thought which does not 'factually' occasion conduct, since the domain of value is entirely separate from the domain of empirical fact. Hampshire objects to such a view because it gives no coherent account of ordinary intentional acts, of the relation of will to ordinary felt desires, and of ordinary assessments of conduct. He concludes that we may return to 'the attempts and tryings which are

[*] Stuart Hampshire, *Freedom of the Individual* (London, 1966).

[193]

recorded in our ordinary speech' and 'the desires and interests that explain them'.

Hampshire agrees with Aristotle in finding *Akrasia* a paradox. Can one 'really intend' what one believes to be mistaken? He argues that intentions and beliefs must at least have plausibility if they are to be properly so called. Believing, unlike fearing or wanting, has a built-in (normative) assertion of the appropriateness of its object. Believing and intending are active states, whereas desires and fears, unless they depend on beliefs, are passive states. Self-alteration by 'techniques' is confined to the latter and only here can we use scientific knowledge. (Getting rid of irrational fears is not like changing one's mind by argument.) Science simply gives us information about the limits of our powers, and it makes no difference whether this information is physical or psychological. Increase in such knowledge does not limit freedom, since the subject can always 'step back' to survey the situation anew in the light of the knowledge; and in general the more we learn of the conditions in which we act the closer the relation will be between intention and achievement. These distinctions between active and passive, intention and induction, normative and observed, beliefs and superstitions, decisions and wishes, are built into our language and are the material of our freedom. A man is free in so far as he is able to 'step back' from his data, including his own mind, and so to achieve what he intends.

*

I wish to make an entry into Professor Hampshire's argument at the point where he dismisses the doctrine of the transcendent will. This doctrine (its forms are very various) is one response to a very old problem in moral philosophy: how is human freedom compatible with the authority of the Good? Definitions and revelations of the Good seem to preclude the spiritual value of a free adherence. Kant inaugurates a new era when he makes a virtue out of this difficulty by pointing out that it is the very mysteriousness and separateness of the spiritual world which renders it spiritual. God (or value) is necessarily an object of faith, not of knowledge. Kant's combination of this insight with his confidence in science produces the dualism which shocks Hampshire. Since we are not just free spirits but also causally determined animals we are not transparent to ourselves and our motivation is both obscure and surprising. (We cannot easily determine beforehand how far idealism may extend our possibilities and how far we may be able to act against our character.) Much modern philosophy (existentialist and analytical) follows Kant here: since value has clearly no place in the empirical (scientific) world it must be given another kind of importance by being attached directly to the operation of the human will. (Wittgenstein's *Tractatus* is the modern classic of this type of empiricism: though I would not myself attribute any quasi-existentialist theory of the will to Wittgenstein. His exasperating hints seem to lead in a different direction.)

Now it is not easy to see at first sight why Hampshire rejects *in toto* this pregnant and various 'doctrine of the transcendent will', since he himself holds, as I shall argue, a view which is a version of this same doctrine. However I think there is a particular feature of the doctrine which Hampshire finds menacing, and that is that it may portray (this is certainly true of Kant and the existentialists) human motivation as mysterious:

> If one dismisses the transcendent will, we are left with the attempts and tryings which are recorded in our ordinary speech, and embodied in action, and with the desires and interests that explain them.

It is for the same reason that Hampshire follows Aristotle in trying to remove the obscurity from the *Akrasia* situation by dividing it up into various cases which do not include the puzzling central one of really judging A better and doing B.

*

It is important to Hampshire's argument that we should be able cleanly to separate willing from believing (a genuine belief is not willed, it is formulated on evidence) and be able to discuss thought-dependent motivation in ordinary public language, free of personal or technical jargon. His distinction of passive from active mind is, although he allows for borderline cases, a dualism as strict as Kant's (and its close relation), and his picture of the formulation of belief in ordinary language and of motivation as a function of ordinary statable interests is intended to exclude from the active area not only any metaphysical or religious view of the mind (for instance, the operation of grace) but also any specialised psychological view.

Recall the structure of his argument. Will depends on desires, some of which depend on beliefs, which depend on thinking which is active and has built-in norms. Science deals with passive mind, and increases in scientific knowledge can be dominated by the agent's 'stepping back' to review the situation. Freedom is a matter of being realistic enough (holding rational enough beliefs) to be able to achieve what we intend. It is the normative (objective, impersonal, unwilled) nature of the formulation of belief which rescues the active (uncaused) side of the mind from its passive (caused) side. And to be able to picture the desires which affect the will as being intelligibly connected with rational norms of belief we must eschew mysterious theories of motivation and allow ordinary public language to be adequate to explain our acts in terms of our statable wants and interests.

Let me try to clarify my objections to this view. The argument depends on the purity of the two dualisms: active and passive, and (within the former) reason and will. Motivation must be explicable in 'ordinary language' (a phenomenon, indeed a *character*, often mentioned in the book) if we are to be able to see transparently the mechanism which connects reason (the formulation of sensible beliefs) with will and allows of the 'stepping back' movement. Hampshire permits no machinery in between the passive states, which he surrenders to empirical psychology, and the active disengaged states which manufacture the free will as he sees it (surely transcendent enough). If there is any murky area of motivation which essentially (and apart from trivial borderline cases) blurs this distinction then the whole argument is damaged.

Hampshire, who is well known to be no enemy of Freud, mentions his name only once in the book, where he says that if a man were to accept a psychological explanation of a fear, 'unless the explanation were a Freudian one, it would give him no place as endorsing, and as responsible for, his fear'. The implication is that a Freudian explanation enables us to attach the fear intelligibly to a more clearly seen structure of motivation which we may endorse or at any rate accept as ours: the explanation is then *ipso facto* a 'stepping back' movement and so can be recruited on to the active side of reason (becomes a part of reason); whereas all other psychological techniques illuminate not reason itself, but the merely passive aspects of mind.

These are large assumptions. It is arguable that psychological methods (such as Freudian methods) which depend on the co-operation and assent of the patient are differently situated from methods which do not have this dependence. But what is the status of the patient's assent (appropriation)? Is it, plus perhaps a therapeutic effect, the only possible verification of any theory which professes to explain our higher (rational) activities? It is at least (especially given the great variety of such theories: Freud, Marx) not obvious without more argument than Hampshire offers (in fact he offers none) that this is so, or that a given theory can always either be dominated by a stepping back movement or be regarded as such a movement. One can only step back if there is somewhere to step back to. If one allows these doubts the purity of the dualism is essentially blurred and the murkiness of the passive invades the active to an indefinite extent. This point, which would need much more discussion, I leave here.

*

What I mainly want to argue is trickier. Hampshire himself uses the strict value-fact dualism which he attributes to the transcendent will merchants, only he draws his line so as to isolate, not value as such, but simply the value of freedom. His system (like most existentialist systems) implies two levels of value. There is the primary value of freedom itself and there are the secondary values which consist of the things chosen. Hampshire does not concern himself with the secondary values. He implies that freedom is an achievement, but a fairly simple and intelligible achievement, since the drama of attempt and motivation is something 'recorded in our ordinary language'. The failure to be free is the failure to operate the machinery of will-desire-belief-reason in such a way as to enjoy the detachment of rational thought. It is that failure and not any more complicated moral failure.

I think in an almost liberal political sense Hampshire would make a merit of these limitations. Freedom, he would say, is how you choose, not what you choose, doing what you intend, not doing what is right. I agree with Hampshire that any definition of freedom must be normative, but it seems to me that the norms involved are more complicated than those to which he appeals; and I do not think that a moral (*as opposed to a purely political*) definition of freedom can successfully separate the two levels of value.

It is significant that Hampshire relegates *imagination* to the passive side of the mind, regarding it as an isolated non-responsible faculty which makes potentially valuable discoveries which reason may inspect and adopt. Hampshire certainly regards imagination as a side issue. It is not even mentioned in his main argument. Why? Philosophical discussion is often obscure because philosophers invent (and have to invent) a limited vocabulary of systematically related terms. The critical reader must not only follow the argument but also scrutinise the assumptions carried by the vocabulary. Hampshire uses words such as 'will', 'desire', and 'reason', and by-passes 'imagination' because this word may be used to name an activity which is awkward for his theory. What is this activity?

Hampshire implies that 'imaginings' are just drifting ideas. I should like to use the word (in a sense more like its normal one) to describe something which we all *do* a great deal of the time. This activity, which may be characterised by a contrast with 'strict' or 'scientific' thinking, is (like so many totally familiar things) not easy to describe, but one might attempt a description as follows: a type of reflection on people, events, etc., which builds detail, adds colour, conjures up possibilities in ways which go beyond what could be said to be strictly factual. When this activity is thought to be bad it is sometimes called 'fantasy' or 'wishful thinking'. That we are all constantly engaged in this activity is something which Hampshire chooses to ignore, and he selects his vocabulary accordingly.

Now Hampshire might say that imagination, if thought to be important, should be seen simply as a passive condition which may impede freedom by making thinking unrealistic. (Recall that Hampshire connects rational thought with doing what we intend, i.e., being free, by assuming that we will not achieve what we intend unless our beliefs are realistic.) That imagination (or 'fantasy', meaning 'bad imagining') may do this is plain: to reflect on an enemy solely in terms of revenge fantasies is not only wrong but likely to cloud the judgement. But should this great human activity be thought of only in these terms? Is there not also a good constructive imagination which plays an important part in our life? Hampshire would be unwilling to allow this for a rather important reason. He can readily admit imaginings which are unwilled, isolated, passive. But if we admit active imagination as an important faculty it is difficult not to see this as an exercise of will. Imagining is *doing*, it is a sort of personal exploring. Now Hampshire's picture depends on a divorce between will and reason (he considers the influence of will upon belief at the level of a man forcing himself to believe in his Leader against his better judgement, that is, it is always improper). Our freedom is said to consist in our ability to remove ourselves into a region where we can assess situations under no pressure from the will.

*

Is Hampshire's neglect of imagination merely a slip which he could remedy without damage to his argument? I do not think so.

The world which we confront is not just a world of 'facts' but a world upon which our imagination has, at any given moment, already worked; and although such working may often be 'fantasy' and may constitute a barrier to our seeing 'what is really there', this is not necessarily so. Many of the beliefs which are relevant to action are unlike disciplined scientific or scholarly beliefs. They are beliefs in the genesis of which active imagination and will play a part which is not necessarily sinister. The formulation of beliefs about other people often proceeds and must proceed imaginatively and under a direct pressure of will. We have to *attend* to people, we may have to have *faith* in them, and here justice and realism may demand the inhibition of certain pictures, the promotion of others. Each of us lives and chooses within a partly private, partly fabricated world, and although any particular belief might be shown to be 'merely fantastic' it is false to suggest that we could, even in principle, 'purge' the world we confront of these personal elements. Nor is there any reason why we should. To be a human being is to know more than one can prove, to conceive of a reality which goes 'beyond the facts' in these familiar and natural ways.

This activity is, moreover, usually and often inevitably, an activity of evaluation. We evaluate not only by intentions, decisions, choices (the events Hampshire describes), but also, and largely, by the constant quiet work of attention and imagination. The image here is not so much that of a body moving (Hampshire's image) but rather of a sort of seeping of colour, or the setting up of a magnetic field. When moments of decision arrive we see and are attracted by the world we have already (partly) made. That is why 'attempts and tryings recorded in ordinary language' (public language) may be inadequate to explain the mysteries of motivation. (Even Hampshire admits that it may be difficult to reproduce a man's unstated beliefs.) This is also (I think) the explanation of *Akrasia*: *Akrasia* is only a paradox if we assume (with Aristotle) that we really desire the good, or (with Hampshire) that we are really rational, that is readily able to become detached and have motives available for inspection in public language. But the good and evil that we dream of may be more incarnate than we realise in the world within which we choose. This too is why (as the existentialists point out but leave unintelligible) deliberation at the moment of choice often seems ineffectual. We are obscure to ourselves because the world we see already contains our values and we may not be aware of the slow delicate processes of imagination and will which have put those values there. This implies, of course, that at moments of choice we are normally less free than Hampshire pictures us as (potentially) being, and that freedom is a more difficult and complex achievement than Hampshire suggests.

*

This is not, of course, to say that the picture offered by Hampshire is unrealistic in all cases. One might grant that the unwilled detachment which he regards as essential to freedom can occur in practical situations; though it seems to me untypical of our most important moral decisions and it would be hard to determine in any particular case that its background was not already 'tainted' by will. But it is true that 'we know what it is like to be convinced by evidence'; this knowledge is one of our most important characteristics, and if Hampshire had claimed to be producing *an* argument against determinism (and not a complete 'phenomenology of freedom') his description of the mind, captioned 'this sometimes happens', could constitute an up-to-date (post-Wittgenstein) version of the 'argument from rationality'.

If what Hampshire describes ever happens then we are potentially free in one, though not to my mind the most important, sense of 'free'. That is, we have a capacity for rational detachment in our decisions; though this would not, in my view, be a guarantee of freedom except in cases where efforts of imagination and will were not, as it happens, also required by the situation. I think Hampshire is right to say that what makes determinism not just unproved but unthinkable is the difficulty of conceiving any total translation of the normative language involved in describing free behaviour into a neutral language of natural law; and I would myself rely on such an argument, though the norms I would refer to are different from those of Hampshire. Meanwhile, empirical psychology can show what it can show.

*

I have been arguing that Hampshire's sharp distinctions of active and passive, reason and will, break down because a constructive activity of imagination and attention 'introduces' value into the world which we confront. We have already partly willed our world when we come to look at it; and we must admit moral responsibility for this 'fabricated' world, however difficult it may be to control the process of fabrication. *On such a view it will be impossible to separate 'pure freedom' as a value untouched by secondary values.* That reality goes beyond 'mere fact' and that to reach it we need strength and refinement of the imagination is not an obscure metaphysical doctrine. Consider any case of knowing another person really well or appreciating a great work of art. And if many of our important beliefs are and have to be products of a willed attention, then realism about the world is seen to require qualities of character (virtues) other than a professedly neutral and simple ability for detached thought. Political freedom may, and indeed should, be defined in terms which exclude questions of realism or meritorious choice. But as Hume wisely remarked, 'something may be true in politics which is false in fact'. Moral freedom, if it is to be defined at all, cannot, it seems to me, be defined without a reference to virtue. A mediocre man who achieves what he intends is not the ideal of a free man. To be free is something like this: to exist sanely without fear and to perceive what is real. I would be prepared to imply that one who perceives what is real will also act rightly. If the magnetic field is right our movements within it will tend to be right.

Hampshire sees the enemy of freedom in what he regards as the sinister influence of will upon belief, the tainting of reason. I would see the enemy of freedom as fantasy, a bad use of imagination: something relentlessly natural to human beings and against which 'pure reason' has little chance. There must also be a willed imaginative reaching out towards what is real.

This is of course to pose a problem, not to solve it. The question of the authority of the Good (which engendered the doctrine of the transcendent will) remains, and must penetrate any ideal theory of freedom. How we picture the realism of the free (if they exist) will be a function of what in general we take to be valuable and real. I would suggest, however, that there is one region in which agreement might be sought. Surely great artists are (in respect of their art) free men. Ethics and aesthetics are not one, but art is the great *clue* to morals.

Review-article in *Encounter*, July 1966.

PART FIVE

Towards a Practical Mysticism, 1959–78

'Art and morality are, with certain provisos . . . one. Their essence is the same. The essence of both of them is love. Love is the perception of individuals. Love is the extremely difficult realisation that something other than oneself is real.'

'The Sublime and the Good', 1959

The Sublime and the Good

Tolstoy complains as follows: 'All the existing aesthetic standards are built on this plan. Instead of giving a definition of true art and then deciding what is and what is not good art by judging whether a work conforms or does not conform to this definition, a certain class of works which for some reason pleases a certain circle of people is accepted as being art, and a definition of art is then devised to cover all these productions.'* I cannot altogether agree with this. Our direct apprehension of which works of art are good has just as much authority, engages our moral and intellectual being just as deeply, as our philosophical reflections upon art in general, and indeed if Tolstoy were right critics would have explicitly to formulate a morality and an aesthetic before they could be sure of their judgements. I cannot believe this to be necessary; and since my own concern here is with defining art in general, and not with judging particular works, I would rather say the opposite thing. Our aesthetic must stand to be judged by great works of art which we know to be such independently; and it is right that our faith in Kant and in Tolstoy should be shaken when we discover shocking eccentricities in their direct judgement of merit in art. So let us start by saying that Shakespeare is the greatest of all artists, and let our aesthetic grow to be the philosophical justification of this judgement. We may note that a similar method can, and in my view should, be used in moral philosophy. That is, if a moral philosophy does not give a satisfactory or sufficiently rich account of what we unphilosophically know to be goodness, then away with it.

Is it possible to offer a single definition of art at all? The same question may be asked concerning morals. Now clearly both art

* All quotations from Tolstoy are from *What Is Art?* [1896].

and morals can be defined in two different ways: either by means of a sort of lower common denominator, asking such questions as 'What distinguishes an art object, regardless of merit, from an object fashioned by nature or chance?' and 'What distinguishes a moral judgement, regardless of the values it expresses, from a statement of fact or a judgement of taste?'; or alternatively art and morals may be defined through a study of their highest manifestations, in order to find what is the essence of 'true' art or the best morality. Equally clear, it is not always easy to separate these two kinds of definition even if one is resolutely seeking one or the other. I am not concerned here with the first kind of definition, the lowest common denominator one. I think that such a definition is worth formulating, and that one can get something (though not as much as some modern philosophers, such as R. M. Hare believe) in answer to the question 'What is in common to all moral judgements?'; and similarly with aesthetic judgements. This investigation is, however, much less important than the other one; and here, of course, in undertaking the other one, one will inevitably be displaying what one takes to be valuable, one will be making (shocking to some philosophers) judgements of value. Tolstoy rightly says, 'The estimation of the value of art ... depends on men's perception of the meaning of life; depends on what they hold to be the good and the evil of life.' Whether we think art is an amusement, or an education, or a revelation of reality, or is for art's sake (whatever that may mean) will reveal what we hold to be valuable and (the same thing) what we take the world to be fundamentally like.

One of the most interesting of recent attempts to define art, and indeed one of the few philosophical attempts which has any interest at all, is that made by Kant in the *Critique of Aesthetic Judgement*; and I propose to work towards my own sketch of a definition through a consideration and criticism of Kant's. I would summarise Kant's view as follows: in speaking of aesthetic judgement Kant distinguishes between the beautiful and the sublime, and in speaking of the beautiful he distinguishes between free and dependent beauty. The true judgement of taste concerns free beauty. Here, according to Kant, the imagination and the understanding are in harmony in the apprehension of a sensuous object which is not brought under any particular concept and is verified in accordance with a rule we cannot formulate. Beauty is 'coupled with the representation through which the object is given, not through which it is thought.' Beauty is a matter of form. What is truly beautiful is independent of any interest, it is not tainted either by the good, or by any pleasure extraneous to the act of representing to ourselves the object itself. It has no concern with charm or with emotion. What is beautiful exhibits 'purposiveness without a purpose'; it is composed as if with a purpose, and yet it has no purpose which we can name. It is also, to use Kant's language, universal though subjective, and necessary though not apodictic. That is, we assume, though we cannot prove, a 'common sense' (*sensus communis*) when laying down a judgement of taste, and we are 'suitors for agreement', holding that everyone ought to hold beautiful what we hold beautiful. But as *ex hypothesi* we cannot formulate the rule according to which the beautiful object is constructed we can never be proved right. Further, the aesthetic judgement is immediate and the pleasure taken in it is inseparable from, is in fact, the synthesis: the putting together of a conceptless representation. What Kant calls aesthetic judgements may be made in relation to either art or nature, and Kant says that art and nature please us by resembling each other; that is, we like nature when it seems to be purposefully constructed and we like art when it seems to be pointless. As examples of free beauty, i.e., true beauty, Kant gives flowers, birds, wallpaper patterns, lines aimlessly intertwining, and 'all music that is not set to words'. He also says that 'a bird's song, which we can reduce to no musical role, seems to have more freedom in it, and thus to be richer for taste, than the human voice singing in accordance with all the rules that the art of music prescribes'. 'In the estimate of a free beauty (according to mere form) we have the pure judgement of taste.' As examples of dependent beauty he gives 'the beauty of man, the beauty of a horse, or of a building' which 'presupposes a concept of the end that defines what the thing has to be, and consequently a concept of its perfection'. Any attempt, for instance, to represent a certain kind of character mars the purity of beauty by the introduction of a concept; and of course any concern with goodness or with a moral content is equally fatal. Any combination of 'intellectual delight with the aesthetic' results in something which is not a pure judgement of taste (though it may be excellent in other ways).

Concerning the sublime, as distinct from the beautiful, Kant has these things to say: Whereas beauty is not connected with emotion, the sense of the sublime is. Strictly, whereas objects may be beautiful, no object is ever sublime. It is rather that certain aspects of nature occasion feelings of sublimity in us. Whereas beauty results from a harmony between imagination and understanding, sublimity results from a conflict between imagination and reason. (Beauty is an intermediate concept of the understanding, sublimity is an indeterminate concept of the reason.) What is vast and formless in nature, or vast and powerful and terrifying, can occasion a sense of sublimity, provided we are not actually afraid. A mountain range, the starry sky, the stormy sea, a great waterfall – these things give us the sublime. Now the sublime is defined by Kant as follows: 'It is an object (of nature) the repesentation of which determines the mind to regard the elevation of nature beyond our reach as equivalent to a presentation of ideas.' It is a feeling which 'renders inevitable the supremacy of our cognitive faculties on the rational side over the greatest faculty of sensibility'. That is, reason imposes upon us as a law the comprehension of what is before us as a totality. Reason for Kant, and also for Hegel, is the faculty which seeks for systematic wholeness and abhors incompleteness and juxtaposition. Confronted with the starry sky, the mountains, imagination strives to its utmost to satisfy this requirement of reason, and fails. So that on the one hand we experience distress at this failure of the imagination to compass what is before us, and on the other hand we feel exhilaration in our consciousness of the absolute nature of reason's requirement and the way in which it goes beyond what mere sensible imagination can achieve. This mixed experience is, Kant remarks, very like *Achtung*, the experience of respect for the moral law. 'The feeling of our incapacity to attain to an idea that is a law for us is Respect.' In *Achtung* we feel pain at the thwarting of our sensuous nature by a moral requirement, and elation in the consciousness of our rational nature; that is, our freedom to conform to the absolute requirements of reason.

The beautiful and the sublime are related to the good, that is also to the idea of freedom, in different ways. Although Kant insists that the beautiful must not be tainted with the good, that is conceptual-ised in any way which would bring it into the sphere of moral judgement, he yet says that the beautiful symbolises the good, it is an analogy of the good. The judgement of taste is a sort of sensuous counterpart of the moral judgement, in that it is independent, disinterested, free. But, as Kant puts it, the freedom of the judgement of taste is more like the freedom of *play*. The experience of sublimity has a much closer relation to morals, since here it is the reason, that is the moral will itself, which is active in the experience. And whereas the experience of beauty is like cognition and is contemplative and restful, the experience of the sublime sets the mind in motion and resembles the exercise of the will in moral judgement. The freedom of sublimity does not symbolise, but *is* moral freedom, only moral freedom not practically active but only, as it were, intuiting itself in an exultant manner.

Now to proceed to some commentary on this. I want first of all to make some minor and obvious comments, comments which if accepted will change Kant's view, in the spirit of many of his own intentions, into a familiar current view of art which would command much greater agreement. I want then to make more radical criticisms and to evoke from them the sketch of what I take to be the true view of art. We note at once that pure art or true art, according to Kant, is a very small area of what we normally think of as art. The paradigm case of aesthetic appreciation for Kant is something like looking at a flower, or better still an abstract pattern of lines, where form can sport playfully to produce a quasi-object with no interference from any concept. Kant does in fact cautiously allow more dubious cases, such as pieces of poetry, into the realm of art, provided they are thought of as simply 'a free play of the imagination', and not as anything like conceptual classification or statement. Poetry conducts 'a free play of the imagination as if it were a serious business of the understanding'. Poetry pleases us by resembling rhetoric while being in fact pure play.

I do not think that the position Kant is trying to hold here is altogether coherent. The extreme nature of what he has had to say about free and dependent beauty (e.g. that the representation of anything of which we can have an ideal or governing concept must result in dependent beauty) is difficult to square with allowing any poetry except the poetry of Mallarmé in the realm of free beauty at all. Kant is more consistent in allowing only *wordless* music to qualify. However that may be, I think very few of us would now accept the extremely narrow conception of art which is implicit here, however exactly we interpret it. We would wish I think to transform, if we are to accept it at all, the notion that the work of art is not governed by a concept. We would not want to share Kant's ideal of the work of art as being if possible, as somehow striving to be, non-significant. The idea that it is in some sense an end in itself need not entail *that*; and we can speak of the work of art as having its own unique self-containing form, being indeed a quasi-object, and having no educational purpose, while at the same time allowing it to *use* concepts, or even *be* a thing with other purposes, such as a church. When I. A. Richards said that a poem does not say anything, he did not mean that it did not consist of intelligible sentences. There will of course be variation of opinion as to how far we should go in letting art have truck with concepts. Some people may feel that in regarding a church as an art-object we should abstract from its usefulness, others would disagree; and equally we may go to varying lengths in allowing the profundity and importance of what is *said* in a poem to affect our judgement of it as a poem. And it may indeed be difficult in such cases to separate aesthetic judgement from other types of judgement. But I think the general and current theory, while still insisting in the spirit of Kantian aesthetics that the art object is independent and for itself, would take a more liberal view of the extent to which it might incarnate or express concepts. A related point is this. Kant treats the aesthetic judgement on the analogy of the perceptual judgement of cognition. That is, it must happen at once, as it were automatically, bringing us its pleasure in the very act of synthesis. This is equally a picture which will suit our apprehension of a rose, but not our apprehension of *King Lear*. But these are minor criticisms. We can keep, if we wish to, a great deal of what Kant has to say about form; absence of a rule we can formulate, disinterestedness, independence, while allowing conceptual content, and allowing too that aesthetic enjoyment is not a momentary quasi-perceptual state of mind. That is, the art object is not just 'given', it is also *thought*.

And with these corrections we have, I suggest, a view which would now be widely accepted, and which has been well expressed, for instance, by Stuart Hampshire in his article 'Logic and Appreciation' in the book *Aesthetics and Language* edited by [William] Elton. '[The artist] did not set himself to create beauty, but some particular thing. The canons of success and failure, of perfection and imperfection, are in this sense internal to the work itself ... Anything whatever may be picked out as an object of aesthetic interest – anything which when attended to carefully and apart altogether from its uses provides, by the arrangement of its elements and their suggestion to the imagination, some peculiar satisfaction of its own. An aesthetic judgement has to point to the arrangement of elements and to show what constitutes the originality of the arrangement in this particular case.'

I want to go on now to the more important criticisms of Kant's position; and to help us here, let us turn first to Shakespeare, in accordance with the principle I laid down at the start, and then to Tolstoy. Why will Kant's view simply not do at all? I suggest, and this is just the beginning of an answer, that it is at least clear that it will not do because it does not in any way account for the greatness of tragedy. Nor does it account for that similar greatness in non-literary arts which may bear other names. Kant prefers bird-song to opera. Kant thinks that art is essentially play. Now Shakespeare is great art, and Shakespeare is not play, so Kant must be wrong. Tolstoy thought that our estimate of art showed our views on good and evil. Let us look at one or two other things which he had to say. Artistic activity, according to Tolstoy, is the communication of feeling. A boy tells of an encounter with a wolf. He is an artist if he can re-create and transmit his feelings. Art proper, however, art in the strict sense, is not the transmission of any feeling, but only of the highest feelings, i.e. feelings flowing from religious perception. 'Art is a human activity having for its purpose the transmission to others of the highest and best feelings to which men have risen.' It is 'a means of union among men joining them together in the same feelings, and indispensable for the life and progress towards well-being of individuals and of humanity'. And 'there is nothing fresher than the feelings springing from the religious consciousness of each age'. These pronouncements are at once promising and serious after the view, in some ways so unnervingly frivolous, held by Kant. They are, however, more the pronouncements of a moralist than of a philosopher. Tolstoy holds in addition a further view which though profound and challenging is difficult to handle. He holds that great art is universal and simple in a way which makes it generally easy to understand. Note that here a sort of profound instinctive religious perception, shared by all, takes the place of Kant's *sensus communis*. 'What distinguishes a work of art from all other mental activity is just the fact that its language is understood by all.' 'Great works of art are only great because they are accessible and comprehensible to everyone.' They are understood because every man's relation to God is the same. Examples of great art: the Iliad, the stories of the Old Testament, the parables, folk tales. Also, some novels by Dickens, George Eliot, Dostoevsky, Victor Hugo. Examples of bad obscure art condemned by Tolstoy: impressionist painting, poems by Mallarmé and Baudelaire, nearly all the music of Beethoven. At this point we may profitably return to the Shakespeare principle. Tolstoy must be wrong here at least. One feels immense sympathy with, one is impressed by, the seriousness of his view that great art must be universal in the sense of simple, non-particular and comprehensible to all – but we know in fact that there is great art which is difficult. So we cannot take Tolstoy's preference as a criterion. Can we however make something of his view that great art expresses religious feeling, or religious *perception*, to put the essence of the matter in a less controversial form; and can we in any way connect this with some of the perhaps acceptable elements of Kant's view?

I return now to Kant and to the sublime. There is something suggestive, indeed intoxicating, in the connection of the sublime via the concept of *Achtung* with Kant's ethical theory, which is itself one of the most beautiful and exciting things in the whole of philosophy. However, when we look closely at this connection it turns out to be more difficult, than might appear at first sight, to extract from it a theory of art more acceptable to us than Kant's theory of the beautiful. The sublime has, of course, according to Kant, nothing to do with art. It is an uplifting emotion experienced in the Alps. This may indeed discourage us, especially since Kant's choice of examples suggests an eighteenth-century cult of the more

Gothic aspects of nature which it does not now occur to us to think of as particularly edifying; and, more seriously, if we consider what may be actual occasions of sublime feelings, these feelings are not at all easy to interpret, and we may suspect them to have to do, in their real complexity, not only with morals but also with sex. *Achtung* itself, I think we may say without disrespect to that great concept, also has its connections with sex. However, in spite of this discouragement I cannot help brooding upon the relation of sublimity to *Achtung* and feeling that it must be pregnant with something marvellous. Let us try again.

The theory of the sublime ought to be Kant's theory of tragedy. It nearly but not quite is Hegel's theory of tragedy. Let us see what is wrong with both of these theories. To put the contrast between Kant and Hegel here in a nutshell: Kant thinks of the sublime as the failure of imagination to compass an abstractly conceived non-historical, non-social, quasi-mathematical totality which is not *given* but only vaguely adumbrated by reason. The sublime is a segment of a circle, grasped by imagination, with the rest of the circle demanded and as it were dreamt of by reason, but not given. The sublime is only occasioned by natural objects (non-historical, non-social, non-human), and the imaginative understanding the lack of which occasions the pain-and-pleasure of sublimity is a kind of vast systematic perception of nature which space and time and the nature of our sensibility forbids. Hegel here, as indeed everywhere else, makes social and historical and human and concrete what Kant has offered as abstract, non-historical, etc. The experience of tragedy, according to Hegel, is the envisaging of a conflict between two incompatible goods. Not a conflict between good and evil but between two goods, which are seen to be such because they incarnate different real social forces with real claims in society. Antigone and Creon are both right, as we see if we understand the total situation which encloses them both. The unity of the ethical substance is given as total, and within it we see and comprehend a conflict of goods. Of modern drama Hegel complains that it is a mere conflict of individuals who do not represent any real concrete good, but merely their own private whims and passions. There is no complete ethical substance within which the play happens. The difference then between Kant and Hegel is that Kant connects sublimity with the dream of an empty non-historical totality which is not given. We have only a segment of the circle. Whereas Hegel connects tragedy with a human historical social totality which is given, within which we see a conflict the resolution and reconciliation of which is the totality itself. We have not just a segment, but the whole circle. Let us put this in terms of freedom. The sublime is an experience of freedom, but of an empty freedom which is the fruitless aspiring demand for some sort of impossible total perceptual comprehension of nature. Hegel humanises the demand of reason. Reason is now demanding a total understanding of a human social situation – but what is unnerving is that, according to him, reason's demand is satisfied. So that the freedom of the tragic characters is only relative to an externally comprehended social whole within which they move. Kant is concerned, though in a very narrow way, with the helplessness of human beings. But Hegel's tragedy does not seem to be tragedy at all, since the spectators are not in the helpless position of the dramatic characters, but comfortably seated at the point of view of the totality. Whatever Aristotle meant by catharsis it was not this. Let me in anticipation say that to my mind the true view of tragedy is a combination of Kantian and Hegelian elements. To use an awkward mixed metaphor, the circle must be humanised but it must not be given. I shall explain, I hope, more clearly what I mean by this.

The short-comings of Kant's aesthetics are the same as the shortcomings of his ethics. Kant is afraid of the particular, he is afraid of history. He shares this fear with Plato, and also in a different way with Tolstoy. Plato's mistrust of art was a mistrust of something which was hopelessly concerned with the senses, with the particular. Plato says (*Republic,* 604E) that 'the fretful part of us presents many and varied occasions for imitation, while the intelligent and temperate disposition, always remaining approximately the same, is neither easy to imitate nor to be understood when imitated'. This might be a commentary on the failure of many novelists. Tolstoy also says, 'Strip the best novels of our time of their details, and what will remain?' Kant's ideal *objets d'art* were flowers and meaningless lines interweaving: simple, clean things not tainted by any historical or human particularity. And this was what he meant by calling them *free.* If we turn from Kant's aesthetics to his ethics the ideal is the same. Kant resented the hold which history has upon ethics. He attempts to make of the act of moral judgement an instantiating of a timeless form of rational activity; and it is this, this empty demand for a total order, which we are required to respect in each other. Kant does not tell us to respect whole particular tangled-up historical individuals, but to respect the universal reason in their breasts. In so far as we are rational and moral we are all the same, and in some mysterious sense transcendent to history. We belong to a harmony of wills which although it is not given here below in some sense exists. Kant's view of ethics contains no place for the idea of tragedy, so it is not surprising that he is unable to give an account of it in his aesthetics. Freedom is our ability to rise out of history and grasp a universal idea of order which we then apply to the sensible world. What we see of Kant's own actual moral views accords with this. We are supposed to live by exceedingly simple and general rules: suppression of history, suspicion of eccentricity. Here we can see more clearly how it is that beauty symbolises the good, is its sensuous counterpart. The aesthetic judgement has the same simple self-contained character as the moral judgement, and it is ideally the response to something which is not complicated or highly individual. Kant's aesthetic tastes mirror his moral preferences. He would like, as it were, by morality to crystallise out of the historical process a simple society living strictly by extremely general rules ('Always tell the truth,' etc.), with no place for the morally complicated or eccentric.

Let me now briefly and dogmatically state what I take to be, in opposition to Kant's view, the true view of the matter. Art and morals are, with certain provisos which I shall mention in a moment, one. Their essence is the same. The essence of both of them is love. Love is the perception of individuals. Love is the extremely difficult realisation that something other than oneself is real. Love, and so art and morals, is the discovery of reality. What stuns us into a realisation of our supersensible destiny is not, as Kant imagined, the formlessness of nature, but rather its unutterable particularity; and most particular and individual of all natural things is the mind of man. That is incidentally why tragedy is the highest art, because it is most intensely concerned with the most individual thing. Here is the true sense of that exhilaration of freedom which attends art and which has its more rarely achieved counterpart in morals. It is the apprehension of something else, something particular, as existing outside us. The enemies of art and of morals, the enemies that is of love, are the same: social convention and neurosis. One may fail to see the individual because of Hegel's totality, because we are ourselves sunk in a social whole which we allow uncritically to determine our reactions, or because we see each other exclusively as so determined. Or we may fail to see the individual because we are completely enclosed in a fantasy world of our own into which we try to draw things from outside, not grasping their reality and independence, making them into dream objects of our own. Fantasy, the enemy of art, is the enemy of true imagination: Love, an exercise of the imagination. This was what Shelley meant when he said that egotism was the great enemy of poetry. This is so whether we are writing it or reading it. The exercise of overcoming one's self, of the expulsion of fantasy and convention, which attends for instance the reading of *King Lear* is indeed exhilarating. It is also, if we perform it properly which we hardly ever do, painful. It is very like *Achtung*. Kant was marvellously near the mark. But he thought of freedom as the aspiration to a universal order consisting of a prefabricated harmony. It was not a tragic freedom. The tragic freedom implied by love is this: that we all have an indefinitely extended capacity to imagine the being of others. Tragic, because there is no prefabricated harmony, and others are, to an extent we never cease discovering, different from ourselves. Nor is there any social totality within which we can come to comprehend differences as placed and reconciled. We have only a segment of the circle. Freedom is exercised in the confrontation by each other, in the context of an infinitely extensible work of imaginative understanding, of two irreducibly dissimilar individuals. Love is the imaginative recognition of, that is respect for, this otherness.

From the point of view of this theory we can offer a pocket history of literature, establishing an order of merit. This pocket history works through the idea of freedom as this idea has been treated at different times. The history of the treatment of freedom falls into five phases. These phases can be taken as roughly chronological, and can also be used independently of chronology.

They are as follows. (1) *Tragic freedom*. This is the concept of freedom which I have related to the concept of love: freedom as an exercise of the imagination in an unreconciled conflict of dissimilar beings. It belongs especially to, was perhaps invented by, the Greeks. The literary form is tragic drama. (2) *Medieval freedom*. Here the individual is seen as a creature within a partly described hierarchy of theological reality. The literary forms are religious tales, allegories, morality plays. (3) *Kantian freedom*. This belongs to the Enlightenment. The individual is seen as a non-historical rational being moving towards complete agreement with other rational beings. The literary forms are rationalistic tales and allegories and novels of ideas. (4) *Hegelian freedom*. This belongs mainly to the nineteenth century. The individual is now thought of as a part of a total historical society and takes his importance from his role in that society. The literary form is the true novel (Balzac, George Eliot, Dickens). (5) *Romantic freedom*. This belongs mainly to the nineteenth and twentieth centuries, though it has its roots earlier. The individual is seen as solitary and as having importance in and by himself. Both Hegelian and Romantic freedom are of course developments of Kantian freedom. Hegel makes the Kingdom of Ends into a historical society; while the Romantic concludes from the unhistorical emptiness of Kant's other rational beings that in fact one may as well assume that one is alone. (This is one line of thought leading to existentialism. *Angst* is the modern version of *Achtung*; we now fear, not the law itself, but its absence.) The literary form is the neurotic modern novel.

This pocket history is of course only a toy, but it does I think suggest some things which are true. It does not work altogether chronologically for obvious reasons, since Shakespeare was not a Greek. We may also note, and this perhaps is one of its perceptions, that this history seems to condemn the novel to fall below the level of tragedy. The novel fails to be tragic because, in almost every case, it succumbs to one of the two great enemies of Love, convention and neurosis. The nineteenth-century novel succumbed to convention, the modern novel succumbs to neurosis. The nineteenth-century novel is better than the twentieth-century novel because convention is the less deadly of the two; and given a society which is in a dramatic phase of its being the mere exploration of that society will take you very far indeed. It will not however take you all the way. We can understand Tolstoy when he says, 'strip the best novels of our time of their details and what will remain?' Yet Tolstoy himself also proves that the novel can be tragic, it can rise to that level. A recent novel which also proves it, though it is well below Tolstoy's achievement, is *Dr Zhivago*. In the case of Tolstoy and Pasternak, it is, I think, not difficult to see that the quality of their greatness should be called compassion, love: the non-violent apprehension of difference. And with what exhilaration do we experience the absense of self in the work of Tolstoy, in the work of Shakespeare. That is the true sublime.

A final word about art and morals. To say that the essence of art is love is not to say, is nothing to do with saying, that art is didactic or educational. It is of course a fact that if art is love then art improves us morally, but this is, as it were, accidental. The level at which that love works which is art is deeper than the level at which we deliberate concerning improvement. And indeed it is of the nature of love to be something deeper than our conscious and more simply social morality, and to be sometimes destructive of it. This is why all dictators, and would-be dictators, from Plato to Khrushchev have mistrusted art. It is a fallacy which has worked confusion in modern philosophy that the only alternative to a sort of Bloomsbury art-for-art's sake theory of art is a sinister theory of didactic art. This is not so. The work of the great artists shows up 'art-for-art's sake' as a flimsy frivolous doctrine. Art is for life's sake, in the sense in which I have tried to indicate, or else it is worthless.

I have gone as far as I can in the direction of identifying art and morals. It remains that they are different for reasons connected with sense and form. I should say at this point that I take my theory to apply to all the arts and not just the literary arts. The notion of a loving respect for a reality other than oneself is as relevant to making a vase as it is to writing a novel, nor does the theory only apply to arts which involve, in the obvious sense, imitation. The highest art is not music, as Schopenhauer, who was not very concerned with particular human beings, imagined, but as I said earlier, tragedy, because its subject-matter is the most important and most individual that we know. We are now in a position to reinterpret the idea of the independence, self-containedness, for itselfness of a work of art which is one of the attractive aspects of Kant's theory and of its Bloomsbury descendants. There are two aspects to this independence. One aspect is this: In the creation of a work of art the artist is going through the exercise of attending to something quite particular other than himself. The intensity of this exercise itself gives to the work of art its special independence. That is, it is an independence and uniqueness which is essentially the same as that conferred upon, or rather discovered in, another human being whom we love. There is however another aspect to the matter. The artist is creating a quasi-sensuous thing. He is more like God than the moral agent. When Catullus writes a poem to Licinius after a night of carousing, he begins by telling Licinius what happened yesterday, which Licinius, however severe his hangover, may be presumed to know. That is, the artist strives to make what he creates self-contained and as far as possible self-explanatory. What makes tragic art so disturbing is that self-contained form is combined with something, the individual being and destiny of human persons, which defies form. A great tragedy leaves us in eternal doubt. It is the form of art where the exercise of love is most like its exercise in morals. But in the end the sublime joy of art is not the same as *Achtung*, respect for the moral law. Art after all is consolation and delight, although really great art gives us a mixed and sombre delight which is akin to our recognition of morality. Perhaps we should give the last austere word to Kant after all. 'It is in this manner . . . that we are to understand those passages of Scripture . . . in which we are commanded to love our neighbour, even our enemy . . . Love, as an affection, cannot be commanded, but beneficence for duty's sake may; even though we are not impelled to it by any inclination – nay, are even repelled by a natural and unconquerable aversion. This is *practical* love and not *pathological* – a love which is seated in the will and not in the propensions of sense – in principles of action and not of tender sympathy' (*Fundamental Principles of the Metaphysic of Morals*). I do not agree that only practical love can be commanded, and I cannot think why Kant, who attributes such majesty to the human soul, should hold that any aversion was strictly 'unconquerable'. Pathological love can be commanded too, and indeed if love is a purification of the imagination, must be commanded. But the fact remains that the love which is not art inhabits the world of practice, the world which is haunted by that incompleteness and lack of form, which is abhorred by art, and where action cannot always be accompanied by radiant understanding, or by significant and consoling emotions. Tragedy in art is the attempt to overcome the defeat which human beings suffer in the practical world. It is, as Kant nearly said, as he ought to have said, the human spirit mourning and yet exulting in its strength. In the practical world there may be only mourning and the final acceptance of the incomplete. Form is the great consolation of love, but it is also its great temptation.

Essay in *Chicago Review*, Autumn 1959.

Existentialists and Mystics

Art represents a sort of paradox in human communication. In order to tell the truth, especially about anything complicated, we need a conceptual apparatus which partly has the effect of concealing what it attempts to reveal. Both Plato and the Zen masters mistrust art for this reason. Art naturally, and often uncritically, purveys all kinds of 'protective symbolism', whose purpose is to clothe our metaphysical nakedness and in general to cheer us up. Such symbolism finds a more systematic expression in theology and philosophy. Art today is in a turmoil partly because we are all unprecedentedly self-conscious about the images and symbols which make our lives supportable. We know too much psychology. Technological changes which used to be slow and invisible are now fast and perceptible. Religion is not what it was. The novel, that great sensitive mirror, or screen, or field of forces, is still one of the most articulate expressions of the dilemmas of its age. I want to use the fairly recent history of the novel as an instrument of diagnosis.

The most obvious difference between nineteenth-century novels and twentieth-century novels is that the nineteenth-century ones are better. Another clear difference lies in a changing attitude to society. The nineteenth-century novelist partly explores society, partly takes it for granted. Even if he attacks it, his thought still moves within it like a fish in water. Even the great romantic individualists in nineteenth-century literature, such as Julien Sorel, are still felt by their authors as part of society. Society is real and the human soul is pretty solid too: the mind, the personality are continuous and self-evident realities. In this confident scene religion and politics make their appearance, but they do not obtrude. Marianne Dashwood says of the faithless Willoughby that though she can never forget him, she will check and regulate his memory 'by religion, by reason, by constant employment'. What a wonderful trio, and how remote they seem now. Religion, reason, and work were indeed the great stays of the nineteenth century and it was typical of that expansive time that the three should associate naturally and equally together, without religion for instance trying to lord it over the other two. Society looked after them all and gave them proper places.

There is a great consoling power in the nineteenth-century novel, a deep relaxing of tension, however alarming or horrible the events which are narrated, because of a sense of the strength of society, and of politics as a natural and ordinary part of the human scene. One might sum this up by saying that there is a profound belief in God, a faith in the absolute significance and *unity* of the moral world. This particular confidence is peculiar to its age. Compare Tolstoy with Shakespeare. How immensely, almost dogmatically, *theological* Tolstoy seems by contrast. Shakespeare investigates society, but does not take it for granted or move within it like a fish in water. He writes marvellously about political power, but he does not take politics for granted and he sees its place in human life as problematic. He conceives of the total breakdown of human order. He writes as one without belief in God. (This is an aspect of his greatness.) He is always on the very edge of things and that we are made happy and not frenzied by what he writes is just the effect of his angelic art.

Nineteenth-century thinkers knew where politics fitted in. There were political problems, but politics itself was not a problem. This, I think, is not what we feel now. An important change has come about, perhaps very recently, in our deep assumptions about politics, which I would express by saying that the Machiavellian era in human history has come to an end. People used to make a clear distinction between the world of morals and the world of politics which because of the advance of modern technology it is no longer appropriate to make. It used to be assumed (in Europe, and of course Europe was the consciousness of the world) that legitimate self-interest abroad and individualism at home would keep the human race going tolerably well, given even a minimum degree of reason and good will. Of course, nineteenth-century thinkers did not conceive of the ferocity and callousness of modern dictatorships. But they also did not conceive of the way in which, even in democratic countries, our situation as political creatures would be altered by nuclear weapons and by television.

In the past it could be assumed that robust individualistic common sense would look after things on the public front, while personal morality, working on quite different principles, would look after the private sector. As far as public affairs were concerned, nations stood up for what they took to be their legitimate interests by diplomacy and if necessary by war. While at home the individual citizen exhibited the vigorous useful egoism of the capitalist era and defended his rights as best he could against the encroachment of governments. Thus the assumptions of European liberal political thinking in the nineteenth century and indeed later. And these assumptions could very roughly work because nations could not do each other any fatal degree of harm and governments could not get very close to individuals. This was true even of governments who were trying to get at individuals, such as the Czarist government. Governments were too remote and clumsy to be very dangerous. As we know, these comforting assumptions can no longer be made. Nuclear weapons have turned the hurly-burly of legitimate self-interest into a sort of Russian roulette; and governments, even fairly nice ones, can dominate and mould the consciousness of their subjects by all kinds of new technical means.

Against this background I want now to suggest, for purposes of diagnosis, a distinction between two types of recent novel. Doubtless many novels may turn out to be both types or neither. But even a ramshackle classification may be instructive and set the imagination in motion. I propose to distinguish between what I shall call 'the existentialist novel' and 'the mystical novel'. (I use the word 'existentialist' in a broad atmospheric sense.) The existentialist novel shows us freedom and virtue as the assertion of will. The mystical novel shows us freedom and virtue as understanding, or obedience to the Good.

The existentialist novel is the natural heir and outcome of Western nineteenth-century thought and is the child of the Romantic movement. It crystallises at a time when confidence in society and in the things which make it so solid, confidence in religion, reason and work, is beginning to wane. Existentialism, or to use an even more general term, voluntarism, philosophy which emphasises and values will-power, is of course an offspring of the thought of Immanuel Kant. It is also a natural mode of being of the capitalist era. It is attractive, and indeed to most of us still natural, because it suggests individualism, self-reliance, private conscience, and what we ordinarily think of as political freedom, in that important sense where freedom means not doing what is right but doing what is desired. The beginnings of capitalism and the age of science both produced and needed free-moving independent people. Protestantism pictures such people as endowed with freedom of conscience, no longer slaves of authority. Only what is freely chosen is genuinely valuable. Political theory too has begun to tell us that we are individuals with rights and should obey the laws out of self-interest and not out of awe. Yet with all this talk of freedom, the individual in the nineteenth century was rarely lonely because he was held secure by God and Reason and Society, powers in which he believed and in which he knew other people believed. So that there was in nineteenth-century thinking a kind of contradiction or paradox: the contradiction which thinkers such as Nietzsche were so anxious to expose. People were supposed to be solitary and self-reliant but really they were not. Industrial conditions made the poorer people into sheep. Social betterment inspired the bolder spirits. Reason held out vistas of improvement, and science preached optimism. God consoled everybody. Politics took its important but on the whole limited place. Politics looked after rational self-interest while Religion and Society looked after private conscience. In England the philosophy of the age was utilitarianism, a modest, humane, and unmetaphysical doctrine.

Change the scene to the twentieth century and much of what Nietzsche wished to happen has happened, though not quite as he intended. God, Reason, Society, Improvement and the Soul are being quietly wheeled off. The individual is more genuinely frightened and alone. The nineteenth-century man used his will to choose and get things which were felt to be valuable independently of his will, for instance because they were approved of by religion or society. Twentieth-century man, outside the Marxist countries, finds his religious and metaphysical background so impoverished that he is in some danger of being left with nothing of inherent value except will-power itself. It is true that now increasingly technological *divertissements* are available to make sheep once more of those who have emerged from the industrial cave. But these are superficial remedies. The deep confidence has gone. The voluntarist or existentialist novel is the document of this anxious modern consciousness.

We know this novel and its hero well. The story of the lonely brave man, defiant without optimism, proud without pretension, always an exposer of shams, whose mode of being is a deep criticism of society. He is an adventurer. He is godless. He does not suffer from guilt. He thinks of himself as free. He may have faults, he may be self-assertive or even violent, but he has sincerity and courage, and for this we forgive him. (D. H. Lawrence, E. Hemingway, A. Camus, J.-P. Sartre, K. Amis . . .) Kant and Protestantism pictured man as divided between his fallen nature and a separate spiritual world. His good will was the tension which connected him to this higher realm. The indubitable claims of duty were the proof that this other world was real. For the modern existentialist descendant of this line of thought, this spiritual elsewhere has ceased to exist. Duty speaks less sternly and a good deal less clearly. Yet man is divided still. His will, that adventurous instrument which makes him so different from sticks and stones and billiard balls and greengrocers and bank managers, his will is separate from the rest of his being and uncontaminated. He *might* do anything.

The mystical novel is both newer and more old-fashioned. What is characteristic of this novel is that it keeps in being, by one means or another, the conception of God. Man is still pictured as being divided, but divided in a new way, between a fallen nature and a spiritual world. I call these novels mystical, not of course as a term of praise, but because they are attempts to express a religious consciousness without the traditional trappings of religion. (Existentialists are not worshippers, mystics are.) No (conventional) God, no Church, no social support or protective institutions. No simple or secure connection with morality. Mystics too have dispensed with these things and have inhabited a spiritual world unconsoled by familiar religious imagery. Mystics who are artists invent their own imagery, which we often find hard to understand. Other mystics are speechless. What I call the mystical novelist may or may not be a good man or a good novelist, but what he is attempting to do, perhaps unsuccessfully, is to invent new religious imagery (or twist old religious imagery) in an empty situation.

Both kinds of novelist have their characteristic defects and temptations. The existentialist may become so obsessed with the powerful self-assertive figure of his hero (or anti-hero) that he presents a mediocre person as being important and valuable simply because he is contemptuous of society and gets his own way. This is a fairly familiar contemporary failure. The mystic on the other hand may be lacking in the existentialist virtues of sincerity and courage, and may merely reintroduce the old fatherly figure of God behind a façade of fantastical imagery or sentimental adventures in cosy masochism. This is familiar too. It is easy to *say* there is no God. It is not so easy to believe it and to draw the consequences. There is, of course, no occasion to conclude that one or other type of novel is *per se* superior. (G. Greene, P. White, S. Bellow, M. Spark, W. Golding . . .) Unhappily for my classification, most mystical novelists have existentialist characteristics, so prevalent is this way of looking at the world.

I have in this exposition put the existentialist first and the mystic second, and I think this order is right both logically and chronologically. The existentialist response is the first and immediate expression of a consciousness without God. It is the heir of nineteenth-century Luciferian pride in the individual and in the achievements of science. It is, or tries to be, cheerfully godless. Even its famous gloom is a mode of satisfaction. From this point of view, man is God. The mystical attitude is a second response, a second thought about the matter, and reflects the uneasy suspicion that perhaps after all man is not God. One might connect this with our gradually changing consciousness of science. Science today is more likely to make us anxious than to make us proud, not only because we are now able to blow up our planet, but because, oddly enough, space travel does not make us feel like gods. It makes us feel rather parochial and frightened.

As we readily recognise and sympathise with the hero of will-power, so we can also recognise and sympathise with the mystical hero. He too is a man in tension, but here the tension is not between will and nature, but between nature and good. This is the man who has given up traditional religion but is still haunted by a sense of the reality and unity of some sort of spiritual world. The imagery here is an imagery of height and distance. Much is required of us and we are far from our goal. The virtue of the mystical hero is humility. Whereas the existentialist hero is an anxious man trying to impose or assert or find himself, the mystical hero is an anxious man trying to discipline or purge or diminish himself. The chief temptation of the former is egoism, of the latter masochism. The philosophical background or protective symbolism is fairly clear in each case. The first hero is the new version of the romantic man, the man of power, abandoned by God, struggling on bravely, sincerely and alone. This image consoles by showing us man as strong, self-reliant and uncrushable. The second hero is the new version of the man of faith, believing in goodness without religious guarantees, guilty, muddled, yet not without hope. This image consoles by showing us man as frail, godless, and yet possessed of genuine intuitions of an authoritative good.

Here, or perhaps earlier, someone might want to object and to point out that this attempted diagnosis of the modern scene is already well out of date. When even Michel Butor* seems remote what are we to say of these two worthies? The existentialist hero, with his choices and his will-power, seems almost Victorian, and as for the mystical hero, he must be at least forty-five by now, and represents a last shadowy hangover from the vanishing era of religious belief. It is an alarming characteristic of our present world that things are *supposed* to go out of date rapidly. Built-in obsolescence is not only accepted but welcomed. 'Oh, that was last year's music', says Paul McCartney of *Sergeant Pepper*. All the arts seem to reflect this tendency. The novel is followed by the anti-novel, art by anti-art. The monumental finished enduring *thingy* character of Western art is no longer taken for granted. The old idea of the artist as the creator of complete things designed to be contemplated is brought into question. Traditional art is under attack because it suddenly seems academic and confined, comfortable, insufficiently sensitive to the present horrors of the world, insufficiently wild and extreme in its reactions. A similar kind of revolutionary exasperation in the 1920s produced, technologically

* [French novelist and critic (1926–), exponent of the *nouveau roman*.]

[227]

before its time, surrealism. Both then and now the visual arts probably represent the most obvious, and in a way most symbolic, form of the movement. Pictures do not live in frames, sculptures ramble about the room. This is indeed a symbol of an important new attitude in art where the aim is no longer to make a reflective statement but rather to invite immediate involvement and participation. Art (good art) used to silence and annihilate the self. We contemplated in quietness something whose authority made us unaware of ourselves. We were 'all eyes'. Now the aim of art is often the opposite. Shall I leave my seat in the theatre and rush up on to the stage? What could be more self-conscious-making than such a thought? From this new viewpoint, how far away the old-fashioned 'committed writer' already seems to be, with his responsible completed statements about man and society. One might indeed say that the modern artist is much closer to the spirit of Lenin, in that his aim is *really* not to explain the world but to change it.

This art or anti-art which gives expression to a revolt against 'the establishment' in all its forms is often alarming. One may well fear and censure an indiscriminate attack upon 'the past', which is often in effect an attack upon the institutions of democracy and the whole tradition of rational thought. On the other hand, the modern movement is also a warning to tyrants: the Russians, when they invaded Czechoslovakia, had got the message. This new scene, so far as I have been able to observe it in England, is singularly unChristian. Christianity is not abandoned so much as simply unknown. A generation has been growing up outside it. What does this mean in terms of what I have called protective symbolism, the instinctive philosophical background of the ordinary person, the background upon which the artist in the past relied for the possibility of communication? The two types of novel of which I was speaking earlier are both in fairly obvious ways continuations of a nineteenth-century tradition, with perhaps new assumptions about society, but with intelligibly traditional assumptions about virtue. Is some very much deeper change now coming about; and what is the place of literature in this scene? There is some profound and rather unnerving question here which haunts one and which is not too easy to formulate. Has literature always depended on a sort of implicit moral philosophy which has been unobtrusively supported by religious belief and which is now with frightful rapidity disappearing? And if this is so, what is the future of literature and indeed of art as we have known it?

It may be said that such fears are exaggerated. Since the beginning (Homer) of our literature there has never been a really deep break. And there is no reason to imagine that there will be a break unless and until our world becomes quite unrecognisably different and we are all born in test tubes and do not have fathers and mothers. We today have no great or essential difficulty in understanding plays written by Greeks in the fifth century BC. We make, in many respects though not in all, the same kinds of moral judgements as the Greeks did, and we recognise good or decent people in times and literatures remote from our own. Patroclus, Antigone, Cordelia, Mr Knightley, Alyosha. Patroclus's invariable kindness. Cordelia's truthfulness. Alyosha telling his father not to be afraid of hell. It is just as important that Patroclus should be kind to the captive women as that Emma should be kind to Miss Bates, and we feel this importance in an immediate and natural way in both cases in spite of the fact that nearly three thousand years divide the writers. And this, when one reflects on it, is a remarkable testimony to the existence of a single durable human nature. Can we then be confident that in spite of modern technology and the fading of religion and in spite of everything, things will go on more or less as before? Or should we, even if only to arm ourselves, admit the possibility that in the long run the virtues as we have known them will turn out to be something local, supported by temporary phenomena such as organised religions and hierarchical societies? Wittgenstein said that talking about ethics was running fruitlessly against the boundaries of language; and it may be that the further implication of this is that there is something fundamentally incoherent and unimaginable in the whole idea of goodness. The mystical novelists, even when they rejected the idea of God, retained images of lofty structures, an unachieved area of real good, making positive spiritual demands upon the human soul. May it not be that this is the last stage of a very long illusion?

In fact, in spite of the great and dreadfully fast changes which are taking place, I do not think that either life or literature is going to be left without its background of moral philosophy. Moral philosophy used to be fed and supported by thought about religion. Now, perhaps I should say if we are lucky, it may be fed and supported by thought about politics. Any Marxist would say that this is a laborious discovery of the obvious. But I think that what is happening is in some ways unexpected. Marx said prophetically, and indeed this still has something of the status of a prophecy, that now for the first time in history the human race had the technical means to cure many of its age-old ills such as hunger and homelessness and poverty. We today are in an even more remarkable situation. We are not only coming into possession of the means to cure the ills, we are in the position of not being able to avoid quite literally seeing them. On television we see the sufferings of the world, we see how other lives go to waste. As our latterday prophets keep telling us, technology is making the world into a village, bringing us closer to each other and generating immense new powers: while at the same time, we see that we are still even now patently unable to set things to rights, unable to stop famine in India or war in Africa. I think this is fundamentally the situation which drives young people into a kind of frenzy.

As a result of these pressures a change is, in my view, coming about in the *place* of politics in human life. And I do not just mean that nuclear weapons make the old limited kind of political thinking inexpedient. Of course morality invades politics when the pursuit of national self-interest can have such indiscriminately widespread effects. We no longer have to build, or only to build, barriers of force against what we fear, we have, as quickly as possible, to build moral barriers. But I think the change is something even deeper, which is rather like this. Moral thinking is, I suggest, in process of executing a kind of somersault. The existentialist thought that what was valuable was freedom, thought of as will-power. The mystic thought that what was valuable was spirit, magnetic and remote. Now we are (perhaps) being driven to think in a much more immediate and, in the philosophical sense, *naturalistic* way that what is valuable is food and shelter and work and peace. Of course the human race has always known in practice, and has theoretically known for centuries, that these were important human goods, so important that they were often spoken of as *rights*. But because of the Machiavellian separation of ends and means, morals and politics, in our thinking about the world, and also because of an evident lack of technological power to alter situations, these fundamental goods were never able to take a central place and to let other values radiate from them. When I was young I thought, as all young people do, that freedom was the thing. Later on I felt that virtue was the thing. Now I begin to suspect that freedom and virtue are concepts which ought to be pinned into place by some more fundamental thinking about a proper quality of human life, which *begins* at the food and shelter level. This philosophical viewpoint is, of course, not new. It is a form of utilitarianism: less optimistic, more desperate, but still recognisable as a relation of the great doctrine of Bentham and John Stuart Mill. And many of the vociferous young people of today are really, though they may not realise it and would consider it too dull a label, utilitarians.

The Marxist critic who has been listening to this argument may say at this point: you mean *Marxists*. When Jean-Paul Sartre stopped being an existentialist and became a utilitarian, it seemed that the only practical thing to do about this was to become a Marxist. Of course Marxism contains a strong admixture of utilitarian doctrine: concern for quite ordinary kinds of happiness. This is one important reason for its appeal. But I do not think that the philosophy in question is a form of Marxism. It is a militant liberalism, it is a doctrine of human rights, a naturalistic unhistoricist untheoretical theory which is closer to Mill (or even to Zen) than to Marx even when it calls to revolution. This untheory says that human good is something which lies in the foreground of life and not in its background. It is not a flickering of will-power, nor a citadel of esoteric virtue, but a good quality of human life: and we know, naturally, where to *begin* thinking about this.

Philosophers since G. E. Moore have been critical of utilitarianism because it was *naturalistic*: that is, it rested value upon what people actually needed and wanted rather than on what they ought to need and want; and also because it seemed to give no place to the idea of virtue. But consideration of what human beings actually need and want is not a bad place to begin a consideration of their duties, nor is that a bad method of consideration, even though to say a man needs shelter is not quite like saying that he needs

Shakespeare. Marx tried to mend a fissure in human nature upon which Kant insisted. Perhaps there are more commonsensical ways of mending it. Because human beings are what they are and have the needs which they do have, freedom, democracy, truth and love are important. And this is, as it were, to see the thing the other way round, with many of the traditional factors but in a different perspective. Of course any extended picture of human nature involves a movement from the obvious to the less obvious. Perhaps this movement can best be argued step by step, without insisting upon the old baffling drama of the gap. These are ancient problems. But there is, especially now in this age of vanishing backgrounds, an obvious good sense in starting in the foreground and trying to see everything from there, and this good sense is what keeps utilitarianism alive as a popular philosophy. It did work in the nineteenth century and it still, in a new way, has work to do. Whether it can be made impeccable as a strict philosophical doctrine I do not know; but neither do I know of any other ethical theory which is thus faultless. Perhaps Wittgenstein is right.

We are, apparently, entering an untheological time. Even the theology of Marxism has lost some of its charm. The old assumptions appear in different guises and in attenuated forms and begin to seem less satisfactory. But we are not left entirely without moral symbolism or without an intelligible relation with our past. We are still part of the civilisation of Homer and Shakespeare. The cult of the 'immediate' is (I think) an instinctive product of the doctrine of the foreground, but I would regard it as a local symptom of a change rather than as being itself the change. Because human nature is what it is, art will probably look after itself and literature will look after itself. The foreground contains, after all, everything that the writer needs to continue his trade, and also provides him with enduring and to some extent traditional motives for doing so. The writer has always been important, and is now *essential*, as a truth-teller and as a defender of words. (There is only one culture and words are its basis.) He is threatened today in both these roles. But I do not think that the will to fight is likely to be weakened by the vanishing of the theologies: perhaps on the contrary. It may be that in the end the novelist will prove to be the saviour of the human race. The story is almost as fundamental a human concept as the thing, and however much novelists may try, for reasons of fashion or of art, to stop telling stories, the story is always likely to break out again in a new form. Everything else may be done by pictures or computers, but stories about human beings are best told in words, and that 'best' is a matter of a response to a deep and ordinary human need.

And if stories are told, virtue will be portrayed, even if the old philosophies have gone away. It may be that the portrayal of virtue is easier against a background of strong society and firm ideology. When we recognise Mr Knightley as an English gentleman and Levin as a conscientious Russian landowner, the role makes the merit more explicit. But great art has also taught us that virtue can be portrayed independently of precise social background through some more general appeal to our knowledge of man and his frailty. Virtue standing out gratuitously, aimlessly, unplaced by religion and society, surprising us as it so often does in real life: the gentleness of Patroclus in the middle of a ruthless war, the truthfulness of Cordelia in a flattering court. The utter chanciness of human life and the fact of death make virtue always, really, perhaps, when the illusory backgrounds are removed, something gratuitous, something which belongs in the absolute foreground of our existence, along with self-evident goods such as eating enough and not being afraid. And it is in this way, I think, that we see it in the greatest literature. Goodness is needful, one has to be good, for nothing, for immediate and obvious reasons, because somebody is hungry or somebody is crying.

It might be argued that the general demythologising of the modern scene puts literature in a new and improved position because it forces it to be more truthful. Just as it might be (and indeed is) argued that the demythologising of religion is a great moral tonic because it asks the ordinary believer to do what only the exceptional one could do in the past, that is live a religious life without illusions. However the optimism would be rash in both cases and for the same reason. Human beings need fantasies. The novelist is potentially *the greatest truth-teller of them all*, but he is also an expert fantasy-monger. This is too cosy an art form not to be often degraded in the interests of the self-indulgent fantasy of both the writer and the reader. As far as we can see into the human future there will doubtless be bad novels, cheering people up and probably not doing them too much harm. It is an index of the fears that sometimes haunt one that even an endless vista of bad novels seems so happy and so humane a prospect. The old subjects are, so far, still there, made even more significant and more poignant by the lack of the consolations of metaphysics: the ordinary familiar world of love and egoism and human need. Perhaps the best that can be said, and that is indeed a great deal, is that the writer can and will in the end resemble the Buddhist master who said that when he was young he thought that mountains were mountains and rivers were rivers, then after many years of study and devotion he decided that mountains were not mountains and rivers were not rivers, and then at last when he was very old and wise he came to understand that mountains are mountains and rivers are rivers.

Essay in *Essays & Poems Presented to Lord David Cecil*, ed. W. W. Robson, 1970.

Salvation by Words

We are told that art is now under attack. Of course it has often been under attack. Tyrants always fear art because tyrants want to mystify while art tends to clarify. The good artist is a vehicle of truth, he formulates ideas which would otherwise remain vague and focuses attention upon facts which can then no longer be ignored. The tyrant persecutes the artist by silencing him or by attempting to degrade or buy him. This has always been so. However it may be admitted that in this age art seems to have rather more enemies than usual. The tyrants of course are still here and we know what they do. But now science, philosophy, and forces arising within art itself threaten this traditional activity: an activity which we are so used to, which we take so much for granted, and which is perhaps more frail and unstable than it might seem.

The Romantics felt instinctively that science was an enemy of art, and of course in certain simple and obvious ways they were right. A technological society, quite automatically and without any malign intent, upsets the artist by taking over and transforming the idea of craft, and by endlessly reproducing objects which are not art objects but sometimes resemble them. Technology steals the artist's public by inventing sub-artistic forms of entertainment and by offering a great counterinterest and a rival way of grasping the world.

Of course science affects the artist not only in his public relations but in his soul. What is called 'anti-art' is not a novel phenomenon. The latest art has often seemed like an anti-art and been so regarded by its friends as well as its enemies. At regular intervals in history the artist has tended to be a revolutionary or at least an instrument of change in so far as he has tended to be a sensitive and independent thinker with a job that is a little outside established society. In this century we have already seen the completed history of a movement, surrealism, which fought art by art on behalf of revolution. The surrealist movement, of course, ended by dividing into two, some of its members returning into art via anti-art and others abandoning art for politics. The motives of surrealism are not unlike the motives of our contemporary anti-art revolutionaries. The artist has a particular way of making his own a very general revulsion against a materialistic reproductive industrial society. He is particularly well equipped to attack and caricature this society, and he may elect to do so by deliberately deforming his own art and turning it into a mockery and a provocation.

*

A motive for change in art has always been the artist's own sense of truth. Artists constantly react against their tradition, finding it pompous and starchy and out of touch. Today's reaction seems only more extreme than before, in that many young artists, especially in the visual arts, seem to want to reject the whole of the European tradition and to challenge the very idea of the work of art, that well-known and well-loved idol of so many past genera-tions. The work of art and the artist as its creator have lost some of their old grandeur and dignity. Writers and painters are not so much revered now as they were, say, in the nineteenth century. And there is a deep crisis of confidence in the very idea of art as the making of completed statements. I think that technological enter-tainment sub-art affects the artist here by showing him how what is utterly ephemeral can have an immensely attractive technical perfection and can be, because it is so unpretentious, curiously honest. European art, the great art upon which we were once brought up, is certainly very grand stuff by comparison, claiming serious attention, professing to purvey universal truths, offering big complicated completed statements about the world. Many people today, especially young people, instinctively mistrust this claim to completeness. They want to challenge the completeness of the art object itself as a way of challenging the authority of the statement it appears to be making. Traditional art is seen as far too grand, and is *then* seen as a half-truth.

There is also, and has been, only now it is stronger than ever, a decent and comprehensible kind of utilitarian reaction against art. Philistines, of course, we have always with us, but I am thinking here not of Mr Gradgrind but of sincere people who feel that in a world reeling with misery it is frivolous to enjoy art, which is after all a kind of play. There is a familiar puritanical and Protestant ancestry to this thinking, which expresses itself in the philosophy of Jeremy Bentham, who refused to allow poetry a dignity which was higher than that of pushpin. Today technology further disturbs the artist and his client not only by actually threatening the world, but by making its wretchedness apparent upon the television screen. The desire to attack art, to neglect it or to harness it or to transform it out of recognition, is a natural and in a way respectable reaction to this display. Western moral philosophy, which has of late been moving quietly from existentialist behaviourism to sociological utilitarianism, has in fact thereby exhibited in philosophical form two of the possible hostile reactions to art. Existentialism, the last fling of liberal Romanticism in philosophy, by putting a value upon sincerity and immediacy, suggests a criticism of old solemn art as being in *mauvaise foi*. The 'happening' is a proper child of existentialism. In fact Romanticism has always held the seeds of anti-art in its cult of sincere feeling. Rousseau: the beginning of the end. While sociological utilitarianism, with a bent that is scientific rather than humanist, represents a certain deliberate and even high-minded philistinism.

*

I cannot here discuss all these multifarious foes of art. I want simply to do two things: to diagnose what I think is a fundamental malaise which afflicts us (in the West) about art; and to make a resultant recommendation. To help the diagnosis I want to draw in two great and notorious, and in many ways sympathetic, critics of art: Plato and Freud. Freud says that 'before the problem of the creative artist psychoanalysis must lay down its arms'. However, Freud does not lay down his arms. He tells us that art is essentially the fantasy life of the artist stimulating the fantasy life of the artist's client. The work of art lies in between, acting as a sort of concealed bribe. The formal and 'innocent' aesthetic charm of the art work leads the client, as it has already led the artist, on towards an end pleasure of quite another sort, a sexual satisfaction in a licensed play of fantasy, which provides the work with a spurious air of completion. Art

[237]

then consoles, but does so by secret and unacknowledged means; the unity and the dignity of the work of art are in a sense sham.

Freud is actually too loyal and traditional a European to make his attack upon art in any savage style. He interlards his criticism with compliments, though the criticism is none the less devastating. No such polite respect for a large established institution hampered Plato when he decided to exclude artists from his ideal state. Plato outlaws the artist for reasons which are remarkably Freudian. He regards art as the base addressing the base, created by and for and about the lowest part of the soul. Art studies the unstable and the various, what we might call the neurotic, which it can easily and amusingly depict. Goodness, which is steady and unified and 'uninteresting', art cannot understand or represent. (Plato is thinking mainly of writers of course.) Art moreover makes us 'relax our guard' (Plato's phrase) and indulge vicariously in adventures of emotion which we would not tolerate as part of our 'real life' activity. Art is a false consolation, celebrating the mediocre and the mean and excusing self-indulgent emotion.

This powerful attack, which occurs at the end of the *Republic*, may be effectively read in conjunction with a remarkable passage in the *Phaedrus* (275), in which Plato criticises writing. I mean the use of a visual symbolism to express words, then of course still a comparative novelty. Plato says that written statements can only properly be reminders of genuinely understood communications which occur *viva voce*, face to face. A written statement, like a picture, is only itself and cannot answer back. It is portable and can be moved from one place to another and so is able to be degraded and misunderstood by ill-wishing and mediocre minds. The written word should always be thought of as ancillary to real direct communication, by which it must be constantly refreshed, and not as an end in itself. Literature then, verbal art, would of course be open to this criticism too if it were written down. Thus Plato anticipates not only Freud (whose therapy depends, incidentally, upon the spoken, not written, word), but existentialist aesthetics and Marshall McLuhan as well.

*

I think these two great critics have suggested an unease about art which perhaps especially afflicts us now. Of course it can be said at once that what Freud and Plato have to say applies with a prime obviousness to bad art: the lowest part of the soul amusing the lowest part of the soul. But what is interesting about it is that it has its application to good art too. Many people, including many artists, feel now that art affects a false dignity and purveys a false consolation, and that the work of art is a false unity. Much visual art exhibits a consciousness of this false unity by an attack upon unity as such. Pictures fall out of frames, objects are made too large or too senselessly complex to be grasped by a unified vision. The printed word too is thought of as somehow essentially insincere, and hence a preference for immediate experience, participation, happenings, which cannot lie.

It may in fact be, in this age of frightful self-consciousness, wise and healthy to admit that art is a sort of conjuring trick and that the work of art is a sort of pseudo-object. Of course works of art are not, though they are linked more or less closely to, 'material objects'. The work of art, however, appears as a *sui generis* 'object' in so far as it appears as a quasi-sensuous self-contained unity. W. H. Auden describes a poem as a 'contraption', but adds that there is a guy inside it. This felicitous image suggests something a good deal less formally complete than many advocates of art would like to think that works of art manage to be. Of course the arts differ among themselves, and certain arts, perhaps music, can attain a degree of formal completeness that is impossible in literature; and I mainly have literature in mind here, though what I say does, I believe, apply *mutatis mutandis* to all the arts. Of course no poem, no play, and *a fortiori* no novel can be as clarified and as non-accidental and complete as it seems, and as it aims at seeming, to us when we are absorbed in it, or when we vaguely brood upon it when not studying it. How small in compass a Shakespeare play often looks when we return to the text from a more vague enjoyment of our general sense of it as an object.

*

There is certainly a conjuring trick. But our discovery of the trick need not discredit the trickster. We in the West have always been perhaps too fascinated by the idea of the work of art, that grand safe authoritative benign resplendent transcendent entity. And now we express uneasiness about art by means of criticism of the art object, and feel that if the object is attacked art is attacked. I myself very much believe in the importance of the work of art as an attempted formal unity and completed statement. There is no substitute for the discipline of this sort of attempt to tell truth succinctly and clearly. This particular effort is uniquely world-revealing. I do not think that the traditional production of works of art is ending or should end. But art is not discredited if we realise that it is based on and partly consists of ordinary human jumble, incoherence, accident, sex. (Sex, though it produces great thought forms, is fundamentally jumble: not even roulette so much as mish-mash.) Great art, especially literature, but the other arts too, carries a built-in self-critical recognition of its incompleteness. It accepts and celebrates jumble, and the bafflement of the mind by the world. The incomplete pseudo-object, the work of art, is a lucid commentary upon itself.

Andrey Sinyavsky has defined art as telling truth by the absurd and leading up to simplicity. These words are important. Art makes a place for precision in the midst of chaos by inventing a language in which contingent details can be lovingly noticed and obvious truths stated with simple authority. The incompleteness of the pseudo-object need not affect the lucidity of the mode of talk which it bodies forth; in fact, the two aspects of the matter ideally support each other. In this sense all good art is its own intimate critic, celebrating in simple and truthful utterance the broken nature of its formal complexity. All good tragedy is anti-tragedy. *King Lear.* Lear wants to enact the false tragic, the solemn, the complete. Shakespeare forces him to enact the true tragic, the absurd, the incomplete.

*

Great art, then, by introducing a chaste self-critical precision into its mimesis, its representation of the world by would-be complete, yet incomplete, forms, inspires truthfulness and humility. (So Plato, though partly right, was partly wrong.) Great art is able to display and discuss the central area of our reality, our actual consciousness, in a more exact way than science or even philosophy can. I want to speak finally about one of the main tools of this exploration: words. If we wish to exhibit to ourselves the unpretentious, un-bogus, piercing lucidity of which art is capable we may think of certain pictures, certain music. (Bach, Piero.) Or we may think of a use of words by Homer or Shakespeare. But there is no doubt which art is the most practically important for our survival and our salvation, and that is literature. Words constitute the ultimate texture and stuff of our moral being, since they are the most refined and delicate and detailed, as well as the most universally used and understood, of the symbolisms whereby we express ourselves into existence. We became spiritual animals when we became verbal animals. The *fundamental* distinctions can only be made in words. Words are spirit. Of course eloquence is no guarantee of goodness, and an inarticulate man can be virtuous. But the quality of a civilisation depends upon its ability to discern and reveal truth, and this depends upon the scope and purity of its language.

Any dictator attempts to degrade the language because this is a way to mystify. And many of the quasi-automatic operations of capitalist industrial society tend also toward mystification and the blunting of verbal precision. Some misguided people even attack the printed word and hence words themselves in the name of sincerity and genuine feeling. But we have to realise that, in our world, the quality of words is the quality of printed words. Of course Plato is right that words are best understood, are most precise and profound, when used in particular face to face contexts. The printed word has inevitable ambiguities. And doubtless there are some things, such as Zen Buddhism or the philosophy of Wittgenstein, which can only be communicated at all by *viva voce* discussion. But since we do not live in a city-state we have to use print, and though this is a danger it can also be an inspiration and a challenge.

We must not be tempted to leave lucidity and exactness to the scientist. Whenever we write we ought to write as well as we can, in order to meet the dangers of which Plato spoke, and in order to defend our language and render subtle and clear that stuff which is the deepest texture of our spirit. When George Jackson deplored time wasted upon Latin that could have been used for maths or science he was wrong from his own point of view. Of course the exactness of science has an importance which is not likely to be underestimated. But the study of a language or a literature or any study that will increase and refine our ability to *be* through words is part of a battle for civilisation and justice and freedom, for clarity and truth, against vile fake-scientific jargon and spiritless slipshod journalese and tyrannical mystification. There are not two cultures. There is only one culture and words are its basis; words are where we live as human beings and as moral and spiritual agents.

*

As I said earlier, I do not think that the art object as would-be complete statement either will or should perish. It is important to try to make such statements because they challenge our ability to discern and express truth and often constitute the only form in which certain truths can be expressed at all. And I think that the work of art, as a pseudo-thing, is profoundly suited to the nature of beings who inhabit a thingy planet and are themselves pseudo-things. I believe that, as in the past, art will take over anti-art and make it its own. This is an anti-metaphysical age in our part of the world. The rejection of art is in many ways an aspect of a general rejection of metaphysics, in philosophy, in religion, and in the popular beliefs which are compounded out of these. This stripping down of the scene certainly produces shock. But it has also perhaps made possible a kind of healing agnosticism, a natural mysticism, a new humility which favours clarity and plain speech and the expression of obvious and unpretentious truths: truths that are often unconnected and unhallowed by system, reflections of the somewhat random creatures that we are. Both art and philosophy constantly re-create themselves by returning to the deep and obvious and ordinary things of human existence and making there a place for cool speech and wit and serious unforced reflection. Long may this central area remain to us, the homeland of freedom and of art. The great artist, like the great saint, calms us by a kind of unassuming simple lucidity, he speaks with the voice that we hear in Homer and in Shakespeare and in the Gospels. This is the human language of which, whenever we write, as artists or as word-users of any other kind, we should endeavour to be worthy.

Part of the Blashfield Address delivered to the American Academy of Arts and Letters at its annual ceremonial, 17 May 1972.

Art is the Imitation of Nature

The quotation with which I am starting is, 'Art imitates nature' or 'Art is the imitation of nature'. Now, the philosopher Wittgenstein, under whose shadow I grew up as a student, sometimes used to start his lectures by saying, 'I feel inclined to say . . .' something or other, and then he would offer some commonplace remark like, 'my thoughts take place in my head', or 'red is inside that object' or something like this which might seem a natural idea but when looked at turned out to be very odd. Well, I feel inclined to say that art imitates nature – art is the imitation of nature. The paradigm here would, presumably, be painting and I think that painting often serves as a sort of explanatory metaphor for the other arts. We look at something which interests us and we reproduce it in another medium; and the image of the painter who sits there at his easel and looks at the landscape is a profound idea, which we carry with us as we think of different forms of art. We transform what we look at; we don't try to produce another landscape – we know perfectly well that we are producing something quite different. On the other hand, the notion of imitation is very deep in this situation. The Greeks spent a hundred years perhaps of the best time in the history of sculpture, as we know it, in trying to learn how to imitate the human form. This is an interesting case of a pure effort of imitation stretching from very, as one might say, primitive, or naïve, often marvellously beautiful imitations towards more naturalistic ones, gradually becoming extremely naturalistic, by which time their art was in decline; and there's some interesting moral there.

But what is imitation exactly and what counts as imitation? It is easy to become confused or to confuse ourselves, rather, as we reflect on this question. Music – and it has been said that all arts aspire to the condition of music (I am not sure whether they do or

[243]

not) – music doesn't seem to imitate nature except in some rather trivial sense. And, one might say, is abstract painting about nature? I am inclined to say, 'Yes it is,' but what does that mean? Does a map look like a countryside, if we move a little bit away from art but remaining within a convention which is certainly related to art? Well, obviously, a map does not resemble a countryside. If one takes fairly ordinary and familiar cases it is clear that 'x' looks like 'y' is subject to all sorts of conventions and historical changes. Do we want to use, here, the word 'realism' to describe the best, whatever that may be, sort of imitation? To take a telling example, we might be inclined to say that the most realistic or truly imitative painting we can imagine is that of the Dutch interior school – and if such a painter were to go in for a *trompe l'oeil* effect, then one might say the imitation would be very complete indeed. And yet, we may ask, what do we actually see? We have all been disturbed by the impressionist painters and we may now be inclined to say something clever like, 'The impressionist paints what he sees, the Dutchman paints what he thinks'; and if we turn to literature, who is the most realistic novelist? Jane Austen, Flaubert, Dickens, Virginia Woolf, Robbe-Grillet? Does not a stream-of-consciousness novel, like an impressionist picture, imitate something absolutely fundamental? Yet, what is fundamental? We don't always live, or have experience at that sort of fundamental level. A novel by Robbe-Grillet often imitates nature, especially our physical surroundings, very exactly indeed. Moreover, we have left quite out of account here questions of aesthetic merit. How do they affect the issue? How is imitation connected with merit, or is it not connected? Now, I want to put into the picture something else which I feel inclined to say, something which, in fact, has already been said by Keats, that Art is Truth, art is some kind of truth, art is true. Keats said that, 'what the imagination seizes as beauty must be truth whether it existed before or not'. What makes art important, what makes art good? If we think of imitation as the only test either of merit in art or of art itself – the identity of art, as distinct from something else – we would be in difficulties, not only because it's not clear what imitation is, but also because some art imitations seem better and worse than others in rather complicated ways. What counts as aesthetic merit in relation to imitation? We want to say something like, 'a picture tells us something, a novel clearly tells us something. We learn from art, we learn to look at the world, art is a kind of statement, it has a strong cognitive aspect.' Yet, can we introduce such a strong concept as truth into the picture here? Is good art true and bad art false? I am inclined to say yes to this rather obscure idea. Let us consider literature here. It is instructive in art to look at the critical vocabulary – what sort of things the critics say, most naturally, about the form of art. Some criticism of literature is purely formal, but very much more of it is, somehow, moral, and, in particular the critic may accuse the writer of some kind of lying or misrepresentation. Words used about novels such as 'sentimental', 'pretentious', 'vulgar', 'trivial', 'banal' and so on, impute a kind of falsehood. Let us look for a moment at some philosophical background to the idea of imitation or 'mimesis', to give it the original name. Plato, of course, regarded art as fundamentally mimetic, or imitative. He was notoriously hostile to art, one might say, roughly, for three sorts of reasons. First, he was afraid, as any absolute ruler might be, of the power of art as persuasion or propaganda, art as irrational emotion, art as attractive lies, or, one might add, art as the telling of inconvenient or subversive truth. Secondly, he regarded art as a prime distraction from the study of nature. Art would inhibit reflection and liberating thought. Goodness and knowledge, for Plato, both lay in the same direction. At the top of the ladder of dialectic were the Ideas or Forms – conceptions of great universality and sources of moral enlightenment – but the products of art were at the bottom of the ladder, since they were unreflective imitations of trivial, particular things, mere reproductions of the world of the senses, upon which we *ought* to be reflecting rationally; and you will remember, in the last book of *The Republic*, the discussion Plato offers of the man who is painting the bed, where he indicates that the painter is pursuing some extraordinarily trivial activity, inferior even to that of the carpenter. Rational reflection – for instance, measurement – would lead us beyond sensible particulars towards understanding and thus, towards goodness. Thirdly, Plato also rejected art for some rather sophisticated psychological reasons, and here he was thinking of the dramatists rather than of the painters. He thought of art as emotional fantasy. It gave expression to the lowest part of the

[245]

mind of the artist and appealed to the lowest part of the mind of the client – I use the word client here to cover the spectator of the drama, the reader of the book, the hearer of the music, the spectator of the picture, and so on. It was an emotional substitute for reality, and this is not unlike the view of art sometimes expressed by Freud.

Freud constantly said that he owed a great deal of his insight to Plato. The concept of Eros, of course, he took from Plato. Art, according to Freud is a substitute, it is a substitute for 'power, riches, and the love of women'. It is the possession in fantasy of what [is] lacked in reality and the obsessive fantasies of the author stir up the obsessive fantasies of the reader. The art work itself appears in this picture of it as rather unimportant – it lies in between the active fantasy mind of the author and the active fantasy of the reader since it is, itself, simply a stimulus, as in the thriller or romance where the hero, alias the author, wins all his battles, triumphs over his enemies and gets the girl he loves – he may have his faults but fundamentally he is honest and lovable, and so on. The limiting case of this idea would of course be the use of art in pornography, and there is no doubt that a great deal of art, including some good art, is used in this way. As W. H. Auden said, 'No poet can prevent his work from being used as magic.' Plato's reaction to art is puritanical, and is a kind of reaction which seems to recur at regular intervals. Art suddenly begins to seem to us too much, too attractive, too sexy, too self-indulgent, too obscure, too pretentious, too full of overflow from the unconscious mind. Plato regarded the unconscious mind as the enemy, though when it was purified, it could be an ally to goodness. He constantly complains that poets do not know what they are doing and they cannot explain their work which has a daemonic source, or, in a purified sense, a divine source; but, for most of us, the source is daemonic and not divine and, in any case, what is divine is always dangerous. Commenting on characters in fiction, Plato remarks, and I think this is a good critical remark, that the bad dynamic or daemonic man who is always agitated, always changing, is a more interesting character to us than the good man who is dull, modest, unobtrusive and always the same. The unconscious mind is the enemy and so, of course, is sex, concerning which Plato took an alarmist and puritanical view, though he also thought that purified sexual energy, the good Eros, could lead us to enlightenment. Aristotle, one might say in passing, of course, also thought of art as mimesis. It seemed obvious, I think to the Greeks, that art was imitation of nature; but he took a more commonsensical view of the matter, as we would expect. He was not frightened of art (I am thinking of the dramatists), he held that presentation of life in art could have an ennobling effect, and this is, of course, a view which is very familiar to us since the Romantic movement which also idealised art in just this sense – in a sense in which, I think nowadays, and this is interesting, art is not idealised. People do not think so well of art, now, as they did in the high days of the Romantic movement. Plato's view, of course, seems to ask to be changed into precisely some opposite, idolising, idealising view of art, by being turned upside-down. Plotinus did this and also, of course, Schopenhauer, whom we may associate with the Romantic movement. In this view art is mimesis all right, but it imitates not particulars but the Ideas or Forms themselves, the things which are at the very top of the ladder of dialectic, its highest products. This is a very lofty view of art. The artist, in Schopenhauer's view, elicits from nature forms of very great universality and intellectual clarity and condensed significance which are lurking there to be discovered. As Shelley put it, 'Forms more real than living man, nurselings of immortality'. Art is a higher truth and the artist is a kind of priest. The Form and the art object are, as it were, universal particulars and are thus giving us privileged information about nature. I find Schopenhauer's view very attractive but I cannot share it. It is too intellectual and unsuspicious a view of art. Plato perhaps is too suspicious but I think his suspicion comes from a much deeper understanding of what art is like. Art is very much to do with accident, with contingency, with detail, with self-expression, with trickery of all kinds, with magic. I think the idea of magic, here, perhaps sums up the extraordinary ambiguity of art, and of this Plato was, of course, very well aware since he was himself a great artist. Art is to do with sex and with the unconscious mind. I spoke of a recurrent, puritanical reaction to the arts: the Romantic movement produced such a reaction in Tolstoy, whose attitude is, in some ways, remarkably like Plato's. Tolstoy too had ambivalent feelings about sex. He hated pretension and obscurity in art. He not only hated

Baudelaire and Verlaine, he also managed to hate Shakespeare, and he condemned almost all his own work. In his book, called *What Is Art?* he says everything he himself has written is bad, except for, *A Prisoner of the Caucasus* and a little story called, *God Knows the Truth and Waits*. *What Is Art?* is actually, though it is certainly an extremely eccentric book, a very good book on art, and there are not all that many good books on the subject. Tolstoy wanted, or said he wanted, literature to be very simple and universally understood: folk tales, moral stories, parables, fables, clear stories about good men, about good and evil. This is very like what Plato wanted too. Works which are simple, unpretentious, unambiguous and improving, not pretentious, sexy, attractive and obscure. Tolstoy added the splendidly high-minded idea that art is fundamentally religious, that it should express the highest religious perceptions of the age, perceptions which have to be reformulated in every generation, and with this view, to which I shall return, I feel a good deal of sympathy.

Puritans want art to do good, they want it to do useful work. Now a critic, such as F. R. Leavis, who has been influential in England over quite a long period, wants literature to be serious and mature, to express profound and interesting views of character and society. An attitude such as this, is, of course, on the way to a utilitarian theory of art. I do not want to discuss utilitarian theories here. The Marxist theory is, no doubt, the strongest and best-known, though the Marxist utilitarian view of art comes, one might say, in more than one variety. Some Marxists think that literature should provide immediate pamphlets or improving stories to serve the present state of the revolution and this, I think, would be quite close to what Plato, in one part of his mind at any rate, thought that art should be doing. Other Marxist critics, for instance Georg Lukács, thought – at any rate, until his comrades corrected him – that some serious bourgeois literature, particularly the great nineteenth-century novels, provided deep, valuable social analysis and might even, *mutatis mutandis*, be taken as models. I cannot myself hold either of these views, [. . .] but I will pass by this tempting by-way which, from the point of view of what I am explaining now, is not on the main track. I think that a free literature does in fact help society very much by telling it a lot of truths and drawing attention to a lot of things which might otherwise not be noticed. But the artist's job is to produce good art and that is a problem, the problem, for each artist, how that can best be done – good art, in a sense which does not necessarily include the idea of serving society. The service to society will no doubt appear then also as an extra or a by-product.

I have been speaking of the periodic desire to purify art, the puritanical reaction, the desire to let blood, as it were, to diminish something which has become too pompous, too bloated, too florid. We have, of course, a recent and more local case of such puritanism in the literary theories developed from structuralism and I shall use the word 'formalism' to cover literary theories of this sort. And of course it is unnecessary to say anything by way of explanation to this audience about formalism since I am sure you all know more about it than I do. Formalism is the latest manifestation of a malaise about language which now goes back a long way – in its present form at least as far as Mallarmé and, if one wants to go back much farther, Plato too expressed a strong uneasiness about literature, which is based on a strong uneasiness about language. Plato saw that sign-using itself was the trouble. We are now accustomed to hearing ourselves described as sign-using, meaning-bestowing animals who must bear the consequences thereof. The work of Anglo-Saxon linguistic philosophers has, of course, long been concerned with these questions, questions for instance asked by Bertrand Russell and answered by Wittgenstein. 'The meaning of a word is its use'. 'What signs fail to express, their application shows' (from The Tractatus). These are structuralist remarks. Wittgenstein's work may, indeed, be described as a process of dissolving of substances into uses of language. As far as literature is concerned, formalism has, of course, attacked many of these old conventions, and these attacks are directed against certain classical assumptions about unity, the unified self, the unified object, the unified story, things which, before we became aware of certain truths about the relation of language to the world, we constructed or imagined as substances lying beyond the net of language – in fact we thought it might be possible to crawl, as it were under the net. Anxiety about the unity of the self is, of course, not very new. It was expressed by the Scottish philosopher David Hume, who said that the self was a bundle of perceptions. Hume's discoveries about the disunity of the self, the disunity of the material object, the peculiar nature of the concept of cause, about how substances were illusions created by nothing stronger than habit were what, according to Kant himself, aroused Kant from his dogmatic slumber and set him to labour to vindicate the idea of unity. Literature has, as we know, not been unaffected by these worries which have usually not arrived in it direct from philosophy although we know that, for instance, Laurence Sterne was interested in the work of John Locke. Novelists such as James Joyce and Virginia Woolf accept, as it were, a challenge from language, the clearly delineated human person vanishes, an impressionistic stream of consciousness flows instead, then even the idea of consciousness itself may seem to vanish, objects and scenes dissolve into words. Jean-Paul Sartre is of course a case of an influence of philosophy upon literature embodied in one man. As philosopher he attacks the idea of the unified self, explores the viscous, insubstantial nature of consciousness, and as a writer he describes his consciousness. Contemporary formalism pursues this line of reflection even farther, and in new ways, as we know. When I was a student of philosophy there was a famous article by an English philosopher called [H. A.] Prichard* which was called, 'Does moral philosophy rest on a mistake?' and one might say the question now asked in many quarters is, 'Does literature rest on a mistake?' The doctrine may be described as literary idealism or literary monism. We must not picture the world as lying separately behind the signs by which we designate, characterise or constitute it; in a sense there is nothing but signs and literature must take up this challenge by no longer producing works which encourage what might be called the realistic fallacy, the illusion of looking through words into another world. The writer must serve the truth of the situation by drawing attention to the medium itself which is not really, in a sense, a medium at all. Such a view would, of course, exclude the notion of art as mimesis in the simple-minded sense in which Plato and Aristotle pictured it – the painter painting the bed, the dramatist imitating a scene from real life. Roland Barthes allows the term 'mimesis', but in a new and

* [See footnote p. 76 above.]

limited sense – 'une mimesis fondée non sur l'analogie des substances (comme dans l'art dit réaliste) mais sur celle des fonctions'.* I am not myself a formalist though I think the movement is of great interest. Its style as revolutionary or anti-bourgeois, which may be related to one of its great ancestors, surrealism, I now leave aside. This is separable from other aspects of the theory and is an aspect which could take us a long way. I think the fundamental thing about formalism is that it expresses, in the form of a new attitude to language and literature, a sense of the loss of the unified self. It is, as one might put it, the disunified self which disunifies the object and the story.

I want to continue against this background to talk about art and I will return, I hope, to the issues which have been raised. Literature is dangerous, it is a kind of magic. It is also something very lofty, it expresses or explains religion to each generation. Or is it perhaps in some way based on a mistake, ought we not to see it as being just words, whatever that might mean? Can all these things be true? I think it would be impossible to over-estimate the magical nature of art. Art is an attempt to achieve omnipotence through personal fantasy. Art is the abode of wish-fulfilment and power mania. One might say that art is a prime producer of illusory unities. It seems to unify the personalities both of the artist and of his client, and this, I think, is one of the deep attractions of art, that it gathers together the personality of the creator and the personality of the reader or spectator into a sense of unified significance which may, of course, be very momentary. This I think happens whether the work of art itself is good or bad. The work of art in so far as its sketchy existence is completed by the ready fantasy of the writer and the reader, that wicked co-operating pair, is an illusory unity and pornography is, again, the pure case of this collusion between the artist and his client. The merest sketch here can do the work, the merest sketch is, indeed, the work. But something like this is also true of great art. This is something the artist usually attempts to conceal, artists are tricksters. Writers try to conceal their obsessions. The presence of obsession in their work is sometimes evident,

* [A mimesis based not on the analogy of substances (as in the art known as realist) but on that of functions.]

sometimes not so evident, and this irrespective of whether the writing is good or bad. They may conceal their obsessions by sentimentality, by the introduction of values which are not fully related to the deep structure of the work. More sophisticated writers may use irony or wit to cool down what might otherwise seem too warm, or they may use abstract ideas, intellectual reflection to produce an air of objectivity. These are familiar dodges, well known both to the author and to the critic. This is a way of suggesting that art is mere trickery. Well, in a way, a lot of it is. It is, in a sense, a battle with the reader, as I think people often want to say nowadays to draw attention to the fact that the artist and his client are natural enemies, and although I have just been saying that they are collusive there is also a sense in which the artist is wary, he is suspicious, he is afraid of his reader or his spectator and knows what sort of things the sophisticated client will look for in his art; and if these are things which are too close to his secret obsessions he will be at great pains to conceal them. Art is a battle with obsessive unconscious forces and in this sense Plato was right to say that the enemy is the unconscious mind, although of course the unconscious mind is also the source of art and the paradox is that if there are no unconscious forces there is no art.

Yet, we must also, in reaction, tell ourselves how ordinary and how natural and how instinctive art is. Literature, which might seem more sophisticated than painting or music, is just as natural – perhaps, given the existence of speech, more natural. The story is a natural unit which we all use every day. We are all story-tellers and in this sense we are all literary artists. We return home and we tell what happened to us during the day, and in doing this we give form and entertainment value to something which was, perhaps, as we experienced it, rather dull and formless. The story is a way of thinking, it is a fundamental mode of consciousness, or self-being. It is, in its primitive form, concerned with the communication of emotion, and I think that art is clearly communication, it needs very great ingenuity to persuade us that it is anything else. Tolstoy takes as a paradigm of literature the situation of the boy who meets the wolf in the forest and comes home and describes the experience. The story as everyday activity is in fact very often emotional, very often funny and very often about people, and the language which it uses is evaluative language. One might say here that almost all language is evaluative language, language is soaked in value. If we were to describe this room we would naturally use many evaluative terms in the description. It is with great difficulty, in artificial situations, for artificial purposes, scientific or legal, for instance, that we attempt to expel value from ordinary language. We are all story-tellers and we tell stories about people, and we tell these stories not only to other people but also to ourselves. We have in our activity as story-tellers a way of judging, a way of evaluating the world that surrounds us, and this gives us in return a sense of our own identity, our own separateness, our own self-being.

Hume who attacked the idea of the unified self and the unified object, admitted that as soon as he left his study and his philosophical work, all his old illusions, his strong, natural beliefs resumed their force. What is this self-being? I think this is something which both writers and philosophers are rather suspicious and uneasy about now, possibly because of having been, as they might feel, in the past, duped by too simple an idea of self awareness as a kind of identity or a kind of unity. When I was reflecting on this I thought to myself, 'Well when do we have self-being or consciousness, or whatever word we choose to cover this extremely nebulous but very important and recognisable condition?' and I thought of myself, first, sitting alone in a garden, then I thought of myself sitting in a pub, and then I remembered, of course, that these are exactly where, in the beginning of Sartre's novel, *La Nausée*, the hero loses his sense of self-identity – and this is interesting. As soon as he sits reflecting in these highly meditative situations, in the park or in the café, he begins first of all to feel 'here I am, here I am' and then he says, 'but what is this "here I am"?' Literature is very natural, both because we are interested in the quality of our own self-being or consciousness – we brood on it – and because we are endlessly interested in other people. Most fiction is about people, and the difficulties of fiction are also about people, about ourselves as entities and about others. The main activity and the main difficulty of the writer of fiction is in creation of character, whatever sort of attitude he may take to this activity, whatever mode he uses in relation to the presence of characters in his work. His chief temptations, in the simplest sense, are to exalt himself, to sentimentalise some characters, to diminish other characters. The whole mystery of human individuality is involved here – how different we are from each other, and why it is that we love one person, we dislike another person and we are indifferent to a third person; and nothing in a way could be more important than this fact about us. Any literary artist, even the man who is telling his wife what happened at the office, is confronted, whether he knows it or not, by questions concerning objectivity, impartiality, truth, justice; and of course as readers of fiction we are offered the choice of following or not following the emotional paths traced out by the author. Are we prepared to identify with those he loves and to despise those he hates? This is a taking of sides which happens, I think, very instinctively and very early on in reading works of fiction.

Our freedom as moral judges in relation to the work of fiction is, of course, one of the pleasures of wide reading. What do we think about Hamlet? What do we think about Fabrice del Dongo, or Madame Bovary? Or what about D. H. Lawrence's treatment of Clifford Chatterley compared with his treatment of Mellors? Does Tolstoy meanly abandon characters such as Sonia and Karenin? Does Henry James abandon Charlotte Stant? Here, I think, we naturally envisage a relation between the author and his character as if the character could turn round and say to the author, 'You have been unfair to me.' Can Mauriac get away with a character as incoherent as that of his Thérèse? Is Fanny Price in *Mansfield Park* really a rather nasty girl or is she a nice girl? We believe that Swann loved Odette but do we believe in the same way that Marcel loved Albertine? As a method of criticism such speculations may seem simple-minded and perhaps old-fashioned, but this is the natural beginning of criticism. This sort of natural reflection about stories and about novels can reveal to us how clearly the author's moral attitude is exhibited, even if he wishes to conceal it, in his attitude to his characters, in what some critics call 'the placing' of his characters. Literature is soaked in the moral, language is soaked in the moral, fictional characters swim in a moral atmosphere. There are, of course, different kinds of moral atmosphere and moral tone, and fiction in this century has explored and exhibited many varieties. I am not sure if a story can have no moral atmosphere.

The practice of any art is, of course, a moral discipline in that it involves a struggle against fantasy, against self-indulgence. But fictional literature has a special moral dimension because it is about people and, I venture to say, it is in however covert, unclear, secret, ambiguous a way, about the struggle between good and evil.

For various reasons contemporary writers are often reluctant to admit this, and it is interesting to see that a work such as Tolkien's *Lord of the Rings*, which is very clearly about the struggle between good and evil, is a great popular success. I want to return here to mimesis, and 'art imitates nature' and 'imagination reveals truth'. I think, myself, that the old-fashioned mimetic paradigm is still a good one whereby to understand the artist. We are inquisitive animals, we are full of curiosity. The satisfaction of social curiosity was one of the charms of the nineteenth-century novel. What are other people really like? People are so very secretive. Sometimes it is said, 'Those characters and that novel are purely fantastic – nobody in real life is like that.' But people in real life are very, very odd, as soon as one gets to know them at all well, and they conceal this fact because they are frightened of appearing eccentric or shocking and so on. What are other people really like? What goes on inside their minds? What goes on inside their houses? Any writer is conscious of a tension between himself and something utterly other than himself, and he is also conscious of the obsessive, self-enclosing strength of his fantasy. Imagination, as opposed to fantasy, is the ability to see the other thing, what one might call, to use those old-fashioned words, nature, reality, the world. This sense of distance and otherness belongs to the good artist as it belongs to the religious man, and it is in this way that one might understand Tolstoy's view of art as something religious. Imagination is a kind of freedom, a renewed ability to perceive and express the truth. And to pick up this word religion and looking back upon the nineteenth-century novel as a great product of religion, one might say that the most important change that we have experienced in this century is the loss of religion as something taken for granted, in the sense in which, to a remarkable degree, the great nineteenth-century writers, whatever they might have called themselves, were religious people and took for granted a religious background to life. It is interesting too that after a phase of comparative atheism or irreligion there are signs of a kind of revival of religion through a change in theology. I do not know how far this is something that people in this country feel, but I think in England we see theology demythologising itself, to use this popular term, confessing that a lot of what was normally or originally thought of as dogma must be regarded as myth. This is something which could have a profound effect on the future, it could bring religion back within the orbit of what an ordinary person can believe. T. S. Eliot said that Christianity has always been adjusting itself to be something which we can believe. So that if one describes art in religious terms I think that these terms are not out of date and indeed one could connect the work of theology now with the work of the artist now. Tolstoy's view of art as religious pictures [and] art as reformulating in every generation something of our relationship to what one might call our metaphysical background.

Imagination is a kind of freedom, a renewed ability to perceive and express truth, and this is to put forward another of these lofty and high-minded views of art. The artist must tell the truth about something which he has understood. This is perhaps the best piece of advice which one can give to the writer. This idea must somehow remain within the work of art however ingenious it is and be felt by the artist and perceived by the critic. Keats's famous remark about 'what the imagination seizes as beauty must be truth' continues, 'whether it existed before or not'; and the paradox of art is that the work itself may, as it were, have to invent the methods by which we verify it, by which we test it for truth, to erect its own interior standards of truthfulness. And one might think in this connection about abstract painting which is so often taken as a paradigm of what is happening to literature now, [a] paradigm often used in formalist criticism because here the notion of the object dissolving into something else is most evident. One sees in paintings by Mondrian, for instance, the way in which what in a first painting in a series looks like a tree becomes something much more like a lot of squares or oblongs in the final version. Good abstract paintings are not just idle daubs or scrawls, forms wandering round at random in spaces, they are somehow about light and colour and space, and I think that this is something that the abstract painter is very conscious of, he is not in a state of total freedom, he is relating himself to something else and his paintings exist for us in a world where we normally take colours to be parts of objects. The painter and the writer confront these curious problems about a reality which is alien and at the same time something which they are bestowing meaning upon, which they are related to in this curious internal relation. Formalism draws our attention to the extent to which we are responsible for what we see. Yet, the otherness of nature is a more important part of the image. We bestow significance but we also constantly test it and we incorporate the tests, the tests of truth, in the work itself. This is very evident in a novel where the reader rightly expects, however odd the work may be, some kind of moral aesthetic sense of direction, some indication of how to read the relation, or apparent lack of relation, to the ordinary world. Works of art are individuals and they are the work of individuals, which is one of many reasons why it is difficult to treat them satisfactorily in a scientific manner. In the case of fiction the subject matter is usually, also, individual people. The work of fiction is not only all that self-contained and, again, usually moral, set of judgements which we think of as making the unity of the critic and the author; it is also concerned with judgements which we make in ordinary life, external judgements, judgements upon real people which are not totally unlike judgements which we make upon people in literature. This openness, this ordinariness may be deplored by some purists but to escape from it requires a good aesthetic excuse as well as a good deal of ingenuity. I see no reason to be worried here. Other people are, after all, the most interesting features of our world and in some way the most poignantly and mysteriously alien. Literature tells us things and teaches us things. In portraying characters the author displays most clearly his discernment, his truthfulness, his justice, or his lack of these qualities, and one of our enjoyments lies in considering and judging his judgements. The highest pleasures of literature and, one might say, of art generally, are in this sense moral pleasures.

This paper was presented in the Anglo-Irish section of a symposium on British writing at the University of Caen, 1978.

PART SIX

Can Literature Help Cure the Ills of Philosophy? 1959–61

'Literature, in curing its own ills, can give us a new vocabulary of experience and a truer picture of freedom.'

'Against Dryness', 1961

The Sublime and the Beautiful Revisited

What I have to say does not fall into the domain of literary criticism, as it is understood nowadays. My subject lies on the borders of literature and philosophy, but it is important to insist that I am not a critic. My remarks will be at times more personal and throughout more abstract than those of a critic; and I would like to say at the start that although what follows may sound like a manifesto and may imply a dogmatic tone of voice, I am not all that sure that what I say is right.

I want to connect a literary problem with a more general political and moral problem. Roughly, I think one may be enlightened by connecting the question: Is the Liberal-democratic theory of personality an adequate one? with the question: What is characteristic of the greatest literary works of art? The latter question could also be put in the form: What, chiefly, makes Tolstoy the greatest of novelists and Shakespeare the greatest of writers? I shall be concerned here mainly with the novel, and I approach the problem as a novelist concerned with the creation of character. Wherein does the reality of a person reside and in what way can one, or should one, display that reality? More precisely, I want to treat recent changes in the portrayal of character in novels as symptoms of some more general change of consciousness. It has for some time now been the fashion to say that we are in a morass, and to attempt to get out of the morass by attacking Romanticism; and I am going to do this too. The word 'Romantic' is best defined by what it is opposed to, and I shall be opposing it to different things from some to which it is usually opposed. But I hope it will become tolerably clear what I mean by it.

I shall pursue my line of thought first in the region of philosophy, and come later, having erected a sort of philosophical structure, to discuss literature; and I shall start by considering certain ideas of Kant. Kant is the father of all modern forms of the problem of freedom, and also incidentally the father of most modern theories of art. To him, even more than to Rousseau or to Hegel, we may impute both the initial strength and the later weakness of the Liberal theory of personality, which is to such an extent also the Romantic theory of personality. I shall argue later that it is desirable to purge the Liberal theory of many of its Romantic elements. I am using the word 'Liberal' here of course in its traditional historical sense, the sense in which the philosophy of John Stuart Mill is a Liberal philosophy.

Kant's moral philosophy rests on the equation that virtue is freedom is reason. Virtue is not a knowledge *of* anything; it is rather an ability to impose rational order. We respect others, not as particular eccentric phenomenal individuals, but as co-equal bearers of universal reason; though it is true (and this is Kant's agnosticism) that we do not *know* reason in ourselves or others, in the same way that we know material objects. Not being purely rational we are not transparent to ourselves. The entire world of our emotions and desires is irrelevant to morality. We turn from the messy and ambiguous region of the emotions to the undoubted clarity of the choice and the act. The only emotion in which Kant interests himself, and which he connects with morality, is the mixed pleasure and pain of *Achtung*, that is, respect for the moral law, which is an *experience* of our freedom – our freedom, as it were, biting into our phenomenal being. This great concept is of course the immediate ancestor of the popular existentialist concept of *Angst*.

Kant's theory of art accords with his theory of morals; but it has one or two special features. Kant makes a distinction, a distinction which has not in my view fascinated philosophers as much as it should, between the sublime and the beautiful. Strictly, Kant's theory of art as such is concerned only with the beautiful, but the distinction is suggestive, as I shall argue later, of a total theory of art which uses his concept of the sublime as well. Kant's theory of the beautiful is explanatory of a great deal of Romantic theory and practice. The beautiful is the experience of a conceptless harmony between the imagination and the understanding. Art, as the production of the beautiful, is not a matter of discovering or imparting truths ('what oft was thought but ne'er so well expressed') – it is rather the production of a certain kind of quasi-thing. It is noteworthy that the work of art is conceived by Kant, and mostly by the Romantics, on the analogy of a fairly small perceptual object. Kant of course construed the judgement of taste precisely on the analogy of the perceptual judgement. What is constructed is a self-contained object, strictly purposeless, yet with an air of purpose, existing for its own sake. In art, we enjoy an immediate intuitive inexplicable understanding of a unique quasi-sensible object. It is remarkable how friendly and familiar this really very obscure theory seems: we take to it like ducks to water.

In constructing the art-object freedom is not involved, since reason is not in play; but Kant says that the beautiful is an analogon of the good, the enjoyment of art is an analogon of the free rational act, in that it is the construction of something clean, free, empty, self-contained, not contaminated by the messiness of emotion, desire, or personal eccentricity. Art is hygienic; but as it is not an activity of the reason, it is a sort of *play* and is connected with morals only by analogy.

Now the sublime is a very different matter. As described by Kant the sublime is not connected with art at all. While the beautiful is an experience of the imagination and the understanding in harmony, the sublime is an experience of the imagination and the reason in conflict. Whereas the beautiful reposes us, the sublime rends us. It is an emotional experience resulting from the defeated yet invigorating attempt of reason to compass the boundlessness and formlessness of nature. Confronted with some vast prospect, the starry sky, or the Alps, the imagination and the senses cannot properly take in what lies before them, that is they cannot satisfy the reason, which demands a total complete ordered picture. Yet in being so defeated the reason gains a fresh sense of its own independence and dignity. Since reason *is* the moral will, the experience of the sublime is a sort of moral experience, that is, an experience of freedom. It is a mark of spiritual power resulting from a serious and amazed survey of the vastness of nature. But since it is not connected with action it is not strictly moral activity. It is the moral will not in action but as it were triumphantly intuiting itself. It is, as Kant puts it, a reminder of our supersensible destiny: an experience analogous to *Achtung*, a mixture of defeat and victory.

With the theory of the sublime we have the distressing feeling of some vast and wonderful idea being attached to a trivial occasion. Who, one might say, cares what sort of emotions Kant experienced in the Alps? There must be more to it: and I shall suggest later that Kant's view is pregnant with a concept of the tragic, and with a theory of the connection between literature and morality.

With the Hegelian descendants of Kant we are in the mainstream of Romanticism. For Kant, neither morality nor art was a matter of knowledge, whereas Hegel pictured reality in terms of a developing range of historical and psychological concepts and implied that complete knowledge of it was possible. Reason was not ultimately defeated; it could close the circle of knowledge: no agnosticism here, no sense of limit. Hegel did picture virtue in terms of knowledge in the sense that progress was measured by increasing self-awareness. Virtue was also freedom in the sense of recognition of necessary process, that is freedom as self-knowledge. For Kant virtue is freedom is rational order; for Hegel virtue is freedom is self-knowledge.

In this universe, art is a stage of self-awareness which we ultimately pass beyond. Tragedy too is a product of appearance not of reality. It is the mutual misunderstanding of parts of the whole. From the point of view of the whole itself there is no tragedy. Meanwhile, however, there is the conflict: the self locked in struggle with itself and evolving as a result of the struggle. There is only one being in the Hegelian universe, the whole which cannot allow anything outside itself and which struggles to realise all that is apparently other. This is Hegel's gift to the Romantic movement, and one from whose effects we have not yet recovered.

The opponents of Hegel may be divided into those who understand him very well and feel a mixture of love and hate as a result, and those who have never read him and would not understand him if they did. We may single out from the former the Kierkegaardian or existentialist Hegelians, who are pure Romantics, and from the latter the Hobbesian empiricists, who are Liberals touched by Romanticism at a certain stage. The Liberal dilemma may be seen as the failure of these two disparate elements to help each other to produce a new post-Hegelian theory of personality.

Kierkegaard, as we know, fought against the swallowing up of the individual human person in the Hegelian system. He fought for the conception of a private individual destiny: the root idea of existentialism, that the individual human existence is not enclosed by a world of essences. However, Kierkegaard is profoundly Hegelian. He retained and used with wonderful versatility the clear, dramatic, solipsistic picture of the self at war with itself and passing in this way through phases in the direction of self-knowledge. Kierkegaard, like the modern existentialists, is anti-system, and even, like them, anti-bourgeois; yet psychologically speaking he may be described as 'totalitarian', in the sense that he is concerned with the whole man and with his isolated struggle for salvation. The individual described by Kierkegaard is alone, except for the mystery of religion. Kierkegaard's agnosticism (like that of Kant, as we see when we look at that a second time) is dramatic rather than resigned. We do not know all – but 'all' is magnetically *there* to be known. Our solitude is completed, the circle is closed, by our relation to a veiled deity. The deity and the solitary self between them enclose the whole of reality.

When we turn from the existentialist Hegelians to the Hobbesian empiricists we breathe a very different air. Whereas Kantian aesthetics is familiar to us as cultured persons and consumers of art, the universe of discourse of Hobbes and Locke is familiar to us as political beings and more generally as ordinary users of common sense. Here are the familiar ideas of our Liberalism, ideas we take for granted, and whose undisputed simplicity makes the Liberalism of the English-speaking world different from other varieties. In the world as envisaged by Hobbes, Locke, and Hume there is a plurality of persons, who are quite separate and different individuals and who have to get along together. Moreover, implicitly for Hobbes and explicitly for Locke, that which has a right to exist, that which is deserving of tolerance and respect, is not the rational or good person, but the actual empirically existing person whatever he happens to be like. The agnosticism out of which this tolerance sprang was the undramatic commonsensical agnosticism of Locke rather than the dramatic agnosticism of Kant and Kierkegaard. It

[265]

just is in fact rather difficult to understand other people and to be certain what is the right thing to do: one is fallible, so one must be patient. This agnostic tolerance was developed most explicitly by Mill, who was indeed touched but by no means overwhelmed by the Romantic movement. Mill retains an eighteenth-century sense of society. His individual is eccentric, unique, holy, pregnant with genius, but *not* alone.

This is the tradition out of which a criticism of Romanticism should have come, but did not. It was partly that Romanticism was from the start absolutely entwined with the Liberal tradition and must have seemed to be its lifeblood. But there were also features in that tradition itself, thinking of it as something with older roots and a separate being, which made it ultimately unable to find as it were a footing, a vantage point from which to criticise, even to *see* the Romantic movement. The empiricists had, it is true, a certain commonsensical picture of society. They recognised a range of virtues corresponding to the range of human impulses and social situations; whereas the Hegelians ultimately recognised only one virtue, progress in self-mastery. But the empiricist picture of society was undynamic and naïve; and this was true even of Mill. The real impetus of the philosophical movement with which Liberalism was connected was not primarily moral or political, it was scientific; and we may say that the simple and powerful Liberal ideas to which we are so attached occurred in a way as a by-product and as a result of what we may call the phenomenal *luck* of our English-speaking societies. What most of all concerned the empiricists, and what drove their theories onward, was the construction of a picture of the material world, the development of that atomic empiricism which has had so strong a hold on our philosophical imagination, and which is only now vanishing from the scene, partly as a result of the development of science as a separate discipline, and partly as a result of the criticism by Wittgenstein of assumptions held in common by Hume and by Bertrand Russell; and with this parcelling out of our intellectual tradition which has been happening of late, we are become uneasily aware of its extreme simplicity and poverty in certain respects. It was indeed the Romantic movement itself which gave it an appearance of colour and body.

Now before turning about, and attempting to use a consideration of literature in a more telling diagnosis of these ills, it is still necessary to say something about the most recent trends in philosophy. Here again I must be, on a very complex subject, very brief. For my purposes, there are two important philosophies, existentialism (here I take the work of Sartre as typical) and linguistic empiricism (the tradition of Moore and Wittgenstein). Both of these, I shall argue, show certain symptoms which may be connected with symptoms of decline in our literature.

Existentialism and empiricism (as I shall call it for short) share a number of motives and doctrines. Both philosophies are against traditional metaphysics, attack substantial theories of the mind, have a touch of puritanism, construe virtue in terms of will rather than in terms of knowledge, emphasise choice, are markedly Liberal in their political bias, are neo-Kantian. But in other ways they are very different.

The inspiration of empiricism is a scientific inspiration which expresses itself in an extreme desire for precision of meaning. Such a desire cannot but be to some extent inimical to words; and one cannot be surprised at the increasing importance and popularity of mathematical logic, which is now regarded in many quarters as the basis of philosophy. On the other hand, empirical concepts have their being in empirical languages, and in their clarification appeal is made to the conception of 'ordinary language', thought of as a really existing network, within which meanings are established for general inspection, so that perfect clarity and conclusiveness can be attained by the making of logical points, i.e. points depending on conventionally accepted definitions. This technique, which produces satisfactory results when used to clarify our concepts of the material world, is less satisfactory when used to clarify moral concepts.

Linguistic moral philosophy, of which one of the most influential exponents is the American philosopher Stevenson, operates by seeking the meaning of moral concepts in the moment of moral choice, through studying the role which words such as 'good' play in choice situations. What is given by this study is, with variations of detail, as follows: moral situations are those in which we give generally comprehensible reasons for choices of a certain degree of importance. Our choices, together with our reasons, display our values, and the moral concept (e.g. the word 'good') is the instrument of commendation whereby we point out what is to be chosen. Note that this picture is conventional, behaviouristic, and Liberal in tendency. It is conventional: the agent is seen as a being subject to rules, surrounded by a civilised society, surrounded in short by the network of ordinary language, that is, for these purposes, by the network of moral conceptual activity at its most common and universally accepted level. It is behaviouristic; and here an anti-substantialist theory of the mind joins hands with a certain Liberal puritan austerity. Since inner acts of the mind only have identity through their conventional connection with outer acts, we may say that morally speaking a man *is* what he observably does. As in the philosophy of Kant, we turn away from the chaos of empirical inwardness to the clarity of overt action. What a man 'feels' is of no interest to us, and even what he believes is of no interest except in so far as his beliefs are defined by his actions. The picture is Liberal (neo-Kantian) in its concern with reasoned choice. Ordinary Language Man, as we may call the person here envisaged, is not overwhelmed by any structure larger than himself, such as might be represented by a metaphysical belief or by an institution. As a moral agent he is completely free, choosing between acts and reasons on his own responsibility; and it has been a major preoccupation of empiricist moral philosophy to depict the agent as totally free and self-sufficient. Even the presence of others is felt, if at all, simply as the presence of rational critics. This man is alone with a loneliness similar to the loneliness of Kant's man.

In the philosophy of Sartre we find the same solitary moral agent, and the same emphasis on the moment of choice, but displayed in terms of a dramatic Hegelian psychology. One might say that whereas Ordinary Language Man represents the surrender to convention, the Totalitarian Man of Sartre represents the surrender to neurosis: convention and neurosis, the two enemies of under-standing, one might say the enemies of love; and how difficult it is in the modern world to escape from one without invoking the help of the other. Sartre's man is like a neurotic who seeks to cure himself by unfolding a myth about himself. Ordinary Language Man is at least surrounded by something which is not of his own creation, viz. ordinary language. But Totalitarian Man is entirely alone. How well we know this man from the pages of modern literature. He suffers from *Angst*, which is *Achtung* minus confidence in universal reason, that is, with its dignified and exultant aspect removed. He makes his choices against the apocalyptic background of the modern world – an apocalyptic world picture favours a total creed – and if he is sincere he knows that he is always in an extreme situation. He is stripped to essentials. Sartre says, speaking of existentialist literary works: 'It is always the whole man that is in question.'

This man on the one hand mistrusts his inner life and finds it insubstantial; to attribute substance to it is to fall into insincerity. On the other hand, he dramatises his situation in a myth. He is Hegel's man, who is a clear-cut piece of drama rather than an individual. He is also Hegel's man who abhors the contingent or accidental. (*La Nausée*, horror of the contingent.) According to Sartre, a desire for our lives to have the form and clarity of something necessary, and not accidental, is a fundamental human urge. In the world inhabited by Totalitarian Man there are other people, but they are not real contingent separate other people. They appear as organised menacing extensions of the consciousness of the subject. A potentially or apparently separate centre of significance is necessarily a menace to a Hegelian, something to be internalised in a battle of consciousnesses just as discrepant centres in oneself are overcome by reflection.

Virtue, for total [Totalitarian] Man, is sincerity, courage, will: the unillusioned exercise of complete freedom. Virtue is not knowledge, since to pretend to any stable knowledge relevant to morality would be a case of bad faith; just as the ordinary bourgeois social virtues, which take society for granted, are cases of bad faith. Existentialism shares with empiricism a terror of anything which encloses the agent or threatens his supremacy as a centre of significance. In this sense both philosophies tend toward solipsism. Neither pictures virtue as concerned with anything real outside ourselves. Neither provides us with a standpoint for considering real human beings in their variety, and neither presents us with any technique for exploring and controlling our own spiritual energy. Ordinary Language Man is too abstract, too conventional: he incarnates the commonest and vaguest network of conventional moral thought; and Totalitarian Man is too concrete, too neurotic: he is simply the

[269]

centre of an extreme decision, man stripped and made anonymous by extremity.

I take these two philosophies, linguistic empiricism and Sartrian existentialism, as representative of the wisdom which philosophy has now to offer to the Liberal tradition. I consider them here as symptoms rather than positively as influences, though I think existentialism has in fact been influential well outside academic circles. The philosopher often clarifies and crystallises something which exists in a less coherent form in the general consciousness: that is, I take the general consciousness today to be ridden either by convention or by neurosis; and there are many features in both these current philosophies in which we can recognise ourselves. There are of course critics, particularly critics within the existentialist tradition, of many of the points I have mentioned. One might think of Gabriel Marcel, and of Simone Weil; but such critics have remained isolated since they do not at all represent what we take ourselves to be like. Nor, and I speak briefly here of something that would need to be discussed at greater length, does it seem to me that the Christian religion has been able to present us in recent times with any satisfying or powerful picture of ourselves and each other. What we take ourselves to be like is, I think, successfully portrayed by Ordinary Language Man on the one hand, and Totalitarian Man on the other. And I shall argue presently that this regrettable situation is to be intimately connected, both as cause and as effect, with the decline of our prose literature.

*

Here I conclude my philosophical introduction and turn to consider literature, hoping to use certain philosophical conceptions in the diagnosis of certain literary ills. Let me say here again that I am not a critic. I am doing what philosophers do, that is putting up an abstract structure to edify, explain, and provoke reflection. In this case mostly the last. And I shall not be unduly dismayed if it is pointed out that this or that particular work does not fit conveniently into my structure. I shall be content if something is clarified, even if something is discussed.

If we take it that a dominant philosophy pictures the consciousness of the age, and if we take it that the dominant philosophy of the nineteenth century, outside England and America, was the philosophy of Hegel, and if with this in mind we turn to look at the nineteenth-century novel, we get an agreeable surprise. There are of course plenty of reasons (obvious ones in our civilisation) why the nineteenth-century novel, although it shared with Hegelianism a historical sense, certainly a social sense, is, in the respect that interests me, so un-Hegelian. All the same it is remarkable, and in ways entirely relevant to its characteristic and pre-eminent merits, how very un-Romantic the great nineteenth-century novel is. I am here using the word 'Romantic' in my own somewhat narrow sense, which will I hope very soon be made clearer. The feature that most interests me in the un-Hegelian nature of those great novels is simply this: that they contain a number of different people.

[. . .] There is in these novels a plurality of real persons more or less naturalistically presented in a large social scene, and representing mutually independent centres of significance which are those of real individuals. What we have here may be called a display of tolerance. A great novelist is essentially tolerant, that is, displays a real apprehension of persons other than the author as having a right to exist and to have a separate mode of being which is important and interesting to themselves. We may decide later that 'tolerance' is too mild a word for this capacity at its highest. But 'tolerance' is a word which links nineteenth-century literature with Liberalism. Here one may see the Liberal spirit at its best and richest, disporting itself in literature, and not yet menaced by those elements of Romanticism which later proved, if I am right, so dangerous. The great novels are victims neither of convention nor of neurosis. The social scene is a life-giving framework and not a set of dead conventions or stereotyped settings inhabited by stock characters. And the individuals portrayed in the novels are free, independent of their author, and not merely puppets in the exteriorisation of some closely locked psychological conflict of his own. The literary work itself is not in the grip of necessity – how soon we sense this in the cases where it is. The great novelist is not afraid of the contingent; yet his acceptance of the contingent does not land him in banality. In respect of this quality, and of others, the writer with whom we are most tempted to compare this novelist is Shakespeare.

The persons whom I have here in mind, and whom I have called the great novelists, are of course Scott, Jane Austen, George Eliot, Tolstoy, especially Tolstoy – one could add other names, but these suffice to make the point. I realise it is paradoxical to call, for instance, Scott an un-Romantic writer; but I do not mind the paradox so long as the meaning is clear. In calling these novelists the great ones I do not exclude other types of greatness – though it is part of my thesis that this is probably the greatest sort of greatness. It is true that we find in the nineteenth century other remarkable novelists (Dostoevsky, Melville, Emily Brontë, Hawthorne) to whom we would not want to deny a first place, and to whom the title 'Romantic', in my sense, could more readily be applied: writers who give the impression of externalising a personal conflict in a tightly conceived self-contained myth; and it would be perverse to argue that they are great in spite of their Romanticism. This is not the place to analyse their merits. But in attempting to elucidate a standard based on the work of what I have called the un-Romantic writers, one may at least provide oneself with a tool to explore that contrast further. Many reasons might be given for the particular qualities of the nineteenth-century novel: reasons which might connect it with particular, now-vanished historical and social conditions. I am not concerned with these either. What I want to discover and assert is a value which I think belongs, or has belonged since at least the eighteenth century, to prose literature as such, and which does not cease to be a value when it becomes more difficult of attainment. We should always beware of doctrines of necessity which show us (with professions of regret) the eminently desirable, the good, as being, alas, the impossible.

I want now, after this brief glance at the nineteenth-century novel, to look at what may be called Romanticism in decline, and to look in particular at a certain literary movement which shows us the Romantic view of art no longer controlled by the forces which had contributed to produce the great novels. I mean the movement connected originally with Symbolism, and represented in our tradition in varying ways by such persons as T. S. Eliot, T. E. Hulme, I. A. Richards, and others. I shall take this movement as a clear and self-conscious symptom of a wider general trend; and I think the influence of this movement on modern literature has in fact been considerable. This is a matter more usually discussed in relation to poetry; but I think we may see the power of Symbolist ideas in the development of prose literature as well.

The Symbolists, as I shall call this heterogeneous group for short, professed of course to be opponents of Romanticism. A position common to Eliot and Hulme, and which they took to be an anti-Romantic position, could be summed up in Hulme's statement that perfection since the Renaissance had been erroneously conceived in human terms. This had resulted in an art and a philosophy which was vague, emotional, formless, and messy. The Symbolists were certainly anti-humanist; and in common with the linguistic empiricists and with the Sartrian existentialists what they most abhorred was messiness. They shared especially with the empiricists an extreme desire for precision and clear definition. 'Everything is what it is and not another thing.' Butler's remark which G. E. Moore prefixed to *Principia Ethica* could equally have been a Symbolist motto; and indeed Hulme hailed Moore as an ally.

But the Symbolist desire to be precise and to escape from the messy took a special form. As Hulme said, 'We must find beauty in small dry things.' The Symbolists were fascinated by the senses, particularly the sense of sight. What they wanted were small, clean, resonant, and self-contained things of which the image or symbol was the type. What is beautiful must be separate, conceived on the analogy of a sensible object. Indeed to create a sensible object – 'to hand over sensations bodily' – but one purged of its contingency, was the Symbolist ideal. What they wanted, one might say, was to have the sensible world, but with the help of art to know it intuitively and not discursively. Prose literature was the form of art which lay furthest from their concerns; and, like the empiricists, and for roughly the same reasons, they were uneasy about the discursive nature of language. Language was a *pis aller* [last resort]. The ideal of a work of art was 'not to mean, but to be'. Art, including literature, should be the creation of unique self-contained things.

Now it is plain that this view is none other than Kant's theory of the beautiful, served up in a fresh form, and as such it is something which had been inside the Romantic movement from the start. The motive here, as in the case of Kant, is a fear of contingency, a yearning to pierce through the messy phenomenal world to some perfect and necessary form and order. An adoration of necessity, more or less concealed, has always been a characteristic of Romanticism, coexisting in the earlier days with the wilder untidy life-loving more purely Rousseau-esque elements, but in later times proving itself more powerful. What is feared is history, real beings, and real change, whatever is contingent, messy, boundless, infinitely particular, and endlessly still to be explained; what is desired is the timeless non-discursive whole which has its significance completely contained in itself. One might say of the Symbol that it is an analogon of an individual, but not a real individual. It has the uniqueness and separateness of an individual, but whereas the real individual is boundless and not totally definable, the symbol is known intuitively to be self-contained: it is a making sensible of the idea of individuality under the form of necessity, its contingency purged away. Plato mistrusted art because it imitated what was various and unreal; the symbolists desired an art which would have satisfied Plato.

It is not at all surprising, when we consider the matter further, to discover that the Symbolist trend is intolerant and anti-Liberal. Its fear of contingency and history is a fear of the real existing messy modern world, full of real existing messy modern persons, with individual messy modern opinions of their own. To this Hulme and Eliot would oppose institutions and dogma, the presumed clarity and cleanliness of the medieval world when, to use Eliot's phrase apropos of Dante, 'thought was orderly and strong and beautiful'. It is odd and sobering that we may discover this extreme horror of the details of modern life expressed not only by Eliot but also by Tolstoy. In *What Is Art?* Tolstoy asks: 'Strip the best novels of our time of their details and what will remain?' And to the hopelessly contingent detail-ridden novel Tolstoy opposes the pure simplicity of the parable or folk tale: the symbol, one might say, of a religious perception. It is as well that Tolstoy did not practise what he preached until later in life. And Eliot, in a mood not unlike that of Tolstoy, says that he would prefer an illiterate audience to one which is but half-educated.

Eliot of course quite explicitly connects his moral criticism of what he calls the Liberal view of personality with his aesthetic criticism of post-seventeenth-century literature which suffers from the 'dissociation of sensibility'. Romantic poetry lacks hardness, is not able directly to present us with things, because Romantic Liberal persons are concerned with the emotional expression of their own personalities, and not with the being and authority of the thing that confronts them. This Romantic cult of personality and denial of external authority Eliot traces back through humanism, the Romantic movement, the Puritans, to the work of Shakespeare, and it is at this point one may attempt to define one's dislike of his attitude.

With certain aspects of Eliot's criticism of the Liberal view of personality I am in sympathy, as I shall explain shortly. What I like about his criticism is that he accuses the Liberal view of a failure to emphasise the discipline involved in realising that something real exists other than oneself. What I dislike about his criticism is his view of *what* it is that we are thus to discover outside ourselves, what we are to oppose to the individual. That which should be respected by the individual is according to Eliot, in literature, that is in poetry, 'the thing', and [in] life, in morality, 'the institution', or 'the dogma'. In neither case is it 'another person' whom we should thus treat as separate and real. This is objectionable both because Mr Eliot's faith in institutions seems to me excessive: I cannot agree with his view that 'it is better to worship a Golden Calf than to worship nothing'; and because Mr Eliot seems so ready to throw overboard what, with the theoretical assistance of Hobbes, Locke, Mill, and others we have established in our tradition, a respect for the individual person as such, however eccentric, private, messy, and generally tiresome he may be. And one aspect of respecting something is being interested enough in it to try to understand it.

This is where literature, especially prose literature, comes in or should come in. I have spoken of Shakespeare as being the greatest exponent of what I called, giving it too humble a name, that tolerance which we find also in the great novelists. The pages of Shakespeare abound in free and eccentric personalities whose reality Shakespeare has apprehended and displayed as something quite separate from himself. He is the most invisible of writers, and in my sense of the word the most un-Romantic of writers. Now it is impossible to give close attention to the novel, either as writer or as reader, without facing the problem of freedom. Let us see how Mr

Eliot faces it in this connection. I am unable to be confident from Mr Eliot's writings that he has ever enjoyed and admired any novel. He does however in *After Strange Gods* make some interesting comments on the nineteenth-century novel. He gives qualified approval to Jane Austen, Dickens, and Thackeray, because with them 'personality ... was more nearly in its proper place. The standards by which they criticized their world, if not very lofty ones, were at least not of their own making.' But with George Eliot the modern decline begins: she exhibits 'the dreary rationalism of the epoch', and 'is of the same tribe as all the serious and eccentric moralists we have had since'. It is not surprising that given a choice between neurosis and convention Mr Eliot should prefer convention. *Some* of the reasons for which he does so are ones which may be respected, as I shall soon argue.

But it is significant, and from my point of view unpardonable, that he should cast his vote against George Eliot. For she, at a level at times almost equal to that of Tolstoy, displays that godlike capacity for so respecting and loving her characters as to make them exist as free and separate beings. It is this freedom which Mr Eliot resents, and which he sees simply in terms of a messy Romantic self-assertion. But this is to confound the categories. The discipline involved in creating characters such as those of George Eliot is the reverse of an uninhibited self-assertion. What Mr Eliot really dislikes here is the modern world, as shown in the independent and unconventional standpoint of some of the characters and of their author. Jane Austen, who exhibits a similar discipline in the creation of separate persons, does not incur his censure because she places her free people within an old conventional world. Mr Eliot fails to distinguish between two senses of 'free': 'free' as meaning 'independent of the author' and 'free' as meaning 'independent-minded'. Yet in fact if we consider his whole position he is really committed to disliking freedom in both these senses, and it is only because he is not interested enough in the novel and does not take it seriously enough, that he fails to see that Jane Austen is just as great a menace, from his point of view, as George Eliot. That is, to put my point in another way, one cannot altogether separate these two senses of 'free'. A society which can produce great novelists and which can appreciate great novelists is a society in which tolerance and respect for the existence of other persons is likely to flourish, with all that that implies of independence of mind. So Mr Eliot is right too from his point of view, to be afraid of Shakespeare and to see in this loving toleration of, indeed delight in, manifold different modes of being, a beginning of the modern world.

I have suggested that Mr Eliot does not really like novels. In fact I think that he does not really like *prose* except when it is used for didactic purposes. This is very important. Eliot remarks, apropos of his own work, 'In one's prose reflection one may be legitimately occupied with ideals, whereas in the writing of verse one can only deal with actuality.' And I suspect that he believes in general that prose is not well able to deal, in that sense, with actuality. Such a belief is of course entirely in the Symbolist manner. The Symbolist ideal of significance, the ideal of the resonant self-contained work of art which made itself as like as possible to a *thing*, made difficulties for the ordinary discursive features of language. Mallarmé, for instance, went to extremes to overcome these difficulties. Language was, as it were, too 'spread out' for the Symbolists. It was only of value to them if they could tie it into a knot. It was 'not to mean, but to be'. Clearly from this point of view, poetry is of far more use than prose – in fact, prose might just as well be written off, banished altogether from the realm of art, and left to do the jobs of explanation and instruction which it is so well fitted to perform.

It is significant that this view is quite explicitly stated by Sartre in his book *What Is Literature?*, where he distinguishes between 'the word which is lived and the word which is met'. Poetry is the word which is met, which lies outside us, separate, thing-like, and complete. Prose is the word which is lived, the language which we inhabit and which we must treat as a tool, and use for making disclosures. That is, poetry is conceived in terms of the Kantian Romantic conception of the work of art, whereas prose should be thought of as useful, informative, and essentially didactic. Sartre imagines that by making this distinction he is defending prose; he is defending it by asserting that it must give information and not attempt to be poetry. There is a place for this assertion, as a protest for instance against certain degenerations, attempted suicides as it were, of prose language. But I shall argue that this is not the best way to defend prose, and is indeed merely another way of betraying it.

We may put Mr Eliot's attitude to language in terms of a distinction which I made earlier, and which may serve as a formula to explain the Symbolist–Romantic position, and to give a clue to much that is, in my view, not well with modern literature. Eliot criticises the Liberal view of personality because it seems to him to encourage a complete self-absorption of the individual. With this criticism I have some sympathy. But one must ask what it is *outside* the individual the reality of which ought to be attended to. Eliot answers: things and institutions. Our attention to things properly takes the form of art, and where language is concerned takes the form of poetry. Our attention to institutions properly takes the form of didactic reflective prose writing. Eliot does *not* say that what we should attend to outside ourselves is other persons. So it is not surprising that he makes no place for imaginative prose literature which is *par excellence* the form of art most concerned with the existence of other persons. And with developments such as these, which take conscious form in critics as wide apart as Eliot and Sartre, the stage is set for the decline of the novel. The Romantic theory of art, now passing triumphantly into its last phase, seems to condemn the novel to being either a poem in disguise or else a piece of informative prose, a pamphlet, a human document, or a piece of journalism.

If we turn now to look at modern literature in England and America it is not, I think, difficult to see the pattern which I have indicated. The modern novel, the serious novel, does tend toward either of two extremes: either it is a tight metaphysical object, which wishes it were a poem, and which attempts to convey, often in mythical form, some central truth about the human condition – or else it is a loose journalistic epic, documentary or possibly even didactic in inspiration, offering a commentary on current institutions or on some matter out of history. We are offered things or truths. What we have lost is persons. Modern French literature offers notable examples in both kinds. It is interesting that Sartre and Simone de Beauvoir, both of whom have admitted that they look to art to transform the contingent into the necessary, have been quite willing to surrender to contingency where their own novels are concerned. They have here readily sacrificed form and 'universal significance' to the formless and the deliberately ephemeral. This is done partly as a result of the nature of their talents, but partly, and this they say themselves, with a definite didactic purpose. So we have on the one hand a novel like *The Mandarins*, which is enormous, formless, topical, and often close to being brilliant journalism, and on the other hand, a novel like *The Stranger* of Camus, which is a small, compact, crystalline, self-contained myth about the human condition, as economical, resonant, and thing-like as it is possible to make any piece of imaginative prose writing to be. There is little point in multiplying examples, though one could amuse oneself by doing so at length; and one thing which would, I think, emerge is that on the whole the small metaphysical novels are better than the social epics. Neurosis pays better dividends than convention. The tightly conceived thing-like books are on the whole better written, more imaginatively conceived, and altogether more inspired and ambitious than the others. Plenty of reasons could be suggested for this. Whereas society in the nineteenth century was either a reassuring place where one lived, or else an exciting, rewarding, interesting place where one struggled, society today tends to appear, by contrast, as menacing, puzzling, uncontrollable, or else confining, and boring. And on the other hand, behind and through society we see the whole apocalyptic scene, the travelling rocket, the hydrogen bomb, and all the things which precisely make us want to think in terms of the human condition and the total man.

Modern literature presents us with the triumph of neurosis, the triumph of myth as a solipsistic form. Our social epics lack creative vitality, and are more concerned with exploration of institutions than with creation of character. While in our metaphysical novels, which represent what is best and most influential in our literature, the hero is alone, with no company, or with only other parts of himself for company. Here Hegel is still king and we have Romanticism in its final, purest, and most undiluted form, where the struggle between persons is really a struggle within the mind of a single character. In such works we feel the ruthless subjection of the characters to the will of their author. The characters are no longer free. The author does not even want them to be free. If they were free they would get in his way. His book is an attempt to work out his own salvation by an exercise in self-discovery. I described the Symbol or image of the Symbolists as the making sensible of an idea of individuality, as being an analogon of the real individual. We may notice that with the dominance of what I have called neurotic Romantic literature the real individual has tended to disappear from the novel, and his place has been taken by the symbolic individual who *is* the literary work itself. The naturalistic conception of character has largely disappeared from the intention of the novelist and from the apparatus of the critic. And indeed how few characters from recent novels can we remember as personalities. We most remember personalities in those cases where a single person has swallowed up the entire book: we remember the hero of *The Stranger*, we remember the hero of *The Catcher in the Rye*. But this is because of an overwhelming presence, not of course necessarily in the autobiographical sense, of the author. What we recall is the author himself, or else something very significant about him. Whereas when we think of the works of Tolstoy or George Eliot, we are not remembering Tolstoy and George Eliot, we are remembering Dolly, Kitty, Stiva, Dorothea and Casaubon.

I cannot feel that we should be resigned to this situation. Indeed the danger is rather, as one looks about, not simply that we should become resigned to it, but that we should positively glory in it. But if we do this we abandon something important which is the special property of prose literature. Poetry may tell us truths or it may attempt to be a thing. It may be *The Vanity of Human Wishes* or *Bâteau ivre*. But the novel has got to face the special problem of the individual *within* the work. It has got to solve that problem; and, if I am right, to solve it by denying freedom to the fictional individual either by making him merely part of his creator's mind, or by treating him as a conventional social unit, is likely to be a sort of failure. To speak of failure here has nothing disgraceful about it. Almost every work of art is a failure. The point is that this particular type of failure is one that we ought never to cease worrying about. What sort of works are most effortlessly and naturally written under present social conditions is quite another matter; and it is another matter too that there are major works which disregard the rules I am suggesting. Though I would venture to say that ultimately we judge the great novelists by the quality of their awareness of others, and that for the novelist this is at the highest level the most crucial test. But whatever one may think about the temper of the age, and about the value of what I have called neurotic works, it remains important to resist certain critical assumptions, and to keep alive certain standards of value and comparison. Unless we do this, and do it, I think, in something like the way I am suggesting, we shall be unable to understand or explain why it is that Walter Scott and Tolstoy are to a staggering degree better than the most praised of contemporary novelists. And what we cannot explain we may cease to believe. We shall lose our sense of distance; and this will be a pity.

Nowadays we no longer demand of people in books that they should be like real people, except in some minimal sense of verisimilitude in a book of a documentary type. And we may be tempted to forget how almost impossibly difficult it is to create a free and lifelike character, or to feel that this particular effort is worth [ma]king. This ready surrender of something which it seems to me is the essential power of prose literature is also dangerous at a moment when science leads us to think of personality in a technical and departmentalised fashion, and when philosophy has left us without a way of envisaging the whole person, and has even popularised a very partial view. Mr Eliot was right to denounce the shallowness of the Liberal concept of personality. And there is a sense here in which literature, for our sake as well as its own, is called on to bear witness.

To ask the novelist to bear these things in mind is not to ask him to become a didactic writer. On the contrary, as I have suggested, didactic writing is, paradoxically, a nemesis of the Romantic view of art, and involves the surrender of the values of which I speak. That literature must be either play (production of self-contained things) or else didactic (discursive statement of truths) is a fallacy which dates from Kant, and which is of the essence of Romanticism. This view, which condemns prose to being either poetry *manqué* or journalism, is I think a misleading view even when applied to poetry. Applied to prose it can be very dangerous indeed. Prose literature can *reveal* an aspect of the world which no other art can reveal, and the discipline required for this revelation is *par excellence* the discipline of this art. And in the case of the novel, the most important thing to be thus revealed, not necessarily the only thing, but incomparably the most important thing, is that other people exist.

We may indeed look back to Kant, not only for the source of the error, but for the clue to its solution. Kant contrasted the experience of beauty, the reposeful contemplation of the purposeless self-contained quasi-object, with the experience of the sublime, the upsetting glimpse of the boundlessness of nature; the latter *only* was a spiritual or moral experience, and for Kant it had nothing to do with art. But one's theory of art must account for the fact that experience of art is spiritual experience. This is more obviously true of some arts than of others, and whether one wants to make it universally true, i.e. to say that *any* art experience is spiritual experience, is too large a question to pursue here. For purposes of my argument, it seems clear enough that experience of the art of the novel is spiritual experience; and where spirit fails, I would want to argue, art fails. Kant creates the error and suggests the cure; for the theory of the sublime can be transformed into a theory of art. 'The sublime' is an enjoyment and renewal of spiritual power arising from an apprehension of the vast formless strength of the natural world. How close this is indeed to being a theory of tragedy, if we think of the spectator as gazing not at the Alps, but at the spectacle of human life.

It is indeed the realisation of a vast and varied reality outside ourselves which brings about a sense initially of terror, and when properly understood of exhilaration and spiritual power. But what brings this experience to us, in its most important form, is the sight, not of physical nature, but of our surroundings as consisting of other individual men. It is the spectacle of this manifold, if we can actually apprehend it, which is not easy, which brings the exhilaration and the power and reminds us, to use Kant's words, of our supersensible destiny. Obviously its apprehension is not solely the concern of art. But art, of certain types at least, is intimately connected with this apprehension, fails where the apprehension fails, and where it succeeds has spiritual power derived from this source.

What is pictured here is very like Kant's idea of the sublime – and yet importantly different too. Kant's man stands alone confronting the mountains or the sea and feels defiant pride in the free power of his reason. His reason, it is true, is at that moment frustrated and conscious of its inability to achieve complete understanding; but there is nothing humbling or regrettable about this frustration. On the contrary, it brings with it a larger consciousness of the dignity of rationality. Whereas the man that I have in mind, faced by the manifold of humanity, may feel, as well as terror, delight, but not, if he really sees what is before him, superiority. He will suffer that undramatic, because un-self-centred, agnosticism which goes with tolerance. To understand other people is a task which does not come to an end. This man will possess 'spirit' in the sense intended by Pascal when he said: 'The more spirit one has the more original men one discovers. Ordinary people do not notice differences between men.' And a better name for spirit here is not reason, not tolerance even, but love.

When Mr Eliot praised Jane Austen because her standards, though not lofty, were not of her own making, he was, I have suggested, confusing the question of her achievement as an artist (her ability to see something other than herself) with the question of her attitude to the society she described (which he likes because it is a conservative one). An artist as great, but not as conservative, George Eliot, meets with his disapproval. Yet when he was thinking of his own work, and when he was thinking simply as an artist and not as a politician, Mr Eliot understood the matter very well, as when he said: 'The progress of an artist is a continual self-sacrifice, a continual extinction of personality.' This is perfectly true. Art is not an expression of personality, it is a question rather of the continual expelling of oneself from the matter in hand. Anyone who has attempted to write a novel will have discovered this difficulty in the special form which it takes when one is dealing with fictitious characters. Is one going to be able to present any character other than oneself who is more than a conventional puppet? How soon one discovers that, however much one is in the ordinary sense 'interested in other people', this interest has left one far short of possessing the knowledge required to create a real character who is not oneself. It is impossible, it seems to me, not to see one's failure here as a sort of spiritual failure. And to look at virtue, morality, as it appears in this context, may perhaps enlighten us concerning its nature in general. Here a diagnosis of literary ills brings us back to moral philosophy and to the philosophy of Liberalism.

Virtue is not essentially or immediately concerned with choosing between actions or rules or reasons, nor with stripping the personality for a leap. It is concerned with really apprehending that other people exist. This too is what freedom really is; and it is impossible not to feel the creation of a work of art as a struggle for freedom. Freedom is not choosing; that is merely the move that we make when all is already lost. Freedom is knowing and understanding and respecting things quite other than ourselves. Virtue is in this sense to be construed as knowledge, and connects us so with reality. The Kantians were wrong to exclude knowledge from virtue, and the Hegelians were wrong to make virtue into a self-knowledge which excluded others. The knowledge and imagination which is virtue is precisely the kind which the novelist needs to let his characters be, to respect their freedom, and to study them themselves in that most significant area of activity, where they are trying to apprehend the reality of others. The artist is indeed the analogon of the good man, and in a special sense he *is* the good man: the lover who, nothing himself, lets other things be through him. And that also, I am sure, is what is meant by 'negative capability'.

I have suggested that it is necessary to detach Liberalism from Romanticism. To do this we must be willing consciously to defend against science, against philosophy, against political theories, against even in some forms literature, a conception of the whole human being, the contingent eccentric fellow, the fellow whom John Stuart Mill lovingly envisaged but whom he was unable philosophically to protect, as having a right to exist. Here prose literature can help our health by not abandoning the naturalistic idea of character; and that this will also be in its own best interests as an art will not be accidental. Literature, morals, and politics must all concern themselves with reality. David Hume uttered perhaps the most important half-truth in the history of political philosophy when he said that something could be true in politics which was false in fact. It seems that what is false in fact cannot go on indefinitely being true in politics; and we have lived for long enough on the notion of the Kantian rational being.

I want to bring this to a close by quoting two remarks by Henry James. The first is his well-known remark concerning Balzac and his characters; that Balzac did not love these people because he knew them, he knew them because he loved them. And this expresses the essence of what I have here wanted to say. The second remark is this, made by James in a letter. He quotes a passage which describes two people falling in love, from a novel by Pierre Loti, and then he says of the passage: 'Perhaps you will find in it something of the same strange *eloquence* of suggestion and rhythm as I do: which is what literature gives when it is most exquisite and which constitutes its sovereign value and its resistance to devouring time.'

This, which reads almost strangely now, comes to remind us that novels are after all written in words. I have suggested that we are still suffering from the results of the Romantic attack on words. The novelist who is either poet or journalist is not using prose as he should. A literature that is written in words, like a literature which really envisages persons, is disappearing. And with Henry James's remark we may turn at last to what finally differentiates art from life, the question of form. Form is the temptation of love and its peril, whether in art or life: to round off a situation, to sum up a character. But the difference is that art has *got* to have form, whereas life need not. And any artist both dreads and longs for the approach of necessity, the moment at which form irrevocably crystallises. There is a temptation for any novelist, and one to which if I am right modern novelists yield too readily, to imagine that the problem of a novel is solved and the difficulties overcome as soon as a form in the sense of a satisfactory myth has been evolved. But that is only the beginning. There is then the much more difficult battle to prevent that form from becoming rigid, by the free expansion against it of the individual characters. Here above all the contingency of the characters must be respected. Contingency must be defended for it is the essence of personality. And here is where it becomes so important to remember that the novel is written in words, to remember that 'eloquence of suggestion and rhythm' of which James spoke. A novel must be a house fit for free characters to live in; and to combine form with a respect for reality with all its odd contingent ways is the highest art of prose.

Essay in *Yale Review*, December 1959.

Against Dryness

The complaints which I wish to make are concerned primarily with prose, not with poetry, and primarily with novels, not with drama; and they are brief, simplified, abstract, and possibly insular. They are not to be construed as implying any precise picture of 'the function of the writer'. It is the function of the writer to write the best book he knows how to write. These remarks have to do with the background to present-day literature, in Liberal democracies in general and Welfare States in particular, in a sense in which this must be the concern of any serious critic.

We live in a scientific and anti-metaphysical age in which the dogmas, images, and precepts of religion have lost much of their power. We have not recovered from two wars and the experience of Hitler. We are also the heirs of the Enlightenment, Romanticism, and the Liberal tradition. These are the elements of our dilemma: whose chief feature, in my view, is that we have been left with far too shallow and flimsy an idea of human personality. I shall explain this.

Philosophy, like the newspapers, is both the guide and the mirror of its age. Let us look quickly at Anglo-Saxon philosophy and at French philosophy and see what picture of human personality we can gain from these two depositories of wisdom. Upon Anglo-Saxon philosophy the two most profound influences have been Hume and Kant: and it is not difficult to see in the current philosophical conception of the person the work of these two great thinkers. This conception consists in the joining of a materialistic behaviourism with a dramatic view of the individual as a solitary will. These subtly give support to each other. From Hume through Bertrand Russell, with friendly help from mathematical logic and science, we derive the idea that reality is finally a quantity of material atoms and that significant discourse must relate itself directly or indirectly to reality so conceived. This position was most picturesquely summed up in Wittgenstein's *Tractatus*. Recent philosophy, especially the later work of Wittgenstein and the work of Gilbert Ryle derivative therefrom, alters this a little. The atomic Humian picture is abandoned in favour of a type of conceptual analysis (in many ways admirable) which emphasises the structural dependence of concepts upon the public language in which they are framed. This analysis has important results in the philosophy of mind, where it issues in modified behaviourism. Roughly: my inner life, for me just as for others, is identifiable as existing only through the application to it of public concepts, concepts which can only be constructed on the basis of overt behaviour.

This is one side of the picture, the Humian and post-Humian side. On the other side, we derive from Kant, and also Hobbes and Bentham through John Stuart Mill, a picture of the individual as a free rational will. With the removal of Kant's metaphysical background this individual is seen as alone. (He is in a certain sense alone on Kant's view also, that is: not confronted with real dissimilar others.) With the addition of some utilitarian optimism he is seen as eminently educable. With the addition of some modern psychology he is seen as capable of self-knowledge by methods agreeable to science and common sense. So we have the modern man, as he appears in many recent works on ethics and I believe also to a large extent in the popular consciousness.

We meet, for instance, a refined picture of this man in Stuart Hampshire's book *Thought and Action*. He is rational and totally free except in so far as, in the most ordinary law-court and commonsensical sense, his degree of self-awareness may vary. He is, morally speaking, monarch of all he surveys and totally responsible for his actions. Nothing transcends him. His moral language is a practical pointer, the instrument of his choices, the indication of his preferences. His inner life is resolved into his acts and choices, and his beliefs, which are also acts, since a belief can only be identified through its expression. His moral arguments are references to empirical facts backed up by decisions. The only moral word which he requires is 'good' (or 'right'), the word which expresses decision. His rationality expresses itself in awareness of the facts, whether about the world or about himself. The virtue which is fundamental to him is sincerity.

If we turn to French philosophy we may see, at least in that section of it which has most caught the popular imagination, I mean in the work of Jean-Paul Sartre, essentially the same picture. It is interesting how extremely Kantian this picture is, for all Sartre's indebtedness to Hegelian sources. Again, the individual is pictured as solitary and totally free. There is no transcendent reality, there are no degrees of freedom. On the one hand there is the mass of psychological desires and social habits and prejudices, on the other hand there is the will. Certain dramas, more Hegelian in character, are of course enacted within the soul; but the isolation of the will remains. Hence *angoisse*. Hence, too, the special anti-bourgeois flavour of Sartre's philosophy which makes it appeal to many intellectuals: the ordinary traditional picture of personality and the virtues lies under suspicion of *mauvaise foi*. Again the only real virtue is sincerity. It is, I think, no accident that, however much philosophical and other criticism Sartre may receive, this powerful picture has caught our imagination. The Marxist critics may plausibly claim that it represents the essence of the Liberal theory of personality.

It will be pointed out that other phenomenological theories (leaving aside Marxism) have attempted to do what Sartre has failed to do, and that there are notable philosophers who have offered a different picture of the soul. Yes; yet from my own knowledge of the scene I would doubt whether any (non-Marxist) account of human personality has yet emerged from phenomenology which is fundamentally unlike the one which I have described and can vie with it in imaginative power. It may be said that philosophy cannot in fact produce such an account. I am not sure about this, nor is this large question my concern here. I express merely my belief that, for the Liberal world, philosophy is not in fact at present able to offer us any other complete and powerful picture of the soul. I return now to England and the Anglo-Saxon tradition.

The Welfare State has come about as a result, largely, of socialist thinking and socialist endeavour. It has seemed to bring a certain struggle to an end; and with that ending has come a lassitude about fundamentals. If we compare the language of the original Labour Party constitution with that of its recent successor we see an impoverishment of thinking and language which is typical. The Welfare State is the reward of 'empiricism in politics'. It has represented to us a set of thoroughly desirable but limited ends, which could be conceived *in non-theoretical terms*; and in pursuing it, in allowing the idea of it to dominate the more naturally theoretical wing of our political scene, we have to a large extent lost our theories. Our central conception is still a debilitated form of Mill's equation: happiness equals freedom equals personality. There should have been a revolt against utilitarianism; but for many reasons it has not taken place. In 1905 John Maynard Keynes and his friends welcomed the philosophy of G. E. Moore because Moore reinstated the concept of experience, Moore directed attention away from the mechanics of action and towards the inner life. But Moore's 'experience' was too shallow a concept; and a scientific age with simple, attainable, empirical aims has preferred a more behaviouristic philosophy.

What have we lost here? And what have we perhaps never had? We have suffered a general loss of concepts, the loss of a moral and political vocabulary. We no longer use a spread-out substantial picture of the manifold virtues of man and society. We no longer see man against a background of values, of realities, which transcend him. We picture man as a brave naked will surrounded by an easily comprehended empirical world. For the hard idea of truth we have substituted a facile idea of sincerity. What we have never had, of course, is a satisfactory Liberal theory of personality, a theory of man as free and separate and related to a rich and complicated world from which, as a moral being, he has much to learn. We have bought the Liberal theory as it stands, because we have wished to encourage people to think of themselves as free, at the cost of surrendering the background.

We have never solved the problems about human personality posed by the Enlightenment. Between the various concepts available to us the real question has escaped: and now, in a curious way, our present situation is analogous to an eighteenth-century one. We retain a rationalistic optimism about the beneficent results of education, or rather, technology. We combine this with a romantic conception of 'the human condition', a picture of the individual as stripped and solitary: a conception which has, since Hitler, gained a peculiar intensity.

The eighteenth century was an era of rationalistic allegories and moral tales. The nineteenth century (roughly) was the great era of the novel: and the novel throve upon a dynamic merging of the idea of person with the idea of class. Because nineteenth-century society was dynamic and interesting and because (to use a Marxist notion) the type and the individual could there be seen as merged, the solution of the eighteenth-century problem could be put off. It has been put off till now. Now that the structure of society is less interesting and less alive than it was in the nineteenth century, and now that Welfare economics have removed certain incentives to thinking, and now that the values of science are so much taken for granted, we confront in a particularly dark and confusing form a dilemma which has been with us implicitly since the Enlightenment, or since the beginning, wherever exactly one wishes to place it, of the modern Liberal world.

If we consider twentieth-century literature as compared with nineteenth-century literature, we notice certain significant contrasts. I said that, in a way, we were back in the eighteenth century, the era of rationalistic allegories and moral tales, the era when the idea of human nature was unitary and single. The nineteenth-century novel (I use these terms boldly and roughly: of course there were exceptions) was not concerned with 'the human condition', it was concerned with real various individuals struggling in society. The twentieth-century novel is usually either crystalline or journalistic; that is, it is either a small quasi-allegorical object portraying the human condition and not containing 'characters' in the nineteenth-century sense, or else it is a large shapeless quasi-documentary object, the degenerate descendant of the nineteenth-century novel, telling, with pale conventional characters, some straightforward story enlivened with empirical facts. Neither of these kinds of literature engages with the problem that I mentioned above.

It may readily be noted that if our prose fiction is either crystalline or journalistic, the crystalline works are usually the better ones. They are what the more serious writers want to create. We may recall the ideal of 'dryness' which we associate with the symbolist movement, with writers such as T. E. Hulme and T. S. Eliot, with Paul Valéry, with Wittgenstein. This 'dryness' (smallness, clearness, self-containedness) is a nemesis of Romanticism. Indeed it *is* Romanticism in a later phase. The pure, clean, self-contained 'symbol', the exemplar incidentally of what Kant, ancestor of both Liberalism and Romanticism, required art to be, is the analogue of the lonely self-contained individual. It is what is left of the other-worldliness of Romanticism when the 'messy' humanitarian and revolutionary elements have spent their force. The temptation of art, a temptation to which every work of art yields except the greatest ones, is to console. The modern writer, frightened of technology and (in England) abandoned by philosophy and (in France) presented with simplified dramatic theories, attempts to console us by myths or by stories.

On the whole: his truth is sincerity and his imagination is fantasy. Fantasy operates either with shapeless day-dreams (the journalistic story) or with small myths, toys, crystals. Each in his own way produces a sort of 'dream necessity'. Neither grapples with reality: hence 'fantasy', not 'imagination'.

The proper home of the symbol, in the 'symbolist' sense, is poetry. Even there it may play an equivocal role since there is something in symbolism which is inimical to words, out of which, we have been reminded, poems are constructed. Certainly the invasion of other areas by what I may call, for short, 'symbolist ideals', has helped to bring about a decline of prose. Eloquence is out of fashion; even 'style', except in a very austere sense of this term, is out of fashion.

T. S. Eliot and Jean-Paul Sartre, dissimilar enough as thinkers, both tend to undervalue prose and to deny it any *imaginative* function. Poetry is the creation of linguistic quasi-things; prose is for explanation and exposition, it is essentially didactic, documentary, informative. Prose is ideally transparent; it is only *faute de mieux* written in words. The influential modern stylist is Hemingway. It would be almost inconceivable now to write like Landor. Most modern English novels indeed are not *written*. One feels they could slip into some other medium without much loss. It takes a foreigner like Nabokov or an Irishman like Beckett to animate prose language into an imaginative stuff in its own right.

[292]

Tolstoy who said that art was an expression of the religious perception of the age was nearer the truth than Kant who saw it as the imagination in a frolic with the understanding. The connection between art and the moral life has languished because we are losing our sense of form and structure in the moral world itself. Linguistic and existentialist behaviourism, our Romantic philosophy, has reduced our vocabulary and simplified and impoverished our view of the inner life. It is natural that a Liberal democratic society will not be concerned with techniques of improvement, will deny that virtue is knowledge, will emphasise choice at the expense of vision; and a Welfare State will weaken the incentives to investigate the bases of a Liberal democratic society. For political purposes we have been encouraged to think of ourselves as totally free and responsible, knowing everything we need to know for the important purposes of life. But this is one of the things of which Hume said that it may be true in politics but false in fact; and is it really true in politics? We need a post-Kantian unromantic Liberalism with a different image of freedom.

The technique of becoming free is more difficult than John Stuart Mill imagined. We need more concepts than our philosophies have furnished us with. We need to be enabled to think in terms of degrees of freedom, and to picture, in a non-metaphysical, non-totalitarian and non-religious sense, the transcendence of reality. A simple-minded faith in science, together with the assumption that we are all rational and totally free, engenders a dangerous lack of curiosity about the real world, a failure to appreciate the difficulties of knowing it. We need to return from the self-centred concept of sincerity to the other-centred concept of truth. We are not isolated free choosers, monarchs of all we survey, but benighted creatures sunk in a reality whose nature we are constantly and overwhelmingly tempted to deform by fantasy. Our current picture of freedom encourages a dream-like facility; whereas what we require is a renewed sense of the difficulty and complexity of the moral life and the opacity of persons. We need more concepts in terms of which to picture the substance of our being; it is through an enriching and deepening of concepts that moral progress takes place. Simone Weil said that morality was a matter of attention, not of will. We need a new vocabulary of attention.

It is here that literature is so important, especially since it has taken over some of the tasks formerly performed by philosophy. Through literature we can re-discover a sense of the density of our lives. Literature can arm us against consolation and fantasy and can help us to recover from the ailments of Romanticism. If it can be said to have a task, that surely is its task. But if it is to perform it, prose must recover its former glory, eloquence and discourse must return. I would connect eloquence with the attempt to speak the truth. I think here of the work of Albert Camus. All his novels were *written*; but the last one, though less striking and successful than the first two, seems to me to have been a more serious attempt upon the truth: and illustrates what I mean by eloquence.

It is curious that modern literature, which is so much concerned with violence, contains so few convincing pictures of evil.

Our inability to imagine evil is a consequence of the facile, dramatic and, in spite of Hitler, optimistic picture of ourselves with which we work. Our difficulty about form, about images – our tendency to produce works which are either crystalline or journalistic – is a symptom of our situation. Form itself can be a temptation, making the work of art into a small myth which is a self-contained and indeed self-satisfied individual. We need to turn our attention away from the consoling dream necessity of Romanticism, away from the dry symbol, the bogus individual, the false whole, towards the real impenetrable human person. That this person is substantial, impenetrable, individual, indefinable, and valuable is after all the fundamental tenet of Liberalism.

It is here, however much one may criticise the emptiness of the Liberal idea of freedom, however much one may talk in terms of restoring a lost unity, that one is forever at odds with Marxism. Reality is not a given whole. An understanding of this, a respect for the contingent, is essential to imagination as opposed to fantasy. Our sense of form, which is an aspect of our desire for consolation, can be a danger to our sense of reality as a rich receding background. Against the consolations of form, the clean crystalline work, the simplified fantasy-myth, we must pit the destructive power of the now so unfashionable naturalistic idea of character.

Real people are destructive of myth, contingency is destructive of fantasy and opens the way for imagination. Think of the Russians, those great masters of the contingent. Too much contingency of course may turn art into journalism. But since reality is incomplete, art must not be too much afraid of incompleteness. Literature must always represent a battle between real people and images; and what it requires now is a much stronger and more complex conception of the former.

In morals and politics we have stripped ourselves of concepts. Literature, in curing its own ills, can give us a new vocabulary of experience, and a truer picture of freedom. With this, renewing our sense of distance, we may remind ourselves that art too lives in a region where all human endeavour is failure. Perhaps only Shakespeare manages to create at the highest level both images and people; and even *Hamlet* looks second-rate compared with *Lear*. Only the very greatest art invigorates without consoling, and defeats our attempts, in W. H. Auden's words, to use it as magic.

Essay in *Encounter*, January 1961.

PART SEVEN

Re-reading Plato, 1964–86

'We need a moral philosophy that can speak significantly of Freud and Marx, and out of which aesthetic and political views can be generated. We need a moral philosophy in which the concept of love, so rarely mentioned now by philosophers, can once again be made central.'

'On "God" and "Good"', 1969

The Idea of Perfection

It is sometimes said, either irritably or with a certain satisfaction, that philosophy makes no progress. It is certainly true, and I think this is an abiding and not a regrettable characteristic of the discipline, that philosophy has in a sense to keep trying to return to the beginning: a thing which it is not at all easy to do. There is a two-way movement in philosophy, a movement towards the building of elaborate theories, and a move back again towards the consideration of simple and obvious facts. McTaggart says that time is unreal, Moore replies that he has just had his breakfast.* Both these aspects of philosophy are necessary to it.

I wish in this discussion to attempt a movement of return, a retracing of our steps to see how a certain position was reached. The position in question, in current moral philosophy, is one which seems to me unsatisfactory in two related ways, in that it ignores certain facts and at the same time imposes a single theory which admits of no communication with or escape into rival theories. If it is true that philosophy has almost always done this, it is also true that philosophers have never put up with it for very long. Instances of the facts, as I shall boldly call them, which interest me and which seem to have been forgotten or 'theorised away' are the fact that an unexamined life can be virtuous and the fact that love is a central concept in morals. Contemporary philosophers frequently connect consciousness with virtue, and although they constantly talk of

---

* [G. E. Moore (1873–1958) and J. E. McTaggart (1866–1925), contemporaries at Cambridge. McTaggart's arguments about the unreality of time – see e.g. *The Nature of Existence* – are said to have driven Moore to philosophising. Moore wrestled with the problem of perception, and that of the objectivity of goodness – see e.g. *Principia Ethica*.]

[299]

freedom they rarely talk of love. But there must be some relation between these latter concepts, and it must be possible to do justice to both Socrates and the virtuous peasant. In such 'musts' as these lie the deepest springs and motives of philosophy. Yet if in an attempt to enlarge our field of vision we turn for a moment to philosophical theories outside our own tradition we find it very difficult to establish any illuminating connection.

Professor Hampshire says, in the penultimate chapter of *Thought and Action,* that 'it is the constructive task of a philosophy of mind to provide a set of terms in which ultimate judgements of value can be very clearly stated'. In this understanding of it, philosophy of mind is the background to moral philosophy; and in so far as modern ethics tends to constitute a sort of Newspeak which makes certain values non-expressible, the reasons for this are to be sought in current philosophy of mind and in the fascinating power of a certain picture of the soul. One suspects that philosophy of mind has not in fact been performing the task, which Professor Hampshire recommends, of sorting and classifying fundamental moral issues; it has rather been imposing upon us a particular value judgement in the guise of a theory of human nature. Whether philosophy can ever do anything *else* is a question we shall have to consider. But in so far as modern philosophers profess to be analytic and neutral, any failure to be so deserves comment. And an attempt to produce, if not a comprehensive analysis, at least a rival soul-picture which covers a greater or a different territory should make new places for philosophical reflection. We would like to know what, as moral agents, we have got to do because of logic, what we have got to do because of human nature, and what we can choose to do. Such a programme is easy to state and perhaps impossible to carry out. But even to discover what, under these headings, we *can* achieve certainly demands a much more complex and subtle conceptual system than any which we can find readily available.

Before going on to consider the problems in philosophy of mind which underlie the inarticulate moments of modern ethics, I should like to say a word about G. E. Moore. Moore is as it were the frame of the picture. A great deal has happened since he wrote, and when we read him again it is startling to see how many of his beliefs are philosophically unstatable now. Moore believed that good was a supersensible reality, that it was a mysterious quality, unrepresentable and indefinable, that it was an object of knowledge and (implicitly) that to be able to see it was in some sense to have it. He thought of the good upon the analogy of the beautiful; and he was, in spite of himself, a 'naturalist' in that he took goodness to be a real constituent of the world. We know how severely and in what respects Moore was corrected by his successors. Moore was quite right (it was said) to separate the question 'What does "good" mean?' from the question 'What things are good?' though he was wrong to answer the second question as well as the first. He was right to say that good was indefinable, but wrong to say that it was the name of a quality. Good is indefinable because judgements of value depend upon the will and choice of the individual. Moore was wrong (his critics continue) to use the quasi-aesthetic imagery of vision in conceiving the good. Such a view, conceiving the good on the analogy of the beautiful, would seem to make possible a contemplative attitude on the part of the moral agent, whereas the point about this person is that he is essentially and inescapably an *agent*. The image whereby to understand morality, it is argued, is not the image of vision but the image of movement. Goodness and beauty are not analogous but sharply contrasting ideas. Good must be thought of, not as part of the world, but as a movable label affixed to the world; for only so can the agent be pictured as responsible and free. And indeed this truth Moore himself half apprehended when he separated the denotation from the connotation of 'good'. The concept 'good' is not the name of an esoteric object, it is the tool of every rational man. Goodness is not an object of insight or knowledge, it is a function of the will. Thus runs the correction of Moore; and let me say in anticipation that on almost every point I agree with Moore and not with his critics.

The idea that 'good' is a function of the will stunned philosophy with its attractiveness, since it solved so many problems at one blow: metaphysical entities were removed, and moral judgements were seen to be, not weird statements, but something much more comprehensible, such as persuasions or commands or rules. The idea has its own obviousness: but it does not depend for its plausibility solely upon its usefulness or upon an appeal to our ordinary knowledge of the moral life. It coheres with a whole moral psychology, much of which has been elaborated more recently. I want now to examine certain aspects of this psychology and to trace it to what I think is its origin and basis in a certain argument of Wittgenstein. First I shall sketch 'the man' which this psychology presents us with, then I shall comment on this man's most important features, and then I shall proceed to consider the radical arguments for such an image.

I shall use for my picture of 'the man' of modern moral philosophy two works of Professor Hampshire, his book *Thought and Action* and his lecture *Disposition and Memory*. Hampshire's view is, I think, without commanding universal agreement, fairly central and typical, and it has the great merit that it states and elaborates what in many modern moral philosophers is simply taken for granted. Hampshire suggests that we should abandon the image (dear to the British empiricists) of man as a detached observer, and should rather picture him as an object moving among other objects in a continual flow of intention into action. Touch and movement, not vision, should supply our metaphors: 'Touching, handling and the manipulation of things are misrepresented if we follow the analogy of vision.' Actions are, roughly, instances of moving things about in the public world. Nothing counts as an act unless it is a 'bringing about of a recognizable change in the world'. What sorts of things can be such recognisable changes? Here we must distinguish between 'the things and persons that constitute the external world and the sensations and impressions that I or anyone else may from moment to moment enjoy'. What is 'real' is potentially open to different observers. The inner or mental world is inevitably parasitic upon the outer world, it has 'a parasitic and shadowy nature'. The definiteness of any thought process depends upon 'the possibility of [its] being recognized, scrutinized and identified by observers from different points of view; this possibility is essential to any definite reality'. 'The play of the mind, free of any expression in audible speech or visible action is a reality, as the play of shadows is a reality. But any description of it is derived from the description of its natural expression in speech and action.' 'The assent that takes place within the mind and in no process of communication when no question has been actually asked and answered is a shadowy assent and a shadowy act.' 'Thought cannot be thought, as opposed to day-dreaming or musing, unless it is directed towards a conclusion, whether in action or in judgement.' Further: thought and belief are separate from will and action. 'We do try, in ordinary speech and thought, to keep the distinction between thought and action as definite as possible.' Thought as such is not action but an introduction to action. 'That which I do is that for which I am responsible and which is peculiarly an expression of myself. It is essential to thought that it takes its own forms and follows its own paths without my intervention, that is, without the intervention of my will. I identify myself with my will. Thought, when it is most pure, is self-directing . . . Thought begins on its own path, governed by its universal rules, when the preliminary work of the will is done. No process of thought could be punctuated by acts of will, voluntary switchings of attention, and retain its status as a continuous process of thought.' These are very important assumptions. It will follow from this that a 'belief' is not something subject to the will. 'It seems that I cannot present my own belief in something as an achievement, because, by so presenting it, I would disqualify it as *belief*.' These quotations are from *Thought and Action*, the later part of Chapter Two.

In the Ernest Jones lecture, *Disposition and Memory*, Hampshire does two things: he puts the arguments of *Thought and Action* more polemically in a nutshell, and he introduces, under the protection of Freud, an idea of 'personal verification' which I shall discuss at length below. From *Disposition and Memory*: 'Intention is the one concept that ought to be preserved free from any taint of the less than conscious.' And 'it is characteristic of mental, as opposed to physical, concepts that the conditions of their application can only be understood if they are analysed genetically'. These are succinct statements of what has already been argued in *Thought and Action*. Hampshire now gives us in addition a picture of 'the ideally rational man'. This person would be 'aware of all his memories as memories . . . His wishes would be attached to definite possibilities in a definite future . . . He would . . . distinguish his present situation from unconscious memories of the past . . . and would find his motives for action in satisfying his instinctual needs within the objectively observed features of the situation.' This ideal man does not exist because the palimpsest of 'dispositions' is too hard to penetrate: and this is just as well because ideal rationality would leave us 'without art, without dream or imagination, without likes or dislikes unconnected with instinctual needs'. In theory, though not in practice, 'an interminable analysis' could lay bare the dispositional machinery and make possible a perfect prediction of conduct; but Hampshire emphasises (and this is the main point of the lecture) that such ideal knowledge would not take the form of a scientific law but would have its basis and its verification in the history of the individual. I shall argue later that the very persuasive image with which Hampshire has presented us contains incompatible elements. Roughly, there is a conflict between the 'logical' view of the mind and the 'historical' view of the mind, a conflict which exists partly because logic is still tied to an old-fashioned conception of science. But this is to anticipate.

I shall find it useful later to define my own view in fairly exact section-by-section contrast with Hampshire's; and as his view is rich in detail, extensive quotation has been necessary. As I have suggested, Hampshire's man is to be found more or less explicitly lurking behind much that is written nowadays on the subject of moral philosophy and indeed also of politics. Hampshire has thoroughly explored a background which many writers have taken for granted: and for this one is grateful. This 'man', one may add, is familiar to us for another reason: he is the hero of almost every contemporary novel. Let us look at his characteristics, noting them as yet without discussion. Hampshire emphasises clarity of intention. He says 'all problems meet in intention', and he utters in relation to intention the only explicit 'ought' in his psychology. We ought to know what we are doing. We should aim at total knowledge of our situation and a clear conceptualisation of all our possibilities. Thought and intention must be directed towards definite overt issues or else they are merely day-dream. 'Reality' is potentially open to different observers. What is 'inward', what lies in between overt actions, is either impersonal thought, or 'shadows' of acts, or else substanceless dream. Mental life is, and logically must be, a shadow of life in public. Our personal being is the movement of our overtly choosing will. Immense care is taken to picture the will as isolated. It is isolated from belief, from reason, from feeling, and is yet the essential centre of the self. 'I identify myself with my will.' It is separated from belief so that the authority of reason, which manufactures belief, may be entire and so that responsibility for action may be entire as well. My responsibility is a function of my knowledge (which tries to be wholly impersonal) and my will (which is wholly personal). Morality is a matter of thinking clearly and then proceeding to outward dealings with other men.

On this view one might say that morality is assimilated to a visit to a shop. I enter the shop in a condition of totally responsible freedom, I objectively estimate the features of the goods, and I choose. The greater my objectivity and discrimination the larger the number of products from which I can select. (A Marxist critique of this conception of bourgeois capitalist morals would be apt enough. Should we want many goods in the shop or just 'the right goods'?) Both as act and reason, shopping is public. Will does not bear upon reason, so the 'inner life' is not to be thought of as a moral sphere. Reason deals in neutral descriptions and aims at being the frequently mentioned ideal observer. Value terminology will be the prerogative of the will; but since will is pure choice, pure movement, and not thought or vision, will really requires only action words such as 'good' or 'right'. It is not characteristic of the man we are describing, as he appears either in textbooks or in fiction, to possess an elaborate normative vocabulary. Modern ethics analyses 'good', the empty action word which is the correlate of the isolated will, and tends to ignore other value terms. Our hero aims at being a 'realist' and regards sincerity as the fundamental and perhaps the only virtue.

The very powerful image with which we are here presented is behaviourist, existentialist, and utilitarian in a sense which unites these three conceptions. It is behaviourist in its connection of the meaning and being of action with the publicly observable, it is existentialist in its elimination of the substantial self and its emphasis on the solitary omnipotent will, and it is utilitarian in its assumption that morality is and can only be concerned with public acts. It is also incidentally what may be called a democratic view, in that it suggests that morality is not an esoteric achievement but a natural function of any normal man. This position represents, to put it in another way, a happy and fruitful marriage of Kantian liberalism with Wittgensteinian logic solemnised by Freud. But this also is to anticipate; what confronts us here is in fact complex and difficult to analyse. Let me now try to sort out and classify the different questions which need to be answered.

I find the image of man which I have sketched above both alien and implausible. That is, more precisely: I have simple empirical objections (I do not think people are necessarily or essentially 'like that'), I have philosophical objections (I do not find the arguments convincing), and I have moral objections (I do not think people *ought* to picture themselves in this way). It is a delicate and tricky matter to keep these kinds of objections separate in one's mind. Later on I shall try to present my own rival picture. But now first of all I want to examine in more detail the theory of the 'inner life' with which we have been presented. One's initial reaction to this theory is likely to be a strong instinctive one: either one will be content with the emphasis on the reality of the outer, the absence of the inner, or one will feel (as I do) it cannot be so, something vital is missing. And if one thinks that somehow or other 'the inner' is important, one will be the more zealous in criticising the arguments concerning its status. Such criticisms may have far-reaching results, since upon the question of 'what goes on inwardly' in between moments of overt 'movement' depends our view of the status of choice, the meaning of freedom, and the whole problem of the relation of will to reason and intellect to desire. I shall now consider what I think is the most radical argument, the keystone, of this existentialist–behaviourist type of moral psychology: the argument to the effect that mental concepts must be analysed genetically and so the inner must be thought of as parasitic upon the outer.

This argument is best understood as a special case of a yet more general and by now very familiar argument about the status of what is 'private'. Our tradition of philosophy, since Descartes until very recently, has been obsessed by an entity which has had various names: the *cogitatio*, the sense-impression, the sense-datum. This entity, private to each person, was thought of as an *appearance* about which the owner had infallible and certain *knowledge*. It was taken by Descartes as the starting point of a famous argument, and was pictured by the British empiricists as an instrument of thought. The conception of the *cogitatio* or sense-datum, oddly attractive and readily grasped, suggests among other things that what is inward may be private in one of two senses, one a contingent sense and one a logical sense. I can tell you, or refrain from telling you, a secret; but I cannot (logically) show you my sense-data.

After a long and varied history this conception has now been largely abandoned by philosophers. The general argument for abandoning it has two prongs. Briefly, the argument against the *cogitatio* is that (a) such an entity cannot form part of the structure of a public concept, (b) such an entity cannot be introspectively discovered. That is, (a) it's no use, (b) it isn't there. The latter point may be further subdivided into an empirical and a logical contention. The empirical contention is that there are very few and pretty hazy introspectabilia, and the logical contention is that there are in any case difficulties about their identification. Of the two moments in the general argument (a) has received more attention than (b), since as (a) has been regarded as knock-down (b) has been treated as subsidiary. If something is no use it does not matter much whether it's there or not. I shall argue shortly that because something is no use it has been too hastily assumed that something else is not there. But let us first look at the argument in more detail.

I said that the argument about mental concepts was a special case of the general argument. The general argument is at its most felicitous when applied to some simple non-mental concept such as 'red'. 'Red' cannot be the name of something private. The structure of the concept is its public structure, which is established by coinciding procedures in public situations. How much success we can have in establishing any given public structure will be an empirical question. The alleged inner thing can neither be known (Descartes) nor used (the British empiricists). Hume was wrong to worry about the missing shade of blue, not because a man could or couldn't picture it, or that we could or couldn't be persuaded that he had, but because the inner picture is necessarily irrelevant and the possession of the concept is a public skill. What matters is whether I stop at the traffic lights, and not my colour imagery or absence of it. I identify what my senses show me by means of the public schemata which I have learned, and in no other way can this be *known* by me, since knowledge involves the rigidity supplied by a public test. Wittgenstein in the *Untersuchungen* sums the situation up as follows: 'If we construe the grammar of the expression of sensation on the model of "object and name", the object drops out of consideration as irrelevant.'

This argument, which bears down relentlessly upon the case of 'red', might seem to be even more relentless in the case of the very much more shadowy inner entities which might be supposed to be the 'objects' of which mental concepts are 'names'. After all, one might say to oneself in a quasi-nonsensical way, my sensation of red does, when I am doing philosophy, look like something which I have privately 'got'; and if I am not allowed to 'keep' even this clear little thing as my own private datum, why should I expect to 'keep' the hopelessly hazy inner phenomena connected with concepts such as 'decision' and 'desire'? Surely I should in the latter cases be even happier to rely upon the 'outer' face of the concept, since the inner one is so vague. Let me clarify this so as to make plain the force of the genetic argument in the case of mental concepts.

Wittgenstein of course discusses in this context mental as well as physical concepts. But his discussion is marked by a peculiar reticence. He does not make any moral or psychological generalisations. He limits himself to observing that a mental concept verb used in the first person is not a report about something private, since in the absence of any checking procedure it makes no sense to speak of oneself being either right or mistaken. Wittgenstein is not claiming that inner data are 'incommunicable', nor that anything special about human personality follows from their 'absence', he is merely saying that no sense can be attached to the idea of an 'inner object'. There are no 'private ostensive definitions'. Whether Wittgenstein is right to say that we can attach no sense to the idea of being mistaken about how things *seem*, and whether any legitimate conclusions about human nature can be drawn from his position I shall consider later. I want now to go on to look at the conclusions which *have* (not by him) been drawn, and at the developed form of the argument as we find it, with variations, in Hampshire, Hare, Ayer, Ryle and others.

As I have said, the argument seems to bear even more strongly in proportion as the alleged inner datum becomes more obviously shadowy and even tends to be irresponsibly absent. In such cases purely empirical considerations (the empirical subdivision of (b) above) are especially strong. I say, 'Well, I must decide. All right. I'll go.' Perhaps nothing introspectible occurs at all? And even if it does *that* is not the decision. Here we see what is meant by speaking of a genetical analysis. How do I *learn* the concept of decision? By watching someone who says 'I have decided' and who then acts. How else could I learn it? And with that I learn the essence of the matter. I do not 'move on' from a behaviouristic concept to a mental one. (Since ordinary language, which 'misleadingly' connects the mental with the inner, straightforwardly connects the physical with the outer, a genetic analysis of physical concepts would not be especially revealing.) A decision does not turn out to be, when more carefully considered, an introspectible movement. The concept has no further inner structure; it *is* its outer structure. Take an even clearer example. How do I distinguish anger from jealousy? Certainly not by discriminating between two kinds of private mental data. Consider how I *learned* 'anger' and 'jealousy'. What identifies the emotion is the presence not of a particular private object, but of some typical outward behaviour pattern. This will also imply, be it noted, that we can be mistaken in the names which we give to our own mental states.

This is the point at which people may begin to protest and cry out and say that something has been taken from them. Surely there is such a thing as deciding and not acting? Surely there are *private* decisions? Surely there are lots and lots of objects, more or less easily identified, in orbit as it were in inner space? It is not, as the argument would seem to imply, silent and dark within. Philosophers will reply coolly to these protests. Of course a sense can be attached to: he decided to but did not. That is, he said he would go, and we had reasons to believe that he would, but a brick fell on his head. Or, the notion of his going cohered with many other things he was doing and saying, and yet he did not go. But all this is just as overt, just as little private, as the actual carrying out of the decision. And it must be admitted to be, when one reflects, difficult to attach sense by any other method to the idea of an unfulfilled decision, in our own case just as much as in the case of someone else. Are there 'private' decisions? I said some words to myself. But did I really decide? To answer that question I examine the *context* of my announcement rather than its private core.

However, it will be said, surely there *are* introspectible objects which we can identify? We *do* have images, talk to ourselves, etc. Does the genetic argument imply that these are nothing? Well, it might be answered, let us look at them. One might roughly divide these data in order of shadowiness into visual images, verbal thoughts, other images, other thoughts and feelings which while not exactly verbal or visual seem nevertheless to be 'entities'. It will be true of all these that I cannot show them to other people. Of course I can to a limited extent describe them, I can describe my imagery or mention words which I 'say' in my head. I can also give metaphorical descriptions of my states of mind.* But what does this amount to? These data, vaguer and more infrequent than one might unreflectively suppose, cannot claim to be 'the thing itself' of which my uttered thoughts are the report. Note that I offer my descriptions in ordinary public words whose meaning is subject to ordinary public rules. Inner words 'mean' in the same way as outer words; and I can only 'know' my imagery because I know the public things which it is 'of'. Public concepts are in this obvious sense sovereign over private objects; I can only 'identify' the inner, even for my own benefit, via my knowledge of the outer. But in any case there is no check upon the accuracy of such descriptions, and as Wittgenstein says, 'What is this ceremony for?' Who, except possibly empirical psychologists, is interested in alleged reports of what is *purely* inward? And psychologists themselves now have grave doubts about the value of such 'evidence' from introspection. Whether I am *really* thinking about so-and-so or deciding such-and-such or feeling angry or jealous or pleased will be properly determined, and can only be determined, by the overt context, however sketchy and embryonic. That I decided to do X will be true if I said sincerely that I was going to and did it, even if nothing introspectible occurred at all. And equally something introspectible might occur, but if the outward context is entirely lacking the something cannot be called a decision. As Wittgenstein puts it, 'a wheel that can be turned though nothing else moves with it is not part of the mechanism'.

---

* Ryle discusses these 'chronicles' and 'histories' of thought in *Aristotelian Society Supplementary Volume*, 1952.

These radical arguments are, it seems to me, perfectly sound over a certain range. They really do clearly and definitively solve certain problems which have beset British empiricism. By destroying the misleading image of the infallible inner eye they make possible a much improved solution of, for instance, problems about perception and about universals. A great deal that was, in Hume and Berkeley, repugnant to common sense can now be cleared away. But, as I have said, while Wittgenstein remains sphinx-like in the background, others have hastened to draw further and more dubious moral and psychological conclusions. Wittgenstein has created a void into which neo-Kantianism, existentialism, utilitarianism have made haste to enter. And notice how plausibly the arguments, their prestige enhanced from undoubted success in other fields, seem to support, indeed to impose, the image of personality which I have sketched above. As the 'inner life' is hazy, largely absent, and any way 'not part of the mechanism', it turns out to be *logically* impossible to take up an idle contemplative attitude to the good. Morality must be action since mental concepts can only be analysed genetically. Metaphors of movement and not vision seem obviously appropriate. Morality, with the full support of logic, abhors the private. Salvation by works is a conceptual necessity. *What* I am doing or being is not something private and personal, but is imposed upon me in the sense of being identifiable only via public concepts and objective observers. Self-knowledge is something which shows overtly. Reasons are public reasons, rules are public rules. Reason and rule represent a sort of impersonal tyranny in relation to which however the personal will represents perfect freedom. The machinery is relentless, but until the moment of choice the agent is outside the machinery. Morality resides at the point of action. What I am 'objectively' is not under my control; logic and observers decide that. What I am 'subjectively' is a footloose, solitary, substanceless will. Personality dwindles to a point of pure will.

Now it is not at all easy to mount an attack upon this heavily fortified position; and, as I say, temperament will play its part in determining whether or not we *want* to attack or whether we are content. I am not content. Let me start cautiously to suggest an alternative view, taking however for a rubric the warning words of

[311]

Wittgenstein: 'Being unable – when we surrender ourselves to philosophical thought – to help saying such-and-such; being irresistibly inclined to say it – does not mean being forced into an *assumption*, or having an immediate perception or knowledge of a state of affairs.'

For purposes of the rest of this discussion it will be useful to have an example before us: some object which we can all more or less see, and to which we can from time to time refer. All sorts of different things would do for this example, and I was at first tempted to take a case of *ritual*, for instance a religious ritual wherein the inner consent appears to be the real act. Ritual: an outer framework which both occasions and identifies an inner event. It can be argued that I make a promise by uttering the words 'I promise': a performative utterance. But do I, in a religious context, repent by sincerely uttering the words 'I repent', am I 'heartily sorry' simply by saying in an appropriate situation that I am heartily sorry? Is this so even if I then amend my life? This is not so clear and is indeed a difficult and interesting question. I decided however not to take a religious example, which might be felt to raise special difficulties, but to take something more ordinary and everyday. So here is the example.

A mother, whom I shall call M, feels hostility to her daughter-in-law, whom I shall call D. M finds D quite a good-hearted girl, but while not exactly common yet certainly unpolished and lacking in dignity and refinement. D is inclined to be pert and familiar, insufficiently ceremonious, brusque, sometimes positively rude, always tiresomely juvenile. M does not like D's accent or the way D dresses. M feels that her son has married beneath him. Let us assume for purposes of the example that the mother, who is a very 'correct' person, behaves beautifully to the girl throughout, not allowing her real opinion to appear in any way. We might underline this aspect of the example by supposing that the young couple have emigrated or that D is now dead: the point being to ensure that whatever is in question as *happening* happens entirely in M's mind.

Thus much for M's first thoughts about D. Time passes, and it could be that M settles down with a hardened sense of grievance and a fixed picture of D, imprisoned (if I may use a question-begging word) by the cliché: my poor son has married a silly vulgar girl. However, the M of the example is an intelligent and well-intentioned person, capable of self-criticism, capable of giving careful and just *attention* to an object which confronts her. M tells herself: 'I am old-fashioned and conventional. I may be prejudiced and narrow-minded. I may be snobbish. I am certainly jealous. Let me look again.' Here I assume that M observes D or at least reflects deliberately about D, until gradually her vision of D alters. If we take D to be now absent or dead this can make it clear that the change is not in D's behaviour but in M's mind. D is discovered to be not vulgar but refreshingly simple, not undignified but spontaneous, not noisy but gay, not tiresomely juvenile but delightfully youthful, and so on. And as I say, *ex hypothesi*, M's outward behaviour, beautiful from the start, in no way alters.

I used above words such as 'just' and 'intelligent' which implied a favourable value judgement on M's activity: and I want in fact to imagine a case where one would feel approval of M's change of view. But of course in real life, and this is of interest, it might be very hard to decide whether what M was doing was proper or not, and opinions might differ. M might be moved by various motives: a sense of justice, attempted love for D, love for her son, or simply reluctance to think of him as unfortunate or mistaken. Some people might say 'she deludes herself' while others would say she was moved by love or justice. I am picturing a case where I would find the latter description appropriate.

What *happens* in this example could of course be described in other ways. I have chosen to describe it simply in terms of the substitution of one set of normative epithets for another. It could also be described, for instance, in terms of M's visual imagery, or in simple or complex metaphors. But let us consider now what exactly 'it' is which is being described. It may be argued that there is nothing here which presents any special difficulty. For purposes of moral judgement we may define 'actions' in various ways. One way in this case would be to say that M decided to behave well to D and did so; and M's private thoughts will be unimportant and morally irrelevant. If however it is desired to include in the list of M's moral acts more than her overt behaviour shows, one will have to ask of the extra material: in what sense 'moral' and in what sense 'acts'? Of course if M's reflections were the prologue to *different* outer acts, then the reflections might be allowed to 'belong' to the acts as their 'shadows' and gain from them their identity and their importance: though the difficulty of discerning the inward part and connecting it with the outer as a condition of the latter could still be considerable. But what are we to say in the present case?

Hampshire tells us: 'Thought cannot be thought as opposed to day-dreaming or musing, unless it is directed towards a conclusion, whether in action or in judgement . . . The idea of thought as an interior monologue . . . will become altogether empty if the thought does not even purport to be directed towards its issue in the external world . . . Under these conditions thought and belief would not differ from the charmed and habitual rehearsal of phrases or the drifting of ideas through the mind.' Let us exclude from this discussion something which might at this point try to enter it, which is the eye of God. If M's mental events are not to depend for being and importance upon this metaphysical witness, do we want to, and if so how can we, rescue them from the fate of being mere nothings, at best describable as day-dreams?

It would be possible of course to give a *hypothetical* status to M's inner life, as follows. ' "M's vision of D has altered" *means* that *if* M were to speak her mind about D now she would say different things from the things she would have said three years ago.' This analysis avoids some difficulties but, like phenomenalism, encounters others. The truth of the hypothetical proposition could be consistent with nothing in the interim having occurred in M's mind at all. And of course a change of mind often does take the form of the simple announcement of a new view without any introspectible material having intervened. But here *ex hypothesi* there is at least something introspectible which has occurred, however hazy this may be, and it is the status of this which is in question. At any rate the idea which we are trying to make sense of is that M has in the interim been *active*, she has been *doing* something, something which we approve of, something which is somehow worth doing in itself. M has been morally active in the interim: this is what we want to say and to be philosophically permitted to say.

At this point the defender of what I have called the existentialist–behaviourist view may argue as follows. All right. Either M has no introspectible material, in which case since M's conduct is constant, it is hard to see what could be meant by saying that she had changed her mind, other than saying that a hypothetical proposition is true which no one could know to be true; or else M has introspectible material and let us see what this might be like. M may imagine saying things to D, may verbally describe D in her mind, may brood on visual images of D. But what do these goings-on mean? What is to count here as serious judgement as opposed to 'the charmed and habitual rehearsal of phrases'? M's introspectabilia are likely on examination to prove hazy and hard to describe; and even if (at best) we imagine M as making clear verbal statements to herself, the identity and meaning of these statements is a function of the public world. She can only be thought of as 'speaking' seriously, and not parrot-like, if the outer context logically permits.

The point can also be made, it may be said in parenthesis, that the identity of inward thoughts is established via the public meaning of the symbolism used in thinking. (See, e.g., Ayer, *Thinking and Meaning*.) This should refute claims to 'ineffable experience', etc. Philosophers have more recently chosen to emphasise the 'shadow' view, that is to consider the particular sense of the thought via context rather than the general sense of the thought via symbols. But I think the points are worth separating. They represent two complementary pictures of the 'self' or 'will' as outside the network of logical rules, free to decide where to risk its tyranny, but thereafter caught in an impersonal complex. I can decide what to say but not what the words mean which I have said. I can decide what to do but I am not master of the significance of my act.

Someone who says privately or overtly 'I have decided' but who never acts, however favourable the circumstances (the existentialist–behaviourist argument continues), has not decided. Private decisions which precede public actions may be thought of as the 'shadow' of the act, gaining their title from being part of a complex properly called 'decision': though even here the term 'decision' if applied to the inner part only would be a courtesy title since there is no check upon the nature or existence of the inner part and its connection with the outer. Still, that is the situation in which we innocuously and popularly speak of 'private decisions' or 'inner acts', i.e., where some kind of outer structure is present and we may if we like picture, perhaps we naturally picture, an inner piece too. In M's case, however, since there is no outward alteration of structure to correspond to an alleged inner change, no sequence of outer events of which the inner can claim to be shadows, it is dubious whether any sense can be given here to the idea of 'activity'. The attempted categorical sense of M's inner progress has to fall back on the hypothetical sense mentioned above. And the hypothetical proposition cannot be known to be true, even by M, and could be true without anything happening in M's mind at all. So the idea of M as *inwardly* active turns out to be an empty one. There is only outward activity, ergo only outward moral activity, and what we call inward activity is merely the shadow of this cast back into the mind. And, it may be bracingly added, why worry? As Kant said, what we are commanded to do is to love our neighbour in a practical and not a pathological sense.

This is one of those exasperating moments in philosophy when one seems to be being relentlessly prevented from saying something which one is irresistibly impelled to say. And of course, as Wittgenstein pointed out, the fact that one is irresistibly impelled to say it need not mean that anything *else* is the case. Let us tread carefully here. In reacting against the above analysis there is certainly one thing which I do *not* wish to maintain, and that is that we have infallible or superior knowledge of our mental states. We can be mistaken about what we think and feel: that is not in dispute, and indeed it is a strength of the behaviourist analysis that it so neatly accommodates this fact. What is at stake is something different, something about *activity* in a sense which does not mean privileged activity.

Let me try in a rough ordinary way and as yet without justification to say what I take to be, in spite of the analysis, the case about M: a view which is not congruent with the analysis and which if true shows that the analysis cannot be correct. The analysis pictures M as defined 'from the outside in': M's individuality lies in her will, understood as her 'movements'. The analysis makes no sense of M as continually active, as making progress, or of her inner acts as belonging to her or forming part of a continuous fabric of being: it is precisely critical of metaphors such as 'fabric of being'. Yet can we do without such metaphors here? Further, is not the metaphor of vision almost irresistibly suggested to anyone who, without philosophical prejudice, wishes to describe the situation? Is it not the natural metaphor? M *looks* at D, she attends to D, she focuses her attention. M is engaged in an internal struggle. She may for instance be tempted to enjoy caricatures of D in her imagination. (There is curiously little place in the other picture for the idea of *struggle*.) And M's activity here, so far from being something very odd and hazy, is something which, in a way, we find exceedingly familiar. Innumerable novels contain accounts of what such struggles are like. Anybody could describe one without being at a loss for words. This activity, as I said, could be described in a variety of ways, but one very natural way is by the use of specialised normative words, what one might call the secondary moral words in contrast to the primary and general ones such as 'good'. M stops seeing D as 'bumptious' and sees her as 'gay', etc. I shall comment later upon the importance of these secondary words. Further again, one feels impelled to say something like: M's activity is peculiarly *her own*. Its details are the details of *this* personality; and partly for this reason it may well be an activity which can only be performed privately. M could not *do this* thing in conversation with another person. Hampshire says that 'anything which is to count as a definite reality must be open to several observers'. But can this quasi-scientific notion of individuation through unspecified observers really be applied to a case like this? Here there is an activity but no observers; and if one were to introduce the idea of potential observers the question of their *competence* would still arise. M's activity is hard to characterise not because it is hazy but *precisely because it is moral*. And with this, as I shall shortly try to explain, we are coming near to the centre of the difficulty.

What M is *ex hypothesi* attempting to do is not just to see D accurately but to see her justly or lovingly. Notice the rather different image of freedom which this at once suggests. Freedom is not the sudden jumping of the isolated will in and out of an impersonal logical complex, it is a function of the progressive attempt to see a particular object clearly. M's activity is essentially something progressive, something infinitely perfectible. So far from claiming for it a sort of infallibility, this new picture has built in the notion of a necessary fallibility. M is engaged in an endless task. As soon as we begin to use words such as 'love' and 'justice' in characterising M, we introduce into our whole conceptual picture of her situation the idea of progress, that is the idea of perfection: and it is just the presence of this idea which demands an analysis of mental concepts which is different from the genetic one.

I am now inclined to think that it is pointless, when faced with the existentialist–behaviourist picture of the mind, to go on endlessly fretting about the identification of particular inner events, and attempting to defend an account of M as 'active' by producing, as it were, a series of indubitably objective little things. 'Not a report' need not entail 'not an activity'. But to elaborate this what is needed is some sort of change of key, some moving of the attack to a different front. Let us consider for a moment the apparently so plausible idea of identity as dependent upon observers and rules, an idea which leads on directly to the genetic analysis of mental concepts. This is really red if several people agree about the description, indeed this is what being really red means. He really decided, roughly, if people agree that he kept the rules of the concept 'decide'. To decide means to keep these rules and the agent is not the only judge. Actions are 'moving things about in the public world', and what these movements *are*, objective observers are actually and potentially at hand to decide.

Wittgenstein, as I have said, does not apply this idea to moral concepts, nor discuss its relation to mental concepts in so far as these form part of the sphere of morality. (That mental concepts enter the sphere of morality is, for my argument, precisely the central point.) But no limit is placed upon the idea either; and I should like to place a limit. What has enabled this idea of identification to go too far is partly, I think, an uncriticised conception of science which has taken on where Hume left off.

Hume pictured a manifold of atoms, hard little indubitable sense-data or appearances, whose 'subsequent' arrangement provided the so-called material world. The Copernican Revolution of modern philosophy ('You can't have "knowledge" of "appearances" ') removes the notion of certainty from the inside to the outside: public rules now determine what is certain. It may still be disputed whether one cannot sometimes give a sense to 'being mistaken about an appearance'. There is certainly an area for discussion here, but this discussion has never become a very radical one. It has remained within the general terms of the revolution; and although it would be impossible to dispute the importance of that revolution it has nevertheless been so far in effect a continuation of Hume by other means. (The work of J. L. Austin for instance is a detailed and brilliant exorcism of the notion of the sense-impression. Yet by substituting an impersonal language-world for the old impersonal atom-world of Hume and Russell he in a way 'saves' the latter.) What the philosopher is trying to characterise, indeed to justify, is still the idea of an impersonal world of facts: the hard objective world out of which the will leaps into a position of isolation. What defines and constitutes fact has been removed from one place to another, but the radical idea of 'fact' remains much the same. Logic (impersonal rules) here obliges science with a philosophical model.

What makes difficulties for this model is the conception of persons or individuals, a conception inseparable from morality. The whole vocabulary, so profoundly familiar to us, of 'appearance' and 'reality', whether as used by the old British empiricists or by modern empiricism, is blunt and crude when applied to the human individual. Consider for instance the case of a man trying privately to determine whether something which he 'feels' is repentance or not. Of course this investigation is subject to some public rules, otherwise it would not be *this* investigation: and there could be doubts or disputes about whether it is this investigation. But these apart, the activity in question must remain a highly personal one upon which the *prise* [grasp] of 'the impersonal world of language' is to say the least problematic: or rather it is an activity which puts in question the existence of such an impersonal world. Here an individual is making a specialised personal *use* of a concept. Of course he derives the concept initially from his surroundings; but he takes it away into his privacy. Concepts of this sort lend themselves to such uses; and what use is made of them is partly a function of the user's *history*. Hume and Kant, the two patron saints of modern philosophy, abhor history, each in his own way, and abhor the particular notion of privacy which history implies. A certain conception of logic and a certain conception of science also abhor history.

But once the historical individual is 'let in' a number of things have to be said with a difference. The idea of 'objective reality', for instance, undergoes important modifications when it is to be understood, not in relation to 'the world described by science', but in relation to the progressing life of a person. The active 'reassessing' and 'redefining' which is a main characteristic of live personality often suggests and demands a checking procedure which is a function of an individual history. Repentance may mean something different to an individual at different times in his life, and what it fully means is a part of this life and cannot be understood except in context.

There is of course a 'science' which concerns itself especially with the history of the individual: psychoanalysis. And with a determination at all costs not to part company with a scientific conception of 'the objective' it is to psychoanalysis that Professor Hampshire finally appeals: he very properly lets in the historical individual, but hopes to keep him by this means upon a lead. Hampshire reads in an impersonal background to the individual's checking procedure with the help of the notion of an ideal analysis. The analyst is pictured as somehow 'there', as the ultimate competent observer playing the part of the eye of God. Hampshire allows that it is possible in theory though not in practice to 'approach complete explanations of inclination and behaviour in any individual case through an interminable analysis'. But why should some unspecified psychoanalyst be the measure of all things? Psychoanalysis is a muddled embryonic science, and even if it were not, there is no argument that I know of that can show us that we have got to treat its concepts as fundamental. The notion of an 'ideal analysis' is a misleading one. There is no existing series the extension of which could lead to such an ideal. This is a *moral* question; and what is at stake here is the liberation of morality, and of philosophy as a study of human nature, from the domination of science: or rather from the domination of inexact ideas of science which haunt philosophers and other thinkers. Because of the lack until fairly recently of any clear distinction between science and philosophy, this issue has never presented itself so vividly before. Philosophy in the past has played the game of science partly because it thought it was science.

Existentialism, in both its Continental and its Anglo-Saxon versions, is an attempt to solve the problem without really facing it:

to solve it by attributing to the individual an empty lonely freedom, a freedom, if he wishes, to 'fly in the face of the facts'. What it pictures is indeed the fearful solitude of the individual marooned upon a tiny island in the middle of a sea of scientific facts, and morality escaping from science only by a wild leap of the will. But our situation is not like this. To put it simply and in terms of the example which we have considered of M and her daughter-in-law: even if M were given a full psychoanalytical explanation of her conduct to D she need not be confined by such an explanation. This is not just because M has a senseless petulant freedom which enables her to be blind, nor is it just because (the more subtle view favoured by Hampshire) she is then enabled to redeploy her psychic forces on a ground of greater knowledge. It is because M is not forced to adopt these concepts at all, in preference say to any particular set of moral or religious concepts. Science can instruct morality at certain points and can change its direction, but it cannot contain morality nor, ergo, moral philosophy. The importance of this issue can more easily be ignored by a philosophy which divorces freedom and knowledge, and leaves knowledge (via an uncriticised idea of 'impersonal reasons') in the domain of science. But M's independence of science, and of the 'world of facts' which empiricist philosophy has created in the scientific image, rests not simply in her moving will but in her seeing knowing mind. Moral concepts do not move about *within* a hard world set up by science and logic. They set up, for different purposes, a different world.

Let me try now to explain more positively what it is about moral concepts which puts them entirely out of relation with the behaviourist view with its genetic explanation of mental phenomena. I want here to connect two ideas: the idea of the individual and the idea of perfection. Love is knowledge of the individual. M confronted with D has an endless task. Moral tasks are characteristically endless not only because 'within', as it were, a given concept our efforts are imperfect, but also because as we move and as we look our concepts themselves are changing. To speak here of an inevitable imperfection, or of an ideal limit of love or knowledge which always recedes, may be taken as a reference to our 'fallen' human condition, but this need be given no special dogmatic sense. Since we are neither angels nor animals but human individuals, our dealings with each other have this aspect; and this may be regarded as an empirical fact or, by those who favour such terminology, as a synthetic *a priori* truth.

The entry into a mental concept of the notion of an ideal limit destroys the genetic analysis of its meaning. (Hampshire allowed the idea of perfection to touch one concept only, that of intention: but he tried to save this concept from morality by making the ideal limit a scientific one.) Let us see how this is. Is 'love' a mental concept, and if so can it be analysed genetically? No doubt Mary's little lamb loved Mary, that is it followed her to school; and in some sense of 'learn' we might well learn the concept, the word, in that context. But with such a concept that is not the end of the matter. (Nor indeed the beginning either.) Words may mislead us here since words are often stable while concepts alter; we have a different image of courage at forty from that which we had at twenty. A deepening process, at any rate an altering and complicating process, takes place. There are two senses of 'knowing what a word means', one connected with ordinary language and the other very much less so. Knowledge of a value concept is something to be understood, as it were, in depth, and not in terms of switching on to some given impersonal network. Moreover, if morality is essentially connected with change and progress, we cannot be as democratic about it as some philosophers would like to think. We do not simply, through being rational and knowing ordinary language, 'know' the meaning of all necessary moral words. We may have to learn the meaning; and since we are human historical individuals the movement of understanding is onward into increasing privacy, in the direction of the ideal limit, and not back towards a genesis in the rulings of an impersonal public language.

None of what I am saying here is particularly new: similar things have been said by philosophers from Plato onward; and appear as commonplaces of the Christian ethic, whose centre is an individual. To come nearer home in the Platonic tradition, the present dispute is reminiscent of the old arguments about abstract and concrete universals. My view might be put by saying: moral terms must be treated as concrete universals. And if someone at this point were to say, well, why stop at moral concepts, why not claim that all universals are concrete, I would reply, why not indeed? Why not consider red as an ideal end-point, as a concept infinitely to be learned, as an individual object of love? A painter might say, 'You don't know what "red" means.' This would be, by a counter-attack, to bring the idea of value, which has been driven by science and logic into a corner, back to cover the whole field of knowledge. But this would be part of a different argument and is not my concern here. Perhaps all concepts could be considered in this way: all I am now arguing is that some concepts must be.

In suggesting that the central concept of morality is 'the individual' thought of as knowable by love, thought of in the light of the command, 'Be ye therefore perfect', I am not, in spite of the philosophical backing which I might here resort to, suggesting anything in the least esoteric. In fact this would, to the ordinary person, be a very much more familiar image than the existentialist one. We ordinarily conceive of and apprehend goodness in terms of virtues which belong to a continuous fabric of being. And it is just the historical, individual, nature of the virtues as actually exemplified which makes it difficult to learn goodness from another person. It is all very well to say that 'to copy a right action is to act rightly' (Hampshire, *Logic and Appreciation*), but what is the form which I am supposed to copy? It is a truism of recent philosophy that this operation of discerning the form is fairly easy, that rationality in this simple sense is a going concern. And of course for certain conventional purposes it is. But it is characteristic of morals that one cannot rest entirely at the conventional level, and that in some ways one ought not to.

We might consider in this context the ambiguity of Kant's position in the *Grundlegung*, where he tells us that when confronted with the person of Christ we must turn back to the pattern of rationality in our own bosoms and decide whether or not we approve of the man we see. Kant is often claimed as a backer of the existentialist view: and these words may readily be taken to advocate that return to self, that concern with the purity of the solitary will, which is favoured by all brands of existentialism. Here I stand alone, in total responsibility and freedom, and can only properly and responsibly do what is intelligible to me, what I can do with a clear intention. But it must be remembered that Kant was a 'metaphysical naturalist' and not an existentialist. Reason itself is for him an ideal limit: indeed his term 'Idea of Reason' expresses precisely that endless aspiration to perfection which is characteristic of moral activity. His is not the 'achieved' or 'given' reason which belongs with 'ordinary language' and convention, nor is his man on the other hand totally unguided and alone. There exists a moral reality, a real though infinitely distant standard: the difficulties of understanding and imitating remain. And in a way it is perhaps a matter of tactics and temperament whether we should look at Christ or at Reason. Kant was especially impressed by the dangers of blind obedience to a person or an institution. But there are (as the history of existentialism shows) just as many dangers attaching to the ambiguous idea of finding the ideal in one's own bosom. The argument for looking outward at Christ and not inward at Reason is that self is such a dazzling object that if one looks *there* one may see nothing else. But as I say, so long as the gaze is directed upon the ideal the exact formulation will be a matter of history and tactics in a sense which is not rigidly determined by religious dogma, and understanding of the ideal will be partial in any case. Where virtue is concerned we often apprehend more than we clearly understand and *grow by looking*.

Let me suggest in more detail how I think this process actually happens. This will I hope enable me to clarify the status of the view I hold and to relate it to linguistic philosophy in particular. I have spoken of a process of deepening or complicating, a process of learning, a progress, which may take place in moral concepts in the dimension which they possess in virtue of their relation to an ideal limit. In describing the example of M and her daughter-in-law I drew attention to the important part played by the normative-descriptive words, the specialised or secondary value words. (Such as 'vulgar', 'spontaneous', etc.) By means of these words there takes place what we might call 'the siege of the individual by concepts'. Uses of such words are both instruments and symptoms of learning. Learning takes place when such words are used, either aloud or privately, in the context of particular acts of attention. (M attending to D.) This is a point to be emphasised. That words are not timeless, that word-utterances are historical occasions, has been noted by some philosophers for some purposes. (Strawson* notes it when attacking the Theory of Descriptions.) But the full implications of this fact, with its consequences for the would-be timeless image of reason, have not, in our modern philosophy, been fully drawn. As Plato observes at the end of the *Phaedrus*, words themselves do not contain wisdom. Words said to particular individuals at particular times may occasion wisdom. Words, moreover, have both spatio-temporal and conceptual contexts. We learn through attending to contexts, vocabulary develops through close attention to objects, and we can only understand others if we can to some extent share their contexts. (Often we cannot.) Uses of words by persons grouped round a common object is a central and vital human activity. The art critic can help us if we are in the presence of the same object and if we know something about his scheme of concepts. Both contexts are relevant to our ability to move towards 'seeing more', towards 'seeing what he sees'. Here, as so often, an aesthetic analogy is helpful for morals. M could be helped by someone who both knew D and whose conceptual scheme M could understand or in that context begin to understand. Progress in understanding of a scheme of concepts often takes place as we listen to normative–descriptive talk in the presence of a common object. I have been speaking, in relation to our example, of progress or change for the better, but of course such change (and this is more commonly to be observed) may also be for the worse. Everyday conversation is not necessarily a morally neutral activity and certain ways of describing people can be corrupting and wrong. A smart set of concepts may be a most efficient instrument of corruption. It is especially characteristic of normative words, both desirable and undesirable, to belong to sets or patterns without an appreciation of which they cannot be understood. If a critic tells us that a picture has 'functional colour' or 'significant form' we need to know not only the picture but also something about his general theory in order to understand the remark. Similarly, if M says D is 'common', although the term does not belong to a technical vocabulary, this use of it can only be fully understood if we know not only D but M.

* [P. F. Strawson (b. 1919), major post-war analytical philosopher, who contributed to the dominant linguistic philosophy of the time. Author of *Individuals* and a powerful study of Kant, *The Bounds of Sense*.]

This dependence of language upon contexts of attention has consequences. Language is far more idiosyncratic than has been admitted. Reasons are not necessarily, and *qua* reasons, public. They may be reasons for a very few, and none the worse for that. 'I can't explain. You'd have to know her.' If the common object is lacking, communication may break down and the same words may occasion different results in different hearers. This may seem on reflection very obvious; but philosophy is often a matter of finding a suitable context in which to say the obvious. Human beings are obscure to each other, in certain respects which are particularly relevant to morality, unless they are mutual objects of attention or have common objects of attention, since this affects the degree of elaboration of a common vocabulary. We develop language in the context of looking: the metaphor of vision again. The notion of privileged access to inner events has been held morally suspect because, among other things, it would separate people from 'the ordinary world of rational argument'. But the unavoidable contextual privacy of language already does this, and except at a very simple and conventional level of communication there is no such ordinary world. This conclusion is feared and avoided by many moralists because it seems inimical to the operation of reason and because reason is construed on a scientific model. Scientific language tries to be impersonal and exact and yet accessible for purposes of teamwork; and the degree of accessibility can be decided in relation to definite practical goals. Moral language which relates to a reality infinitely more complex and various than that of science is often unavoidably idiosyncratic and inaccessible.

Words are the most subtle symbols which we possess and our human fabric depends on them. The living and radical nature of language is something which we forget at our peril. It is totally misleading to speak, for instance, of 'two cultures', one literary-humane and the other scientific, as if these were of equal status. There is only one culture, of which science, so interesting and so dangerous, is now an important part. But the most essential and fundamental aspect of culture is the study of literature, since this is an education in how to picture and understand human situations. We are men and we are moral agents before we are scientists, and the place of science in human life must be discussed in *words*. This is why it is and always will be more important to know about Shakespeare than to know about any scientist: and if there is a 'Shakespeare of science' his name is Aristotle.

I have used the word 'attention', which I borrow from Simone Weil, to express the idea of a just and loving gaze directed upon an individual reality. I believe this to be the characteristic and proper mark of the active moral agent. 'Characteristic' and 'proper' suggest in turn a logical and a normative claim; and I shall discuss below how far what I say is to be taken as recommendation and how far as description. In any case a theory, whether normative or logical, is the more attractive the more it explains, the more its structure may be seen as underlying things which are familiar to us in ordinary life. I want now to go on to argue that the view I am suggesting offers a more satisfactory account of human freedom than does the existentialist view. I have classified together as existentialist both philosophers such as Sartre who claim the title, and philosophers such as Hampshire, Hare, Ayer, who do not. Characteristic of both is the identification of the true person with the empty choosing will, and the corresponding emphasis upon the idea of movement rather than vision. This emphasis will go with the anti-naturalistic bias of existentialism. There is no point in talking of 'moral seeing' since there is nothing *morally* to see. There is no moral vision. There is only the ordinary world which is seen with ordinary vision, and there is the will that moves within it. What may be called the Kantian wing and the Surrealist wing of existentialism may be distinguished by the degree of their interest in *reasons* for action, which diminishes to nothing at the Surrealist end.

Our British philosophers are of course very interested in reasons, emphasising, as I have said, the accessibility, the non-esoteric nature of moral reasoning. But the production of such reasons, it is argued (and this is indeed the point of emphasising their impersonal character), does not in any way connect or tie the agent to the world or to special personal contexts within the world. He freely chooses his reasons in terms of, and after surveying, the ordinary facts which lie open to everyone: and he acts. This operation, it is argued, *is* the exercise of freedom. This image of man as a highly conscious self-contained being is offered by some philosophers as a *donné* and by others, e.g. Hampshire, as a norm; although Hampshire is careful to give the norm a scientific background.

Let us now ask quite simply if this is realistic, if this is what, in our experience, moral choice is like. It might seem at first that the existentialists have an advantage in that they do account for a peculiar feature of moral choice, which is the strange emptiness which often occurs at the moment of choosing. Of course choices happen at various levels of consciousness, importance, and difficulty. In a simple easy unimportant choice there is no need to regard 'what goes on' as anything beyond the obvious sequence of reason, decision, action, or just reason, action; and such choices may properly be regarded as 'impersonal'. 'Shall I go? Oh yes, I promised to.' I receive my bill and I pay it. But difficult and painful choices often present this experience of void of which so much has been made: this sense of not being determined by the reasons. This sensation is hailed with delight by both wings of existentialism. The Kantian wing claims it as showing that we are free in relation to the reasons and the Surrealist wing claims it as showing that there are no reasons. Indeed this experience of emptiness seems perfectly to verify the notion that freedom is simply the movement of the lonely will. Choice is outward movement since there is nothing else there for it to be.

But is this the case, and ought we really to be so pleased about this experience? A more sombre note concerning it is struck at one point by Sartre, who on this problem veers wildly between Kantianism and Surrealism. *Quand je délibère les jeux sont faits.* If we are so strangely separate from the world at moments of choice are we really choosing at all, are we right indeed to identify *ourselves* with this giddy empty will? (Hampshire: 'I identify myself with my will.') In a reaction of thought which is never far from the minds of more extreme existentialists (Dostoevsky for instance), one may turn here towards determinism, towards fatalism, towards regarding freedom as a complete illusion. When I deliberate the die is already cast. Forces within me which are dark to me have already made the decision.

This view is if anything less attractive and less realistic than the other one. Do we really have to choose between an image of total freedom and an image of total determinism? Can we not give a more balanced and illuminating account of the matter? I suggest we can if we simply introduce into the picture the idea of *attention*, or looking, of which I was speaking above. I can only choose within the world I can *see*, in the moral sense of 'see' which implies that clear vision is a result of moral imagination and moral effort. There is also of course 'distorted vision', and the word 'reality' here inevitably appears as a normative word. When M is just and loving she sees D as she really is. One is often compelled almost automatically by what one *can* see. If we ignore the prior work of attention and notice only the emptiness of the moment of choice we are likely to identify freedom with the outward movement since there is nothing else to identify it with. But if we consider what the work of attention is like, how continuously it goes on, and how imperceptibly it builds up structures of value round about us, we shall not be surprised that at crucial moments of choice most of the business of choosing is already over. This does not imply that we are not free, certainly not. But it implies that the exercise of our freedom is a small piecemeal business which goes on all the time and not a grandiose leaping about unimpeded at important moments. The moral life, on this view, is something that goes on continually, not something that is switched off in between the occurrence of explicit moral choices. What happens in between such choices is indeed what is crucial. I would like on the whole to use the word 'attention' as a good word and use some more general term like 'looking' as the neutral word. Of course psychic energy flows, and more readily flows, into building up convincingly coherent but false pictures of the world, complete with systematic vocabulary (M seeing D as pert-common-juvenile, etc.) Attention is the effort to counteract such states of illusion.

On this view we are certainly in a sense less free than we are pictured as being on the other view, in that the latter presents a condition of perfect freedom as being either our unavoidable fate (the Surrealists) or our conceivably attainable goal (the Kantians). Freedom for Hampshire is a matter of having crystal-clear intentions. But on the view which I suggest, which connects morality with attention to individuals, human individuals or individual realities of other kinds, the struggle and the progress is something more obscure, more historically conditioned, and usually less clearly conscious. Freedom, itself a moral concept and not just a prerequisite of morality, cannot here be separated from the idea of knowledge. That *of* which it is knowledge, that 'reality' which we are so naturally led to think of as revealed by 'just attention', can of course, given the variety of human personality and situation, only be thought of as 'one', as a single object for all men, in some very remote and ideal sense. It is a deep paradox of moral philosophy that almost all philosophers have been led in one way or another to picture goodness as knowledge: and yet to show this in any sort of detail, to show 'reality' as 'one', seems to involve an improper prejudging of some moral issue. An acute consciousness of this latter difficulty has indeed made it seem axiomatic to recent philosophers that 'naturalism is a fallacy'. But I would suggest that, at the level of serious common sense and of an ordinary non-philosophical reflection about the nature of morals, it is perfectly obvious that goodness *is* connected with knowledge: not with impersonal quasi-scientific knowledge of the ordinary world, whatever that may be, but with a refined and honest perception of what is really the case, a patient and just discernment and exploration of what confronts one, which is the result not simply of opening one's eyes but of a certainly perfectly familiar kind of moral discipline.

What then of the 'void', the experience of *Angst* of which the existentialists have told us so much? If it cannot be understood in their sense as an experience of pure freedom, what is it, and does it really occur at all? Perhaps there are several different conditions involved here. But the central one, the heart of the concept, I think I would describe rather as a kind of fright which the conscious will feels when it apprehends the strength and direction of the personality which is not under its immediate control. Innumerable 'lookings' have discovered and explored a world which is now (for better or worse) *compulsively* present to the will in a particular situation, and the will is dismayed by the feeling that it ought now to be everything and in fact is not. *Angst* may occur where there is any felt discrepancy between personality and ideals. Perhaps very simple people escape it and some civilisations have not experienced it at all. Extreme *Angst*, in the popular modern form, is a disease or addiction of those who are passionately convinced that personality resides solely in the conscious omnipotent will: and in so far as this conviction is wrong the condition partakes of illusion. It is obviously, in practice, a delicate moral problem to decide how far the will can coerce the formed personality (*move* in a world it cannot *see*) without merely occasioning disaster. The concept of *Angst* should of course be carefully distinguished from its ancestor, Kant's *Achtung*, in which dismay at the frailty of the will is combined with an inspiring awareness of the reality which the will is drawn by (despair at the sensuous will, joy in the rational will). The loss of that awareness, or that faith, produces *Angst*, which is properly a condition of sober alarm. Those who are, or attempt to be, exhilarated by *Angst*, that is by the mere impotence of the will and its lack of connection with the personality, are, as I have suggested above, in danger of falling into fatalism or sheer irresponsibility.

The place of choice is certainly a different one if we think in terms of a world which is *compulsively* present to the will, and the discernment and exploration of which is a slow business. Moral change and moral achievement are slow; we are not free in the sense of being able suddenly to alter ourselves since we cannot suddenly alter what we can see and ergo what we desire and are compelled by. In a way, explicit choice seems now less important: less decisive (since much of the 'decision' lies elsewhere) and less obviously something to be 'cultivated'. If I attend properly I will have no choices and this is the ultimate condition to be aimed at. This is in a way the reverse of Hampshire's picture, where our efforts are supposed to be directed to increasing our freedom by conceptualising as many different possibilities of action as possible: having as many goods as possible in the shop. The ideal situation, on the contrary, is rather to be represented as a kind of 'necessity'. This is something of which saints speak and which any artist will readily understand. The idea of a patient, loving regard, directed upon a person, a thing, a situation, presents the will not as unimpeded movement but as something very much more like 'obedience'.

Will and reason then are not entirely separate faculties in the moral agent. Will continually influences belief, for better or worse, and is ideally able to influence it through a sustained attention to reality. This is what Simone Weil means when she says that 'will is obedience not resolution'. As moral agents we have to try to see justly, to overcome prejudice, to avoid temptation, to control and curb imagination, to direct reflection. Man is not a combination of an impersonal rational thinker and a personal will. He is a unified being who sees, and who desires in accordance with what he sees, and who has some continual slight control over the direction and focus of his vision. There is nothing, I think, in the foreground of this picture which is unfamiliar to the ordinary person. Philosophical difficulties may arise if we try to give any single organised background sense to the normative word 'reality'. But this word may be used as a philosophical term provided its limitations are understood. What is real may be 'non-empirical' without being in the grand sense systematic. In particular situations, 'reality' as that which is revealed to the patient eye of love is an idea entirely comprehensible to the ordinary person. M knows what she is doing when she tries to be just to D, and we know what she is doing too.

I said that any artist would appreciate the notion of will as obedience to reality, an obedience which ideally reaches a position where there is no choice. One of the great merits of the moral psychology which I am proposing is that it does not contrast art and morals, but shows them to be two aspects of a single struggle. The existentialist–behaviourist view could give no satisfactory account of art: it was seen as a quasi-play activity, gratuitous, 'for its own sake' (the familiar Kantian–Bloomsbury slogan), a sort of by-product of our failure to be entirely rational. Such a view of art is of course intolerable. In one of those important movements of return from philosophical theory to simple things which we are certain of, we must come back to what we know about great art and about the moral insight which it contains and the moral achievements which it represents. Goodness and beauty are not to be contrasted, but are largely part of the same structure. Plato, who tells us that beauty is the only spiritual thing which we love immediately by nature, treats the beautiful as an introductory section of the good. So that aesthetic situations are not so much analogies of morals as cases of morals. Virtue is *au fond* the same in the artist as in the good man in that it is a selfless attention to nature: something which is easy to name but very hard to achieve.

[332]

Artists who have reflected have frequently given expression to this idea. (For instance, Rilke praising Cézanne speaks of a 'consuming of love in anonymous work'. Letter to Clara Rilke, 13 October 1907.)

Since the existentialist–behaviourist view wished to conceive of will as pure movement separated from reason and to deprive reason of the use of normative words (since it was to be 'objective'), the moral agent so envisaged could get along, was indeed almost forced to get along, with only the most empty and general moral terms such as 'good' and 'right'. The empty moral words correspond here to the emptiness of the will. If the will is to be totally free the world it moves in must be devoid of normative characteristics, so that morality can reside entirely in the pointer of pure choice. On my view it might be said that, *per contra*, the primary general words could be dispensed with entirely and all moral work could be done by the secondary specialised words. If we picture the agent as compelled by obedience to the reality he can see, he will not be saying, 'This is right', i.e., 'I choose to do this', he will be saying, 'This is A B C D' (normative-descriptive words), and action will follow naturally. As the empty choice will not occur the empty word will not be needed. It would however be far from my intention to demote or dispense with the term 'good': but rather to restore to it the dignity and authority which it possessed before Moore appeared on the scene. I have spoken of efforts of attention directed upon individuals and of obedience to reality as an exercise of love, and have suggested that 'reality' and 'individual' present themselves to us in moral contexts as ideal end-points or Ideas of Reason. This surely is the place where the concept of good lives. 'Good': 'Real': 'Love'. These words are closely connected. And here we retrieve the deep sense of the indefinability of good, which has been given a trivial sense in recent philosophy. Good is indefinable not for the reasons offered by Moore's successors, but because of the infinite difficulty of the task of apprehending a magnetic but inexhaustible reality. Moore was in a way nearer the truth than he realised when he tried to say both that Good was *there* and that one could say nothing of what it essentially was. If apprehension of good is apprehension of the individual and the real, then good partakes of the infinite elusive character of reality.

I have several times indicated that the image which I am offering should be thought of as a general metaphysical background to morals and not as a formula which can be illuminatingly introduced into any and every moral act. There exists, so far as I know, no formula of the latter kind. We are not always the individual in pursuit of the individual, we are not always responding to the magnetic pull of the idea of perfection. Often, for instance when we pay our bills or perform other small everyday acts, we are just 'anybody' doing what is proper or making simple choices for ordinary public reasons; and this is the situation which some philosophers have chosen exclusively to analyse. Furthermore, I am well aware of the *moral* dangers of the idea of morality as something which engages the whole person and which may lead to specialised and esoteric vision and language. Give and take between the private and the public levels of morality is often of advantage to both and indeed is normally unavoidable. In fact the 'conventional' level is often not so simple as it seems, and the quaintly phrased hymn which I sang in my childhood, 'Who sweeps a room as for Thy laws makes that and the action fine', was not talking foolishly. The task of attention goes on all the time and at apparently empty and everyday moments we are 'looking', making those little peering efforts of imagination which have such important cumulative results.

I would not be understood, either, as suggesting that insight or pureness of heart are more important than action: the thing which philosophers feared Moore for implying. Overt actions are perfectly obviously important in themselves, and important too because they are the indispensable pivot and spur of the inner scene. The inner, in *this* sense, cannot do without the outer. I do not mean only that outer rituals make places for inner experiences; but also that an overt action can release psychic energies which can be released in no other way. We often receive an unforeseen reward for a fumbling half-hearted act: a place for the idea of grace. I have suggested that we have to accept a darker, less fully conscious, less steadily rational image of the dynamics of the human personality. With this dark entity behind us we may sometimes decide to act abstractly by rule, to ignore vision and the compulsive energy derived from it; and we may find that as a result both energy and vision are unexpectedly given. To decide when to attempt such leaps is one of the most difficult of moral problems. But if we do leap ahead of what we know, we still have to try to catch up. Will cannot run very far ahead of knowledge, and attention is our daily bread.

Of course what I have been offering here is not and does not pretend to be a 'neutral logical analysis' of what moral agents or moral terms are like. The picture offered by, e.g., Hampshire is of course not neutral either, as he admits in parenthesis. (*Thought and Action*, Chapter Two.) 'A decision has to be made between two conceptions of personality ... It may be that in a society in which a man's theoretical opinions and religious beliefs were held to be supremely important, a man's beliefs would be considered as much part of his responsibility as his behaviour to other men.' And he contrasts this with 'a utilitarian culture'. Hampshire speaks here of a 'decision'; and there is always an existentialist 'short way' with any rival theory: to say, 'You use that picture, but you *choose* to use it.' This is to make the existentialist picture the ultimate one. I would wish to exclude any such undercutting of my theory. To say that it is a normative theory is not to say that it is an object of free choice: modern philosophy has equated these ideas but this is just the equation I am objecting to. I offer frankly a sketch of a metaphysical theory, a kind of inconclusive non-dogmatic naturalism, which has the circularity of definition characteristic of such theories. The rival theory is similarly circular; and, as I have explained, I do not find that its radical arguments convincingly establish its sweeping moral and psychological conclusions.

Philosophers have always been trying to picture the human soul, and since morality needs such pictures and as science is, as I have argued, in no position to coerce morality, there seems no reason why philosophers should not go on attempting to fill in a systematic explanatory background to our ordinary moral life. Hampshire said, and I quoted this at the start, that 'it is the constructive task of the philosophy of mind to provide a set of terms in which ultimate judgements of value can be very clearly stated'. I would put what I

EXISTENTIALISTS AND MYSTICS

think is much the same task in terms of the provision of rich and fertile conceptual schemes which help us to reflect upon and understand the nature of moral progress and moral failure and the reasons for the divergence of one moral temperament from another. And I would wish to make my theory undercut its existentialist rivals by suggesting that it is possible in terms of the former to explain why people are obsessed with the latter, but not vice versa. In any case, the sketch which I have offered, a footnote in a great and familiar philosophical tradition, must be judged by its power to connect, to illuminate, to explain, and to make new and fruitful places for reflection.

Based upon the Ballard Matthews Lecture, delivered at the University College of North Wales, 1962.

On 'God' and 'Good'

To do philosophy is to explore one's own temperament, and yet at the same time to attempt to discover the truth. It seems to me that there is a void in present-day moral philosophy. Areas peripheral to philosophy expand (psychology, political and social theory) or collapse (religion) without philosophy being able in the one case to encounter, and in the other case to rescue, the values involved. A working philosophical psychology is needed which can at least attempt to connect modern psychological terminology with a terminology concerned with virtue. We need a moral philosophy which can speak significantly of Freud and Marx, and out of which aesthetic and political views can be generated. We need a moral philosophy in which the concept of love, so rarely mentioned now by philosophers, can once again be made central.

It will be said, we have got a working philosophy, and one which is the proper heir to the past of European philosophy: existentialism. This philosophy does so far pervade the scene that philosophers, many linguistic analysts for instance, who would not claim the name, do in fact work with existentialist concepts. I shall argue that existentialism is not, and cannot by tinkering be made, the philosophy we need. Although it is indeed the heir of the past, it is (it seems to me) an unrealistic and over-optimistic doctrine and the purveyor of certain false values. This is more obviously true of flimsier creeds, such as 'humanism', with which people might now attempt to fill the philosophical void.

The great merit of existentialism is that it at least professes and tries to be a philosophy one could live by. Kierkegaard described the Hegelian system as a grand palace set up by someone who then lived in a hovel or at best in the porter's lodge. A moral philosophy should be inhabited. Existentialism has shown itself capable of becoming a popular philosophy and of getting into the minds of those (e.g. Oxford philosophers) who have not sought it and may even be unconscious of its presence. However, although it can certainly inspire action, it seems to me to do so by a sort of romantic provocation rather than by its truth; and its pointers are often pointing in the wrong direction. Wittgenstein claimed that he brought the Cartesian era in philosophy to an end. Moral philosophy of an existentialist type is still Cartesian and egocentric. Briefly put, our picture of ourselves has become too grand, we have isolated, and identified ourselves with, an unrealistic conception of will, we have lost the vision of a reality separate from ourselves, and we have no adequate conception of original sin. Kierkegaard rightly observed that 'an ethic which ignores sin is an altogether useless science', although he also added, 'but if it recognizes sin it is *eo ipso* beyond its sphere'.

Kant believed in Reason and Hegel believed in History, and for both this was a form of a belief in an external reality. Modern thinkers who believe in neither, but who remain within the tradition, are left with a denuded self whose only virtues are freedom, or at best sincerity, or, in the case of the British philosophers, an everyday reasonableness. Philosophy, on its other fronts, has been busy dismantling the old substantial picture of the 'self', and ethics has not proved able to rethink this concept for moral purposes. The moral agent then is pictured as an isolated principle of will, or burrowing pinpoint of consciousness, inside, or beside, a lump of being which has been handed over to other disciplines, such as psychology or sociology. On the one hand a Luciferian philosophy of adventures of the will, and on the other natural science. Moral philosophy, and indeed morals, are thus undefended against an irresponsible and undirected self-assertion which goes easily hand in hand with some brand of pseudo-scientific determinism. An unexamined sense of the strength of the machine is combined with an illusion of leaping out of it. The younger Sartre, and many British moral philosophers, represent this last dry distilment of Kant's views of the world. The study of motivation is surrendered to empirical science: will takes the place of the complex of motives and also of the complex of virtues.

The history of British philosophy since Moore represents intensively in miniature the special dilemmas of modern ethics. Empiricism, especially in the form given to it by Russell, and later by Wittgenstein, thrust ethics almost out of philosophy. Moral judgements were not factual, or truthful, and had no place in the world of the *Tractatus*. Moore, although he himself held a curious metaphysic of 'moral facts', set the tone when he told us that we must carefully distinguish the question 'What things are good?' from the question 'What does "good" mean?' The answer to the latter question concerned the will. Good was indefinable (naturalism was a fallacy) because any offered good could be scrutinised by any individual by a 'stepping back' movement. This form of Kantianism still retains its appeal. Wittgenstein had attacked the idea of the Cartesian ego or substantial self and Ryle and others had developed the attack. A study of 'ordinary language' claimed (often rightly) to solve piecemeal problems in epistemology which had formerly been discussed in terms of the activities or faculties of a 'self'. (See John Austin's book on certain problems of perception, *Sense and Sensibilia*.)

Ethics took its place in this scene. After puerile attempts to classify moral statements as exclamations or expressions of emotion, a more sophisticated neo-Kantianism with a utilitarian atmosphere has been developed. The idea of the agent as a privileged centre of will (for ever capable of 'stepping back') is retained, but, since the old-fashioned 'self' no longer clothes him he appears as an isolated will operating with the concepts of 'ordinary language', so far as the field of morals is concerned. (It is interesting that although Wittgenstein's work has suggested this picture to others, he himself never used it.) Thus the will, and the psyche as an object of science, are isolated from each other and from the rest of philosophy. The cult of ordinary language goes with the claim to be neutral. Previous moral philosophers told us what we ought to do, that is they tried to answer both of Moore's questions. Linguistic analysis claims simply to give a philosophical description of the human phenomenon of morality, without making any moral judgements. In fact the resulting picture of human conduct has a clear moral bias. The merits of linguistic analytical man are freedom (in the sense of detachment, rationality), responsibility, self-aware-ness, sincerity, and a lot of utilitarian common sense. There is of course no mention of sin, and no mention of love. Marxism is ignored, and there is on the whole no attempt at a *rapprochement* with psychology, although Professor Hampshire does try to develop the idea of self-awareness towards an ideal end-point by conceiving of 'the perfect psychoanalysis' which would make us perfectly self-aware and so perfectly detached and free.

Linguistic analysis of course poses for ethics the question of its relation with metaphysics. Can ethics be a form of empiricism? Many philosophers in the Oxford and Cambridge tradition would say yes. It is certainly a great merit of this tradition, and one which I would not wish to lose sight of, that it attacks every form of spurious unity. It is the traditional inspiration of the philosopher, but also his traditional vice, to believe that all is one. Wittgenstein says, 'Let's see.' Sometimes problems turn out to be quite uncon-nected with each other, and demand types of solution which are not themselves closely related in any system. Perhaps it is a matter of temperament whether or not one is convinced that all is one. (My own temperament inclines to monism.) But let us postpone the question of whether, if we reject the relaxed empirical ethics of the British tradition (a cheerful amalgam of Hume, Kant and Mill), and if we reject, too, the more formal existentialist systems, we wish to replace these with something which would have to be called a metaphysical theory. Let me now simply suggest ways in which I take the prevalent and popular picture to be unrealistic. In doing this my debt to Simone Weil will become evident.

Much of contemporary moral philosophy appears both unambi-tious and optimistic. Unambitious optimism is of course part of the Anglo-Saxon tradition; and it is also not surprising that a philosophy which analyses moral concepts on the basis of ordinary language should present a relaxed picture of a mediocre achieve-ment. I think the charge is also true, though contrary to some appearances, of existentialism. An authentic mode of existence is presented as attainable by intelligence and force of will. The atmosphere is invigorating and tends to produce self-satisfaction in the reader, who feels himself to be a member of the élite, addressed by another one. Contempt for the ordinary human condition, together with a conviction of personal salvation, saves the writer from real pessimism. His gloom is superficial and conceals elation. (I think this to be true in different ways of both Sartre and Heidegger, though I am never too sure of having understood the latter.) Such attitudes contrast with the vanishing images of Christian theology which represented goodness as almost impossibly difficult, and sin as almost insuperable and certainly as a universal condition.

Yet modern psychology has provided us with what might be called a doctrine of original sin, a doctrine which most philosophers either deny (Sartre), ignore (Oxford and Cambridge), or attempt to render innocuous (Hampshire). When I speak in this context of modern psychology I mean primarily the work of Freud. I am not a 'Freudian' and the truth of this or that particular view of Freud does not here concern me, but it seems clear that Freud made an important discovery about the human mind and that he remains still the greatest scientist in the field which he opened. One may say that what he presents us with is a realistic and detailed picture of the fallen man. If we take the general outline of this picture seriously, and at the same time wish to do moral philosophy, we shall have to revise the current conceptions of will and motive very considerably. What seems to me, for these purposes, true and important in Freudian theory is as follows. Freud takes a thoroughly pessimistic view of human nature. He sees the psyche as an egocentric system of quasi-mechanical energy, largely determined by its own individual history, whose natural attachments are sexual, ambiguous, and hard for the subject to understand or control. Introspection reveals only the deep tissue of ambivalent motive, and fantasy is a stronger force than reason. Objectivity and unselfishness are not natural to human beings.

Of course Freud is saying these things in the context of a scientific therapy which aims not at making people good but at making them workable. If a moral philosopher says such things he must justify them not with scientific arguments but with arguments appropriate to philosophy; and in fact if he does say such things he will not be saying anything very new, since partially similar views have been expressed before in philosophy, as far back as Plato. It is important to look at Freud and his successors because they can give us more information about a mechanism the general nature of which we may discern without the help of science; and also because the ignoring of psychology may be a source of confusion. Some philosophers (e.g. Sartre) regard traditional psychoanalytical theory as a form of determinism and are prepared to deny it at all levels, and philosophers who ignore it often do so as part of an easy surrender to science of aspects of the mind which ought to interest them. But determinism as a total philosophical theory is not the enemy. Determinism as a philosophical theory is quite unproven, and it can be argued that it is not possible in principle to translate propositions about men making decisions and formulating viewpoints into the neutral languages of natural science. (See Hampshire's brief discussion of this point in the last chapter of his book *The Freedom of the Individual*.) The problem is to accommodate inside moral philosophy, and suggest methods of dealing with the fact that so much of human conduct is moved by mechanical energy of an egocentric kind. In the moral life the enemy is the fat relentless ego. Moral philosophy is properly, and in the past has sometimes been, the discussion of this ego and of the techniques (if any) for its defeat. In this respect moral philosophy has shared some aims with religion. To say this is of course also to deny that moral philosophy should aim at being neutral.

What is a good man like? How can we make ourselves morally better? *Can* we make ourselves morally better? These are questions the philosopher should try to answer. We realise on reflection that we know little about good men. There are men in history who are traditionally thought of as having been good (Christ, Socrates, certain saints), but if we try to contemplate these men we find that the information about them is scanty and vague, and that, their great moments apart, it is the simplicity and directness of their diction which chiefly colours our conception of them as good. And if we consider contemporary candidates for goodness, if we know of any, we are likely to find them obscure, or else on closer inspection full of frailty. Goodness appears to be both rare and hard to picture. It is perhaps most convincingly met with in simple people – inarticulate, unselfish mothers of large families – but these cases are also the least illuminating.

It is significant that the idea of goodness (and of virtue) has been

[342]

largely superseded in Western moral philosophy by the idea of rightness, supported perhaps by some conception of sincerity. This is to some extent a natural outcome of the disappearance of a permanent background to human activity: a permanent background, whether provided by God, by Reason, by History, or by the self. The agent, thin as a needle, appears in the quick flash of the choosing will. Yet existentialism itself, certainly in its French and Anglo-Saxon varieties, has, with a certain honesty, made evident the paradoxes of its own assumptions. Sartre tells us that when we deliberate the die is already cast, and Oxford philosophy has developed no serious theory of motivation. The agent's freedom, indeed his moral quality, resides in his choices, and yet we are not told what prepares him for the choices. Sartre can admit, with bravado, that we choose out of some sort of pre-existent condition, which he also confusingly calls a choice, and Richard Hare holds that the identification of mental data, such as 'intentions', is philosophically difficult and we had better say that a man is morally the set of his actual choices. That visible motives do not necessitate acts is taken by Sartre as a cue for asserting an irresponsible freedom as an obscure postulate; that motives do not readily yield to 'introspection' is taken by many British philosophers as an excuse for forgetting them and talking about 'reasons' instead. These views seem both unhelpful to the moral pilgrim and also profoundly unrealistic. Moral choice is often a mysterious matter. Kant thought so, and he pictured the mystery in terms of an indiscernible balance between a pure rational agent and an impersonal mechanism, neither of which represented what we normally think of as personality; much existentialist philosophy is in this respect, though often covertly, Kantian. But should not the mystery of choice be conceived of in some other way?

We have learned from Freud to picture 'the mechanism' as something highly individual and personal, which is at the same time very powerful and not easily understood by its owner. The self of psychoanalysis is certainly substantial enough. The existentialist picture of choice, whether it be surrealist or rational, seems unrealistic, over-optimistic, romantic, because it ignores what appears at least to be a sort of continuous background with a life of its own; and it is surely in the tissue of that life that the secrets of good and evil are to be found. Here neither the inspiring ideas of freedom, sincerity and fiats of will, nor the plain wholesome concept of a rational discernment of duty, seem complex enough to do justice to what we really are. What we really are seems much more like an obscure system of energy out of which choices and visible acts of will emerge at intervals in ways which are often unclear and often dependent on the condition of the system in between the moments of choice.

If this is so, one of the main problems of moral philosophy might be formulated thus: are there any techniques for the purification and reorientation of an energy which is naturally selfish, in such a way that when moments of choice arrive we shall be sure of acting rightly? We shall also have to ask whether, if there are such techniques, they should be simply described, in quasi-psychological terms, perhaps in psychological terms, or whether they can be spoken of in a more systematic philosophical way. I have already suggested that a pessimistic view which claims that goodness is the almost impossible countering of a powerful egocentric mechanism already exists in traditional philosophy and in theology. The technique which Plato thought appropriate to this situation I shall discuss later. Much closer and more familiar to us are the techniques of religion, of which the most widely practised is prayer. What becomes of such a technique in a world without God, and can it be transformed to supply at least part of the answer to our central question?

Prayer is properly not petition, but simply an attention to God which is a form of love. With it goes the idea of grace, of a supernatural assistance to human endeavour which overcomes empirical limitations of personality. What is this attention like, and can those who are not religious believers still conceive of profiting by such an activity? Let us pursue the matter by considering what the traditional object of this attention was like and by what means it affected its worshippers. I shall suggest that God was (or is) a *single perfect transcendent non-representable and necessarily real object of attention*; and I shall go on to suggest that moral philosophy should attempt to retain a central concept which has all these characteristics. I shall consider them one by one, although to a large extent they interpenetrate and overlap.

[344]

Let us take first the notion of an object of attention. The religious believer, especially if his God is conceived of as a person, is in the fortunate position of being able to focus his thought upon something which is a source of energy. Such focusing, with such results, is natural to human beings. Consider being in love. Consider too the attempt to check being in love, and the need in such a case of another object to attend to. Where strong emotions of sexual love, or of hatred, resentment, or jealousy are concerned, 'pure will' can usually achieve little. It is small use telling oneself 'Stop being in love, stop feeling resentment, be just.' What is needed is a reorientation which will provide an energy of a different kind, from a different source. Notice the metaphors of orientation and of looking. The neo-Kantian existentialist 'will' is a principle of pure movement. But how ill this describes what it is like for us to alter. Deliberately falling out of love is not a jump of the will, it is the acquiring of new objects of attention and thus of new energies as a result of refocusing. The metaphor of orientation may indeed also cover moments when recognisable 'efforts of will' are made, but explicit efforts of will are only a part of the whole situation. That God, attended to, is a powerful source of (often good) energy is a psychological fact. It is also a psychological fact, and one of importance in moral philosophy, that we can all receive moral help by focusing our attention upon things which are valuable: virtuous people, great art, perhaps (I will discuss this later) the idea of goodness itself. Human beings are naturally 'attached' and when an attachment seems painful or bad it is most readily displaced by another attachment, which an attempt at attention can encourage. There is nothing odd or mystical about this, nor about the fact that our ability to act well 'when the time comes' depends partly, perhaps largely, upon the quality of our habitual objects of attention. 'Whatsoever things are true, whatsoever things are honest, whatsoever things are just, whatsoever things are pure, whatsoever things are lovely, whatsoever things of good report; if there be any virtue, and if there be any praise, think on these things.'

The notion that value should be in some sense *unitary*, or even that there should be a single supreme value concept, may seem, if one surrenders the idea of God, far from obvious. Why should there not be many different kinds of independent moral values? Why should all be one here? The madhouses of the world are filled with people who are convinced that all is one. It might be said that 'all is one' is a dangerous falsehood at any level except the highest; and can that be discerned at all? That a belief in the unity, and also in the hierarchical order, of the moral world has a psychological importance is fairly evident. The notion that 'it all somehow must make sense', or 'there is a best decision here', preserves from despair: the difficulty is how to entertain this consoling notion in a way which is not false. As soon as any idea is a consolation the tendency to falsify it becomes strong: hence the traditional problem of preventing the idea of God from degenerating in the believer's mind. It is true that the intellect naturally seeks unity; and in the sciences, for instance, the assumption of unity consistently rewards the seeker. But how can this dangerous idea be used in morals? It is useless to ask 'ordinary language' for a judgement, since we are dealing with concepts which are not on display in ordinary language or unambiguously tied up to ordinary words. Ordinary language is not a philosopher.

We might, however, set out from an ordinary language situation by reflecting upon the virtues. The concepts of the virtues, and the familiar words which name them, are important since they help to make certain potentially nebulous areas of experience more open to inspection. If we reflect upon the nature of the virtues we are constantly led to consider their relation to each other. The idea of an 'order' of virtues suggests itself, although it might of course be difficult to state this in any systematic form. For instance, if we reflect upon courage and ask why we think it to be a virtue, what kind of courage is the highest, what distinguishes courage from rashness, ferocity, self-assertion, and so on, we are bound, in our explanation, to use the names of other virtues. The best kind of courage (that which would make a man act unselfishly in a concentration camp) is steadfast, calm, temperate, intelligent, loving . . . This may not in fact be exactly the right description, but it is the right sort of description. Whether there is a single supreme principle in the united world of the virtues, and whether the name of that principle is love, is something which I shall discuss below. All I suggest here is that reflection rightly tends to unify the moral world, and that increasing moral sophistication reveals increasing unity. What is it like to be just? We come to understand this as we come to understand the relationship between justice and the other virtues. Such a reflection requires and generates a rich and diversified vocabulary for naming aspects of goodness. It is a shortcoming of much contemporary moral philosophy that it eschews discussion of the separate virtues, preferring to proceed directly to some sovereign concept such as sincerity, or authenticity, or freedom, thereby imposing, it seems to me, an unexamined and empty idea of unity, and impoverishing our moral language in an important area.

We have spoken of an 'object of attention' and of an unavoidable sense of 'unity'. Let us now go on to consider, thirdly, the much more difficult idea of 'transcendence'. All that has been said so far could be said without benefit of metaphysics. But now it may be asked: are you speaking of a transcendent authority or of a psychological device? It seems to me that the idea of the transcendent, in some form or other, belongs to morality: but it is not easy to interpret. As with so many of these large elusive ideas, it readily takes on forms which are false ones. There is a false transcendence, as there is a false unity, which is generated by modern empiricism: a transcendence which is in effect simply an exclusion, a relegation of the moral to a shadowy existence in terms of emotive language, imperatives, behaviour patterns, attitudes. 'Value' does not belong inside the world of truth functions, the world of science and factual propositions. So it must live somewhere else. It is then attached somehow to the human will, a shadow clinging to a shadow. The result is the sort of dreary moral solipsism which so many so-called books on ethics purvey. An instrument for criticising the false transcendence, in many of its forms, has been given to us by Marx in the concept of alienation. Is there, however, any true transcendence, or is this idea always a consoling dream projected by human need on to an empty sky?

It is difficult to be exact here. One might start from the assertion that morality, goodness, is a form of realism. The idea of a really good man living in a private dream world seems unacceptable. Of course a good man may be infinitely eccentric, but he must know certain things about his surroundings, most obviously the existence of other people and their claims. The chief enemy of excellence in

[347]

morality (and also in art) is personal fantasy: the tissue of self-aggrandising and consoling wishes and dreams which prevents one from seeing what is there outside one. Rilke said of Cézanne that he did not paint 'I like it', he painted 'There it is.' This is not easy, and requires, in art or morals, a discipline. One might say here that art is an excellent analogy of morals, or indeed that it is in this respect a case of morals. We cease to be in order to attend to the existence of something else, a natural object, a person in need. We can see in mediocre art, where perhaps it is even more clearly seen than in mediocre conduct, the intrusion of fantasy, the assertion of self, the dimming of any reflection of the real world.

It may be agreed that the direction of attention should properly be outward, away from self, but it will be said that it is a long step from the idea of realism to the idea of transcendence. I think, however, that these two ideas are related, and one can see their relation particularly in the case of our apprehension of beauty. The link here is the concept of indestructibility or incorruptibility. What is truly beautiful is 'inaccessible' and cannot be possessed or destroyed. The statue is broken, the flower fades, the experience ceases, but something has not suffered from decay and mortality. Almost anything that consoles us is a fake, and it is not easy to prevent this idea from degenerating into a vague Shelleyan mysticism. In the case of the idea of a transcendent personal God the degeneration of the idea seems scarcely avoidable: theologians are busy at their desks at this very moment trying to undo the results of this degeneration. In the case of beauty, whether in art or in nature, the sense of separateness from the temporal process is connected perhaps with concepts of perfection of form and 'authority' which are not easy to transfer into the field of morals. Here I am not sure if this is an analogy or an instance. It is as if we can see beauty itself in a way in which we cannot see goodness itself. (Plato says this at *Phaedrus* 250E.) I can *experience* the transcendence of the beautiful, but (I think) not the transcendence of the good. Beautiful things contain beauty in a way in which good acts do not exactly contain good, because beauty is partly a matter of the senses. So if we speak of good as transcendent we are speaking of something rather more complicated and which cannot be experienced, even when we see the unselfish man in the concentration camp. One might be tempted to use the word 'faith' here if it could be purged of its religious associations. 'What is truly good is incorruptible and indestructible.' 'Goodness is not in this world.' These sound like highly metaphysical statements. Can we give them any clear meaning or are they just things one 'feels inclined to say'?

I think the idea of transcendence here connects with two separate ideas, both of which I will be further concerned with below: *perfection* and *certainty*. Are we not certain that there is a 'true direction' towards better conduct, that goodness 'really matters', and does not that certainty about a standard suggest an idea of permanence which cannot be reduced to psychological or any other set of empirical terms? It is true, and this connects with considerations already put forward under the heading of 'attention', that there is a psychological power which derives from the mere idea of a transcendent object, and one might say further from a transcendent object which is to some extent mysterious. But a reductive analysis in, for instance, Freudian terms, or Marxist terms, seems properly to apply here only to a degenerate form of a conception about which one remains certain that a higher and invulnerable form must exist. The idea admittedly remains very difficult. How is one to connect the realism which must involve a clear-eyed contemplation of the misery and evil of the world with a sense of an uncorrupted good without the latter idea becoming the merest consolatory dream? (I think this puts a central problem in moral philosophy.) Also, what is it for someone, who is not a religious believer and not some sort of mystic, to apprehend some separate 'form' of goodness behind the multifarious cases of good behaviour? Should not this idea be reduced to the much more intelligible notion of the interrelation of the virtues, plus a purely subjective sense of the certainty of judgements?

At this point the hope of answering these questions might lead us on to consider the next, and closely related 'attributes': *perfection* (absolute good) and *necessary existence*. These attributes are indeed so closely connected that from some points of view they are the same. (Ontological proof.) It may seem curious to wonder whether the idea of perfection (as opposed to the idea of merit or improvement) is really an important one, and what sort of role it can play. Well, is it important to measure and compare things and know just how good they are? In any field which interests or concerns us I think we would say yes. A deep understanding of any field of human activity (painting, for instance) involves an increasing revelation of degrees of excellence and often a revelation of there being in fact little that is very good and nothing that is perfect. Increasing understanding of human conduct operates in a similar way. We come to perceive scales, distances, standards, and may incline to see as less than excellent what previously we were prepared to 'let by'. (This need not of course hinder the operation of the virtue of tolerance: tolerance can be, indeed ought to be, clear-sighted.) The idea of perfection works thus within a field of study, producing an increasing sense of direction. To say this is not perhaps to say anything very startling; and a reductionist might argue that an increasingly refined ability to compare need not imply anything beyond itself. The idea of perfection might be, as it were, empty.

Let us consider the case of conduct. What of the command 'Be ye therefore perfect?' Would it not be more sensible to say 'Be ye therefore slightly improved?' Some psychologists warn us that if our standards are too high we shall become neurotic. It seems to me that the idea of love arises necessarily in this context. The idea of perfection moves, and possibly changes, us (as artist, worker, agent) because it inspires love in the part of us that is most worthy. One cannot feel unmixed love for a mediocre moral standard any more than one can for the work of a mediocre artist. The idea of perfection is also a natural producer of order. In its *light* we come to see that A, which superficially resembles B, is really better than B. And this can occur, indeed must occur, without our having the sovereign idea in any sense 'taped'. In fact it is in its nature that we cannot get it taped. This is the true sense of the 'indefinability' of the good, which was given a vulgar sense by Moore and his followers. It lies always beyond, and it is from this beyond that it exercises its *authority*. Here again the word seems naturally in place, and it is in the work of artists that we see the operation most clearly. The true artist is obedient to a conception of perfection to which his work is constantly related and re-related in what seems an external manner. One may of course try to 'incarnate' the idea of perfection by saying to oneself 'I want to write like Shakespeare' or 'I want to paint like Piero'. But of course one knows that Shakespeare and Piero, though almost gods, are not gods, and that one has got to do the thing oneself alone and differently, and that beyond the details of craft and criticism there is only the magnetic non-representable idea of the good which remains not 'empty' so much as mysterious. And thus too in the sphere of human conduct.

It will be said perhaps: are these not simply empirical generalisations about the psychology of effort or improvement, or what status do you wish them to have? Is it just a matter of 'this works' or 'it is as if this were so'? Let us consider what, if our subject of discussion were not Good but God, the reply might be. God exists *necessarily*. Everything else which exists exists contingently. What can this mean? I am assuming that there is no plausible 'proof' of the existence of God except some form of the ontological proof, a 'proof' incidentally which must now take on an increased importance in theology as a result of the recent 'de-mythologising'. If considered carefully, however, the ontological proof is seen to be not exactly a proof but rather a clear assertion of faith (it is often admitted to be appropriate only for those already convinced), which could only confidently be made on the basis of a certain amount of experience. This assertion could be put in various ways. The desire for God is certain to receive a response. My conception of God contains the certainty of its own reality. God is an object of love which uniquely excludes doubt and relativism. Such obscure statements would of course receive little sympathy from analytical philosophers, who would divide their content between psychological fact and metaphysical nonsense, and who might remark that one might just as well take 'I *know* that my Redeemer liveth', as asserted by Handel, as a philosophical argument. Whether they are right about 'God' I leave aside: but what about the fate of 'Good'? The difficulties seem similar. What status can we give to the idea of certainty which does seem to attach itself to the idea of good? Or to the notion that we must receive a return when good is sincerely desired? (The concept of grace can be readily secularised.) What is formulated here seems unlike an 'as if' or an 'it works'. Of course one must avoid here, as in the case of God, any heavy material connotation of the misleading word 'exist'. Equally, however, a purely subjective conviction of certainty, which could receive a ready psychological explanation, seems less than enough. Could the problem really be subdivided without residue by a careful linguistic analyst into parts which he would deem innocuous?

A little light may be thrown on the matter if we return now, after the intervening discussion, to the idea of '*realism*' which was used earlier in a normative sense: that is, it was assumed that it was better to know what was real than to be in a state of fantasy or illusion. It is true that human beings cannot bear much reality; and a consideration of what the effort to face reality is like, and what are its techniques, may serve both to illuminate the necessity or certainty which seems to attach to 'the Good'; and also to lead on to a reinterpretation of 'will' and 'freedom' in relation to the concept of love. Here again it seems to me that art is the clue. Art presents the most comprehensible examples of the almost irresistible human tendency to seek consolation in fantasy and also of the effort to resist this and the vision of reality which comes with success. Success in fact is rare. Almost all art is a form of fantasy-consolation and few artists achieve the vision of the real. The talent of the artist can be readily, and is naturally, employed to produce a picture whose purpose is the consolation and aggrandisement of its author and the projection of his personal obsessions and wishes. To silence and expel self, to contemplate and delineate nature with a clear eye, is not easy and demands a moral discipline. A great artist is, in respect of his work, a good man, and, in the true sense, a free man. The consumer of art has an analogous task to its producer: to be disciplined enough to see as much reality in the work as the artist has succeeded in putting into it, and not to 'use it as magic'. The appreciation of beauty in art or nature is not only (for all its difficulties) the easiest available spiritual exercise; it is also a completely adequate entry into (and not just analogy of) the good life, since it *is* the checking of selfishness in the interest of seeing the real. Of course great artists are 'personalities' and have special styles; even Shakespeare occasionally, though very occasionally, reveals a personal obsession. But the greatest art is 'impersonal' because it shows us the world, our world and not another one, with a clarity which startles and delights us simply because we are not used to looking at the real world at all. Of course, too, artists are pattern-makers. The claims of form and the question of 'how much form' to elicit constitutes one of the chief problems of art. But it is when form is used to isolate, to explore, to display something which is true that we are most highly moved and enlightened. Plato says (*Republic*, VII, 532) that the *technai* have the power to lead the best part of the soul to the view of what is most excellent in reality. This well describes the role of great art as an educator and revealer. Consider what we learn from contemplating the characters of Shakespeare or Tolstoy or the paintings of Velasquez or Titian. What is learnt here is something about the real quality of human nature, when it is envisaged, in the artist's just and compassionate vision, with a clarity which does not belong to the self-centred rush of ordinary life.

It is important too that great art teaches us how real things can be looked at and loved without being seized and used, without being appropriated into the greedy organism of the self. This exercise of *detachment* is difficult and valuable whether the thing contemplated is a human being or the root of a tree or the vibration of a colour or a sound. Unsentimental contemplation of nature exhibits the same quality of detachment: selfish concerns vanish, nothing exists except the things which are seen. Beauty is that which attracts this particular sort of unselfish attention. It is obvious here what is the role, for the artist or spectator, of exactness and good vision: unsentimental, detached, unselfish, objective attention. It is also clear that in moral situations a similar exactness is called for. I would suggest that the authority of the Good seems to us something necessary because the realism (ability to perceive reality) required for goodness is a kind of intellectual ability to perceive what is true, which is automatically at the same time a suppression of self. *The necessity of the good is then an aspect of the kind of necessity involved in any technique for exhibiting fact.* In thus treating realism, whether of artist or of agent, as a moral achievement, there is of course a further assumption to be made in the fields of morals: that true vision occasions right conduct. This could be uttered simply as an enlightening tautology: but I think it can in fact be supported by appeals to experience. The more the separateness and differentness of other people is realised, and the fact seen that another man has needs and wishes as demanding as one's own, the harder it becomes to treat a person as a thing. That it is realism which makes great art great remains too as a kind of proof.

If, still led by the clue of art, we ask further questions about the faculty which is supposed to relate us to what is real and thus bring us to what is good, the idea of compassion or love will be naturally suggested. It is not simply that suppression of self is required before accurate vision can be obtained. The great artist sees his objects (and this is true whether they are sad, absurd, repulsive or even evil) in a light of justice and mercy. The direction of attention is, contrary to nature, outward, away from self which reduces all to a false unity, towards the great surprising variety of the world, and the ability so to direct attention is love.

One might at this point pause and consider the picture of human personality, or the soul, which has been emerging. It is in the capacity to love, that is to *see*, that the liberation of the soul from fantasy consists. The freedom which is a proper human goal is the freedom from fantasy, that is the realism of compassion. What I have called fantasy, the proliferation of blinding self-centred aims and images, is itself a powerful system of energy, and most of what is often called 'will' or 'willing' belongs to this system. What counteracts the system is attention to reality inspired by, consisting of, love. In the case of art and nature such attention is immediately rewarded by the enjoyment of beauty. In the case of morality, although there are sometimes rewards, the idea of a reward is out of place. Freedom is not strictly the exercise of the will, but rather the experience of accurate vision which, when this becomes appropriate, occasions action. It is what lies behind and in between actions and prompts them that is important, and it is this area which should be purified. By the time the moment of choice has arrived the quality of attention has probably determined the nature of the act. This fact produces that curious separation between consciously rehearsed motives and action which is sometimes wrongly taken as an experience of freedom. (*Angst.*) Of course this is not to say that good 'efforts of will' are always useless or always fakes. Explicit and immediate 'willing' can play some part, especially as an inhibiting factor. (The daemon of Socrates only told him what not to do.)

In such a picture sincerity and self-knowledge, those popular

[354]

merits, seem less important. It is an attachment to what lies outside the fantasy mechanism, and not a scrutiny of the mechanism itself, that liberates. Close scrutiny of the mechanism often merely strengthens its power. 'Self-knowledge', in the sense of a minute understanding of one's own machinery, seems to me, except at a fairly simple level, usually a delusion. A sense of such self-knowledge may of course be induced in analysis for therapeutic reasons, but 'the cure' does not prove the alleged knowledge genuine. Self is as hard to see justly as other things, and when clear vision has been achieved, self is a correspondingly smaller and less interesting object. A chief enemy to such clarity of vision, whether in art or morals, is the system to which the technical name of sado-masochism has been given. It is the peculiar subtlety of this system that, while constantly leading attention and energy back into the self, it can produce, almost all the way as it were to the summit, plausible imitations of what is good. Refined sado-masochism can ruin art which is too good to be ruined by the cruder vulgarities of self-indulgence. One's self is interesting, so one's motives are interesting, and the unworthiness of one's motives is interesting. Fascinating too is the alleged relation of master to slave, of the good self to the bad self which, oddly enough, ends in such curious compromises. (Kafka's struggle with the devil which ends up in bed.) The bad self is prepared to suffer but not to obey until the two selves are friends and obedience has become reasonably easy or at least amusing. In reality the good self is very small indeed, and most of what appears good is not. The truly good is not a friendly tyrant to the bad, it is its deadly foe. Even suffering itself can play a demonic role here, and the ideas of guilt and punishment can be the most subtle tool of the ingenious self. The idea of suffering confuses the mind and in certain contexts (the context of 'sincere self-examination' for instance) can masquerade as a purification. It is rarely this, for unless it is very intense indeed it is far too interesting. Plato does not say that philosophy is the study of suffering, he says it is the study of death (*Phaedo*, 64 A), and these ideas are totally dissimilar. That moral improvement involves suffering is usually true; but the suffering is the by-product of a new orientation and not in any sense an end in itself.

I have spoken of the real which is the proper object of love, and of knowledge which is freedom. The word 'good' which has been moving about in the discussion should now be more explicitly considered. Can good itself be in any sense 'an object of attention'? And how does this problem relate to 'love of the real'? Is there, as it were, a substitute for prayer, that most profound and effective of religious techniques? If the energy and violence of will, exerted on occasions of choice, seems less important than the quality of attention which determines our real attachments, how do we alter and purify that attention and make it more realistic? Is the *via negativa* of the will, its occasional ability to stop a bad move, the only or most considerable conscious power that we can exert? I think there is something analogous to prayer, though it is something difficult to describe, and which the higher subtleties of the self can often falsify; I am not here thinking of any quasi-religious meditative technique, but of something which belongs to the moral life of the ordinary person. The idea of contemplation is hard to understand and maintain in a world increasingly without sacraments and ritual and in which philosophy has (in many respects rightly) destroyed the old substantial conception of the self. A sacrament provides an external visible place for an internal invisible act of the spirit. Perhaps one needs too an analogy of the concept of the sacrament, though this must be treated with great caution. Behaviouristic ethics denies the importance, because it questions the identity of anything prior to or apart from action which decisively occurs, 'in the mind'. The apprehension of beauty, in art or in nature, often in fact seems to us like a temporally located spiritual experience which is a source of good energy. It is not easy, however, to extend the idea of such an influential experience to occasions of thinking about people or action, since clarity of thought and purity of attention become harder and more ambiguous when the object of attention is something moral.

It is here that it seems to me to be important to retain the idea of Good as a central point of reflection, and here too we may see the significance of its indefinable and non-representable character. *Good, not will, is transcendent.* Will is the natural energy of the psyche which is sometimes employable for a worthy purpose. Good is the focus of attention when an intent to be virtuous co-exists (as perhaps it almost always does) with some unclarity of vision. Here, as I have said earlier, beauty appears as the visible and accessible aspect of the Good. The Good itself is not visible. Plato pictured the good man as eventually able to look at the sun. I have never been sure what to make of this part of the myth. While it seems proper to represent the Good as a centre or focus of attention, yet it cannot quite be thought of as a 'visible' one in that it cannot be experienced or represented or defined. We can certainly know more or less where the sun is; it is not so easy to imagine what it would be like to look at it. Perhaps indeed only the good man knows what this is like; or perhaps to look at the sun is to be gloriously dazzled and to see nothing. What does seem to make perfect sense in the Platonic myth is the idea of the Good as the source of light which reveals to us all things as they really are. All just vision, even in the strictest problems of the intellect, and *a fortiori* when suffering or wickedness have to be perceived, is a moral matter. The same virtues, in the end the same virtue (love), are required throughout, and fantasy (self) can prevent us from seeing a blade of grass just as it can prevent us from seeing another person. An increasing awareness of 'goods' and the attempt (usually only partially successful) to attend to them purely, without self, brings with it an increasing awareness of the unity and interdependence of the moral world. One-seeking intelligence is the image of 'faith'. Consider what it is like to increase one's understanding of a great work of art.

I think it is more than a verbal point to say that what should be aimed at is goodness, and not freedom or right action, although right action, and freedom in the sense of humility, are the natural products of attention to the Good. Of course right action is important in itself, with an importance which is not difficult to understand. But it should provide the starting point of reflection and not its conclusion. Right action, together with the steady extension of the area of strict obligation, is a proper criterion of virtue. Action also tends to confirm, for better or worse, the background of attachment from which it issues. Action is an occasion for grace, or for its opposite. However, the aim of morality cannot be simply action. Without some more positive conception of the soul as a substantial and continually developing mechanism of attachments, the purification and reorientation of which must be the task of morals, 'freedom' is readily corrupted into self-assertion and 'right action' into some sort of *ad hoc* utilitarianism. If a scientifically minded empiricism is not to swallow up the study of ethics completely, philosophers must try to invent a terminology which shows how our natural psychology can be altered by conceptions which lie beyond its range. It seems to me that the Platonic metaphor of the idea of the Good provides a suitable picture here. With this picture must of course be joined a realistic conception of natural psychology (about which almost all philosophers seem to me to have been too optimistic) and also an acceptance of the utter lack of finality in human life. The Good has nothing to do with purpose, indeed it excludes the idea of purpose. 'All is vanity' is the beginning and the end of ethics. The only genuine way to be good is to be good 'for nothing' in the midst of a scene where every 'natural' thing, including one's own mind, is subject to chance, that is, to necessity. That 'for nothing' is indeed the experienced correlate of the invisibility or non-representable blankness of the idea of Good itself.

I have suggested that moral philosophy needs a new and, to my mind, more realistic, less romantic, terminology if it is to rescue thought about human destiny from a scientifically minded empiricism which is not equipped to deal with the real problems. Linguistic philosophy has already begun to join hands with such an empiricism, and most existentialist thinking seems to me either optimistic romancing or else something positively Luciferian. (Possibly Heidegger is Lucifer in person.) However, at this point someone might say, all this is very well, the only difficulty is that none of it is true. Perhaps indeed all is vanity, *all* is vanity, and there is no respectable intellectual way of protecting people from despair. The world just is hopelessly evil and should you, who speak of realism, not go all the way towards being realistic about this? To speak of Good in this portentous manner is simply to speak of the old concept of God in a thin disguise. But at least 'God' could play a real consoling and encouraging role. It makes sense to speak of loving God, a person, but very little sense to speak of loving Good, a concept. 'Good' even as a fiction is not likely to inspire, or even be comprehensible to, more than a small number of mystically minded people who, being reluctant to surrender 'God', fake up 'Good' in his image, so as to preserve some kind of hope. The picture is not only purely imaginary, it is not even likely to be effective. It is very much better to rely on simple popular utilitarian and existentialist ideas, together with a little empirical psychology, and perhaps some doctored Marxism, to keep the human race going. Day-to-day empirical common sense must have the last word. All specialised ethical vocabularies are false. The old serious metaphysical quest had better now be let go, together with the outdated concept of God the Father.

I am often more than half persuaded to think in these terms myself. It is frequently difficult in philosophy to tell whether one is saying something reasonably public and objective, or whether one is merely erecting a barrier, special to one's own temperament, against one's own personal fears. (It is always a significant question to ask about any philosopher: what is he afraid of?) Of course one is afraid that the attempt to be good may turn out to be meaningless, or at best something vague and not very important, or turn out to be as Nietzsche described it, or that the greatness of great art may be an ephemeral illusion. Of the 'status' of my arguments I will speak briefly below. That a glance at the scene prompts despair is certainly the case. The difficulty indeed is to look at all. If one does not believe in a personal God there is no 'problem' of evil, but there is the almost insuperable difficulty of looking properly at evil and human suffering. It is very difficult to concentrate attention upon suffering and sin, in others or in oneself, without falsifying the picture in some way while making it bearable. (For instance, by the sado-masochistic devices I mentioned earlier.) Only the very greatest art can manage it, and that is the only public evidence that it can be done at all. Kant's notion of the sublime, though extremely interesting, possibly even more interesting than Kant realised, is a kind of romanticism. The spectacle of huge and appalling things can indeed exhilarate, but usually in a way that is less than excellent. Much existentialist thought relies upon such a 'thinking reed' reaction which is nothing more than a form of romantic self-assertion. It is not this which will lead a man on to unselfish behaviour in the concentration camp. There is, however, something in the serious attempt to look compassionately at human things which automatically suggests that 'there is more than this'. The 'there is more than this', if it is not to be corrupted by some sort of quasi-theological finality, must remain a very tiny spark of insight, something with, as it were, a metaphysical position but no metaphysical form. But it seems to me that the spark is real, and that great art is evidence of its reality. Art indeed, so far from being a playful diversion of the human race, is the place of its most fundamental insight, and the centre to which the more uncertain steps of metaphysics must constantly return.

As for the élite of mystics, I would say no to the term 'élite'. Of course philosophy has its own terminology, but what it attempts to describe need not be, and I think is not in this case, removed from ordinary life. Morality has always been connected with religion and religion with mysticism. The disappearance of the middle term leaves morality in a situation which is certainly more difficult but essentially the same. The background to morals is properly some sort of mysticism, if by this is meant a non-dogmatic essentially unformulated faith in the reality of the Good, occasionally connected with experience. The virtuous peasant knows, and I believe he will go on knowing, in spite of the removal or modification of the theological apparatus, although what he knows he might be at a loss to say. This view is of course not amenable even to a persuasive philosophical proof and can easily be challenged on all sorts of empirical grounds. However, I do not think that the virtuous peasant will be without resources. Traditional Christian superstition has been compatible with every sort of conduct from bad to good. There will doubtless be new superstitions; and it will remain the case that some people will manage effectively to love their neighbours. I think the 'machinery of salvation' (if it exists) is essentially the same for all. There is no complicated secret doctrine. We are all capable of criticising, modifying and extending the area of strict obligation which we have inherited. Good is non-representable and indefinable. We are all mortal and equally at the mercy of necessity and chance. These are the true aspects in which all men are brothers.

On the status of the argument there is perhaps little, or else too much, to say. In so far as there is an argument it has already, in a compressed way, occurred. Philosophical argument is almost always inconclusive, and this one is not of the most rigorous kind. This is not a sort of pragmatism or a philosophy of 'as if'. If someone says, 'Do you then believe that the Idea of the Good exists?' I reply, 'No, not as people used to think that God existed.' All one can do is to appeal to certain areas of experience, pointing out certain features, and using suitable metaphors and inventing suitable concepts where necessary to make these features visible. No more, and no less, than this is done by the most empirically minded of linguistic philosophers. As there is no philosophical or scientific proof of total determinism the notion is at least allowable that there is a part of the soul which is free from the mechanism of empirical psychology. I would wish to combine the assertion of such a freedom with a strict and largely empirical view of the mechanism itself. Of the very small area of 'freedom', that in us which attends to the real and is attracted by the good, I would wish to give an equally rigorous and perhaps pessimistic account.

I have not spoken of the role of love in its everyday manifestations. If one is going to speak of great art as 'evidence', is not ordinary human love an even more striking evidence of a transcendent principle of good? Plato was prepared to take it as a starting point. (There are several starting points.) One cannot but agree that in some sense this is the most important thing of all; and yet human love is normally too profoundly possessive and also too 'mechanical' to be a place of vision. There is a paradox here about the nature of love itself. That the highest love is in some sense impersonal is something which we can indeed see in art, but which I think we cannot see clearly, except in a very piecemeal manner, in the relationships of human beings. Once again the place of art is unique. The image of the Good as a transcendent magnetic centre seems to me the least corruptible and most realistic picture for us to use in our reflections upon the moral life. Here the philosophical 'proof', if there is one, is the same as the moral 'proof'. I would rely especially upon arguments from experience concerned with the realism which we perceive to be connected with goodness, and with the love and detachment which is exhibited in great art.

I have throughout this paper assumed that 'there is no God' and that the influence of religion is waning rapidly. Both these assumptions may be challenged. What seems beyond doubt is that moral philosophy is daunted and confused, and in many quarters discredited and regarded as unnecessary. The vanishing of the philosophical self, together with the confident filling in of the scientific self, has led in ethics to an inflated and yet empty conception of the will, and it is this that I have been chiefly attacking. I am not sure how far my positive suggestions make sense. The search for unity is deeply natural, but, like so many things which are deeply natural, may be capable of producing nothing but a variety of illusions. What I feel sure of is the inadequacy, indeed the inaccuracy, of utilitarianism, linguistic behaviourism, and current existentialism in any of the forms with which I am familiar. I also feel sure that moral philosophy ought to be defended and kept in existence as a pure activity, or fertile area, analogous in importance to unapplied mathematics or pure 'useless' historical research. Ethical theory has affected society, and has reached as far as to the ordinary man, in the past, and there is no good reason to think that it cannot do so in the future. For both the collective and the individual salvation of the human race, art is doubtless more important than philosophy, and literature most important of all. But there can be no substitute for pure, disciplined, professional speculation: and it is from these two areas, art and ethics, that we must hope to generate concepts worthy, and also able, to guide and check the increasing power of science.

Essay in *The Anatomy of Knowledge*, ed. Marjorie Grene, 1969.

The Sovereignty of Good Over
Other Concepts

The development of consciousness in human beings is inseparably connected with the use of metaphor. Metaphors are not merely peripheral decorations or even useful models, they are fundamental forms of our awareness of our condition: metaphors of space, metaphors of movement, metaphors of vision. Philosophy in general, and moral philosophy in particular, has in the past often concerned itself with what it took to be our most important images, clarifying existing ones and developing new ones. Philosophical argument which consists of such image-play, I mean the great metaphysical systems, is usually inconclusive, and is regarded by many contemporary thinkers as valueless. The status and merit of this type of argument raises, of course, many problems. However, it seems to me impossible to discuss certain kinds of concepts without resort to metaphor, since the concepts are themselves deeply metaphorical and cannot be analysed into non-metaphorical components without a loss of substance. Modern behaviouristic philosophy attempts such an analysis in the case of certain moral concepts, it seems to me without success. One of the motives of the attempt is a wish to 'neutralise' moral philosophy, to produce a philosophical discussion of morality which does not take sides. Metaphors often carry a moral charge, which analysis in simpler and plainer terms is designed to remove. This too seems to me to be misguided. Moral philosophy cannot avoid taking sides, and would-be neutral philosophers merely take sides surreptitiously. Moral philosophy is the examination of the most important of all human activities, and I think that two things are required of it. The examination should be realistic. Human nature, as opposed to the natures of other hypothetical spiritual beings, has certain discoverable attributes, and these should be suitably considered in any discussion of morality. Secondly, since an ethical system cannot but commend an ideal, it should commend a worthy ideal. Ethics should not be merely an analysis of ordinary mediocre conduct, it should be a hypothesis about good conduct and about how this can be achieved. How can we make ourselves better? is a question moral philosophers should attempt to answer. And if I am right the answer will come partly at least in the form of explanatory and persuasive metaphors. The metaphors which I myself favour and the philosopher under whose banner I am fighting, I will make clear shortly.

First, however, I wish to mention very briefly two fundamental assumptions of my argument. If either of these is denied what follows will be less convincing. I assume that human beings are naturally selfish and that human life has no external point or τέλος. That human beings are naturally selfish seems true on the evidence, whenever and wherever we look at them, in spite of a very small number of apparent exceptions. About the quality of this selfishness modern psychology has had something to tell us. The psyche is a historically determined individual relentlessly looking after itself. In some ways it resembles a machine; in order to operate it needs sources of energy, and it is predisposed to certain patterns of activity. The area of its vaunted freedom of choice is not usually very great. One of its main pastimes is day-dreaming. It is reluctant to face unpleasant realities. Its consciousness is not normally a transparent glass through which it views the world, but a cloud of more or less fantastic reverie designed to protect the psyche from pain. It constantly seeks consolation, either through imagined inflation of self or through fictions of a theological nature. Even its loving is more often than not an assertion of self. I think we can probably recognise ourselves in this rather depressing description.

That human life has no external point or τέλος is a view as difficult to argue as its opposite, and I shall simply assert it. I can see no evidence to suggest that human life is not something self-contained. There are properly many patterns and purposes within life, but there is no general and as it were externally guaranteed pattern or purpose of the kind for which philosophers and theologians used to search. We are what we seem to be, transient mortal creatures subject to necessity and chance. This is to say that there is, in my view, no God in the traditional sense of that term; and the traditional sense is perhaps the only sense. When Bonhoeffer says that God wants us to live as if there were no God I suspect he is misusing words. Equally the various metaphysical substitutes for God – Reason, Science, History – are false deities. Our destiny can be examined but it cannot be justified or totally explained. We are simply here. And if there is any kind of sense or unity in human life, and the dream of this does not cease to haunt us, it is of some other kind and must be sought within a human experience which has nothing outside it.

The idea of life as self-enclosed and purposeless is of course not simply a product of the despair of our own age. It is the natural product of the advance of science and has developed over a long period. It has already in fact occasioned a whole era in the history of philosophy, beginning with Kant and leading on to the existentialism and the analytic philosophy of the present day. The chief characteristic of this phase of philosophy can be briefly stated: Kant abolished God and made man God in His stead. We are still living in the age of the Kantian man, or Kantian man-god. Kant's conclusive exposure of the so-called proofs of the existence of God, his analysis of the limitations of speculative reason, together with his eloquent portrayal of the dignity of rational man, has had results which might possibly dismay him. How recognisable, how familiar to us, is the man so beautifully portrayed in the *Grundlegung*, who confronted even with Christ turns away to consider the judgement of his own conscience and to hear the voice of his own reason. Stripped of the exiguous metaphysical background which Kant was prepared to allow him, this man is with us still, free, independent, lonely, powerful, rational, responsible, brave, the hero of so many novels and books of moral philosophy. The *raison d'être* of this attractive but misleading creature is not far to seek. He is the offspring of the age of science, confidently rational and yet increasingly aware of his alienation from the material universe which his discoveries reveal; and since he is not a Hegelian (Kant, not Hegel, has provided Western ethics with its dominating image) his alienation is without cure. He is the ideal citizen of the liberal

[365]

state, a warning held up to tyrants. He has the virtue which the age requires and admires, courage. It is not such a very long step from Kant to Nietzsche, and from Nietzsche to existentialism and the Anglo-Saxon ethical doctrines which in some ways closely resemble it. In fact Kant's man had already received a glorious incarnation nearly a century earlier in the work of Milton: his proper name is Lucifer.

The centre of this type of post-Kantian moral philosophy is the notion of the will as the creator of value. Values which were previously in some sense inscribed in the heavens and guaranteed by God collapse into the human will. There is no transcendent reality. The idea of the good remains indefinable and empty so that human choice may fill it. The sovereign moral concept is freedom, or possibly courage in a sense which identifies it with freedom, will, power. This concept inhabits a quite separate top level of human activity since it is the guarantor of the secondary values created by choice. Art, choice, decision, responsibility, independence are emphasised in this philosophy of puritanical origin and apparent austerity. It must be said in its favour that this image of human nature has been the inspiration of political liberalism. However, as Hume once wisely observed, good political philosophy is not necessarily good moral philosophy.

This impression is indeed an austere one, but there is something still to be added to it. What place, one might ask, is left in this stern picture of solitary all-responsible man for the life of the emotions? In fact the emotions have a rather significant place. They enter through a back door left open by Kant and the whole Romantic movement has followed after. Puritanism and Romanticism are natural partners and we are still living with their partnership. Kant held a very interesting theory about the relation of the emotions to the reason. He did not officially recognise the emotions as part of the structure of morality. When he speaks of love he tells us to distinguish between practical love which is a matter of rational actions, and pathological love which is a mere matter of feeling. He wants to segregate the messy warm empirical psyche from the clean operations of the reason. However, in a footnote in the *Grundlegung* he allows a subordinate place to a particular emotion, that of *Achtung,* or respect for the moral law. This emotion is a kind of suffering pride which accompanies, though it does not motivate, the recognition of duty. It is an actual experience of freedom (akin to the existentialist *Angst*), the realisation that although swayed by passions we are also capable of rational conduct. A close relation of this concept is Kant's handsome conception of the Sublime. We experience the Sublime when we confront the awful contingency of nature or of human fate and return into ourselves with a proud shudder of rational power. How abject we are, and yet our consciousness is of an infinite value. Here it is Belial not Satan who speaks.

> For who would lose,
> Though full of pain, this intellectual being,
> Those thoughts that wander through eternity* . . .

The emotions are allowed to return to the scene as a kind of allowable, rather painful, thrill which is a by-product of our status as dignified rational beings.

What appears in Kant as a footnote and a side issue takes, however, a central place in the development which his philosophy underwent in the Romantic movement. I would sum this up by saying that Romanticism tended to transform the idea of death into the idea of suffering. To do this is of course an age-old human temptation. Few ideas invented by humanity have more power to console than the idea of purgatory. To buy back evil by suffering in the embrace of good: what could be more satisfying, or as a Romantic might say, more thrilling? Indeed the central image of Christianity lends itself [to] just this illegitimate transformation. The *Imitatio Christi* in the later work of Kierkegaard is a distinguished instance of Romantic self-indulgence on this theme, though it may seem unkind to say this of a great and most endearing writer who really did suffer for telling his society some truths. The idea of a rather exciting suffering freedom soon began to enliven the austerity of the Puritan half of the Kantian picture, and with this went a taming and beautifying of the idea of death, a cult of pseudo-death and pseudo-transience. Death becomes *Liebestod*, painful and exhilarating, or at worst charming and sweetly

* [John Milton, *Paradise Lost*, BK II.]

tearful. I speak here of course, not of the great Romantic artists and thinkers at their best, but of the general beaten track which leads from Kant to the popular philosophies of the present day. When the neo-Kantian Lucifer gets a glimpse of real death and real chance he takes refuge in sublime emotions and veils with an image of tortured freedom that which has been rightly said to be the proper study of philosophers.

When Kant wanted to find something clean and pure outside the mess of the selfish empirical psyche he followed a sound instinct but, in my view, looked in the wrong place. His enquiry led him back again into the self, now pictured as angelic, and inside this angel-self his followers have tended to remain. I want now to return to the beginning and look again at the powerful energy system of the self-defensive psyche in the light of the question, How can we make ourselves better? With such an opponent to deal with one may doubt whether the idea of the proud, naked will directed towards right action is a realistic and sufficient formula. I think that the ordinary man, with the simple religious conceptions which make sense for him, has usually held a more just view of the matter than the voluntaristic philosopher, and a view incidentally which is in better accord with the findings of modern psychology. Religion normally emphasises states of mind as well as actions, and regards states of mind as the genetic background of action: pureness of heart, meekness of spirit. Religion provides devices for the purification of states of mind. The believer feels that he needs, and can receive, extra help. 'Not I, but Christ.' The real existence of such help is often used as an argument for the truth of religious doctrines. Of course prayer and sacraments may be 'misused' by the believer as mere instruments of consolation. But, whatever one thinks of its theological context, it does seem that prayer can actually induce a better quality of consciousness and provide an energy for good action which would not otherwise be available. Modern psychology here supports the ordinary person's, or ordinary believer's, instinctive sense of the importance of his states of mind and the availability of supplementary energy. Psychology might indeed prompt contemporary behaviouristic philosophers to re-examine their discarded concepts of 'experience' and 'consciousness'. By opening our eyes we do not necessarily see what confronts us. We are anxiety-ridden animals. Our minds are continually active, fabricating an anxious, usually self-preoccupied, often falsifying *veil* which partially conceals the world. Our states of consciousness differ in quality, our fantasies and reveries are not trivial and unimportant, they are profoundly connected with our energies and our ability to choose and act. And if quality of consciousness matters, then anything which alters consciousness in the direction of unselfishness, objectivity and realism is to be connected with virtue.

Following a hint in Plato (*Phaedrus*, 250) I shall start by speaking of what is perhaps the most obvious thing in our surroundings which is an occasion for 'unselfing', and that is what is popularly called beauty. Recent philosophers tend to avoid this term because they prefer to talk of reasons rather than of experiences. But the implication of experience with beauty seems to me to be something of great importance which should not be by-passed in favour of analysis of critical vocabularies. Beauty is the convenient and traditional name of something which art and nature share, and which gives a fairly clear sense to the idea of quality of experience and change of consciousness. I am looking out of my window in an anxious and resentful state of mind, oblivious of my surroundings, brooding perhaps on some damage done to my prestige. Then suddenly I observe a hovering kestrel. In a moment everything is altered. The brooding self with its hurt vanity has disappeared. There is nothing now but kestrel. And when I return to thinking of the other matter it seems less important. And of course this is something which we may also do deliberately: give attention to nature in order to clear our minds of selfish care. It may seem odd to start the argument against what I have roughly labelled as 'Romanticism' by using the case of attention to nature. In fact I do not think that any of the great Romantics really believed that we receive but what we give and in our life alone does nature live, although the lesser ones tended to follow Kant's lead and use nature as an occasion for exalted self-feeling. The great Romantics, including the one I have just quoted, transcended 'Romanticism'. A self-directed enjoyment of nature seems to me to be something forced. More naturally, as well as more properly, we take a self-forgetful pleasure in the sheer alien pointless independent existence of animals, birds, stones and trees. 'Not how the world is, but that it is, is the mystical.'

I take this starting point, not because I think it is the most important place of moral change, but because I think it is the most accessible one. It is so patently a good thing to take delight in flowers and animals that people who bring home potted plants and watch kestrels might even be surprised at the notion that these things have anything to do with virtue. The surprise is a product of the fact that, as Plato pointed out, beauty is the only spiritual thing which we love by instinct. When we move from beauty in nature to beauty in art we are already in a more difficult region. The experience of art is more easily degraded than the experience of nature. A great deal of art, perhaps most art, actually is self-consoling fantasy, and even great art cannot guarantee the quality of its consumer's consciousness. However, great art exists and is sometimes properly experienced and even a shallow experience of what is great can have its effect. Art, and by 'art' from now on I mean good art, not fantasy art, affords us a pure delight in the independent existence of what is excellent. Both in its genesis and its enjoyment it is a thing totally opposed to selfish obsession. It invigorates our best faculties and, to use Platonic language, inspires love in the highest part of the soul. It is able to do this partly by virtue of something which it shares with nature: a perfection of form which invites unpossessive contemplation and resists absorption into the selfish dream life of the consciousness.

Art however, considered as a sacrament or a source of good energy, possesses an extra dimension. Art is less accessible than nature but also more edifying since it is actually a human product, and certain arts are actually 'about' human affairs in a direct sense. Art is a human product and virtues as well as talents are required of the artist. The good artist, in relation to his art, is brave, truthful, patient, humble; and even in non-representational art we may receive intuitions of these qualities. One may also suggest, more cautiously, that non-representational art does seem to express more positively something which is to do with virtue. The spiritual role of music has often been acknowledged, though theorists have been chary of analysing it. However that may be, the representational arts, which more evidently hold the mirror up to nature, seem to be concerned with morality in a way which is not simply an effect of our intuition of the artist's discipline.

These arts, especially literature and painting, show us the peculiar sense in which the concept of virtue is tied on to the human condition. They show us the absolute pointlessness of virtue while exhibiting its supreme importance; the enjoyment of art is a training in the love of virtue. The pointlessness of art is not the pointlessness of a game; it is the pointlessness of human life itself, and form in art is properly the simulation of the self-contained aimlessness of the universe. Good art reveals what we are usually too selfish and too timid to recognise, the minute and absolutely random detail of the world, and reveals it together with a sense of unity and form. This form often seems to us mysterious because it resists the easy patterns of the fantasy, whereas there is nothing mysterious about the forms of bad art since they are the recognisable and familiar rat-runs of selfish day-dream. Good art shows us how difficult it is to be objective by showing us how differently the world looks to an objective vision. We are presented with a truthful image of the human condition in a form which can be steadily contemplated; and indeed this is the only context in which many of us are capable of contemplating it at all. Art transcends selfish and obsessive limitations of personality and can enlarge the sensibility of its consumer. It is a kind of goodness by proxy. Most of all it exhibits to us the connection, in *human* beings, of clear realistic vision with compassion. The realism of a great artist is not a photographic realism, it is essentially both pity and justice.

Herein we find a remarkable redemption of our tendency to conceal death and chance by the invention of forms. Any story which we tell about ourselves consoles us since it imposes pattern upon something which might otherwise seem intolerably chancy and incomplete. However, human life is chancy and incomplete. It is the role of tragedy, and also of comedy, and of painting to show us suffering without a thrill and death without a consolation. Or if there is any consolation it is the austere consolation of a beauty which teaches that nothing in life is of any value except the attempt to be virtuous. Masochism is the artist's greatest and most subtle enemy. It is not easy to portray death, real death, not fake prettified death. Even Tolstoy did not really manage it in *Ivan Ilyich*, although he did elsewhere. The great deaths of literature are few, but they show us with an exemplary clarity the way in which art invigorates us by a juxtaposition, almost an identification, of pointlessness and value. The death of Patroclus, the death of Cordelia, the death of Petya Rostov. All is vanity. The only thing which is of real importance is the ability to see it all clearly and respond to it justly which is inseparable from virtue. Perhaps one of the greatest achievements of all is to join this sense of absolute mortality not to the tragic but to the comic. Shallow and Silence. Stefan Trofimovich Verhovensky.

Art then is not a diversion or a side issue, it is the most educational of all human activities and a place in which the nature of morality can be *seen*. Art gives a clear sense to many ideas which seem more puzzling when we meet with them elsewhere, and it is a clue to what happens elsewhere. An understanding of any art involves a recognition of hierarchy and authority. There are very evident degrees of merit, there are heights and distances; even Shakespeare is not perfect. Good art, unlike bad art, unlike 'happenings', is something pre-eminently outside us and resistant to our consciousness. We surrender ourselves to its *authority* with a love which is unpossessive and unselfish. Art shows us the only sense in which the permanent and incorruptible is compatible with the transient; and whether representational or not it reveals to us aspects of our world which our ordinary dull dream-consciousness is unable to see. Art pierces the veil and gives sense to the notion of a reality which lies beyond appearance; it exhibits virtue in its true guise in the context of death and chance.

Plato held that beauty could be a starting point of the good life, but he came to mistrust art and we can see played out in that great spirit the peculiarly distressing struggle between the artist and the saint. Plato allowed to the beauty of the lovely boy an awakening power which he denied to the beauty of nature or of art. He seems to have come to believe that all art is bad art, a mere fiction and consolation which distorts reality. About nature he seems, in the context of the theory of forms, to have been at least once in doubt. Are there forms of mud, hair and dirt? If there are then nature is redeemed into the area of truthful vision. (My previous argument assumes of course, in Platonic terms, that there are.) Another starting point, or road, which Plato speaks of more often however is the way of the τέχναι, the sciences, crafts, and intellectual disciplines excluding the arts. I think there is a way of the intellect, a sense in which intellectual disciplines are moral disciplines, and this is not too difficult to discern. There are important bridge ideas between morality and other, at first sight different human activities, and these ideas are perhaps most clearly seen in the context of the τέχναι. And as when we use the nature of art as a clue, we may be able to learn more about the central area of morality if we examine what are essentially the same concepts more simply on display elsewhere. I mean such concepts as justice, accuracy, truthfulness, realism, humility, courage as the ability to sustain clear vision, love as attachment or even passion without sentiment or self.

The τέχνη [science, craft] which Plato thought was most important was mathematics, because it was most rigorous and abstract. I shall take an example of a τέχνη more congenial to myself: learning a language. If I am learning, for instance, Russian, I am confronted by an authoritative structure which commands my respect. The task is difficult and the goal is distant and perhaps never entirely attainable. My work is a progressive revelation of something which exists independently of me. Attention is rewarded by a knowledge of reality. Love of Russian leads me away from myself towards something alien to me, something which my consciousness cannot take over, swallow up, deny or make unreal. The honesty and humility required of the student – not to pretend to know what one does not know – is the preparation for the honesty and humility of the scholar who does not even feel tempted to suppress the fact which damns his theory. Of course a τέχνη can be misused; a scientist might feel he ought to give up a certain branch of study if he knew that his discoveries would be used wickedly. But apart from special contexts, studying is normally an exercise of virtue as well as of talent, and shows us a fundamental way in which virtue is related to the real world.

I suggested that we could see most clearly in the case of the τέχναι the nature of concepts very central to morality such as justice, truthfulness or humility. We can see too the growth and the inter-connection of these concepts, as when what looks like mere accuracy at one end looks more like justice or courage, or even love at the other. Developing a *Sprachgefühl* is developing a judicious respectful sensibility to something which is very like another organism. An intellectual discipline can play the same kind of role as that which I have attributed to art, it can stretch the imagination, enlarge the vision and strengthen the judgement. When Plato made mathematics the king τέχνη he was regarding mathematical thought as leading the mind away from the material world and enabling it to perceive a reality of a new kind, very unlike ordinary appearances. And one might regard other disciplines, history, philology, chemistry, as presenting us with a new kind of subject matter and showing us a new reality behind appearance. These studies are not only an exercise in virtue, they might be thought of as introductory images of the spiritual life. But they are not the spiritual life itself and the mind which has ascended no farther has not achieved the whole of virtue.

I want now to make a closer approach to the central subject of my argument, the Good. Beauty and the τέχναι are, to use Plato's image, the text written in large letters. The concept Good itself is the much harder to discern but essentially similar text written in small letters. In intellectual disciplines and in the enjoyment of art and nature we discover value in our ability to forget self, to be realistic, to perceive justly. We use our imagination not to escape the world but to join it, and this exhilarates us because of the distance between our ordinary dulled consciousness and an apprehension of the real. The value concepts are here patently tied on to the world, they are stretched as it were between the truth-seeking mind and the world, they are not moving about on their own as adjuncts of the personal will. The authority of morals is the authority of truth, that is of reality. We can see the length, the extension, of these concepts as patient attention transforms accuracy without interval into just discernment. Here too we can see it as natural to the particular kind of creatures that we are that love should be inseparable from justice, and clear vision from respect for the real.

That virtue operates in exactly the same kind of way in the central area of morality is less easy to perceive. Human beings are far more complicated and enigmatic and ambiguous than languages or mathematical concepts, and selfishness operates in a much more devious and frenzied manner in our relations with them. Ignorance, muddle, fear, wishful thinking, lack of tests often make us feel that moral choice is something arbitrary, a matter for personal will rather than for attentive study. Our attachments tend to be selfish and strong, and the transformation of our loves from selfishness to unselfishness is sometimes hard even to conceive of. Yet is the situation really so different? Should a retarded child be kept at home or sent to an institution? Should an elderly relation who is a trouble-maker be cared for or asked to go away? Should an unhappy marriage be continued for the sake of the children? Should I leave my family in order to do political work? Should I neglect them in order to practise my art? The love which brings the right answer is an exercise of justice and realism and really *looking*. The difficulty is to keep the attention fixed upon the real situation and to prevent it from returning surreptitiously to the self with consolations of self-pity, resentment, fantasy and despair. The refusal to attend may even induce a fictitious sense of freedom: I may as well toss a coin. Of course virtue is good habit and dutiful action. But the background condition of such habit and such action, in human beings, is a just mode of vision and a good quality of consciousness. It is a *task* to come to see the world as it is. A philosophy which leaves duty without a context and exalts the idea of freedom and power as a separate top level value ignores this task and obscures the relation between virtue and reality. We act rightly 'when the time comes' not out of strength of will but out of the quality of our usual attachments and with the kind of energy and discernment which we have available. And to this the whole activity of our consciousness is relevant.

The central explanatory image which joins together the different aspects of the picture which I have been trying to exhibit is the concept of Good. It is a concept which is not easy to understand partly because it has so many false doubles, jumped-up intermediaries invented by human selfishness to make the difficult task of virtue look easier and more attractive: History, God, Lucifer, ideas of power, freedom, purpose, reward, even judgement are irrelevant. Mystics of all kinds have usually known this and have attempted by extremities of language to portray the nakedness and aloneness of Good, its absolute for-nothingness. One might say that true morality is a sort of unesoteric mysticism, having its source in an austere and unconsoled love of the Good. When Plato wants to explain Good he uses the image of the sun. The moral pilgrim emerges from the cave and begins to see the real world in the light of the sun, and last of all is able to look at the sun itself. I want now to comment on various aspects of this extremely rich metaphor.

The sun is seen at the end of a long quest which involves a reorientation (the prisoners have to turn round) and an ascent. It is real, it is out there, but very distant. It gives light and energy and enables us to know the truth. In its light we see the things of the world in their true relationships. Looking at it itself is supremely difficult and is unlike looking at things in its light. It is a different kind of thing from what it illuminates. Note the metaphor of 'thing' here. Good is a concept about which, and not only in philosophical language, we naturally use a Platonic terminology, when we speak about seeking the Good, or loving the Good. We may also speak seriously of ordinary things, people, works of art, as being good, although we are also well aware of their imperfections. Good lives as it were on both sides of the barrier and we can combine the aspiration to complete goodness with a realistic sense of achievement within our limitations. For all our frailty the command 'be perfect' has sense for us. The concept Good resists collapse into the selfish empirical consciousness. It is not a mere value tag of the choosing will, and functional and casual uses of 'good' (a good knife, a good fellow) are not, as some philosophers have wished to argue, clues to the structure of the concept. The proper and serious use of the term refers us to a perfection which is perhaps never exemplified in the world we know ('There is no good in us') and which carries with it the ideas of hierarchy and transcendence. How do we know that the very great are not the perfect? We see differences, we sense directions, and we know that the Good is still somewhere beyond. The self, the place where we live, is a place of illusion. Goodness is connected with the attempt to see the unself, to see and to respond to the real world in the light of a virtuous consciousness. This is the non-metaphysical meaning of the idea of transcendence to which philosophers have so constantly resorted in their explanations of goodness. 'Good is a transcendent reality' means that virtue is the attempt to pierce the veil of selfish consciousness and join the world as it really is. It is an empirical fact about human nature that this attempt cannot be entirely successful.

Of course we are dealing with a metaphor, but with a very important metaphor and one which is not just a property of philosophy and not just a model. As I said at the beginning, we are creatures who use irreplaceable metaphors in many of our most important activities. And the decent man has probably always, if uncertainly and inexplicably, been able to distinguish between the real Good and its false double. In most ideological contexts virtue can be loved for its own sake. The fundamental metaphors as it were carry this love through and beyond what is false. Metaphors can be a mode of understanding, and so of acting upon, our condition. Philosophers merely do explicitly and systematically and often with art what the ordinary person does by instinct. Plato, who understood this situation better than most of the metaphysical philosophers, referred to many of his theories as 'myths', and tells us that the *Republic* is to be thought of as an allegory of the soul. 'Perhaps it is a pattern laid up in heaven where he who wishes can see it and become its citizen. But it doesn't matter whether it exists or ever will exist; it is the only city in whose politics [the good man] can take part' (*Republic*, 592).

I want now to continue to explain the concept of the Good and its peculiar relation to other concepts by speaking first of the unifying power of this idea, and secondly of its indefinability. I said earlier that as far as I could see there was no metaphysical unity in human life: all was subject to mortality and chance. And yet we continue to dream of unity. Art is our most ardent dream. In fact morality does actually display to us a sort of unity, though of a peculiar kind and quite unlike the closed theoretical unity of the ideologies. Plato pictures the journeying soul as ascending through four stages of enlightenment, progressively discovering at each stage that what it was treating as realities were only shadows or images of something more real still. At the end of its quest it reaches a non-hypothetical first principle which is the form or idea of the Good, which enables it then to descend and retrace its path, but moving only through the forms or true conception of that which it previously understood only in part (*Republic*, 510–11). This passage in the *Republic* has aroused a great deal of discussion but it seems to me that its general application to morality is fairly clear. The mind which has ascended to the vision of the Good can subsequently see the concepts through which it has ascended (art, work, nature, people, ideas, institutions, situations, etc., etc.) in their true nature and in their proper relationships to each other. The good man knows whether and when art or politics is more important than family. The good man sees the way in which the virtues are related to each other. Plato never in fact anywhere expounds a systematic and unitary view of the world of the forms, though he implies that there is a hierarchy of forms. (Truth and Knowledge, for instance, come fairly closely underneath Good, *Republic*, 509 A). What he does suggest is that we work with the idea of such a hierarchy in so far as we introduce order into our conceptions of the world through our apprehension of Good.

This seems to me to be true. Plato's image implies that complete unity is not seen until one has reached the summit, but moral advance carries with it intuitions of unity which are increasingly less misleading. As we deepen our notions of the virtues we introduce relationship and hierarchy. Courage, which seemed at first to be something on its own, a sort of specialised daring of the spirit, is now seen to be a particular operation of wisdom and love. We come to distinguish a self-assertive ferocity from the kind of courage which would enable a man coolly to choose the labour camp rather than the easy compromise with the tyrant. It would be impossible to have only one virtue unless it were a very trivial one such as thrift. Such transformations as these are cases of seeing the order of the world in the light of the Good and revisiting the true, or more true, conceptions of that which we formerly misconceived. Freedom, we find out, is not an inconsequential chucking of one's weight about, it is the disciplined overcoming of self. Humility is not a peculiar habit of self-effacement, rather like having an inaudible voice, it is selfless respect for reality and one of the most difficult and central of all virtues.

Because of his ambiguous attitude to the sensible world, of which I have already spoken, and because of his confidence in the revolutionary power of mathematics, Plato sometimes seems to imply that the road towards the Good leads away from the world of particularity and detail. However, he speaks of a descending as well as an ascending dialectic and he speaks of a return to the cave. In any case, in so far as goodness is for use in politics and in the market place it must combine its increasing intuitions of unity with an increasing grasp of complexity and detail. False conceptions are often generalised, stereotyped and unconnected. True conceptions combine just modes of judgement and ability to connect with an increased perception of detail. The case of the mother who has to consider each one of her family carefully as she decides whether or not to throw auntie out. This double revelation of both random detail and intuited unity is what we receive in every sphere of life if we seek for what is best. We can see this, once more, quite clearly in art and intellectual work. The great artists reveal the detail of the world. At the same time their greatness is not something peculiar and personal like a proper name. They are great in ways which are to some extent similar, and increased understanding of an art reveals its unity through its excellence. All serious criticism assumes this, though it might be wary of expressing it in a theoretical manner. Art reveals reality and, because there is 'a way in which things are', there is a fellowship of artists. Similarly with scholars. Honesty seems much the same virtue in a chemist as in a historian and the evolution of the two could be similar. And there is another similarity between the honesty required to tear up one's theory and the honesty required to perceive the real state of one's marriage, though doubtless the latter is much more difficult. Plato, who is sometimes accused of over-valuing intellectual disciplines, is quite explicit in giving these, when considered on their own, a high but second place. A serious scholar has great merits. But a serious scholar who is also a good man knows not only his subject but the proper place of his subject in the whole of his life. The understanding which leads the scientist to the right decision about giving up a certain study, or leads the artist to the right decision about his family, is superior to the understanding of art and science as such. (Is this not what καίτοι νοητῶν ὄντων μετὰ ἀρχῆς means? *Republic*, 511D.) We are admittedly specialised creatures where morality is concerned and merit in one area does not seem to guarantee merit in another. The good artist is not necessarily wise at home, and the concentration camp guard can be a kindly father. At least this can seem to be so, though I would feel that the artist had at least got a starting point and that on closer inspection the concentration camp guard might prove to have his limitations as a family man. The scene remains disparate and complex beyond the hopes of any system, yet at the same time the concept Good stretches through the whole of it and gives it the only kind of shadowy unachieved unity which it can possess. The area of morals, and ergo of moral philosophy, can now be seen, not as a hole-and-corner matter of debts and promises, but as covering the whole of our mode of living and the quality of our relations with the world.

Good has often been said to be indefinable for reasons connected with freedom. Good is an empty space into which human choice may move. I want now to suggest that the indefinability of the good should be conceived of rather differently. On the kind of view which I have been offering it seems that we do really know a certain amount about Good and about the way in which it is connected with our condition. The ordinary person does not, unless corrupted by philosophy, believe that he creates values by his choices. He thinks that some things really are better than others and that he is capable of getting it wrong. We are not usually in doubt about the direction in which Good lies. Equally we recognise the real existence of evil: cynicism, cruelty, indifference to suffering. However, the concept of Good still remains obscure and mysterious. We see the world in the light of the Good, but what is the Good itself? The source of vision is not in the ordinary sense seen. Plato says of it, 'It is that which every soul pursues and for the sake of which it does all that it does, with some intuition of its nature, and yet also baffled' (*Republic*, 505). And he also says that Good is the source of knowledge and truth and yet is something which surpasses them in splendour (*Republic*, 508–9).

There is a sort of logical, in the modern sense of the word, answer to the question but I think it is not the whole answer. Asking what Good is is not like asking what Truth is or what Courage is, since, in explaining the latter, the idea of Good must enter in, it is that in the light of which the explanation must proceed. 'True courage is . . .' And if we try to define Good as X we have to add that we mean of course a good X. If we say that Good is Reason we have to talk about good judgement. If we say that Good is Love we have to explain that there are different kinds of love. Even the concept of Truth has its ambiguities and it is really only of Good that we can say 'it is the trial of itself and needs no other touch'. And with this I agree. It is also argued that all things which are capable of showing degrees of excellence show it in their own way. The idea of perfection can only be exemplified in particular cases in terms of the kind of perfection which is appropriate. So one could not say in general what perfection is, in the way in which one could talk about generosity or good painting. In any case, opinions differ and the truth of judgements of value cannot be demonstrated. This line of argument is sometimes used to support a view of Good as empty and almost trivial, a mere word, 'the most general adjective of commendation', a flag used by the questing will, a term which could with greater clarity be replaced by 'I'm for this.' This argument and its conclusion seem to me to be wrong for reasons which I have already given: excellence has a kind of unity and there are facts about our condition from which lines converge in a definite direction; and also for other reasons which I will now suggest.

A genuine mysteriousness attaches to the idea of goodness and the Good. This is a mystery with several aspects. The indefinability of Good is connected with the unsystematic and inexhaustible variety of the world and the pointlessness of virtue. In this respect there is a special link between the concept of Good and the ideas of Death and Chance. (One might say that Chance is really a subdivision of Death. It is certainly our most effective *memento mori.*) A genuine sense of mortality enables us to see virtue as the only thing of worth; and it is impossible to limit and foresee the ways in which it will be required of us. That we cannot dominate the world may be put in a more positive way. Good is mysterious because of human frailty, because of the immense distance which is involved. If there were angels they might be able to define good but we would not understand the definition. We are largely mechanical creatures, the slaves of relentlessly strong selfish forces the nature of which we scarcely comprehend. At best, as decent persons, we are usually very specialised. We behave well in areas where this can be done fairly easily and let other areas of possible virtue remain undeveloped. There are perhaps in the case of every human being insuperable psychological barriers to goodness. The self is a divided thing and the whole of it cannot be redeemed any more than it can be known. And if we look outside the self what we see are scattered intimations of Good. There are few places where virtue plainly shines: great art, humble people who serve others. And can we, without improving ourselves, really see these things clearly? It is in the context of such limitations that we should picture our freedom. Freedom is, I think, a mixed concept. The true half of it is simply a name of an aspect of virtue concerned especially with the clarification of vision and the domination of selfish impulse. The false and more popular half is a name for the self-assertive movements of deluded selfish will which because of our ignorance we take to be something autonomous.

We cannot then sum up human excellence for these reasons: the world is aimless, chancy, and huge, and we are blinded by self. There is a third consideration which is a relation of the other two. It is *difficult* to look at the sun: it is not like looking at other things. We somehow retain the idea, and art both expresses and symbolises it, that the lines really do converge. There is a magnetic centre. But it is easier to look at the converging edges than to look at the centre itself. We do not and probably cannot know, conceptualise, what it is like in the centre. It may be said that since we cannot see anything there why try to look? And is there not a danger of damaging our ability to focus on the sides? I think there is a sense in trying to look, though the occupation is perilous for reasons connected with masochism and other obscure devices of the psyche. The impulse to worship is deep and ambiguous and old. There are false suns, easier to gaze upon and far more comforting than the true one.

Plato has given us the image of this deluded worship in his great allegory. The prisoners in the cave at first face the back wall. Behind them a fire is burning in the light of which they see upon the wall the shadows of puppets which are carried between them and the fire and they take these shadows to be the whole of reality. When they turn round they can see the fire, which they have to pass in order to get out of the cave. The fire, I take it, represents the self, the old unregenerate psyche, that great source of energy and warmth. The prisoners in the second stage of enlightenment have gained the kind of self-awareness which is nowadays a matter of so much interest to us. They can see in themselves the sources of what was formerly blind selfish instinct. They see the flames which threw the shadows which they used to think were real, and they can see the puppets, imitations of things in the real world, whose shadows they used to recognise. They do not yet dream that there is anything else to see. What is more likely than that they should settle down beside the fire, which, though its form is flickering and unclear, is quite easy to look at and cosy to sit by?

I think Kant was afraid of this when he went to such lengths to draw our attention away from the empirical psyche. This powerful thing is indeed an object of fascination, and those who study its power to cast shadows are studying something which is real. A recognition of its power may be a step towards escape from the cave; but it may equally be taken as an end-point. The fire may be mistaken for the sun, and self-scrutiny taken for goodness. (Of course not everyone who escapes from the cave need have spent much time by the fire. Perhaps the virtuous peasant has got out of the cave without even noticing the fire.) Any religion or ideology can be degraded by the substitution of self, usually in some disguise, for the true object of veneration. However, in spite of what Kant was so much afraid of, I think there is a place both inside and outside religion for a sort of contemplation of the Good, not just by dedicated experts but by ordinary people: an attention which is not just the planning of particular good actions but an attempt to look right away from self towards a distant transcendent perfection, a source of uncontaminated energy, a source of *new* and quite undreamt-of virtue. This attempt, which is a turning of attention away from the particular, may be the thing that helps most when difficulties seem insoluble, and especially when feelings of guilt keep attracting the gaze back towards the self. This is the true mysticism which is morality, a kind of undogmatic prayer which is real and important, though perhaps also difficult and easily corrupted.

I have been speaking of the indefinability of the Good; but is there really nothing else that we can say about it? Even if we cannot find it another name, even if it must be thought of as above and alone, are there not other concepts, or another concept, with which it has some quite special relation? Philosophers have often tried to discern such a relationship: Freedom, Reason, Happiness, Courage,

History have recently been tried in the role. I do not find any of these candidates convincing. They seem to represent in each case the philosopher's admiration for some specialised aspect of human conduct which is much less than the whole of excellence and sometimes dubious in itself. I have already mentioned a concept with a certain claim and I will return to that in conclusion. I want now to speak of what is perhaps the most obvious as well as the most ancient and traditional claimant, though one which is rarely mentioned by our contemporary philosophers, and that is Love. Of course Good is sovereign over Love, as it is sovereign over other concepts, because Love can name something bad. But is there not nevertheless something about the conception of a refined love which is practically identical with goodness? Will not 'Act lovingly' translate 'Act perfectly', whereas 'Act rationally' will not? It is tempting to say so.

However I think that Good and Love should not be identified, and not only because human love is usually self-assertive. The concepts, even when the idea of love is purified, still play different roles. We are dealing here with very difficult metaphors. Good is the magnetic centre towards which love naturally moves. False love moves to false good. False love embraces false death. When true good is loved, even impurely or by accident, the quality of the love is automatically refined, and when the soul is turned towards Good the highest part of the soul is enlivened. Love is the tension between the imperfect soul and the magnetic perfection which is conceived of as lying beyond it. (In the *Symposium* Plato pictures Love as being poor and needy.) And when we try perfectly to love what is imperfect our love goes to its object *via* the Good to be thus purified and made unselfish and just. The mother loving the retarded child or loving the tiresome elderly relation. Love is the general name of the quality of attachment and it is capable of infinite degradation and is the source of our greatest errors; but when it is even partially refined it is the energy and passion of the soul in its search for Good, the force that joins us to Good and joins us to the world through Good. Its existence is the unmistakable sign that we are spiritual creatures, attracted by excellence and made for the Good. It is a reflection of the warmth and light of the sun.

Perhaps the finding of other names for Good or the establishing of special relationships cannot be more than a sort of personal game. However I want in conclusion to make just one more move. Goodness is connected with the acceptance of real death and real chance and real transience and only against the background of this acceptance, which is psychologically so difficult, can we understand the full extent of what virtue is like. The acceptance of death is an acceptance of our own nothingness which is an automatic spur to our concern with what is not ourselves. The good man is humble; he is very unlike the big neo-Kantian Lucifer. He is much more like Kierkegaard's tax collector. Humility is a rare virtue and an unfashionable one and one which is often hard to discern. Only rarely does one meet somebody in whom it positively shines, in whom one apprehends with amazement the absence of the anxious avaricious tentacles of the self. In fact any other name for Good must be a partial name; but names of virtues suggest directions of thought, and this direction seems to me a better one than that suggested by more popular concepts such as freedom and courage. The humble man, because he sees himself as nothing, can see other things as they are. He sees the pointlessness of virtue and its unique value and the endless extent of its demand. Simone Weil tells us that the exposure of the soul to God condemns the selfish part of it not to suffering but to death. The humble man perceives the distance between suffering and death. And, although he is not by definition the good man, perhaps he is the kind of man who is most likely of all to become good.

Delivered as the Leslie Stephen Lecture, 1967.

The Fire and the Sun: Why Plato
Banished the Artists

To begin with, of course, Plato did not banish all the artists or always suggest banishing any. In a memorable passage in the *Republic* (398 A) he says that should a dramatic poet attempt to visit the ideal state he would be politely escorted to the border. Elsewhere Plato is less polite, and in the *Laws* proposes a meticulous system of censorship. Scattered throughout his work, from the beginning to the end, there are harsh criticisms, and indeed sneers, directed against practitioners of the arts. This attitude is puzzling and seems to demand an explanation. However, what sounds like an interesting question may merit an uninteresting answer; and there are some fairly obvious answers to the question why Plato was so hostile to art. He speaks in the *Republic* (607 B) of 'an old quarrel between philosophy and poetry'. The poets had existed, as prophets and sages, long before the emergence of philosophers, and were the traditional purveyors of theological and cosmological information. Herodotus (ii, 53) tells us that the Greeks knew little about the gods before Homer and Hesiod taught them; and Heraclitus (fr. 57) attacks Hesiod, whom he calls 'the teacher of most men', as a rival authority. Also of course any political theorist who is particularly concerned about social stability (as Plato, like Hobbes, had good reason to be) is likely to consider the uses of censorship. Artists are meddlers, independent and irresponsible critics; literary genres affect societies (*Republic*, 424 C) and new styles of architecture bring changes of heart. A further and related possibility is that Plato simply did not value art (not all philosophers do); he sometimes calls it 'play', and if he thought it, however dangerous, essentially trivial, he would have less hesitation in harassing it. Certainly the Greeks in general lacked our reverential conception of 'fine art', for which there is no separate term in Greek, the word *techné* covering art, craft, and skill.

However, after such considerations one is still uneasy. We, or at any rate we until recently, have tended to regard art as a great spiritual treasury. Why did Plato, who had before him some of the best art ever created, think otherwise? He was impressed by the way in which artists can produce what they cannot account for (perhaps this suggested certain ideas to him), and although he sometimes, for instance in the *Apology* and the *Ion*, holds this against them, he does not always do so. He speaks more than once of the artist's inspiration as a kind of divine or holy madness from which we may receive great blessings and without which there is no good poetry (*Phaedrus*, 244–5). Technique alone will not make a poet. Poets may intuitively understand things of the greatest importance (*Laws*, 628 A), those who succeed without conscious thought are divinely gifted (*Meno*, 99 D). And although, as the jokes in the *Protagoras* suggest, Plato thought poorly of literary critics ('Arguments about poetry remind me of provincial drinking parties', 347 C), he was obviously familiar with the most cultivated and even minute discussions of taste and literary evaluation. (Soup should be served with a wooden, not a golden, ladle. *Hippias Major*, 291 A). He even dubiously allows (*Republic*, 607 D) that a defence of poetry might one day be made (as indeed it was by Aristotle) by a poetry lover who was not a poet. Yet although Plato gives to beauty a crucial role in his philosophy, he practically defines it so as to exclude art, and constantly and emphatically accuses artists of moral weakness or even baseness. One is tempted to look for deeper reasons for such an attitude; and in doing so to try (like Plotinus and Schopenhauer) to uncover, in spite of Plato, some more exalted Platonic aesthetic in the dialogues. One might also ask the not uninteresting question whether Plato may not have been in some ways right to be so suspicious of art.

Plato pictures human life as a pilgrimage from appearance to reality. The intelligence, seeking satisfaction, moves from uncritical acceptance of sense experience and of conduct, to a more sophisticated and morally enlightened understanding. How this happens and what it means is explained by the Theory of Forms. Aristotle (*Metaphysics*, 987 A–B) represents the theory as having a double origin – in Socrates's search for moral definitions, and in Plato's early Heraclitean beliefs. He also (990 B) puts this in terms of the 'one over many' argument and the 'argument from the sciences'. How is it that many different things can share a common quality? How is it that although sensa are in a flux we can have *knowledge*, as opposed to mere opinion or belief? Further: what is virtue, how can we learn it and know it? The postulation of the Forms (Ideas) as changeless eternal non-sensible objects for the seeking mind was designed to answer these questions. It is characteristic of human reason to seek unity in multiplicity (*Phaedrus*, 249 B). There must be things single and steady there for us to know, which are separate from the multifarious and shifting world of 'becoming'. These steady entities are guarantors equally of the unity and objectivity of morals and the reliability of knowledge. *Republic*, 596 A, tells us that there are Forms for all groups of things which have the same name; however, Plato only gradually interprets this large assertion. The earliest dialogues pose the problem of the one and the many in the guise of attempted definitions of moral qualities (courage, piety, temperance), and the first Forms to which we are introduced are moral ones, although very general non-moral Forms such as 'size' appear in the *Phaedo*. Later, mathematical and 'logical' Forms make their appearance, and at different times Forms of sensa are also admitted. The Form of Beauty is celebrated in the *Symposium* and the *Phaedrus*, and the Form of the Good appears in the *Republic* as an enlightening and creative first principle. (The light of the Good makes knowledge possible and also life.) In the *Phaedrus* and the *Phaedo* the Forms become part of an argument for the immortality of the soul. We are aware of the Forms, and so are able to enjoy discourse and knowledge, because our souls were before birth in a place where they were clearly *seen*: the doctrine of recollection or *anamnesis*. The incarnate soul tends to forget its vision, but can be reminded by suitable training or prompting. (The slave in the *Meno* is able to solve the geometrical problem.) The relation between the single Form and its many particulars or instances is explained variously, and never entirely satisfactorily, by metaphors of participation and imitation. On the whole, the early dialogues speak of a 'shared nature', and the later ones of imperfect copies of perfect originals.

The use of the Forms in the doctrine and argument of *anamnesis* tends to impose a picture of entities entirely separated from the sensible world ('dwelling elsewhere') and this 'separation' is increasingly emphasised. (An aesthetic conception.) The pilgrimage which restores our knowledge of this real world is explained in the *Republic* by the images of the sun and the quadripartite divided line, and by the myth of the cave (514). The prisoners in the cave are at first chained to face the back wall where all they can see are shadows, cast by a fire which is behind them, of themselves and of objects which are carried between them and the fire. Later they manage to turn round and see the fire and the objects which cast the shadows. Later still they escape from the cave, see the outside world in the light of the sun, and finally the sun itself. The sun represents the Form of the Good in whose light the truth is seen; it reveals the world, hitherto invisible, and is also a source of life.

There is of course a vast literature upon the interpretation of this myth, on the relation between 'the line' and 'the cave', and on how strictly we are to take the distinctions which Plato makes concerning the lower stages of the enlightening process. I shall take it that the cave illuminates the line, and that we are to attach importance to these distinctions. The details of what happens in the cave are to be studied seriously; and the 'lower half' of the story is not just an explanatory image of the 'higher half', but is significant in itself. The pilgrim is thus seen as passing through different states of awareness whereby the higher reality is studied first in the form of shadows or images. These levels of awareness have (perhaps: Plato is not prepared to be too clear on this, 533 E, 534 A) objects with different degrees of reality; and to these awarenesses, each with its characteristic mode of desire, correspond different parts of the soul. The lowest part of the soul is egoistic, irrational, and deluded, the central part is aggressive and ambitious, the highest part is rational and good and knows the truth which lies beyond all images and hypotheses. The just man and the just society are in harmony under the direction of reason and goodness. This rational harmony also gives to the (indestructible) lower levels their best possible satisfaction. Art and the artist are condemned by Plato to exhibit the lowest and most irrational kind of awareness, *eikasia*, a state of vague image-ridden illusion; in terms of the cave myth this is the condition of the prisoners who face the back wall and see only shadows cast by the fire. Plato does not actually say that the artist is in a state of *eikasia*, but he clearly implies it, and indeed his whole criticism of art extends and illuminates the conception of the shadow-bound consciousness.

I shall look first at Plato's view of art, and later at his theory of beauty. His view of art is most fully expounded in Books III and X of the *Republic*. The poets mislead us by portraying the gods as undignified and immoral. We must not let Aeschylus or Homer tell us that a god caused Niobe's sufferings, or that Achilles, whose mother after all was a goddess, dragged Hector's body behind his chariot or slaughtered the Trojan captives beside the funeral pyre of Patroclus. Neither should we be led to picture the gods as laughing. Poets, and also writers of children's stories, should help us to respect religion, to admire good people, and to see that crime does not pay. Music and the theatre should encourage stoical calmness, not boisterous uncontrolled emotion. We are infected by playing or enjoying a bad role. Art can do cumulative psychological harm in this way. Simple harmonious design, in architecture or in furniture, the products of wholesome craftsmanship enjoyed from childhood onward, can do us good by promoting harmony in our minds; but art is always bad for us in so far as it is mimetic or imitative. Take the case of the painter painting the bed. God creates the original Form or Idea of bed. (This is a picturesque argument: Plato nowhere else suggests that God makes the Forms, which are eternal.) The carpenter makes the bed we sleep upon. The painter copies this bed from one point of view. He is thus at three removes from reality. He does not understand the bed, he does not measure it, he could not make it. He evades the conflict between the apparent and the real which stirs the mind toward philosophy. Art näively or wilfully accepts appearances instead of questioning them. Similarly a writer who portrays a doctor does not possess a doctor's skill but simply 'imitates doctors' talk'. Nevertheless, because of the charm of their work such people are wrongly taken for authorities, and simple folk believe them. Surely any serious man would rather produce real things, such as beds or political activity, than unreal things which are mere reflections of reality. Art or imitation may be dismissed as 'play', but when artists imitate what is bad they are adding to the sum of badness in the world; and it is easier to copy a bad man than a good man, because the bad man is various and entertaining and extreme, while the good man is quiet and always the same. Artists are interested in what is base and complex, not in what is simple and good. They induce the better part of the soul to 'relax its guard'. Thus images of wickedness and excess may lead even good people to indulge secretly through art feelings which they would be ashamed to entertain in real life. We enjoy cruel jokes and bad taste in the theatre, then behave boorishly at home. Art both expresses and gratifies the lowest part of the soul, and feeds and enlivens base emotions which ought to be left to wither.

The ferocity of the attack is startling, though of course it is urbanely uttered. One can scarcely regard it as 'naïve'. Nor is it surely (as Bosanquet suggested in *A History of Aesthetic*, Chapter III*) intended as an ironic *reductio ad absurdum* ('if this is all art is, it's a failure'); though the deliberation is sometimes almost gleeful. Of course the Greeks lacked what Bosanquet calls the 'distinctively aesthetic standpoint', as presumably everyone did with apparent impunity until 1750, and this being so, their attitude to art tended to be rather more moralistic than formalistic, and this is also true of Aristotle. Tolstoy exaggerates only slightly when he says (in *What Is Art?*), 'the Greeks (just like everybody else always and everywhere) simply considered art (like everything else) good only when it served goodness'. Socrates offers it as obvious (*Republic*, 400 E) that good writing and good rhythm and good design depend on good character. We might just entertain this as a hypothesis. The notion that tales which glorify bad men or art which stirs unworthy emotions may do moral damage is certainly familiar to us today, nor are we unaware of the social role of children's stories. The point about 'imitating doctors' talk' is also a shrewd one. The pseudo-authority of the writer (for instance the novelist) may indeed mislead the unwary. However, one is dismayed to learn that the censor is to remove one's favourite bits of Homer; and it may seem odd that Plato is unwilling to admire a clever imitation even as craft, unlike Homer who marvels at the verisimilitude of Achilles's shield at *Iliad*, XVII, 584. (Bosanquet again, in search of Greek

---

* [B. A. Bosanquet, *A History of Aesthetic* (London, 1892).]

aesthetic attitudes. See *A History of Aesthetic*, Chapter II.) Moreover, to regard art as simple reduplication (like dull photography) seems to beg the whole question of what art is to an extent which seems to demand comment, even granted the lack of the 'aesthetic standpoint'. By contrast, Aristotle's remarks appear like luminous common sense. Surely art transforms, is creation rather than imitation, as Plato's own praise of the 'divine frenzy' must imply. To revert to the case of the bed, the painter can reveal far more than the 'one viewpoint' of the ordinary observer. The painter and the writer are not just copyists or even illusionists, but through some deeper vision of their subject matter may become privileged truth-tellers. The tempting correction was made by Plotinus when he suggested that the artist does not copy the material object but copies the Form: a view which on examination turns out to be even more unsatisfactory.

Some of the views developed in the *Republic* are given a trial run in the *Ion*, a dialogue regarded by scholars as very early; the earliest, according to Wilamowitz.* Socrates questions Ion, a rhapsode (poetry reciter), who specialises in Homer. Socrates wonders whether Ion's devotion to Homer is based upon skilled knowledge (*techné*) or whether it is merely intuitive or, as Socrates politely puts it, divinely inspired. Ion lays claim to knowledge, but is dismayed when Socrates asks him what Homeric matters he is expert on. What, for instance, does he know of medicine, or sailing or weaving or chariot racing, all of which Homer describes? Ion is forced to admit that here doctors, sailors, weavers, and charioteers are the best judges of Homer's adequacy. Is there then any Homeric subject on which Ion is really an expert? With unspeakable charm Ion at last says, yes, generalship, though he has not actually tried it of course: a conclusion which Socrates does not pursue beyond the length of a little sarcasm. Ion, though lightly handled by Socrates, is presented as both naïve and something of a cynic, or sophist. He may not know much about chariots but he does know how to make an audience weep, and when he does so he laughs to himself as he thinks of his fee. Socrates finally consoles Ion by allowing that it

---

* [Ulrich F. M. von Wilamowitz-Moellendorff (1848–1931), major pioneer in Greek studies, and biographer of Plato.]

must then be by divine inspiration (θείᾳ μοίρᾳ) that he discerns the merits of the great poet. Plato does not suggest in detail that Homer himself 'does not know what he is talking about', although he speaks in general terms of the poet as 'nimble, winged, and holy', and unable to write unless he is out of his senses. He confines his attack here to the secondary artist, the actor-critic; and in fact nowhere alleges that Homer made specific mistakes about chariots (and so on). In the *Ion* Homer is treated with reverence and described in a fine image as a great magnet which conveys magnetic properties to what it touches. Through this virtue the silly Ion is able to magnetise his clients. The question is raised, however, of whether or how artists and their critics need to possess genuine expert knowledge; and it is indeed fair to ask a critic, with what sort of expertise does he judge a poet to be great? Ion, looking for something to be expert on, might more fruitfully have answered: a general knowledge of human life, together of course with a technical knowledge of poetry. But Plato does not allow him to pursue this reasonable line. The humane judgement of the experienced literary man is excluded from consideration by Socrates's sharp distinction between technical knowledge and 'divine intuition'. The genius of the poet is left unanalysed under the heading of madness, and the ambiguous equation 'insanity – senseless intuition – divine insight' is left unresolved. It is significant that these questions, this distinction and equation, and the portrait of the artist as a sophist, make their appearance so early in Plato's work. Shelley translated this elegant and amusing dialogue. *He* did not mind its implications.

In the *Laws*, a treatise which describes a completely stable society, Plato pays the arts the compliment (and it is a compliment) which they now receive in totalitarian states. Didactic uses of art are studied in detail; even children's games are to be controlled (797 B). Music and song are to be sanctified and rendered changeless, as in Egypt (657, 799), where the paintings and sculptures of ten thousand years ago are no better and no worse than those of today. The most important citizen in the state will be the Minister of Education (765 D). The Muses and the gods of games will help out fear, law, and argument (783 A), and the citizenry will be 'compelled to sing willingly, as it were' (670 D). People must be trained from earliest years to enjoy only good pleasures, and poets will be forced to explain that the just man is always happy (659 D, 660 E). The best literary paradigm for the writer to look to (this has the resonance of Kafka) is the book of the Laws itself (957 D). The *Laws* proves how seriously Plato took the power of the arts, but it adds little of relevant philosophical interest.

In the *Philebus*, however, one gets a glimpse of art in the context of beauty, and it is possible to construct a limited aesthetic out of materials found in this dialogue. The *Philebus*, in which aesthetic imagery is freely used to describe the workings of the mind, is a discussion of pleasure. Plato has already (in the *Gorgias*) attacked the view that pleasure is the only good and has made known in earlier dialogues (especially in the *Republic*) his objections to gross or simple-minded hedonism. Greed, πλεονεξία, the violation of modest sense, is the typical fault of the pleasure-seeker. In fact Plato's conception of pleasure is, and must be, as we shall see, far more complex than these formal arguments, including that of the *Philebus*, suggest. It is agreed at the beginning of the dialogue that the good life must contain both pleasure and reason, the question being which of these makes it good. Pleasure is described as 'essentially unlimited' (31 A), and Philebus (who rarely speaks: some charming peevish boy no doubt) argues that it is its unlimited character which gives it its supreme value (27 E). Socrates, however, wants to connect goodness with limit, an idea which is associated with the Forms, here somewhat inconclusively present. Our human arrangements are a mixture of various sorts of unlimited material (τὸ ἄπειρον) with orderly limits which are imposed in the creation of the world by divine cosmic intelligence (26). (The implication here is that these original mixtures are fundamentally good; that divine intelligence faces insoluble problems is admitted in the *Timaeus*.) We too bring about what is good by a right communion or association (ὀρθὴ κοινωνία) of the unlimited with rational limitation. The argument proceeds to suggest that only rationally controlled pleasures are good, and that intelligence, most kin to divine order, is the good-making ingredient in the good life. A distinction is made between true and false pleasures which is then carefully blended into a distinction between pure and impure pleasures (62–3). The clearer value of truth moves in to assist the obscurer value of good, and is joined in turn by the idea of the pure, always so dear to Plato. (The separated Forms are pure objects of spiritual vision.) Examples of impure pleasures would be those which are really a blend of pleasure and pain, depending upon physical contrast (cessation of discomfort) or upon mental contrast (envy, spite), or those which involve false judgements, where the falsity of the judgement infects the pleasure. Socrates says that some anti-hedonist thinkers have wished to argue that all pleasures are thus impure (false, bad); but he wishes to establish the existence of at last some pure pleasures. The first items upon his list are aesthetic. Quality of pleasure is here linked with quality of beauty. Some things are absolutely (truly, purely) beautiful, others only relatively so (depending upon falsity or contrast). Through sensation we pleasurably experience pure beauty when we see certain colours or simple geometrical figures or listen to single series of pure notes (51 C–D). Such pleasures are evidently never extreme or excessive. Beauty of animals (allowed at *Republic*, 401 A) or of pictures is specifically excluded, and human beauty is not discussed. The list goes on to mention some pure non-aesthetic pleasures, such as smells (admitted to be 'less divine'), pleasures of learning (which are also lauded as attentive to reality, unlike fleeting contrast pleasures, at *Republic*, 585), and certain pleasures connected with health and temperance and virtue generally (63 E) which are not described here, though they are bodied forth elsewhere in Plato's work. In fact the aesthetic examples, meagre as they are (and of course not intended as a formal 'aesthetic'), are designed to establish beauty in the crucial mediating role which it occupies in the dialogue. Socrates tries to 'save' pleasure by attaching it to reason and truth in the form of beauty, here narrowly defined through satisfaction in measure, moderation, and harmony. 'The power of good has fled away into the nature of the beautiful; for measure and proportion are everywhere connected with beauty and virtue' (64 E). Truth is pure and small in extent and not extreme (52 D), and pleasures which consort with truth and with the experience of beauty must be restrained and rational. Pleasure in general and apart from reason is the biggest impostor (ἀλαζονίστατον), and the greatest pleasures tend to be ridiculous and ugly (65 E). (Excessive pleasure and pain are said at *Timaeus*, 86 A to be among the worst diseases of the mind.) Beauty enters the argument as something pleasant, but the dialogue ends with an attack upon the general conception of pleasure. Pleasure is by nature immoderate and indefinite and inimical to right proportion, and is thereby a prime cause of the breakdown in human affairs of the good compositions designed by the cosmic intelligence. Beauty is allowed only an extremely narrow connection with the pleasures of sense, though, in so far as it is a proportion-bearing feature of the cosmos, it is an aspect of Good, and as such properly attracts our love.

In reflections upon art it is never as easy as it might seem at first sight to separate aesthetic from non-aesthetic considerations. Much of what Plato says about art is concerned with the results of its consumption expressed in terms which are obviously moral or political rather than aesthetic. And even when it seems that he is clearly concerned with what is aesthetic ('contemplative') as opposed to what is grossly didactic ('practical'), it must be remembered that for him the aesthetic is the moral since it is of interest only in so far as it can provide therapy for the soul. The *Philebus* does appear to offer us, though with ulterior metaphysical intentions, an aesthetic method of judgement, though a very restricted one. There is nothing here about divine inspiration, except in the sober sense that it appears to be our duty to imitate the cosmic Mind. We should imitate only God, and that by sorting out and emphasising and attending to harmonious patterns which are already latent in the universe. The area of acceptable art where pure pleasure, true beauty, and sense experience overlap is very small. Decent art must obey truth; and truth is expressive of reality (the two ideas blend in the word ἀλήθεια), and is pure, small in extent, and lacking in intensity. At 58 c philosophical truth is compared to a small piece of pure white colour. Art should thus take its humble quiet place in a life of virtuous moderation.

It may be said that Plato is a puritan and this is a puritanical aesthetic. Plato is of course a puritan; and doubtless had mixed feelings about the great artist inside himself. There is in all his work, and not only in the later dialogues, a recurring tone of sometimes almost vehement rejection of the joys of this world. Human life is not μέγα τι, anything much (*Republic*, 486 A). The flesh is mortal trash (*Symposium*, 211 E). We are shadows (*Meno*, 100 A), chattels

[396]

of the gods (*Phaedo*, 62 B). Of course the Greeks in general always took a fairly grim view of the human situation, and the Pythagoreans regarded the body as a prison. But Plato's own austere observations have an unmistakably personal note. This is most evident of course in the *Laws* where we are told that men are sheep, slaves, puppets, scarcely real, possessions of the gods, lucky to be their toys. Human affairs are not serious, though they have to be taken seriously. We exist for the cosmos, not the cosmos for us. (644 B, 713 D, 803 B–C, 804 B, 902 B, 903 C.) ('You don't think much of men,' says Megillus. 'Sorry, I was thinking about God,' says the Athenian.) To be happy men must be abject (meek, lowly) before God (716 A). E. R. Dodds (*Greeks and the Irrational*, p. 215) comments upon this un-Greek use of the word ταπεινός, usually a term of abuse. Of course, by the time he wrote the *Laws* Plato had plenty of reasons for thinking poorly of mankind; but the tone suggests a religious attitude rather than a resentful one. God, not man, is the measure of all things (716 B).

It can certainly be argued that only simple, even naïve, forms of art can be unambiguous companions of a thoroughly sober life. Like all puritans Plato hates the threatre. (And we can understand his feelings from as near to home as *Mansfield Park*.) The theatre is the great home of vulgarity: coarse buffoonery, histrionic emotion, slanderous ridicule such as Aristophanes directed against Socrates. Good taste is outraged by trendy showmanship, horrible naturalistic sound effects, and the raucous participation of the audience. (*Republic*, 396 B, 397 A; *Laws*, 670 A, 700 E.) We are told in the *Philebus* (48) that the playgoer experiences impure emotion, φθόνος, spiteful pleasure, and delights in τὸ γελοῖον, the ludicrous, which is a kind of vice, in direct opposition to the Delphic precept; and such impure pleasure is characteristic not only of the theatre but of 'the whole tragedy and comedy of life' (50 B). In the *Laws* too (656 B) our easy-going amusement in the theatre is compared to the tolerance of a man who only playfully censures the habits of wicked people amongst whom he lives. The serious and the absurd have to be learnt together; but ludicrous theatrical buffoonery is fit only for foreigners and slaves: virtue is not comic (816 E). Words lead to deeds and we ought not to brutalise our minds by abusing and mocking other people (935 A). After the banishment of the dramatic poet in the *Republic* we are urged (398 B) to be content with 'the more austere and less amusing writer who would imitate the speech of the decent man'. Any gross or grotesque mockery would be regarded as a form of falsehood; and although Plato's work is full of jokes (even bafflingly so), one may sometimes get the impression that the good man (like the gods) never laughs. Plato is of course right in general (and his words are well worth our attention today) about the cheapening and brutalising effect of an atmosphere where everything can be ridiculed. The question is also worth asking: what may I properly laugh at, even in my private thoughts?

The dangerous political role of the theatre would of course not be absent from Plato's mind. In the *Laws* (701 A) he deplores the 'vile theatrocracy' of an unruly auditorium. In all this there could even be an element of envy. (Plato often condemns envy; philosophers attack their own faults.) He had been himself a writer of poetry; and when a man with two talents chooses (or at any rate concentrates upon) one, he may look sourly upon the practitioners of the other. In the *Symposium* (176 E) Socrates congratulates Agathon upon his success in the theatre 'in the presence of thirty thousand Greeks'. ('You are being sarcastic,' says Agathon.) No philosopher commanded such an audience, or would presumbly wish for one; only philosophers are not always consistent. Plato often speaks bitterly about the lack of respect for philosophers and the inability of ordinary people to distinguish them from sophists. As a political realist (in the *Laws* for instance) Plato tolerates the theatre, but it pleases him to imagine a simple moderate life devoid of all such artificial nonsense. Consider the delightful, and surely not ironic, description in the *Republic* (372) of the small natural ideal state where men live modestly upon cheese and figs and olives, and recline garlanded drinking their wine upon couches of bryony and myrtle. Glaucon says, 'You are describing a city of pigs!' The arts do not make their appearance until Socrates sarcastically amends this picture for Glaucon's benefit. Greed damages societies and men. The best *technai* are those which remain modestly close to and 'co-operate with nature' (*Laws*, 889 D), such as farming, physical training, simple cooking, and unfussy medicine. The *Timaeus* (88-9) recommends exercise and a natural regime rather than drugs; and the sensible carpenter (at *Republic*, 406 D) who consults a doctor, accepts a simple immediate remedy but rightly has no time for elaborate treatment and so either recovers naturally or dies and is rid of his trouble.

The other aspect of the puritanical Plato is the passionate Plato. He commends homosexual love but says that it should be chaste, and in the *Laws* forbids homosexual practices. (*Laws*, 837–7, 636 C; *Symposium*, 210; *Phaedrus*, 256 C.) He doubtless had his own experience of the divided soul. One may recall the sufferings of the bad horse in the *Phaedrus* (254 E) and the extreme and shameful pleasures mentioned in the *Philebus* (66 A) which are ugly and ridiculous and kept hidden in the hours of darkness. Of course much bad art deliberately and much good art incidentally is in league with lower manifestations of erotic love; therefore art must be purged. What art would the aesthetic of the *Philebus* allow the good state to possess? Plato's dictum that some colours and mathematical figures, imagined or bodied forth in objects (51 C), are absolutely beautiful and sources of pure pleasure is not on the face of it very clear. His words suggest entities too abstract or too simple to be able to hold the attention in the way usually associated with the experience of beauty. His frequent examples elsewhere may show us what he had in mind. Simple wholesome folk melodies would be acceptable, and certain straightforward kinds of military music. Plato was interested in music and in the Pythagorean discovery that the intervals of the scale could be expressed numerically. He often uses musical metaphors, and treats audible harmony as an edifying aspect of cosmic order (*Timaeus*, 47 E). He takes the symbolic role of music for granted (for instance at *Republic*, 400). However, perhaps because of the nature of Greek music, or because he feared its 'unlimited' expressive powers, he never seems to have been tempted to raise its status by regarding it as a branch of mathematics. (Other more recent censors have paid discriminating tribute to the importance of our emotional response to music, even while favouring this art because it seems void of ideas.) The pure colours envisaged by Plato would be wedded to simple mathematical patterns (that the forms would not be elaborate is made clear at 51 C), such as could appear on pottery, or on buildings which could themselves be plainly designed objects of beauty, or upon the embroideries of which Plato more than once speaks. Above all the spirit of the work must be modest and unpretentious. The paintings of (for instance) Mondrian and Ben Nicholson, which might be thought of as meeting his requirements, would I think be regarded by Plato as histrionic and dangerously sophisticated. All represention would of course be barred. In general, folk art and simple handicrafts would express the aesthetic satisfactions of his ideal people. The didactic poetry permitted by the *Republic* and the *Laws* ('hymns to the gods and praises of good men') would be justified by its effective operation upon the soul, although it might no doubt promote a pleasure less than pure.

We may pause here for a moment and compare Plato's views, as expressed in the *Philebus*, with those of two other great puritans, Tolstoy and Kant. Plato's fear of art, and theirs too, is to some extent a fear of pleasure. For Tolstoy, art should be defined not through the pleasure it may give, but through the purpose it may serve. Beauty is connected with pleasure, art is properly connected with religion, its function being to communicate the highest religious perceptions of the age. The kind of art which Tolstoy particularly disliked (and which he freely criticised by the 'can't make head or tail of this stuff' method), the inward-looking art-fostered art of the later Romantics (Baudelaire, Mallarmé, Verlaine), is deliberately obscure and 'the feelings which the poet transmits are evil'. Tolstoy also condemned Shakespeare for lack of moral clarity. Elaborate art tends to be a kind of lying. Tolstoy would agree with *Philebus*, 52 D: intensity and bulk are not connected with truth. Academic aesthetic theories are pernicious because they present art as some sort of complex lofty mystery. But there is no mystery. Purity, simplicity, truthfulness, and the absence of pretence or pretension are the marks of sound art, and such art is universally understood, as are simple folk tales and moral stories. Ordinary people know instinctively that art becomes degraded unless it is kept simple. By these criteria Tolstoy was quite prepared to dismiss almost all his own work as bad. (He excepted *A Prisoner of the Caucasus* and *God Sees the Truth and Waits. What Is Art?*, Chapter VI.) Tolstoy particularly detested opera. Plato would have detested it too. Complex or 'grand' art affects us in ways we do not understand, and even the artist has no insight into his own activity, as Socrates says with sympathetic interest in the *Apology* and airy ridicule in the *Ion*.

Both Plato and Kant, because they are so well aware of the frightful devious egoism of the human soul, are anxious to build metaphysical barriers across certain well-worn tracks into depravity; and to keep apart certain ideas which are longing to merge. Kant's almost fanatical insistence on strict truthfulness has its counterpart in Plato, only this is to some extent obscured by Plato's artful playfulness. Plato wants to cut art off from beauty, because he regards beauty as too serious a matter to be commandeered by art. He allows morality to enter art but only at a simple level (as a reminder of higher harmonies) or under the eye of the censor. Kant, on the other hand, wants to cut beauty off from morals. Kant restricts beauty for the same reason for which Plato restricts art, to get it cleanly out of the way of something more important.

Plato constantly uses the image of the harmonious whole which determines the proper order of its parts. This indeed is one of his prime images. The soul, the state, the cosmos, are such organic wholes; and he speaks (for instance at *Phaedrus*, 286 D) of the way in which inspired imagination goes beyond technique in art to produce a kind of completeness. But whereas Aristotle discusses aesthetic structure in terms entirely familiar to us (*Poetics*, VII, VIII: 'A whole is what has a beginning, a middle and an end.' 'That whose presence or absence makes no perceptible difference is not an integral part of the whole'), Plato never sets up any such definition of a 'work of art', nor indeed does he, except ostensively, define art as opposed to craft. He tends to discuss the effects of styles and patterns rather than the nature of complete objects. We think of art primarily as objects, but there are whole art traditions, notably that of Islam, which do not. Kant does offer a definition, when he describes beauty as coming about when the imagination composes sense experience under the general, orderly, object-forming guidance of the understanding, but without a concept. Beauty has an objective formal occasion, but is a unique subjective composition with an air of purposeful organisation, but no purpose. In the *Critique of Judgement* Kant offers two accounts of beauty. One is narrow and formalistic (as it were what beauty ought to be like); the other, taking more account of actual works of art, and developing the idea of the artist as the inspired 'genius', is wider and more confused. (Genius does not know its method.) Almost all 'real' art turns out to be 'impure'; Kant would certainly agree with Plato that the pleasures of literature are. In the stricter account, the pure judgement of taste bears upon formal properties only; desire, charm, or moral or intellectual content are excluded. Colour is merely charming. Geometrical figures as such are not beautiful because they are constituted by a concept. Kant's examples of pure conceptless beauty, in art or nature, have a Platonic simplicity: birds, flowers (tulips for instance, of which Kant appears to have been fond), Greek-style designs, patterns of foliage on wallpaper. (Plato would not have objected to unpretentious wallpaper.) Though pure beauty has no moral message, the instinctive enjoyment of natural beauty is the mark of a good soul: the forms of natural beauty are spiritually superior to those of art.

Plato distinguishes between very simple permissible beauty in art, and beauty in nature which, as I shall explain, he regards as very important. Kant admits pure beauty in nature only at levels of satisfaction in simple forms, such as leaves and flowers. Beauty in nature is always in danger of becoming merely charming: the song of the nightingale conjures up the 'dear little bird', and is spoilt for us if we are then told that it is produced by a boy hidden in the grove. The wilder aspects of nature have for him a higher role to play. In distinguishing the sublime from the beautiful, Kant gears his whole machine to the attempt to keep the claims of the spiritual world quite separate from the simpler more egoistic and undemanding enjoyment of beauty. We apprehend beauty and rest in the contemplation thereof when sense experience inspires the imagination to formulate some unique non-conceptual pattern. The sublime, on the other hand, is a disturbing feeling (which we regard as an attribute of its cause) which arises in us when reason's authoritative demand for intelligible unity is defeated by the formless vastness or the power of nature; its aspect as 'unlimited', to use the language of the *Philebus*: the starry heavens, mountains, waterfalls, the sea. It is a kind of aesthetic and yet moral feeling of mixed pleasure and pain, akin to the respect which the moral law inspires: pain at reason's defeat, but pleasure at our responding sense of reason's dignity and spiritual value. The sublime stirs and wakens our spiritual nature. In this experience we are not led into theoretical studies of natural form, but receive a shock from nature's lack of form, and our inspiriting pleasure is a pure product of our moral faculty. The sublime, not the beautiful, connects us through purified emotion with the highest good and is an active agent of enlightenment. This metaphysical separation, insisted on by Kant, is inimical both to common-sense egoism (which rejects the sublime or treats it as beautiful) and to Hegelian idealism (which demands the reduction of the two areas to intelligible unity). Thus for instance Bosanquet: 'With Turner and Ruskin before us we do not comprehend the aesthetic perception to which, as to Kant, the stormy sea was simply horrible' (*History of Aesthetic*, Chapter x). This evades Kant's whole point; and the Romantic movement shockingly cheated him in taking over the sublime. Kant is attempting, as Plato is, clearly and finally to separate unresting spiritual aspiration from a restful satisfaction in the pleasing forms of art or nature. Plato too gives nature a stirring spiritual role, only here it is nature as beautiful which awakes the dreaming captives. Plato is of course indifferent to many of the show-pieces of the Kantian sublime (mountains, sea) as well as to the more ordinary charms of nature. Socrates says in the *Phaedrus* (230 D) that fields and trees have nothing to teach him. Plato would agree with Kant about the edifying role of the starry heavens; only Kant would be edified by reason's defeat (theoretical studies do not thus enlighten us), whereas for Plato the stars would properly inspire us to geometry (*Republic*, 530 A), thus to philosophy (*Timaeus*, 47 C) shining as evidence of a divine hand, endowed with souls (*Timaeus*, 41 E), or as visible gods (*Laws*, 899 B). 'Can we then deny that everything is full of gods?' Plato asks here, quoting Thales.

Plato temperamentally resembles Kant in combining a great sense of human possibility with a great sense of human worthlessness. Kant is concerned both with setting limits to reason, and with increasing our confidence in reason within those limits. Though he knows how passionate and how bad we are, Kant is a moral democrat expecting every rational being to be able to do his duty. Plato, on the other hand, is a moral aristocrat, and in this respect a puritan of a different type, who regards most of us as pretty irrevocably plunged in illusion. Plato (except mythically in the

Timaeus) sets no theoretical limits to reason, but the vast distance which he establishes between the good and the bad makes him as alien to Hegel as Kant is. Plato is accused of moral 'intellectualism', the view that we are saved not by ordinary morality but somehow by thinking. Let us now look more closely at what Plato considered thinking to be like. He was concerned throughout with how people can change their lives so as to become good. The best, though not the only, method for this change is *dialectic*, that is, philosophy regarded as a spiritual discipline. The aim of Socrates was to prove to people that they were ignorant, thus administering an intellectual and moral shock. In the *Sophist* (230 C), dialectic is described as a purgation of the soul by ἔλεγχος, argument, refutation, cross-questioning; and in the *Phaedo* (67 E) true philosophers are said to 'practise dying'. Philosophy is a training for death, when the soul will exist without the body. It attempts by argument and the meticulous pursuit of truth to detach the soul from material and egoistic goals and enliven its spiritual faculty, which is intelligent and akin to the good. Now what exactly is philosophy? Some might say that philosophy is certain arguments in certain books, but for Plato (as indeed for many present-day philosophers) philosphy is essentially talk. *Viva voce* philosophical discussion (the ψιλοὶ λόγοι of *Theaetetus*, 165 A) is the purest human activity and the best vehicle of truth. Plato *wrote* with misgivings, because he knew that truth must live in present consciousness and cannot live anywhere else. He expressed these misgivings in the *Phaedrus* and (if he wrote it) in the *Seventh Letter*.

The remarks about writing in the *Phaedrus* are very striking and cannot but have relevance to Plato's view of art, not only because some writing is art. Of course in Plato's time books were still rather rare luxury articles. Phaedrus says (257, D) that many people hesitate to leave written speeches behind them for fear of being called sophists. Socrates (274-5) proceeds to explore the propriety or impropriety of writing by means of a myth. Theuth (Thoth, alias Hermes, also mentioned in the *Philebus*), a deity living in Upper Egypt, whom Plato here credits with the invention of number, arithmetic, geometry, astronomy, draughts, and dice, comes to Thamous, who is King and God, and says: 'My lord, I have invented this ingenious thing, it is called *writing*, and it will improve both the wisdom and the memory of the Egyptians.' Thamous (God is always doing geometry, but he cannot write) replies that, on the contrary, writing is an inferior substitute for memory and live understanding. Men will be led to think that wisdom resides in writings, whereas wisdom must be in the mind. A book cannot answer back or distinguish wise or foolish readers. (Plato expresses this view as early as *Protagoras*, 329 A.) It needs its parent to speak for it. Like a painting, it says always one thing and cannot explain. The gardens of literature produce ephemeral flowers, for amusement only. The wise man will plant in suitable souls seeds which are not sterile, when properly understood thought is conveyed in live discussion. ('How easily you make up stories from Egypt or any country you please!' says Phaedrus admiringly. 'In the past, dear boy,' says Socrates, 'people were content to listen to an oak or a rock provided it spoke the truth.') Only words inscribed on the soul of the hearer enable him to learn truth and goodness; such spoken truths are a man's legitimate sons. Writing spoils the direct relationship to truth in the present. Since truth (relation to the timeless) exists for incarnate beings only in immediate consciousness, in live dialectic, writing is precisely a way of absenting oneself from truth and reality. The *Seventh Letter* makes the same point even more emphatically. What is really important in philosophy cannot be put into written words and scarcely indeed into words. (Language itself may be a barrier.) Written words are the helpless victims of men's ill will, and encourage inferior exposition at second hand. Writing can easily become a kind of lying, something frivolously pursued for its own sake, in fact an art form. True understanding comes suddenly to trained thinkers after sustained and persistent discussion; and there is little danger of a man forgetting the truth once he has grasped it since it lies within a small compass.

The spirit of this tirade is curiously contemporary, and may remind us of familiar existentialist arguments and their more recent offspring in the form of attacks upon literacy and art, mounted by literate people and artists. These demonstrations, even at their least serious or most naïve, are conceived in the interests of truth, which here appears variously in the guises of sincerity, genuine feeling, freedom, and so on. A truer heir of Plato's argument is to be found within philosophy in the form of an attack upon system, jargon, grandeur, and the development of wordy theories which prevent a simple lively relationship with truth. (The dialogue form itself is of course a slight precaution against monolithic system.) Modern thinkers as unlike each other as Kierkegaard and Wittgenstein have felt acutely what Plato gives expression to. Kierkegaard, fighting Hegel, attempted to use art itself as an anti-theoretical mystification in order to scare off disciples and promote live thought. Wittgenstein scared disciples by the direct method and also wrote with reluctance because he feared that his books would fall into the hands of fools. He too thought that there was little danger of forgetting what had once been properly understood. Criticising some of his own work he is reported as saying in conversation: 'No. If this were philosophy you could learn it by heart.' What has been clearly seen is appropriated and cannot be lost.

It is necessary before discussing this further to fill in some metaphysical background to it. Writing, invented by the god who invented numbers and games, so sadly remote from reality, may be viewed as a case of an even more general Platonic problem. Here we must look for a moment first at the doctrine of *anamnesis* (recollection), and then at the adventures and misadventures of the Theory of Forms. Plato asks the question, which so many philosophers have asked since (Hume and Kant asked it with passion): how do we seem to know so much upon the basis of so little? We know about perfect goodness and the slave in the *Meno* knows geometry because the soul was once separate from the body (and will presumably be so again) and saw these things clearly for itself. Learning is recollection (*Phaedo*, 91 E). Now when incarnate it is confused by ordinary sense perception, but can gain some refreshment from the contemplation of eternal objects to which it is akin and which it feels prompted to rediscover; although of course (*Phaedo*, 66) such contemplation must always be imperfect so long as the soul and the body remain together.

The idea of unconscious knowledge goes very far back in Plato and was in some original form no doubt adopted by him from those (Pythagoreans) mentioned at *Phaedo*, 62 B who held that the soul is imprisoned in the body and has a home elsewhere to which it goes and from which it returns. The divinely inspired prophet was of course in Greece (as elsewhere) a familiar figure, the man who mysteriously knows more than he can explain or understand. The human mind is potentially connected with an obscure elsewhere; and traditionally the poets, as inspired beings, could also count as seers. The Muses are after all the daughters of Memory, and Apollo (*Cratylus*, 405 A) is both prophet and musician. Prophetic and poetic madness are juxtaposed in the *Phaedrus*. Plato was clearly fascinated by the unconscious nature of the artist's inspiration, which he constantly mocks, but which he also uses as a clue. In the *Protagoras* (347 E) he prefers the company of philosophers to that of poets, since poets never know what they are talking about, and neither does anybody else. In the *Meno*, however, he asks: can virtue be taught? No, not even by Themistocles or Aristides or Pericles. Some things are teachable (διδακτόν), others must be 'remembered' (ἀναμνηστόν, 87 B). Even statesmen who are wise are like the poets in that they do not know the source of their wisdom. Plato concludes that wisdom comes to us somehow 'by divine dispensation' (θείᾳ μοίρᾳ, 100 B). There is indeed no limit to the power of remembering since 'all nature is akin and the soul has learnt everything' (81 D), so through recovering one thing we can by this mysterious process go on to recover others. The creative mind instinctively connects, and a profound idea joins the far-fetched to the familiar and illuminates its own evidence. Plato (for instance, at *Republic*, 572 A) tells of soothing anger by deliberately falling asleep with quiet thoughts; and the discussion of education in the *Laws* shows how much he had reflected upon the powers of 'subliminal' persuasion.

The world rediscovered in *anamnesis* is the world of the Forms, and the Forms have in Plato's thought a history which is both complex and obscure. The most beautiful vision of the Forms as objects of veneration and love is given to us in the *Phaedrus* (250) where (in a myth) they are referred to as 'realities' or 'entities' (ὄντα), quasi-things which can be seen as passing in procession. They are seen 'by the soul alone' when it seeks 'by itself' (*Phaedo*, 66 D, 79 D), and are therefore associated with the hope of the soul's immortality. The Form of Beauty (*Symposium*, 211) shines forth by and in itself, singular and eternal, whereas the Forms 'with us' are infected and fallen 'trash'. The 'lovers of sights and sounds', including connoisseurs of art, at *Republic*, 476 are 'dreaming' because they take a resemblance for a reality. One does not have to read far in Plato to see that the Aristotelian explanation of the origin of the Theory of Forms in terms of 'logic' is only part of the picture. From the start the need for the Forms in Plato's mind is a moral need. The theory expresses a certainty that goodness is something indubitably real, unitary, and (somehow) simple, not fully expressed in the sensible world, therefore living elsewhere. The eloquence and power of Plato's evocation may in itself persuade us, in particular contexts, that we understand, but of course it is never very easy to see what the Forms are supposed to be, since in speaking of them Plato moves continually between ontology, logic, and religious myth. F. M. Cornford argues that when the theory first appears 'the process of differentiating concepts from souls has not yet gone very far in Plato's mind' (*From Religion to Philosophy*, section 132). On this view the Form was originally conceived as a piece of soul-stuff or a daemonic group-soul. It is scarcely possible to develop any such idea with precision; Plato speaks of the Forms with a remarkable combination of absolute confidence and careful ambiguity. In so far as the historical Socrates was interested in studying moral concepts it might seem that the first Forms were definitions or (in the modern sense) universals. Yet the tendency to reify them also begins early. The Form represents the *definiendum* as it is 'in itself' (αὐτὸ καθ' αὐτὸ); and *Protagoras*, 330 C even tells us that Justice is just. The early Forms also 'participate' in particulars and thus give them definition and some degree of reality. But from the *Phaedo* onward Plato develops, especially in moral and religious contexts, a picture of the Forms as changeless and eternal and *separate* objects of spiritual vision known by direct acquaintance rather than through the use of language (propositions). The mediocre life is a life of illusion. The discovery of truth and reality, the conversion to virtue, is through the unimpeded vision of the transcendent Forms. At the same time, in his more logical metaphysical contexts, Plato criticises and even attacks this picture, without however abandoning it; it reappears in a splendid mythological guise in the *Timaeus*, and evidently expresses something for which Plato cannot find any other formulation. The last reference to the Forms is the sober one at *Laws*, 965. 'Can there be

any more accurate vision or view of any object than through the
ability to look from the dissimilar many to the single idea?' Here the
language of vision seems plainly metaphorical. A mysterious late
unwritten doctrine is said to associate the Forms with numbers (the
Good is the One), but of this little can be said. Plato played in many
ways with the concepts of one, many, limit, and it seems unlikely
that the 'number' doctrine represents anything entirely new.
Dialectic (philosophy) follows the varying fates of the Forms, thus
appearing sometimes as mystical vision, sometimes as meticulous
classification, the ability to make distinctions and discern relevant
differences (*Politicus*, 285 A, *Philebus*, 16–17).

The most radical doubts concerning the reified or visionary
Forms occur in the *Parmenides*, *Theaetetus*, and *Sophist*. In the
Parmenides the youthful Socrates attempts to expound a doctrine of
Forms which is subjected to damaging criticism by Parmenides. No
sense can be made of the idea of 'participation', the relation
between a particular and a 'similar' Form leads to a vicious regress
(the 'third man' argument), and it is in general impossible to
establish how Forms can be known. Parmenides also presses upon
Socrates the question: what are there Forms of? The theory has
thriven upon a consideration of the great moral Forms, the
mathematical Forms of the *Republic*, and certain other respectable
Forms of great generality. But are there Forms of everything, even
of trivial things such as mud, hair, and dirt? (As *Republic*, 596 A,
where Forms are associated with common names, would suggest.)
When Socrates inclines to say no, Parmenides rightly points out that
if he gives up here he is not yet a philosopher. At the same time, and
in spite of his criticisms and questions, Parmenides holds that
(somehow) Forms are necessary for knowledge and discourse, since
'you must always mean the same thing by the same name' (147 D).
The *Theaetetus* does not refer directly to the Forms, though certain
important 'common qualities' are discussed (185 C). The dialogue
mainly concerns the absolute difference between knowledge and
opinion, which was an original founding idea of the theory. In
discussing the quarrel between the followers of Parmenides and of
Heraclitus (the One men and the flux men) Socrates, rejecting 'total
motion' and 'total rest', anticipates the arguments of the *Sophist*;
and we are told at 182 B that nothing is one 'all by itself' (αὐτὸ καθ'

αὐτό). 'False opinion' is considered (how is it that we make mistaken judgements?), and there is a long and inconclusive attempt to define 'knowledge'. The argument rejects the view that knowledge is perception (the evident presence of the known where the mind 'touches' it) or that it is true opinion, or true opinion with an explanation (*logos*) attached; the ability to distinguish particulars always involves more insight into relevant differences than can be unambiguously expressed, so the particulars lie inaccessibly under the net of the mode of expression.

The *Sophist* (where Theaetetus is questioned by a visiting follower of Parmenides and Zeno) returns to the Forms and picks up problems left unsolved in the *Parmenides* and the *Theaetetus*. What is knowledge? What are negation and falsehood? How is it that the Forms are essential to thought? How does Being enter Becoming, how can it? Plato also makes an important move in allowing (248) that what knows (soul, ψύχη) must be as real as what is known (Forms). This leaves the way open for the *Timaeus* and for the much enhanced role of ψύχη in that dialogue and in the *Laws*, where real truth-knowing Soul appears as a mediator between changeless being and the world of sense, whose status as real is from now on quietly upgraded. Being must accommodate both motion and rest; and Plato here concedes the necessity of a theory of motion as part of a theory of the real, and thus comes closer to the scientific interests of his predecessors, interests which he himself pursues in the *Timaeus*. The formal pretext of the *Sophist* is the use of the dialectical method of 'division' to define 'sophist'. This raises questions about kinds of imitation and fake, then about the more general problem of negation, where in the course of a complex discussion the 'Eleatic stranger' criticises views held by 'the Friends of the Forms' (probably Plato's own earlier doctrine). How can we say what is not? How are false judgements meaningful, how can there be false opinions, imitations, images, pictures, deceptions, copies, products of mimesis? These are the stock-in-trade of the sophist, who is at last defined as an ironical, ignorant, fantastical image-maker who attempts to escape censure by denying the existence of falsehood and the validity of reason. He runs away into the darkness of not-being and feels his way about by practice (254 A). The dialogue explains that if we are to see how

[410]

false judgements are significant we must avoid the old Eleatic confrontations of absolute being with absolute not-being. (The stranger admits to being a bit of a parricide where Father Parmenides is concerned.) Theaetetus is led to agree that not-being does seem to be rather interwoven with being (240 C), and the stranger explains that not-being is not the opposite of being, but that part of being which is different or other (257–8). When we deny that something is X, we are not denying that it *is*, but asserting that it is other. This is possible because the world is neither a dense unity nor an inapprehensible flux, but an orderly network of samenesses and differences (249). This network (συμπλοκή) makes possible falsehood and deception, and also truth and language. What are thus systematically connected are the Forms, here figuring as classes. 'We derive significant speech from the inter-weaving of the Forms' (259 E). This interweaving depends upon the pervasive presence of certain 'great kinds', very general structural concepts or logical features: existence, same, different, rest, motion. These are compared to vowels which join other letters together in a limited number of permissible groupings (253 A). Reality is such that some things are compatible, others incompatible, some arrangements are possible, others impossible (253 C). (Wittgenstein, solving the same problem, offers similar arguments in the *Tractatus*. On the relation between *Theaetetus* and *Sophist*, with some mention of Wittgenstein, see McDowell's commentary on *Theaetetus*, 201–2.*) The question of the Forms is not just a question about one and many to be answered by a dialectic of classification, as mentioned at *Philebus*, 16 and *Phaedrus*, 266 B and *Laws*, 965. It is a question of logical structure, meaning. This is the structure desiderated by Socrates at *Parmenides*, 130 A. It is also glanced at (but without reference to Forms) in the *Theaetetus* (185–6) as part of the argument against regarding knowledge as perception. In the *Republic* an interlocking network (σύμπλοκη, 476 A) of Forms is rather obscurely indicated (they have 'necessary relations' as in mathematics?), and the liberated mind is pictured (511 C) as moving about among them with no intermediary. ('I don't quite understand', says Glaucon. The idea of Good as first principle is never

---

* [John McDowell, *Commentary on Theaetetus* (Oxford, 1973).]

really explained.) In the *Phaedo* (99 E) Socrates admitted that he could not look at the sun and had to turn to *logoi* (propositions, discourse), which he added were not to be thought of as images. (That is, speech, not objects of perception.)

What the *Sophist* at last makes clear is that the Form system is available to us only in discourse. Thinking is inner speech, 263 E, 264 A, and *Theaetetus*, 190 A. (Plato's argument does not in fact depend on this identification which is rightly denied by Wittgenstein, *Investigations*, p. 217. See also *Tractatus*, 4.002.) This is where truth and knowledge live, and plausibility and falsehood too. Because reality is thus systematic (because of the orderly intrusion of not-being into being), writing and imitation and forgery and art and sophistry are possible, and we are able meaningfully and plausibly to say what is not the case: to fantasise, speculate, tell lies, and write stories. In such a world the sophist, as charlatan and liar, is a natural phenomenon, since for truth to exist falsehood must be able to exist too. Moreover, if knowledge lives at the level of discourse we cannot (as far as the *Sophist* is concerned), in the ultimate perhaps mystical (quasi-aesthetic) sense envisaged earlier, know the Forms. The *Phaedo* speaks of an escape from the body and even the *Theaetetus* (176 B) tells us to flee to the gods. The *Sophist* discusses knowledge without insisting upon such removals. The image of knowledge as direct acquaintance, as seeing with the mind's eye (although Plato does use it again later) here gives way to the conception of knowledge as use of propositions and familiarity with structure. Truth lies in discourse not in visions; so neither the little individual particulars (whose unknowability the *Theaetetus* ended by admitting) nor the Forms as separated supersensible individuals, are directly accessible to the mind. The sophist is pictured at 254 A as being in the cave. But the imagery of spiritual progress is absent, and the dialogue makes a less strong claim for knowledge than that rejected in the *Theaetetus* (that knowledge is perception) or put forward in the *Republic* (that it is, somehow, being face to face with the Forms).

It is now perhaps possible to see deeper reasons for Plato's hostility to writing and to the practice of imitation, including mimetic art. One is struck by the similarity of the venomous description of the sophist to the descriptions of the artist which are found elsewhere. If falsehood has to be possible then a whole art of deceiving can exist (264 D). The ideal of knowledge is to see face to face, not (*eikasia*) in a glass darkly. However, truth involves speech and thought is mental speech, so thought is already symbolism rather than perception: a necessary evil. (On the ambiguity of necessary evils, and the problems of the *Sophist* generally, see Jacques Derrida's brilliant essay *La Pharmacie de Platon*.) The best we can hope for is the flash of ultra-verbal understanding which may occur in live philosophical discussion when careful informed trained speech has set the scene. (*Seventh Letter*, 341 C.) Language itself, spoken, is already bad enough. Writing and mimetic art are the introduction of further symbols and discursive *logoi* or quasi-*logoi* which wantonly make a poor situation even worse and lead the mind away in the wrong direction. (Derrida comments on Plato's frequent use of the word φάρμακον, drug, to mean what can kill or cure. Writing is described as a φάρμακον at *Phaedrus*, 275 A.) The sophist is odious because he plays with a disability which is serious, glories in image-making without knowledge, and, living in a world of fictions, blurs the distinction between true and false (260 D). He is a subjectivist, a relativist, and a cynic. In the process of division which leads to the definition of the sophist, even the artist-copyist is allotted a slightly higher place in the realm of *eikasia*, the shadow world of the cave. The sophist is described as an εἰρωνικὸς μιμητής, an ironical imitator. (εἰρωνικὸς is sometimes translated 'insincere', but 'ironical' best conveys the idea of curious intelligent double-talk which is required here.) Ironical, as opposed to naïve, imitators have been disturbed by philosophy and (286 A) through experiences of the hurly-burly of argument uneasily suspect that they are really ignorant of what they publicly profess to understand. We may recall here the ἀδολεσχίας καὶ μετεωρολογίας φύσεως πέρι, the discussion and lofty speculation about the nature of things, mentioned in the *Phaedrus* (269 E), of which all great art stands in need, and which Pericles was so lucky to pick up a smattering of from Anaxagoras. We are also reminded of the description of the artist in Book X of the *Republic* (599 C) as a false plausible know-all who can 'imitate doctors' talk'. The artist begins indeed to look like a special sort of sophist; and not the least of his crimes is that he directs our attention to particulars which he presents as intuitively knowable, whereas concerning their know-ability philosophy has grave and weighty doubts. Art undoes the work of philosophy by deliberately fusing knowledge by acquaintance and knowledge by description.

*

The argument so far has been about art, and it is time now to talk about beauty, to which Plato gives by contrast such an important role. Beauty as a spiritual agent, in Plato, excludes art. Plato's work is, as I said, largely concerned with ways to salvation. We may speak of a (democratic) 'way of justice' which, without necessarily leading to true enlightenment, is open to anyone who is able to harmonise the different levels of his soul moderately well under the general guidance of reason. The characteristic desires of each level would not be eliminated, but would in fact, under rational leadership, achieve their best general satisfaction. The baser part is really happier if rationally controlled. This reasonable egoism would be accessible to the lower orders in the *Republic*. Plato certainly thought that few could be 'saved', but allowed that many might lead a just life at their own spiritual level. (The doubts raised at the end of Book IX of the *Republic* concern surely the existence of the ideal state as a real state, and not any dubiety about its far more important efficacy as an allegory of the soul.) The *Laws* presents a somewhat grimmer picture of the status of the ordinary just man. Plato remarks that most people want power not virtue (687 C) and must be trained by pleasure and pain to prefer justice. (Art can help here.) Of course justice is in fact pleasanter as well as better than injustice, but even if it were not it would be expedient to say that it was (653, 663). Political systems make men good or bad. The way of justice is subservient to two higher ways, which I shall call 'the way of Eros', and 'the way of Cosmos'. In so far as justice involves a harmony of desires, and if all desires are (as Plato tells us at *Symposium*, 205 E) for the good in the guise of the beautiful, then the way of justice could lead into higher ways, and even the humblest citizen could suffer a divine disturbance. In the *Republic*, although 'the beautiful' is mentioned (for instance at 476 B), mathematical studies rather than science or love of beauty introduce us to the highest wisdom; and although mathematics too is 'beautiful' this is not yet emphasised.

In his conception of the beautiful Plato gives to sexual love and transformed sexual energy a central place in his philosophy. Sexual love (Aphrodite) as cosmic power had already appeared in Presocratic thought in the doctrines of Empedocles (fr. 17). Plato's Eros is a principle which connects the commonest human desire to the highest morality and to the pattern of divine creativity in the universe. Socrates more than once claims to be an expert on love (*Symposium*, 177 E, 212 B; *Phaedrus*, 257 A). In spite of Plato's repeated declaration that philosophers should stay chaste and his requirement that the soul must try to escape from the body, it is the whole Eros that concerns him, and not just some passionless distillation. The Eros described to Socrates by Diotima in the *Symposium* is not a god but a daemon, a mediating spirit of need and desire, the mixed-up child of Poverty and Plenty. He is poor and homeless, a sort of magician and sophist, always scheming after what is good and beautiful, neither wise nor foolish but a lover of wisdom. We desire what we lack. (Gods do not love wisdom since they possess it.) This Eros, who is lover not beloved, is the ambiguous spiritual mediator and moving spirit of mankind. Eros is the desire for good and joy which is active at all levels in the soul and through which we are able to turn toward reality. This is the fundamental force which can release the prisoners and draw them toward the higher satisfactions of light and freedom. It is also the force which finds expression in the unbridled appetites of the tyrant (who is described in Books VIII–IX of the *Republic*). There is a limited amount of soul-energy (*Republic*, 458 D), so, for better or worse, one desire will weaken another. Eros is a form of the desire for immortality, for perpetual possession of the good, whatever we may take the good to be. No man errs willingly; only the good is always desired as genuine (*Republic*, 505 D), and indeed only the good is desired. This desire takes the form of a yearning to create in and through beauty (τόκος ἐν καλῷ, *Symposium*, 206 B), which may appear as sexual love (*Laws*, 721 B) or love of fame (the poets have immortal children) or love of wisdom. (These are the three levels of desire explored in the *Republic*. Desire must be purified at all levels.) Diotima goes on to tell Socrates of these erotica into which even he may be initiated, although the true mysteries lie beyond. The initiate is not to rest content with beauty in one

[415]

embodiment, but to be drawn onward from physical to moral beauty, to the beauty of laws and *mores* and to all science and learning and thus to escape 'the mean slavery of the particular case'. Carnal love teaches that what we want is always 'beyond', and it gives us an energy which can be transformed into creative virtue. When a man has thus directed his thoughts and desires toward beauty of the mind and spirit he will suddenly receive the vision, which comes by grace, θεία μοίρα, of the Form of Beauty itself, absolute and untainted and pure, αὐτὸ καθ' αὐτὸ μεθ' αὐτοῦ μονοειδὲς ἀεὶ ὄν. F. M. Cornford (*The Unwritten Philosophy*) excellently says 'the best commentary on the *Symposium* is to be found in the *Divine Comedy*'. He quotes the end of *Purgatorio*, Canto XXVII. As Dante parts from the human wisdom of Virgil, and experiences the magnetic pull of divine wisdom in the person of Beatrice, he feels (like the soul in the *Phaedrus*) the growth of wings. Virgil tells him that happiness, which mortals seek in so many forms, will now at last let all his hunger rest, and henceforth his own perfected will and desire will be his rightful guide. *Tratto t'ho qui con ingegno e con arte: lo tuo piacere omai prendi per duce.*

The *Symposium* and the *Phaedrus* are two of the great erotic texts of literature. The *Phaedrus* describes spiritual love in the most bizarre and intense physical terms. (How the soul grows its wings, 251.) Plato is here too in softened mood toward poetry, since he allows that the good poet is a divinely inspired madman. However the highest form of divine madness is love of beauty, that is, falling in love (249 D). We love beauty because our soul remembers having seen it when before birth it saw the Forms unveiled: 'perfect and simple and happy visions which we saw in the pure light, being ourselves pure' (250 C). But when the soul becomes incarnate it partially forgets, and is but confusedly reminded when it sees the earthly copies of the Forms. The copies of wisdom, justice, temperance are usually obscure to the mind of the incarnate soul, but beauty in its instances is most clearly seen (ἐκφανέστατον), most moving, most reminiscent of the vision of it in heavenly purity. What a frenzy of love wisdom would arouse if it could be looked at with such clarity. Plato continues his exposition with the image of the soul as a charioteer with a good and a bad horse. As they approach the beloved the bad lustful horse rushes forward and has to be savagely restrained while the good horse is obedient and modest. Beauty shows itself to the best part of the soul as something to be desired yet respected, adored yet not possessed. Absolute beauty, as the soul now recalls it, is attended by chastity. Love prompts *anamnesis* and the good comes to us in the guise of the beautiful, as we are also told in the *Philebus*.

This account, half mythical, half metaphysical, graphically suggests both the beginning and the end of the awakening process. We restlessly seek various 'goods' which fail to satisfy. Virtue in general may not attract us, but beauty presents spiritual values in a more accessible and attractive form. The beautiful in nature (and we would wish to add in art) demands and rewards attention to something grasped as entirely external and indifferent to the greedy ego. We cannot acquire and assimilate the beautiful (as Kant too explains): it is in this instructive sense transcendent, and may provide our first and possibly our most persisting image (experience) of transcendence. 'Falling in love', a violent process which Plato more than once vividly describes (love is abnegation, abjection, slavery) is for many people the most extraordinary and most revealing experience of their lives, whereby the centre of significance is suddenly ripped out of the self, and the dreamy ego is shocked into awareness of an entirely separate reality. Love in this form may be a somewhat ambiguous instructor. Plato has admitted that Eros is a bit of a sophist. The desire of the sturdy ego (the bad horse) to dominate and possess the beloved, rather than to serve and adore him, may be overwhelmingly strong. We want to de-realise the other, devour and absorb him, subject him to the mechanism of our own fantasy. But a love which, still loving, comes to respect the beloved and (in Kantian language again) treat him as an end not as a means, may be the most enlightening love of all. Plato's insistence that (homosexual) love should be chaste may be read literally, but also as an image of the transcendent and indomitable nature of beauty. That chaste love teaches is indeed a way of putting the general moral point of the erotic dialogues. Plato commends orderly married love in the *Laws*, and announces equality of the sexes. But family life did not touch his imagination and he does not suggest that here essentially unselfishness is to be learnt: a fact which has earned him the hostility of some critics. The metaphysical contention which is so passionately enveloped in the erotic myths is to the effect that a sense of beauty diminishes greed and egoism and directs the energy of the soul in the direction of the real and the good. In so far as this contention is argued by Plato via the Theory of Forms (which he himself admits to be riddled with difficulties), it may appear obscure and less than convincing. What is more convincing and very much more clear (and to some extent separable from the full-dress metaphysical system) is the moral psychology which we are offered here and in the *Republic*: a psychology which implicitly provides a better explanation of evil (how good degenerates into egoism) than Plato's more strictly philosophical arguments have been able to give us elsewhere, for instance in the *Philebus*. Eros is the desire for good which is somehow the same even when a degenerate 'good' is sought.

The comparison with Freud is an interesting and an obvious one, and would suggest itself even without Freud's own clear announcement, made several times, of his debt to Plato, and also to Empedocles. 'The enlarged sexuality of psychoanalysis coincides with the Eros of the divine Plato' (*Three Essays on the Theory of Sexuality*, preface to the third edition). Freud certainly follows an important line in Plato's thought when he envisages sex as a sort of universal spiritual energy, an ambiguous force which may be destructive or can be used for good. Freud also makes a tripartite division of the soul and pictures the health of the soul as a harmony of the parts. Freud like Plato (*Republic*, 439), and following Empedocles (Love and Strife), first divided the soul in two, picturing it as a horseman or a class-divided state. His reasons for preferring a trio are the same as Plato's: an unmediated fight does not present a realistic picture of human personality. Kant had his own clear reasons for refusing mediation. Hume's attempts to mediate produce some of his best work. Plato's psychology would have benefited from a more prolonged study of the central area. Plato often speaks of the soul as being sick and in need of therapy. Both Plato and Freud wish to heal by promoting awareness of reality. Only Freud holds that we grasp reality through the ego and not through the 'critical punishing agency' of the ideal; whereas Plato holds that, above a reasonable egoism, there is a pure moral faculty which discerns the real world and to which sovereignty properly belongs. To put it another way, Plato is in favour of religion and the Father: it would be hard to overestimate the effect upon him of the death of Socrates, and although he never 'invents' a full-dress Father-God, his work abounds in images of paternity; while Freud is against religion and against fathers. Freud bars the way to the top and gives the ego the right to supreme control. Of course Plato's Eros, the daemonic negotiator between God and man, represents a sexuality which is almost entirely (perhaps for incarnate beings never entirely) able to be transfigured. Since the real is the good our energy is 'originally' pure. Freud, on the other hand, sees sexual energy as (rather precariously) climbing from a natural to an ideal level. Both thinkers share the important idea of the soul (mind) as an organic totality, strongly internally related and with a limited available material. 'Anyone who knows anything of the mental life of human beings is aware that hardly anything is more difficult for them than to give up a pleasure they have once tasted. Really we never can relinquish anything, we only exchange one thing for something else. When we appear to give something up, all we really do is to adopt a substitute.' (*The Relation of the Creative Writer to Day-Dreaming, Collected Papers*, vol. IV.) Plato would agree. Never has a philosopher more clearly indicated that salvation concerns the whole soul: the soul must be saved entire by the redirection of its energy away from selfish fantasy toward reality. Plato does not imagine that dialectic can save us, and indeed it will not be possible, unless the whole soul, including its indestructible baser part, is in harmony. Plato is in this respect a relentless psychological realist and more than once describes the soul as governed by mechanical gravitational forces which make change for the better very difficult. In morose moments in the *Laws* Plato even speaks like a determinist (we are puppets dangling from strings of impulse, 732 E), but elsewhere (904 B) he makes the growth of character depend on our will and the general trend of our desires. The transmigration myth at *Phaedrus*, 247 pictures the aspiring soul as subject to some kind of natural gravity, and so does the rather grim last judgement at the end of the *Republic*. How far Plato 'believed' these and other doctrines which he inherited from the Pythagoreans and used for his own purposes has been much debated. But whatever his dogma, there is little doubt about his psychology. Justice is in this respect automatic. It does not seem to me that Plato has softened the old 'justice of Zeus' (see Hugh Lloyd-Jones's interesting argument in his book of that name); he has made its operation more sophisticated and considerably more just. We cannot escape the causality of sin. We are told in the *Theaetetus* (176–7) that the inescapable penalty of wickedness is simply to be the sort of person that one is, and in the *Laws* (904 C, D) that evil-doers are in Hades in this world. Wittgenstein said of Freud that 'he was influenced by the nineteenth-century idea of dynamics' (*Conversations on Freud*). Perhaps he was; but the dynamic model is already in Plato. Nor can one doubt that the concept of *anamnesis* influenced Freud's idea of the timeless and inaccessible unconscious mind. When Freud was twenty-three he translated an article bearing on *anamnesis* by J. S. Mill.* However, I know of no explicit reference by him to the doctrine.

Plato's Eros inspires us through our sense of beauty, but Eros is a trickster and must be treated critically. We have been told in the *Laws* (687 B) that the human soul desires omnipotence. The energy which could save us may be employed to erect barriers between ourselves and reality so that we may remain comfortably in a self-directed dream world. Freud's condition of neurosis represents this refusal of reality in favour of magical self-deception. The neurotic 'mistakes an ideal connection for a real one' and 'over-estimates the psychic process as opposed to reality'. Let us here, still led by Freud, look back again from Eros to art. Freud says in *Totem and Taboo*, 'only in art has the omnipotence of thought been retained in our civilization'. He shares Plato's deep mistrust of art, as well as his interest in the nature of inspiration, only of course Freud, confronted with the grandeur of the European tradition at its most confident (it is less confident now) does not dare to be too rude to art. 'Before the problem of the creative artist analysis must, alas, lay down its arms' (*Dostoevsky and Parricide, Collected Papers*, vol. v). However, Freud does not in fact leave art unharassed. He offers us elsewhere (in the paper on *The Relation of the Creative Writer to Day-Dreaming*) a striking and far from flattering definition of the work of art. Everyone has personal fantasies which are concealed

* See [Philip] Rieff, *Freud* [: *The Mind of the Moralist* (London)], 1959, p. 364.

and would be repulsive if uttered. 'The essential *ars poetica* lies in the techique by which our feeling of repulsion is overcome . . . The writer softens the egotistical character of the day-dream by changes and disguises, and he bribes us by the offer of a purely formal, that is aesthetic, pleasure in the presentation of his fantasies.' The aesthetic bribe is described by Freud as a 'fore-pleasure' (*Vorlust*) similar to those which lead onward to orgasm. (This concept is discussed at more length in *Three Essays on the Theory of Sexuality*, III, I.) The work of art is then a magical pseudo-object (or εἰκών) placed between the artist and his client whereby they can both, separately, pursue their private fantasy lives unchecked. 'True enjoyment of literature proceeds from the release of tensions in our minds. Perhaps much that brings about this result consists in the writer putting us into a position in which we can enjoy our day-dreams without reproach or shame.'

Plato says in the *Republic* (606 A) that the artist makes the best part of the soul 'relax its guard'. One of the subtleties of Freud's definition is that it is indifferent to the 'formal value' of the art work, since what is really active and really attractive is the concealed fantasy. As W. H. Auden says, a remark which could have been made by Plato, 'no artist . . . can prevent his work being used as magic, for that is what all of us, highbrow and lowbrow alike, secretly want art to be' ('Squares and Oblongs', *Poets at Work*). One could hardly wish for a more thorough characterisation of art as belonging to the lower part of the soul and producing what are essentially shadows. (The art object as material thing, a piece of stone or paper etc., would be classed with ordinary visible sensa; what the artist and his client 'see' would be the shadow.) W. D. Ross says that 'Plato is no doubt in error in supposing that the purpose of art is to produce illusion.' In fact Plato's view of art as illusion is positive and complex. Images are valuable aids to thought; we study what is higher first 'in images'. But images must be kept within a fruitful hierarchy of spiritual endeavour. What the artist produces are 'wandering images'. In this context one might even accuse art of specialising in the degradation of good desires, since the trick of the aesthetic veil enables the good to descend. The art object is a false whole which owes its air of satisfying completeness to the licensing of a quite other process in the quasi-mechanical fantasy life of the client, and also of the artist, who, as Plato frequently pointed out, probably has little idea of what he is at. The formal properties of the art object are delusive. The relation of art to the unconscious is of course at the root of the trouble. Put in Platonic terms, art is a sort of dangerous caricature of *anamnesis*. The 'unlimited' irrational nature of pleasure makes it suspect, and art has a conspiracy with pleasure which is the more damaging since it is partly secret. As explained in the *Philebus* the pleasures of any art except the very simplest are impure. (This is likely to be true upon any reasonable definition of 'pure' and 'impure'.) As escapism, art is an expert in 'pleasure by contrast', which though doubtless welcome to wretched suffering mortals, compares poorly with (for instance) the pure and positive pleasures of learning. The highest pleasure lies in the contemplation of the changeless, where there is calm clear perception. The element of the 'unlimited' in art pleasure comes from its connection with the purely egoistic unconscious (in Freudian terms) and privily robs art of ἀλήθεια, truthfulness and realism. Art has no discipline which ensures veracity; truth in art is notoriously hard to estimate critically. Human beings are natural liars, and sophists and artists are the worst. Art undermines our sense of reality and encourages us to believe in the omnipotence of thought. Thus the supposed 'content' of art leaks away into the 'unlimited' and no genuine statement is made. Truth must be very sure of herself (as she is in mathematics) before she allows any connection with art: so, if there must be art, better to stick to embroidery and wallpaper.

Plato was not unaware of neurosis as mental disease, as distinct from moral depravity or the wilful ignorance for which ἐλεγχος, ruthless questioning, was the suitable purge. Although he usually took a rather tough view of the θερεπεία ψυχῆς [care of the soul], he says at *Timaeus*, 86 B that folly is a disease of the soul, and at *Laws*, 731 tells us to talk gently to remediable offenders; it is repeated in both contexts that no man errs willingly. The profound action of music upon the soul is of course often mentioned, and there is a reference in the *Laws* (790) to art as a cure for anxiety states.* This is of course an aspect of the magical nature of art so

* On this see E. R. Dodds, *The Greeks and the Irrational* [Berkeley, 1951], Chapter III.

often emphasised by Plato. Freud saw how art can stabilise neurosis without removing it. The artist comes to terms with his frailties (even with his vices) by using them in art, thus producing a stability which may be (from the point of view of mental health) less than satisfactory. The destructive power of the neurosis is foiled by art; the art object expresses the neurotic conflict and defuses it. This sort of (as it might be seen by Freud or Plato) 'imperfect' and misleading transformation or pseudo-cure would especially characterise the artist as 'ironical copyist' (as opposed to naïve fantasist) who has been disturbed by argument and speculation: a little knowledge of philosophy or psychology. Such a 'cure' may be seen as arresting progress. (Freud of course did not envisage perfect cures, and would doubtless have regarded many artists as solving their problems quite inadequately.) There is an element here of *corruptio optimi pessima*. The poet is a menace because he can corrupt even the good man, and the more sophisticated the art the more potentially dangerous. To revert to the imagery of the cave, we might think of the ironical artist as having moved out of the shadowy region of *eikasia* as far as the fire, which he takes as his sun. (The fire in the cave corresponds to the sun in the outside world, *Republic*, 517 B.) Here he can recognise for what they are the objects which cast the shadows. The bright flickering light of the fire suggests the disturbed and semi-enlightened ego which is pleased and consoled by its discoveries, but still essentially self-absorbed, not realising that the real world is still somewhere else. (The 'lower' general education offered in the *Republic* could promote a moderate and fairly rational egoism.) The Delphic precept does not enjoin that kind of self-knowledge. The true self-knower knows reality and sees, in the light of the sun, himself as part of the whole world. In spite of their different aims, it is arguable that Plato and Freud mistrust art for the same reason, because it caricatures their own therapeutic activity and could interfere with it. Art is pleasure-seeking self-satisfied pseudo-analysis and pseudo-enlightenment.

Beauty then is too important a matter to be left to artists, or for art to meddle with at all except at a controllably simple level of, for instance, mathematical pattern. Nature educates us, art does not. This means: not statues, but boys. (We learn reality through the pains of rationally controlled human love, *Symposium*, 211 B.) It also means a proper attention to the physical world around about us. The nature which Plato here regards as so educational is not of course the nature of the Romantics (trees and fields have no message), nor is it Kant's Sublime. Even to say that the perishable aspect of the natural scene defeats possessive ends is to take up a later viewpoint. What interests Plato in nature is pattern, necessity which is the test of truth: what turns opinion into certainty. Study of form liberates the mind, but it must be hard non-pliable real form, not the complicit pliable disingenuous forms of art. Encounter with the necessary leads to knowledge of the eternal and changeless. This educational truthful 'hardness' of the real is seen by Plato at first most evidently in mathematics, which plays the crucial mediating role in the education system of the *Republic*. Mathematics leads us beyond the lower (softer) education (described in Book III) which consists of (carefully selected) stories, music, poetry, where an uncriticised imagery is the best available vehicle of such truth as can be grasped. Understanding of how mathematics is independent of sense experience leads us to understand how the Forms are; and necessary mathematical relations suggest necessary relations between Forms. The early Socrates of the *Apology* and the *Phaedo* rejected scientific studies, and at *Republic*, 529–30 we are told to use the tapestry of the heavens to remind us of geometry, but not to imagine that the stars can be objects of knowledge. Later Plato finds this necessary 'hardness' in the 'logical' rigidity of the Form world (*Sophist*), and later still in certain intimations of cosmic reason (*Timaeus*), where the stars (47 A) now suggest number and time and also researches into the nature of the universe. In the *Laws* astronomy has become a respectable subject, since the divine intelligence is revealed in all things (966 A) and science will not necessarily lead to atheism. The Athenian regrets not having studied astronomy when he was young (821). The gods are not jealous of their secrets, but glad if we can become good through studying them (*Epinomis*, 988 B). Already however in the *Republic*, and in the context of the attack on art, Plato has set the cosmic 'way' within the reach of the craftsman. Measuring and counting are 'felicitous aids' (602 D) by which reason leads the soul from appearance to reality. The paradoxes of sense experience inspire us to philosophy, and our respect for and satisfaction in necessary form, whether in mathematics or in nature, tend to fortify our rational faculties. (Philosophy since Plato has largely favoured just these starting points.) The object which appears to bend as it enters water provokes a lively puzzlement about what is real, and 'that part of the soul which trusts measuring and calculating is the best' (*Republic*, 602 C, 603 A). How our satisfaction in measurement and symmetry and harmony in the world about us is our sense of its reality and beauty has been explained in the *Philebus*; and the truth-loving Eros can inspire the carpenter as well as the mathematician. But art always wants to take over the natural scene, and indeed affects how we see it. The self-indulgent imagination of the artist and his client tend to smooth out the contradictions of the world of natural necessity. The painter is content with the 'bent' object and prepared to celebrate it as it is (and in literature *mutatis mutandis*). Art baffles the motive to probe. It fascinates and diverts the Eros which should, whether through love of people or of cosmic form, conduct us to philosophy. Art gives magically induced satisfaction to the lower part of the soul, and defaces beauty by mixing it with personal sorcery. Beauty gives us an immediate image of good desire, the desire for goodness and the desire for truth. We are attracted to the real in the guise of the beautiful and the response to this attraction brings joy. To overcome egoism in its protean forms of fantasy and illusion (*per tanti rami cercando*) is automatically to become more moral; to see the real is to see its independence and ergo its claims. The proper apprehension of beauty is joy in reality through the transfiguring of desire. Thus as we respond we experience the transcendence of the real and the personal ego fades as, in the words of the *Symposium* (210 D), we 'escape from the mean petty slavery of the particular case and turn toward the open sea of beauty'.

Plato's connection of the good with the real (the ambiguous multiform phenomenon of the ontological proof) is the centre of his thought and one of the most fruitful ideas in philosophy. It is an idea which at an instinctive level we may readily imagine that we understand. We do not have to believe in God to make sense of the motto of Oxford University, displayed upon an open book, *Dominus illuminatio mea*. And I shall argue later that, for all its sins, art can show us this connection too. But what is the 'reality' to which Eros moves us and from which art allegedly diverts us? The Theory of Forms was invented to explain this, and the *Parmenides* and the *Sophist* exhibited some of the resultant difficulties. The relation of Forms to particulars remains persistently problematic as Plato moves uncertainly from a metaphor of participation to one of imitation, and increasingly emphasises that the Forms are 'separate'. The Forms are more like 'imminent universals' at the start, and 'transcendent models' later on. The theory is in evident process of transition in the *Parmenides*. The *Sophist* represents a moment of discovery and offers a new theory. What is of importance here is not the puzzling relation of Forms to particulars, but the now more comprehensible relation of Forms to each other. Because of what is possible and impossible in the Form world, reality has deep rigid structure and discourse is possible. Dialectic, becoming more specialised, can thenceforth operate more confidently though less ambitiously. The philosopher in the *Republic* returns to the cave, and once he is used to it, can manage better than the captives (520 C). (He gives up studying and goes into politics, for which his studies have trained him.) Later on (*Theaetetus* 172–4, *Philebus* 58 C, *Seventh Letter*, 344 E) the implication is that dialectic is 'for its own sake', and the philosopher is confused by practical life. The Form of the Good in the *Republic* is a first principle of explanation and also (if we follow the image of the sun), some sort of general first cause. The *Sophist* is concerned with the logical rather than the moral Forms, and although 'soul' makes its appearance as a principle of life and movement, this idea still lacks moral and theological development, and Plato's earlier 'psychology' still best explains the role of goodness. Art, of course, comes under this 'psychological' heading, together with the problem of appearance and reality as originally envisaged. It remains Plato's (surely correct) view that the bad (or mediocre) man is in a state of illusion, of which egoism is the most general name, though particular cases would of course suggest more detailed descriptions. Obsession, prejudice, envy, anxiety, ignorance, greed, neurosis, and so on and so on *veil* reality. The defeat of illusion requires moral effort. The instructed and morally purified mind sees reality clearly and indeed (in an important sense) provides us with the concept. The original role of the Forms was not to lead us to some attenuated elsewhere but to show us the real world. It is the dreamer in the cave who is astray and elsewhere.

What here becomes of the problem of the relation of Forms to particulars, and is it still important? If dialectic is a kind of logic, together with a kind of classification involving a pursuit to *infimae species*, then the problem posed at the end of the *Theaetetus* about the unknowability of the particular may indeed remain, but may also be deemed trivial. In the early dialogues sense experience seems to be at least partly veridical in so far as particular things 'partake' of the Forms; and later on *Theaetetus*, 155–7 offers a fairly straightforward (realistic) discussion of perception. In the *Republic*, where the Forms are transcendent, the objects of opinion diminish near the lower end of the scale from 'being' toward 'not-being' (478–9). The *Sophist* turns this awkward ontological distinction into a 'logical' one. But supposing what interests us is the reality which is penetrable to moral insight? (Logic can look after itself; ethics cannot.) What about mud, hair, and dirt (*Parmenides*, 130 C), and in what sense if any are they to be 'given up'? The metaphor of knowledge as vision is not so easily eliminated, at either end of the scale of being. When the veil is removed and the rational and virtuous man sees reality, how much – indeed what – does he see? Are there things which somehow exist but which are irrelevant to serious thought, as Socrates was inclined to say in the *Parmenides*? Is it possible to *see* beyond the 'formal network'? (Instinct says yes.) What does the light of the sun reveal; and who sees the most minute particulars and cherishes them and points them out? As one batters here at the cage of language it is difficult to keep the artist out of the picture even when one is attempting to describe the good man. Of course we are in trouble here through doing what Parmenides told Socrates he must do if he was really to be 'grabbed' by philosophy (*Parmenides*, 130 D, E), that is let nothing go and see if what is true of one is true of all. From the point of view of the moralist it looks as if the argument which culminates in the *Sophist* has destroyed too much, since notably it has removed our direct vision of the Forms and their positive role as (somehow) sources of light and being. However Plato does not here abandon the problem of the reality and intelligibility of the sensible world, but begins to envisage it in a new way.

The early picture of the Forms is unsatisfactory not only because of the unclarified relation of these separate changeless perfect entities to a changing imperfect world, but also because the Forms are supposed to be the only realities. The transmigrating souls of the *Phaedo* and the *Phaedrus* are of unexplained and lesser dignity, although they 'resemble' the changeless (*Phaedo*, 786); and in the *Phaedo* the sensible world appears as a fallen realm which is a gross irrelevant hindrance to true knowledge, philosophy, and virtue. Hence philosophers 'practise dying' (67 E). The earlier dialogues emphasise a contrast between what is moving and unreal and what is motionless and real. Vice is restless, so is art (*Republic*, 605 A). The bad man and the artist see shifting shadows (εἴκονες), not a steady reality. The *Sophist*, however (248 E), exclaims with passion, 'Surely we shall not readily allow ourselves to be persuaded that motion and life and soul and intelligence are not really there in absolute being and that it neither lives nor thinks, but all solemn and holy and mindless is motionless and fixed.' Plato, led by the epistemological arguments of the *Parmenides* and the *Theaetetus*, is not ready fully to separate the psychological-moral idea that vice is a state of illusion from the problem of the reality and physical nature of the sensible cosmos. He has already, in Eros, established an authoritative active principle which can relate everything to the Forms. (The low Eros is the high Eros.) But Eros as mediator, and as 'redeemer', of the trivia of the ordinary world, is still a detached insight and a psychological myth. The attribution of life and movement to ultimate being in the *Sophist* brings this 'mediation' into the area of philosophical argument; though inconclusively so since Plato soon returns again to 'explanation' by myth. To extend the possibility of knowledge (as opposed to opinion), he here conjures up a moving knower to follow a moving known, and gives a more definite status to the problem of the origin of motion. In doing so he creates a fundamental division in the structure of the ultimately real since κίνησις and ζωή and ψύχη and φρονήσις (movement, life, soul, intelligence) are now allowed somehow into the company of the still changeless Forms. This 'fissure', and the attempt to relate Forms to particulars by this method, raises its own insoluble problems, though it has also proved a great fountainhead of metaphysical imagery. Soul has already been described as the only self-mover and thus as the origin of motion at *Phaedrus*, 245–6 and *Politicus*, 272 B; and creative intelligence or mind (φρόνησις, νοῦς) now comes forward to be the supreme guide of soul, as life and movement are allowed to be intelligible. One result of this mediation is the extension of the power of Good into the details of the sensible world through a technique of active creation. Throughout his work Plato uses the imagery of *mimesis*, which the Theory of Forms necessitates but cannot explain. In a magnificent myth he at last frankly embraces the image and sanctifies the artist, while giving to the Forms a final radiant though mysterious role. There is only one true artist, God, and only one true work of art, the Cosmos.

In Raphael's divine vision of the School of Athens, Plato, holding the *Timaeus*, points with a single finger upward, while Aristotle, holding the *Ethics*, stretches out his extended hand toward the world. The *Timaeus* is an account of the creation of the world by God, wherein Christian thinkers from Origen to Simone Weil have had no difficulty in discerning the doctrine of the Trinity, and other thinkers 'with a little good will' (Paul Shorey) have been able to see quite a lot of modern physics. The rational and good Demiurge creates the cosmos and endows it with a discerning Soul. He works as well as he can, gazing at a perfect model (the Forms), to create a changing sensible copy of an unchanging intelligible original. He cannot, however, create perfectly because he is using pre-existent material which contains irrational elements, the 'wandering causes', which represent irreducible qualities tending toward some minimal non-rational order of their own. The activity of these causes is called 'necessity' (ἀνάγκη), meaning not mechanical system but a semi-random interruption of rational purposes.* The purposeful Demiurge is not omnipotent and cannot subdue the wandering causes, but *persuades* them, so as to create the best possible world. In this process the Forms remain entirely separate and untouched as they have always been. Their copied reflections appear ephemerally

---

* See [F. M.] Cornford's commentary [on the *Timaeus*, in *Plato's Cosmology* (London, 1937)] pp. 47–8. The Greeks were familiar with tools, not with machines.

in the medium of space which is eternal and uncreated. (There is no Form of space, though there is a Form of time.) The Demiurge creates junior gods and human souls, and delegates to the gods the task of creating us. He is also a just judge, allotting destinies according to conduct. We, who belong both to being and to becoming, find our moral guidance in the cosmos itself, the work of the divine hand. The Demiurge creates the world because, being good and without envy, he wishes all things to be as like himself as possible, and he desires for human creatures that they shall achieve the best possible life.

Socrates said in the *Phaedo* (97–9) that he gave up reading Anaxagoras because no account was given of purposeful causation. The *Timaeus*, deliberately taking issue with Plato's evolutionary 'materialist' predecessors, offers a carefully modified quasi-teleological cosmogony in the form of a myth, wherein moral imagery and scientific speculation are remarkably blended. The Demiurge (Plato's portrait of the artist and a most attractive figure) is a new conception, palely foreshadowed in the *Philebus*. Plato's predecessors ('the wise' mentioned at *Gorgias*, 508 A) had of course already pictured the universe as 'order' (*Kosmos*); and Greek theology had been tending gradually toward the separation of a morally good sovereign Zeus from the other Olympian gods. Plato's God is not, however, to be identified with this new Zeus. Plato regarded the Olympians with a detached but not totally irreverent scepticism. (See *Timaeus*, 40 A, also *Cratylus*, 400 D, *Phaedrus*, 246 C, *Epinomis*, 984 D.) Nor is he at all like the cosmic 'gods' of the Presocratics. And although Plato quotes Pherecydes saying that Zeus became Eros to create the world, the Demiurge is not Plato's Eros, though he is related to him. The Demiurge looks towards the Forms with rational passion and with a yearning to create (τόκος ἐν κάλῳ), but he is a free divine being, not a needy daemon. He is morally perfect (though not omnipotent) and lacks the envious spite (φθόνος) which the Olympians so often felt toward mortals. (The Greeks always feared this spite and constantly expressed the fear in their literature.) On the other hand he is unlike Jehovah and the Christian God in that he does not require, or receive, worship or gratitude. He wishes us well and hopes for our salvation (he admonishes human souls at 42 D), but we are not necessarily at the centre of his concern. He is probably more interested in the stars. As *Laws*, 903 C tells us, the cosmos does not exist for our sake, we are not its end. And the message of the *Timaeus*, as indeed of other dialogues including the *Republic*, is that we exist, and must seek such perfection as may be available to us, as parts of a whole.

The World Soul, developed from ideas in the *Sophist*, completes Plato's Trinity. This mysterious Soul is an incarnation of spirit which pervades the whole sensible cosmos and is created for this purpose by the Demiurge. At 44 A–B it is hinted that the World Soul may not be entirely rational, and it is certainly the most junior and least authoritative of the trio, its two partners being uncreated. In terms of the (not unrelated) Christian Trinity the artist figure, the creative Demiurge, occupies of course the position of the Holy Ghost, not of God the Father. The Demiurge is active νοῦς, best translated here as 'mind'. Absolute original authority rests in the Forms, and the World Soul, incarnate spirit in the realm of sense, is, it is implied, somewhat 'fallen' thereby (as the incarnate Forms are 'fallen' in the *Phaedo*). If one may here respond simply and naïvely to something so complex, I confess that I find Plato's Trinity more morally radiant than that of the Church. The theology of the *Timaeus* is also more splendid than Plato's own further theological speculations in *Laws*, x. To suggest that God is not omnipotent has always been a prime Christian heresy. The image of a morally perfect but not all-powerful Goodness seems to me better to express some ultimate (inexpressible) truth about our condition. The Jehovah of Genesis is totally unlike the artist, human or divine, in that he creates out of nothing and expects perfection. (Perhaps the Demiurge more intelligently realised his limitations at the start, whereas Jehovah realised his later and was correspondingly bad-tempered?) Also, the eternal separate inviolate Forms seem to me a more profound image of moral and spiritual reality than the picture of a personal Father, however good. The Forms represent the absolute and gratuitous nature of the moral demand, so splendidly though so differently emphasised by Kant, who also separated God from our knowledge of moral perfection. The mythical Demiurge creates because active mind must move (that movement belongs to ultimate being was recognised in the *Sophist*), and he is moved by love for the Forms to attempt to imitate them in another medium.

Like the mortal artist he fails, both because the other medium cannot (as he is well aware) reproduce the original, and because the material resists his conceptions and his powers. The result is a quite different entity, which is the 'best possible'. The Platonic Trinity is a development, and sub-division, of the concept of Eros. It relates Eros to Cosmos, and expresses in an alternative and more complex way the idea that Good attracts, an ingredient of the ontological proof. A live force moves through the created world towards Good. The Demiurge is here the mediating figure between Being and Becoming. Good is seen as beautiful in the purified or even semi-purified gaze of active mind. We are kin to νοῦς and no one errs willingly. In the Christian Trinity love passes continually between the three persons all of whom are in motion. In Plato's Trinity two partners are busy while one is still. The Demiurge is intelligently busy (and as independent causes proliferate, his work must go on), while the World Soul is not quite sure what it is at, but does the best it can. Incarnate spirit, even in saints and geniuses, is muddled and puny. The Forms remain changeless, and eternal. I am sure that one should resist the Christianising view that the Forms yearn for realisation or tend towards it. Such 'yearning' belongs entirely to the mythical Demiurge. Good is 'beyond being' as Plato says at *Republic*, 509 B, and never really explains the idea. The question of course remains and must remain, why does the sensible world exist at all? Creation myths are not philosophical explanations. Plato never thought that they were, and he never philosophically clarified the relation between Forms and sensa.

The *Philebus* spoke of the difficulty of locating Good, and of how Good took refuge in the character of the Beautiful. The *Timaeus* exhibits this creative movement of Good into Beauty, as it also establishes as first cause Mind that looks to Good, and not Good itself. The Demiurge is in a state of activity while the Forms are in a state of rest. Beauty comes about through the persuasion of necessity by divine intelligence; everything that exists has both a necessary and a divine cause. Beauty belongs to God and must be sought only in him, as he makes it visible through the cosmos. The cosmos is in the highest and exemplary sense an aesthetic object, and indeed the only one. The Demiurge's satisfactions and his relation to his material are those of an artist. The material resists organisation not as a scientist's material resists, when systems cannot yet be discerned, but as an artist's material resists, because it is in part fundamentally a jumble of which nothing can be made. (Possibly modern physics feels itself closer to the situation of the artist.) Of course the Demiurge is a mythical being (to describe God is impossible, 28 C), but his partial defeat represents the failure of an earlier requirement: the availability to intelligence of perfect knowledge such as that envisaged in the *Republic*. There, what could be known could be known perfectly, and what could not be known was in danger of being deemed unreal and therefore nothing: a problem which was met in the *Sophist* by an explanation of God's logical limitations. Here, in the *Timaeus*, we see his corresponding difficulties as an applied physicist.

Plato, who at first rejected natural science, had by this time learnt a good deal more about it and cannot resist some scientific speculation, although he still distinguishes as strictly as ever between knowledge of being and opinion about becoming, and admits the latter with a smiling apology. We may 'for amusement' lay aside 'arguments about reality' and consider 'probable accounts of becoming' (59 C). This apology introduces some detailed and admittedly 'probable' explanations of natural phenomena. The more general and large-scale proceedings of the Demiurge are offered to us more confidently, together with clear indications of the limited scope of his power. The raw stuff of creation has inherent causal tendencies and the medium of space in which it is worked is also not made by the Demiurge, and though eternally real is not in fact entirely intelligible (52 B), but apprehended by a 'bastard reasoning' which leads us to 'dream' that 'everything is somewhere'. (A foreshadowing of Kant's problem: we experience space without understanding it.) Space is the reality which carries the transient flux and lends some being to even the most shadowy of appearances; though how this happens is admitted at 52 C to be somewhat astonishing and hard to describe. The Demiurge understands time since he creates it as a 'moving image of eternity' (time is circular), but it is not entirely clear that he understands space. A creative Soul is present in the *Laws*, again named as first cause (889 C), and we are told that *physis* is brought about by *techné* and *nous* (892 A–B), but these problems, which are grasped in the *Timaeus* in a great *élan* of sometimes half-playful artistry, are brought to no conclusion.

The interest of the dialogue is of course fundamentally moral, and the scientific conjectures never stray too far from a moral concern. Plato is not here discussing (and indeed never really discusses again) his persistent problem about the definition of knowledge and its limitations. The implication of the myth is that our claims must ever be modest ones, but this does not make the vision less inspiring. The *Timaeus* declares the intelligible reality of the whole material universe, not hitherto clearly asserted by Plato. His descriptions of it relate to our ordinary experience as do the descriptions offered by the modern physicist, and are not totally unlike these. The privilege of knowing by direct perception is transferred to the Demiurge, who can see both ends of the scale of being, the great uncreated Particulars and the little created ones. Through this image Plato is able, in a masterpiece of art which is radiant with joy, to 'solve' some of his old problems by relating creative Eros directly to the eternal authority of Good, and through it to the world. It is hard for the moralist to abandon the idea of this connection as something potentially direct, however difficult it may be to explain how we can 'know' anything of the sort. Art and the artist may indicate what lies just beyond the explanations offered by 'plain words', once the words have carefully made a place for revelation. And although 'officially' we humans may not be able to see into these mysteries, one mortal artist at least is self-contradictorily telling us about them.

In the context of his great mythical reconciliation, Plato assumes rather than demonstrates the Forms. An argument for their existence is given in the most curtailed but essential version at 51 D–E, where we are also told that only gods and very few men can possess knowledge. No other arguments, as such, are offered, but the position allotted to the Forms is in many ways more intelligible, at this point where perhaps Plato realises the insolubility of the problems which they pose, than that which they occupied in the *Republic*, where Good was supposed to play a creative role (509 B). This role is taken over by the Demiurge who makes the cosmos as we experience it (including mud, hair, and dirt) upon an intelligible model, joining in every instance his divine causation to the necessary causation of the original stuff, and thereby sanctifying the cosmos and rendering it potentially penetrable to human reason. Beauty can then be discerned everywhere, though this is not emphasised by either Plato or the Demiurge whose interests tend to be rather grandiose. So it turns out that the artist copies the Forms after all, but he has to be God and even then cannot succeed perfectly. The separateness of the Forms is stated in the most uncompromising terms at 52 A. Their authority is absolutely unimpaired by the presence of the Demiurge; and in the mysterious magnificence of this assertion lies part of the deep sense of the whole theory.

This splendidly complex mythical image of the creative process suggests and indeed demands interesting analogies with art of the mortal variety, and these will be considered later. The Demiurge presents himself of course not only as an engineer with a knowledge of physics and chemistry, but as a geometer, architect, and as a musician (37 C). Vision is the most uplifting of human senses (47 B), but the fine art preferred by God is music, inaudible of course. (All art aspires to this condition?) The audible kind is allowed (47 C) to be of benefit to us. The construction of the human body interests the Demiurge, but he delegates the process of incarnation, together with the invention of a workable incarnate psyche, to his young subordinates, who are described (69 D) as infusing in generous quantities the 'dreadful and necessary' emotions required for human survival. (It sounds as if this is rather a perfunctory job.) In spite of some interesting and sympathetic remarks about psychosomatic disorders (89–90), Plato does not here concern himself much with our moral psychology: which does not mean that he has abandoned his earlier views on the subject. In the *Timaeus* he is looking at the situation from God's point of view, where evil appears as a failure to impose rational order. It must however be admitted that the later dialogues are less sanguine about human perfectibility. (Most orderings of the dialogues put *Phaedrus* before *Sophist*, *Sophist* before *Timaeus*, and *Laws* last.) The human species is perhaps (on any view) not the most successful or edifying ingredient of the cosmic art object.

Our best task (68–9) is to distinguish in created things between the divine and the necessary cause and seek to understand and conform ourselves to the divine cause, and to seek the necessary cause for the sake of the divine, since we cannot see the divine without the necessary; and thus to gain whatever happiness and holiness our nature admits of. In doing this we see the beauty of the world through studying the structural work of the divine architect, including his geometry and his logic. Our position, both as created beings and as, in our little way, creators, is however a humble one. The Creator who gazes at the eternal and intelligible produces what is good, but he who without intelligence simply copies the world of becoming produces something worthless (28 A). An intelligent use should be made of the arts (τέχναι), not to give irrational pleasure but to reduce disharmony, and for this purpose speech and music exist (47 C–D). The *Timaeus* takes a modest view of human insight and creative ability. The proper activity of the human artist is in simple ways to discern and emphasise and extend the harmonious rhythms of divine creation: to produce good design rather than pretentious rival objects. (Consider much Islamic art.) Such artists should, like other craftsmen, meticulously study the world so as to distinguish its appearance from its reality. Our relation to the divine pattern thus discerned must not be ambitiously mimetic (mimesis apes appearance), but rather participatory and continuous. The decent artist patiently sorts order out of disorder. To put it (as Plato does not) in terms with a Kantian ring: a good man does not copy another good man, playing him as an actor plays a role, but attempts to become himself a part or function of the divine intelligence. We were never told to 'copy' the Forms by producing something else, but only to become able to see them and thus in a sense to become like them. In the *Timaeus* myth they are more remote from us, seen by God and by him creatively transformed into another medium. Our humbler task, as part of creation, is to understand the Forms through the cosmic intelligence which is akin to our own. The artist must surrender his personal will to the rhythm of divine thought, as in the oriental doctrine of the Tao. If he practises mimetic art he may be guilty of a kind of blasphemy, as has always been recognised in Islam and in Judaism. The second commandment: Thou shalt not make unto thee any graven image, or any likeness of any thing that is in heaven above, or that is in the earth beneath, or that is in the water under the earth (Exodus 20:4).

Of this Kant says, 'There is no more sublime passage in the Jewish law' (*Critique of Judgement*, II, 274). There must be no picturesque mediator, no cue for egoistic drama. In the *Grundlegung* Kant firmly sets aside even Christ as mediator. Our sovereign and accessible guide is reason, and God is a remote object of faith. In the *Phaedo* Socrates fears that the sun will blind him, but in the *Republic* (516 B) the perfectly just man looks at the sun and 'is able to see what it is, not by reflections in water or by fantasms of it in some alien abode, but in and by itself in its own place'. This is the direct perception which the *Theaetetus* rejects as a possible description of knowledge. The God of the *Phaedrus* condemns writing because it interposes a speechless medium between the knower and the known. However, in the *Parmenides* the Forms as objects of knowledge are in trouble, and in the *Sophist* knowledge appears as familiarity with interwoven structure rather than acquaintance with individual realities. In the *Philebus* and the *Timaeus* Plato develops the idea, present mythically in the *Symposium* and the *Phaedrus*, of beauty as the mediator between us and Good; and is then the more meticulously anxious to keep this precious instrument away from the tarnishing hands of art.

Throughout his work Plato understands intellectual activity as something spiritual, the *love* of learning spoken of in the *Symposium* and the *Philebus*. Mediation through the beautiful takes place not only in intellectual studies but also through personal love and through the various *technai*, all kinds of craft and skill (excluding mimetic art) to which Plato at different times attaches importance. Love of beauty and desire to create inspire us to activities which increase our grasp of the real, and because they diminish our fantasy-ridden egoism are self-evidently good. Any *techné* gives us knowledge of reality through experience of necessity, and love of people does this too. Plato does not analyse in detail how selfish love changes into unselfish love, but the asides in the early dialogues do not suggest that this should simply be thought of as a transference of affection to philosophy. The wise lover does not only love the glamorous, but discerns the spiritual beauty of the unglamorous, a process movingly described by Alcibiades in his homage to Socrates at *Symposium*, 215. Plato is more concerned in his later work, and indeed in the *Republic* to show how the great structural features of the world, the subject matter of logic and mathematics and (as he later sees it) of science, are beautiful and spiritually attractive. It is the attraction of beauty (good as harmony and proportion) which leads us into studies of the *a priori* and (to use a subsequent terminology) the synthetic *a priori*: pure studies yielding pure pleasures. In the mythology of the *Timaeus*, only passionate selfless unenvious mind can understand the world since passionate selfless unenvious mind made it, and we see in the light of the Good, to return to the image of the sun. The cosmogony of the *Timaeus* is 'teleological' in that the Demiurge works purposively, but in doing so he seems to satisfy Kant's definition in that his purposiveness is without ulterior purpose. Order is obviously more beautiful and good than disorder, and 'self-expression' of the Demiurge, who is generous and without envious φθόνος, takes place under the authority of an independent Model. Our participation in these joys must, however, be seen as modest. The contact with changeless truth brought about through insight into pure living mind can only for incarnate beings be limited and occasional, and we are likely to see more of necessary causes than of divine causes. The truth which we can grasp is something quiet, small in extent (*Philebus*, 52 c), and to be found only in the lived real moment of direct apprehension out of which the indirectness of mimetic art and writing and perhaps language and discursive thought itself always tends to remove us. Those who want to be saved should look at the stars and talk philosophy, not write or go to the theatre.

How far Plato's own religious experience and practice remained separate from his philosophy and (as he more than once hints) ineffable, we are never likely to know. At *Phaedo* 69 D the 'enlightened ones' (βάκχοι) are identified with the true philosophers. It is a fair guess that his attitudes, as distinct from his arguments, owe much to 'the mysteries', and from this source he drew a confidence in divine providence and divine justice which he then expressed in philosophical and mythical form.* In some ways his 'pessimism' seems to increase as his theology is more consciously formulated. He never thought that we were μέγα τι, anything much, and the created beings of the *Timaeus* appear as small and helpless

---

* See [F.] Solmsen, *Plato's Theology*, Chapter VII.

(seen of course by God), activated by 'necessary passions', and foreshadowing the 'puppets' of the *Laws*. The persuasion of the necessary by the divine is indeed not something into which we can see very far. Even to think of this as a Kantian 'idea of reason' is to view it in too rosy a light. Plato, for all his 'rationalism', never established reason as Kant does. Kant says that we gain enlightenment from the shock of reason's defeat by promptly feeling the strength and superior value of the 'defeated'. Plato does not console us with any readily available human reason (even incarnate reason in the form of the World Soul has its limitations), and as his thought develops the spiritual world gradually recedes. In the *Republic* we meet the spiritual in the guise of the necessary when paradoxes of sense experience disturb thoughtless acceptance and lead the mind to seek for tests of truth; and we are encouraged by the encounter with changeless knowable entities in mathematics. We are no better off in the *Timaeus* where active cosmic voῦς has taken the place of the non-hypothetical first principle of the *Republic*. Indeed, though it must be kept in mind that the *Timaeus* is a theocentric myth, we seem to be worse off, in that there is no intelligible ladder of ascent, such as we have in the *Republic*, and the unimpeded vision of Good is reserved for the Demiurge. By the time the cosmic God arrives we seem to be further away from him than from the Zeus of the *Phaedrus* to whom Plato, in such lyrical and happy mood, declares his allegiance.

Plato allowed the image of a perfect unmixed good, which was the sole true object of desire, to summon up the (mythological) idea of a perfect creator-ruler. He never identified this 'God' with the Form of the Good. What the intellect seeks as perfect is, in thought at any rate, to be kept separate from the concept of God. The metaphor of moral vision, so important in the *Republic*, is maintained, but now while God sees the Forms, we see the stars (47 B). The cosmic deity seems more to express the inaccessibility of the absolutely real than its accessibility. In the early dialogues the spiritual world is so close that we seem to be God's children. In the *Timaeus* we are his grandchildren. In the *Laws* we are his toys. Our frailty is insisted upon. We are scarcely real (like, 889 C, the products of art), we are abject creatures, ταπεινοί, dangling from strings of pleasure and pain (*Laws*, 644, 716, 902-7). In the *Phaedo* and the *Theaetetus* Plato uses images of escape to God. In the *Laws* the imagery is often of almost total separation and slavery. Plato's remarks about slaves (777) are (perhaps) surprisingly harsh, (perhaps) emotionally charged. Slaves should be addressed only with orders. ([G.] Vlastos comments on Plato's use of δουλεία [slavery] for other forms of submission: *Slavery in Classical Antiquity* [ed. Moses I. Finley.) The earlier part of the dialogue contains some scanty discussions of religious observance and popular cult, the more pictorial forms of religion suitable for those who can see the truth only 'in images'; and of course the rulers in the *Laws* are to use the charms of religion and art in the service of social stability, as the Egyptians did with such remarkable success (657, 799). Plato's own 'negative theology' appears as it were accidentally in grim asides which, like many important things in his work, often appear as jokes. Only God is a serious matter. We should not see our lives as serious toil for the sake of unserious play. For us, only play is 'serious' since we are playthings of the gods. Thus art (music) is valuable as an aid to divine grace (803). (These are deep words about the nature of play, religion, and art.) 'Everything is full of gods' (899 B); yet also God seems to have receded to an astronomical distance.

One of Plato's evident aims, both here and in the *Republic*, is the moral reform of religious concept and religious practice. Traditional city state religion was now undergoing a crisis of 'demythologisation' not totally unlike that of present-day Christianity. So the *Laws* is not 'wantonly' exploring the possibility of new religious ideas. That such radical change was under general consideration we can see from the dramatists. Book X of the dialogue is devoted to more positive and theoretically coherent theological speculation, mythical in style though picking up a number of familiar philosophical themes. The cosmos again appears, and even more evidently so than in the *Timaeus*, as a harmoniously organised work of art wherein the parts are subservient to the total design. The supreme figures of the *Timaeus* appear here in altered guise, with the function of Soul much increased, and the Forms in eclipse. The many and the One receive mention at 965, in connection with the unity of virtue; and 895 D shows that Plato was still reflecting upon problems raised by the Forms, though we are not given the fruit of the reflection. Soul is now the cause of all things, including the details of sensible qualities, and is active everywhere. But although what it brings about resembles an art object, Soul is not, like the Demiurge, an artist-copyist, and our world is at last real and not a copy. There is, moreover, bad Soul as well as good Soul. This dualism is not new in Plato's thought (*Republic*, 397 B, *Politics*, 270 A), though it is nowhere discussed at length. Soul is still properly subject to the authority of Mind, but may join itself with unreason (897 B). The best 'prelude' to the *Laws* (887 C) is refutation of atheism, and especially of the view that the gods do not care. Being their 'property', we are carefully and justly and indeed lovingly looked after. Chattels are not necessarily despised, and the image is a pious one, mentioned as a 'mystery' at *Phaedo*, 62 B. Divine providence is just and good, even though evil men may prosper. (Plato often muses upon the success of evil.) The gods care for even the smallest things, but they do so also with a view to the whole: just as a doctor looks at the part in relation to the whole body, and statesmen look to the whole state and craftsmen to the whole object (902). Individual souls matter, and, as essential parts of the cosmic art object, move to their appropriate places under the guidance of the divine gamester (πεττευτής, 903 D). (God is not only always doing geometry, he is always playing draughts.)

The intermittent, not uninvigorating gloom of the *Laws* need not to be construed as the cynicism of an ageing man, though it is true that Plato's political adventures had miscarried and the great philosophical game of patience had failed to come out. In fact the dialogue is not a tale of gloomy repression, even if Plato's last State is in many ways one which we would detest. The authoritarianism of the *Laws* has been more publicised, especially of late, than has its humane moral and political wisdom. (Modern criticism of Plato as 'reactionary' is too often historically naïve.) Plato does not here attempt the major philosophical problems to which he constantly returns in other dialogues, but his extremely minute discussions often illuminate his earlier more generally stated theories. The practical detail is remarkable, the advice often good, whether the talk is of property, law and justice, or of exercises for pregnant women and the importance of tidy hair and shoes. The life of moderation, of physical fitness and rational virtue, so often lauded earlier, is here exemplified in detail, and in this picture we may see how it is that the just are happier than the unjust. Art, within the limits of censorship, is treated with interest and even with a sort of fresh respect. Music and dance are described in animated detail, and *techné* is said (921 B) to be 'naturally clear and truthful'. The plain clear sustained relaxed eloquence of the moralising is new and impressive, where here at last Plato speaks to us of morality without worrying about background theory, but taking it for granted and illustrating it out of his wide experience of states and peoples. We all suffer from self-love, so we must be gentle with remediable criminals and try to see how, in their case too, there was a sense in which they did not err willingly (731). Apparent 'equality' means real inequality if men do not receive what is appropriate; however, a more meticulous justice must always be tempered by tolerance and common sense (757). The *Laws* also contains (805) not only the earliest but probably the most uncompromising declaration ever made by a major philosopher of the equality of the sexes. Women can even do philosophy.

Plato, who treated the Olympians with such careful detachment, was of course well aware of the ambiguous nature of a busy personified 'God' or gods except as either necessary cult, or explanatory myth in a philosophical context. He always feared magic and almost the whole of his philosophy is a running fight against misleading and uncriticised images, some of them his own. Any seriously envisaged 'God', once liberated from Zeus, has to recede, since anything said about him is likely to mislead us. 'To find out the maker and father of all things is indeed a task, and having found him to explain him to all men is an impossibility' (*Timaeus*, 28 C). In the *Laws* God appears as a theological device, as quasi-philosophical quasi-mythical theological speculation, or as an absence prompting bitter jokes. Escape from the cave and approach to the Good is a progressive discarding of relative false goods, of hypotheses, images, and shadows, eventually seen as such. However, even the most enlightened discourse involves language, and dealing with the world is, as Plato usually envisages it, dealing with instances or copies of the Forms whose relation to their great originals can never be satisfactorily pictured. The glory of the Demiurge never dims that of the Form of the Good as it appears in splendour in the *Republic*. As difficulties emerged Plato changed his imagery, sometimes and finally abandoning philosophical argument altogether. He was always conscious of the possibility of being misunderstood, and the writer of the *Seventh Letter* expresses this anxiety with vehemence. St John of the Cross says that God is the abyss of faith into which we fall when we have discarded all images of him. This is the point at which Plato starts making jokes.

*

We are now in a position to see the fundamentally religious nature of Plato's objections to art, and why he so firmly relegated it to the mental level of *eikasia*. Art is dangerous chiefly because it apes the spiritual and subtly disguises and trivialises it. Artists play irresponsibly with religious imagery which, if it must exist, should be critically controlled by the internal, or external, authority of reason. Artists obscure the enlightening power of thought and skill by aiming at plausibility rather than truth. Art delights in unsavoury trivia and in the endless proliferation of senseless images (television). Art is playful in a sinister sense, full of (φθόνος) a spiteful amused acceptance of evil, and through buffoonery and mockery weakens moral discrimination. The artist cannot represent or celebrate the good, but only what is daemonic and fantastic and extreme; whereas truth is quiet and sober and confined. Art is sophistry, at best an ironic *mimesis* whose fake 'truthfulness' is a subtle enemy of virtue. Indirectness and irony prevent the immediate relationship with truth which occurs in live discourse; art is thus the enemy of dialectic. Writing and painting introduce an extra distancing notation and by charm fix it in place. They create a barrier of imagery which arrests the mind, rigidifies the subject matter, and is defenceless against low clients. The true *logos* falls silent in the presence of the highest (ineffable) truth, but the art object cherishes its volubility, it cherishes itself, not the truth, and wishes to be indestructible and eternal. Art makes us content with appearances, and by playing magically with particular images it steals the educational wonder of the world away from philosophy and confuses our sense of direction toward reality and our motives for discerning it. Through an unpurified charm masquerading as beauty, art is 'most clearly seen'. 'Form' thus becomes the enemy of knowledge. (See the end of *Death in Venice*.) Art localises the

[443]

intelligence which should be bent upon righting the proportions of the whole of life. Form in art is for illusion and hides the true cosmic beauty and the hard real forms of necessity and causality, and blurs with fantasy the thought-provoking paradox. Art objects are not real unities but pseudo-objects completed by the fantasising mind in its escape from reality. The pull of the transcendent as reality and good is confused and mimicked. The true sense of reality as a feeling of joy is deceitfully imitated by the 'charm-joy' of art. There is very little good art, and even that (*corruptio optimi pessima*) is dangerous. Enjoyment of art deludes even the decent man by giving him a false self-knowledge based on a healthy egoism: the fire in the cave, which is mistaken for the sun, and where one may comfortably linger, imagining oneself to be enlightened. Art thus prevents the salvation of the whole man by offering a pseudo-spirituality and a plausible imitation of direct intuitive knowledge (vision, presence), a defeat of the discursive intelligence at the bottom of the scale of being, not at the top. Art is a false presence and a false present. As a pseudo-spritual activity, it can still attract when coarser goals are seen as worthless. We seek eternal possession of the good, but art offers a spurious worthless immortality. It thus confuses the spiritual pilgrimage and obscures the nature of true *catharsis* (purification). Its pleasures are impure and indefinite and secretly in league with egoism. The artist deceives the saving Eros by producing magical objects which feed the fantasy life of the ego and its desire for omnipotence. Art offers itself as 'a mechanism of sensibility which could devour any experience'. (T. S. Eliot on the undissociated sensibility. Plato, perhaps rightly, regards such sensibility as primary in artists.) The separateness, the otherness of art is a sham, a false transcendence, a false imitation of another world. (The negress who sings upon the gramophone record in *La Nausée*.) Art may thus become a magical substitute for philosophy, an impure mediator professing to classify and explain reality. But there is no short cut to enlightenment, and as the *Philebus* (16) tells us, we must sort out the world with patience, not hastily producing a pseudo-unity or *eikon*. Art practises a false degenerate *anamnesis* where the veiled something which is sought and found is no more than a shadow out of the private storeroom of the personal unconscious. The work of art may even be thought of as a pernicious caricature of the Form, as the Form was originally conceived, the pure daemonic particular, timeless, radiant, reality-bestowing, separate, directly knowable, and unique.

Plato often makes jokes about his philosophical predecessors in whom the distinction between myth and *logos* is less clearly marked than it is in his own work. An uneasy awareness of the perhaps essential intrusion of (in some sense) myth is no doubt for Plato a part of his old 'quarrel between philosophy and poetry'. Socrates in the *Phaedo* (100 A) says that when he rejected science and turned to *logoi* he was not just using images: and Plato is constantly scrupulous to distinguish clearly between 'pictures' and 'conversations'. However, the artist (or is it the philosopher?) in him still urges him to explain by using images. 'Is it a metaphor?' is of course a fundamental question to be asked about metaphysical explanation, about for instance what we are told in the *Critique of Pure Reason* and the *Phenomenology of Mind*; and indeed such works could not exist at all without the help of metaphor. Plato is right to exclaim (*Timaeus*, 47 B) that sight (vision) is our greatest blessing, without which we would not reach philosophy. Our ability to use visual structures to understand non-visual structures (as well as other different visual ones) is fundamental to explanation in any field. The Theory of Forms, when read in conjunction with the explanatory tropes of the line and the cave (which may be an Orphic myth colonised by Plato), can certainly produce some blazingly strong imagery in the mind which may well in the long run obstruct understanding. Some of the difficulties of philosophical explanation may be seen in the fact that although Plato at first treats the Forms as quasi-things (what a word means, perfect particulars, 'soul-stuff') and later as attributes, he yet preserves them as objects of divine vision (though we are not told what they 'look like') in the *Timaeus*, because there is something essential that can only be explained by this image. Plato spent some extremely valuable time (*Parmenides, Theaetetus, Sophist*) dismantling his earlier imagery, but then invented some more, marvellous, entirely new, mythological but still explanatory images in the *Timaeus*. As F. M. Cornford remarks, the Greeks (of Socrates's time) had immense confidence in reason because of advances in geometry. Part of the drama of that confidence was played out in Plato's philosophical life. However, his failures do not lead him (as they might lead a later,

Christian or liberal, thinker) to conclude humbly or tolerantly that the human mind is essentially limited and fallible. They lead rather to a firmer sense of hierarchy. Wisdom is *there*, but belongs to gods and very few mortals (*Timaeus, Laws*). After all, Plato was continuously involved in politics and even in his middle life was not optimistic about the generality of men. He lived as an active participant through some of the most horrible and harrowing historical events ever recorded in detail, and of which (except in so far as they concerned the death of Socrates) there is almost no direct mention in the dialogues. (The *Theaetetus* opens with the news of Theaetetus, dying of wounds and dysentery after the battle of Corinth, being carried up from the harbour; but the argument then quickly removes us into the past.) Life and (what one must in this context call) art are held in a remarkable tension. The dramatic dating of the dialogues is aesthetically brilliant.

Throughout his work, including the more cheerful earlier writings, Plato emphasises the height of the objective and the difficulty of the ascent. On the other hand, even at his gloomiest he is never in essentials a sceptic. The Good (truth, reality) is absent from us and hard of access, but it is there and only the Good will satisfy. This fact is concealed by the consoling image-making ego in the guise of the artist whom every one of us to some extent is. Art with its secret claim to supreme power blurs the distinction between the presence and the absence of reality, and tries to cover up with charming imagery the harsh but inspiring truth of the distance between man and God. This void may of course also be concealed by the metaphysical ladders of the philosopher; it is all very well to tell us to throw away the ladder: the ladder is interesting. Art, in and out of philosophy, may ignore the journey and persuade us we are already there and deny the incommensurabilities of reality and mind. A softening romanticism dogs philosophy in the guise of art. 'Poetic pluralism is the corollary to the mysticism of the One.'* But awareness of the gap is not itself the bridge. Plato knew the dangers of his own artistry, and the exasperated bitter theological remarks in the *Laws* may express his realisation that as soon as philosophy abandons ψιλοί λόγοι, cool unadorned non-jargon prose, it too is in danger of being used as magic. The strongest motive to

---

* Edgar Wind, *Pagan Mysteries in the Renaissance* ([London] 1958) p. 176.

philosophy is probably the same as the strongest motive to art: the desire to become the Demiurge and reorganise chaos in accordance with one's own excellent plan.

Any release of spirit may be ambiguous in its power, and artists, both visual and literary, love this area of ambiguity, for reasons well understood by both Plato and Freud. There has always been a dangerous relationship between art and religion, and, where theology hesitates, art will eagerly try to explain. Art may here be seen as the more 'dangerous' where 'pure thought' is the less powerful. No wonder (from his own point of view) that Plato, who must by then have felt a diminished faith in the 'high dialectic', kept the artists under such rigid control in the *Laws*, where private speculation is discouraged and picturesque popular religion is an instrument of state power. In fact, unless specifically prevented from doing so, art instinctively materialises God and the religious life. This has been nowhere more true than in Christianity, which has been served by so many geniuses. The familiar figures of the Trinity have been so celebrated and beautified in great pictures that it almost seems as if the painters were the final authorities on the matter, as Plato said that the poets seemed to be about the Greek gods. Partly because of the historical nature of Christianity, Christian images tend to be taken 'for real'. Art contributes, in a perhaps misleadingly 'spiritual' way, the material gear of religion; and what should be a mediating agency may become in effect a full-stop barrier. Many modern theologians are attempting to remove this great rigidified and now often unacceptable mythological barrier which divides Christianity from ordinary sophisticated people. Whether Christian belief can survive this process remains to be seen. Art fascinates religion at a high level and may provide the highest obstacle to the pursuit of the whole truth. A rigid high pattern of integrated 'spiritual' imagery arrests the mind, prevents the free movement of the spirit, and fills the language with unclear metaphor. (The abyss of faith lies beyond images and beyond *logoi* too.) Kierkegaard, as I mentioned earlier, forerunner of much modern unease about art, sensed these problems and deliberately used art as a destructive anti-theoretical mystification, to promote a more direct relationship to the truth and to prevent the dogmatic relaxation of tension brought about by a hard aesthetically burnished theology. (But art is tricky stuff: did he succeed?)

In the East (an area so shockingly close to the founders of European rationalism) art is seen as a humbler and more felicitously ambiguous handmaid of religion. Whereas Western art, becoming separated and grand and 'an authority', just as Plato feared, has surreptitiously lent its power to an ossifying of the religion it purports to serve. (The sin of pride.) Although art in the East is even more generally (loosely) connected with religion than it is in the West, the imagery is usually, though significant, less highly specialised, less rationally clarified, less relentlessly literary. The magnificent Hindu deities, however clearly and lovingly rendered, are more mysterious. Eastern religions lack the terrible historical clarity of Christianity. Eastern art is humbler, less 'grand', and has a quieter and perhaps for that reason deeper relation to the spiritual. We may perhaps find a parallel to Plato's attitude in the dignified puritanism of Islam with its reservations about 'figures' and 'objects' and its rejection of role-playing theatre. Zen Buddhists, who are Platonic in their use of the *technai*, but who reject philosophy, actually employ art as anti-art, the favoured images being not only, however skilful, absurdly simple, but also often deliberately incomplete. Many modern visual artists feel an evident sympathy with such attitudes, though they differ about how much skill is required to make anti-art art effective. (This will partly depend of course upon its exact purpose.) Zen also makes use of educational paradoxes (*koan*). Plato's paradoxes (the 'bent' object in water) lead on to measurement, and thus to the cosmic Eros, whereas the paradoxes of Zen are designed to smash rational thought in the interests of a more true and direct understanding. Zen is prepared to use art so long as art does not take itself too seriously; and Zen is well aware of the way in which art imagery may provide false resting places. Pure unpretentious very simple art is the best companion for the religious man. Plato would agree. Zen emphasises skill but favours throwaway products. Plato (*Laws*, 956 B) says that artefacts offered to the gods should be such as can be made in a single day.

Gilbert Ryle describes Plato as an Odysseus rather than a Nestor, and there are of course elements of inconsistency and sheer accident in the work of any persisting thinker. There does, however, seem to be a unity of both thought and feeling in Plato's reactions to art, during the changing pattern of his attitudes to other philosophical questions, and during the momentous history (not discussed here) of his non-philosophical life, including his agonisingly mixed feelings about taking part in politics. That the *Apology* contains an attack on the poets is doubtless significant. *Phaedo* 61 tells how Socrates, although not *mythologikos*, obeyed his dream command to 'make music'. Plato, the heir, so eminently able in this department, puzzled as his master had done about how best to obey. The politically motivated hostility to a free art, which Plato shares with modern dictators, is separable from more refined objections which are both philosophical and temperamental; and although we may want to defend art against Plato's charges we may also recognise, in the context of the highest concern, how worthy of consideration some of these charges are. There is a kind of religious life which excludes art and it is not impossible to understand why.

In fact Plato himself supplies a good deal of the material for a complete aesthetic, a defence and reasonable critique of art. The relation of art to truth and goodness must be the fundamental concern of any serious criticism of it. 'Beauty' cannot be discussed 'by itself'. There is in this sense no 'pure aesthetic' viewpoint. Philosophy and theology have to reject evil in the course of explaining it, but art is essentially more free and enjoys the ambiguity of the whole man; hence the doubleness which of course it shares with Plato's Eros. Where philosophy and theology are purists, art is a shameless collaborator, and Plato rightly identifies irony and laughter as prime methods of collaboration. The judging mind of the skilful artist is a delicate self-effacing instrument; the tone or style by which the writer or painter puts himself 'in the clear' may be very close to a subtle insincerity. (As for instance in what critics call the 'placing' of characters in a novel.) Hence Plato's insight reaches to the deepest levels of our judgement of worth in art. And since his philosophy is largely concerned with how the attractiveness of beauty turns out to be the moral pull of reality, we might expect to be able to extract, in spite of Plato's own negative and often contemptuous attitudes, some positive aesthetic touchstone from his writings. In pursuit of this let us consider for a moment one of his more shocking positions, and one which we might be inclined to dismiss as some sort of 'idle' puritanism: his view of τὸ γελοῖον, the ludicrous or absurd.

Although it may be said in general that philosophy is witty rather than funny and that the same is true of religion (Christ makes witty remarks but not jokes), Plato's work is in fact full of pleasing jokes and is pervaded by a light of humour and sweet-tempered amusement. However, he rejects the ludicrous as πονηρία τις, a kind of vice (*Philebus,* 48 C), and says that it signals a lack of self-knowledge. His censor would remove the marvellous description of the gods laughing at the beginning of the *Iliad* (*Iliad,* I, 599, *Republic,* 389 A). The laughter is perhaps not very good-natured, but that is not Plato's point. Laughter (as distinct from amused smiles) is undignified, explosive, something violent and extreme, offending against the modest sobriety which is, with such an impressive backing of theory, commended in the *Philebus.* Of course there is something anti-authoritarian about violent laughter, and there are even today societies, and not primitive ones, where public laughter is frowned upon. The frightened or guilty mind will always wonder: what are they laughing at? Plato more positively, at intervals throughout the dialogues, in the *Republic* as well as in the *Laws,* seems to equate an absurdity-rejecting dignity with some sort of virtuous self-respect. In this he contrasts with his Zen colleagues who (alone of moralists?) take the funny as central to the human pilgrimage. The *koan* often appears as some sort of wild joke. Of course there is a bad absurd (degrading, hurtful), but is there not also a good absurd? Loss of dignity need not be loss of moral stature, can be surrender of vanity, discovery of humility; and a sense of the ludicrous is a defence against pretensions, not least in art. Plato, however, in one of the earliest European attempts to define the good man, as opposed to the hero, attaches importance to his dignity; and the Judaeo-Christian tradition in general has shunned presentation of the good man as absurd. (Job is not absurd.) This may seem natural to us, although it is worth asking the question whether one can be humble with unimpaired dignity. And of course modern (bourgeois) literature has delighted in the absurd, attractive, good-seeming hero, a figure whom Plato would no doubt, and perhaps rightly, view with distaste. Laughter, and the art which produces it, may notoriously have no *logos*. We laugh wildly without knowing quite why (lack of self-knowledge) at situations and absurd jokes which resist analysis. In the *Philebus* (65–6) Plato seems to suggest that the absurdity of sex is repugnant. Freud, discussing jokes (*Jokes and Their Relation to the Unconscious*, IV, 2), refers to what he calls the 'fore-pleasure principle' which he also uses in his general description (already referred to) of the mysterious pleasures of art. The gentle though often profound jesting of the dialogues often takes place in situations where love relationships are glanced at, as for instance in the charming picture of Zeno and Parmenides smiling at each other as they listen to the youthful Socrates holding forth. These were 'fore-pleasures' whose possible conclusions the artist Plato keeps out of view for reasons which closely mingle the aesthetic and the moral. The dignified tact with which the whole subject of love is handled is one of the highest effects of Plato's art.

'Order is beautiful (good), disorder is bad.' The *Republic* seems to assume a world where what is really real is harmonious, and we can reasonably attempt to know ourselves and the world. In the *Timaeus* the Demiurge cannot entirely subdue disorder, and we mortals are victims of 'necessary passions'. In one of the significant throwaway asides in the *Laws* (923 A) the citizens are addressed as 'creatures of a day' who cannot 'know themselves'. The paradigmatic image of the clarified world of mathematics, to which the *Republic* gave so high a place, gives way to a more realistic picture of the mind confronting a confused world. The Demiurge is an instructive portrait of the artist in that he is dealing with material which, though endowed with causal properties, is recalcitrant not through being mechanically systematic but through being partly fundamentally jumbled. F. M. Cornford (*Thucydides Mythistoricus*, vol. VI, quoted in his comments on *Timaeus* 47–8) speaks of how Thucydides contrasted the field of ordinary human foresight not with an area of causal law but with an unknown territory of chance full of inscrutable activities of gods and spirits, in the face of which human motives tended to count as absolute beginnings. This, even for us children of a scientific age, is not wholly unlike the way in which we sometimes view the field of our fortunes. The Demiurge has to accept a degree of 'absurdity' (jumble), but he retains the ideal of harmony, and the disorder which faces him is to be deplored, and neither exaggerated nor celebrated.

The discussion in *Philebus*, 49–50 connects the ludicrous or absurd with one variety at least of the gleeful envious malice (φθόνος) which Plato associates especially with the theatre, but then extends to 'the whole tragi-comedy of life'. φθόνος is hard to render in English because it contains (as we must understand it in the *Philebus*) an element of sado-masochistic glee which is not fully present in either 'malice' or 'envy'. The narrator of Dostoevsky's *Notes from Underground* (II, 2) both expresses and analyses the concept, as well as providing a loving description of the 'use' of art by the baser mind. 'Everything always finished up to my satisfaction in an entrancingly lazy transition into art, that is into the most delightful forms of existence, all available and ready for me, heartily pinched from poets and novelists, and adaptable to every possible demand and use. For example, I triumph over everybody . . .' etc. The artist, ideally, if he is to proceed beyond the wallpaper stage, should imitate the calm unenvious Demiurge who sees the recalcitrant jumble of his material with just eyes, and with a commanding sense of proportion: that sense of proportion and right order which *Philebus*, 16–17 tells us is fostered by dialectic. But Plato will not allow that this is possible. The bad artist (who resides in all of us) as naïve fantasist, to use the distinction of the *Sophist* and the imagery of the cave, sees only moving shadows and construes the world in accordance with the easy unresisted mechanical 'causality' of his personal dream-life. (The bad thriller or facile romance and its client.) The mediocre artist (the ironical man by the fire, if we may so characterise him), who thinks he 'knows himself but too well', parades his mockery and spleen as a despairing dramatic rejection of any serious or just attempt to discern real order at all. This figure (a fairly familiar one in the pages of Plato's dialogues, where he is criticised, and of modern literature, where he is indulged) is on the road toward the 'all is permitted' and 'man is the measure of all things' of the cynical sophist. Neither of these, as artist or as man, possesses true self-knowledge or a just grasp of the hardness of the material which resists him, the necessity, the ἀνάγκη of the world. Confronted with semi-chaos the Demiurge is steadied (if he needs it) by the presence of the Forms. But must the mortal artist, condemned to some variety of self-indulgence, be either a dreamer or a cynic; and can he not attempt to see the created world in the pure light of the Forms?

It is tempting to 'refute' Plato simply by pointing to the existence of great works of art, and in doing so to describe their genesis and their merits in Platonic terms. Kant, though suspicious of beauty because of its possible lapse into charm, was prepared to treat it as a symbol of the good (*Critique of Judgement*, I, 59); and could not art at least be so regarded, even if we take Plato's objections seriously? Good art, thought of as symbolic force rather than statement, provides a stirring image of a pure transcendent value, a steady visible enduring higher good, and perhaps provides for many people, in an unreligious age without prayer or sacraments, their clearest *experience* of something grasped as separate and precious and beneficial and held quietly and unpossessively in the attention. Good art which we love can seem holy and attending to it can be like praying. Our relation to such art though 'probably never' entirely pure is markedly unselfish. The calm joy in the picture gallery is quite unlike the pleasurable flutter felt in the saleroom. Beauty is, as Plato says, visibly transcendent; hence indeed the metaphor of vision so indispensable in discussions of aesthetics and morality. The *spectacle* of good in other forms, as when we admire good men and heroes, is often, as experience, more mixed and less efficacious. As Kierkegaard said, we admire and relax. Good art, on the other hand, provides work for the spirit. Of course morality is quite largely a matter of action, though what we look at profoundly affects what we do. (Whatsoever things are honest . . . whatsoever things are pure . . . think on these things.' Philippians 4:8.) And of course the practice of personal relations is the fundamental school of virtue. The spiritual revelations involved in dealing with people are in an evident sense more important than those available through art, though they tend to be less clear. What are motives and do they matter? When is altruism an exercise of power? (etc. etc. etc.) Of course such questions need, in particular cases, answers. But art remains available and vivid as an experience of how egoism can be purified by intelligent imagination. Art-beauty must in a sense be detached from good because art is not essential. Art, though it demands moral effort and teaches quiet attention (as any serious study can do) is a kind of treat; it is, like Kant's Sublime, an extra. We can be saved without seeing the Alps or the Cairngorms, and without Titian and Mozart too. We have to make moral choices, we do not have to enjoy great art and doubtless many good people never do. But surely great art points in the direction of the good and is at least more valuable to the moralist as an auxiliary than dangerous as an enemy. How, when, whether bad art (of which of course there is a great deal) is morally damaging is, as we know, a deep question not easily answered. For great art to exist a general practice of art must exist; and even trivial art is a fairly harmless consolation, as Plato himself seems prepared to admit in the *Laws*.

Of course art is huge, and European philosophy is strangely small, so that Whitehead scarcely exaggerates in calling it all footnotes to Plato. General talk about 'art', to which one is driven when discussing Plato's view, is always in danger of becoming nonsense. There is no science of criticism; any so-called critical 'system' has in the end to be evaluated by the final best instrument, the calm open judging mind of the intelligent experienced critic, unmisted, as far as possible, by theory. Confronted with academic aesthetics as he knew it, Tolstoy's instincts were sound, and his reply to the effect that all we need to know is that good art promotes good, is one with which we can sympathise. However one is tempted, and partly in order to do justice to Plato's argument, to try to explain in more detail just how great art is good for us, and in doing so to take our best material out of Plato himself. Art is a special discerning exercise of intelligence in relation to the real; and although aesthetic form has essential elements of trickery and magic, yet form in art, as form in philosophy, is designed to communicate and reveal. In the shock of joy in response to good art, an essential ingredient is a sense of the revelation of reality, of the really real, the ὄντως ὄν: the world as we were never able so clearly to see it before. When Burne-Jones is reported as saying, 'I mean by a picture a beautiful romantic dream of something that never was, never will be – in a light better than any light that ever shone – in a land no one can define or remember, only desire – and the forms divinely beautiful', we are embarrassed, not least because this does indeed seem to describe many of his pictures in an aspect which marks them as delightful or marvellous but not exactly great.* One would not think of applying such language to the work of (for instance) Seurat or Cézanne, or to remoter and apparently 'fanciful' art, such as mythological subjects treated by Botticelli or Titian. When Artemis speeds by as Actaeon falls, the revelation remains mysterious but somehow true, and with the 'hardness' of truth. A reading of Plato helps us to see how good art is truthful. Dream is the enemy of art and its false image. As pictured in the *Republic*, the higher level is reflected as an image in the lower level. The high-temperature fusing power of the creative imagination, so often and eloquently described by the Romantics, is the reward of the sober truthful mind which, as it reflects and searches, constantly says no and no and no to the prompt easy visions of self-protective self-promoting fantasy. (Like the daemon of Socrates which said only 'No'.) The artist's 'freedom' is hard won, and is a function of his grasp of reality. To adapt Plato's image, the Demiurge creates time as an, interestingly transformed, image of eternity, but finds the mysterious essential medium of space already existing. The images which body forth the truth come spontaneously, in the end, into the space which it is so hard to apprehend and accept, and to keep empty against the pressures which are tending to collapse it. (The *Vorlust* is always impatient for a conclusion.) The imagination fuses, but in order to do so it must tease apart in thought what is apart in reality, resisting the facile merging tendencies of the obsessive ego. The prescription for art is then the same as for dialectic: overcome personal fantasy and egoistic anxiety and self-indulgent day-dream. Order and separate and distinguish the world justly. Magic in its unregenerate form as the fantastic doctoring of the real for consumption by the private ego is the bane of art as it is of philosophy. Obsession shrinks reality to a single pattern. The artist's worst enemy is his eternal companion, the cosy dreaming ego, the dweller in the vaults of *eikasia*. Of course the highest art is powered by the force of an individual unconscious mind, but then so is the highest philosophy; and in both cases technique is useless without divine fury.

What is hard and necessary and unavoidable in human fate is the subject-matter of great art. To use a mixture of Platonic and

* See F. de Lisle, *Burne-Jones* ([London,] 1904), p. 173, quoted by John Christian in Hayward Gallery Burne-Jones Exhibition Catalogue, 1975.

Kantian language, we see in a dream that art is properly concerned with the synthetic *a priori*, the borderland of *dianoia* and *noesis*, the highest mental states described in the *Republic*. Art is about the pilgrimage from appearance to reality (the subject of every good play and novel) and exemplifies in spite of Plato what his philosophy teaches concerning the therapy of the soul. This is the 'universal', the high concern which Tolstoy said was the proper province of the artist. The divine (intelligent) cause persuades the necessary cause so as to bring about the best possible. It is the task of mortals (as artists and as men) to understand the necessary for the sake of the intelligible, to see in a pure just light the hardness of the real properties of the world, the effects of the wandering causes, why good purposes are checked and where the mystery of the random has to be accepted. It is not easy to do justice to this hardness and this randomness without either smoothing them over with fantasy or exaggerating them into (cynical) absurdity. Indeed 'the absurd' in art, often emerging as an attempt to defeat easy fantasy, may merely provide it with a sophisticated disguise. The great artist, while showing us what is not saved, implicitly shows us what salvation means. Of course the Demiurge is attempting against insuperable difficulties to create a harmonious and just world. The (good) human artist, whom Plato regards as such a base caricature, is trying to portray the partially failed world as it is, and in doing so to produce something pleasing and beautiful. This involves an intelligent disciplined understanding of what may be called the structural problems of the Demiurge. There is a 'sublime absurd', comic or tragic, which depends on this insight into where the 'faults' come. (Both *Henry IV* Part 2, III, ii and *King Lear*, V, iii.) Forgivably or unforgivably, there is a partly intelligible causality of sin. The good artist helps us to see the place of necessity in human life, what must be endured, what makes and breaks, and to purify our imagination so as to contemplate the real world (usually veiled by anxiety and fantasy) including what is terrible and absurd. Plato said at *Republic*, 395 A that no one can write both comedy and tragedy. As the *Symposium* ends Socrates is telling Agathon and Aristophanes that this can be done. One would like to have an account of this conversation. Plato, with a perverse negligence, never favours us with any serious literary criticism.

Moral philosophers, attempting to analyse human frailty, have produced some pretty unrealistic schemata, usually because they were trying to do too many things at the same time. The contemporary philosopher is in this respect more modest. The question, at what level of generality am I to operate? is of course one which faces both the artist and the philosopher. Great discoveries are made at great levels of generality, as when Plato subjects the profound idea that no one errs willingly to a number of transformations within a general picture of the human soul as knower and agent. On the other hand, the lack of detail can leave the reader unconvinced that he is really seeing 'human life' and not the 'ghostly ballet of bloodless categories', the vision of which haunted another and more recent Platonist, F. H. Bradley. To take one example, Plato, wishing to make the different levels of the soul correspond to different tasks in society and different types of state, connects his concept of θυμοειδές, the central transformational region of the soul, especially with honour and ambition, and thereby oversimplifies a concept which is essential to his analysis of moral change. The *Republic*, like many other great ethical treatises, is deficient in an account of positive evil. The 'tyrannical man' has to prove too much. A portrayal of moral reflection and moral change (degeneration, improvement) is the most important part of any system of ethics. The explanation of our fallibility in such matters as seeing the worse as the better is more informatively (though of course less systematically) carried out by poets, playwrights, and novelists. It has taken philosophy a long time to acknowledge this: the famous 'quarrel' is indeed of long standing, and the suspicion that art is fundamentally frivolous. It is only comparatively recently that moral philosophers have condescended to enlist the aid of literature as a mode of explanation.

The sight of evil is confusing, and it is a subject on which it is hard to generalise because any analysis demands such a battery of value judgements. One would like to think that the just man sees the unjust man clearly. ('God sees him clearly.') Art is (often too) jauntily at home with evil and quick to beautify it. Arguably however, good literature is uniquely able publicly to clarify evil, and emulate the just man's private vision without, such is his privilege, the artist having to be just except in his art. That this separation is possible seems a fact of experience. Art accepts and enjoys the ambiguity of the whole man, and great artists can seem to 'use' their own vices for creative purposes without apparent damage to their art. This mystery belongs indeed to the region of the unmeasured and unlimited. Plato understands what criticism must be constantly aware of, how the bad side of human nature is secretly, precariously, at work in art. There is a lot of secret cruelty there and if the art is good enough (consider Dante, or Dostoevsky) it may be hard to decide when the disciplined 'indulgence' of the cruelty damages the merit of the work or harms the client. But to see misery and evil justly is one of the heights of aesthetic endeavour and one which is surely sometimes reached. How this becomes beautiful is a mystery which may seem very close to some of the central and most lively obscurities in Plato's own thought. (The divine cause is always touching the necessary cause.) Shakespeare makes not only splendour but beauty out of the malevolence of Iago and the intolerable death of Cordelia, as Homer does out of the miseries of a pointless war and the stylish ruthlessness of Achilles. Art can rarely, but with authority, show how we learn from pain, swept by the violence of divine grace toward an unwilling wisdom, as described in the first chorus of the *Agamemnon* in words which somehow remind us of Plato, who remained (it appears) so scandalously indifferent to the merits of Aeschylus. (A case of envy?) And of course art can reveal without explaining and its justice can also be playful. The docility of necessity to intelligence may be as vividly evident in non-mimetic non-conceptual art ('pure contraption' and 'absolute gift'), which fleetingly illuminates deep structures of reality, as if the artist could indeed penetrate the creative reverie of the Demiurge where truth and play mysteriously, inextricably mingle.

One might, in praising art to Plato, even add that if there is, as an effective persuasion, an ontological proof (Plato's main idea after all), art provides a very plausible version of it. Perhaps in general art *proves* more than philosophy can. Familiarity with an art form and the development of taste is an education in the beautiful which involves the often largely instinctive, increasingly confident sorting out of what is good, what is pure, what is profoundly and justly imagined, what rings true, from what is trivial or shallow or in some way fake, self-indulgent, pretentious, sentimental, meretriciously obscure, and so on. Most derogatory critical terms impute some kind of falsehood, and on the other hand (Keats) 'what the imagination seizes as beauty must be truth'. Bad art is a lie about the world, and what is by contrast seen as good is in some important evident sense seen as *ipso facto* true and as expressive of reality: the sense in which Seurat is better than Burne-Jones, Keats than Swinburne, Dickens than Wilkie Collins, etc. Plato says in the *Philebus* that an experience of pleasure may be infected with falsity. Learning to detect the false in art and enjoy the true is part of a life-long education in moral discernment. This does not mean living in an aesthetic cloister. Good art, however complex, presents an evident combination of purity and realism: and if we think at once of moral teachings which do the same (the Gospels, St Augustine, Julian of Norwich, parts of Plato), it has to be admitted that these too are in their own perfectly natural way art. The development of any skill increases our sense of (necessity) reality. Learning an art is learning all sorts of strange tricks, but fundamentally it is learning how to make a formal utterance of a perceived truth and render it splendidly worthy of a trained purified attention without falsifying it in the process. When Plato says (*Philebus*, 48 D) that to enjoy the ridiculous is to obey the command: do not know thyself, he is using (though perversely) an important principle of literary criticism: that which militates against self-knowledge is suspect. To know oneself *in the world* (as part of it, subject to it, connected with it) is to have the firmest grasp of the real. This is the humble 'sense of proportion' which Plato connects with virtue. Strong agile realism, which is of course not photographic naturalism, the non-sentimental, non-meanly-personal imaginative grasp of the subject-matter is something which can be recognised as value in all the arts, and it is this which gives that special unillusioned pleasure which is the liberating whiff of reality; when in high free play the clarified imaginative attention of the creative mind is fixed upon its object. Of course art is playful, but its play is serious. τῆς σπουδῆς ἀδελφὴ παιδιά. Freud says that the opposite of play is not work but reality. This may be true of fantasy play but not of the playfulness of good art which delightedly seeks and reveals the real. Thus in practice we increasingly relate one concept to another, and see beauty as the artful use of form to illuminate truth, and celebrate reality; and we can then experience what Plato spoke of but wished to separate from art: the way in which to desire the beautiful is to desire the real and the good.

It may be tempting here to say that the disciplined understanding, the just discernment, of the good artist must depend (if one wants to play further with the *Timaeus* myth) upon some kind of *separate* moral certainty. Again the metaphor of vision: a source of light. However it is difficult to press the idea beyond the status of a tautology. Good artists can be bad men; the virtue may, as I said earlier, reside entirely in the work, the just vision be attainable only there. After all, however much we idolise each other, we are limited specialised animals. Moreover, even the work itself may be less perfect than it seems. We are creatures of a day, nothing much. We do not understand ourselves, we lack reality, what we have and know is not ὄντως ὄν [what truly is], but merely ὄν πως [what is in one way or another]. We are cast in the roles of Shallow and Silence; and must not, in favour of art or philosophy, protest too much. (The best in this kind are but shadows, and the worst are no worse, if imagination amend them.) Because of the instinctive completing activity of the client's mind, its 'unlimited' co-operation with the artist, we often do not see how unfinished even great work may be; and if the artist presses this upon our attention we are shocked since we so much want to believe in perfection. Great works of art often do seem like perfect particulars, and we seem here to enjoy that 'extra' knowledge which is denied to us at the end of the *Theaetetus*. But because of the muddle of human life and the ambiguity and playfulness of aesthetic form, art can at best only explain partly, only reveal almost: and of course any complex work contains impurities and accidents which we choose to ignore. Even the Demiurge will never entirely understand. Although art can be so good for us, it does contain some of those elements of illusion out of which its detractors make so much of their case. The pierced structure of the art object whereby its sense flows into life is an essential part of its mortal nature. Even at its most exquisite art is incomplete. Simone Weil, that admirable Platonist, said that a poem is beautiful in so far as the poet's thought is fixed upon the ineffable. Art, like (in Plato's view) philosophy, hovers about in the very fine air which we breathe just beyond what has been expressed.

One need not, however, enter into metaphysical or psychological arguments to diminish art or to defend it either. Its simpler solider merits are obvious: a free art is an essential aspect of a free society, as a degraded lying art is a function of a tyrannical one. Art as the great general universal informant is an obvious rival, not necessarily a hostile one, to philosophy and indeed to science, and Plato never did justice to the unique truth-conveying capacities of art. The good or even decent writer does not just 'imitate doctors' talk', but attempts to understand and portray the doctors' 'world', and these pictures, however modest, of other 'worlds' are interesting and valuable. The spiritual ambiguity of art, its connection with the 'limitless' unconscious, its use of irony, its interest in evil, worried Plato. But the very ambiguity and voracious ubiquitousness of art is its characteristic freedom. Art, especially literature, is a great hall of reflection where we can all meet and where everything under the sun can be examined and considered. For this reason it is feared and attacked by dictators, and by authoritarian moralists such as the one under discussion. The artist is a great informant, at least a gossip, at best a sage, and much loved in both roles. He lends to the elusive particular a local habitation and a name. He sets the world in order and gives us hypothetical hierarchies and intermediate images: like the dialectician he mediates between the one and the many; and though he may artfully confuse us, on the whole he instructs us. Art is far and away the most educational thing we have, far more so than its rivals, philosophy and theology and science. The pierced nature of the work of art, its limitless connection with ordinary life, even its defencelessness against its client, are part of its characteristic availability and freedom. The demands of science and philosophy and ultimately of religion are extremely rigorous. It is just as well that there is a high substitute for the spiritual and the speculative life: that few get to the top morally or intellectually is no less than the truth. Art is a great international human language, it is for all. Of course art has no formal 'social role' and artists ought not to feel that they must 'serve their society'. They will automatically serve it if they attend to truth and try to produce the best art (make the most beautiful things) of which they are capable. The connection of truth with beauty means that art which succeeds in being for itself also succeeds in being for everybody. And even without the guarantee of a Platonic aesthetic, art need not be too humble. Hear the words of Jane Austen (*Northanger Abbey*, Chapter v). ' "And what are you reading Miss –?" "Oh, it is only a novel", replies the young lady; while she lays down her book with affected indifference, or momentary shame. – "It is only Cecilia, or Camilla, or Belinda"; or, in short, only some work in which the greatest powers of the mind are displayed, in which the most thorough knowledge of human nature, the happiest delineation of its varieties, the liveliest effusion of wit and humour are conveyed to the world in the best chosen language.'

The most obvious paradox in the problem under consideration is that Plato is a great artist. It is not perhaps to be imagined that the paradox troubled him too much. Scholars in the land of posterity assemble the work and invent the problems. Plato had other troubles, many of them political. He fought a long battle against sophistry and magic, yet produced some of the most memorable images in European philosophy: the cave, the charioteer, the cunning homeless Eros, the Demiurge cutting the *Anima Mundi* into strips and stretching it out crosswise. He kept emphasising the imageless remoteless of the Good, yet kept returning in his exposition to the most elaborate uses of art. The dialogue form itelf is artful and indirect and abounds in ironical and playful devices. Of course the statements made by art escape into the free ambiguity of human life. Art cheats the religious vocation at the last moment and is inimical to philosophical categories. Yet neither philosophy nor theology can do without it; there has to be a pact between them, like the pact in the *Philebus* between reason and pleasure.

Plato says (*Phaedrus*, Letter VIII) that no sensible man will commit his thought to words and that a man's thoughts are likely to be better than his writings. Without raising philosophical problems about what a man's thoughts *are*, one may reply that the discipline of committing oneself to clarified public form is proper and rewarding: the final and best discoveries are often made in the actual formulation of the statement. The careful responsible skilful use of words is our highest instrument of thought and one of our highest modes of being: an idea which might seem obvious but is not now by any means universally accepted. There may in theoretical studies, as in art, be so-called ultra-verbal insights at any level; but to call ultimate truth ineffable is to utter a quasi-religious principle which should not be turned round against the careful verbalisation of humbler truths. Nor did Plato in practice do this. He wanted what he more than once mentions, immortality through art; he felt and indulged the artist's desire to produce unified, separable, formal, durable objects. He was also the master, indeed, the inventor, of a pure calm relaxed mode of philosophical exposition which is a high literary form and a model for ever. Of course he used metaphor, but philosophy needs metaphor and metaphor is basic; how basic is the most basic philosophical question. Plato also had no doubt a strong personal motive which prompted him to write. Socrates (*Theaetetus*, 210 C) called himself a barren midwife. Plato often uses images of paternity. Art launches philosophy as it launches religion, and it was necessary for Plato, as it was for the evangelists, to write if the Word was not to be sterile and the issue of the Father was to be recognised as legitimate.

Plato feared the consolations of art. He did not offer a consoling theology. His psychological realism depicted God as subjecting mankind to a judgement as relentless as that of the old Zeus, although more just. A finely meshed moral causality determines the fate of the soul. That the movement of the saving of Eros is toward an impersonal pictureless void is one of the paradoxes of a complete religion. To present the idea of God at all, even as myth, is a consolation, since it is impossible to defend this image against the prettifying attentions of art. Art will mediate and adorn, and develop magical structures to conceal the absence of God or his distance. We live now amid the collapse of many such structures, and as religion and metaphysics in the West withdraw from the embraces of art, we are it might seem being forced to become mystics through the lack of any imagery which could satisfy the mind. Sophistry and magic break down at intervals, but they never go away and there is no end to their collusion with art and to the consolations which, perhaps fortunately for the human race, they can provide; and art, like writing and like Eros, goes on existing for better and for worse.

Based upon the Romanes Lecture, 1976.

Art and Eros:
A Dialogue about Art

Characters in order of appearance

CALLISTOS *a beautiful youth*
ACASTOS *a serious youth*
MANTIAS *a political man, in love with Callistos*
DEXIMENES *a cynical man*
PLATO
SOCRATES

Athens in the late fifth century BC.

At the time of the dialogue, Plato is about twenty years old, Socrates about sixty.

Acastos, Callistos, Mantias and Deximenes are fictional characters.

At the house of Deximenes.
Enter Callistos, Acastos, Mantias, Deximenes and Plato. Callistos
carries an actor's mask. Plato sits apart. They have just come from
the theatre.

CALLISTOS: Oh wasn't it great? That last scene was just – *perfect* –
Oh I did enjoy the play! Didn't you, Acastos?

ACASTOS: I'm not sure.

DEXIMENES: Acastos never knows what he feels.

CALLISTOS: You must know what you feel, who else could?

MANTIAS: Is Socrates coming?

CALLISTOS: Oh I do hope Socrates will come!

MANTIAS: Stop jumping around!

CALLISTOS: Did you like the play, Plato?

DEXIMENES: Did you like it?

MANTIAS: No, I never do.

DEXIMENES: Why do you go then?

MANTIAS: One must keep an eye on the theatre, it's an influence.

CALLISTOS: I believe it all when it is happening.

ACASTOS: They say you shouldn't do that, you should sort of realise
that it's a play, and –

MANTIAS: How can you not with actors speaking in those
pretentious unnatural voices!

DEXIMENES: Plays aren't serious. The theatre is cheap magic. Toys
for conceited directors. A chance for half-educated people to
think they've understood something. It's unimportant.

MANTIAS: Nothing people like so much is unimportant.

CALLISTOS: Yes, everybody loves the theatre, not just us intellectuals.

Laughter

DEXIMENES: Art is all in the mind. It's not in the play. We invent the
art experience ourselves.

ACASTOS: So we all have different ones?

MANTIAS: I must say I think the theatre's done everything now, after
what we've had today. We've seen it all!

[465]

DEXIMENES: People always think their art is the end of art.

Callistos, who has been playing with his actor's mask, suddenly puts it on and begins to declaim:

CALLISTOS: Zeus, whoever he may be,

If he cares to bear this name –

MANTIAS: Oh shut up!

DEXIMENES: The theatre is humbug. But who wants it to be like life, it's escape.

CALLISTOS: Yes, who wants it to be like horrid old life? It's a dream world.

DEXIMENES: Monkey business on the stage and private fantasies in the audience!

MANTIAS: It's magic all right. Did you see that audience? How many people? Ten thousand? All sitting absolutely silent and spellbound. Why should they? Why do they *stay* there? Theatre is a kind of miracle, it's an *influence*. Magic can be very useful.

CALLISTOS: You want everything to be useful. Why don't you just enjoy it?

DEXIMENES: He's a politician!

Callistos starts eating some fruit.

MANTIAS: That isn't just for you. Can't you wait? Don't play with it!

CALLISTOS: Oh, you're so socially minded! I think politics should know its place.

MANTIAS: In our society its place is everywhere.

CALLISTOS: Sometimes I think a tyranny would be so relaxing, you wouldn't have to think about politics at all.

ACASTOS: We'll never have tyranny here, after all we *invented* democracy – Yes, I did enjoy the play, and it moved me – but I don't know why.

MANTIAS: Precisely.

ACASTOS: But all sorts of things move us and we don't know why.

MANTIAS: I think we should find out why people are moved.

DEXIMENES: You mean some of us should, so as to control the others!

CALLISTOS: All beauty is like that – it's mysterious –

ACASTOS: Yes – And aren't we forgetting that the plays are a religious festival?

DEXIMENES: Of course we are!

ACASTOS: I don't like seeing the gods portrayed on the stage – after all, how do we know what the gods are like? It's irreverent –

CALLISTOS: You are so old-fashioned. We know what we think about the gods.

ACASTOS: Do we? I don't.

MANTIAS: Religion is important. We shouldn't become too familiar with our gods.

CALLISTOS: There's nothing wrong with irreverence, look at Aristophanes.

DEXIMENES: Well, look at him! (*gesture of disgust*)

MANTIAS: Satire can be influential, it matters what people laugh at.

ACASTOS: I don't think people should laugh at religion, but I think it's good if they can laugh at politicians!

MANTIAS: He who laughs at religion one day will despise his rulers the next. Democracies can perish because in the end people don't believe in anything and don't revere anything.

Enter Socrates. They all rise.

SOCRATES: Well, my dears, did you enjoy the play?

ACASTOS: We were just arguing about it, sir.

CALLISTOS: Bags I sit next to Socrates!

SOCRATES: It's my lucky day!

DEXIMENES: Yes, I saw who you were sitting next to in the theatre.

SOCRATES: I have always worshipped beauty. Who's over there?

CALLISTOS: Plato, he's got one of his moods!

SOCRATES: What was your argument about?

DEXIMENES: Here we go!

CALLISTOS: Deximenes thinks the theatre is magic so it's *not* important, and Mantias thinks the theatre is magic so it *is* important, and Acastos thinks we shouldn't portray the gods, and Mantias thinks it's bad to laugh at people and –

SOCRATES: And what do you think?

CALLISTOS: I think it's fun!

MANTIAS: We were wondering what the theatre was for.

DEXIMENES: Need it be for anything?

CALLISTOS: Everything is for something, isn't it, Socrates?

DEXIMENES: What are you for?

MANTIAS: Need you ask?

SOCRATES: He is young and will have many uses!

ACASTOS: Deximenes says the theatre is false. Can one say that art is true or false?

MANTIAS: I'd rather say good or bad, that is, good or bad for us.

ACASTOS: But you're assuming –

SOCRATES: Wait, wait, not so fast. This is a difficult question. Shall we try to sort it out?

DEXIMENES: You sort it out, Socrates, we'll listen.

SOCRATES: Shall I ask questions and get someone to answer?

DEXIMENES: Who is to stop you, my dear?

SOCRATES: Who shall answer? Let us have the youngest, then if he makes mistakes he need not blush.

DEXIMENES: Who is the youngest?

MANTIAS: Callistos is.

CALLISTOS (*alarmed*): No, no, Plato is younger.

SOCRATES: I think Plato is communing with a god and we should not interrupt him. You shall answer.

CALLISTOS: Well, all right, but please don't be cross if –

DEXIMENES: Socrates is never cross.

SOCRATES: Dear child! Perhaps we should start by considering art in general, and then move from the general to the particular. Do you agree?

MANTIAS: Yes, yes, yes.

SOCRATES: We speak, don't we, of 'the arts' as a *family*. But isn't it *odd* that we should classify them together when they are so unlike? It seems that we can see a common quality. Shall we attempt a definition of art?

ACASTOS: Oh yes!

SOCRATES: Then later we can see whether it can be called true or false, or good or bad, or whether it has a use. This won't be easy, I think. Now since you are the victim today, how would you define art?

CALLISTOS: Well, art is the *Odyssey* and the *Agamemnon* and the *Antigone* and the statue of Athena in the Parthenon and music and –

SOCRATES: Wait a moment, this list could go on for ever! These are *examples* of art. But what is the 'artiness' which makes all these different things art?

CALLISTOS: You mean all art, any art?

SOCRATES: Yes.

CALLISTOS: Well – art is copying.

MANTIAS: Why do you suddenly say that?

SOCRATES: What do you mean by copying?

CALLISTOS: I mean like – like paintings – or like imitations of men and animals like you see on the Acropolis. Art tries to be like what things are really like.

SOCRATES: And the best art is the most like?

CALLISTOS: Yes.

MANTIAS: You're contradicting what you said just now –

SOCRATES: So is sculpture a better art than painting?

CALLISTOS: Well – er –

SOCRATES: Painters represent men in two dimensions whereas sculptors represent them in three dimensions.

DEXIMENES: Be brave!

CALLISTOS: Yes, that's better – and the theatre is the best of all because the actors are real men imitating real men.

ACASTOS (*very fast*): That can't be right, if you mean imitation like comparing a statue with a man. Old statues which don't look like real people are often much better art – and if we just want to imitate real things why have art at all? Real men are more like men than marble men are. Or why not just put a cooking pot on a pedestal and call it art, or a few old bricks or – ?

DEXIMENES: If they were called art at least we'd look at them.

MANTIAS: What does music imitate?

SOCRATES: Don't bully him. Perhaps you would like to restate your definition.

CALLISTOS: Yes, well music doesn't seem to copy anything. A play tells a story of course, and that's like life –

DEXIMENES: Is it?

SOCRATES: Go on, my child, try again.

CALLISTOS: Art is like a sort of form or diagram, it's like life only sort of *different*, like summarised or simplified or –

SOCRATES: Do you want to give up your idea that art is copying, imitation of life?

CALLISTOS: No, but it's copying into a world where everything

[469]

looks different and clearer, and there's no muddle and no horrid accidental things like in life.

ACASTOS: No horrid accidental things!

CALLISTOS: It's like a map.

DEXIMENES: How dull.

SOCRATES: Art is a sort of formal copying into a medium where things look similar but clearer and simpler?

CALLISTOS: Yes!

MANTIAS: Before you came Callistos was saying art was fabulous and marvellous and beautiful and made him happy and so on! Why don't you say that now? Why did you suddenly say that art is copying?

CALLISTOS (*smugly*): Because I know Socrates likes a clear answer even if it's wrong.

SOCRATES: Why did you start by talking about painting?

CALLISTOS: It seems most like what art's really like, I mean here's the thing and here's the picture and you can sort of measure the one against the other.

MANTIAS: Do stop saying 'sort of'!

SOCRATES: Yes, and we often express ideas in visual images, as when we say of music that it's high or low. I'm touched that you tried to please me by saying something clear. But perhaps your idea is still too simple. You spoke of an exact copy, then you spoke of a schematic copy, like a map. Don't you want to add something? When you came out of the theatre you were excited and happy –

MANTIAS: I think we should start again –

Mantias is trying from now on to take over the argument. Acastos also wants to speak and keeps raising his hand. Socrates checks them with a gesture.

CALLISTOS: Yes, when I said about forms and maps that sounds dull, and art isn't dull, it's emotion and excitement and some art is thrilling like music or when you're in the theatre and you don't know what on earth it's about but your heart *beats* and – of course painting isn't exciting like that –

DEXIMENES: Oh come on – isn't it – sometimes?

CALLISTOS (*puzzled for a moment*): You mean like pictures, like

[470]

those *special* pictures in Derkon's house which show – ? Yes, but that's *sex*.

DEXIMENES: Isn't art about sex?

CALLISTOS: Well –

DEXIMENES: Don't blush, you can't shock Socrates.

SOCRATES: He looks charming.

ACASTOS: Of course we all have kinds of pictures of – But those horrible erotic scenes in Derkon's house aren't art at all, they're just designed to –

DEXIMENES: Acastos is such a puritan, almost as bad as Plato.

ACASTOS: Well, what does Plato think?

He turns to Plato, but Plato ignores him.

MANTIAS: What's the matter with him?

DEXIMENES: Jealousy. He wants Socrates all to himself.

MANTIAS: I see he's taking notes again. Socrates told him not to.

SOCRATES: Go on, hold on to your idea, you've just discovered something you want to add, so perhaps you might now restate your definition.

CALLISTOS: You mean with sex in?

SOCRATES: Anything you like in.

DEXIMENES: You needn't call it sex, call it passion.

SOCRATES: What does music do?

CALLISTOS: It expresses feelings and emotions and makes you feel as if the musical pattern went straight into your heart, into your body.

SOCRATES: Don't you want to put something like that into your definition?

DEXIMENES: Oh come on!

CALLISTOS: Art is the expression of feeling, the communication of emotion. All art is like music really.

SOCRATES: You said it was like painting. Now you say it is like music. You used the word pattern. *Now* do you want to give up your idea that art imitates the world, in some way?

CALLISTOS: It won't do for music – unless music copies something we can't see or hear.

SOCRATES: Some say that the gods are always doing geometry. Perhaps they are always composing music too.

ACASTOS: I like that – and we sometimes overhear a little.

CALLISTOS: But art *is* about the world, how real things are changed into a sort of feeling-pattern, a feeling – thought or – sorry, I'm in a muddle –

SOCRATES: Go on, dear boy, don't give up, try to catch something here. Remember, you are doing philosophy – and sometimes when you've been trying really hard to get a glimpse of an idea you can only talk about it in a kind of nonsense. So stop trying to be clear and just talk honest nonsense.

CALLISTOS (*trying hard*): Art is a sort of copying or imitating, because it *is* about the real world somehow, though I'm not sure about music, and it has a pattern and form, so it does change things, it's sort of neater and clearer than life, but it shows us real things with great – *force* – with *emotion* – and through seeing and hearing and imagining – and it's not sort of *analysed*, it's all condensed into one, like a *thing* – and it's exciting and sexy and – oh dear –

SOCRATES: No, no, you've done very well. You've talked most excellent nonsense and helped our argument along splendidly. You said art was like a realistic picture, then you said it was like a map, then you said it was like music where an emotional pattern enters into the body. And just now you spoke of seeing and hearing and imagining. Are all arts something to do with the senses?

CALLISTOS: Yes, I think so –

ACASTOS: But –

SOCRATES: Acastos has been waving his hand at me for some time, let us hear what he has to say.

ACASTOS: I agree that art is to do with the senses – I mean poetry has rhythms and sounds and pictures have shapes and colours, and the body is involved, I don't mean like sex –

DEXIMENES: Why not?

ACASTOS: But really art is *thinking*. I mean, good art is deep wise thinking. And bad art is bad because it's stupid or depraved thinking. Callistos said something about a 'feeling-thought'. I don't know what that is. But I'm sure good art *tells* us something. It isn't just a dose of emotion. It's like vision – insight – knowledge –

SOCRATES: Good, good, you are continuing Callistos's splendid nonsense! Copying, maps, feeling, thinking. Yes, we use all these ideas to help each other out, as each one by itself seems helpless. But still the ideas remain obscure, they stand as it were in a ring holding hands and each idea tries to support the next but cannot support itself. Do you want to keep Callistos's idea that art is imitation of the world?

ACASTOS: Yes, but not simple like a real man and a marble man, it's *indirect*.

CALLISTOS: I said it was different!

ACASTOS: The artist puts thoughts in, he's a judge of reality.

SOCRATES: A judge suggests justice – truth –

ACASTOS: Yes, the idea of copying and judging means *truth* and *morality*. Art has got to be *true*. Deximenes said art is trickery and fantasy and perhaps bad art is, but good art is wisdom and truth. Art is looking at the world and explaining it in a *deep* way and when we understand the explanation or even half understand it we feel oh – such joy – and I think that's what *beauty* is –

DEXIMENES: What about beauty in nature? Nature doesn't explain! *Callistos, let off the hook, pats himself on the back, plays with the mask, tries to put it onto Mantias, who thrusts him away. Plato is listening attentively to what Acastos is saying.*

ACASTOS: A man could copy cleverly, like in pornographic pictures, but if there's no moral judgement and no thought the thing is dead and false. Callistos said art was sexy and I suppose it is sometimes, but I'd rather say it was to do with love, with really loving the world and seeing what it's like. I think good art is passionate and holy.

SOCRATES: I like that, I like that –

ACASTOS: And it's *somehow* true – I'm certain of that –

SOCRATES: Hold on to that certainty, my dear young friend.
Slight pause. Socrates glances at Plato, but Plato will not be drawn in. He drops his head sulkily.
I like your instincts. The good artist is wise, compassionate, just – but we're in deep waters. You'll have to think more carefully about what you mean by saying that good art is true.

DEXIMENES: *Poetry* isn't *true*! This is getting too awfully high-minded for me.

ACASTOS (*increasingly excited by his ideas but confused*): I mean, I think good art is *good* for us, it *teaches* us – great poetry is *wise* –

CALLISTOS (*he has donned the mask again and begins to declaim*): Zeus, whoever he may be,

If he cares to bear this name –

MANTIAS: All this woolly talk has simply brought us to the obvious point which I wanted to make at the start! At last Acastos has quite accidentally said something sensible! He says good art is good for us! That's the whole thing in a nutshell. It's educational. Socrates said your ideas were standing in a circle holding hands and each trying to explain the next and couldn't. My idea breaks the circle. If we think of art as education everything becomes clear, it answers all the questions – it's clear why we classify the arts together, it makes sense of music, it clarifies this notion of morality which Acastos has introduced –

ACASTOS: I don't mean that art is education.

MANTIAS: You said so!

ACASTOS: I said it was good for us.

MANTIAS: What's the difference? I'm concerned with politics and social life, unlike some who are only interested in their own little messy private feelings. Politics is not self-centred, it's to do with other people, with caring, with society. The essence of politics is explanation, that is persuasive explanation.

DEXIMENES: I thought the essence of politics was coercion.

MANTIAS: I said *persuasive* explanation, another name for this is rhetoric. And this explains the nature of art. Art is rhetoric. Not copying or music or thought. Rhetoric.

SOCRATES: You stun us with the simplicity of your idea.

MANTIAS: Well it's so clear. And that's how we distinguish between good and bad art. Good art makes good citizens, bad art makes bad citizens. It's as simple as that.

SOCRATES: Do you *define* good art as art which benefits society?

MANTIAS (*after hesitation but firmly*): Yes.

ACASTOS: Oh no!

CALLISTOS: Horrid!

MANTIAS: The really useful and valuable arts are the ones which make plain statements, stuff you can understand.

DEXIMENES: Lots of poetry is very obscure, or personal, or erotic.

MANTIAS: Art which is private and obsessive is bad, it distracts people from the real world, the *public* world. I should have thought that's obvious and should be of interest to Acastos with his concern for truth! And erotic art makes people think that sex is the whole point of life!

CALLISTOS: Isn't it?

DEXIMENES: All art can be used as pornography. Art happens in the mind. Even great art isn't sacred. We all have obsessions.

MANTIAS: *You* have.

CALLISTOS: Sex is *funny*!

MANTIAS: An art which is solely concerned with sex and personal relations is selfish and untruthful. Wouldn't you agree, Acastos? *Acastos is not sure.*

SOCRATES: Isn't it the nature of art to explore the relation between the public and the private? Art turns us inside out, it exhibits what is secret. What goes on inwardly in the soul is the essence of each man, it's what makes us individual people. The relation between that inwardness and public conduct *is morality*. How can art ignore it?

DEXIMENES: Mantias doesn't believe in individual people.

MANTIAS: Yes, I do! That's just what I do believe in and you don't! Art must overcome the *alienation* of men from each other. It should try to make *sense* of society. (*To Acastos*) That's better than private fantasy, isn't it?

DEXIMENES: If you ban private personal relations you ban the whole of art.

MANTIAS: Our painting and our sculpture represent people who are physically healthy. I think our arts should represent people who are morally healthy!

SOCRATES: Who are these people?

MANTIAS: Good citizens.

DEXIMENES: I know, healthy handsome young men performing valuable social duties!

MANTIAS: All right, you jeer at the idea of the good citizen! What have *you* ever done with all that cleverness and idealism you had when we were *their* age?
Deximenes is hurt.

I'm sorry. This society is full of injustice and misery. Isn't it, Acastos? Yes or no?

ACASTOS: Yes.

MANTIAS: Won't the whole man, the decent man, try to change this, won't he devote all he has to changing it? Why should artists be exempt? Why shouldn't they use their talents to help their society? Art is a thought concealed in an emotional package, as Acastos said –

ACASTOS: I didn't – I don't think I did –

MANTIAS: Emotion is important but it must be simplified –

SOCRATES: Callistos made a distinction between realistic copying, and formal schematic representation, like a map. What would your simplified art be like?

MANTIAS: Formal and schematic, but realistic enough to be plausible. The meaning must be clear to everybody.

DEXIMENES: And not just to us intellectuals, as Callistos would say!

MANTIAS: Precisely. Intellectuals are usually self-indulgent people who think refined private thoughts and neglect the public good.

ACASTOS: But you're an intellectual!

DEXIMENES: He's a boss-type intellectual.

ACASTOS: You want art to be propaganda!

MANTIAS: Art is education. All education propagates values. They may as well be the right values. No?

ACASTOS: But if it's propaganda and persuasion it isn't true!

MANTIAS: Socrates told you to think what you mean by 'true'. When we make moral judgements on people we're trying to persuade them, we're trying to affect their conduct, aren't we – *aren't* we?

ACASTOS: Well –

MANTIAS: You admire Pericles, don't you?

ACASTOS: Yes.

MANTIAS: Wasn't he a persuader, a great rhetorician, all those marvellous speeches – You've got to *encourage* your citizens, make them confident, proud of their state –

DEXIMENES: Give them a glorious past!

MANTIAS: It matters how we see our past, that's obvious.

DEXIMENES: Some things are better forgotten, some things must never be forgotten!

ACASTOS: We never let anyone forget that we defeated the Persians!

MANTIAS: All right! Every country has a selective tradition. Most Persians have probably never heard of the Battle of Marathon!

ACASTOS: What you call selective tradition is lying! We ought to tell the truth about the past.

MANTIAS: You keep on using the word 'truth' as if it were some sort of decisive weapon, or even a reasonably clear idea. History is persuasive speculation, it's fabulation. What can we know about 'what really happened'? Literature *invents* the past, that's why it's so important, it must go on inventing the past that the present needs!

ACASTOS: You make it all sound like lying!

MANTIAS: It's bound to be what you call lying, I want it to be useful purified lying.

DEXIMENES: Purified lying – that's good!

MANTIAS: Art isn't like nature, even 'realism' isn't, words can't express things, they can't go out and touch them, words aren't names –

SOCRATES: Wait a moment. You say we can't know the past, we can only make up useful stories about it. Now you're talking about language generally. You mean words can't picture reality at all?

MANTIAS: That's what I mean!

SOCRATES: How do you know? Do you look at words and then at reality and –

MANTIAS (*floundering*): I mean – really there's no such thing as 'reality' or 'nature', it's not just sitting there, we *make* it out of words – ideas – concepts –

ACASTOS: So language doesn't refer to the world?

SOCRATES: Wait, we must see what Mantias is up to, what he really *wants*, metaphysicians usually *want* something or other. Of course words are not just names, the operation of language is very complicated, we use all sorts of conceptual tricks to relate to our surroundings, we often disagree about how to do it. It certainly does *not* follow from this, that there is no independent world such as common sense takes for granted.

DEXIMENES (*knocking a table*): Of course there's an independent world.

SOCRATES: Not a bad argument!

MANTIAS: It's a stupid argument, as you perfectly well know.

Language has meaning through internal coherence, it's not like a window we look through.

SOCRATES: Well, sometimes it's like a window, and often it's not coherent. Perhaps you are thinking of mathematics or of some language used by the gods. Our natural mortal language is a much more messy business and very difficult to theorise about. Let us say that your hypothesis is interesting but rather far-fetched! Our language is being broken and tested and altered all the time in relation to *something else* which certainly *seems* to be 'just sitting there', quite pleased with itself, and indifferent to our ingenuity and our wishes! This is our most evident and primary experience. Of course it is mysterious, consciousness itself is the most mysterious thing of all, and philosophers feel challenged by mysteries. But philosophy can't always say something systematic and universal and marvellous! Faced with something so very – difficult – I think we should be careful and modest and hold on to common sense and our ordinary conceptions of truth. Reality resists us, it is contingent, it transcends us, it surprises us, language is a *struggle*, we live on a borderline –

ACASTOS (*bursting in*): We must have words *and* reality or we can't distinguish true and false!

SOCRATES: I think Mantias would like to blur or reinterpret that distinction, that is his point, that is what his metaphysical theory is *for*. He would like to substitute useful or useless, or coherent or non-coherent, or perhaps significant-now and not significant-now. He would regard this as a *political* idea of some importance.

MANTIAS: Yes, and an obvious one too! Language makes men, it *speaks* men, it determines what they see and understand – it's not just an adventure playground for writers – it must be made to *work* in the present and *serve* society –

SOCRATES: So really language is not description, it's more like orders?

MANTIAS: Well, yes – I mean, we don't want to explain the world, we want to change it!

ACASTOS: But if words aren't true or false what are *we* doing now arguing with each other?

DEXIMENES: We are exempt, Acastos! People who talk like Mantias always exclude themselves from their generalisations! It's only the simple folk who talk like parrots!

MANTIAS: All right, but let's not be too modest, very few people can *invent* concepts and ideas –

DEXIMENES: That's the new tyranny in a nutshell, a programme for tyrants! A few rules manipulating the language, and the mass of ordinary chaps enjoying plausible simple social art! Words perish, and nobody can speak the truth!

ACASTOS (*fast*): Socrates says we live on a borderline, yes we're *all* out there, using words and inventing concepts and struggling with reality and keeping the language alive and making it say true things, and that's why literature is so important, and –

CALLISTOS: Jokes are works of art too!

SOCRATES: Yes, good! (*Everyone is trying to talk*) Be quiet, my children! I don't want this argument to become too abstract and lose its bite. In philosophy you must locate your problem (*gestures*) and then hold it firmly and turn it round to see its different faces. Now – Acastos sees art as essentially free reflection and truth-telling. Mantias sees it as carefully planted signposts to good and bad, or rather useful and useless –

MANTIAS: Yes, that's what I mean by good and bad. Writers should take sides with good. (*To Acastos*) You can't disagree with that!

ACASTOS: If you detach writers from ordinary free truth they'll just play with language!

MANTIAS: They should portray good men in a clear intelligent way, and show them overcoming bad men.

SOCRATES: So they will portray bad men too?

MANTIAS: Yes, but the bad men must not be interesting or attractive, they must be schematically represented –

ACASTOS: You mean caricatured?

MANTIAS: And never shown as successful.

SOCRATES: Yet in real life bad men are often both interesting and successful. And good men are often dull, because they are quiet and steady, whereas bad men are unstable and odd.

ACASTOS: Surely there are plenty of interesting good men in literature.

SOCRATES: Name some.

DEXIMENES: Who are our great literary heroes? Crooks to a man.

Achilles, the biggest egoist ever. Odysseus, a swindler and a liar. The whole cast of the stupid pointless Trojan war are one lot of ruthless thugs against another lot.

ACASTOS: Hector.

DEXIMENES: Proves my point, a nonentity. Who doesn't side with Achilles?

ACASTOS: I don't.

CALLISTOS: My dear, Achilles is a Greek!

DEXIMENES: Agamemnon, a power-crazy general, Clytemnestra, a murderer, Antigone, a selfish opinionated trouble-maker. And some of the greatest crooks of all are the gods. No wonder no one believes in them any more.

ACASTOS: I believe in the gods.

CALLISTOS: So does Socrates.

DEXIMENES: No, the religious era is over. Who's going to believe those stories now? Who really thinks that Zeus is an old man with a beard somewhere up there?

CALLISTOS (*softly*): Zeus, whoever he may be –

ACASTOS: Some people say the myths are true but sort of symbolic. What do you think, Socrates?

SOCRATES: I think that religion will always be with us, and we shall continually remake it into something we can believe. You see, we want to be certain that goodness rests upon reality. And as this desire will never go away, we shall always be searching for the gods. We want to love what is pure and holy, and to know that it is *safe*.

ACASTOS: Safe?

SOCRATES: Inviolable, indestructible, *real*.

CALLISTOS: But do the gods exist?

SOCRATES: Here we reach the end of what words can do. The gods concern the inmost heart of each man – and about this he can only speak to himself – and to them.

ACASTOS: Can't we always invent language, like poets do?

SOCRATES: There is a very great distance between the human and the divine. We must hope the gods will come to us. Perhaps there is something in us which belongs to them and which they will claim – in their own way. A man should follow virtue and look toward the good – and be content to *know* what he cannot *say*.

ACASTOS: But – *does* goodness rest upon reality?

SOCRATES (*just for Acastos*): Yes, my dear.

MANTIAS: No sensible politician wants to destroy religion. Religion is an image of authority. People must take the exercise of authority for granted. That is the mystery of government, that men will obey other men, and that many men will obey few men. Nothing could be more disastrous for a state than the disappearance of a generally accepted religion. As soon as the myth of government is challenged the state descends into anarchy.

ACASTOS: You call it a myth.

MANTIAS: It's the most important myth of all. *Obedience.*

ACASTOS: You talk as if ordinary people were stupid or semi-criminal.

MANTIAS: Any practical politician assumes that! Of course the state must control art. If it doesn't it is wasting a precious source of power. All that emotion in the theatre today, wasted, just rising up uselessly into the sky! What an energy loss!

SOCRATES: What is such control usually called?

MANTIAS: Censorship.

ACASTOS: I'm against it.

CALLISTOS: Me too.

SOCRATES: We must not be afraid of names.

MANTIAS: Every state exercises some censorship. (*To Acastos*) Do you want pornographic muck to circulate, like those pictures you hate so? Would you like children to see them?

ACASTOS: Well – no – but –

MANTIAS: And you're so keen on the rights of minorities, under-privileged groups or whatever jargon you use. Would you like to see plays in our theatres which encourage people to be unkind to slaves and women?

DEXIMENES: They don't need encouragement.

MANTIAS: You say slavery is contrary to nature. Don't you want to silence people who say slaves are just animals?

DEXIMENES: Acastos thinks animals have rights too!

MANTIAS: Well things then.

DEXIMENES: Things lib!

MANTIAS: Art must not stir up useless violence or make us hate people just because they're foreigners –

CALLISTOS: Can't we hate anyone, not even bloody Spartans?

DEXIMENES: Arguments like this are futile because they assume that we can change things – we can't. None of us can control the state, even tyrants can't. We always talk as if *we* could, we, the intellectuals. But no one controls it – it's a machine that rolls on under its own laws. Who understands economics? The economists don't, how can we? We are passengers not drivers in this chariot. There are no drivers.

MANTIAS: People say that who haven't the wit to see who the drivers are! That sort of talk leads straight to tyranny or mob rule!

DEXIMENES: What about you – You'd be arresting poets because you couldn't understand their poems!

ACASTOS: I suppose your dull bad art could do some good –

DEXIMENES: Like stories telling children to wash!

MANTIAS: Then you agree with me!

ACASTOS: No! I don't want to argue your argument at all – I meant – Oh help me, Socrates!

SOCRATES: Well, we could discuss whether censorship or freedom is better – but I think Acastos wants to say that we have lost sight of our original objective. If we could discover what art really is we would also see how it relates to society.

CALLISTOS: Oh let's forget society!

SOCRATES: Now you wish to *define* art in terms of its social role, and this is what Acastos objects to. (*Acastos is nodding agreement.*) Now would you agree that art is a skill?

MANTIAS: Yes.

SOCRATES: And properly to understand a skill one must understand what it is to exercise it well? Very well?

MANTIAS (*dubiously*): Yes.

ACASTOS: That's it, Mantias won't really *look* at what I call good art.

SOCRATES: You have different views of what the skill *is*. So you must reject his definition.

ACASTOS: I do, I refuse to define good art as good-for-society art. Art must be free and on its own because that's how it will tell us the truth and show us the things that are really – high – and real – I mean, it's like the human spirit talking – good art just can't help being good for society, but artists mustn't think about that. Good

[482]

artists are trying to understand something and show something which they see – their duty is to be good artists. Good art explains to us how the world is changing and it judges change, it's the highest wisest choice of morality, it's something spiritual – without good art a society dies. It's like religion really – it's our best speech and our best understanding – it's a proof of the greatness and goodness which is in us and –

DEXIMENES: And everything follows from that, I suppose, including the liberation of slaves and women!

ACASTOS: Yes!

SOCRATES: What a Protean monster our art turns out to be! Copies, maps, thoughts, music, games, rhetoric, social service, and now religion!

CALLISTOS: My head's spinning. Pass the wine, old cock.

DEXIMENES: Old cock!

ACASTOS: You see – what we call inspiration –

DEXIMENES: He's off again.

Plato utters a low groan.

SOCRATES: Did I hear a sound? Did young Plato utter an observation? Or did some passing god groan over our follies?

PLATO: Oh what nonsense you all talk! I don't mean Socrates but he's just making you hold forth and not correcting you.

DEXIMENES: You correct us then, *dear* boy!

SOCRATES: We have so far lacked the benefit of your opinion.

PLATO: Oh it's so –

CALLISTOS: Plato's so emotional and extreme, he gets so cross!

DEXIMENES: You mean he takes it all seriously.

CALLISTOS: There's no need to be rude.

SOCRATES: Would you like to join our conversation?

PLATO: Yes.

DEXIMENES: Yes, please.

SOCRATES: Then be a little kind to us. If you roar at us like a wild beast we shall be too frightened to talk to you.

DEXIMENES: I'd box his ears for him.

CALLISTOS: Of course we are philosophers and Plato is a poet so we must make allowances –

ACASTOS: At least you can tell us who you agree with.

PLATO: I agree with Deximenes.

Laughter.

CALLISTOS: You can't!

DEXIMENES: I'm touched by this unexpected tribute.

PLATO: Art is lies, it's fantasy, it's play, it's humbug, it's make-believe, the theatre is rubbish, it's –

SOCRATES: Dear boy, don't shout at us. Either talk seriously and honestly or go away.

PLATO: And I think philosophy is lies too.

ACASTOS: How can you say that in front of Socrates!

PLATO: I'm sorry –

SOCRATES: That can be argued also, by a philosophical argument. If you want to talk to us you must join this discussion, not start another one. You have been listening to us and even thought some of our nonsense worth writing down. But please don't say what you don't mean.

PLATO: I'm very sorry, but really, you're all so unserious about art, as if it were a sort of side issue. As if one could say there's the navy and the silver mines and the war and the latest news about Alcibiades and this and that and then of course there's art and – But art is – in a way it's almost *everything* – you don't see how deep art is, and how *awful* it is!

CALLISTOS: I think your poems are rather nice.

SOCRATES: Explain yourself, my dear Plato, since you've found your tongue at last, and do it *quietly*.

PLATO: Art is full of horrible things which it makes us accept –

DEXIMENES: Life is full of horrible things, why shouldn't art be?

PLATO: Life is accidental, art isn't. You were talking about Achilles and how we all love him and we *identify* with him. But he slaughters all those Trojan prisoners beside the funeral pyre of Patroclus. And Odysseus whom everyone admires, when he comes home he hangs all the servant girls just because they went to bed with the suitors. And he murders all the suitors, and this ghastly blood bath is supposed to be great art –

DEXIMENES: Why shouldn't he kill the suitors?

PLATO: There you are! Because it's art you stop thinking! Because it's art you can murder prisoners and hang silly helpless women and slaughter a lot of people who haven't done any harm except hang around your house and propose honourable marriage to your widow, they didn't rape her!

DEXIMENES: But such things happen in life –

PLATO: Yes, but why celebrate them in art? And I agree with Mantias about malicious laughter being evil. So why does Homer show us the gods laughing spitefully at Hephaistos? And this is the poet whom we're all supposed to admire and love.

DEXIMENES: You admire and love him.

PLATO: Yes, but I'm irrational (*laughter*). And we're all waiting for Agamemnon to be murdered, we're licking our lips at the idea of Clytemnestra using an axe on her husband –

ACASTOS: You said you agree with Deximenes –

PLATO: Yes, art is erotic, all art is erotic.

CALLISTOS: He means all good art.

DEXIMENES: No, he means all bad art.

PLATO: Even Sophocles –

SOCRATES: Wait, wait, wait, don't just deluge us with examples. You have asked some interesting questions, but let us go along slowly as we have to do in philosophy and not just rush away after every new thing. Let us review our argument so far, and then Plato can leap off the end of it and spread his wings in the air. Callistos said that art was copying, then he said that it was like a map, then he said that it stirred up the emotions and was like music. And Acastos said that it was thinking and truthful vision. And Mantias said that it was rhetoric or propaganda. And Acastos was so shocked by this that he said it was religion.

DEXIMENES: And don't forget my view, which Plato says he agrees with, that art is fantasy. Art objects are fake objects, we invent them ourselves, it's just private fantasy in our minds. Callistos said that art aspires to the condition of music, Acastos said it aspires to the condition of religion, I say it aspires to the condition of pornography.

SOCRATES: Before we proceed I am going to be a little unkind to somebody.

CALLISTOS: Oh not to me!

SOCRATES: No, to Mantias.

MANTIAS: Oh!

SOCRATES: I am going to ask you to put aside your definition of art as a socially useful craft.

MANTIAS: Why?

SOCRATES: Just now I distinguished your question of the *use* of art and Acastos's question about what art is.

MANTIAS: But I define art by its use.

SOCRATES: Many things are socially useful. You say art is a socially useful craft – and if we ask what *sort* of socially useful craft, the answer is, an *artistic* one. But to understand this we must first have a more fundamental idea of what art really is.

MANTIAS: I don't follow –

SOCRATES: Much of what you said about the *effect* of art is important. But we cannot define art by its effect without *first* considering its nature, since other things could produce the same effect.

MANTIAS: Oh all right –

Callistos embraces him.

SOCRATES: Now, my dear splendid clever boy, try to put your thoughts in order, don't just pour them over us like a bath attendant. Think, my child, think, you *can* think.

PLATO (*after holding his head for a moment*): Of course we must ask about good and bad art in order to see what art is. Bad art is nothing, it's fantasy, like we have when we imagine ourselves great and wonderful – or like sentimental rubbish or Mantias's dull improving stories. And of course bad art can be harmful like pornographic muck or like stories designed to make people hate each other – you know – But to see how dangerous and terrible art is we have to see what *good* art is like, why we tolerate it, why we *love* it, why we sit in the theatre –

ACASTOS: What about inspiration?

PLATO: All right, good art is not just selfish fantasy and that's why you want to call it 'true'. But what is this inspiration and how does it differ from what makes us have stupid fantasies and daydreams? It's something so *deep* –

DEXIMENES: You mean it's erotic.

PLATO: I don't want to use that word, sometimes words are spoilt. I mean something which can be either bad or good –

SOCRATES: Sometimes when words fail us we have to turn to the gods and utter their holy and untainted names.

PLATO: Yes. Let us call it Eros. Art comes from the deep soul where a great force lives, and this force is sex and love and desire – desire for power, desire for possession, sexual desire, desire for beauty, desire for knowledge, desire for God – what makes us good, or bad – and without this force there is no art, and no science either, and no – no man – without Eros man is a ghost. But with Eros he can be – either a demon or – Socrates.

DEXIMENES: Socrates is a good demon.

CALLISTOS: But you do mean sex, don't you?

PLATO: Not in your sense.

ACASTOS: Love, then.

PLATO: Love, what's that? A tyrant loves power, a lecher loves women, Deximenes loves music, or it can be intellectual –

SOCRATES: Theaetetus loves mathematics

ACASTOS: You mean art comes out of a passion which can be either good or bad, and good art comes out of a good passion, but that's just what I was saying, why it tells truth, and why it must be *free*, and why it does serve society, but not in Mantias's way. Because of this passion, which is a kind of *vision*, artists can see truth and tell truth, they can tell more truth than anyone else, they can *communicate* it –

PLATO: So you think, I would like to agree, but art is more terrible, more ambiguous, no wonder rulers fear it and want to tame it, as Mantias does, and make it little and mean and small. Art's so attractive, poetry transforms horror and wickedness into beauty. Art can make terrible things into wonderful things and that's the biggest lie of all.

DEXIMENES: Call it a half-truth. Can human beings bear more than half the truth? They're lucky to have half. That's what's called escape and thank God for it!

PLATO: Escape! But we must not escape. Art is the highest escape route, it's the last exit, and that is why it is the most dangerous.

DEXIMENES: Since few people ever get as far as your last exit I don't think it matters very much.

CALLISTOS: But what are we escaping *from*?

PLATO: Art is dangerous to philosophy, it's dangerous to religion. It masquerades as the whole truth and makes us content with something less. And people idolise it so, Deximenes said the theatre makes fools think they've understood something. The language of art can also make people who are not fools think they have understood something, it can make them stop going on.

CALLISTOS: Going on *where*?

PLATO: I think – I think that the human mind, the human soul is a vast region most of which is dark. There are different parts, different levels. There are dark low levels where we are hardly individual people at all –

Plato has come nearer to Socrates and speaks to him eloquently, almost like a lover. Socrates smiles.

ACASTOS (*intently listening*): Is *that* Eros?

PLATO: Eros is there. This darkness is sex, power, desire, inspiration, *energy* for good or evil. Many people live their whole lives in that sort of darkness, seeing nothing but flickering shadows and illusions, like images thrown on a screen – and the only energy they ever have comes from egoism and dreams. They don't know what the real world is like at all. Not only could they not understand any difficult thought, they cannot even *see* ordinary things – like that wine cup or the face of Socrates – because anxiety and selfishness are making them blind, they live behind a dark veil.

ACASTOS: Do you mean evil people?

DEXIMENES: Sounds like most of us!

PLATO: Then there's another level where people understand a little about the world and live by habits and a few simple ideas.

CALLISTOS: Dull people.

PLATO: They have illusions too, like accepting conventions and prejudices without thinking about them, and being selfish in an orderly prudent sort of way, buying things for their houses and so on –

DEXIMENES: That sounds like most of us too!

PLATO: All these people are like – like living in a cave. They see only shadows, they don't see the real world or the light of the sun. But then sometimes some people can get out of the cave –

CALLISTOS: This all sounds rather élitist to me.

PLATO: When they get out they're *amazed*, they see real things in the sunlight, their minds are awakened and they understand – and oh – the world, when you understand it and can see it, even a little – can be so beautiful – and the anxiety and the mean egoism go away and your eyes are unveiled – perhaps it's only for a short time, because the light of the sun dazzles you – and you begin to know about what Acastos calls the truth, and see the difference between truth and falsehood in the clear light of truth itself –

ACASTOS: Like when you really understand mathematics.

PLATO: Yes, like when you *really* understand anything – And that's *difficult* – I don't just mean slick cleverness, I mean something which shakes the whole soul and opens it out into some large brightness and this is love too, when we love real things and see them distinctly in a clear light.

MANTIAS: What about the people they've left behind in the dark?

PLATO: And when we begin to know and to find out, it's wonderful, it's like remembering, as if we were coming home to a spiritual world where we really belong.

MANTIAS: Is this some sort of *religious* theory?

PLATO: And then the highest thing of all, there's wisdom, and all the things you understand, the hard things, come together somehow, and you see that they're *connected*, and that's real wisdom, which is goodness and virtue and freedom – real freedom like what most people who talk about freedom can't conceive of – and this isn't just intellectual understanding, it's spiritual, it's what we really think in our hearts about the gods, like Socrates said – and that's Eros too, the high, the heavenly Eros, love made perfect and wise and good – and that far far point, that's truth, seeing everything in the light of the sun – and then – seeing the sun itself – and that's goodness – and joy –

DEXIMENES: Dear me.

CALLISTOS: It's those mystery religions, they take drugs, you know.

ACASTOS: This is a bit like something Socrates said once, but you make it all sound different. Socrates never said that everything was connected.

DEXIMENES: May I ask, are we all living at these different levels all the time?

PLATO: I'm not sure –

ACASTOS: I like your picture – very much – though I can't understand it.

DEXIMENES: Neither can he.

ACASTOS: But where does art come in? Of course I see that a lot of art is just shadows and illusions, images on a flickering screen –

DEXIMENES: The fantasy of the artist arousing the fantasy of the viewer.

ACASTOS: But what about good art?

PLATO: Is there any?

DEXIMENES: Oh come – !

ACASTOS: Yes, of course!

PLATO: Don't we deceive ourselves? We want to worship artists because they save us trouble. They give the illusion of thinking great thoughts. But art is never far from fantasy, and the people who enjoy it degrade it even further! Art isn't something up in heaven in an airtight box looked after by Apollo, it's just words or pictures which people find attractive!

ACASTOS (*confused*): But language does refer to a separate reality, and –

PLATO: That reality is *separate* is my point! Any language depends on some sense of true and false, but language is as good as its user. Most people only believe in themselves, they don't *really* think other people exist, they don't *explore* the real world, it's too difficult and painful, and their language is weak and limited, just a network of illusions. And of course many *high* things can be hard to express, hard to say at all except to somebody else who understands. Language travels with the soul, it becomes purer through trying to tell truth. Reality is difficult to get to, we have to try –

DEXIMENES: You mean we ought to try. But can't we separate truth and goodness?

PLATO: No. They're interlocked. That's just where art misleads us, it seems to remove the difficulty, it produces such a strong impression that we imagine we've arrived, that we're in the presence of something real! Good art can be a kind of image or *imitation* of goodness. That's how it deceives enlightened people and stops them from trying to become better. It's a kind of sacrilege. If you believe in the gods, whatever they may be, you know that they make some absolute pure demand – the highest thing of all – it's like when an athlete in the Games is strained almost beyond endurance, almost to dying. Art softens the demand of the gods. It puts an attractive veil over that *final* awful demand, that final transformation into goodness, the almost impossible *last step* which is what human life is really all about. *Pause.*

DEXIMENES: That's what you meant by the last exit.

MANTIAS: I'm all for religion but this is crazy.

CALLISTOS: I think Plato hates art because he's envious. He's envious of the great poets, he wishes he was one.

PLATO: Art is the final cunning of the human soul which would rather do anything than face the gods.

Pause. Then Socrates chuckles. Plato, who has been exalted, now smiles, spreads his arms, falls on one knee before Socrates.

SOCRATES: You have spoken beautifully and given praise to that and to those, to whom praise is due and perhaps with this hymn of praise we ought to end our discussion.

ACASTOS: Oh, no!

SOCRATES: I'm afraid that the simple and homely things which any of us might now wish to say would seem an anti-climax after this paean of eloquence. But since art has found such a potent enemy, perhaps a humble devotee might just say one or two brief things in her defence. We must not be too stunned by our young friend's rhetoric – for he is a persuasive fellow – and he does what persuaders often do, he makes different things seem the same, he says good art is 'really' the same as bad art. Whereas Acastos thinks the difference between them is very great and important. When we find a generally held distinction we are wise not to blur it before we look to see if it shows something true. It may be that the only art you would praise is practised in heaven when Apollo and the Muses delight the ears of the other gods. But here below the difference between good and bad art as we know it remains significant. It is true that we do often prefer illusions and magic to the hard task of thinking – and that the *half-truth* may be the comforting place where we stop trying.

CALLISTOS: I don't see why we should try at all.

SOCRATES (*stroking Callistos's hair*): Callistos asks a good question.

PLATO: We try because our home is elsewhere and it draws us like a magnet.

SOCRATES: This too is a poetic image and may be a comforting one. You yourself said earlier that art is everywhere. Callistos unkindly suggested that you envy the great poets, perhaps you do. Art is a fundamental method of explanation, and this is what Acastos was trying to say to us when he talked so well earlier on. And it is a *natural* mode of explanation for human beings and one which, in your eloquence, you use yourself. Our home may be elsewhere, but we are condemned to exile, to live here with our fellow exiles. And we have to live with language and with words. You have spoken reverently about what is highest, and whatever belief we hold about the gods we may understand you. You say art consoles us and prevents us from taking the final step. You say art is a last exit or a second best. It may be that human beings can only achieve a second best, that second best is our best. (*Plato is shaking his head.*) Perhaps not only art but all our highest speculations, the highest achievements of our spirit, are second best. Homer is imperfect. Science is imperfect. Any high thinking of which we are capable is faulty. Not everything connects, my dear Plato. We are not gods. What you call the whole truth is only for them. So our truth must include, must *embrace* the idea of the second best, that all our thought will be incomplete and all our art tainted by selfishness. This doesn't mean there is no difference between the good and the bad in what we achieve. And it doesn't mean not trying. It means trying in a humble modest truthful spirit. *This* is our truth.

PLATO: You mean we can't get all the way.

SOCRATES: No.

PLATO: Philosophy can get all the way.

SOCRATES: No.

PLATO: If I thought that, I could not imagine wanting to be a philosopher at all.

DEXIMENES: You will never be a philosopher, you are far too emotional.

SOCRATES: It may even be that, as Acastos says, good art tells us more truth about our lives and our world than any other kind of thinking or speculation – it certainly speaks to more people. And perhaps the language of art is the most universal and *enduring* kind of human thought. We are mixed beings, as you said yourself, mixed of darkness and light, sense and intellect, flesh and spirit – the language of art is the highest native natural language of that condition. And you were right to say that art is not just a rare skill. We are all artists, we are all story-tellers. We all have to live by art, it's our daily bread – by what our language gives us, by what we invent for ourselves, by what we steal from others. And we should thank the gods for great artists who draw away the veil of anxiety and selfishness and show us, even for a moment, another world, a real world, and tell us a little bit of truth. And we should not be too hard on ourselves for being comforted by art.

ACASTOS: Hear, hear!

CALLISTOS (*teasing Plato*): Give in, give in!

Plato laughs. The gathering is beginning to break up.

ACASTOS: You spoke of Eros. Don't you think that – on that *path* – that way – whether we can ever reach the end of it or not – that just loving each other – I mean loving as we love – and not only as lovers – is something that is – wonderful and – perhaps teaches most of all?

PLATO: Human love is so selfish.

CALLISTOS: Plato won't love until he has become a god and can love another god!

PLATO (*to Acastos, laughingly*): Yes, yes, of course – you are right.

They all laugh, touching each other.

MANTIAS: You should go into politics, young fellow. You could go far. Come round to my place some time, we'll talk about it.

Callistos, who has been putting his mask on again, sees his chance and leaps up on to a table and begins to recite.

CALLISTOS: Zeus whoever he may be
If he cares to bear this name
By it I will clamour to
Zeus – no other can I see

[493]

To lift from soul the sullen weight,
But only he, who writes in thought
His fierce decree
That wisdom must be bought by pain.
As the slow ache comes again
Dripping grief on sleeping men,
So will wisdom come unsought
To those who never wanted to be taught.

Plato listens in anguish, tries to cover his ears. The others smile, allowing themselves to be moved by the poetry. At last Plato rushes at Callistos and drags him down and pulls the mask off.

PLATO: Oh stop – stop –

CALLISTOS: Don't be so rough!

DEXIMENES: Envy – envy – Plato knows he will never be a great poet.

PLATO: I'm going to destroy all my poems – tonight – I'll tear them up!

SOCRATES: Now, now, my children, be at peace, and don't tear things up, especially not poems. Our talk has moved under its own laws to a conclusion and has left us many things to talk about on another day. Let me thank you all – Deximenes, I thank you for your hospitality and this excellent and inspiring wine, I thank Mantias for so generously holding back his argument, I thank Acastos for being so certain that art is truth – and I thank Plato, who is youngest, for producing such a great shower of hazy, golden thoughts.

CALLISTOS: What about me?

SOCRATES: I thank you for being the most beautiful.

MANTIAS: I think he did very well.

DEXIMENES: You are the most beautiful, Socrates.

SOCRATES: And let us thank the gods for the gift of love, which Acastos spoke so truly of just now, and thank the god who *is* love, whom Plato praised with so much poetic eloquence. In truly loving each other we learn more perhaps than in all our other studies.

Laughing and embracing each other they begin to go away. Plato and Socrates are last.

PLATO: Oh –

SOCRATES: What?

PLATO: I'm so happy. I don't know why. I love you so much.

SOCRATES: I'm so glad, Come – and – dear boy –

PLATO: Yes?

SOCRATES: Don't write it all down!

Plato laughs. Socrates puts his arm round him and leads him off.

Art and Eros received its first three performances as National Theatre Platform events, directed by Michael Kustow, in February 1980, with Andrew Cruikshank as Socrates, Greg Hicks as Plato, Adam Norton as Acastos, Robin McDonald as Callistos, Anthony Douse as Mantias, Michael Beint as Deximenes. It was published in *Acastos: Two Platonic Dialogues*, 1986.

Above the Gods:
A Dialogue about Religion

Characters in order of appearance

A SERVANT
ANTAGORAS *a sophist, in love with Timonax*
TIMONAX *a socially conscious youth*
ACASTOS *a serious questing youth*
SOCRATES
PLATO
ALCIBIADES

Athens in the late fifth century BC.

Socrates is about sixty years old, Alcibiades about forty, Plato about twenty.

Acastos, Antagoras and Timonax are fictional characters.

At the house of Antagoras. The servant is arranging wine and fruit. Enter, garlanded after a religious festival, Antagoras, Timonax and Acastos. Acastos smiles at the servant, who bows and withdraws. They fiddle with their garlands.

ACASTOS: I love religious festivals, they're such fun.

TIMONAX: *Fun?*

ACASTOS: Well, of course it's serious, it's a solemn occasion –

TIMONAX: I thought you didn't believe in fun!

ANTAGORAS: Religious people always have to pretend they enjoy it, it's their least elegant form of hypocrisy!

TIMONAX: Let's have a drink.

Enter Socrates. They all rise and wait till he is seated. They sit. Antagoras pulls Timonax to sit with him.

SOCRATES (*To Antagoras*): How kind of you to invite us.

ANTAGORAS: My house is honoured.

SOCRATES: Where's young Plato?

TIMONAX: Please not Plato, he's so emotional, he always spoils the argument, he gets cross when he can't explain his ideas.

ACASTOS: My garland is full of fleas!

TIMONAX: So is mine!

Hasty removal of garlands.

ANTAGORAS: They recycle these things. What an image of human life, flowers full of fleas!

ACASTOS (*watching the fleas with sympathy*): Ah, look at them!

ANTAGORAS: Animal lover!

SOCRATES: Acastos, did I hear you say you thought the festival was fun, and then you felt you had to say it was 'a solemn occasion'.

TIMONAX: Off we go!

SOCRATES: Did you mean to contradict yourself? Ought we all to have had long faces?

ACASTOS (*tense*): No. Yes. Perhaps we should. People were laughing and playing about.

TIMONAX: Including you.

ANTAGORAS: Horse play. Our people have no dignity.

TIMONAX: It was a holiday!

SOCRATES (*to Acastos*): You disapprove?

ACASTOS: I *think* I disapprove. I mean, it's not *just* a holiday, we're supposed to be honouring the gods.

ANTAGORAS: You don't believe in the gods.

ACASTOS: Well – yes, I do –

TIMONAX: Come off it, Acastos!

ACASTOS: In a way – sort of – I believe in *religion*.

SOCRATES: Can we distinguish religion from belief in gods?

Enter Plato. He clicks his heels and bows to Socrates.

ACASTOS: Oh, Plato, hello. Here – (*indicating a place beside him*)

TIMONAX: Do you believe in the gods, Plato?

Plato ignores him, sits beside Acastos.

Plato's garland's full of fleas. Why don't you wash sometimes?

ACASTOS: They all are!

Plato, irritated, unamused, removes his garland and tosses it away.

TIMONAX: Plato –

ANTAGORAS: Shut up.

SOCRATES (*to Antagoras*): May I suggest we celebrate this holy day by talking about religion? (*Antagoras bows assent.*) When I was young I was privileged to hear Zeno and Parmenides discussing religion –

ANTAGORAS: Those were godlike men!

SOCRATES: I was struck by their humility in the face of this awesome subject. So let us lesser beings be humble too. Suppose we start from a personal confession, that seems right when we speak of what is supposed to concern the individual soul. Tell me, Antagoras, do you believe in the gods?

ANTAGORAS: No, of course not! That's all fable, superstitious belief in the supernatural, mythology, suitable for childish primitives.

SOCRATES: Quite a lot of educated people believe in gods.

ANTAGORAS: Yes, but fewer and fewer, it's all going out. This is a time of transition. Our civilisation is growing up, we're scientific and factual, we can analyse the old superstitions and see how they arose. God is not the measure of all things, man is the measure of all things, we invented the gods.

SOCRATES: Why? Why did we invent the gods?

ANTAGORAS: Well, originally out of fear of nature, fear of thunder for instance, people thought it was Zeus being angry. Religion is essentially magic, a desire for power over hostile forces. 'Religious experience' is just a comfortable feeling that the gods know all about us, there's a higher sense to it all, the gods have fixed the meaning of everything, so nothing is really dreadful or accidental or –

SOCRATES: You don't believe in divine spiritual beings?

ANTAGORAS: No! And if there were such beings *we* would be their *judges*. Any god who *existed* would be just a thing in our world, which *we* could decide about. It's not that God *must* exist, or *might* exist, it's that he can't *exist*. *We* are the source of morality and rational judgement. Once we understand this we *can't* believe in gods. We can't go back once we've become rational and free, it's an irreversible move.

SOCRATES: We are the gods now?

ANTAGORAS: Yes, if you like. The gods were just ideal pictures of us; we have to get rid of them to realise our own possibilities.

SOCRATES: The old philosophers, whom we think of as so wise, I mean like Thales and Heraclitus, saw the whole cosmos as a sort of spiritual being, everything was holy, religion was a harmony with the whole of nature.

ANTAGORAS: Yes, but that was really science. They wanted to find out what the universe was made of, atoms and so on. Myth was mixed up with science in those days. Those were great men in their time but we've moved on.

SOCRATES: So religion is magic and primitive science – and primitive morality too? Since we've now discovered that we are the only source of value.

ANTAGORAS: Yes, religion has always been concerned with morals and social conduct, that's why it's been so important.

SOCRATES: Important?

ANTAGORAS: An important phenomenon. Morality was mixed up with mythology like science was, it was all one big thing, now we cut the thing into three pieces, throw away the mythology, and have a proper science and a proper morality. You must approve of that!

SOCRATES: What's 'proper'?

ANTAGORAS: More pure, more true, not mixed up with lies. Now we can *separate fact from value*, give each its proper place in life, get rid of the supernatural on both sides. Instead of cosmic mythology we have science, instead of picturesque god fables, we have independent moral men making up their minds and choosing their values. *We* are the lords of meaning, there isn't any higher meaning set up somewhere else. There's nothing high, there's nothing deep, there's nothing hidden – but that is *obvious*, it's what everybody in this room believes.

SOCRATES: Don't be impatient with me. I am not at all sure what everybody in this room believes. Not all intelligent people think that religion is just superstition. For instance someone might say that the old stories are not literally true, but that they can *convey* truth – and that there are not many gods but only one, called, perhaps, Zeus, or God, a spiritual power, which is perfectly good –

ANTAGORAS: Whether you call it Zeus or God or anything, it's still a supernatural person with a name and modern people can't believe in such a person.

SOCRATES: Can there be religion without gods or a personal god?

ANTAGORAS: No. Religion is *essentially* superstition.

SOCRATES: But has been closely connected with morality.

ANTAGORAS: People thought the gods would punish them for being bad and reward them for being good. A pretty debased sort of morality! Surely *you*, Socrates, would say that virtue is for its own sake and not for a reward!

SOCRATES: Let's go slowly. In philosophy if you aren't moving at a snail's pace you aren't moving at all. Perhaps inside that connection with morality we may find many different things wrapped up.

ACASTOS: A pious superstitious peasant could be a better man than I am.

ANTAGORAS (*quickly*): I wonder if you really believe that, Acastos? Superstitious belief is degrading, it's corrupting, it prevents thought, it's the acceptance of a lie.

SOCRATES: So you think religion is over, finished by the age of science. And this is a good thing?

ANTAGORAS: Well, yes – *and* no – Now this is *quite* another argument, it's a *political* argument. We intellectuals, we understand the situation, we can bear the burden –

SOCRATES: Of being gods.

ANTAGORAS: Of freedom and value and a responsible unaided morality. But considered simply as a social phenomenon religion can be a useful stabilising factor. We're living in a period of intellectual and psychological *shock*, a time of deep change, an interregnum, a *dangerous interim*. Public morality could break down, some would say it *is* breaking down.

SOCRATES: If you were a tyrant you wouldn't abolish religion?

ANTAGORAS: Not until I had found a substitute! Of course as you know I detest tyrants. But if people worshipped the gods and kept quiet this might save the state from worse things. So long as there's an uneducated mob, there's a place for something like religion. Personally, I don't like the smell of it, religiosity is in bad taste, 'religious experience' is infantile fantasy; it's a matter of style. But this doesn't mean one should disrupt society to put people right. Religious sanctions, even rather vague ones, support popular morality and social order. Let's face it, ordinary morals are full of superstition, fear of the gods, fear of your neighbour, fear of the state. When young people lose that fear and become fearless, when they lose all respect for authority, things can really fall apart. It's a dangerous time. Religion is ritual and ritual is a symbol of order. Religion carries moral tradition. It's dying a natural and inevitable death, but the majority of people are slow in growing up. Meanwhile the state may have to take the place of the gods. (*Looking at Timonax.*) It's this *transition* that we intellectuals must try to *think* about. And we mustn't let sentimental modern political attitudes stop us from thinking.

During Antagoras's increasingly passionate speech Timonax has become extremely restive. He now bursts out.

TIMONAX: This is cynicism, it's élitism – !

ANTAGORAS: Public morality needs a popular background.

TIMONAX: I agreed with you before, but this – !

ANTAGORAS: Something with a bit of *colour* in it –

TIMONAX: You mean military parades!

ANTAGORAS: People must have faith in their society. Nationalism, patriotism, why not? Those are natural emotions.

TIMONAX: I shall go mad!

ANTAGORAS: The deification of the state is being forced upon us. I don't like it – but the alternative is anarchy!

By this time Antagoras, who is almost shouting, is thoroughly upset by his own logic, and Timonax is angry. Socrates makes pacifying gestures.

SOCRATES: This is indeed a new argument, a *political* argument about means to an end, means to a stable and orderly society. I think our original argument is more fundamental because it relates to values which can put political means and ends into question.

TIMONAX: He despises the morality of ordinary people, he thinks he's got a superior morality which justifies him treating them as puppets!

SOCRATES (*with a gesture towards Antagoras*): This would bring us back to Acastos's question about the superstitious but virtuous peasant. Is there not such a person?

ANTAGORAS: He might be virtuous but not in respect of his superstition.

SOCRATES: It's not so easy to separate a good man from his superstition. Might not someone who delayed his decision by praying to a god, come to a wiser decision?

ANTAGORAS: I prefer rational thought!

SOCRATES: You say this is a time of transition. Religious dogma is also changing. Could there not be a good religious way of life without the supernatural beliefs?

ACASTOS (*vigorously nodding assent to this question*): Yes!

ANTAGORAS: I wouldn't call that religion. I see what you are at, Socrates, but I won't let you do it. You want to smuggle religion back as some sort of refined morality. I shouldn't have allowed you and Acastos to posit this virtuous peasant, and I won't let my political argument be undercut by your moral argument. I don't believe in goodness in your grand solemn sense. I don't believe in moral perfectionism. Morality is a profoundly relative matter, the concept is irremediably confused, it's not something glorious and eternal, *that's* what we've learnt from getting rid of the gods! *If we go beyond the simplest ideas about morality we land in nonsense.* Philosophers always try to invent some impressive background or 'underlying reality'. But morality has no background except the actual continuance of human society, it's practically important, but in a theoretical sense it's a superficial phenomenon. *There isn't anything deep or high.* You want to separate out a part of religion to do with perfect virtue or salvation or something, to make religion go on existing without supernatural beliefs, but there is no such part. We're all the same, only some of us are more rational and free. Anything else is pure hypocrisy!

SOCRATES: My dear Antagoras, please don't be cross with me. You imagine I am up to all kinds of trickery, I assure you I am not. I am simply trying to hold on to the strands of what has already become quite a complicated argument. Do you mind if we now let Timonax join in? He has been bursting to for some time.

ANTAGORAS: He won't be happy until he's attacking me, he's such a pugnacious boy. But he won't agree with you either.

TIMONAX (*incoherent with annoyance and conviction, to Antagoras*): It's nothing to do with *you*, it isn't *personal*, it's a matter of *truth* and – and how things *are* – you deny morality –

ANTAGORAS (*cooler*): I don't, I just define it in a modest manner.

TIMONAX: But you take a high moral line when it suits you! Socrates seems to want religion to go on as virtue or something –

ACASTOS: Socrates hasn't said –

TIMONAX: And you want it to go on as a drug to stop people from resisting tyranny –

ANTAGORAS: No, I don't –

SOCRATES: Stop, let him talk.

TIMONAX (*very fast*): Of *course* the old stories are lies, but they're lies that have got to be *destroyed*. Religion is *immoral*, it stops people from thinking about how to change society. Yes, we are at the end of our childhood, and we must get rid of that old primitive past and *kick* it to *pieces*. I think *men* should be gods, not the state. I happen to believe in democracy and that means making *everybody* capable of thinking and distinguishing true and false. I believe in brotherhood and equality and all those things which modern science makes possible at last. Religion has always been a reactionary force, it makes people lazy and stupid, it consoles them for their rotten lives, they can think about heaven and not care about changing the world –

ANTAGORAS: I'm all for changing the world, I just think it can't be done in ten days!

TIMONAX: You're a cynic!

ANTAGORAS: I'm a pragmatist.

TIMONAX: Your pragmatism leads straight into tyranny, you say religiosity is in bad taste, you say morality is a matter of style –

ANTAGORAS (*under Timonax's flow*): I don't –

TIMONAX: You say there's nothing deep and nothing high, but there is, *truth* is, and *caring about people* is, morality *matters*, it isn't relative, it's absolute, we can't be *relaxed* about all this. Religion is false, it's degrading, it makes real morality impossible, now for the first time we can have *real* morality which is just for itself. If we're gods we must be good truthful gods and make society more moral and good, and another thing, religion isn't just dream stuff, it's a political force, it commits terrible crimes, intolerance and persecution and cruelty, it's like a political party, it *is* a political party, and even people who don't believe in religion are sentimental about it. Religious leaders may have lots of charm, what everyone now calls 'charisma', I hate that word, but look what they *do*, they interfere with social arrangements and tell us what to do in our private lives, and what we can *read*, they even prevent their own thinkers from thinking –

ANTAGORAS: If you imagine that all religious leaders are hypocrites you are being dangerously naïve.

TIMONAX: You don't deny that the Delphic Oracle is a political fraud, do you? Do you, Acastos?

ACASTOS: No.

TIMONAX: Religion is the enemy of morality, anything that rests on lies must be, the basis of morality is making people happier and freer and better, more equal, more tolerant, more truthful, more just, that's *absolutely* important, and it's as high and as deep as you please, that's what I mean by *idealism*. Who disagrees with that?

Timonax has by now risen to his feet in his excitement. Acastos is upset and confused.

SOCRATES: Perhaps we shall agree that these are moral *aims*, but this

[504]

is not to say that such aims are the *basis* or *definition* of morality. And, dear Timonax, please sit down, your eloquence is making me feel quite tired. You see, we are in deep waters. Antagoras and Timonax seem to be agreeing about religion but differing about morality. If, as Antagoras put it, there is 'nothing high and nothing deep' this takes away an important part of the traditional conception of religion, that part which *connects morality* with some absolute background. Antagoras also of course denies the absolute status which Timonax gives to morals.

ANTAGORAS: Timonax contradicts himself, he is taking up a religious attitude, his 'absolute' is just God, it can't be anything else!

SOCRATES (*to Timonax, who has dismissed this remark with a derisive gesture*): Do you want to add anything now?

TIMONAX: No, but I shall speak again if I hear anybody talking nonsense.

SOCRATES: I'm sure you will, dear boy. Now let's hear a different voice, I suspect there's one not far off. Plato? (*Plato shakes his head slightly.*) Acastos, I think it's your task to help us now. (*Acastos makes a helpless gesture.*) Never mind if you've nothing clear to say, just try to say your unclear thing as directly as possible.

ACASTOS: I agree with lots of things they said, I don't believe in the old myths and stories, and of course religion does a lot of bad things –

SOCRATES: But – ?

ACASTOS: I suppose it's a silly argument, but all those people who believed in religion for so long can't just have been mistaken, I mean it's not a bit like an ordinary factual mistake.

SOCRATES: It's not necessarily easy to say what an ordinary factual mistake is. Our whole way of seeing the world is changing exceptionally fast.

ACASTOS: Yes, we've found out *hundreds* of things, like what people in the past would never have dreamt of –

SOCRATES: And might not all these new methods of explanation affect our whole outlook, change our perspective, so that now we simply *can't* believe things which people did in the past? Religion is a mode of explanation, it explained the world, it guaranteed morality, it made it all look *real*. Now our sense of reality has shifted, we explain the world in new ways which cohere with all our new knowledge.

ACASTOS: Yes, it all looked so solid and impressive *then* and doesn't *now*. We have science and – and morality is (*touches his chest*) our own judgement – I suppose – I'm not clear about that. And the whole atmosphere is getting anti-religious as if religion couldn't breathe any more. We know so much – but not about ourselves – we're so – each one of us – so *amazing* (*expressive gestures*) – I mean more amazing than the stars, or anything – and we seem to *need* something – there's a part of us that *wants* –

TIMONAX: Wants God!

ANTAGORAS: Illusions, dear child.

ACASTOS: Well, people like to feel that they can talk to God – but religion can't be slavish subjection to some supernatural person, it's got to be freely accepted.

SOCRATES: There is a saying of Heraclitus that 'he who alone is wise wants and does not want to be called Zeus'. What do you think that means?

ACASTOS (*with gestures*): I think it means that we're drawn to the idea of a sort of central – good – something very real – after all morality *feels* more like discovering something than just inventing it – and we want to sort of *assert* this central thing – by giving it a *name* – but at the same time we see this is wrong, it makes it like a material thing, we can't conceive it in this way, and it's as if it itself forbids us to.

SOCRATES: Yes, truth forbids what also seems a natural even inevitable way of formulating something important. We put the truth into a conceptual picture becuse we feel it can't be expressed in any other way; and then truth itself forces us to criticise the picture.

Slight pause.

Is this unusual? Isn't it rather like what artists are doing all the time?

ACASTOS: You mean using images, and then trying to improve them, and –

SOCRATES: In a way we are all artists, we all use metaphors and symbols and figures of speech, and we can't always explain what they mean in other terms, any more than we can with a work of art. We're surrounded by statues and pictures of gods and stories about them. Religion has always used art, and art has helped to make the mythology look so real. But at times religion has also rejected art, and perhaps it's doing so now. Do you want religion to go on existing?

ACASTOS: Yes, but not with lying. Yet I feel that if we lose traditional religion now we may lose *all* religion because – it can't use the old language and concepts – and it can't make new ones in time – and many people find it empty and senseless – and then when the priests change the old-fashioned language into modern words it sounds so ugly and awkward, it loses its spiritual force – it's as if the gods can't speak to us any more, they are silent, they've hidden themselves. But I don't want worship and ritual and prayer and so on just to *go* – there's a valuable – precious – thing somewhere inside it all.

SOCRATES: Well, that's the thing that we want to find.

ANTAGORAS: Your precious thing is just a dream of morality. Morality with flowers round its neck and fleas in the flowers.

ACASTOS: No, no – religion is having an intense attitude and no time off. (*Laughter, in which Plato does not join.*) I mean, it's *more* like life, like *real* life. Life is awful, terrible, like in war, and we're always at war, and then death comes to us all and – religion is about those awful deep things.

ANTAGORAS: *There's nothing deep*, Acastos, that's the message of the modern world and we've got to live with it!

ACASTOS: Religion is – something that stays put when you're terribly unhappy or – guilty. It's like being sure that in spite of all evil – and selfishness – and pain – there really is goodness, and that it matters – more than anything else – all the time and everywhere, and it's true – more than our ordinary – dreamy life – and so morality isn't just what we happen to think – it's like discovering the truth, or remembering it.

TIMONAX: But religious people think they're going to live for ever in heaven!

ACASTOS: We can't know that, so it has nothing to do with us. I think immortality is an anti-religious idea, as if there were

[507]

rewards or anything happening somewhere else. It's all got to be *now* and *here*.

ANTAGORAS: What has?

ACASTOS: That sort of – absolute seriousness.

TIMONAX: But that *is* morality.

ANTAGORAS: Religion is just morality plus a tragic feeling.

ACASTOS: No! (*voices raised*)

SOCRATES: Wait, wait! I want Acastos to tell us how he thinks religion relates to morality. Some people might say that morality is just public social rules and that there are a lot of serious private things which have nothing whatever to do with morals. Would you say that, Timonax?

TIMONAX (*after a moment's reflection*): Yes, so long as that doesn't make morality unimportant.

SOCRATES (*to Acastos*): And isn't that a sensible view, isn't that common sense?

ANTAGORAS: It's certainly *political* common sense!

ACASTOS: I think religion *contains* morality. It goes beyond common sense, it goes beyond that sort of limited attitude, dividing the world into manageable bits. Religion is believing that your life is a *whole* – I mean that goodness and morality and duty are just *everywhere* – like *always* looking further and deeper – and feeling *reverence* for things – a religious person would care about everything in that sort of way, he'd feel everything mattered and every second mattered.

SOCRATES: No time off!

TIMONAX: Oh come, you must draw the line somewhere!

SOCRATES: Perhaps for Acastos religion means not drawing the line.

ACASTOS: That's what one would mean by saying that Zeus is always watching.

TIMONAX: You don't believe that Zeus is always watching!

ACASTOS: No, I mean it's *as if*! It's like we're (*expressive gesture*) *immersed.*

ANTAGORAS: 'All is one' is the oldest lie in the philosophy book.

SOCRATES (*while Acastos nods*): So a religious attitude sees our life as an interconnected whole and a religious man would feel responsible for the *quality* of all his thoughts and experiences, even his perceptions, as if everything were significant and worthy of justice?

ACASTOS: Yes, this sort of – *perpetual work* – seems to me what religion is.

SOCRATES: You approve of such an attitude.

ACASTOS: Yes, it's – as I see it – it's like – it's humility and unselfishness – and setting yourself aside to make room for other things, and people –

TIMONAX: But you can't care about everything, that's a ridiculous conceited idea, not a bit humble, anyway you'd go mad! You're talking about states of mind all the time, lofty private emotions, what about actions, actions are what matter –

ACASTOS: I don't mean *just* emotions – actions come out of states of mind and how we *see* the world, we can only move in the world we can see, we have to change ourselves and become better and understand more –

ANTAGORAS: We can't change ourselves, we've always known that, only now we know why!

SOCRATES: You said religion contained morality. Do you want to say that religion is the *basis* of morality?

ACASTOS (*obviously exhausted by his ordeal*): I don't know. Lots of religious people are bad and lots of non-religious people are good.

SOCRATES: Does that tend to disprove your position?

ACASTOS: I don't think so.

SOCRATES: You've done very well, Acastos, but you haven't told us how to distinguish between morality and religion. Perhaps religion is just a 'refined' sort of morality which some people choose to invent?

TIMONAX: Neurotic people!

ACASTOS: Well, part of it is that you don't invent it, it's absolutely *there*, like a – *judgement*.

SOCRATES: Now gather yourself together for a final assault.

ACASTOS (*struggling*): I can't –

SOCRATES: Can there be religion without mythology, without stories and pictures? Should we be trying now to think of it like that?

ACASTOS: I don't know!

SOCRATES: Is a certain opaqueness, a certain *mystery*, necessary to it?

ACASTOS (*almost tearful*): *I don't know!*

SOCRATES: Would you say that religion is something *natural*?

TIMONAX: Socrates, do stop, let's have an interval, let's drink and not think! Acastos says there is no time off from religion, but do let's have some time off from philosophy!

Socrates relaxes and smiles, signs assent.

ANTAGORAS: When it gets difficult he wants a drink.

TIMONAX: I *love* arguing!

ANTAGORAS: Only when you win.

TIMONAX: Socrates, defend me.

SOCRATES (*petting him*): One who is so beautiful needs no other defence.

ANTAGORAS: I think we should go on, otherwise we'll lose the thread, we'll lose the *intensity*, to use Acastos's favourite word. (*He claps his hands for the servant.*)

TIMONAX (*pleasantly*): Acastos isn't religious, he's just a prig, aren't you, dear?

The servant enters bringing more wine. Typical behaviour of each character to him. Socrates is relaxed and amiable, Acastos would-be friendly but awkward, Timonax perfunctory, Antagoras indifferent. Plato observes and frowns.

TIMONAX (*indicating the servant*): Well, if you want to go on and we want to rest why not question this chap? I know Socrates never needs a rest.

SOCRATES: What does Antagoras think?

ANTAGORAS: Whatever you like. He's not very bright and he can't speak the language very well.

As they discuss the servant Acastos is uncomfortable, looks at Plato, who remains impassive.

TIMONAX: Has he got a religion?

ANTAGORAS: I don't know, better ask him.

SOCRATES: I would like Acastos to question him.

ACASTOS: Oh no, please not!

SOCRATES: I won't always be here to ask questions, others must learn. Besides you are young and gentle and won't upset him. Go on, my dear.

ACASTOS (*nervous*): We're talking about religion. (*It takes a moment for him to attract the servant's attention.*) Look – excuse me –

ANTAGORAS: He lives in a dream. He isn't even listening.

ACASTOS: Do you have a *religion*?

SERVANT: A what, sir? No, I don't think so, sir.

The servant is a graceful youth. He is a little timid at first.

TIMONAX: That shows it isn't natural.

SOCRATES: Tell him what it is.

ACASTOS: Oh dear – I mean when you go to services, rituals, acts of worship.

SERVANT: I don't know what is that –

SOCRATES: Don't use difficult words.

ACASTOS: When you sing hymns, you sing –

SERVANT (*cheering up*): Oh, yes, sing hymns, yes, and music, noise, yes, beat, your heart beat, and your feet – (*He moves a few steps*).

ACASTOS (*as they all smile*): So you believe in God, you think that perhaps there is a God?

SERVANT: Oh no –

TIMONAX: Fun, but no God. Hooray!

SERVANT: Not like that – I don't think – I *know* there is God.

ANTAGORAS: Ask him what he's like.

ACASTOS: What is your God like?

SERVANT: I don't understand. *Everybody* knows that, sir.

ANTAGORAS: Well, we don't, so please tell us.

ACASTOS (*with an encouraging gesture*): Go on.

SERVANT: How can I say, he is everywhere, he knows all things, he made all things, he is God, he is here in this room –

ANTAGORAS: I can't see him. (*Socrates checks him with a gesture.*)

ACASTOS: How do you know about God?

SERVANT: I have always known, sir, ever since I was a tiny baby, my first words were about God. I knew him at once.

ACASTOS: You mean your mother taught you?

SERVANT: My mother – (*assenting gesture*) but I know it already, he was there, in my little body, in all I see when I open my eyes, when I was a child, and now, in my heart and my soul – so is God in all men.

ACASTOS: And you worship God.

[511]

SERVANT: I don't know – He is with me always, I sing to him, I laugh to him, I cry to him. And when I die I shall go to God. That makes me happy. Whatever happen, I am happy man.

TIMONAX: Lucky old you!

ACASTOS: You pray to God sometimes?

SERVANT (*scornful*): Not sometimes, all the time! I talk to him, I tell him my life, I tell him all troubles, all what I want.

ACASTOS: Does he give you what you want?

SERVANT: He knows best, oh he knows best. He knows what is my good. I am humble man, small man. But God blesses me.

ACASTOS: So you love him because he is kind?

SERVANT: Not therefore! I love him because he is God. Even if he kill me, I love him. I love him more than anything, not anybody more I love than God.

ACASTOS: But why?

SERVANT (*who thinks this is obvious*): He loves me, he made me to be, he keeps me to be. Like little fish in sea am I in God's love! All I eat, sleep, work, do, inside his love. Because I exist there is God. Without his love I become small like – like this – and wither away, and become – no thing (*gestures*).

ANTAGORAS: Gift of language these fellows have.

TIMONAX: Don't you ever pray to God to make you rich and grand, like him? (*He points to Antagoras.*)

SERVANT: I am well-off man inside God's love, that is all I know.

TIMONAX: I don't believe you. Aren't you cross with God because he made you like this?

SERVANT (*upset*): I am not good man, I have many sin, many fault, many, many. I need my God. I am all bad, he is all good, I have bad thoughts –

TIMONAX (*interrupting*): So if you –

SOCRATES (*stopping the conversation with a gesture*): Thank you, thank you, you spoke very well.

At a nod from Antagoras the servant goes. Socrates rises and stands a little apart.

ANTAGORAS: I suppose he's what they call a natural mystic!

ACASTOS: So you *do* think religion is natural?

ANTAGORAS: Superstition is! He believes it all literally.

[512]

TIMONAX: Whatever happens I am happy man. Perhaps *that's* religion.

ACASTOS: I liked that!

TIMONAX: No wonder it inhibits social progress!

ANTAGORAS: I was afraid he was going to confess he'd stolen something, most embarrassing!

TIMONAX: With God standing there looking at him accusingly!

ANTAGORAS: There you are, not a bad idea if it stops people from stealing!

TIMONAX: He's rather adorable, would you sell him to me!

ANTAGORAS: What do you want him for?

Socrates returns to the group and stands in front of Plato, studying him. Plato is uneasy, rises, moves. The others watch.

SOCRATES: Well, what do you think, young Plato? We don't seem to have heard from you.

PLATO (*after a moment, cool, almost impertinent*): Do you really want to know what I think?

They stare at each other. Then Socrates turns away and sits down, beckoning to Acastos. They are all seated except for Plato, who is left out.

SOCRATES (*to Acastos*): Well, my child, we are still without a definition of religion which separates it clearly from morality.

ACASTOS: I think that –

PLATO (*vehemently interrupting, very fast*): Religion isn't just a feeling, it isn't just a hypothesis, it's not like something we happen not to know, a God who might perhaps be there isn't a God, it's got to be necessary, it's got to be certain, it's got to be proved by the whole of life, it's got to be the magnetic centre of everything –

SOCRATES: Wait a minute! So you want to talk?

PLATO: Yes. (*pause*) Please.

SOCRATES: All right. Sit down. And don't be in such a hurry. You say 'it's got to be certain.' There are different kinds of certainty.

TIMONAX: Intolerance, dogmatism, persecution.

SOCRATES: And what is one to be certain of? You used the word God.

PLATO (*still fast*): That was just a figure of speech, of course there are no gods, they are just images, religion is above the gods, there *can't* be gods, but that doesn't mean it's anything we happen to think, it doesn't mean *we're* the gods, that's just the *opposite*, it's beyond us, it's more real than us, we have to come to it and let it change us, religion is spiritual change, *absolute* spiritual change.

SOCRATES: Not so fast please. Moral ideas can change people too.

PLATO: Not so deeply, not in the way that's *required* of us, this isn't something optional, we're not volunteers, we're conscripts. We're bad, we have to become good, it's a long way. Anyhow morality, if it's anything serious, is something religious.

SOCRATES: Whether it knows it or not?

PLATO: Yes. I mean, what I'd *call* religion is what can really *change* us. Morality is derivative, it's a shadow of religion, the gods are shadows of religion, *we* are shadows, looking for the light, looking for the sun, for what's *real* and *necessarily* true.

SOCRATES: Many people would say that *necessity* belongs to mathematics and logic. In the real world things aren't necessarily true, they may or may not be true, we have to look and see.

PLATO: That's just where religion is *different*, it's unique, it's about what's *absolute*, what *can't* not be there. If we conceive it at all we see that it must be real.

SOCRATES: What is this 'it' that you're certain of in this special unique way, which isn't God and which has to exist and is proved by everything and is seen in the clear light beyond the shadows?

PLATO: Good.

ANTAGORAS: What did he say?

PLATO: *Good.*

TIMONAX: That's an abstract idea.

ANTAGORAS: It's an empty box into which we put whatever takes our fancy.

SOCRATES: By 'good' do you mean virtue?

PLATO: Virtue under a necessity to which everything points. I mean – to become virtuous is the absolute goal of human life –

ANTAGORAS: Oh – ! (*Derisive moan*)

PLATO (*ignoring him*): But we can't switch it on by empty will power. We have to *learn* what's true and what's real and that *is* understanding and loving what's good, that's how *everything* teaches us, everything *proves* it –

SOCRATES: *Wait* – Timonax said that good is an abstract idea, and

Antagoras called it an empty box. Perhaps what they meant is
that it must leave us *free* to call *all* sorts of things good.

PLATO: I don't think freedom is very important.

ACASTOS: Oh really! (*Timonax and Antagoras also exclaim.*)

PLATO: Choosing just anything you like –

ANTAGORAS: That's *political* freedom and it *is* important.

PLATO: Real spiritual freedom is very difficult. I'd rather give it
some other name like – truth.

ACASTOS: Truth.

PLATO: Truth isn't just *facts*, its a *mode of being*. It's finding out
what's real and responding to it – like when we really see other
people and know they exist. You see I think there are different
levels in the soul, only a bit of us is real and knows truth, the rest
is fantasy, anxiety, resentment, envy, all selfish tricks – *you* know.
We live in a dream, we're wrapped up in a dark veil, we think
we're omnipotent magicians, we don't believe anything *exists*
except ourselves. Magic is the opposite of goodness. Belief in
magic is slavery. We have to change ourselves, change what we
want, what we desire, what we love, and that's difficult. But if we
even *try* to love what's good our desires can improve, they can
change direction, *that's* what I call freedom. *That's* becoming
morally better, and it's possible and that's *why* it's possible. Real
freedom is not to be a slave of selfish desires. It's when you have –
you know – a feeling of reality –

ACASTOS (*nodding, softly*): Yes.

ANTAGORAS: I never heard such high-minded rubbish! And I don't
like this talk about 'the soul'!

PLATO: Well, the psyche then, a perfectly good Greek word!

ANTAGORAS: You mean we stop being individual people and vanish
into a golden haze?

PLATO: No! We *become* individual people, and stop being self-
absorbed mucky dreamers!

ACASTOS: Mucky dreamers –

PLATO: We become more real –

TIMONAX: You say 'love good'. How do we find out what *is* good?

PLATO: All truth-seeking teaches that, everybody knows something
about it really –

[515]

SOCRATES: You connect goodness with truth-seeking and knowledge. But mightn't we just be idle spectators of what we know, why should it affect what we do?

PLATO: That's where love and desire come in, what Acastos left out. Think of what learning something is like, something difficult like mathematics. You know how that feels when you're trying so hard to see something which *isn't yourself*, something *else*. You forget yourself. All your being and emotions are involved in trying to *understand*, and that's the sort of *desire* that actions come out of too, when you can't help responding because you really care.

SOCRATES: You choose an intellectual example, but it needn't be intellectual learning, it could be a craft.

PLATO: Almost anything – like carpentry – when the carpenter begins to understand, to *see*, to learn some mathematics. (*Turning to Antagoras.*) *That's* deep.

SOCRATES: Or learning about other people, you do what's right when you've forgotten yourself and really understand them.

PLATO: Learning other people, that's much harder. What's easiest is – is beauty – when you see beautiful things and just want them to exist outside, in themselves, so that you can love them and understand them. Beauty is a clue, it's the nearest thing, it's the only spiritual thing we love by instinct –

ANTAGORAS: What's all this got to do with religion?

PLATO: It *is* religion and it's happening all the time. If it's not everywhere, in the air we breathe, it isn't what I mean. If it's something whose non-existence is possible it isn't what I mean! It's to do with life being a whole and not a lot of random choices. Religion must be proved by the whole of life, it isn't a sort of oddity or side issue or one choice among others, it isn't weird like magic. If it's anything it must be everything, it must be proved by loving people and learning things and looking at things. It's not abstract, it's all *here*. It's not retiring from the world, it's knowing the world, the real world, *this* world as it really is, in all its – details –

TIMONAX: You mean *everything*, bits of hair, and mud, and dirt, and fleas and – ?

PLATO (*after a moment*): Yes.

SOCRATES: But what about this 'learning other people', which is so difficult, and so important?

PLATO: Yes, we seem to be naturally good about beauty and bad about people.

TIMONAX: What about beautiful people, what about falling in love!

ANTAGORAS: Don't change the subject.

SOCRATES (*smiling*): He isn't changing the subject!

PLATO: Well, falling in love! It's suddenly as if you didn't exist any more, there's nothing in the world but the other person, all reality has gone somewhere else, he's like a god, it's the most violent experience we ever have –

SOCRATES: A good experience?

PLATO: It can be –

ANTAGORAS: It can be *hell*.

SOCRATES: Lovers are often jealous and selfish and cruel.

TIMONAX: *Usually*, in my experience.

PLATO: Yes, like when you want to *cage* the other person and *dominate* him and *crush* him – but I think falling in love is a sort of *picture* of something good. I mean *as if* one could love very much but without selfishness.

TIMONAX: Impossible.

SOCRATES: You mean one ought ideally to care for everybody in an unselfish way, even to love them. Perhaps the lover might learn to understand spiritual beauty as the carpenter learns to understand mathematics.

PLATO (*gradually becoming excited and rising to his feet*): We can't. And yet we can. We *can* change. You see, love is energy. The soul is a huge vast place, and lots of it is dark, and it's full of energy and power, and this can be bad, but it *can* be good, and *that's* the *work*, to change bad energy into good, when we desire good things and are attracted magnetically by them –

ANTAGORAS: I think your magnetic Good isn't God after all, it's just sex, all this dark energy is sex.

PLATO: All right, it's sex, or sex is it – it's the whole drive of our being and that includes sex.

SOCRATES: Perhaps there is a god there after all. I would call him Eros.

PLATO: Eros! Yes!

[517]

SOCRATES: Only your Eros isn't exactly a god, he's a holy passionate spirit that seeks for God, what you call Good.

PLATO: Yes! He's *in love* with Good!

ANTAGORAS: But your Good is an *idea*.

SOCRATES: Do sit down, Plato!

PLATO (*sits*): Ideas *work* in life, they can become incarnate in how we live, that's how they become real!

ANTAGORAS: These are just attractive metaphors.

PLATO: Metaphors aren't just ornaments, they're fundamental modes of knowledge – it's like – what's at a higher more difficult level appears to us first as a shadow, or an image – then we break through the image and move on and –

SOCRATES: Like the carpenter learning mathematics. (*Plato nods.*) But can we get beyond images and *see* your Good, which you said was like the sun?

PLATO: I don't know. In a way, goodness and truth seem to come out of the depths of the soul, and when we really know something we feel we've always known it. Yet also it's terribly distant, farther than any star. We're sort of – stretched out – It's like beyond the world, not in the clouds or in heaven, but a light that *shows* the world, this world, as it really is –

SOCRATES: You want your Good, your source of true light to be separate and pure and perfect –

PLATO: It's like what Acastos said when in spite of all wickedness, and in all misery, we are certain that there really *is* goodness and that it matters *absolutely*.

SOCRATES: But you wouldn't call it God.

PLATO: *No*, it's not a *person*, we don't have dialogues with it, it won't reward us, we must be good for nothing, it's an *idea*, it's the closest thing (*gesture*) –

SOCRATES: And the farthest thing.

ACASTOS: What about prayer? In your picture can we pray?

PLATO: Yes, but not to a person. Learning can be praying, breathing can be praying. Prayer is keeping quiet and hoping for the light.

ANTAGORAS: Why should ultimate reality be something nice and good? It might be something thoroughly nasty. Either your Good is a thing existing outside us like God, or it's a picture inside us which some people choose to play about with.

PLATO: Now *you're* using metaphors –

ANTAGORAS: What metaphors?

PLATO: Inside and outside! Of course Good doesn't exist like chairs and tables, it's not (*gestures*) either outside or inside. It's in our whole way of living, it's fundamental like truth. If we have the idea of value we necessarily have the idea of perfection as something real.

SOCRATES: So you think everybody knows this?

PLATO: Instinctively, yes. People know that good is real and absolute, not optional and relative, all their life proves it. And when they choose false goods they really know they're false. We can think everything else away out of life, but not value, that's in the very – ground of things.

ACASTOS (*to himself, thinking*): We can't think material objects away out of life – or can we? Or causal connections? Or is that different?

SOCRATES: Is this where you distinguish morality from religion?

PLATO: Yes, except that I don't. Religion is the love and worship of the good, and that's the real basis of morality. Duty, that's what we feel when we want the good but love other things more –

SOCRATES: So some people are religious without knowing it? They mightn't like that.

PLATO: I suppose so. I don't like the word religion actually.

TIMONAX: So after all you're giving up?

PLATO: Nowadays people think of religion as something exotic and formal, and a bit aside from life, whereas what I mean is everywhere, like breathing.

SOCRATES (*thoughtfully*): Sometimes in philosophy we come up against questions which we can't answer, as if our language were a cage and we were right up against the bars. Acastos said he wanted religion to go on, as if it might or mightn't go on. What you call the ground of things, proved by everything, *if* it exists, is bound to go on, it can't not. But how is it to be expressed? Even your phrase 'the ground of being', or whatever, is a metaphor which is understood in a tradition. Religion expressed this idea very strongly, very picturesquely. Now it seems like something much harder to explain, *you* find it hard to explain. Perhaps it needs new metaphors, a new way of thought. But that hasn't happened yet. People still think of religion in the old way, as something formal, with certain rituals, symbols, familiar pictures. You said religion was spiritual change. What changes people must reach their minds and their hearts. Can religion survive without a *mythology*? Perhaps the concept is simply breaking up? Concepts don't live for ever, you yourself said you didn't like the word 'religion'. Isn't that symptomatic?

PLATO: I don't know. I think of mythology as a whole set of false stories. Human life is coherent enough. There are *lots* of ways of talking about the – absolute – however you put it, with *true* images, *true* pointers, natural – sacraments – One thing can stand for another, that's as deep as what's deepest. People have always known this.

ACASTOS (*not expecting an answer*): So it's about what *ordinary* people can believe? It couldn't just be a secret – No, of course not.

SOCRATES: Your Good, your sun, your holy light shining from outside existent being and yet also emerging from deep inside the soul. Aren't these mythological pictures? Would you say it's *as if* this were so?

PLATO (*visibly tiring now*): Not 'as if'. Learning and loving just are *like that*!

SOCRATES: One way of describing the world, perhaps, not an obvious one?

PLATO: When you see things in that light –

SOCRATES: Another metaphor.

TIMONAX: Give up Plato, you're cornered!

SOCRATES: I don't think he's cornered!

PLATO (*making a new move*): It's *got* to be like that otherwise we won't survive. The spirit must have something *absolute*, otherwise it goes crazy. Only religion can carry us through the – horrors – of the future –

SOCRATES: That's a different point. We've had plenty of horrors in the recent past – you think there are more to come?

PLATO: Yes.

SOCRATES: Then your 'ground of things', your 'it must be so', is really 'I want it to be so', it's a cry of fear?

PLATO: No –

SOCRATES: Perhaps you yourself are being too absolute. Religion naturally uses myth and art. These things too are instinctive, and perhaps religion will look after itself better than you imagine. You spoke of beauty – ritual is art, and art is the celebration of beauty. You say we're not gods. But you expect us as thinkers to *clarify* these things which must perhaps always be mysterious and even *fundamentally* muddled. You say spirit must have absolute. Perhaps we are now entering a time when *spirit cannot have any absolute.*

PLATO: Oh – *no* – but it will be different later?

SOCRATES: Who knows what will happen later (*pause*). I like what you say, I love what you say and I love you as you say it.

PLATO: Don't you love me all the time?

SOCRATES: Yes, but especially in this. Now I want you to go on –

PLATO: I can't go on!

SOCRATES: My dear good clever boy, now just try quietly to tell us –

Enter Alcibiades drunk, supported by the servant. Alcibiades puts on a 'camp' manner, but must be seen to be a tough dominating figure, a soldier and a leader. He could be wearing some sort of uniform.

ALCIBIADES: Socrates! I've been looking for you all over. Darling!

SOCRATES (*obviously pleased to see him*): Alcibiades, come in, sit down. (*To Antagoras*) May he join us?

Antagoras makes a helpless humorous gesture.

ALCIBIADES (*to Socrates*): My *love*! He's blushing. Oh you sweet one! The wisest man in the world and he blushes like a boy! Hello, Antagoras, I see you've still got goldilocks, lucky you! And this pretty animal (*stroking the servant*), nice good animal! Oh *Plato*, written any poems lately, dear? Love poems? (*Plato turns his head away.*) Oh sulky! What a sulky pussy! What have you been discussing?

During his speech Alcibiades has inserted himself into the group, sitting beside Socrates and causing the others to move up. A little horseplay, pulls Timonax's hair etc.

ANTAGORAS: Religion.

ALCIBIADES: My favourite subject!

SOCRATES: I imagine you wouldn't call yourself a religious man?

ANTAGORAS: Was it you who castrated all those statues of the gods?

ALCIBIADES: Ssssh! The gods deserve to be castrated. Who are they

[521]

to flaunt their organs at us? But have you really been talking about *them*? (*pointing upwards*)

SOCRATES: I think we've passed beyond the gods. No one seems to want to defend them except me.

TIMONAX: Socrates!

ALCIBIADES: He's a deep one. We don't know how to have him! But where are we if we're beyond the gods?

SOCRATES: Plato has been telling us about being in love.

ALCIBIADES: My subject too!

TIMONAX: He's in love with Good.

ALCIBIADES: Is it mutual?

ANTAGORAS: He thinks that goodness is the same as knowledge.

ALCIBIADES: But I think that too!

PLATO (*tense, very hostile*): No, you don't. We can't possibly be agreeing. Religion is the love and worship of goodness and truth, it's a magnetic power, it's absolute, and if we really love what's good we become good, and –

ALCIBIADES: Oh *Pusskins* –

PLATO: You're drunk!

SOCRATES: Let him say what he means. Come on, and *please* be serious.

ALCIBIADES: Oh, I am, it comes from the heart, to which dear Pusskins here attaches such importance. I will tell you what religion is. It is the love and worship of power.

PLATO: That's –

SOCRATES (*silencing Plato with a gesture*): Power?

ALCIBIADES: What is vulgarly called magic, but what I mean is something deep, as deep as you please, as deep as Plato.

SOCRATES: You'll have to perform some magic yourself if you are to persuade us that power is the object, or essence, of religion.

ALCIBIADES: Well, call it other names. Plato's very good at that, he's a juggler, a magician, a little apprentice magician who had better scuttle back to poetry and leave philosophy to stronger heads. He says religion is the worship of the good, then he calls it truth and knowledge, and it's magnetic and it's absolute and – it's all done by mirrors – by *equations* which hang miraculously in the air!

SOCRATES: Well, what are *your* other names, since you admit you can play the game as well?

[522]

ALCIBIADES: The game is called me-ta-phy-sics. But about religion, surely you are in the secret? I am sure Plato is, for all his priggish talk.

SOCRATES: Stop playing about, my dear, talk clearly, or we'll declare you drunk and throw you out!

ALCIBIADES: My *angel*, your *slave* –

ANTAGORAS: Oh shut up, get on with it.

ALCIBIADES: Religion is knowledge, as Plato said. It's the knowledge of good and evil. There!

PLATO: It's the *fight* between good and evil –

ALCIBIADES: Oh, no –

SOCRATES: What about power?

ALCIBIADES (*solemn and sonorous*): Knowledge is power, as we all know. Power is the *knowledge* that good and evil are *not* enemies, they are *friends*. The human soul is the seat of their harmony. The great chamber of the perfect soul enshrines the secret love of good for evil and evil for good. *That* union is what is absolute, and beautiful, and real. We cannot overcome the darkness within, it's fundamental and indestructible, we must cherish it, we must understand it and love it. Good needs evil, it can only *exist* by contrast, wise Heraclitus told us that, the struggle between the dark and the light is a kind of life-giving play, a game played by lovers. So evil isn't really evil, good isn't really good, we pass beyond the ordinary childish abstract notions of good and evil, and enter into the unity of the world! *Then* we are kings, *then* we are gods, the unified soul is the lord of reality. *That's* religion, *that's* the mystery which the initiated know, and *now is the new era* when at last it will be made plain.

PLATO (*furious*): That's a damned lie, the worst lie of all, Good must *never* make peace with evil, never, never! It must *kill* evil!

ALCIBIADES: You *are* bloodthirsty! Don't you want *harmony*, don't you want to make something *creative* out of all that warfare that's going on inside you? Why be always tearing yourself to pieces? Don't you want human life to *work*, to *function*?

PLATO (*incoherent*): That's perfect *muck*! Good must be pure and separate and – absolute – and – only what's completely good can – save us –

ALCIBIADES: But your perfectly pure good thing does not exist, that's the trouble, dear, all the world proves *that*!

PLATO: It *does*, it *must* – it's *more real* – I can't explain –

ALCIBIADES: My dear little one, I can see that you can't!

Plato hurls himself at Alcibiades. They fight. Alcibiades is stronger, twists Plato's arm.

ACASTOS: Don't hurt him!

ANTAGORAS (*amused*): Sexual jealousy, I'm afraid!

Socrates is amused for a moment, then annoyed.

SOCRATES: Stop it, *stop it!*

He interferes, they separate. Socrates slaps Plato.

ALCIBIADES (*laughing*): Creative strife! Homage to Heraclitus!

PLATO: I hate your ideas, I'd like to kill them!

SOCRATES: You can't kill ideas, you must learn to *think*.

ALCIBIADES: He will never think, he's a dreamy poet, that's what's so charming. What a fierce little kitten it is, pretty pussy!

SOCRATES: Don't torment him. (*To Plato*) I know you want to understand, perhaps you want to understand too much, you want to know too much. In philosophy we have to respect what we can't understand, just *look* at it and *describe* it.

ACASTOS: How do you mean?

SOCRATES: Stay close to what's obviously true, what people call common sense, what clever people may miss entirely. We've been told that religion is superstition, that it's socially useful, that it's the love of goodness, and now that it's the harmony of good and evil. But instead let's say something simple. The most important thing in life is virtue, and virtue isn't a mystery, it's truthfulness and justice and kindness and courage, things we understand. Anybody can *try* to be good, it's not obscure!

ACASTOS: But isn't religion the most important thing, if there is such a thing, *mustn't* it be?

SOCRATES: Beware in philosophy of things which 'must be so', at least look at them with a cool eye. Religion and virtue are not always allies, religion is many things and must be subject to justice and truth. We can't always learn virtue from loving good, we often have to live by external rules. But we are lovers and symbol-makers and that is our talent for religion, which displays the absolute charm of virtue and how we can love it. Religious symbols are a natural, holy use of art. But of course, religion mustn't become magic. There's no secret knowledge, no complete explanation, we must be humble and simple and see what we know and respect what we don't know. Man is not the measure of all things, we don't just invent our values, we live by a higher law, yet we can't fully explain how this is so. (*To Plato*) Everything is in a way less deep and in a way deeper than you think. You want a long explanation, but in the end your explanation repeats what you knew at the start. You said yourself it was like remembering.

PLATO: But the unknown – isn't that the end of the way?

SOCRATES: There is no way, we are here now at the end, we have to do the nearest thing. We are not gods, we are absurd limited beings, we live with affliction and chance. The most important things are close to us, the truth is close, in front of our noses, like the faces of our friends, we need no expert to tell us. Religion is our love of virtue lightening the present moment. It is respect for what we know, and reverence for what we don't know, what we can only *approach*, where our not-knowing must be our mode of knowing, where we make symbols and images, and then destroy them, and make other ones, as we see now in our own time. Images are natural, art is natural, sacraments and pictures and holy things are natural, the inner and the outer reflect each other, there is a reverence which finds what is spiritual everywhere in the world, *he* is right (*pointing to the servant*), God is everywhere. If we love whatever God we know and speak to Him truthfully we shall be answered. Out at the very edge of our imagination the spirit is eternally active. Respect the pure visions which speak to the heart, find there what is absolute. That is why we go to a holy place and kneel down. There is nothing more ultimate than that. (*Pause*)

PLATO: You, who know so much, tell us this!

SOCRATES: Because I do not know so much.

PLATO: But we *can* change, we *can* be enlightened, we *can* be saved?

SOCRATES: If we do good things which are near to us we may improve a little; don't make a drama of it, my dear. To tell the truth, that is an exercise which is always available. Goodness is simple, it's just very difficult.

Socrates is now smiling. He turns to Alcibiades.

ALCIBIADES: Oh you and your simplicity and your ignorance, how you drive us, you *herd* us into thinking!

SOCRATES: So – young Plato –

PLATO: I will kneel at this shrine.

SOCRATES: Well – by Zeus, if we want to see that torchlight procession we should go now! Let us enjoy our gods while we can. Come, Alcibiades. (*To Antagoras*) Thank you. (*To all*) Come, dear friends.

They rise for Socrates's departure. He goes, affectionately arm in arm with Alcibiades.

TIMONAX (*to Antagoras*): I want that boy!

Antagoras and Timonax depart arm in arm. Plato covers his face.

ACASTOS: You're jealous!

PLATO: It can't be so simple. Somehow I couldn't bear it to be simple! If only I could get it *clear*! (*He holds his bursting head.*)

ACASTOS: You never will. Anyway, let's be happy. Come, dear Plato.

Acastos puts his arm round Plato's waist. Plato resists, then accepts the gesture. Acastos pulls him away by the hand. The servant is left alone. He smiles, raising his arms as if in prayer.

AUTHOR'S NOTE

The dialogues are designed to be performed either in modern dress or in period costume. In a period performance the servant in Above the Gods *will of course be a slave, and the following text may be preferred.*

TIMONAX: Well, if you want to go on and we want to rest why not question this black fellow? I know Socrates never needs a rest.
SOCRATES: What does Antagoras think? May we question the slave?
ANTAGORAS: Of course, Socrates, whatever you like.
SOCRATES: Does he speak Greek?
ANTAGORAS: Yes, he was bred on our country estate.
    As they discuss the slave Acastos is uncomfortable, looks at Plato, who remains impassive.
TIMONAX: Has he got any religion?
ANTAGORAS: His mother was a Nubian, she probably had some superstitious belief. But he's a simple chap, he hasn't a single idea in his head, you see he isn't even listening, he's in another world.
TIMONAX: At least we can find out if religion is something natural!
SOCRATES: I would like Acastos to question the slave.
ACASTOS: Oh no! Please not!
SOCRATES: I won't always be here to ask questions, others must learn. Besides you are young and gentle and won't upset him. Go on, my dear.
ACASTOS (*very nervous*): We are talking about religion. (*It takes a moment for him to attract the slave's attention.*) Look – excuse me – we're – talking about *religion*. You know what religion is? *The slave is a graceful youth. He is a little timid at first but soon shows no fear or embarrassment.*

[527]

SLAVE: No, sir.

TIMONAX: End of conversation.

SOCRATES: Go on, tell him what it is.

ACASTOS: Oh dear! I mean – when you go to the temples –

SLAVE: I never go to the temples, sir.

ACASTOS: Do you pray? Pray? say prayers?

SLAVE: I don't know, sir, I do not know what is that.

TIMONAX: Lucky fellow, no religion, that shows it isn't natural!

ACASTOS: Shall we stop here?

SOCRATES (*observing the scene with some amusement*): No, go on.

ACASTOS: You know people believe in worship, and holy and sacred things and places –

SLAVE: I don't know, sir.

TIMONAX: He's simple-minded.

ANTAGORAS: You're getting nowhere with religion, try morality.

ACASTOS (*with a glance at Socrates*): Do you know what morality is, morals, duty –

SLAVE: No, sir.

SOCRATES: Explain it.

ACASTOS: Morality is – well (*Antagoras and Timonax giggle.*) Let me see. When your conscience – no – when you feel something's *right*, and you want to do it because it's right and good, and not just because it's pleasant – For instance, when you make a promise – (*Slave looks blank*) I mean – you do make promises – sometimes, promise somebody something?

SLAVE: No. (*Explains*) I don't make, I don't know what is that thing.

ACASTOS (*getting desperate*): But do you ever feel you *ought* to do something, that it's an *obligation*, when your heart tells you something *must* be done whether you like it or not?

SLAVE: No, sir, certainly not, sir.

ACASTOS: Why certainly not?

SLAVE (*who thinks this is obvious*): I only do what I am told.

ACASTOS: I can't bear this!

ANTAGORAS: You see, they have no sense of duty, no idea of obligation, this is an important element in their condition, a merciful disability, like women, they simply lack the concept!

SOCRATES: Try to get back to religion.

ACASTOS: You know about rites and rituals, when people –

ANTAGORAS: He doesn't know these words.

ACASTOS: Like the procession this afternoon.

SLAVE (*animated*): Oh yes, sir, the procession, that's good, when they dress up, so, and there is such music, and the tambourines, bom bom, and the flowers, it is so beautiful, and my heart goes bom bom, and my feet go, go, go, oh yes, oh yes!

He takes a few steps. Timonax and Antagoras laugh, Socrates smiles. Acastos is touched and upset, Plato frowns slightly.

ANTAGORAS: I'm afraid this isn't getting us anywhere.

SOCRATES: Ask him about the gods.

TIMONAX: What's the use!

ACASTOS: Do you know what the gods are – have you heard of God or the gods?

SLAVE: Gods –

TIMONAX: Never heard of them.

SLAVE: Oh yes, sir, the gods, oh yes!

ACASTOS: Tell me about the gods, do you believe in them?

SLAVE: I don't understand, sir.

ACASTOS: So you don't believe in the gods, you think there are no gods?

SLAVE (*amazed*): No gods?

ACASTOS: That's what you think?

SLAVE: How could I think that when I see them all the time?

ACASTOS: You *see* them? You mean their statues?

SLAVE: No, no, not statues, the *gods*, they are everywhere, you cannot help seeing them!

ANTAGORAS: Well, well!

ACASTOS: Where do you see them?

ANTAGORAS: Are they here?

SLAVE: No, sir, but they are in the garden and in the vineyard and in the trees and beside the river, oh so many gods!

ACASTOS (*fascinated*): What are they like?

SLAVE: They are beautiful, oh so beautiful, the most beautiful of all!

ACASTOS: Are they good?

SLAVE (*puzzled*): I don't know. They are gods.

ACASTOS: Do you talk to them?

SLAVE: Oh yes, I talk to them, much, much talk.

[529]

ACASTOS: And do they answer?

SLAVE: Well, sir, sometimes they laugh, they are often laughing, oh they are so happy!

ACASTOS: Do you pray to them? I mean do you ask them to give you things?

SLAVE: No, sir. What could they give me better than just to be there with me?

TIMONAX: Don't you ask them to make you free one day and not a slave?

SLAVE (*suddenly upset*): I don't know – that –

ACASTOS (*to Socrates*): Can we let him go?

Socrates nods, Antagoras makes a dismissive gesture, the slave departs. Acastos looks accusingly at Timonax.

ACASTOS: You shouldn't have said that!

TIMONAX (*ruefully*): All right! Let's just hope he hasn't got that concept either! But of course he was just putting on an act.

ANTAGORAS: No, no, there you have the childish superstitions of primitive people, they're like children.

ACASTOS: I don't think it's superstition.

TIMONAX: You think there really are gods and he really sees them? You should have asked him how large they are!

SOCRATES: Acastos means that for him there are gods. He is fortunate, he has happy gods. Thales tells us there are gods everywhere.

ANTAGORAS: That's poetic, just a metaphor.

SOCRATES: There are deep metaphors, perhaps there are bottomless metaphors.

At this point Socrates withdraws a little from the others and stands motionless in thought. They are used to this habit of his and lower their voices respectfully. They glance at him occasionally, put fingers to lips. Plato, watching Socrates intently, ignores their conversation.

ANTAGORAS: That slave, he's not much of a worker, he's too dreamy, we've put him on the list for the silver mines, they pay a lot for a healthy one.

TIMONAX: You're going to send that beautiful animal to the silver mines?

ACASTOS: You care because he's beautiful. You ought to care because he's human. They die like flies in the mines.

ANTAGORAS: There are things one doesn't talk about in polite society. There's nothing we can do, moaning about it is just sentimental hypocrisy. Without slavery our economy would collapse.

ACASTOS: I think slavery is retarding our economy. Anyway it's immoral.

TIMONAX: I don't like slavery but we've got to have it, it's a fact of life, always was, always will be.

ACASTOS: Slavery is contrary to nature.

ANTAGORAS: Slavery is a matter of fate.

ACASTOS: That's superstition!

ANTAGORAS: Slavery is a man's fate. It could be yours, it could be mine, where he is we might be. It's a humbling thought.

ACASTOS: But as it happens we're not where he is, and –

ANTAGORAS: There are those upon whom no light falls, it cannot be otherwise.

TIMONAX: Would you sell me that slave?

ANTAGORAS: What do you want him for?

Published in *Acastos: Two Platonic Dialogues*, 1986.

Acknowledgements & Sources

The editor and publisher wish to thank the original publishers of the essays collected in this volume. Details of publishers and previous publication are given below. Every effort has been made to seek permission from publishers and controllers of copyright material, where appropriate, but there are some whom we have been unable to contact. The publishers will be pleased to hear from anyone whose permission to use such material should be obtained.

PART ONE
'Literature and Philosophy: A Conversation with Bryan Magee': Originally shown on BBC Television, 28 October 1977. This substantially reworked version was published in *Men of Ideas* by Bryan Magee (London, BBC Books, 1978). Reprinted here by permission of The Peters Fraser & Dunlop Group Ltd, © Bryan Magee 1978.

PART TWO
'Thinking and Language': From a symposium entitled 'Thinking and Language', between Iris Murdoch, Gilbert Ryle and A. C. Lloyd. Published in *Proceedings of the Aristotelian Society*, no. 25 (1951), pp. 25–34, © the Aristotelian Society 1951.

'Nostalgia for the Particular': Paper read at a meeting of the Aristotelian Society at 21 Bedford Square, London, 9 June 1952. Published in *Proceedings of the Aristotelian Society*, no. 52 (1952), pp. 243–60, © the Aristotelian Society 1952.

'Metaphysics and Ethics': Published in *The Nature of Metaphysics*, ed. D. F. Pears (London, Macmillan, 1957), pp. 99–123. Reprinted here by permission of Macmillan Publishers Ltd.

'Vision and Choice in Morality': Published in *Proceedings of the Aristotelian Society: Dreams and Self-Knowledge*, Supplement no. 30 (1956), pp. 32–58, © the Aristotelian Society 1956.

PART THREE
'The Novelist as Metaphysician': Broadcast on the BBC Third Programme, March 1950. Published in *The Listener* (16 March 1950), pp. 473, 476.

'The Existentialist Hero': Broadcast on the BBC Third Programme, March 1950. Published in *The Listener* (23 March 1950), pp 523–4.

'Sartre's *The Emotions: Outline of a Theory*': Published in *Mind*, no. 59, (April 1950), pp. 268–71.

'De Beauvoir's *The Ethics of Ambiguity*': Published in *Mind*, no. 59 (April 1950), pp. 127–8.

'The Image of Mind': Review of Gabriel Marcel's first volume of Gifford Lectures, *The Mystery of Being: Reflection and Mystery*. Published in *University: A Journal of Enquiry* (Summer 1951), pp. 130–5.

'The Existentialist Political Myth': Published in *Socratic Digest*, no. 5 (1952), pp. 52–63.

'Hegel in Modern Dress': Review of Jean-Paul Sartre's *Being and Nothingness*. Published in *New Statesman and Nation* (25 May 1957), pp. 675–6.

'Existentialist Bite': Review of E. W. Knight's *Literature Considered as Philosophy: The French Example*. Published in *The Spectator* (12 July 1957), pp. 68–9.

PART FOUR
'Knowing the Void': Review of Simone Weil's *Notebooks*. Published in *The Spectator* (2 November 1956), p. 613–4.

'T. S. Eliot as a Moralist': Published in *T. S. Eliot: A Symposium for his 70th Birthday*, ed. N. Braybrooke (London, Rupert Hart-Davis, 1958), pp. 152–60.

'A House of Theory': Published in *Conviction*, ed. N. Mackenzie (London, MacGibbon & Kee, 1958), pp. 218–33; reprinted in *Power and Civilisation*, ed. D. Cooperman and E. V. Walter (New York, Crowell, 1962), pp. 442–55; reprinted *Partisan Review* (Winter 1959), pp. 17–31.

'Mass, Might and Myth': Review of Elias Canetti's *Crowds and Power*. Published in *The Spectator* (7 September 1962), pp. 337–8.

'The Darkness of Practical Reason': Review of Stuart Hampshire's *Freedom of the Individual*. Published in *Encounter* (July 1966), pp. 46–50.

PART FIVE

'The Sublime and the Good': Published in *Chicago Review* (Autumn 1959), pp. 42–55.

'Existentialists and Mystics: A Note on the Novel in the New Utilitarian Age': Published in *Essays & Poems presented to Lord David Cecil*, ed. W. W. Robson (London, Constable, 1970), pp. 169–83. Reprinted here by permission of Constable Publishers.

'Salvation by Words': Part of the Blashfield Address delivered to the American Academy of Arts and Letters, 17 May 1972. Published in *The New York Review of Books*, (15 June 1972), pp. 3–5.

'Art is the Imitation of Nature': Paper presented at a symposium on British writing at the University of Caen, 1978. Published in *Cahiers du Centre de Recherches sur les Pays du Nord et du Nord-Ouest*, no. 1 (Faculté des Lettres et Sciences Humaines, Université de Caen, 1978), pp. 59–65.

PART SIX

'The Sublime and the Beautiful Revisited': Published in *Yale Review* (December 1959), pp. 247–71.

'Against Dryness': Published in *Encounter* (January 1961), pp. 16–20; reprinted in *The Novel Today*, ed. Malcolm Bradbury (Manchester, Manchester University Press, 1977); reprinted in *Revisions*, ed. S. Hauerwas and A. MacIntyre (Notre Dame, University of Notre Dame Press, 1981); reprinted in *Iris Murdoch*, ed. H. Bloom (New York, Chelsea House, 1986).

PART SEVEN

'The Idea of Perfection': Based on the Ballard Mathews Lecture delivered at the University College of North Wales, 1962. Published in *Yale Review* (Spring, 1964), pp. 342–80; reprinted in *The Sovereignty of Good*, Iris Murdoch (London, Routledge, 1970). Reprinted here by permission of Routledge Ltd.

'On "God" and "Good" ': Published in *The Anatomy of Knowledge*, ed. Marjorie Grene (London, Routledge and Kegan Paul, 1969), pp. 233–55; reprinted in *The Sovereignty of Good*, Iris Murdoch (London, Routledge, 1970). Reprinted here by permission of Routledge Ltd.

'The Sovereignty of Good Over Other Concepts': Delivered as the Leslie Stephen Lecture, 1967. Published, courtesy of the Syndics of the Cambridge University Press, in *The Sovereignty of Good*, Iris Murdoch (London, Routledge, 1970). Reprinted here by permission of Routledge Ltd.

'The Fire and the Sun: Why Plato Banished the Artists': Based on the Romanes Lecture, 1976. Published as *The Fire and the Sun: Why Plato Banished the Artists*, Iris Murdoch (Oxford, Clarendon Press, 1977); reprinted (London, Chatto & Windus, 1990).

'Art and Eros: A Dialogue about Art': First performed as National Theatre Platform Performance, National Theatre, London, February 1980. Published in *Acastos: Two Platonic Dialogues*, Iris Murdoch (London, Chatto & Windus, 1986).

'Above the Gods: A Dialogue about Religion': Published in *Acastos: Two Platonic Dialogues*, Iris Murdoch (London, Chatto & Windus, 1986).

Index

Pasternak, Boris, *Dr Zhivago*, 218
Pears, D. F., xxviii
perfection, 207, 370, 376; the idea of, 299–336, 348, 349–50; *see also* good
Pericles, 407, 413, 476
personality, 290; cult of, 162, 275; liberal view of, 261, 262, 265, 274–5, 278, 281, 289, 290; literary, 8–9, 10
pesanteur (solid weight), xiii
phenomenalism, 314
phenomenology, xiv, 23, 55, 87n, 101–3, 106, 116–21, 122, 123, 126, 128, 131, 148, 200, 289; *see also* existentialism
The Philosopher's Pupil, xi, xxiii
'Philosophy and Beliefs' (symposium), xxviii &n
physics, 429, 433, 435
Piero della Francesca, 351
Plato, xi, xii, xv, xvi, xvii, xxiii, xxvii, 3, 6, 23, 74, 158, 159, 160, 214, 218, 241, 245, 322, 332, 341, 344, 357, 358, 361, 370, 372–3, 374, 375, 377–9, 380, 382–3, 386–463; *The Analogy*, 449; *The Apology*, 386, 401, 424; cave myth, 389–90, 413, 423, 426, 427, 445, 451, 462, 488; *Cratylus*, 407, 430; *Epinomis*, 424, 430; *Gorgias*, 394, 430; *Hippias Major*, 387; *Ion*, 387, 392–3, 401; *Kosmos*, 430; *Laws*, xvi, 386, 387, 393–4, 397, 398, 399, 400, 403, 407, 408–9, 410, 411, 414, 415, 417, 419, 420, 422, 424, 431, 433, 435, 439–40, 441–2, 447, 448, 449, 451, 454; *Meno*, 387, 388, 396, 406, 407; *Parmenides*, 409, 410, 411, 426, 427, 428, 437, 445; *Phaedo*, 355, 388, 396, 404, 406, 407, 408, 412, 424, 428, 430, 431, 437, 438, 440, 441, 445, 449, 451; *Phaedrus*, 238, 325, 348, 369, 387, 388, 399, 401, 403, 404–5, 407, 411, 413, 416, 419, 428, 429, 430, 435, 437, 439, 462; *Philebus*, 394, 396, 397, 399, 400, 402, 404, 409, 411, 418, 421, 425, 426, 430, 432, 437, 438, 444, 449, 450, 452, 459, 462; *Politicus*, 409, 429; *Protagoras*, 387, 405, 407, 408; *The Republic*, 214, 238, 245, 353, 377–8, 379, 380, 386–400 *passim*, 403, 407, 408, 409, 411, 412, 413, 414, 415, 418, 419, 421, 423, 424,

425, 426, 427, 428, 431, 432, 433, 434, 437, 438, 439, 443, 449, 451, 455, 456, 457; *Seventh Letter*, 404, 405, 413, 426, 443; *The Sophist*, 404, 409, 410–11, 412, 413, 424, 426, 427, 428, 431, 432, 433, 435, 437, 445, 452; *Symposium*, 5, 384, 388, 396, 398, 399, 407, 414, 415, 416, 425, 437, 438, 456; *Theaetetus*, 404, 409–10, 411, 412, 426, 427, 428, 437, 440, 445, 446, 460, 463; theory of beauty, 388, 390, 394, 395–6, 399, 401, 414–18, 420, 423–5, 435, 436, 437–8, 448, 449, 452, 457, 459; Theory of Forms, 15, 245, 372, 378, 387–9, 390, 394, 395, 406, 407–12, 416, 418, 426–36, 439, 440–1, 442–3, 444–5, 452–3; *Timaeus*, 394, 395, 398, 399, 403, 404, 408, 410, 422, 424, 429, 430, 431, 432, 434, 435, 436, 437, 438, 439, 440, 442, 445, 446, 451, 460; views on art, 13, 15, 214, 221, 237, 238–9, 245–7, 248, 249, 250, 252, 274, 372, 386–7, 389–414, 420, 421–3, 424–5, 426, 428, 434, 435, 440, 442, 443–9, 450–63; *see also Acastos: Two Platonic Dialogues*
Platonism, x, xi, xiii, xxiii–xxiv, xxv &n, 102, 158
play, 281, 440; and art, 209, 211, 263, 386, 390, 459
pleasure, 393, 394–6, 399, 400, 421, 438, 459
Plotinus, 247, 387, 392
poetics, formalist theory of, 24
poetry, 5, 13, 36, 37, 40, 209–10, 212, 237, 239, 246, 277, 280, 292, 386, 387, 390, 393–4, 400, 407, 416, 445, 446, 448, 460, 472, 473–4, 482, 487, 492, 494; and T. S. Eliot, 163, 164–5, 166, 169–70
political myth, the existentialist, 130–45
political philosophy/theory, 98, 171–86, 366, 386
politics, 22–3, 224, 230–1, 236, 474; of adolescence, 141
Popper, Karl, 178
pornography, 14, 246, 251, 473, 475, 481, 485, 486
Pound, Ezra, 165
power, 193, 522–3; Canetti's theory of,

vision, 301, 302, 311, 316, 326, 363,
435, 439, 445, 453, 460; and
'looking' or 'gazing', xxiv, 76–98
passim
'Vision and Choice in Morality', xxviii,
76–98
Vlastos, G., 440
void, 158, 159, 327, 330
Voltaire, 18, 20
voluntarism, 223–4, 225, 368

Warnock, Mary, xxii, xxviii
Waugh, Evelyn, 109
Weil, Simone, xiii–xiv, xxvii, xxx, 157,
270, 293, 327, 331–2, 340, 385, 429,
460; *L'Enracinement*, 159; *The
Notebooks*, 157–60
Weldon, T. D., 69, 178; *The
Vocabulary of Politics*, 83n, 178
Welfare State, 172, 182, 185, 287,
289–90, 291, 293
Wells, H. G., 162
White, Patrick, 226
Whitehead, Alfred North, 6, 454
Wilamowitz, , 392
will, 194–6, 198, 223, 224, 225, 226,
230, 263, 267, 288, 301, 302, 303,
304–5, 306, 316, 328, 330, 331–3,

338, 339, 345, 352, 354, 356, 366;
free, xxvi, xxvii, xxix; good as
function of, 301; heteronomy of the,
78; weakness of (*Akrasia*), 193, 194,
195, 200
Wittgenstein, Ludwig, ix, xi, xiii, 5, 22,
61, 73, 97, 166, 187, 193, 229, 232,
241, 243, 249, 266, 267, 292, 302,
306, 308, 310, 311, 312, 316, 318,
338, 339, 340, 406, 420;
Conversations on Freud, 420;
Investigations, 307, 412; *Tractatus*,
35, 38, 105, 195, 249, 288, 339, 411,
412; *Untersuchungen, see
Investigations*
Woolf, Virginia, 244, 250
words, 33–6, 44, 79, 165, 240–2, 322,
324, 325, 326; *see also* language
working class movement, 172, 181–2
writing, 404–5, 412, 413, 443; *see also*
literature; novels; poetry

Yeats, W. B., xix, 112

Zen Buddhism, 221, 231, 241, 448,
450; *see also* Buddhism
Zeno, 410, 451, 498